Norwich City

The Modern Era

– A Complete Record –

Desert Island Football Histories

Club Histories	ISBN
Aberdeen: A Centenary History 1903-2003	1-874287-49-X
Aberdeen: Champions of Scotland 1954-55	1-874287-65-1
Aberdeen: The European Era – A Complete Record	1-874287-11-2
Bristol City: The Modern Era – A Complete Record	1-874287-28-7
Bristol City: The Early Years 1894-1915	1-874287-74-0
Cambridge United: The League Era – A Complete Record	1-874287-32-5
Cambridge United: 101 Golden Greats	1-874287-58-9
The Story of the Celtic 1888-1938	1-874287-15-5
Colchester United: Graham to Whitton – A Complete Record	1-874287-27-9
Coventry City: The Elite Era – A Complete Record	1-874287-51-1
Coventry City: An Illustrated History	1-874287-59-7
Dundee: Champions of Scotland 1961-62	1-874287-72-4
Dundee United: Champions of Scotland 1982-83	1-874287-71-6
History of the Everton Football Club 1878-1928	1-874287-14-7
Halifax Town: From Ball to Lillis – A Complete Record	1-874287-26-0
Hereford United: The League Era – A Complete Record	1-874287-18-X
Huddersfield Town: Champions of England 1923-1926	1-874287-66-X
Ipswich Town: The Modern Era – A Complete Record	1-874287-43-0
Ipswich Town: Champions of England 1961-62	1-874287-56-2
Luton Town: The Modern Era – A Complete Record	1-874287-05-8
Luton Town: An Illustrated History	1-874287-37-6
Matt Busby: A Complete Man U Record 1945-1971	1-874287-53-8
Motherwell: Champions of Scotland 1931-32	1-874287-73-2
Norwich City: The Modern Era – A Complete Record	1-874287-67-8
Peterborough United: The Modern Era – A Complete Record	1-874287-33-3
Peterborough United: Who's Who?	1-874287-48-1
Plymouth Argyle: The Modern Era – A Complete Record	1-874287-54-6
Plymouth Argyle: 101 Golden Greats	1-874287-64-3
Portsmouth: From Tindall to Ball – A Complete Record	1-874287-25-2
Portsmouth: Champions of England – 1948-49 & 1949-50	1-874287-38-4
The Story of the Rangers 1873-1923	1-874287-16-3
The Romance of the Wednesday 1867-1926	1-874287-17-1
Stoke City: The Modern Era – A Complete Record	1-874287-76-7
Stoke City: 101 Golden Greats	1-874287-55-4
West Ham: From Greenwood to Redknapp	1-874287-19-8
West Ham: The Elite Era – A Complete Record	1-874287-31-7
Wimbledon: From Southern League to Premiership	1-874287-09-0
Wimbledon: From Wembley to Selhurst	1-874287-20-1
Wimbledon: The Premiership Years	1-874287-40-6
Wrexham: The European Era – A Complete Record	1-874287-52-X

World Cup Histories	
England's Quest for the World Cup – A Complete Record	1-874287-61-9
Scotland: The Quest for the World Cup – A Complete Record	1-897850-50-6
Ireland: The Quest for the World Cup – A Complete Record	1-897850-80-8

Miscellaneous	
Red Dragons in Europe – A Complete Record	1-874287-01-5
The Book of Football: A History to 1905-06	1-874287-13-9
Football's War & Peace: The Tumultuous Season of 1946-47	1-874287-70-8

NORWICH CITY

The Modern Era

— A Complete Record —

Series Editor: Clive Leatherdale
Series Consultant: Leigh Edwards

Rob Hadgraft

Desert Island Books

First Published in 2003

DESERT ISLAND BOOKS LIMITED
89 Park Street, Westcliff-on-Sea, Essex SS0 7PD
United Kingdom
www.desertislandbooks.com

British Library Cataloguing-in-Publication Data
A catalogue record for this book is available from the British Library

ISBN 1-874287-67-8

Printed in Great Britain
by Biddles Ltd

Photographs in this book are reproduced by kind permission
of Jim Brown and Roger Wash

Contents

Preface

Norwich City has been such a large part of my life that I can only reflect on my time at Carrow Road with happy memories. To know I was part of the team that won the club its first major trophy, through good management and team spirit, leaves a permanent memory. I can refer back to those high standards even in today's football.

My earliest recollection of joining Norwich is of meeting manger Ken Brown at Norwich Station with Norfolk covered by snow. I had agreed to come on loan from West Brom. 'No worries,' Ken assured me. 'I've arranged a friendly against Ipswich at Great Yarmouth so that we can have a look at you and you can get to know the lads.' I scored with my first touch and went on to score four goals as we won 5-1. Ken said there was a good chance I'd get a permanent move if I kept that average going! He had a great sense of humour.

Earlier I played in the League Cup final for Aston Villa in 1977 but had no recollections of that day. So when Norwich beat Ipswich with Brucie's last-minute header to reach the 1985 final, I spent the build-up to the game with Sunderland encouraging everyone to enjoy and remember the day. I was able to do this myself, and can still remember my view past skipper Watto as he lifted the cup and turned to face our supporters. Magic!

My second coming at Carrow Road was the start of another special chapter in the history of Norwich City. As coach, I sat down in a Norwegian hotel with Gary Megson, who had just arrived on my recommendation, and we assessed what we had at our disposal. Mid-table if we are lucky, was our verdict. Few would have argued with that when the first game of the season saw us go 2-0 down by half-time at Arsenal. What unfolded during the second-half was fairytale stuff (a 4-2 victory) and by the end of November we had an eight-point lead at the top of the Premiership in its inaugural year. We qualified for Europe and all Norwich fans will have their own special memories of Arnhem, Munich and Milan.

I was honoured to be made manager in 1994, but I found out within two days exactly how difficult it would be. Chairman Robert Chase sold Ruel Fox to Newcastle and, from then until the time I left, that was how the club was run. We failed to re-invest after goalkeeper Gunny broke his leg at a time the club was sixth in the table. Although we took on loan players, we might have qualified again for Europe if we had elected to be more positive about our position at that time.

One player who brought more joy than any other over that period was Jeremy Goss, and he came up trumps for me when we played at Anfield in the final game before the famous Kop was demolished. 'Go out and enjoy yourselves,' was my instruction to the players – and Gossy came up with another cracking goal to enable us to finish the season with a 1-0 win.

On the ball City!

JOHN DEEHAN

199 games, 70 goals (January 1982 – May 86)

Coach (June 1992 – January 1994)

Manager (January 1994 – April 1995)

Author's Note

Norwich City first arrived among football's elite in 1972 – and there's rarely been a dull moment since. Since that breakthrough, the Canaries have played in five major finals, five losing semi-finals, celebrated promotion three times, suffered relegation four times, had a run in the UEFA Cup, and finished among the country's top five on three occasions. There have also been some amazing off-the-field episodes.

Eleven vastly different characters have managed the club since 1972 and the playing staff has featured famous names, such as: MacDougall, Peters, Chivers, Osgood, Fashanu, Channon, Royle, O'Neill, Watson, Bruce, Woods, Townsend, Fleck, Sherwood, Fox, Sutton and Bellamy.

The remarkable modern history of this club clearly demanded to be laid down in detail alongside the others in Desert Island Books' soccer history series. I hope my efforts have done justice to the fascinating progress the club has made over the past 30 years or so.

The source material for my research included *the Eastern Daily Press, Eastern Evening News* and *Eastern Football News (Pink 'Un),* plus books such as *Canary Citizens* (Davage, Eastwood & Platt), *Norfolk'n'Good* and *The Second Coming* (Kevin Baldwin), *Martin O'Neill – The Biography* (Alex Montgomery), *Man On The Run* (Mike Channon), *100 Great Football Memories* (ed Peter Rogers), *Survival of the Fattest* (Volumes 1-5), *Rothmans Football Yearbooks* and official club handbooks.

To complete the statistical section of this book I had to search out the facts and figures behind 1,320 Norwich league games and 222 cup-ties. All the essential details from these games are here, including the line-up of both teams and a 50-word summary of each and every match. Websites and bookshelves offer all manner of football paraphernalia these days, but I am confident this book provides unprecedented detail as far as Norwich City is concerned.

I would like to thank Roger Wash and Jim Brown for providing many of the pictures used, John Deehan for taking the time to write a Preface, the staff of the British Newspaper Library at Colindale and Eastern Daily Press library in Norwich for their help, and – last but not least – my wife Katie, for not objecting to this long and arduous project!

ROB HADGRAFT
September 2003

Publishers' Note:
This book contains full details – line-ups for both sides, goalscorers, goal-times, referees, attendances, League positions after each game, cumulative points totals, plus a 50-word summary of key moments – of every first-team match Norwich City have played in the League, FA Cup, League Cup, and Europe, beginning with 1972-73. Minor cups have been excluded for reasons of space.

Introduction

Given the recent success of Delia Smith's Canary Catering emporium at Carrow Road, it's hardly surprising to discover that Norwich City FC was formed amid the clinking cups and excited chatter of a popular restaurant.

The gathering took place at the Criterion Café in White Lion Street on a summer's day in 1902 and was organised by schoolmasters Robert Webster and Joseph Nutchey. This energetic, moustachioed duo were leading lights at a local team known as Norwich Church of England Young Men's Society. But they had bigger things in mind.

They recruited another prominent local sportsman, Arthur Turner, and unfolded plans to create the biggest and best football club for miles around. The new Norwich City FC subsequently made its home on Newmarket Road and gained admission to the Norfolk and Suffolk League. Within weeks the first match took place, a 1-1 friendly with Harwich.

City wore blue and white in those days and were known as The Citizens. By 1905 they had won the regional league title but became the subject of an FA inquiry and were found guilty of 'professional practices'. Officials were suspended for paying for gym facilities, advertising for players, supplying kit and travel expenses. The club's inevitable next step was to turn professional and enter the Southern League.

These were exciting times and enthusiastic fans adopted the anthem 'On the Ball City', apparently pinching it from another Norwich team. The popular local pastime of breeding canaries also became associated with the club and subsequently provided a new nickname, with club colours changing to yellow and green.

Bigger crowds and leasing difficulties meant a new ground had to be found. The Canaries took flight and landed at The Nest. This was part of a disused chalk-pit in Rosary Road and required the grandstands from Newmarket Road to be transported there by horse and cart. The new home was christened with a friendly against Fulham in 1908.

Shortly afterwards, Reading objected to playing a cup-tie at The Nest, claiming the pitch was too small. Their complaint was upheld but City beat the Berkshire side and went on to cause a major shock in the next round, beating Liverpool 3-2. FA Cup history was also created in 1915 in a replay against Bradford City, played on neutral turf at Lincoln. Because the War effort was in full flow, the game was staged behind closed doors so that munitions workers were not distracted from their labours. The official attendance was therefore zero, although police let some fans in to prevent trouble outside.

Norwich's debts grew during the 1914-18 War. The club went into voluntary liquidation but reformed after hostilities ceased. The Football League introduced Third Division Southern and Northern sections in 1920, inviting Norwich to join the former. With crowds still on the rise, a move away from The Nest became imperative. The Colman company's offer of the Carrow Road site was gratefully accepted.

When League football resumed after the 1939-45 War, City twice had to apply for re-election, but by the early 1950s were challenging strongly for promotion to Division Two. There was more FA Cup excitement as Liverpool were beaten in 1951 and Arsenal humbled on their own ground three years later. The giant-killing reputation was consolidated in 1959 when Matt Busby's Manchester United were beaten 3-0 at snowbound Carrow Road and then Cardiff overturned 3-2. Around 20,000 City fans saw a thrilling draw at Tottenham, followed by an even better replay victory. In the quarter-final at Sheffield United, keeper Ken Nethercott dislocated his shoulder but the brave Canaries forced a replay. Another 3-2 win meant Third Division City were in the FA Cup semi-finals. Only Luton stood between a visit to Wembley. The Canaries had the better of a 1-1 draw at White Hart Lane, and also the replay at St Andrews, but Billy Bingham's goal shattered the dream.

Archie Macauley masterminded promotion to Division Two in 1960 and less than two years later the Canaries won the League Cup, a competition then shunned by the top clubs. Fourth Division Rochdale were beaten in a two-legged final and long-serving Ron Ashman capped a great career by lifting the trophy.

In the harsh winter of 1963, Terry Allcock scored four as City hammered Newcastle in the FA Cup and a club record crowd of 43,984 packed the ground for a subsequent tie with Leicester. In 1967, City were at it again, beating champions-elect Manchester United 2-1 at Old Trafford.

In the summer of 1969, Oxford's Ron Saunders became Norwich manager and his third season in charge saw the dream of top-flight football realised. Promotion was clinched at Orient in April 1972 and the title at rain-sodden Watford five days later. A place among the elite beckoned.

Chapter One

The Great Adventure: Peaks & Troughs 1972-76

LEAGUE DIVISION 1	**1972-73**
Division 1	20th
League Cup	Finalists
FA Cup	3rd round
Texaco Cup	Runner-up

The Canaries' first campaign in the top flight was eagerly awaited, with Ron Saunders and his single-minded skipper Duncan Forbes determined not to play second fiddle to the more famous clubs over the next eight months. Famed for its cup exploits down the years, City now wanted to make a real impact in the league. But, as things turned out, it would be cup excitement taking centre stage again.

Since manager Saunders' arrival, Norwich had gained a reputation for being dour and uncompromising, the sort of side that gave little away and lacked attacking flair. The partnership of Forbes and Stringer in central defence was an inspirational rock and the doubts about City's ability to survive at top level concerned their offensive department. In clinching the Second Division title they'd scored a modest 60 goals and winger Ken Foggo was leading scorer with a meagre thirteen. However, Saunders didn't strengthen his forward line in the summer and began the new season with lanky David Cross and energetic Jimmy Bone as his front two.

A draw with Everton kicked off the First Division era, but highlight of the opening weeks was undoubtedly the satisfying victory at Ipswich, City's first triumph over the old enemy in more than five years. Huge interest was generated by the autumn visits of London giants Tottenham and Arsenal, both returning to the capital pointless, much to Norfolk glee. The honeymoon period that many newly promoted clubs enjoy endured for Norwich until mid-November. After hitting the heady heights of the top six, their winning form deserted them. And how.

The distractions of the League and Texaco Cups might have been a hindrance, but Saunders was not the type to make excuses. The unsmiling manager looked grimmer as the winter weeks went by, as his team slid further down the table. Between mid-November and mid-April, Norwich failed to record a single league victory in nineteen games, and hurtled down from sixth to 22nd place.

DID YOU KNOW?

'On The Ball City' is thought to be the world's oldest football supporters' song still in use. It was first heard around 1906.

During this five-months of purgatory, one City player whose enthusiasm levels never dropped was Calcutta-born goalkeeper Kevin Keelan. Enjoying his first taste of top-flight football at the age of 31, he was flamboyant, agile and a true entertainer. He pulled off some sensational saves and fully merited the Player of the Year accolade that would come his way later. Arriving from Wrexham in 1961, Keelan, with jet-black hair and intense eyes, became known for occasional hot-headedness and moments of rashness. He had been the first Norwich keeper ever to be sent off, but having passed 30, now seemed more mature and dependable.

The men directly in front of Keelan were not the flamboyant type. Muscular Forbes, his shorts yanked high and his sleeves rolled up, was the archetypal burly Scottish centre-half. Brave and determined, some of his challenges made teammates wince. First Division referees and forwards soon got to know him well. Like Keelan, Forbes arrived in the First Division at a late stage of his career and wanted to make his presence felt. It would take a punctured lung and cracked ribs to put him out of the side, and it was no coincidence that City's mid-season slump began after 'big Dunc' was hospitalised.

As the run without a league win stretched into 1973, Saunders resolutely stuck to 4-4-2, but dipped into the transfer market. He made captures that would ultimately play a major role in turning the tide. Skilful Colin Suggett from West Brom instantly pepped the low-scoring attack, lanky winger Ian Mellor arrived from Manchester City, and battling bearded midfielder Trevor Hockey was recruited from Sheffield United ('the Blade without a razor', as he was once memorably described). Hockey came in exchange for Jimmy Bone, who'd been popular with the crowd, but not consistent enough for Saunders.

The sight of their beloved Canaries in relegation trouble was counter-balanced for most fans by the cup excitement. The League Cup saw Norwich stride comfortably into the quarter-finals at the expense of Leicester, Hull and Stockport. The tie at Edgeley Park was refereed by Clive Thomas, who, 25 years earlier, had been a Carrow Road groundstaff boy. The home club raised eyebrows over this revelation, but the League saw no reason to cancel Thomas's appointment. A memorable quarter-final night at Highbury saw Arsenal humbled 3-0, thanks to a splendid hat-trick from Graham

Paddon. The former Coventry man may have looked like a Californian hippie, with his long blond hair and beard, but his small frame packed a fierce shot. Three weeks later it was back into London for the semi-final first leg and a comfortable 2-0 win over Chelsea. Never mind the grim league form, City had one foot at Wembley.

The second leg at Carrow Road was hit by fog, but not abandoned until the 84th minute. City were leading 3-2 at the time and felt robbed by referee Gordon Hill's decision – particularly as the fog lifted shortly afterwards! Happily the re-arranged game saw young Govier head a winner to ensure Wembley remained on the itinerary. As the Canary hordes celebrated, few realised they were in the presence of a rather shaken HRH Prince Andrew. With fans battling in the streets outside, the Prince had been welcomed into the boardroom just as a stone crashed through a nearby window. Damage was minimal, save for the pride of red-faced club officials providing royal 'hospitality'. Out on the terraces, the anthem 'On The Ball City' filled the air and even Saunders – who had earlier described the song as a 'dirge' – had to admit it sounded marvellous that night.

The FA Cup proved less enjoyable, with City hammered emphatically by a Leeds side at the peak of its powers, albeit in a second replay. In addition to the ten ties that made up City's involvement in FA and League Cups, another eight dates had to be fulfilled in the Texaco Cup. No wonder the league form suffered. Dundee, Leicester and Motherwell were narrowly beaten to set up a two-legged Texaco final in early May, against neighbours Ipswich, of all people. The Leicester tie was settled through a tense penalty shoot-out, Keelan making two brilliant saves and then tucking one away himself. The competition injected funds into City coffers and the final attracted 65,000-plus over the two games. Ipswich schemer Colin Viljoen echoed an all-too-popular view when he labelled Norwich 'too negative for my liking', but his criticism failed to sting City into a winning response, and they lost both legs by 1-2.

The Texaco Cup was a bridge too far for a team exhausted by the fight to stay in the top division. The league campaign had concluded at Carrow Road in thrilling fashion, with 36,668 urging the players towards the two points needed for safety. By a twist of fate, opponents that night were Malcolm Allison's Crystal Palace, who would be doomed themselves if the result went Norwich's way. Winger Don Rogers put Palace ahead but a fine late Dave Stringer goal won the contest and decided both clubs' fates. Three wins from the closing five league games had proved enough to save Norwich. Those late-season arrivals (Suggett, Hockey and Mellor) had certainly invigorated an exhausted and anxious team.

Match of the Season 1972-73

Norwich 0 Tottenham 1

League Cup final, 3 March 1973

Norwich's first Wembley appearance involved pre-match build-up on a scale not seen in Norfolk since the 1959 FA Cup run. It must have distracted the players, for the semi-final victory was followed by five straight league defeats. At Wembley, they looked relaxed enough as they strode out behind Ron Saunders, but the big day promptly turned sour thanks to a real anti-climax of a game.

A week earlier Trevor Hockey and Colin Suggett had made their debuts but, as they were cup-tied, Ron Saunders brought back Briggs and Anderson and recalled fit-again Forbes. Trevor Howard, a bit-part player in 1972-73, also squeezed in as substitute – a reward for eight years' service by the little utility man from King's Lynn. His opposite number on the Spurs bench was England cap Ralph Coates, whose big-money move from Burnley was not proving a huge success.

It soon became clear that this was not to be a Wembley classic. Too often play became bogged down in midfield; there were few clear-cut chances and even fewer moments of inspiration. Flair players like Paddon and Spurs' Martin Chivers were subdued and rarely got sight of goal. For the most part, Spurs had the slight edge and City fans puzzled over why their heroes apparently 'froze' on the big day.

Spurs' industrious midfielder John Pratt limped off after a drab first half and was replaced by Coates, with City's Howard getting the nod in place of the quiet Jim Blair. The latter, a rangy forward signed from St Mirren, failed to make an impact at Carrow Road. In a 10-month stay he would make just eleven appearances – two of them in cup finals. The subs helped raise the game a little, and – with 73 minutes on the clock – the deadlock was finally broken.

Chivers, tall and elegant but enigmatic, took a long throw which sailed into a crowded Norwich box. It found Martin Peters and was nodded towards Alan Gilzean. The balding Scot laid it back to big Mike England, but the Welsh skipper missed his kick under challenge from Cross. The ball ran to the edge of the box where Coates, twenty yards out, half-volleyed with the outside of his right boot. Anderson's attempt to block failed and the ball arrowed low into the corner. Coates, his wispy hair flapping wildly in the wind, wheeled away with fist pumping.

Stunned Norwich at last exerted pressure on Pat Jennings' goal. Their best chance fell to skipper Forbes, but his header flew over.

The final whistle came all too soon. It was a miserable trek back up the A11 for thousands of drooping Canaries.

LEAGUE DIVISION 1	**1973-74**
Division 1	22nd (relegated)
League Cup	Semi-finals
FA Cup	3rd round
Texaco Cup	Semi-finals

Inevitably as Norwich's second season at top level approached, noises were made about building on the 'consolidation' of the previous campaign. But there was a shock in store less than 48 hours before the big kick-off when chairman Geoffrey Watling tendered his resignation after nearly seventeen years at the helm.

Watling was the club's longest-serving leader. He'd seen his ambition of Division One football realised in spite of years of mountainous difficulties, illness and occasional heavy criticism. He made way for a very different character in Arthur South, popularly known as 'Citizen South of Norwich'. South was the Labour leader of the City Council and a former Lord Mayor of Norwich. Typically, this straight-talker began his tenure with words of warning aimed at manager Ron Saunders. He predicted some 'sharp talking' between them, as they were two men with 'a hard streak'. Less than three months later their relationship would end in dramatic and very public fashion. Clearly an explosion waiting to happen.

A season of turmoil that saw eleven players make senior debuts, began at Wolves. It was a season when Norwich's world would crumble, so it was rather portentous when the opening day saw a Molineux goal frame collapse on top of City keeper Keelan. It happened as Derek Dougan clipped a shot past Keelan, who chased back to keep the ball out, only to finish in the back of net with the goal collapsing around him. As police, first-aiders and manager Saunders rushed to his aid, it became apparent that not only was Keelan trapped, he was also injured. He was eventually stretchered away to sympathetic applause as groundstaff carried out repairs and the players headed for the dressing rooms. When the players reappeared after a fifteen-minute delay, Keelan was among them and he received a warm ovation from home fans as he returned gingerly to his line.

The game ended in defeat and set the tone for an autumn of discontent. By the time Everton came to Carrow Road in November, only two league games from sixteen had been won and the Canaries were third from bottom. That was a perilous position, for three up and three down had been introduced between the top two divisions. The match was preceded by speculation over Manchester City's alleged interest in Saunders. Both manager and Chairman South issued unconvincing denials on the morning of the game.

Desperate for points, City scored first, but crumbled late in the game and by the end the crowd was voicing its disapproval The final straw came when Saunders sent on substitute Clive Payne – a full-back – in place of striker Paul Cheesley. But the cushions that rained on to the field were nothing compared to what took place in the boardroom after the final whistle.

A bust-up between Messrs South and Saunders led to the manager resigning on the spot and storming out. When tempers cooled later, there was no changing of minds, and Mr South didn't appear to be moving heaven and earth to keep his manager anyway.

Disciplinarian Saunders, a robust and prolific goalscorer in his day, had learned the managerial ropes at Yeovil and Oxford. His emphasis on fitness, workrate and discipline won him few friends, but it had got little Norwich into the top division. Crew-cut and thin-lipped, he didn't suffer fools gladly and wasn't a man for compromise. The acrimonious departure of popular striker Jim Bone in early 1973 was just one example of his lack of subtlety or diplomacy. Local reporter Keith Skipper said few people would grieve Saunders' loss because he was 'a distant figure'.

In the event Saunders left Carrow Road saying there was no chance of Norwich going down as he'd taught them too much for that to happen. Within a week he'd been installed at Manchester City and Mr South was identifying potential replacements.

The admirable South, 59, was one of Norwich's most dedicated public servants. He had led the City Council through eighteen turbulent years and was its youngest councillor and Lord Mayor during a colourful political career. His passion for politics was matched by his passion for football. Locally born, in 1956 he had led a successful public appeal that saved the Canaries from financial ruin. A furrier by trade, he was declared bankrupt following the collapse of his business, after a decline which he blamed on changing attitudes towards fur. He would be knighted in 1974, but for now needed some of the skills acquired in business and politics to steady the managerless Norwich City ship.

John Bond, the bright young manager of AFC Bournemouth, suited the South style far more than dour Saunders, and the East Anglian-born Bond was approached and duly installed. In some ways, Bond mirrored his chairman, being outspoken, flamboyant and positive in everything he did. He was given the go-ahead to bring in fresh blood and within months had recruited four familiar faces from his Bournemouth days – Ted MacDougall, Mel Machin, John Benson and Phil Boyer. He also picked up winger John Sissons and shipped out established stars like Graham Paddon, David Cross and Alan Black.

DID YOU KNOW?

When goalkeeper Bryan Gunn broke his leg at Nottingham Forest in 1995, his hospital nurse turned out to be former international Viv Anderson's mother.

However, results failed to improve and City slumped to the bottom, albeit playing a more attacking style that was welcomed. That style paid dividends in cup ties and City reached the last four of the League Cup, losing narrowly to bogey side Wolves. In the Texaco Cup another run was ended in the semi-finals by Burnley.

When Bond's tall, smartly-suited figure breezed into Carrow Road, hopes had been high that the team would see off the threat of relegation. But Bond had to wait for his tenth league game before securing a win, by which time there was much ground to make up. Shortly after that breakthrough win over QPR, Bond splashed a club record £145,000 on Phil Boyer. The new man's all-action front-running quickly won over the fans and revitalised the attack. The Canaries went through March unbeaten in five games, with a 4-0 hammering of relegation rivals Stoke thrown in for good measure.

Manchester United at home in early April proved a crunch game with both sides facing the drop. An hour of deadlock had passed when United's Lou Macari, looking offside, broke clear to score. From that moment even the most ardent Norwich fan seemed to accept the inevitability of relegation. The axe fell, ironically, on the day City chalked up a win over Burnley. Southampton picked up a point elsewhere and could not be overtaken. Not that it did the Saints much good: they became the first club finishing 20th to be relegated from the top division. Norwich ended up bottom.

Relegation is always a bitter pill, but for Norwich fans there was a sense that better times were around the corner. Bond had transformed public relations at Carrow Road, events such as an 'open night' giving the fans a voice. Bond was proving to be a better communicator than his predecessor and he'd put his money where his mouth was to transform the team. He clearly needed time for his ideas to bed in, but there was reason to believe a new-look attacking Canaries would rise again.

Match of the Season 1973-74

Norwich 1 Liverpool 1

Division 1, 15 December 1973

The first home match under the control of John Bond aroused huge interest and 20,000-plus braved wintry conditions to see how the revitalised Canaries would cope against Bill Shankly's high-flying Liverpool.

Goal machine Ted MacDougall, signed in a swap deal with West Ham involving Graham Paddon, was making his home debut and his former Bournemouth colleagues Mel Machin and John Benson were also pulling on the yellow and green shirt for the first time.

The game, on a snow-covered pitch, started in sensational fashion when 20-year-old Paul Cheesley cracked in a marvellous goal in the first minute. It was his first goal in 23 City appearances and a moment to treasure. From the kick-off, Liverpool had advanced but lost possession and a long Norwich clearance saw defenders struggling in the snow as Cheesley streaked clear. He blasted a thunderous drive past the advancing England keeper Ray Clemence.

After months of gloom, this taste of life under Bond was just what the doctor ordered and the roar that greeted the goal must have travelled many miles down the River Wensum. Unfortunately, the opposition was a side who tended not to panic in such situations and Bill Shankly's men responded positively to the shock. With less than twenty minutes on the clock, Kevin Keegan headed on an Ian Callaghan corner and the slim-line Scot Peter Cormack nipped in to beat Keelan from close range.

The pitch caused both sides foothold problems, but City certainly deserved the point that came their way. New full-back Machin looked stylish, especially in the way he linked with the attack, but poor Benson's debut lasted just 30 minutes before he picked up a hip injury. Skipper Duncan Forbes gave his usual uncompromising display and one physical challenge annoyed lanky striker Alan Waddle to such an extent that when no free-kick was awarded he threw a snowball at referee Derek Nippard in protest. Waddle was booked instead, and likewise Alec Lindsay, who sent Max Briggs tumbling into the snow.

MacDougall showed some neat touches but looked like he might need time for to settle in with new colleagues. His attack partner Colin Suggett got clear late on but couldn't summon a proper shot and Clemence smothered the ball. It was the last clear opportunity, but nothing could dampen the spirits of the home fans whose renditions of *On The Ball City* echoed around the ground as they celebrated the start of a new era.

LEAGUE DIVISION 2	**1974-75**
Division 2	3rd (promoted)
League Cup	Finalists
FA Cup	3rd round
Texaco Cup	Group stage

John Bond's first summer in charge of the Canaries saw him busy in the transfer market and boldly predicting his squad had nothing to fear in their new Second Division surroundings. New arrivals included muscular midfielder Peter Morris from neighbours Ipswich, polished defender Tony Powell from Bournemouth and Plymouth's marauding full-back Colin Sullivan. With the MacDougall-Boyer strike force raring to go, Bond felt his forward line was in good shape. His main concern was the supply line. Having sold winger John Sissons, he soon decided little Steve Grapes wasn't right for the job and by the autumn had imported Ipswich flanker Johnny Miller.

With only one defeat in City's first nineteen league and cup games, a quick return to the top flight looked likely. Phil 'Charlie' Boyer was justifying his big fee with fine displays and was boosted by praise from England boss Don Revie, who said he was the most complete striker he'd seen over the first half of 1974-75. Boyer and MacDougall, working in tandem at their third club (after York and Bournemouth), looked a cut above Second Division standard.

From the outset Bond sought to make City a more attractive side and despite relegation his efforts were warmly applauded in Norfolk. Entertaining football from Ron Saunders' sides only came in small doses, but with Bond in charge there was clearly more than just the result to consider. Did this make him a dreamer? An idealist who would win friends but not trophies? Only time would tell. Bond had created a unit able to turn defence into attack quickly and smoothly. His trust in Stringer and Forbes in central defence looked well placed for now, although both men would be the wrong side of 30 by the end of 1974. New signing Powell could play in defence, but found himself in left midfield. Bond's 4-4-2 formation looked well balanced and capable of achieving things.

After a good start, cracks began to appear with the grey skies of November. Putting aside progress in the League Cup, only one win from a spell of seven league games had Bond scratching his head and looking closely at his midfield engine-room. He introduced Coventry's Mick McGuire in January and McGuire proved to be a consistent performer.

But the final piece in the jigsaw didn't arrive until mid-March – and what a capture it proved to be! Martin Peters, holder of 67

England caps, was snapped up for £50,000 from Spurs, an astonishing bargain as it turned out. At the age of 31, Peters was as slim and fit as ever and his attitude exemplary. His class and know-how gave Norwich the extra quality that turned a decent team into a good one, and over the next five years he would repay his fee many times over. Signing a big-name player past his 'prime' is a risky business, but in Peters' case it was a Bond master-stroke. The two men had been colleagues at West Ham in the 1960s and Bond knew he wasn't signing a 'has-been' lacking motivation. A little piece of Ron Greenwood's Upton Park 'academy' began to flower in the fields of Norfolk.

Bond was proving a strong character and lived up to a reputation established at Bournemouth for being no stranger to controversy. At Dean Court he had pulled PR stunts like changing the club's name from Bournemouth & Boscombe Athletic to 'AFC Bournemouth'. He had no plans to tamper with the Norwich name, but did make it clear he wasn't afraid to make himself unpopular if necessary.

This was illustrated after a disappointing home defeat by Bristol Rovers. The fans vented their frustration by barracking utility player John Benson, a Scot playing at full-back, and demanding he be substituted. Bond was furious, and stubbornly left the sub kicking his heels despite the obvious need for new blood on the pitch. He later warned the fans that barracking was destructive and he would never cave in to pressure from the boo-boys. No doubt grateful for Bond's loyalty, the unprepossessing Benson departed a few weeks later to become player-manager of Bournemouth.

Bond soon made headlines again, when he condemned Leicester forward Keith Weller for a petulant walk-out. The player wanted to quit Filbert Street, but his club refused to grant a transfer. The matter came to a head when Weller came off the pitch at half-time during a match with Ipswich, and promptly left the ground. Bond subsequently wrote to all First and Second Division managers, urging them to blacklist Weller. He urged managers to unite and show they would not be party to that sort of behaviour. Bond said players could destroy a manager far faster than vice versa, and if Weller got his way, there would be nothing to stop other players who fancied a move doing the same thing.

Meanwhile, two polished performers who were enjoying life at Carrow Road were Colin Suggett and Mel Machin. Suggett only missed one match and was voted Player of the Year for classy displays as an attacking midfielder, having been converted to this role from striker by Bond. Machin was used in midfield and at full-back and did a good job in both positions. He stunned Nottingham

Forest with a second-half hat-trick at the County Ground – the first time he had hit an opponents' net in 51 games for Norwich. He wasn't smiling later in the season, though, for a sending-off in a thrilling win over West Brom saw him lose his place in the side.

Three successive defeats in January suggested the League Cup run might be distracting the team from its main objective of achieving promotion. One of these was an embarrassing 2-3 home reverse to York, who scored twice in the first 95 seconds.

This slip came just three days after a wonderful night at Old Trafford, when Manchester United were held 2-2 in the first leg of the League Cup semi-final, thus giving City a fine chance of reaching Wembley.

The second leg arrived a few days after the York debacle and produced a tense 1-0 victory, courtesy of Suggett's diving header and several sensational saves by ever-dependable Kevin Keelan. City fans celebrated long and loud, just as they had earlier when Ipswich were beaten on their own turf in the quarter-final replay, thanks to two Miller goals. Miller had only recently left Ipswich to join City, which seemed to make the win all the sweeter. Ipswich were flying high in Division One at the time and Norwich's gleeful smash-and-grab victory would live long in the memory.

Once the final with Aston Villa was out of the way in early March, Norwich still had eleven games left in the race for promotion. Manchester United and Aston Villa looked safe in the first two spots and the remaining place became a battle between Norwich and Sunderland. The two sides met at Carrow Road in March and a bad-tempered goalless affair saw Boyer and Ron Guthrie sent off after squaring up to each other. Bond pulled a cute trick to avoid losing Boyer to suspension, appealing to a tribunal and thus freeing him to play during the run-in.

City's results were marginally better than Sunderland's as the climax loomed and everything came down to the final Saturday of the season. Sunderland's last match was at Villa, while City entertained lowly Portsmouth and still had a further game to come. A Norwich win and Sunderland defeat would see the Canaries promoted. Nearly 60,000 packed into Villa Park, where two second-half goals floored Sunderland. Meanwhile a much smaller, but no less enthusiastic, crowd roared Norwich to a straightforward 3-0 win. The job was done.

The celebration party continued four days later when Villa came to Carrow Road and 35,999 squeezed inside the ground. With both sides safely promoted, the result was academic – but not for Villa boss Ron Saunders who savoured every minute of Norwich's 1-4 hammering.

DID YOU KNOW?

In 1993, Canaries scout Richard Everson offered a talented youngster from Wales a trial at Carrow Road. It was withdrawn when the player turned out to be female.

Match of the Season 1974-75

Aston Villa 1 Norwich 0

League Cup final, 1 March 1975

Lightning does strike twice. Just ask Norwich fans who witnessed the club's second League Cup final in less than 24 months. If the first, against Tottenham, was an anti-climax, this all-Second Division affair was even more so. After all, nobody expected another mediocre affair, but the only real excitement was limited to a brief flurry near the end. One wry observer said that the highlight of the day was the marching bands. Others voted for John Bond's black velvet suit.

Bond had pledged that his players would not benefit by selling on their allocation of tickets, but insisted nevertheless that they were entitled to perks from advertising and interviews. One thing they didn't walk away with was a set of winners' medals. For Villa boss Ron Saunders it was the third successive year he had guided a team to the final, and he had lost the first two.

The only score was a bizarre effort ten minutes from time. Villa winger Frank Carrodus sped past Powell down the right, but was halted by Forbes at the expense of a corner. Chico Hamilton floated the kick over and Keelan rashly ventured off his line, failing by a country mile to reach the ball. He was beaten by a towering header from Chris Nicholl. The ball was heading goalwards until Machin, standing on the line, flung himself to his right and pushed it around the post. It was a magnificent save, right out of Keelan's book, but left Machin with cramp in his calf and City facing a penalty. Under today's rules, Machin would also have been sent off.

Ray Graydon stepped up, but Keelan guessed correctly and dived to his right to push his waist-high effort against the post. Sadly no Norwich player anticipated a loose ball and Graydon was first to the rebound, controlling it and netting comfortably.

LEAGUE DIVISION 1	**1975-76**
Division 1	10th
League Cup	2nd round
FA Cup	5th round

Summer time and the living is easy. Canaries fans spent the scorching summer of 1975 looking forward to their return to the big time. Some felt the heat had got to manager Bond, however, for he seemed in no hurry to bolster his squad for the challenge ahead. The club was happily splashing out on improving facilities, but not the team. The chairman, these days a be-knighted Sir Arthur South, wanted a stadium befitting a top-flight club. He sanctioned a six-figure sum to be spent on projects such as seating in the South Stand and improvements to the Trowse training ground.

It took the early-season sale of midfielder Doug Livermore to Cardiff to free up cash for the purchase of Nottingham Forest's David Jones, a solid, dependable centre-half whom Bond had worked with during their Bournemouth days. Jones was the seventh ex-Cherries man to come to Norfolk in the twenty months since Bond's arrival. With defensive stalwarts Forbes and Stinger both well into their 30s, Jones looked an astute purchase.

Pre-season results can be notoriously misleading, so nobody was overly worried by Anglo-Scottish Cup defeats by Fulham and Bristol City. Of more concern, however, was the way in which Manchester City brushed the Canaries aside 3-0 on the first day of the league programme. A chance for revenge soon came along when the clubs were paired together in the League Cup. Alas, after 210 minutes of deadlock, a second replay ended in an horrendous 1-6 hammering on a rainy night at Stamford Bridge. After the first tie at Carrow Road, Bond had publicly rubbished the Light Blues' defensive attitude, but he wasn't quite so vocal when six goals flew past Kevin Keelan three weeks later.

The Manchester City disasters aside, Bond seemed happy with life as the season unfolded and Norwich bobbed along between mid-table and eighteenth, rarely looking likely to sink into serious danger. A major reason for his contentment was the form of Ted MacDougall. The 28-year-old Scot had showed he was getting back to his best with seventeen league goals in the promotion season, and now he had a point to prove. His previous Division One experience, after becoming the UK's first half-million pound player, had been largely unproductive. At Manchester United and West Ham he had been an expensive flop, totalling ten goals in 42 games. His reputation as a marksman had been forged earlier at Bournemouth, where his achievements included nine goals in a single FA

Cup-tie. Often regarded as a moody and nomadic character, he now seemed content under Bond's command. Although he already had 150-plus goals to his name, he still desperately craved a high-scoring season in the top division.

Even before the autumn leaves had finished falling it looked like MacDougall would get his wish. In a spell of six games he managed eleven goals, including two hat-tricks, and looked razor-sharp. Alongside him, Phil Boyer worked tirelessly and within months he would gain his first England cap. The pair complemented each other perfectly. Boyer was all energy and bustle, while MacDougall was a wild-eyed predator, lurking dangerously and waiting for his moment. Not for him 90 minutes of running up and down the pitch, chasing possession or putting opponents under pressure. He was there to score goals, nothing else. And no goal this season gave him greater pleasure than the winner he scored against former club West Ham. The gestures he made at the Hammers' bench weren't clever or dignified, but spoke volumes about his intensity and desperation to succeed.

MacDougall would end the campaign with 28 goals all told, but even this wasn't enough to prevent Martin Peters winning City's Player of the Year award. The former England star was a marvellous influence on those around him. In an interview given in 2002 Bond had no hesitation in naming Peters as the best signing he ever made as a manager. Peters oozed quality and chipped in with vital goals. And he wouldn't be the last big name to find his career revitalised by a spot of Norfolk air.

Although long-serving Dave Stringer missed the start of the season with an ankle injury, his No 6 shirt was capably filled by Tony Powell. With his flowing blond locks, Powell didn't cut the same sort of macho figure as craggy Duncan Forbes alongside him. But looks can be deceptive and 'Knocker' Powell loved to get stuck in. Meanwhile, big Forbes may have been in his 35th year, but he was still holding his own. He was at his colourful best in a 5-3 thriller with Aston Villa. Attempting to cope with some nippy opposition, he managed to concede a penalty, made amends by heading one in at the other end, and sported a spectacular bloodied nose for good measure. He will have gone home happy that night.

Even the Villa goal bonanza was usurped by events at Anfield a few weeks later, though, when City's marvellous 3-1 victory ended a run of four successive defeats. The Kop was subdued by a great second-half display, featuring a 25-yard blockbuster from Colin Suggett. Bond was beaming with delight, and had an even bigger smile later on when his side completed a double over West Ham, the club he'd served for more than sixteen years and 400 games.

DID YOU KNOW?

Duncan Forbes spent 33 years with Norwich City: thirteen as a player, seven on the commercial staff, and thirteen as chief scout.

With Norwich steering well clear of the relegation zone for most of the winter, the only serious blot on the landscape was an inglorious FA Cup exit at the hands of Bradford City, who won a fifth round tie at Carrow Road with a late goal. It was only the third time a Fourth Division side has ever reached the last eight. The tie had been twice postponed because of flu at Valley Parade, but it was Norwich who felt unwell after the 87th-minute winning goal. Although unlucky in front of goal that evening, Norwich could reflect that Lady Luck certainly had been on their side earlier, when they overcame Fourth Division Rochdale in the third round. It took three games to see them off, but in a goalless first replay the Spotlanders had hit the woodwork three times.

City fans were jubilant when Arsenal and Spurs were sent back down the A11 smarting from 3-1 defeats. And Carrow Road was rocking again just before Easter, when over 31,000 squeezed in to see local rivals Ipswich beaten by a Martin Peters goal. The biggest crowd of all, however, assembled for the visit of championship-challengers QPR in April, an occasion that would see Norwich exert a major say in the destination of the title.

Finishing tenth represented excellent progress. This squad was clearly better equipped than the bunch who took Norwich up in 1972 and Bond felt they could have done even better with a little more self-confidence. With hindsight, a mid-season break by the sea seems to have been pivotal. It was preceded by four defeats, but followed by that confidence-inspiring win at Anfield.

A stricter disciplinary code imposed by the FA seemed to have an impact at Norwich, for the number of bookings fell dramatically over the course of the season. The episode in March 1975 when Phil Boyer exploited a loophole in the rules in order to delay a ban was one of the factors behind the FA clampdown on foul play.

Match of the Season 1975-76

Norwich 3 QPR 2

Division 1, 17 April 1976

QPR arrived at Carrow Road on the back of a marvellous run of eleven wins and a draw, which had propelled them to the top of the table. They had Liverpool snapping at their heels just a point behind, but knew that three wins from their final three games would clinch their first League title, however the rest fared. For mid-table Norwich the result was of far less importance.

Dave Sexton's Rangers, featuring the brilliant but wayward Stan Bowles, brought a huge following and the turnstiles clicked well past the 30,000 mark. Boosted by the atmosphere and free of pressure to get a result, the Canaries looked lively in the opening half-hour and went ahead through a typical piece of MacDougall poaching. Boyer went up for a Suggett cross, the loose ball falling to full-back Dave Clement who attempted to shepherd it back to keeper Phil Parkes. His touch was indecisive and MacDougall pounced.

Rangers were back on terms just before the interval when a fine Bowles pass saw winger Dave Thomas jink round two defenders before cutting into the box and netting a delightful goal. After this the visitors threatened to take control, until an unlikely figure suddenly intervened.

Veteran midfielder Peter 'Diesel' Morris – no goals in 83 games – stepped forward as a corner was punched clear by Parkes and half-volleyed a magnificent shot that nearly burst the Rangers net. It was a stunning goal and a fitting way for Morris to bid farewell to Carrow Road. This would be his last home game before becoming player-manager of his first club, Mansfield.

Following a nasty flare-up between Powell and Bowles, things got worse for the title-chasers when Boyer nodded home, following a fine crossfield ball from Peters. Rangers pulled one back when Don Givens put Powell under pressure and the City defender hooked the ball into the net instead of the crowd as he had intended.

Desperate late pressure failed to yield a third Rangers goal, and their misery deepened when they discovered Liverpool had won and knocked them off the top after six weeks in pole position. The Londoners bounced back to win their final two games, but Liverpool did likewise and captured the title. It was ironic that John Bond should have a say in depriving Rangers of the championship, for he had been fulsome in his praise of their stylish football and critical of their rivals from Merseyside.

Chapter Two

Marooned in Mid-Table 1976-80

LEAGUE DIVISION 1	**1976-77**
Division 1	16th
League Cup	3rd round
FA Cup	3rd round

A revolving door would have been useful at the players' entrance to Carrow Road in 1976-77. John Bond made up for last year's lack of activity in the transfer market in a big way. Some of the deals he pulled off had Canaries fans catching their breath: who would have expected MacDougall, Forbes and Stringer to be heading for pastures new, for example? And who would have predicted nine players making their City debuts over the season?

Bond's first swoop was upon Second Division Luton, where he picked up 29-year-old John Ryan for £46,000. This tall, attacking full-back was a modern version of Bond himself – but with the bonus of ferocious shooting power. The hot summer of 1976 also saw striker Roger Gibbins arrive on a free from Oxford and several fringe players leave the squad. The transfer activity would step up another gear as the season got under way, Bond constantly juggling his options amid a succession of injuries. First of the walking wounded was midfielder McGuire, who collected a serious Achilles problem playing tennis, which ruled him out for the entire season.

Norwich had relied heavily on the goals of MacDougall for more than two years now, but had to start the season without the Scot, who was serving a suspension for being sent off during a close season tour of Norway. He wasn't replaced for the opening game at Anfield, allowing Bond to play an extra midfielder. The ploy worked to an extent, limiting mighty Liverpool to a 1-0 win. City were a tad more positive for the first home match, against Arsenal, but were beaten again and a few days later sank to the bottom of the table after defeat at West Brom. Players like Davies, Grapes and Gibbins simply didn't look ready for Division One yet, and Bond again turned to the transfer market.

It came as a big shock for the fans when MacDougall was sold to the Second Division FA Cup holders Southampton for a bafflingly small sum of £50,000. The player was said to be keen on the move in order to be near his south-coast business interests. Even so, he had won seven Scotland caps while at Norwich and his departure was puzzling and disappointing to most supporters. Perhaps the drop into Division Two was outweighed in his mind by higher pay and the chance to play alongside Mick Channon and Peter Osgood. MacDougall was quickly replaced at Norwich by the younger and more robust Viv Busby. The former Luton and Fulham front man was a lively performer but had fewer goals to his name than MacDougall and would have to work hard to get the Norwich public on his side.

Next in was Jimmy Neighbour from Tottenham, exactly the type of direct winger the team cried out for and a well-known name to excite the fans. With David Jones established at No 5, old-stagers and fan-favourites Forbes and Stringer were allowed to depart on loan to Torquay and Cambridge respectively. Peters took over the captaincy from Forbes, but Carrow Road without the ebullient Scot around was a very different place. As it turned out, the big man's absence only lasted one month. Torquay conceded thirteen goals during this time, but no doubt Forbes taught their other defenders a thing or two about handling centre-forwards during that period. Stringer's sojourn at Cambridge under Ron Atkinson turned into a permanent move, and he played a major role in their drive towards the Fourth Division title.

As Norwich results slowly picked up after the poor start, Boyer decided to come off the transfer list, but this good news was later offset when the player picked up an injury that would keep him out for nearly half the season. It was one of a catalogue of injuries, the blame for which cannot be put down to heavy fixture commitments. Early exits were made from all three cup competitions, meaning the players rarely had to contend with more than one match per week. Three draws in the Anglo Scottish Cup – against Orient, Chelsea and Fulham – meant goodbye to that competition, and a League Cup exit was suffered at the hands of Aston Villa. Biggest cup flop of all came at Elland Road in the FA Cup when Leeds made the most of sloppy defending to cruise into a 5-1 lead by half-time. The Canaries stemmed the flow after this, but Jimmy Armfield's men were happy to take it easy anyway.

To revitalise things in midfield, Bond recruited ex-England star Peter Osgood for a brief loan spell, but he made little impact. Then came the return of Graham Paddon for £110,000 from West Ham for his second spell at Carrow Road. In only his second game Paddon broke his leg at Sunderland. This awful injury came in a tackle with big Jim Holton, which angered the Norwich bench to such an extent that they sprinted on to the pitch, partly to confront Holton and partly to comfort Paddon.

DID YOU KNOW?

Managers John Bond and Ken Brown both selected their own sons – Kevin and Kenny respectively – for the Norwich right-back No 2 shirt during the 1980s.

The injury crisis had reached such proportions by February that Bond asked for the league game at Ipswich to be postponed. Unsuccessful, his patched-up side were hammered 0-5, with Norfolk-born Trevor Whymark reaping a hat-trick. With all the comings, goings and injuries, it was hardly surprising that results were mixed. In several away games City caved in: the lack of points on their travels ensured a near-permanent berth in the bottom half.

One bright spot was the promise shown by teenager Kevin Reeves, signed from Bournemouth for an initial fee of £50,000 and plunged into the side to replace the injured Boyer. The 19-year-old had mustered twenty goals in two seasons at Dean Court and looked a good investment once he had settled into his new environment. Once he was established in the team, Reeves was partnered by either Gibbins or Busby. The latter did not enjoy the best of luck and blew hot and cold. But occasionally Busby would explode into life: his goal-bursts destroyed Leicester and Coventry.

The manager sprang a surprise in April when he made wholesale changes following a 1-3 loss at Everton. Among those axed was keeper Keelan, dropped for the first time in thirteen years. Signed in 1963 for a bargain £6,500, Keelan had become a Norwich institution. Although he was now 36, he had looked as sharp as ever and some fans wondered if Bond had lost his mind. However, with the team clear of relegation worries, the manager felt the time was right to give the patient Roger Hansbury some valuable experience.

Highlights of the generally indifferent league season were 2-1 victories over Liverpool and Manchester United, particularly as Liverpool were on their way to winning the League title and European Cup, and United had been unbeaten in three months. The catalogue of casualties was a valid excuse for inconsistency, but at Bristol City and Newcastle in particular, the team gave dreadful displays – suggesting weaknesses in mental approach.

Match of the Season 1976-77

Norwich 2 Manchester U 1

Division 1, 2 April 1977

The unsavoury aspect attending a visit by Manchester United in the 1970s was the scale of 'hooligan' trouble that could be expected, not only inside the stadium, but also in the town centre of the home club. On this occasion, Norfolk police were ready for the influx, but struggled to cope with fighting inside Carrow Road which forced hundreds flee to safety on the pitch.

United came to East Anglia on the back of a fifteen-match unbeaten run. Their last defeat had been at Ipswich in early January and this run had shot them from below halfway and into the top six. In addition they had forced their way into the FA Cup semi-finals.

Norwich had conceded a combined eight goals in thumpings at Newcastle and Leeds prior to entertaining Manchester United, yet Bond named an unchanged defence, confident they could rise to the occasion, as they had done a few weeks earlier when Liverpool were vanquished at Carrow Road. Suggett returned after injury and imposed himself on the game early, crashing a shot past Alex Stepney with just seven minutes on the clock. The ball had fallen for him after a skirmish resulting from Peters getting on the end of a Sullivan free-kick.

Tommy Docherty's side were pressed back for much of the first half and young Reeves, with just eleven First Division games under his belt, looked at home in this exalted company. He justified the recent faith shown in him by netting City's crucial second goal after 33 minutes. It was a marvellous move, with Peters supplying Gibbins, whose first-time pass allowed Reeves to cleverly round Martin Buchan before drawing Stepney out and netting with cool efficiency for one so young.

United came out with all guns blazing after the break and twelve minutes after the re-start hauled themselves back into the contest. With Keelan a long way off his line, Powell, under pressure from Stewart Houston, looped a header back over his colleague and into his own net. City had to work hard to stay ahead after this, but everyone played their part – not least winger Neighbour, who tracked back on countless occasions to help a beleaguered defence.

LEAGUE DIVISION 1	**1977-78**
Division 1	13th
League Cup	2nd round
FA Cup	3rd round

Concerns over Norwich City's financial state were eased just before the season started when Phil Boyer left the club for £135,000 to rejoin his former strike partner MacDougall at Southampton. The Saints needed someone to replace the departed Mick Channon and took a chance on 28-year-old 'Charlie', who had spent much of the previous season on the treatment table. At the time this deal was being thrashed out, Norwich were engaged on a pre-season tour of the West Country, where they played friendlies against Exeter, Torquay and Plymouth – scoring just once and conceding nine goals. Canaries fans could have been forgiven for feeling a little pessimistic at this stage about what lay ahead.

Undaunted by such negative indicators, the manager named an attack-minded line-up for the opening match at West Ham, and City roared to an excellent 3-1 win, all the goals, strangely enough, coming from defenders. These points kick-started Norwich's season superbly and over the opening weeks things continued to go reasonably well. After ten matches the Canaries were sixth in the table, just three behind surprise-packet leaders Nottingham Forest. Brian Clough had steered Forest into the top flight by the skin of their teeth a few months earlier and now they were riding high at a pace few expected them to maintain. Clough scoffed at the doubters and subsequently led his team to the title, finishing seven points clear of European champions Liverpool.

Unlike Forest, Norwich failed to build on their early-season momentum. It turned into a campaign of fluctuating fortunes which promised much but yielded little. Results at Carrow Road were generally good, but the away form became a cause for concern. The triumph at Upton Park proved to be the only away win of the entire season – and that amounts to 27 fixtures, if all the cups and pre-season friendlies are included. It wasn't as if Norwich had become a 'soft touch' on their travels, for many games were drawn. Indeed, the total of eighteen league draws, home and away, meant City were by some distance the First Division's draw specialists, to the delight of pools punters across the country. Perhaps it would be more judicious to look at the bigger picture and consider the impressive fact that – despite their away-win phobia – City managed to stay in the top ten from August all the way through to early April. Not bad for a club who couldn't compete with the profligate spending going on around them.

DID YOU KNOW?

England captain David Beckham had a trial with Norwich City. He was eleven years old at the time, but his visit came to nothing.

Norwich City were said to be £250,000 in the red at the start of the season – a substantial amount by 1977 standards – but measures taken by the board and manager over the course of the season saw things stabilised by the spring. However, a disturbing trend was the drop in attendances by an average of 3,000 per match. This was a puzzler. The team was not playing less attractive football than twelve months earlier. Indeed, the conversion of full-back Ryan into an attacking midfielder had given City a potent new dimension. After seven years with Luton, and now nearing his 30th birthday, the likeable Ryan was enjoying a new lease of life. The goals began to flow for him and his raking passes, tremendous work-rate and powerful shooting delighted Canaries fans. He modestly claimed that in midfield he did all the running while the more cultured Peters did all the playing.

Ryan's only real low point of the season came when he fluffed a last-minute penalty kick at Highfield Road that would have given Norwich an improbable 5-5 draw against Coventry over Christmas. Another thrilling goal bonanza was served up at home to champions-elect Nottingham Forest a few weeks later. Enjoying a long unbeaten run, Clough's men cruised into a 3-0 lead, but the Canaries never let their heads drop and thrilled a bumper crowd by clawing their way back to finish on equal terms.

Moving Ryan upfield was a Bond master-stroke. The change happened early in the season and compensated for the disappointing contributions from midfielders Paddon and McGuire, who were plagued by injuries. Aside from Ryan and the ever-green skipper Peters, another two players whose season went particularly well were Jones and Reeves. Both began to make an impact on the international scene, with Reeves called into the England Under-21 squad and Jones winning full Welsh caps.

Bond was more than content with young Reeves' progress. The manager's main problem was identifying the right man to play alongside him in attack. Busby filled this role early on, but he was not what Bond wanted and the player went on the transfer list in the autumn, subsequently moving to Stoke for £50,000 in December. Gibbins got an extended run in the No 9 shirt before he too was sold – for £60,000 to the New England Teamen in the USA. Some of this cash was released for Bond's use, and he took a chance on Keith Robson, an aggressive front-runner who had had many disciplinary problems in his seven years as a pro. Robson was signed from Cardiff, who had put him up for sale after an unseemly punch-up with coach Alan Sealey in the Ninian Park car park.

The full-back role vacated by Ryan was filled by Bond's 20-year-old son Kevin. Although a little raw and awkward in his early appearances, Bond junior clearly had talent. It inevitably took a while before he established himself and won the approval of the home fans who were probably extra critical because of who he was.

As one promising career got under way, another reached its twilight stages. Former skipper Forbes completed ten years with the club and was afforded a testimonial against a side made up of the 1972 promotion heroes. Forbes was then recalled for what looked like a swansong in the final game against West Brom. In comic-book fashion the big man ventured upfield to score a last-minute leveller. Rarely has a Carrow Road goal been more rapturously received.

In all, half-a-dozen players made their Norwich debuts this season, one of them – midfielder Mark Halsey – spoiling his big day by getting sent off. It happened at St James' Park, but ten-man City held out for a point thanks to marvellous goals by Ryan and Reeves. The game was watched by fewer than 8,000, relegation-bound Newcastle's lowest crowd since the 1914-18 war.

For the second successive season Norwich suffered early exits in all cup competitions. Eventual semi-finalists Orient nicked an FA Cup victory at Carrow Road, and their fellow Second Division side Burnley ousted City from the League Cup. The Anglo-Scottish tournament was another flop as far as City were concerned, with draws against Orient and Chelsea, plus defeat by Fulham, curtailing progress beyond the preliminary stages.

Bond could reflect on a reasonable season's work overall, however, despite that discouraging drop in attendances. During the campaign he was the target of mid-table rivals Birmingham City, whose stop-gap manager Sir Alf Ramsey had resigned. The Blues' overtures came to nothing and they subsequently appointed Jim Smith to the job. From a supporter's point of view, Norwich's final position of thirteenth wasn't too disappointing – after all, they had finished higher than Ipswich for the first time in twelve years!

Match of the Season 1977-78

Coventry 5 Norwich 4

Division 1, 27 December 1977

One of the joys of football is that even the most unpromising of fixtures can sometimes throw up a real thriller. A match that will never be forgotten. So it was on this Bank Holiday Tuesday, shortly after Christmas 1977.

Both Coventry and Norwich had fought out tension-packed and exhausting local derbies 24 hours earlier, so defenders had a ready-made excuse for the fact that this match produced nine goals, three penalties and a host of near misses. Fabulous entertainment for a 21,578 crowd who simply could not afford to blink in case they missed something.

Gordon Milne's Coventry were an unpredictable side, eighth in the table that morning. During 1977-78 they seemed to spend weeks in the shadows before emerging with a splendid victory or two, only to go back into their shell again. Opponents never quite knew which Coventry they would encounter on any given day.

The fun started with an early Barry Powell penalty, given after Bond brought down Ian Wallace. After 25 minutes a tremendous overhead kick by Wallace, the goal of a lifetime, increased the home side's lead. The game was then turned on its head by three Norwich goals in just twelve minutes. Terry Yorath chopped down Neighbour to give Ryan his chance from the spot. A superb lob by Reeves dropped over stranded keeper Jim Blyth and then, just before half-time, Reeves sensationally headed Norwich 3-2 ahead from a Neighbour cross.

Ten minutes after the break the Canaries failed to clear a bouncing ball and Mick Gooding stepped in to equalise. Coventry regained the lead nine minutes on when Bobby McDonald rifled a fierce drive past helpless Keelan. City hit back gamely yet again, this time Peters touching home a fine Reeves cross for 4-4. Another tame clearance let Norwich down and they were punished by Ray Graydon putting Coventry ahead ten minutes from time. The thrills and spills continued right to the death, City narrowly failing to make it 5-5 with Peters hitting a post, and Ryan seeing his second penalty of the game superbly saved by Blyth.

LEAGUE DIVISION 1	**1978-79**
Division 1	16th
League Cup	4th round
FA Cup	3rd round

The season following the Argentine World Cup became one of great interest to statistically minded Norwich fans. The Canaries created a club record by drawing 23 of their league games (seven in succession) and didn't win a single away match. By the time the campaign ended, the team was on a run of 41 away trips in Division One without a single victory. Tracking back even further, between August 1976 and May 1979, three whole seasons, City only won three of 63 away fixtures.

John Bond was typically bullish when confronted by these statistics. He said the away results were of no real concern to him, and people should really consider the bigger picture. But the problem seemed to be self-perpetuating, for the longer the run without away success went on, the more the pressure increased on the team. An example was the trip to Everton in March 1979, when a brace of goals from Kevin Reeves put City 2-0 ahead, but they seemed unable to cope with the situation and caved in to late pressure, eventually drawing 2-2.

Twenty-three drawn games and just seven victories over this 42-game season tells its own story. Although City steered well clear of relegation with this record, they would have been in far greater trouble had the three-points-for-a-win system been in operation in 1978-79.

On the positive side, promising young talent emerged onto the first-team scene. Take a bow attacking full-back Ian Davies, tigerish midfielder Peter Mendham, versatile Richard Symonds and target-man Justin Fashanu. Despite the shortage of victories, Bond generally fielded a well-balanced side which was only made to look really inferior by runaway leaders Liverpool. His major headache of the season came after an appalling FA Cup defeat at Leicester, more of which later.

Pre-season saw City tackle two minor competitions with limited success. In the Anglo-Scottish Cup they drew with Orient and Mansfield and lost to Notts County, while in the Willhire Cup they beat Colchester and Cambridge before losing to Ipswich. Elsewhere in the league, enormous interest greeted the summer arrival of Argentines Osvaldo Ardiles and Ricky Villa at Tottenham, Alex Sabella at Sheffield United, and, later in the season, the Dutch duo Arnold Muhren and Frans Thijssen at Ipswich. This new trickle of foreigners into the English game would soon become a flood.

DID YOU KNOW?

After the first three months of the 1993-94 season, Norwich had only scored three goals at home, but had netted 21 away.

With his centre-half, David Jones, a long-term injury victim, Bond signed Orient's Phil Hoadley as replacement. Hoadley had approached the club through his own initiative and this so-called 'D-I-Y transfer' attracted national attention. A tribunal fixed his fee at £110,000, which Bond grumpily felt was much too high. Incidentally, the inactive Jones must have set some sort of record in 1978-79 by managing to get booked during a campaign in which he didn't play a single game! He was cautioned against Ipswich for abusive language from the sidelines.

As ever, money was tight. Offsetting some of the Hoadley fee was £60,000 from Newcastle for Suggett, but funds had to be found to accommodate Martin Chivers, the former Spurs and England striker recruited from Servette in Switzerland. On the income side, the club pocketed £63,000 from a new state-funded grant to develop community-related facilities. The arrival of the ageing but talented Chivers aroused great interest, particularly after he scored on his debut against former club Southampton on the opening day. But the big man's contribution to the cause seemed to dwindle as the weeks went by, not helped by an Achilles injury. Bond signed former Aberdeen striker Davie Robb from Tampa Bay Rowdies in September and he too scored on his debut, only to fade from the scene soon afterwards.

With Bond still preaching a stylish, attacking game, there were plenty of goals (at both ends) through the autumn and City's manager was rewarded with a nine-year contract in November. But soon after this the goals dried up and subsequently an unexpected first-team chance was given to former Barnardo's boy Justin Fashanu, still a month short of his eighteenth birthday. Although he looked raw and unrefined, Fashanu clearly had the strength and commitment to make an impact, and he ended the season with five goals to his credit.

City became the pools punter's favourites for their regular score-draws, accumulating enough points to stay above the relegation zone. Shortly after selling full-back Sullivan to Cardiff in January, Bond found himself with a goalkeeping crisis. Keelan and Baker were both put out for the season by injury – the former breaking his thumb in a 0-6 thrashing at Anfield. It meant an extended run for Roger Hansbury, who fared well and only conceded eighteen goals in seventeen games (Keelan had let in 36 in 22).

Not so lucky was Yugoslav keeper Petar Borota, bought by Chelsea to replace the ageing Peter Bonetti. Borota kept a clean sheet on his debut against Liverpool, but in his second match – at Norwich – he felt the full force of a rampant Fashanu and was carried off after 27 minutes with facial injuries. Tommy Langley went in goal and only conceded one goal – a Peters header – as City won 2-0. Managed by Danny Blanchflower, who had re-entered football after years in journalism, Chelsea spent most of the season in the bottom three and were ultimately relegated.

City were as high as tenth by mid-April, but then dropped six places as the season petered out. The Player of the Year award deservedly went to defender Tony Powell, who was ever-present and had perhaps his best season in a City career encompassing 275 senior games. Powell always gave opposing forwards a good physical battle, but was generally regarded as hard but very fair. He would later leave the club for the USA, where he became an elusive figure. He could not be located in time for the 2002 centenary players' re-union and this, bizarrely, led to rumours in the tabloid press that the Norwich City hard-man was living a secret life as a woman, following a sex-change operation.

Those who scoffed were subsequently proved right when the *Daily Mail* tracked Powell down in Los Angeles, where he was found to be managing a hotel. He was vastly amused to hear the stories of a sex-swap. He admitted he had lost contact with the world of football, but still bought English papers to check Norwich's results.

Match of the Season 1978-79

Leicester 3 Norwich 0

FA Cup, 3rd round, 6 January 1979

This cup-tie is chosen because of its impact on the rest of the season, and the way in which it brought matters to a head at Norwich City. The club had gained a reputation as a 'soft touch' away from home, and this limp display at Filbert Street was simply one surrender too many for furious manager Bond.

He acted decisively to stop the rot and slapped three players on the transfer list: former England striker Chivers, leading scorer Ryan, and crowd favourite Paddon. Bond read the riot act and demanded 'blood and commitment' from his squad in future. He was said by many to have picked the wrong side to face lowly Second Division Leicester – but his uncompromising actions in the aftermath were applauded by his critics.

The match was televised, meaning the whole nation saw Norwich's tame capitulation to a side 23 league places below them. Jock Wallace had problems of his own at Filbert Street and had launched his own revolution by plunging youngsters into the fray. Gary Lineker had debuted for the Foxes a week earlier aged eighteen, and against Norwich Andy Peake made his senior debut at seventeen, while David Buchanan became Leicester's youngest FA Cup player at sixteen years and 197 days. In addition, half-a-dozen of their side were 22 or under, and one was a part-time student.

Bond had only given the City No 9 shirt to Chivers after the player telephoned from London pleading to play, and giving assurances that his Achilles injury was no longer a problem. Sadly he was a massive let-down over the 90 minutes, and Bond publicly accused him of not trying. With hindsight, Bond wished he'd selected the less-talented, but highly motivated Keith Robson.

The Leicester youngsters were orchestrated by experienced Keith Weller. Wearing black tights to combat the cold, Weller oozed quality as he set up Larry May's opener on fifteen minutes and scored a superb solo goal himself nine minutes later. The tie went completely out of lackadaisical Norwich's reach fifteen minutes from time when Derek Henderson swooped for the third.

After the game, Bond was in no mood for flimsy excuses and he announced Chivers' imminent departure, regretting the fact he had allowed the 33-year-old to live and train in London while on Norwich's books. It was all a tad embarrassing for skipper Peters, a former Spurs teammate of Chivers, who had been instrumental in bringing his old pal to the club. Via the local paper, Peters apologised to the fans for the team's awful display, and expressed his sadness at the Chivers situation. Chivers had been a great player in his heyday, but was a mere shadow of his old self in a Norwich shirt. He was offloaded a few weeks later for £15,000 to Brighton, but only made five appearances for the Seagulls before moving on again.

Only once in an eleven-year period had Norwich gone beyond the fourth round of the FA Cup and the players felt the full force of Bond's wrath. He gave young Fashanu a debut the following week and was repaid by a rip-roaring display against West Brom, in which Norwich were unrecognisable from the limp team of seven days earlier.

LEAGUE DIVISION 1	**1979-80**
Division 1	12th
League Cup	Quarter-finals
FA Cup	4th

Even a brash optimist like John Bond couldn't have foreseen the 1979-80 season getting off to such a wonderful start. On the opening day, Norwich's dreadful record of 41 winless away games was blasted out of sight with an emphatic display at Everton's Goodison Park. A week later came victory over Leeds – two goals by his son, Kevin – to see the Canaries top the Football League for the first time ever.

Bond had wheeled and dealed over the summer to give his squad the extra something needed to rise above the mid-table mediocrity of recent seasons. He splashed nearly £200,000 on tried and trusted Hammers John McDowell and Alan Taylor, plucked Roger Brown from Fourth Division obscurity at Bournemouth, and ensured that Keelan and Ryan – on their regular busman's holiday in the USA – would be back for the big kick-off. His transatlantic message to veteran goalkeeper Keelan was effectively an SOS, for Hansbury, now vying to be the first choice, had broken his leg in training.

To balance the books, promising full-back Ian Davies departed for Newcastle, and winger Neighbour joined West Ham. Best news of all for Canaries fans was the club's refusal in August to accept a £1 million bid from Manchester City for striker Kevin Reeves. It was a rare sign that perhaps the club was no longer ready to dispose of its biggest assets whenever a chequebook hove into view.

The 4-2 win at Everton was a launch-pad for an eventful season at Carrow Road. It was the first away win in the league for two years and only marred slightly by an ugly feud between Bond Junior and the home team's Brian Kidd. The incident infuriated Bond Senior, and he was later put on a disrepute charge for ranting to pressmen about Kidd's behaviour. 'I could have throttled Kidd,' was one of his less colourful statements. The FA took a lenient view, perhaps understanding his position as a protective parent as well as manager. The younger Bond would go on to have a fine season, even achieving a feat thought to be unique – scoring for both sides in two successive games.

After seven days basking at the top of the League, City were brought back to earth by Coventry, signalling a period of mixed results. They held their place in the top ten until February, by which time victories had become few and far between. The slide back into mid-table after such a promising start was disappointing, if predictable, particularly as local rivals Ipswich were once again challenging near the top.

The Canaries did have their moments, however. Splendid wins over Nottingham Forest and Brighton, plus a magnificent 3-3 derby thriller with Ipswich had the fans in raptures. The latter was a tense, see-saw contest that remains one of the best-remembered East Anglian derbies of all time. There was further cause for celebration when Reeves won his first full England cap, stepping in for Kevin Keegan against Bulgaria. In addition, keeper Keelan, a month short of his 40th year, passed the all-time club appearance record of Ron Ashman, pulling on the green jersey for his 673rd competitive match. He marked the occasion with a clean sheet at Derby.

A suspension for defender Hoadley gave new signing Roger Brown the chance of a run in the first team. This hefty, blond-haired centre-back from the Midlands was an interesting character. He had only turned professional at the age of 25, after starting a career in industry and was spotted by Bournemouth playing part-time for AP Leamington. He was a strong, brave and single-minded stopper in the Duncan Forbes mould, making up for a lack of pace with aerial power. His stay at Carrow Road would be short and not particularly sweet, for he was sold to Fulham after just eight months and 21 games. At Craven Cottage he would be a big success, however, leading a promotion charge and becoming a big favourite for his up-and-at-'em style. Big things were later predicted for him as a coach, but he would ultimately quit the game in 1988 after an unhappy spell as Colchester manager. At Layer Road he was unable to inspire a side whose previous leader was Mike Walker – more of whom later.

This was a pivotal season for teenage striker John Fashanu, who had burst on the scene in January 1979 and now had to establish himself as a genuine top-flight contender. Nobody doubted his athleticism and ability to unsettle defences, but his temperament and lack of discipline was still a concern. His behaviour against Bristol City, for example, angered the Norwich management – let alone the opposition – coming as it did after an ugly episode in the home match with Aston Villa. That day Fash tangled with wily Allan Evans and was sent off for pole-axing the Scottish defender. Fashanu had been a boxing champion as a schoolboy, and seemed to occasionally feel the need to demonstrate this on the football field. Norwich fans became agitated with Evans, his Villa team-mates and the referee, and keeper Jimmy Rimmer was pelted by coins, leading to both managers appealing for calm. This stormy encounter ended with Denis Mortimer sent off for dissent after City had drawn level with a late penalty.

DID YOU KNOW?

Mike Walker won two Manager of the Month awards in a row. One at Colchester, one at Norwich, with the sack at Layer Road coming in between.

Fashanu failed to find net for long spells over the course of the season, but battled on impressively and did well enough to win England Under-21 recognition. His finest hour – ask any Norwich City fan of a certain age to describe it – was the extraordinary goal he fired into the far corner of Liverpool's net in February. It won him the BBC Goal of the Season award and the game is featured in more detail below.

Another forward who made an impact was Alan Taylor, the 1975 Wembley hero for West Ham, even though he spent some weeks on the injured list with knee trouble. His front-running partner, Kevin Reeves, was the subject of continuing interest from Manchester City and by March Norwich could no longer resist the £1 million offered, and Reeves duly headed to Maine Road. Inevitably, there was dissent among the fans over this, but chairman South explained that money simply had to be raised as gates were now regularly below 20,000.

Bond spent some of the money received from the transfer of Reeves on veteran Ipswich winger Clive Woods, a lifelong Canaries fan who had spent eleven years commuting from his Norwich home to play for the old enemy. It was a treat for Carrow Road fans to have an old-fashioned winger again, and evergreen Woods did not let them down. In fact, his enthusiasm still hadn't waned by 2003, for he could still be found playing in local football at the age of 55.

There was no shortage of cup excitement during 1979-80, with a run to the quarter-finals of the League Cup, plus three intriguing FA Cup ties, to be enjoyed. Gillingham, Manchester United and West Brom were soundly beaten before Liverpool came to Carrow Road and ended City's League Cup ambitions at the quarter-final stage, while in the more senior competition Wolves put the Canaries out after ruthlessly exploiting City's three first-half defensive blunders.

On a sad note, many former players and officials from the club attended the funeral of Terry Anderson in February. The 35-year-old winger, who had accumulated 279 games over a nine-year period for Norwich between 1965 and 1974, was found drowned on a beach near his Great Yarmouth home. A week earlier he had gone missing after setting out on a training run. The exact details of how he met his end will presumably never be known.

Match of the Season 1979-80

Norwich 3 Liverpool 5

Division 1, 9 February 1980

This breathless 90 minutes of scintillating action had everything – except two points for City. The mighty Reds, managed by Bob Paisley, were heading for their fourth league championship in five seasons, but were given a fearful fright in a game packed with goals and near misses.

Martin Peters headed City into a surprise lead in only the second minute and it quickly became clear this would be no ordinary game. Liverpool responded in style to the early shock, scoring twice through David Fairclough before twenty minutes had passed. His second was a gem of a goal, created cleverly by Alan Hansen. Reeves blasted City level again to cap a lively first half.

Kenny Dalglish set up Fairclough for an impressive hat-trick with just fifteen minutes left, but the fighting Canaries simply refused to give in. They equalised again with a wonder goal by Fashanu, a strike so impressive it has been repeated time and again on TV ever since.

With his back to goal, the 18-year-old received a pass 25 yards out from the marauding Ryan, who kept motoring down the flank, no doubt expecting the ball to be laid back to him. Fashanu was tightly marked and seemed to have few other options, but something made him try the unexpected. Instead of using Ryan, he juggled the ball, swivelled and cracked it goalwards – a manoeuvre so outrageous it caught everyone by surprise. However, he caught the dropping ball perfectly with his left foot and it sped goalwards, dipping over the startled Ray Clemence and just under the crossbar. There seemed to be a split-second of disbelieving silence before Carrow Road erupted. The goalscorer reacted to the wall of sound by simply striding towards the centre circle, briefly raising one figure to acknowledge his feat. In such moments are legends made. Has their ever been a better Norwich goal?

Sadly for Norwich, this supreme sequence was not enough to subdue their famously resilient visitors. In the dying moments Jimmy Case and Dalglish pounced expertly to climax an unbelievable 90 minutes of classic action.

Chapter Three

Twice Up, Twice Down, & Success at Wembley: 1980-87

LEAGUE DIVISION 1	**1980-81**
Division 1	20th (relegated)
League Cup	3rd round
FA Cup	4th round

This was to be a season of fascinating twists and turns. It brought a change of manager, controversy, plenty of in-fighting behind the scenes, big-money transfer activity – and, best of all, everything was topped off by the entire season's work being dependent on results of the final day.

The summer of 1980 saw four players depart from Carrow Road. These included the much-admired Martin Peters, who left to become player-manager at Sheffield United. The Blades had finished halfway down the Third Division and had parted company with Harry Haslam. Peters would get off to a winning start at Bramall Lane, but just three victories after Christmas 1980 saw his men relegated to the basement division and he quickly followed in Haslam's footsteps.

Meanwhile, Alan Taylor left Norwich for Vancouver Whitecaps, Doug Lythgoe for Oxford, and David Jones was forced to retire because of injury. With Kevin Keelan now settled in the USA, manager John Bond stuck with Roger Hansbury and Clive Baker as his goalkeepers and the only new face for the big kick-off was former Everton and England striker Joe Royle, now 31, who cost £60,000 from Bristol City. The opening day produced a highly enjoyable 5-1 thrashing of Alan Durban's Stoke City, featuring a fine Justin Fashanu hat-trick. Thereafter came four successive league defeats and Bond plunged into the transfer market to try and stop the rot.

The manager's choice looked to be an exciting one. A club record £300,000 was shelled out for Hadjuk Split's skilful midfielder Drazen Muzinic. With 36 full caps for what was then called Yugoslavia, his credentials were never in doubt, but adjusting to English football proved difficult. He spoke no English and the club recruited an interpreter from the University of East Anglia, who on at least one occasion had to spend 90 minutes on the touchline passing on instructions.

DID YOU KNOW?

Full-back Mark Bowen missed two penalties for Norwich in the 1992-93 season – both after 'delaying tactics' were employed by the opposition.

Muzinic's debut helped terminate the losing run, but it was only temporary relief and by early October City were in the bottom three following a 1-6 thrashing at Middlesbrough. Something clearly had to be done fast, but the subsequent turn of events could not have been predicted. When Norwich took the field at home to Wolves on 11 October, manager Bond was nowhere to be seen. It emerged that earlier in the day Manchester City chairman Peter Swales had made a formal approach for his services. The Maine Road club was without a win all season and even lower in the table than Norwich. Nevertheless, the job was clearly an attractive one for Bond, given the greater resources and fan-base of the Manchester club.

After City earned a scrappy draw with Wolves, events off the field unfolded dramatically over the next few days. There were tense and emotional scenes at Carrow Road and the training ground as the various comings and goings were sorted out. Bond agreed to take over at Maine Road and opted to take coaches Benson and Sainty with him. Unfortunately, Sir Arthur South had been under the impression that assistant manager Ken Brown would be accompanying Bond (as, it seems, was Brown himself at one stage) and the job of Norwich caretaker manager was offered to Benson. South was forced into an embarrassing U-turn and switched his job offer to Brown, who would be assisted by coach Mel Machin.

South and Bond initially appeared on good terms regarding the departure, but the complex events of the final few days saw things turn sour and Bond eventually left under a cloud. It turned into a real soap opera, particularly when Bond's son Kevin – by now team skipper – publicly criticised his chairman for treating dad badly, and vowed never to play for Norwich again. Somehow things were smoothed over and Bond the younger remained in the side. He was put on the transfer list, however, and a lengthy saga unravelled regarding a proposed move to join his father at Maine Road, albeit after a spell in the USA with Seattle Sounders. Kevin finally left the club for £400,000 in February 1980. Defender Powell also left for the USA and Bond's captain's armband passed to Paddon.

Bond the elder would be remembered for his emotional outbursts and explosive temperament, as much as for the good times and attacking flair he brought to Carrow Road. There was speculation over whether he would be a success elsewhere without the calming influence of Ken Brown at this side. Brown was known as one of football's nice guys and, given Bond's later traumas at various clubs, many felt he ought to have taken Brown to Maine Road instead of Benson.

Brown and Machin inspired the Canaries to beat Coventry in the wake of all this fuss, and this was enough for them to be confirmed as the full-time managerial team. Tim Shepherd became the new physio, while former players Livermore and Stringer returned as coaches. Life wasn't easy, but by the turn of the year the new regime managed to scrape together five wins from fifteen league games to keep the club just above the bottom three.

Brown could not quite fathom what to do with the talented but ineffective Muzinic, although he did pull off a coup by recruiting Liverpool reserve centre-half David Watson. Watson debuted in a Boxing Day defeat at Ipswich and never looked back. Things were just starting to look brighter when a double blow in January set off an awful run of results. First came a dreadful display at fellow strugglers Sunderland. Then followed an FA Cup pairing that no one really needed – at Bond's Manchester City, who were improving fast under their new supremo. The tie ended in an humiliating 0-6 thrashing: hugely satisfying for Bond, of course, who was no longer on speaking terms with the likes of Chase and Brown.

Seven defeats in a row left City in serious danger of relegation, despite the sterling efforts of veteran Royle and the emerging Mark Barham. Things turned back City's way when Brown dipped into the transfer market again and came up with three fine signings. Martin O'Neill from Nottingham Forest, Steve Walford from Arsenal and keeper Chris Woods on loan from QPR all added a touch of class and helped inspire a four-match winning run. It would have been enough for safety had City's rivals not started winning too.

O'Neill, an intelligent young man who had studied law at university, insisted on a contract that would allow him to leave if Norwich were relegated. He was certainly no shrinking violet and the fact that he failed to get along with Forest manager Brian Clough undoubtedly helped Norwich sign him. Brown was surprised and pleased that Forest allowed him to leave.

The battle for survival meant unfamiliar pressures on Brown and he showed the strain when snubbing an invitation to speak to the Capital Canaries supporters' club. He told them he wouldn't attend because of 'unconstructive' material they published in their newsletters. It was uncharacteristic and illustrated the tension in the air at the time.

As in most good sagas, the final twist to 1980-81 came on the last page. Would City live to fight another day in the top flight? More than 25,000 headed for the Norwich v Leicester match to find out.

Match of the Season 1980-81

Norwich 2 Leicester 3

Division 1, 2 May 1981

To avoid relegation, the Canaries had to beat already doomed Leicester and hope that either Sunderland or Brighton would fail to win their final matches on the same afternoon. Sunderland had a stiff task at Liverpool, but Brighton's looked easier at home to mid-table Leeds. The other club in danger was Wolves, who had two games left and would drop if Norwich won and they lost both their fixtures.

It was complicated, but the bottom line was that if Norwich lost to Leicester they were definitely down, whatever happened elsewhere. The Canaries were also hampered by a considerably worse goal-difference than their rivals.

The pre-match tonic of Woods and Fashanu passing fitness tests was quickly forgotten when disaster stuck during a tense opening half-hour. City fell two behind to Jock Wallace's carefree side and were suddenly facing a mountain to climb. After twenty minutes, Jim Melrose burst into the Norwich box to force the ball past Woods, and two minutes later shrugged off a Walford challenge to lob a second.

But, just as home fans were thinking about next season's fixture list, nippy Barham went on a run and sent over a fine cross for McGuire to head home. It was helter-skelter stuff, and moments later Steve Lynex had the ball in Norwich's net, only for the effort to be ruled out. Both teams looked vulnerable at the back and it didn't help the Norwich cause when the injured John McDowell failed to reappear for the second half.

Norwich continued to look anxious and ragged at times, but managed to pull themselves level just after the hour mark. Greg Downs made a fine tackle to win possession and released Fashanu, who danced round John O'Neill and Mark Wallington to slot the ball in and bring the house down. Norwich powered forward after this, spurred on by the optimistic crowd. Fashanu missed a great chance when he headed over a Downs cross that was cleverly dummied by Royle.

The moment that ended the fight and hushed the crowd came with twelve minutes remaining. With Norwich throwing men forward, Leicester played the ball into space and Melrose raced forward to complete his hat-trick. It was only the second time Leicester had scored three in a match all season. It was 4.30 on the final day and the season was now well and truly over. It later emerged that even a win would not have been enough, for Brighton and Sunderland both triumphed anyway.

LEAGUE DIVISION 2	**1981-82**
Division 2	3rd (promoted)
League Cup	3rd round
FA Cup	5th round

Relegation from the top flight inevitably led to the departure of key players. Worse, the loss of Martin O'Neill and Justin Fashanu was quickly followed by news of crippling debts, and then an opening day hammering at unglamorous Rotherham. Welcome to the real world, Norwich City.

It was hardly the August that Canaries fans had wished for, and there was more grumbling when the manager replaced young Justin Fashanu with ex-Ipswich front-runner Keith Bertschin. From a footballing point of view he was a useful acquisition – but the partisan fans found it difficult to welcome someone connected to the local enemy. Poor Bertschin, an enthusiastic and hard-running striker, would have to work twice as hard as usual to win over the fans. To his credit, he achieved it.

Fashanu had left for Brian Clough's Nottingham Forest for £1 million, a move that would prove disastrous. Fashanu was a fascinating and ultimately tragic figure. Born in London on a day so foggy the Woolwich ferry was suspended, Fashanu's parents – Pearl and Patrick – were Nigerian immigrants. They parted in the mid-1960s, abandoning little Justin and his younger brother John to the care of Dr Barnardo's neo-gothic orphanage at Barkingside. The lads were later fostered by a middle class couple in the Norfolk village of Shropham. They became local curiosities, the only black people for miles around.

Justin joined the choir at the thirteenth-century local church and became a boxer, fighting his way to national schoolboy finals. At fourteen he signed schoolboy forms with Norwich City, and although he made the first team at seventeen, it was the move to Forest that signalled the start of real pressures in his life. His form dipped under the intolerant Clough and following off-field troubles he was offloaded to Notts County. After selling a story to a tabloid newspaper proclaiming his homosexuality – an unprecedented step by a top British footballer – his nomadic and downwardly spiralling career took him to the USA. In 1998, apparently fleeing criminal allegations, he returned to the UK and took his own life in a London lock-up garage. This tragic decline clearly began in 1981, just as younger brother John was starting out at Carrow Road on a career that would go from strength to strength.

At eighteen, John had a handful of first-team games in the autumn and his physical presence and aerial strength marked him as one for the future. With the older Fashanu gone and Joe Royle injured, Ken Brown knew he needed a couple of new faces to mount a promotion challenge. After failing to land Bolton's Tony Henry, he recruited ex-Manchester City stalwart Willie Donachie from the USA and the nightmare start at Millmoor was soon forgotten when four odd-goal wins were chalked up in September.

Overall it was an up and down autumn, however, and by early December rumours were circulating that Brown's position was under threat. Geoff Hurst, Martin Peters and Mike England were all mentioned as potential replacements. City were languishing in mid-table and the dire financial situation didn't help. After announcing an annual loss of £327,000 the club was forced to lay off seven backroom staff – despite the relatively recent £1 million windfalls for Fashanu and Reeves. It all contributed to unrest at Carrow Road and this eventful season reached a nadir at around 3.15pm on 28 December. City welcomed league leaders Luton to Carrow Road, but after just fourteen minutes' play found themselves 0-3 down. A little dignity was restored in the second half, but the defeat led to a major 'clear the air' meeting at which chairman Sir Arthur South gave Brown a vote of confidence and called for everyone to pull together.

Other troubles included an incident against QPR when the referee was hit by a cigarette lighter thrown from the Barclay End. The incident led to wire fencing being erected, but on sunny days the glare from the mesh blinded spectators and it was soon taken down again. This was also an unhappy time for reigning 'Player of the Year' Joe Royle. A local specialist said his troublesome knee would no longer stand up to regular 90 minutes of football and, after seeking a second opinion in London, the 33-year-old striker accepted the inevitable and announced his retirement. With three children to support, Royle spent a number of worrying weeks in the wilderness before one of many letters received a response – and led to his appointment as manager of Oldham.

With Royle hobbling around miserably, the arrival of forward John Deehan from West Brom, followed by the surprise return of Martin O'Neill from Manchester City, boosted morale at Carrow Road. After exiting the FA Cup in the fifth round at West Brom, and with a dozen league games left, Norwich were still in mid-table, but not completely cut off from the leading contenders. Luton and Watford looked set fair for the top two places, but with a win now worth three points, the third promotion slot might just be attainable if a few victories could be strung together. It looked a long shot, but Deehan was hungry and dangerous in attack and O'Neill in inspirational form. Perhaps Norwich could still do it.

DID YOU KNOW?

Justin Fashanu nearly won BBC Sports Personality of the Year in 1996 after a mass vote by students. BBC bosses spotted the prank in time.

Deehan was signed after an impressive four-goal tally in a friendly with Ipswich. The game was staged at Great Yarmouth at the height of the wintry weather that wrecked the league programme for several weeks. Brown was impressed and recruited Deehan on loan, and after a month made it permanent. He was less fortunate when chasing New Zealander Wynton Ruyfer, despite the help of Norwich MP David Ennals in attempting to secure a work permit. The final piece in the jigsaw, however, was Northern Ireland captain O'Neill, who jumped ship at Manchester City after six unhappy months and returned to Norwich for a cut-price fee.

The other players respected O'Neill for his ability and also learned to be wary of his sharp wit and impressive intellect. They got used to his unusual ways and captain for the season Mick McGuire recalled O'Neill's fascination with reading about crime and murder. Before the crucial 1-0 win at Barnsley, O'Neill apparently urged McGuire to accompany him on a trip to see the Yorkshire Ripper's house, but McGuire preferred to put his feet up at the team's hotel. O'Neill was also an acknowledged expert on the A6 murder case which led to the hanging of James Hanratty.

Triggered by O'Neill's fortunate late winner at Bolton (McGuire reckoned the shot bounced seventeen times before finding the net), Norwich set off on a magnificent run which was only briefly interrupted by defeat at champions-elect Luton. In a matter of a few weeks, the Canaries soared into the top six. With just half-a-dozen games left they were very much the form team and giving those above them the jitters. Promotion back to Division One at the first attempt was no longer a distant dream but a real possibility.

A 4-1 win at Leicester set things up for a tense and thrilling final fortnight. With just one game left – at Sheffield Wednesday – City could reflect on a fantastic run of ten victories from eleven games, an achievement that put them on the brink of promotion.

Match of the Season 1981-82

Sheffield Wednesday 2 Norwich 1

Division 1, 15 May 1982

Nearly 10,000 Norwich supporters headed for Hillsborough on the season's final day, hoping to celebrate promotion back to the top division after a remarkable late run of victories. But had the run come too late?

A point would ensure success. The only way the party could be spoiled would be defeat for City, coupled with Leicester winning their final two games – starting with a home fixture against lowly Shrewsbury on the same afternoon. If Leicester failed to win, then the Canaries would go up, regardless of their own result.

Three months earlier such a climax looked a million miles away as City toiled in mid-table. That gloomy mid-winter scene was now long forgotten and the fans who had barracked Ken Brown and jeered Keith Bertschin had completely changed their tune.

The game was deadlocked until the hour mark, when Andy McCulloch hit the City crossbar and Paul Haylock knocked the ball out for a corner. From Terry Curran's flag-kick, Gary Shelton headed back for McCulloch to nod home and silence the Canary hordes. False information circulated that Leicester were beating Shrewsbury and a sense of desperation crept in as the game entered its final five minutes.

The roller-coaster of emotions turned to joy on 86 minutes when a move started by 'Player of the Year' Greg Downs saw Bertschin steam in to power home a Dave Bennett cross. But with City fans still leaping and dancing, Gary Bannister headed a Mel Sterland cross past Woods at the other end. A marauding Wednesday fan was in the penalty area at the time, but nobody seemed to notice. The goal signalled a pitch invasion by other Owls fans, causing a five-minute stoppage. When the final whistle finally came, there was confusion until it was established that Leicester had only drawn, meaning City were up.

Promotion was remarkable achievement. And how strange that Brown should be celebrating just a year after relegation, while his predecessor John Bond was being hounded out of Manchester City a year after leading his men to Wembley. Promotion had been a narrow squeak and Norwich even benefited from the new system of three points for a win. Had the old rules still been in place, Sheffield Wednesday would have been promoted instead of City.

LEAGUE DIVISION 1	**1982-83**
Division 1	14th
Milk Cup	4th round
FA Cup	Quarter-finals

As the return of top-flight football at Carrow Road loomed in the summer of 1982, Norwich fans enjoyed the sight of their man Martin O'Neill skippering Northern Ireland to some notable triumphs in the World Cup in Spain. He was later awarded an MBE for his efforts.

While O'Neill was toiling under a scorching sun in Madrid, Valencia and Zaragoza, his club was clearing the decks for the challenges ahead. A number of fringe players departed, including Yugoslav Drazen Muzinic. The exodus reduced the wage bill, but no fee was recouped for record-signing Muzinic and continuing financial problems at the club meant there was no cash for Ken Brown to strengthen his side. Inevitably many pundits predicted a season of struggle as the squad clearly lacked depth.

In the hope of raising a few bob, City entered the new Football League Trophy and recorded three comfortable wins in August over Northampton, Peterborough and Mansfield. The competition failed to capture the public's imagination, however, and a combined attendance of less than 6,000 saw the three ties. The stay-aways missed a Ross Jack hat-trick in twenty minutes in the 6-2 win over Posh. Later in the season City were ousted at Lincoln in a match that saw John Deehan sent off.

The serious business got under way with a visit from former boss John Bond and his Manchester City side in August. Anglia TV's Gerry Harrison tried to get Bond and his successor Brown to end their long running personal feud, but the pair refused to be interviewed in the same studio. Bond told viewers that Brown was bitter and twisted over the circumstances of Bond's departure to Manchester, comments which horrified Brown. Bond had managed to stir up trouble again, but this time followed up with a public apology and buried the hatchet after the match with his old pal. One wonders whether he would still have done so had his team not run out 2-1 winners.

Apart from the 5-1 thrashing of a poor Birmingham side, Norwich made an indifferent start to the season and were hampered by injuries to key defender Dave Watson. Mick Walsh arrived on loan from Everton to fill the breach, and later Norwegian Aage Hareide was recruited from Manchester City. Dave Jones was no longer available due to his career-ending injury and a testimonial was staged for him in November.

DID YOU KNOW?

Ipswich sports journalist Dave Allard beat full-back Greg Downs in a dressing room contest to find the best impersonator of Norwich boss John Bond.

In the week prior to Christmas, with City languishing in the bottom three, Brown decided to make changes in a bid to arrest the decline. He axed skipper McGuire and took his chairman's advice by recruiting a famous name who most experts felt was on his last legs. Thirty-four-year-old former England front-runner Mick Channon was contemplating quitting football when Brown's call came. Channon was spending most of his time tending his horses and only training once a week with Third Division Bristol Rovers. He had played a handful of games for The Pirates, mostly as substitute, basically as a favour to their manager Bobby Gould. He was overweight and under-motivated and knew his career was nearly over. But, while many folk were busy doing last-minute Christmas shopping, Channon was taking a phone call asking if he fancied another crack at the First Division. Once he got over the shock, Channon agreed to come to Norwich to discuss a one-month deal to help out the struggling Canaries.

Channon found himself spending most of Christmas Eve crawling in heavy traffic along the A11 between London and Norwich. The unexpected opportunity to play at top level again fired his imagination and even the notoriously slow road into Norfolk could not dim his enthusiasm. Nor did the fact that chairman Sir Arthur South was the man who really wanted him at Norwich, rather than the ambivalent Brown. Although he confessed to being unfit, Channon played matches back to back over the next few days and made major contributions. His month with Norwich would ultimately turn into two-and-a-half happy years – far longer than he, or anyone else, expected. Throughout his stay, Channon remained on a month-to-month contract and never moved to the region, which meant his Mercedes clocked up nearly 200,000 miles and eventually 'blew up', to use Channon's own description.

The Boxing Day fixture at Ipswich ended in memorable victory. City kicked off 21st in the table after six defeats in eight games, while Town were in the top ten. Brown pulled a real surprise by dropping skipper McGuire and replacing him with Peter Mendham. McGuire had been a victim of the Carrow Road boo-boys in recent weeks and would soon be on his way to Barnsley after falling out with Brown. Channon made his debut at Portman Road and a lively opening spell saw Mendham head a Barham cross firmly past Paul Cooper. Later, the same player netted a hit-and-hope volley in off the underside of the bar. Ipswich equalised both goals quickly, but the points went to City thanks to a superb last-minute free-kick from O'Neill. Alan Brazil went close to snatching a third equaliser, but by the final whistle all the smiles were on Canary faces. The following day Channon netted a winning goal against Luton at Carrow Road to complete a marvellous holiday double.

The side now looked in better shape for the battles ahead, but with hindsight it is clear that the real turning point of the campaign came at Coventry in January. In a fourth-round FA Cup tie, the Canaries battled superbly to come back from two down. A few days later the inconsistent league form bottomed out with defeat at Southampton and things improved steadily form then on. The renaissance included an enjoyable fifth-round FA Cup win over Ipswich to take City to the last eight for the first time since 1959. Sadly, Norwich tumbled out in a tense and dramatic quarter-final at Jimmy Melia's Brighton. A hotly disputed Jimmy Case goal did the damage.

In early March, with survival still far from secured, Dennis Van Wijk learned he would be dropped for the home match with Watford. But, on the morning of the game, Aage Hareide fractured his cheekbone in a training session collision with coach Dave Stringer. The downcast Dennis Van Wijk had to be recalled and, inevitably, had a fine game and scored in the 3-0 victory.

An unbeaten run of ten league games during the early spring pushed Norwich clear of the danger zone. One of the quintet of victories in this period came against Sunderland in a game featuring a dreadful injury to visiting keeper Chris Turner. He fractured his skull after colliding with Bertschin and falling badly, and was treated on the field for more than seven minutes before being taken to hospital, where he was kept overnight. Nick Pickering took over in goal, but could not prevent two excellent strikes from Deehan giving City the points.

Events elsewhere were a source of entertainment to Norwich fans. For example, John Bond quit relegation-bound Manchester City, leaving his former Norwich colleague John Benson in charge. And £1 million exports Reeves and Fashanu had troubled times in their new surroundings, managing a paltry seventeen goals between them during 1982-83.

In addition to avoiding the drop, there was further good news when City's directors announced a profit following the huge loss the previous year. And a significant event at the end of the season was the election of businessman Robert Chase to the board. Here was a man who would play a very significant role in the club's affairs over the coming years.

Another boost was victory in the FA Youth Cup, with Everton overcome in the final. The Player of the Year award went to defender Watson, by now strongly tipped for England honours, an achievement which would cost the club £100,000 as part of his transfer agreement, if that were to happen. One man who did debut for England was winger Mark Barham, called up on an end-of-season tour to Australia.

Match of the Season 1982-83

Liverpool 0 Norwich 2

Division 1, 23 April 1983

Norwich gate-crashed a big party at Anfield in superb style. Liverpool, with four games left after this encounter, needed just one point to make absolutely sure of retaining their title and 37,000-plus turned out expecting to see Norwich humbled. Bob Paisley, who before kick-off accepted his 21st Manger of the Month award, had led his side to a run of just one defeat in twenty games, including a Wembley win in the Milk Cup.

Although Ian Rush was out injured, few expected anything other than an emphatic home victory. But Liverpool had not bargained on City goalkeeper Woods having a magnificent game, defying the red invaders time and again. After 52 minutes it was Norwich who took the lead when Barham nipped to the bye-line and rammed over a near-post cross. Bertschin and Mark Lawrenson went to meet it and the ball flew in off the defender for an embarrassing own-goal.

The mighty Reds tried desperately to get back on terms, but after 73 minutes O'Neill picked up a loose ball 35 yards from their goal and moved forward several paces before curling a delightful goal past Bruce Grobbelaar. Even the home fans applauded.

Liverpool continued to throw everything at City, but to no avail. While the action continued at the other end of the pitch, Grobbelaar conducted his own private party and answered Norwich fans taunts by performing handstands and other bizarre antics.

With the three-points-for-a-win system now two seasons old, this result meant Norwich had become the first team ever to take six points off Liverpool in a single season. And despite all Liverpool's furious attacking, it was a richly deserved victory in which the underdogs had looked an accomplished outfit.

LEAGUE DIVISION 1	**1983-84**
Canon Division 1	14th
Milk Cup	Quarter-finals
FA Cup	5th round

Norwich fans could have been forgiven for being just a little concerned as 1983-84 got started. The squad had for some months looked in serious need of strengthening, yet the two major events of the summer at Carrow Road involved the departure of two consistent performers – Martin O'Neill and Steve Walford.

Interest was shown in signing injury-plagued Ipswich defender Kevin Beattie, but eventually Brown settled on former Arsenal stopper Willie Young as Walford's replacement. However, the 32-year-old former Scottish international's stay in Norfolk would be little short of disastrous. A handful of undistinguished displays, various injury problems and disputes with the management led to his contract being terminated within a matter of weeks. His former Arsenal team-mate John Devine was another arrival at Carrow Road, and proved a much shrewder capture. Devine's versatility saw him go on to play in virtually every outfield position over the next two years. An Irish international, Devine gave good service to Norwich, despite being the victim of barracking in some games. He later made the news for his exploits as a musician and for marrying the runner-up in a Miss Universe beauty contest.

Walford, the reliable defensive partner of skipper Watson, left for West Ham for a six-figure fee days before the big kick-off. And O'Neill, by now 31, followed him out of Norfolk a few days later, joining Notts County after a pay dispute. Robert Chase, then a director, recalled these events when he granted a rare interview to O'Neill's biographer, Alex Montgomery, in 2003. He said the directors were discussing the O'Neill situation when the player suddenly burst into the boardroom uninvited. O'Neill issued some polite but firm advice on how to handle his move to Notts County and his remuneration. It seems the stunned meeting was won over by the way articulate O'Neill delivered his case, despite the element of gate-crashing involved. After O'Neill had left, chairman Sir Arthur South apparently commented: 'If only he could play football as well as he can talk.'

Although they picked up rookie striker Robert Rosario from Hillingdon Borough, an 'A' level student at the time, Norwich lacked back-up in the striking department. Reserve forwards Greg Shepherd, Ross Jack and John Fashanu were all shipped out to lower division clubs. Given Fashanu's rise to the top later on, releasing him in 1983 now seems a mistake, but at the time he was very raw and looked a million miles from becoming an England centre-forward. Some might say his emergence as a showbiz celebrity would have been easier to predict at the time. With money tight, Brown and coach Machin had to keep faith with Channon, Bertschin and Deehan as their principal attackers, with pacy but untried youngster Louie Donowa waiting for his chance. With Walford's replacement, Willie Young, clearly not up to the task, Brown tried to sign Derby's Paul Futcher, but the deal fell through.

Highlight of the early weeks was the scintillating comeback from 0-3 down at home to Manchester United, detailed more fully below. A low point was the knee injury to winger Barham, during an entertaining victory over Tottenham, which would keep him out for twelve months. After an indifferent start to their league programme, City clawed their way to mid-table by Christmas. Most of the interest among supporters surrounded the progress in the Milk Cup, however, particularly a fourth-round win at neighbours Ipswich. The winner came from old warhorse Channon, enjoying a new lease of life in Division One at the age of 35.

Channon, a bullish character, won many friends and admirers for his refreshingly straightforward approach to life and football. He didn't suffer fools gladly and gave as good as he got on the field. In a miserable 0-3 home defeat by QPR, mounting frustration led to him committing a badly mistimed tackle on Rangers feisty midfielder Gary Waddock. Channon was sent off for only the second time in his long career and banned for two matches.

And the old-stager suffered more traumas after the turn of the year after City crashed out of the FA Cup at Second Division crisis club Derby County. Although The Rams' 2-1 victory was aided by a hotly disputed penalty, coach Machin felt the players had not applied themselves properly and had let the fans down. He gave the team a heated lecture just before they took the field for the next match, a home fixture with West Ham. Channon objected to the nature and timing of Machin's outburst, and stood up and returned the verbal attack with interest. Hardly the best way to prepare for a vital First Division match, you might think, but City beat The Hammers anyway. In his autobiography, Channon reveals that Machin wanted him sacked after this episode, but the pair eventually cooled down and Channon was generous in his praise of Machin's coaching abilities.

He described Machin as the brains behind the team and the one who 'kicked backsides'. Manager Brown, meanwhile, took the role of nice guy, a popular front man with infectious enthusiasm and an attacking outlook on the game. Channon suspected, however, that Brown was never entirely comfortable with him in the side and he accuses his boss of sometimes being indecisive. Evidence of some unrest behind the scenes, then, but probably no worse than at most clubs.

The mauling by QPR and Channon's red card provided a miserable afternoon for Canaries fans that would only be matched at Carrow Road by the visit of Notts County in March. Although heading for relegation, ex-Canary O'Neill inspired his new team to victory, cashing in on a Greg Downs mistake to fire the winning goal himself.

City departed both cup competitions at the fifth round stage. An early head injury to Watson disrupted things against Aston Villa and Tony Barton's men eased into the semi-finals of the Milk Cup with a 2-0 success at Carrow Road. The cup exits were followed by a mid-season break in Malta, but this blast of sun on their backs didn't bring any sparkle to City performances. Just the reverse, in fact, for they were seventh in the table when they caught the plane out, but after returning slid as low as seventeenth. A 6-1 hammering of Watford – a club record win in the top flight – featured four goals by leading marksman Deehan, but turned out to be the only victory in the final thirteen league games. The table shows that City ultimately avoided the drop by a mere three points.

With three games left they knew that one point would ensure their safety, and it was duly captured in a rather undistinguished home draw with strugglers Birmingham. After silencing the Koppites at Liverpool the previous season, City repeated the feat in the final game of this campaign. Now under Joe Fagan's command, the Merseysiders had already retained the First Division title, but once again found Norwich in party-pooping mood. Devine netted a cracking goal to put City in front and although Ian Rush levelled, Norwich took home a well-earned point.

The Anfield result saw the season end on a happy note and there was further good news when Watson and goalkeeper Woods were called into the England squad for a tour of South America. Behind the contented smiles, however, it was clear the club needed to strengthen the squad. Sir Arthur South publicly agreed with this view and promised to help Brown find the new men he wanted.

Match of the Season 1983-84

Norwich 3 Manchester U 3

Division 1, 1 October 1983

Manchester United's visits to Norfolk often prove tempestuous and incident-packed affairs and this was no exception.

DID YOU KNOW?

In 1974 the ref booked a Sheffield United player for repeatedly rolling the ball 'backwards' at the kick-off. He hadn't realised they were kicking the other way!

The omens were never good for Norwich, with the two sides sitting at opposite ends of the table and City fielding teenage debutant Louie Donowa in attack and emergency loanee Mike Pickering on the bench.

An even contest swung the way of Ron Atkinson's Reds just before the interval. They broke swiftly forward and England midfielder Ray Wilkins, known for his crab-like insistence on passing sideways, chose a more positive route and 'nutmegged' Bennett before finding winger Arthur Graham. Graham swung over a fine cross and there was Norman Whiteside, already an established star at the age of eighteen, to sweep the ball beyond Chris Woods.

United powered further ahead shortly after the break when another Graham cross was thundered into the net by Frank Stapleton. With City rocking on their heels, three minutes later Whiteside tucked home a near-post flick by Paul McGrath. There seemed no way back for the home side.

Midway through the second half, City fans felt a glimmer of hope when the lead was reduced to 1-3, Bennett looping a far-post header over Gary Bailey from Devine's cross. Twelve minutes before the end, United really began to sweat as Norwich pulled another back. A foul by McGrath saw Mendham's curling free-kick headed firmly home by Channon. Now the atmosphere was transformed and Norwich players were all pumping fists and grim determination.

Cometh the hour, cometh the man. Eighteen-year-old Ipswich-born Donowa was making his full debut and fate decreed it would be his name on everyone's lips as this game drew to a thrilling climax. With seconds remaining, Mendham sent a shrewd chip into the danger area, leaving Bailey and his defenders in a flap. In slid Donowa to net the ball from an almost horizontal position. The unflappable young man from an Ipswich council estate found himself hero of the hour and completely buried under celebrating teammates.

LEAGUE DIVISION 1	**1984-85**
Canon Division 1	20th (relegated)
Milk Cup	Winners
FA Cup	4th round

Football is full of highs and lows, and sometimes joy and misery comes in equal measure over the course of a single season. This would become one such season at Carrow Road. Rarely in football have cup winners been relegated in the same season.

Highly rated Gillingham defender Steve Bruce signed for £135,000 but on his high-profile debut on the opening day against Liverpool he netted an own-goal after less than two minutes! He overcame this nightmare start, however, and went on to become Player of the Year. One winger departed and another arrived in August, with Dave Bennett quitting due to knee trouble while promising Yarmouth youngster Dale Gordon was introduced to the side. 'Disco Dale' was a skilled crowd-pleaser who had turned down bigger fish to join his local club.

Ken Brown was happy to give youth a chance and also introduced Jeremy Goss and Mark Farrington, the latter doing well after being warned that his future depended on him cutting out his trademark rough stuff. Results were not particularly promising in the early weeks, however, and 'Dixie' Deehan didn't get off the mark until the seventh game, when he repeated his hat-trick of the previous season at home to Watford. That match featured moronic outbursts of racist abuse against certain visiting players, which led to condemnation in the Norfolk press.

Reliable goalkeeper Chris Woods picked up an injury in the Watford game and was forced to drop out after 171 consecutive games. Brown brought in big Joe Corrigan to cover the loss and soon afterwards swooped for another celebrated veteran in Scottish international Asa Hartford. The tough midfielder – who eleven years previously had landed in trouble for spitting at a Norwich supporter – scored twice on his debut against Preston in the Milk Cup.

Five wins in a seven-match spell lifted City into the top half of the table by Christmas and progress was made into the quarter-finals of the Milk Cup. By now the club was without a main stand after a huge night-time blaze, apparently sparked by an electrical fault. The boardroom, dressing rooms and other important areas were all destroyed. On match days it meant the two teams would have to change in an adjoining public house. Plans were soon in place to rebuild the stand and name it after former chairman Geoffrey Watling.

Naturally the blaze was big news the next morning and when the players assembled at the training ground, discussion centred on the serious problems it would pose the club. But the mood was instantly lightened when joker Deehan arrived, racing into the building in full fireman's uniform, brandishing a watering can.

The run up to Christmas 1984 featured a series of milestones. Victory at Sheffield Wednesday represented the first away win in the league for eleven months and was the Hillsborough club's first home defeat for a similar period. A week earlier evergreen Channon had played his 850th senior game and would soon register his 300th career goal. Channon still had plenty to offer at 36 and, if he was starting to lose pace, he made up for it with physical commitment. In a bad-tempered win over Southampton, Channon went in high and late on former England colleague Peter Shilton and inflicted injuries that would sideline the keeper. It only evened things up, however, for Joe Jordan had also put City skipper Dave Watson on a stretcher with a nasty challenge.

After Christmas, events in the Milk Cup seemed to take priority and after chugging contentedly in mid-table for many weeks City slowly slid down the table. Their final eighteen league games produced just three wins, even though things were going swimmingly in the Milk Cup. A narrow quarter-final victory over Grimsby set up a two-legged semi with local rivals Ipswich. The first tie at Portman Road was nearly a disaster, but an appalling first-half display went largely unpunished and City came in trailing by just one goal. In his autobiography, Channon recalls that the manager then told his troops they should knock the ball around and play their way back into the tie – an opinion the outspoken Channon vehemently disagreed with. Poor Brown was shouted down by the player, who insisted they should shut up shop and keep the score down, so that things could be put right in the second leg. Whether or not this was 'player power' in action, City did indeed tighten up and Ipswich failed to increase their lead. It set up a wonderful night at Carrow Road for the return.

After Deehan's deflected shot levelled the aggregate scores, Bruce stormed into the Ipswich box in the dying moments to net a thundering header and book a Wembley place. Carrow Road erupted and the noise nearly brought down what was left of the charred main stand. What a way to reach Wembley – a dramatic late goal in front of the Barclay end, and against the old enemy, too. Life didn't get much better than this.

The final (see below) prompted a civic reception involving the Lord Mayor, meaning Norwich's subsequent league form really was a case of 'after the Lord Mayor's show'. The final twelve games produced just two wins, one of which was the closing game at rainy Stamford Bridge. That 2-1 victory looked enough to ensure safety as City now had 49 points – eight more than Coventry. However, because of a virus around Easter, the Sky Blues still had three games to play. They could overhaul Norwich and send them down if they won all three. It seemed a lot to ask of Coventry, who were hardly in winning ways. Moreover, their final match was against champions Everton, who had been virtually unbeatable for months and had reached two cup finals. On top of this, Coventry had not achieved three straight wins for several years.

It seemed impossible that Don Mackay's side could suddenly turn on the winning style under such pressure. However, strange things happen in football and Norwich fans began to get fidgety when the Midlanders scraped through 1-0 at bottom club Stoke and then beat David Pleat's in-form Luton by the same score. Two wins under their belt and one to go.

So Norwich's future rested on a game at Highfield Road on a warm Sunday morning at the end of May. Howard Kendall unhelpfully rested four of his championship-winning side and Everton were a pale shadow of their normal selves. Coventry overcame their nerves to storm to a 4-1 win and could have scored many more. With disbelief, Milk Cup winners Norwich faced up to the reality of relegation.

A furious Channon lashed out at the League's staging of key games long after the official end of the season. He said Coventry had the advantage of knowing exactly what they needed for survival and their opposition had been tired and unmotivated. Others clearly agreed, for soon the fixture-makers would create a system whereby all clubs' final games have to be played simultaneously. The bizarre climax to 1984-85 would never be repeated.

To rub salt into their wounds, a few days after relegation Norwich's UEFA Cup place – secured by winning at Wembley – was snatched away. Tragic events in Brussels' Heysel Stadium meant English clubs were now banned from Europe. Norwich appealed to the High Court over this, but the ban was confirmed.

Match of the Season 1984-85

Norwich 1 Sunderland 0

Milk Cup final, 24 March 1985

Norwich City's first Wembley win, at the third time of asking, will be remembered by many as the 'friendly final'. Encouraged by club officials and media attention, the two sets of fans made unprecedented efforts to co-operate and mingle with each other on the big day. The idea had a snowball effect and lasting friendships were forged between the two clubs. A feature of the love-in was a 60-a-side football match between the two clubs' supporters in the Wembley car park.

City were playing on a Sunday and before live TV cameras for the first time and the 100,000 full house paid a record £860,935 to witness the occasion. Both sides had enjoyed thrilling semi-final wins – Sunderland overcoming Chelsea – but both were having a poor season in the league and sliding towards relegation to Division Two.

Norwich's Hartford became the first player to appear in League Cup finals with three different clubs and he would take centre stage just after half-time in the game's pivotal moment. Deehan chased a lost cause and managed to dispossess inexperienced David Corner on the bye-line. He slipped the ball back to Hartford, who cracked a shot goalwards from a tight angle and saw the ball deflect wickedly past keeper Chris Turner off Gordon Chisholm.

Minutes later Dennis Van Wijk needlessly handled and referee Neil Midgley pointed to the spot. But winger Clive Walker had the Sunderland hordes groaning as he stroked the penalty against the outside of the post and City's lead remained intact. The Mackems looked ill-at-ease on the big stage – exactly as Norwich had on their previous Wembley appearances – and the Canaries had little serious difficulty in holding on for a deserved victory.

City's old stagers Hartford and Channon particularly enjoyed the occasion, as did winger Barham, recently returned from a year's injury absence. Channon even made it a family occasion by smuggling his young son, Michael junior, into Wembley's inner sanctum. With Brown's blessing, the lad – clad in Norwich tracksuit – watched the game from the bench and even joined the subsequent lap of honour. Victory celebrations spilled into the next day with the traditional parade and civic reception attracting a huge turnout despite appalling weather.

LEAGUE DIVISION 2	**1985-86**
Canon Division 2	Champions
Milk Cup	4th round
FA Cup	3rd round
Screen Sport Super Cup	Semi-final

As had happened four years earlier, relegation from the top flight inevitably meant a summer of change at Carrow Road. Brown and coach Machin drew up their shopping list and made what would prove to be three excellent captures in striker Kevin Drinkell from Grimsby, Burnley's versatile Mike Phelan, and former Bristol Rovers player-manager David Williams.

Gary Brooke, Ian Culverhouse and Wayne Biggins also arrived, the latter after efforts to sign Reading goal ace Trevor Senior came to nothing. Drinkell, in particular, proved to be money well spent. An affable character, who became fond of Norwich pub life, he was a brave and determined front-runner who maintained the consistent goalscoring that marked his Grimsby days.

The campaign got off to a tentative opening, but a 4-0 victory over Sheffield United in September kick-started things nicely and City muscled into the top four before the end of November. By this time, the club had been making headlines regularly for off-the-field affairs, notably when the board of directors resigned *en bloc* at the height of a row over the building of a new main stand.

The turmoil began in September when director Jimmy Jones quit in protest after the board awarded a £1.5 million contract to a building firm not favoured by Jones. Chairman Sir Arthur South had personal links with this firm, although he had quite correctly withdrawn from the voting because of this. Nevertheless, it emerged that there had been procedural errors at the meeting, apparently involving proxy voting. Although these errors were acknowledged and subsequently corrected, it was enough for Jones – a Yarmouth amusements arcade businessman with a 20 per cent shareholding in the club – to propose a vote of no confidence in the board. This would have come to the boil in December, but in the meantime the board decided discretion was the better part of valour and – after a six-hour Sunday night meeting – decided to quit *en bloc*. An emergency board was put in place to run the club until a new seven-man board could be formally created.

A small core of shareholders then tried to prevent Jones getting back on the new board, but were comfortably outvoted in a secret ballot. The new set-up comprised Messrs Chase (chairman), Abbs, Lockwood, Munby, Paterson, Scholes and Jones. The whole messy saga represented a victory for Jones over Sir Arthur and was viewed by many as more of a personality clash than a dispute purely over the re-building plans. Although Sir Arthur had been a popular club figurehead for many years, many supporters sided with Jones, who declared that his objective had always been to try and prevent money being wasted that could otherwise be used to strengthen the team.

The departure of the old board – in particular Sir Arthur and Geoffrey Watling – was a sad turn of events given this pair's marvellous service and personal contributions to the rise of Norwich City FC over a 30-year period. When Sir Arthur died some years later, the tributes poured in thick and fast. Ken Brown called him 'a legend – the best chairman I ever worked for,' while ex-manager John Bond said he was forthright and ruthless, but would be remembered with fondness. Bond admitted he should never have left Norwich and its father-figure chairman when Manchester City came calling for him in 1980.

The stormy events behind the scenes and the lop-sided appearance of the stadium failed to deflect the team from its objective of a quick return to Division One. With Drinkell knocking in the goals on a regular basis, City were an attack-minded team to be feared and enjoyed a run of ten straight league victories. It commenced on 23 November and was only halted by a late and hotly disputed Barnsley equaliser on the first day of February. The fourth of these ten wins – against Oldham at Boundary Park – saw City go top of the table for the first time. They held on to this position for the rest of the season and never looked remotely like relinquishing it after main rivals Portsmouth were seen off 2-0 in mid-January.

The club record run of ten straight wins featured a stunning 6-1 demolition of Millwall. Four goals were scored in a devastating first-half of attacking football that deservedly won a standing ovation at the break. Another club record fell in February when a 3-0 triumph at Shrewsbury represented the tenth away trip in a row without loss.

It was only a matter of time before promotion was clinched. With six games still to go, a win over Sunderland would have done the trick, but the champagne had to be put back on ice after City let their standards drop and the visitors sneaked away with a 0-0 draw in front of a large and disappointed crowd. Three days later and the required points were in the bag as Norwich became probably the first and only football club to win promotion at a rugby and speedway stadium. After the Valley Parade fire, Bradford City were temporarily playing their home matches at nearby Odsal Stadium and it was here that promotion was clinched with a 2-0 win – albeit in front of a disappointingly low turnout of Canaries fans. A far bigger contingent made their way to Grimsby a fortnight later to celebrate the clinching of the divisional championship.

A memorable season was completed in appropriate fashion when Leeds were hammered 4-0 amid a party atmosphere at Carrow Road on the final Saturday. Sadly, some Leeds fans soured the day by causing problems in the city centre, but the Yorkshire team's defender Brendan Ormsby entered the party spirit by heading a comical own-goal to get the goal-scoring underway.

After the instant promotions of 1975 and 1982, this championship win represented the third time Norwich had bounced straight back after relegation from the top flight. It was an impressive habit that would soon become much harder to achieve due to the changing financial structure of the game in subsequent years.

A feature of the 1985-86 campaign was the staging of the League's new Screen Sports Super Cup, with £254,000 sponsorship from the satellite TV sports channel. It was designed to benefit clubs deprived of income by the European ban, although many observers felt the number of fixtures should be kept to a minimum to help Bobby Robson prepare for the Mexico World Cup. A high number of clubs had pulled out of the Full Members Cup, and crowds in that competition remained low, but the Super Cup managed to attract relatively healthy attendances. Norwich managed to reach the semi-finals by virtue of a win and a defeat against Everton plus two draws with Manchester United. The first leg of the semi-final ended 1-1 against Liverpool in front of 15,000-plus at Carrow Road, but the Anfield side prevailed in the return and eased through to the final.

Match of the Season 1985-86

Norwich 2 Portsmouth 0

Division 2, 18 January 1986

From mid-December onwards it seemed certain that the two main contenders for the Second Division title would be Norwich and Portsmouth. The clash of the two in January at Carrow Road was therefore anticipated with relish.

There was added spice because former Norwich favourite Mick Channon now plied his trade at Fratton Park at the grand old age of 37. Another reason for the Carrow Road faithful to feel antagonistic towards Pompey was the fact that their manager, Alan Ball, had won December's Manager of the Month in controversial style ahead of City's Ken Brown. Pompey had lost twice that month yet City boasted a 100 per cent record. Where was the justice in that?

DID YOU KNOW?

Norwich goalkeeper Kevin Keelan was stretchered off at Molineux in 1973 after the frame of the goal collapsed and trapped him underneath.

Portsmouth, who had a reputation for direct and physical football, welcomed back winger Kevin O'Callaghan and midfield destroyer Mick Kennedy for the big match, but had to make do without injured keeper Alan Knight and suspended defender Billy Gilbert. City took the field unchanged for an eleventh successive game and the contest was a red-hot pulsating affair, watched by an enthralled crowd of 20,000-plus.

Proceedings were conducted at a frenzied pace early on. Culverhouse, enjoying a fruitful first season at Norwich, sent in a thrilling 35-yard volley which almost caught Andy Gosney off his line, but the deputy keeper produced an acrobatic save to turn it away. Paul Wood and Channon were booked as tempers flared and the tricky O'Callaghan constantly looked dangerous until City finally achieved a late and welcome breakthrough. Local product Barham did the honours, smartly volleying in Van Wijk's deep cross, following an error by defender Mick Tait. Nine minutes later the points were made safe when Drinkell netted from close range after Phelan's effort on goal was blocked by Gosney. The win stretched Norwich's lead at the top to five points and broke the previous club record of eight successive wins.

Portsmouth picked themselves up afterwards and continued to battle away in second place, only to crumble in the final run in. They'd been either first or second in the table for the entire season and it was only over the final eight days or so that they slipped out of contention, thanks to a disastrous run of three successive defeats in April. Meanwhile the Canaries were soaring back into the top division alongside Charlton and surprise-packets Wimbledon.

LEAGUE DIVISION 1	**1986-87**
Today Division 1	5th
Littlewoods Cup	4th round
FA Cup	4th round
Full Members Cup	Semi-final

This season would see Norwich City do far more than merely consolidate their newly achieved top-flight status. Despite selling their two most valuable assets during the summer, the ensuing campaign would be one of great progress. The final resting place of fifth was the best in club history and reward for years of work by manager Ken Brown and coach Mel Machin. Fifth would have been good enough for a UEFA Cup place had the ban on English clubs not remained in place.

For a second successive season Drinkell topped the goalscoring charts and was again voted Player of the Year. His haul included a wonderful effort at Newcastle, which involved a solo run of 70 yards before he hit the net. He was ably supported by fast-maturing Robert Rosario and hard-working Wayne Biggins, a new signing from Burnley. Known to all as 'Bertie', Biggins was already well-known in Norfolk after an earlier stint at King's Lynn. Burnley had rescued him from a building site when they needed to replace ex-Canary Kevin Reeves and now he came to Carrow Road full of the enthusiasm of someone grateful for an unexpected opportunity.

Many Canaries fans had approached the new season with trepidation after the loss of star performers Chris Woods and Dave Watson. Woods joined the new Graeme Souness regime at Glasgow Rangers for £600,000 – a British record for a goalkeeper. He debuted for the Ibrox club alongside another expensive import from East Anglia – Ipswich's Terry Butcher – in a game which saw Souness sent off amid a series of ugly punch-ups. Skipper Watson's move to Everton for £1.2 million was a protracted affair only settled 48 hours before the big kick-off.

Brown had a tough task replacing these two major talents. He recruited Trevor Putney from Ipswich in exchange for John Deehan, and signed the Spurs reserve midfielder Ian Crook, plus Sunderland duo David Hodgson and Shaun Elliott. The latter replaced Watson in defence, but former Liverpool star Hodgson had to wait a little longer for his debut. Hodgson was at a crossroads after an unproductive time at Roker Park and was trying to shake off an image as an overweight 'Champagne Charlie'. When Brown gave him a full debut in the Littlewoods Cup-tie with Millwall, he repaid the manager's faith with a hat-trick, scoring with his very first touch and inspiring a 4-1 win. It was the first debut hat-trick by a Norwich player since Laurie Sheffield twenty years earlier. Sadly Hodgson could not reproduce his spectacular early form and was last seen in a first-team shirt in November against Manchester United, leaving the pitch in agony after his back seized up.

The other signings proved wiser investments, particularly Putney and Crook, who coincidentally both started out in non-league football in the same part of Essex. Tenacious midfielder Putney was a reliable cog in the engine room, who manfully shrugged off barracking, presumably prompted by his Ipswich connections. The skilled Crook blossomed after six years of limited opportunities at Tottenham. Another new face was Ian Butterworth from Nottingham Forest who established himself in defence during a late autumn injury crisis.

Woods was initially replaced in goal by inexperienced Graham Benstead, but the manager had his eye on Aberdeen youngster Bryan Gunn, understudy at Pittodrie to Jim Leighton. Although Aberdeen accepted Brown's bid, Dons manager Alex Ferguson would not release the player until Leighton was fully recovered from injury. Gunn eventually arrived in October and once in the side never looked back. It was the start of a long and happy association with Norwich: seventeen years later, in 2003, Gunn was still working for the club and held the civic position of Sheriff of the city. The sale of Gunn was Ferguson's last significant act at Aberdeen before he replaced Ron Atkinson at Manchester United in November 1986.

A big talking point at Norwich was the newly completed Main Stand, which cost £1.7 million and seated 2,700. It was in use at the first game – a dramatic 4-3 win over Southampton – but not officially opened until the Duchess of Kent attended the fixture with Manchester City. Chairman Robert Chase was proud of this turnstile-free edifice and said using it was like a visit to the theatre, only with the stage covered in grass. With the Woods and Watson sales yielding nearly £2 million, many Norwich fans were not so lovingly disposed towards expensive ground improvements. They would have preferred strengthening of the team. Mr Chase would, in the coming years, meet massive opposition to his policy of investing heavily in bricks and mortar ahead of flesh and bones.

City got off to a good start, despite the chopping and changing caused by a glut of injuries. After a goalless draw on Luton's synthetic pitch in October, Norwich rose to top of the league. Sadly this was a short-lived pleasure and a run of two wins in the next ten games brought the Canaries back to earth. Six goals conceded at Liverpool dented confidence during this sticky patch, but proved a temporary blip. Indeed, the Christmas holiday period was fruitful, with a Boxing Day victory over bogey side Nottingham Forest, followed the next day by a 1-0 win at Manchester United – City's first at Old Trafford in sixteen visits. During the Forest game somebody in the crowd uttered a remark that annoyed Brian Clough and the Forest supremo emerged from his dug-out to issue a lengthy diatribe. Witnesses reckoned Clough turned his back on the game for at least two minutes to deliver the admonishment.

There was further controversy a week later when Charlton were visitors. After a late Biggins effort was ruled to have crossed the goal-line, to make it 1-1, incensed Charlton players caused a melee in which referee David Axcell was jostled to the floor. He was carried from the field with concussion, but to Charlton's relief later insisted his fall had not been due to any malicious action.

The three domestic cups brought a mixed bag of results. An embarrassing flop in the FA Cup at Third Division Wigan was counter-balanced by progress in the Full Members' competition. After wins over Coventry, Southampton and Portsmouth, City were mere seconds from Wembley when they took the lead in the 89th minute of the semi-final against Charlton. But, amazingly, Paul Walsh levelled immediately and then Butterworth put through his own goal in extra-time to seal City's fate.

Norwich played some sparkling football after Christmas and established a well-deserved top-six place. Arsenal and Liverpool each led the table for several weeks before being overhauled by a phenomenal late run by Everton. The Toffeemen clinched the title by winning 1-0 at Norwich, and some over-enthusiastic celebrations by their fans caused damage in the new stand.

An excellent season ended on a high note for Norwich with victory at Arsenal, but a blot on the landscape was highly regarded coach Mel Machin packing his bags to become manager of Manchester City. Another man on the move around this time was ex-Canaries boss John Bond. Sacked by Second Division strugglers Birmingham, he admitted he was now considering quitting the game altogether – a mere seven years after he left Norwich in search of greater glories.

Match of the Season 1986-87

Norwich 2 Liverpool 1

Division 1, 11 April 1987

An oft-repeated fact, beloved of TV and radio commentators prior to this game, was that Liverpool never lose when Ian Rush scores. No longer true.

DID YOU KNOW?

Winger Clive Woods, a lifelong Norwich City fan, finally signed for his favourite club at the age of 32. He was still playing locally in 2003 aged 55.

Liverpool, top of the league by a narrow margin from neighbours Everton, had half a dozen fixtures left and could not afford to lose if they were to remain serious title contenders. It looked like being their day when Rush tried a first-time shot eight minutes before the interval and saw the bill skid in off a post. It was his 30th of the season and came after City had posed plenty of problems at the other end.

Bruce Grobbelaar had to be alert to save a Rosario header and an effort by Gordon. Norwich continued to press after the break and were finally rewarded with twenty minutes left. Leading scorer Drinkell showed a touch of class by curling in a delicate and precise cross which was met first time by the effervescent Putney. The former Ipswich man swept the ball home for his first Carrow Road goal and set up a thrilling climax.

Both sides went close as the end drew near, but with two minutes left it was Norwich and not the title-chasers who joyfully snatched a winner. Drinkell picked up the ball on the edge of the Liverpool box and bided his time, moving square across the front of the area before suddenly unleashing a ferocious shot that zipped past a surprised Grobbelaar.

Reds boss Kenny Dalglish, well-known for his miserable post-defeat interviews, was clearly depressed about the outcome, but most observers agreed City deserved the points for their patience and enterprise. Everton crushed West Ham 4-0 the same day, which meant Dalglish's men were off the top spot and the initiative with their neighbours. This was the beginning of the end for Liverpool's title quest.

Chapter Four

The Stringer Years: Holding Their Own 1987-92

LEAGUE DIVISION 1	**1987-88**
Barclays Division 1	14th
Littlewoods Cup	3rd round
FA Cup	3rd round
Simod Cup	Quarter-finals

A season full of promise – there was even fanciful talk of a serious championship challenge – would turn into a stormy nine months during which a new management team had to pull out all the stops to prevent Norwich being relegated.

More or less the same group of players that cruised into the top five the previous season inexplicably found themselves floundering badly just months later. It would take a radical change of personnel and a dramatic post-Christmas revival to halt this Carrow Road slump. Three wins from the first eighteen league games left City in 21st place by the start of December. Things hit rock bottom when they lost at home to fellow strugglers Portsmouth in a dreadful game which prompted the question: Where did it all go wrong?

Long-serving Peter Mendham quit full-time football with a pelvic injury and joined King's Lynn as player-manager, but this was one of very few comings and goings at the start of 1987-88. But the settled squad that had flourished a season earlier just couldn't get it together when the new campaign got under way. The pressure quickly began to build on manager Ken Brown, now working alongside coaches David Williams and Dave Stringer after Machin's departure. Williams himself was tried at sweeper more than once, but the experiment met with little success, notably at Oxford where the home side won 3-0.

Six of Norwich's first seven away games in Division One were lost and a Littlewoods Cup defeat at Second Division Stoke pushed the fans patience to breaking point. A bad start was made in the next away game at fellow-strugglers Charlton. Defensive blunders quickly saw City 0-2 down and the travelling fans decided enough was enough. *En masse*, they began waving white handkerchiefs, a mocking reflection that their team had surrendered once again.

Whether influenced by the fans or not, the board acted immediately after this game and Brown was summoned to a meeting on the

Sunday. He reportedly left this meeting not knowing his fate and turned up the next morning at a press conference called by the board. It seems it was only now – shortly before facing the hungry media pack – that Brown realised he was being shown the door. It seemed an unnecessary ordeal for this popular man as he sat, glum-faced, cameras flashing around him, listening to the announcement of his own sacking.

Predictably this bizarre event sparked a barrage of protest. Even those who wanted a change of manager seemed shocked that Brown had been publicly humiliated in this way. There was admiration for the way he handled the moment, clearly close to tears as he spoke of his love for the club and defended his record.

When the bald facts were considered, it was impossible not to sympathise with Brown. He had overseen the club's first Wembley win and its highest-ever league finish. In partnership with Machin he had assembled Norwich's best-ever side. He reflected ruefully that people seemed to expect even better things now that the club was so well set up. He showed courage and dignity and the whole affair ensured that the many fans already unhappy with chairman Chase now turned on him even more viciously. An intense anti-Chase campaign, that would last several years, began in earnest.

One of Brown's last acts as manager had been appointing Mike Walker as reserve coach, just days after Walker had been surprisingly sacked by Fourth Division table-toppers Colchester. Football management had clearly reached new depths as a precarious and unpredictable way of making a living. So now it was Brown's turn to concentrate on a bit of gardening – but at least he had a reported pay-off of £52,000 to fall back on. Coincidentally, Brown left Norwich under a cloud exactly as John Bond had done seven years earlier, leaving in his wake a son who continued to play in the No 2 shirt after his father's departure. And, in the same manner as Kevin Bond, Kenny Brown junior would subsequently leave Norwich a few months later to link up with dad at a different club.

According to press reports, the Norwich board wanted Machin to return from Manchester City to become the new manager, but Brown's former assistant turned them down. Another potential candidate was Mick Channon, who publicly put his own name forward, saying he'd loved his time at Norwich and would initially work for free to prove his worth. The board ignored this offer and plumped for coach and long-serving defender Stringer as caretaker-boss, with Williams as his senior coach.

Dave Stringer's first few weeks in charge were a living nightmare. Through no fault of his own, he found himself in a sort of no-man's land, with the unpopular chairman on one side, and the hostile, protesting supporters on the other. His first match in charge – a 2-4 home defeat by Arsenal – was dominated by the angry chants of the dissatisfied fans. His second home game – that debacle against Portsmouth – was played out in an even more ugly atmosphere.

But Stringer was made of stern stuff and, knowing the supporters had no grudge against him personally, he slowly turned things round. The critical period was a hectic couple of days in mid-December. Out of the club went popular skipper Steve Bruce – sold for £900,000 to Manchester United – and in came striker Robert Fleck from Rangers and central defender, John O'Neill, from QPR. Fleck cost a club record £580,000 and was an instant hit as he quickly hit the goalscoring trail. O'Neill's start was drastically less successful. A tackle involving ex-Canary John Fashanu, after just 34 minutes of his debut against Wimbledon, caused horrendous damage to his knee, from which he would never recover. His career in tatters, O'Neill would later take legal action over Fashanu's fierce challenge.

Stringer could hardly believe this sort of ill-luck. Nevertheless, things were about to improve and he would be rewarded for his strength of character in the face of adversity. Fleck's first Norwich goal set up victory at Derby and when this was followed two days later by an excellent 3-0 thumping of Chelsea, the board confirmed Stringer as full-time manager. By now the supporters had been won over by the new boss, but they continued their anti-Chase campaign, with some shareholders organising a motion of no confidence in the chairman.

Stringer brought stalwart Duncan Forbes back to Carrow Road as chief scout, and within a few weeks had solved the central defence problem by recruiting Andy Linighan from Oldham for a six-figure fee. A 4-1 drubbing of West Ham on New Year's Day meant Stringer had overseen three victories in just seven days. The revival was well and truly in motion and safety from relegation was all but guaranteed when the Canaries went on a run of just one defeat in ten games.

As City climbed to mid-table by March 1988, coach Williams even took time out to act as Wales' temporary manager, but subsequently gave up this role in order to give Norwich his full attention. A stormy season petered out fairly quietly, although it began to look as if a big clear-out of players was on the cards. At least half-a-dozen first-teamers apparently felt their futures lie elsewhere and the atmosphere of unrest was maintained on the terraces, even though that no-confidence vote in Robert Chase turned into a non-event.

DID YOU KNOW?

Norwich central defender Andy Linighan came from a footballing family. Two brothers, his father and an uncle were all professionals.

Match of the Season 1987-88

Tottenham 1 Norwich 3

Division 1, 12 March 1988

Recent trips to the capital had yielded little success for Norwich, but they blasted any suggestion of a London hoodoo in great style on this visit to White Hart Lane.

It was a stunning success and particularly enjoyed by City's trio of ex-Tottenham players – Culverhouse, Bowen, and Crook. Kevin Drinkell must have been pleased with the outcome, as the home side had reportedly been watching him in advance of bidding for his services. Earlier in the campaign, City had beaten Tottenham 2-1 at Carrow Road, since when both managers – Brown and David Pleat – had been replaced. Since that first meeting in October, Terry Venables had guided Tottenham a few places up the table and today the White Hart Lane faithful expected them to be too strong for Norwich.

However, it was Norwich who drew first blood. Trevor Putney's cross was met by the in-rushing Goss, whose brave flying header soared into the net past Bobby Mimms and left the scorer injured. Belgian Nico Claesen was introduced to pep the Spurs attack but Putney took centre stage again and set up Fleck, who let fly with a left-foot effort that Mimms could only help on its way into the net.

Venables looked on despairingly from the dug-out as his side looked increasingly ragged and dispirited. Fifteen minutes from time Mimms came off his line in a bid to deny the rampant Fleck, but Drinkell pounced on the loose ball and drilled home from twelve yards. The travelling fans were jubilant and hardly noticed as Brian Statham's hopeful shot struck Claesen and deflected in for a late consolation.

After the pre-Christmas misery and turmoil, things were now looking far healthier at Norwich and this victory – a week after a 1-0 success over title-chasing Manchester United – left the club in a safe-looking fourteenth place with ten games to go.

Linighan was shaping up well as replacement for the departed skipper Bruce and the strike partnership of Drinkell and new-boy Fleck looked potent. On the field there was now genuine reason for optimism again, despite the dissatisfaction over other matters.

LEAGUE DIVISION 1	**1988-89**
Barclays Division 1	4th
Littlewoods Cup	3rd round
FA Cup	Semi-finals
Simod Cup	2nd round

Norwich had relied heavily on the goals of Kevin Drinkell for three years now, so his close-season departure to Glasgow Rangers was not welcome news in the pubs and clubs of Norfolk. He was one of half a dozen players to leave in the summer as Dave Stringer prepared for his first full season by trimming the squad.

The cash raised from his sales was spent on three new faces. Welsh striker Malcolm Allen arrived from Watford and midfielder Paul Cook from Wigan for relatively modest fees, while Southampton midfielder Andy Townsend signed for £300,000. Hard-running Luton forward David Oldfield turned down a £500,000 move to Carrow Road, leaving many Canaries fans worried that their squad might be short of fire-power.

There were no complaints, however, after the team roared off to a magnificent start, with four successive wins representing the club's best start to a season and hoisting them to the top of the league by mid-September. Stringer, with David Williams now his official right-hand man, won the Manager of the Month award for September and surprised the doubters and cynics by keeping his team at, or near, the top of the table well beyond Christmas.

City's success was based on superb away form. The team won all their opening six away games and demolished the club's reputation of being a soft touch on their travels. But, despite this fine run, Stringer and Williams weren't completely happy with their strike force. Allen was in and out of the side and the Fleck-Rosario partnership never quite established itself as a long-term proposition.

In November, there was the unexpected sight of much-travelled Alan Taylor returning to first-team action at the grand old age of 35. Taylor owned land at nearby Trowse and wanted to settle in an area he loved. He had been released by Bury and asked to train with Norwich to keep himself fit. Eventually he was asked to play for the reserves and impressed Stringer so much that he gave him a monthly contract and called him up for first-team duty.

Taylor's return to the big time was, predictably, a short and sweet affair and he was never going to be the long-term partner for fiery Robert Fleck in attack. Fleck's first full season in the side saw him establish himself firmly as a crowd favourite, his mischievous ways and ability to play to the gallery forming an irresistible alliance with his goalscoring talents.

DID YOU KNOW?

Ipswich cried 'foul' in 2003 when a tannoy announcement was made at Carrow Road, just as one of their players broke clear on Norwich's goal.

Another facet of Robert Fleck was his notorious off-field exploits. Although some of the stories may be apocryphal, Fleck certainly got into a number of scrapes on account of his taste for the high life. Indeed, he had joined Norwich shortly after incurring a substantial fine for a fracas with fellow Glasgow Rangers players in an Airdrie bar. Newspapers would later reveal how he had allegedly left a trail of debts behind in Scotland, at a time when he was living it up in his new East Anglian surroundings. There were lurid tabloid tales of maintenance payment disputes and mounting debts. It subsequently emerged that Norwich City took hold of the situation by loaning him funds and directing a proportion of his wages directly towards his creditors. With a nice line in understatement, Fleck's solicitor suggested that this 'lovable rogue' was perhaps not a financially astute person.

For his part, Fleck revelled in being a big name in the English First Division and spoke openly of how he had failed to get on with Rangers manager Graeme Souness. The Ibrox club's former Canaries keeper Chris Woods had 'sold' Norwich to Fleck, and the move to a completely alien environment subsequently changed his life. By 2003, some sixteen years after abandoning Glasgow, a mellowed Fleck could be found happily settled in the region.

While Fleck was grabbing most of the headlines as Norwich forged onwards at the top of the table, Andy Townsend was establishing himself as a star performer alongside the unfussy and reliable Mike Phelan. Townsend really looked the part and proved to be a shrewd purchase. Before joining Southampton, Townsend had been a computer operator, playing part-time with Weymouth. His office phone rang one day and, to his astonishment, Lawrie McMenemy was at the other end, offering him the chance of a new career. He grabbed it with both hands and now, in the autumn of 1988, was having the time of his life. People really began to sit up and take notice when he grabbed a superb late winner at Old Trafford in a game City had been losing until the 84th minute.

To many observers' surprise, City's early season promise was maintained, and by early April, with around 40 league and cup games under their belt, they were still in with a chance of a 'double'. It was stirring stuff for the supporters, who knew that whatever happened in the home straight, this would go down as a season never to be forgotten. League victories at Manchester United and Liverpool, and a thrilling FA Cup run, would live long in the memory.

Norwich were top of the table after the final whistle on no fewer than fourteen different occasions, and were never lower than second between 10 September and 1 April. In March, Stringer attempted to pep the attack by signing Dean Coney from QPR for £350,000. Coney worked hard but struggled to win the approval of the hard-to-please fans. The manager had earlier shown an interest in promising youngster Alan Shearer of Southampton, but sadly for Norwich this came to nothing!

The championship dream only began to fade after a home defeat by Liverpool on April Fool's Day. City could justifiably point to tiredness, for this was their fifth big match in just fifteen days. The bubble seemed to burst that afternoon and then defeat in the following two games all but killed the title hopes. With four games to go, a 0-5 hammering at Arsenal – the worst loss in eight years – was the final nail in the coffin.

The exciting FA Cup run featured a club record 8-0 thumping of non-league Sutton, in which Allen scored four and Fleck three, plus rousing Carrow Road wins over Sheffield United and West Ham. The dream came to an end on a day of tragedy in mid-April, described more fully below.

Despite the disappointments of the closing weeks, it was a marvellous season overall, and the finishing place of fourth was a best ever. Townsend and Phelan had been superb in midfield and both deserved their international call-ups. It was not all good news, however, for defender John O'Neill had to absorb the news that he would never play again following that tackle by Wimbledon's John Fashanu in December 1987. He made plans to open a health club and restaurant in his native Derry. The tackle had snapped all the tendons in his knee and severed a nerve which made his foot all but useless, leaving him with a permanent limp.

Match of the Season 1988-89

Everton 1 Norwich 0

FA Cup, semi-final, 15 April 1989

Norwich's bid to appear in an FA Cup final for the first time took a serious knock before a ball had even been kicked. News came through on the eve of the game that leading scorer Fleck's father had died suddenly aged only 44, and the player immediately withdrew from the squad to join his bereaved family. The next setback came when key schemer Phelan failed a fitness test on a hamstring.

Nevertheless, it was a noisy and optimistic army of 20,000-plus Norwich fans who made their way along the M6 to Villa Park to tackle an Everton side eight places below them in the table. More than 10,000 City fans filled the famous Holte End, and the bright yellow inflatable Canaries and other paraphernalia made a remarkable sight and helped create a unique semi-final atmosphere.

As a tense and scrappy game got under way, news began filtering through of events at the other semi-final between Liverpool and Nottingham Forest at Hillsborough. What at first sounded like a tiresome outbreak of crowd trouble unfolded into British football's worst tragedy. The match was abandoned and 96 people lost their lives due to the crush at the Leppings Lane End. City players revealed afterwards that they knew nothing of the tragedy until their game had finished, but this was not the case among the crowd and it certainly had an effect on the general atmosphere. Many Everton fans and staff had friends and relatives at the other game and City squad member Paul Cook was another Scouser who spent a worrying time listening to the awful news unfolding.

The pivotal moment in the Villa Park game came on 26 minutes when a cross was arrowed into the Norwich box towards Kevin Sheedy. Ian Crook, attempting to clear, deflected a spinning ball onto his own crossbar. As City fans held their breath, it dropped on the goal-line and was poked over the line at the second attempt by little Pat Nevin.

A Townsend shot and a Linighan header went close as City tried to fight back. Allen saw an overhead kick gathered by Neville Southall. City engineered some promising moves but lacked genuine penetration. After Gunn made a great save from Tony Cottee to keep the game alive, a last-minute effort by Crook was deflected wide.

Norwich's gloom at the final whistle was soon put into perspective when news of the Hillsborough situation unfolded fully. Everton's celebrations were quickly cut short. In the aftermath of this dreadful day, chairman Robert Chase called on the authorities to allow Norwich to remove the 'cage' in front of the Barclay Stand.

LEAGUE DIVISION 1	**1989-90**
Barclays Division 1	10th
Littlewoods Cup	3rd round
FA Cup	4th round
Zenith-Data Systems Cup	3rd round

Not for the first time, the pre-season transfer activity at Carrow Road left Canaries fans disappointed rather than optimistic about the upcoming season. This time the reason was the departure of skipper Mike Phelan, who joined Manchester United for £750,000 having just led City to their best-ever league finish.

His replacement was Coventry's David Phillips, a year younger than Phelan, a dead-ball expert and possessor of a fierce shot. In addition, Tim Sherwood, a skilful young midfielder, arrived from Watford, and Colchester goalkeeper Mark Walton was signed as cover for Gunn. The other deal involved Trevor Putney departing for Middlesbrough, meaning the books showed a net profit of around £250,000 on pre-season business.

Manager Stringer hoped to repeat the fine start of the previous season. His wish was granted, with the side remaining unbeaten in the first eleven league and cup games. A club record was set when the defence kept a clean sheet on the first five away trips. A sparkling memory from this period came at Old Trafford, Phelan's new stamping ground. United had £2.3 million Gary Pallister making his debut and Stringer decided to give the new boy a tall, awkward opponent by selecting Rosario in place of Coney. Just before the break Townsend's pass was headed on by Fleck for Gordon to burst through and slot past Jim Leighton. Twelve minutes from time, Crook's through ball saw Rosario skip past Pallister, only to be hauled down by the world's most expensive defender. Fleck drove the penalty into the corner and a famous victory was complete.

There was even more excitement a week later when Southampton came to Carrow Road for a real thriller which featured eight top-quality goals for the fans to enjoy. After Paul Rideout had put the Saints ahead, Rosario let rip with a 30-yard dipping volley that gave Tim Flowers no earthly chance. Not only was it Rosario's first in ten months, it would later win ITV's goal of the season award. It set the tone for a marvellous game that ebbed and flowed and ended as a breathless 4-4 draw.

Strangely the goals always seemed to dry up whenever City took on Liverpool, however, and this was again the case the following week. At Anfield the sides chalked up their fifth goalless draw in seven meetings – with the other two games having ended 1-0. One man delighted with this state of affairs was Bryan Gunn, whose record for clean sheets against the mighty Liverpool was second to none.

While City were chasing a place in the top three of the table, chairman Robert Chase had his eyes on the prestigious role of President of the Football League. He missed out, however, coming last in a contest between four candidates: Bill Fox of Blackburn got the job.

City's unbeaten run came to an end in October on the synthetic surface at Luton's Kenilworth Road. Fox, Allen and Goss made their first league appearances of the season on the plastic, but City stumbled to a 1-4 defeat by the nimble-footed Hatters. This result seemed to shake Norwich's confidence and saw them embark on a run of six games in which only one win was recorded. This spell included the controversial 3-4 defeat at Arsenal, covered in detail below.

Danish Under-21 international forward Henrik Mortensen joined the club from Aarhus for a hefty £360,000 in October. He needed to be patient, for his league debut was delayed for more than eight weeks – and when he did get a chance he was unable to pin down a regular spot. Another forward whose patience was tested was Coney, who found himself a target of the Carrow Road boo-boys. This was presumably due to his lack of goals rather than any lack of effort. It seemed harsh as Coney seldom wasted a pass and was a good target man. Later in the season he decided enough was enough and asked for a transfer, saying the fans 'had it in for him'. Stringer was furious over the treatment Coney received.

Stringer must have also found food for thought in the goings-on elsewhere involving ex-Norwich colleagues. Up at Barnsley, Mel Machin was sacked in late November, a few weeks later John Bond found himself out of work, and then Ken Brown parted company with Plymouth. Bond seemed in a very unhappy frame of mind and confessed he had become disillusioned with football and wished he had never left Norwich. Living in an apartment in the stockbroker belt of Cheshire, Bond admitted he was happy to be out of the management game. His spells at Burnley, Swansea and Birmingham had been little short of disastrous and, apart from brief success at Manchester City, he had never repeated the achievements of his Bournemouth and Norwich eras.

For the second successive season, a slow decline in Norwich's results set in after Christmas. Only three league games out of eighteen had been lost before Yuletide, but once the players had got their plum pudding out of the way they were beaten eight times in twenty matches. The club finished up in a highly respectable, yet rather disappointing, tenth place. Having finished fourth a year previously, Canaries supporters now had high expectations and few were happy with the outcome of 1989-90. City were evidently still a long way short of establishing themselves as one of the really big guns.

Among the playing successes of the season was Mark Bowen, an overlapping left-sided player whose sorties forward and powerful shooting became a key weapon in the City armoury. Keeper Bryan Gunn enjoyed another excellent campaign, too, although he sparked a strange sequence of events one evening in April when his wife went into labour earlier than expected. Hubby was away with the City party in the West Midlands, but understandably he dashed home when he heard the news of his wife's condition. City were playing Aston Villa the next day and an SOS went out for reserve keeper Walton to get himself up the M6. Walton had played for the reserves that evening and went home to bed unaware of the fuss going on miles away in the West Midlands. Nobody in the Norwich party had Walton's phone number and eventually the police had to be asked to locate him. An officer duly made a night-time trip to his home and awakened him with the news. Walton drove to Birmingham very early the next morning and made a busy debut in a 3-3 thriller.

Within a few weeks of the season ending, City's most valuable assets – Townsend and Linighan – were sold to Chelsea and Arsenal, respectively, for £1.2 million each. The money was too good to turn down, of course, but many Norwich fans were becoming sick and tired of the club's inability to hang on to its best players. Were they right to think City lacked genuine ambition, or was this a case of economic realities having to take priority?

Match of the Season 1989-90

Arsenal 4 Norwich 3

Division 1, 4 November 1989

Norwich arrived at Highbury keen to banish memories of a 0-5 humiliation on this ground six months earlier. Within twenty minutes their prospects were looking bright after Allen nodded home a Gordon corner. Both sides then had a goal disallowed before Phillips curled a precision free-kick past John Lukic on the half-hour, after the lively Allen had been brought down.

But the two-goal lead disappeared shortly after the interval, thanks to Niall Quinn's first goal of the season and a disputed spot-kick from virgin penalty-taker Lee Dixon. It came from a debatable handball decision against defensive rock Linighan.

DID YOU KNOW?

Malcolm Allen was Norwich's top FA Cup scorer of the 1980s – even though his seven goals all came in the same season.

With less than fifteen minutes to go, a Gordon corner was met by a powerful Linighan header which was parried by Lukic. Sherwood, who had replaced the injured Townsend, blasted home from an acute angle. The Gunners quickly squared things again when David O'Leary, making a record-breaking 622nd appearance, knocked in only his ninth club goal following a Nigel Winterburn free-kick.

The action was breathless and moments after Phillips had gone agonisingly close to a fourth Norwich goal, referee George Tyson gave a second dubious penalty against the disbelieving visitors in the last minute. Michael Thomas seemed to back into Butterworth, knocking him over and then apparently stumbling over his legs. It looked an outrageous injustice. Dixon's second penalty of the day was brilliantly saved by Gunn, but after a scramble Dixon forced the rebound in. A tangle of bodies in the goalmouth were pushing and shoving and it quickly developed into a full-blown wrestling match. Some Arsenal players who had been celebrating their winning goal many yards away decided to sprint across and join in. In no time there were fully 21 players involved.

It was an ugly scene, captured in colour close-up by the TV cameras, and both clubs inevitably found themselves reported to the FA. An inquiry would later fine Norwich £50,000 and Arsenal £20,000 for the episode, which again gave vent to feelings of injustice in the City camp. Although Bowen had appeared to 'help' Alan Smith into the net to spark the whole thing off, many Arsenal players had piled in from some distance away, which seemed totally unnecessary. David Cuffley of the *Eastern Football News* suggested Norwich had been harshly dealt with and pointed out that their fine was 22 times greater than the one received by Portsmouth in 1987 for a tally of 64 yellow cards, six red cards, two players arrested and another jailed!

The only people happy about the whole episode were reportedly Norwich shirt sponsors Asics, who were delighted by the coverage their logo received as a result of all the TV close-ups.

LEAGUE DIVISION 1	**1990-91**
Barclays Division 1	15th
Rumbelows Cup	3rd round
FA Cup	Quarter-finals
Zenith-Data Systems Cup	Area finalist

The ban on English clubs competing in Europe was now lifted, giving Norwich City a realistic target to aim at, following successive top-ten finishes in Division One. The introduction of a new 'get-tough' policy on professional fouls was another important feature of the new campaign.

The massive task of replacing the two Andys – Linighan and Townsend – occupied the mind of manager Dave Stringer over the summer. His answer was to spend more than £1 million on a trio of defenders: Tottenham's John Polston, Derby's Paul Blades, and Chester's Colin Woodthorpe.

Norwich could still be counted upon to play attractive football, but would they have enough consistency and steel about them this year? Lingering doubts were to prove justified early on in the season. Convincing defeats by teams like Crystal Palace and Luton upset the Canaries faithful, although things did seem to be improving when a sweeper system was abandoned.

However, all the discontent came to a head in early December when Wimbledon romped into a four-goal lead at Carrow Road after less than half-an-hour's play. Norwich's flimsy resistance was brushed aside by the notoriously physical Dons and after ex-Canary John Fashanu netted the fourth goal, a large section of the Barclay End staged an unprecedented sit-down protest in response. It was an extraordinary sight. Some harsh words from Stringer and Williams saw City tighten up after half-time to prevent any further damage. The team even pulled together sufficiently to win the subsequent three games, but this would to prove be something of false dawn.

Comprehensive defeats over the Christmas period by Manchester United and Coventry halted the mini-revival and the scars from the Wimbledon mauling were cruelly re-opened when Nottingham Forest smashed six goals at Carrow Road in the opening game of 1991. City had become one of the most unpredictable sides in the division. They scraped together enough points to bob around the halfway point for much of the season, but couldn't shake off a habit of looking vulnerable and short on confidence when things didn't go their way.

Four successive clean sheets in the early spring was encouraging, but the spell was broken when former skipper Steve Bruce returned to Carrow Road with Manchester United and hit the net twice in inflicting a 3-0 defeat. United's visit signalled the start of the final quarter of the season, and City sill required nearly 30 points to have any chance of qualifying for Europe. It was a task way beyond them, of course, and their final record showed just two victories from the last eleven games – one of these against a weakened Spurs side preparing for the FA Cup final.

The manner in which the season fizzled out perplexed Stringer. He and assistant Williams knew a lot of hard thinking would need to be done to inject some new sparkle for 1991-92. There were rumblings of discontent around the Trowse training ground and within Carrow Road. Chairman Chase said he was disappointed City had not built on the success of the late 1980s and, ominously, he saw a need to reorganise. These were unconvincing words for most fans, for the problem appeared to lie in the fact that the fine side built by Stringer in 1988-89 was being broken up due to the policy of cashing in on assets. Stringer's task required him to not only overcome the loss of his best players, but to actually build on the success they had brought. A 'mission impossible' if ever there was one.

A five-goal drubbing at Nottingham Forest in April brought more woe, with stand-in goalkeeper Walton rightly cleared of any blame for this particular collapse. The only real high point of the season was the exciting FA Cup fifth-round win over Manchester United on a memorable evening in February. This win set up a quarter-final date with Nottingham Forest, who were actually lower in the table than Norwich, despite the eleven goals they hammered into the Canaries net over the two league encounters. The tie pulled in by far the biggest home gate of the season, but the afternoon turned into a huge anti-climax. Compared to the pulsating United game, this was a strangely sluggish affair with little goalmouth action and nothing to generate genuine excitement in the big crowd. Roy Keane's second-half goal killed the game and Norwich simply couldn't rise to the occasion and hit back.

Interesting sidelines from the season included the putting up of a 'Friendship Trophy' for the winners of the game at Sunderland in December. This was introduced in recognition of the spirit of goodwill created between the two clubs at the 1985 Milk Cup final. The trophy went into Norwich's cabinet after a late Gordon goal ensured a 2-1 win.

A flutter of excitement was generated by the much-maligned Zenith Data Systems Cup, when City overcame Millwall (on penalties) and Southampton to qualify for a regional semi-final with neighbours Ipswich. The 2-0 win over the old enemy marked City's sixteenth cup-tie at home without defeat. A crowd of over 16,000 saw an overhead kick by Fleck hit the Town net, followed by a late second goal from twenty yards by Gordon, who confessed to being an Ipswich fan during his boyhood. The subsequent area final with Crystal Palace ended in a 1-3 aggregate defeat, however. The London club's boss, Steve Coppell, provided some light relief at the post-match press conference by asking: 'What is this Zenith Dating System anyway? My lads want to know where all the birds are.'

During the weeks when things were not going well during 1990-91, the fans often directed their ire towards individual players. Sherwood, a prominent figure with his foppish blond hair, was singled out for the sort of barracking that Coney had suffered a year or so earlier. It led to defiant gestures by the player after he had scored against Coventry. Bowen, who took over the captaincy from Butterworth in February, was prompted to hit out publicly over a 'lack of atmosphere' at many home games. Fleck was also critical of the fans, although some months later the fiery Scot apologised for this and appealed to supporters to forgive and forget past disagreements.

Lanky attacker Robert Rosario left the club for £650,000 during the season to try his luck at Coventry and had a few harsh words to say as he departed. Perhaps justifiably, he considered himself under-used by Norwich, and accused the management of tarnishing his name by suggesting he had an attitude problem. Sensibly, Stringer refused to be drawn into a slanging match when invited to respond.

Against this background of discontent among players and fans, the club quietly announced that season ticket prices were to be increased for 1991-92 – hardly a move to bring a smile back to punters' faces. Nevertheless, it was becoming clear that the following campaign would be an important one, for the clubs relegated out of Division One would miss out on a new 'Super' League being launched in 1992.

Match of the Season 1990-91

Norwich 2 Manchester U 1

FA Cup, 5th round, 18 February 1991

United may have been unbeaten in sixteen matches, but Norwich were not quaking in their boots when Alex Ferguson's men arrived at Carrow Road on this chilly Monday night. Over recent years results against the Red Devils had been good, although understandably the visitors were made hot favourites by the bookies.

DID YOU KNOW?

After scoring against Brighton in 1980, Alan Taylor had to wait nine years for his next Norwich goal. In between, he played for five other clubs.

In a fabulous atmosphere under the floodlights, a frantic Cup-tie ensued. From a purist's point of view there was probably too much scrappy football, but the game was always absorbing and on a knife-edge. A classic English cup-tie, in other words.

It was the type of night tailor-made for little Fleck, a player who loved to take centre-stage on the major occasions. His big moment came on 26 minutes when Sherwood nodded down a Gordon corner and Fleck found himself with the time and space to swivel and hammer a handsome shot past Les Sealey.

The game ebbed and flowed, and some 30 minutes later the visitors pulled themselves level. A superb twist and cross by Lee Sharpe saw the ball brush Polston on its way to the composed Brain McClair, who netted the equaliser. The excitement level was cranked up even higher and within nine minutes there was a third goal.

A low cross from Culverhouse was dummied by Gordon and, after a shrewd touch by sub Fox, Gordon hungrily grabbed the chance to shoot firmly under Sealey's body. The scenes of jubilation featured Gordon's speciality dance of celebration – a sort of shimmy followed by the pulling of imaginary six-shooters from his hips. He had first unveiled this popular routine some four years earlier and its return showed he had recaptured the confidence and arrogance that was such an important part of his play.

Substitute Ruel Fox's contribution was vital to the outcome. He had been out for several weeks, but was one of several players who rose to the occasion and he linked up superbly with Fleck after coming on in place of skipper Butterworth. Fox's golden 25 minutes of action spanned the precise period in which the game turned firmly in Norwich's favour.

LEAGUE DIVISION 1	**1991-92**
Barclays Division 1	18th
Rumbelows Cup	Quarter-finals
FA Cup	Semi-finals
Zenith-Data Systems Cup	2nd round

Money was made available for team strengthening before the start of the new season and Dave Stringer splashed out £1.5 million on striker Darren Beckford from Port Vale and midfielder Rob Newman from Bristol City. The former cost a club record £925,000 and was a big burly target-man in the John Fashanu mould.

With a new Premier League being planned for twelve months hence, Division One had been enlarged back to a 22-club format for the first time since 1987. City kicked off the campaign against Sheffield United with their new men wearing the Nos 9 and 10 shirts, but there was no sign of Tim Sherwood, apparently out in the cold for failing to attend a pre-season friendly. The talented 22-year-old would later briefly return to the side – probably as a means of putting him in the shop window – and a substantial fee from Division Two leaders Blackburn was accepted for his services.

It was rumoured that Stringer had originally wanted Robbie Earle when he went shopping at Port Vale, and only signed Beckford when Earle opted for Wimbledon instead. Whatever the background to the deal, everyone was agreed that it did not prove hugely successful. The size of the fee, which was fixed by a tribunal, undoubtedly weighed heavily on 24-year-old Beckford, who was a fine athlete with genuine pace. Sadly the goals didn't flow though, and it wasn't until October that Carrow Road could breathe a collective sigh of relief at the sight of a successful Beckford strike. By this time he had been rested for a spell as City found themselves in the lower half of the table.

A 3-0 win at Chelsea halted the slide, but Canaries fans heard some bad news before this game when it was announced that local favourite Dale Gordon would be leaving for Glasgow Rangers for £1.2 million. The chairman recouped the money spent on Beckford and he raised a few more pounds by sanctioning a November trip to Kuwait to play a money-spinning friendly. City thus became the first team to visit that country since the overthrow of the Iraqi invasion earlier in the year.

Results in the league followed a similar pattern to the previous season and City rarely threatened to rise much above halfway and challenge for a UEFA Cup place. The occasional notable win would always be quickly cancelled out by a grim defeat. For example, a 3-0 crushing of Liverpool at Carrow Road was soon followed by three games without a goal against modest opposition. Twice in a matter of three weeks, however, Canaries fans enjoyed see-saw thrillers that ended in 4-3 triumphs. The first was at Selhurst Park, where Norwich bagged four goals before half-time, including one from promising young Chris Sutton, who was starting a league match for the first time. Twenty-one days later a crowd of only 11,900 at Carrow Road thrilled to another 4-3 win when Beckford at last got the run of the ball and banged in a hat-trick against Everton.

Since joining from Chester, Colin Woodthorpe had been little used by Stringer, but in February he replaced skipper Mark Bowen at No 3, a move which led to a public outburst from the latter. Bowen said he was proud to be skipper and would battle to get back, but he objected to the manager's words that he had needed a hefty 'kick up the backside'. Stringer, in turn, was angry to see this reported in the local paper, and relations with the sports desk at the *Eastern Daily Press* became a little strained.

The lack of league consistency was frustrating, but for most of the season the focus of attention was on cup matters anyway. City made good progress in both major competitions, reaching the last eight of the Rumbelows Cup and the semi-finals of the FA Cup. In the former, comfortable wins over Charlton and Brentford set up an entertaining fourth round victory over West Ham, but the slippery figure of Spurs' Gary Lineker scored a late winner at White Hart Lane to prevent a semi-final appearance.

The biggest single day of the season was the FA Cup semi-final appearance at Hillsborough, an occasion made possible by a vintage thriller under the Carrow Road floodlights against Southampton. It needed extra-time to dispose of the feisty Saints, who went down to nine men after internationals Matt Le Tissier and Barry Horne were sent off. The path to this quarter-final clash had been relatively trouble-free with City being drawn at home three times against modest opposition.

Although all-seater stadiums had yet to become compulsory, City chairman Robert Chase decided to replace the Barclay End terracing. This area had always been popular with the more noisy element of the home support and its upgrading was another move guaranteed to increase the anti-Chase animosity. Those opposed to the project placed a wreath pitch-side and conducted a sit-down protest during the visit of Arsenal in April. Chase patiently explained that this was the 50th season of League football at Carrow Road and his plan involved creating a suitably modern £2 million double-decker edifice. The blueprint looked impressive, but there was little doubt that the special Barclay atmosphere would be missed in future.

DID YOU KNOW?

Norwich forward Jamie Cureton took the field for a 1995-96 local derby against Ipswich with his hair dyed bright green.

In common with many seasons during the modern era, Norwich ended their campaign with a serious dip in league form. Although they generally produced attractive and watchable football, only one of the last dozen games yielded victory. Inevitably by mid-April this meant relegation had become a serious possibility. However, others near the trap-door continued to drop points too, and a 1-1 draw with Wimbledon in the penultimate match meant enough points had been secured for survival.

Having steered the club rather shakily to safety, Dave Stringer shocked all and sundry by announcing his resignation on the eve of the season's final game. Apart from a four-year stint at Cambridge United, he had been part of the furniture at Carrow Road for 30 years. It emerged that he had visited the chairman a day or two after the Wimbledon game and turned down an extension to his contract. He said the time was right for a new man to take over as 'I've passed my sell-by date'. He admitted that even if City had reached Wembley he would still have taken this decision. He had clearly had enough of the stress and the effects that such a high-profile job had on his family life. He could depart in the knowledge that he had become arguably the club's most successful manager, guiding them to a highest-ever top-flight finish and two FA Cup semi-finals.

Match of the Season 1991-92

Norwich 0 Sunderland 1

FA Cup, semi-final, 5 April 1992

With two Second Division sides having made it through to the FA Cup semi-finals, City found themselves second favourites to win the competition. A 17,000-strong yellow and green army descended on Hillsborough convinced that Norwich's first FA Cup final appearance was a formality.

Managed on a caretaker basis by Malcolm Crosby since the mid-season departure of Denis Smith, Sunderland were having a disappointing season in Division Two, where they had spent virtually the entire campaign in the lower half of the table. Nevertheless, heroic Cup victories over West Ham and Chelsea, both after replays, had got them to Hillsborough.

Stringer was desperate to get his strongest side out for the big game and Fleck and Crook spent the build-up to the match in hyperbaric therapy units – sometimes known as oxygen chambers – in a bid to heal their injures. It worked for Fleck, but Crook had to stay sidelined along with fellow midfielder Phillips.

Slack defending just after the half-hour mark cost Norwich badly. John Byrne combined with David Rush to send young Brian Atkinson sprinting down the right wing and his floated cross wrong-footed keeper Walton and was headed home by Byrne, amid desperate but unheeded pleas for offside. City toiled valiantly in search of an equaliser but it would not come and the workmanlike Wearsiders held on grimly. The closest to a City goal came when a Sutton chip just cleared the bar and a Bowen drive was superbly saved by Tony Norman.

The opposition were clearly not world beaters, but for some reason Norwich simply could not reproduce the attacking flair they were often capable of in less important games. The sense of anti-climax was massive and midfielder Goss later spoke of the awful atmosphere in the dressing room where several of his experienced team-mates were reduced to tears.

Nobody could offer a reasonable explanation as to why Norwich simply didn't perform against such modest opposition. Fleck had had a quiet game and Crook and Phillips were both missed, but the Canaries should still have had enough talent on the park to give Crosby's men far more problems.

Chapter Five

Europe & A Managerial Merry-go-Round 1992-98

FA PREMIER LEAGUE	**1992-93**
Premier League	3rd
Coca-Cola Cup	3rd round
FA Cup	4th round

Reserve-team boss Mike Walker was promoted to manager in the summer of 1992 to replace Dave Stringer, ending weeks of speculation involving various well-known names. Former England stalwarts Bryan Robson and Phil Neal were among those mentioned, and it was reported that Neal was actually offered the job, only for a late change of heart to take place due to disagreements over moving house to Norfolk.

Walker, a former goalkeeper with 656 league games to his name, was seen as a 'safe pair of hands' by the board, but was a surprise appointment to those expecting a bigger name. City fan Kevin Baldwin, who published a witty account of the season's events called *Norfolk and Good*, even suggested the new manager 'was not even a household name in his own household'. Joking aside, the 46-year-old Walker would ultimately prove an inspired choice and attain legendary status in Norwich for his work over the next two years.

Walker had honed his managerial skills with Colchester, where his reward for leading the cash-strapped U's to the top of Division Four in 1987 had been the sack! Apparently his chairman thought Walker's brand of passing football was too soft for the lower leagues. They parted company in the same week that Walker was named Manager of the Month. Within days of that calamity, Walker was offered a job on Norwich's coaching staff by sympathetic Ken Brown, who, ironically, was only days away from losing his own job.

Walker recruited former Canary John Deehan as his deputy at Carrow Road and they immediately faced an unwanted distraction – protracted transfer talks involving leading scorer Robert Fleck. After weeks of unrest, the Scot eventually joined Chelsea for £2.1 million on the eve of the new season. Fleck was quickly replaced by Mark Robins, who cost less than half that amount from Manchester United. Walker also signed experienced Gary Megson, a free-transfer midfielder from Manchester City and made defender Butterworth his skipper. Work at the stadium was completed to make it all-seater in time for the start of the first FA Premier League season. Many Barclay End regulars were unhappy about having to sit, but clearly had little choice in the matter.

Fleck's impending departure was mourned by many die-hard fans. The player and his wife, Jayne, later said they were forced to flee their Norwich home due to the level of speculation and attention he was getting. Fleck missed the pre-season photo-call and for a while his plans were not clear to anybody. It was a very unhelpful situation for the new manager, but the board already knew that nothing seemed to go smoothly where Fleckie was concerned. It was well documented that the club had loaned him a substantial sum to pay off personal debts, for example. When he finally signed on the dotted line for Chelsea, Norwich wisely demanded a clause be inserted in his contract to prevent him playing when the two clubs met at Carrow Road a week later.

All this off-field intrigue was nothing compared to the drama to come, however. It was excitement all the way in the 1992-93 season. Even a hiccup in the first half at Highbury on the opening day proved to be a mere false start, as City sprinted to top of the table and stayed there until well beyond Christmas. Walker proved that he not only talked a good game (he was a journalist's dream with his long pre- and post-match chats), but could transfer his style to the pitch, too. City played a smooth, pass-and-move style of football that made some of the more established clubs look sluggish by comparison.

For more than an hour of that opening game at Arsenal, another routine defeat seemed on the cards after the Gunners had eased into a two-goal lead. But the introduction of new signing Robins as sub sparked an amazing transformation. Four City goals in the final 21 minutes, including an exquisite 30-yard chip from Robins, turned the game on its head and set a memorable season in motion. A month later, former Canaries Fleck and Townsend played a major part in putting Norwich 0-2 down at Chelsea, but, unbelievably, the comeback kids struck again and forced an unlikely win that kept the club top of the table.

Cynics who believed the great start was a flash in the pan were looking smug when City were demolished 1-7 by a rampant Blackburn, but the side recovered its composure superbly, winning five of the next seven games. One of these, against QPR, featured a courageous display by keeper Bryan Gunn, days after he had lost his young daughter to leukaemia. He was given a huge ovation and there was hardly a dry eye in the house.

DID YOU KNOW?

Former Norwich midfielder Martin O'Neill has a fascination with crime and the law. Before one match in the north he slipped away to visit the Yorkshire Ripper's home.

Norwich's lead at the top widened as winter arrived, and a serious title challenge was clearly under way. The fixture at Old Trafford in mid-December looked like being a real test of their credentials. City went into that game eight points clear of Blackburn at the top, knowing that victory would leave them twelve points ahead of United, who were on the fringe of the race. However, the game's decisive moment was a rare error by Daryl Sutch, who accidentally set up the winner for Mark Hughes when he could have cleared the danger by being more decisive.

Although that defeat did not herald a major collapse in Norwich's season, it proved to be, with hindsight, a pivotal moment. The failure to hit the net at Old Trafford was repeated in the next four games. In the last of these, defeat at Sheffield Wednesday knocked City temporarily off the top of the table, with the winner hammered in by future Canaries manager Nigel Worthington. Many fans appeared to believe the title dream was now over, for fewer than 14,000 watched the two January home games. Nevertheless, a place in the top three alongside United and Villa was maintained and on four separate occasions after Christmas the top spot was regained, albeit briefly. As keeper Gunn would later say: 'People said the bubble would burst – but it never really did.' Just before the transfer deadline, record-signing Darren Beckford departed for Oldham, and Bournemouth's Efan Ekoku joined the Canaries as his replacement.

One of the best displays of the season came at home to Villa and featured a dramatic late winner from defender John Polston. It left the title race open again and put City in great heart for the massive forthcoming clash with Manchester United at Carrow Road (see below). But the damage inflicted by a 1-3 defeat was serious and was only too evident four days later when City succumbed to a 1-5 hammering at Tottenham. The Canaries' title hopes finally disappeared under the rainy North London sky.

A place in the UEFA Cup remained up for grabs, however. Splendid wins over Leeds and Liverpool left City needing a point from their final game at Middlesbrough to secure third spot. A topsy-turvy thriller ended 3-3, which meant that City now had to sit and wait nervously for the FA Cup final outcome. Arsenal had already won the Coca-Cola Cup to gain the UEFA slot, but an FA Cup win would qualify them for the Cup Winners' Cup, thus freeing up their UEFA place for Norwich. Appropriately, ex-Canary Andy Linighan's towering header did the trick for the Gunners and celebrations could begin in Norfolk.

It had been a wonderful season. Third in the new Premier League was the club's highest finish ever, and they'd also scored in their first eighteen matches of the season – another club record. Walker twice won the Manager of Month awards and the campaign was littered with memorable goals, notably from the boots of Robins, Phillips and Crook.

Match of the Season 1992-93

Norwich 1 Manchester U 3

Premier League, 5 April 1993

Although the Canaries had lost their substantial lead at the top of the table and were now generally regarded as third favourites for the title, they went into this game knowing that victory could still upset the apple cart. After all, they were only two points behind leaders Aston Villa and two ahead of United, who had a game in hand.

A narrow win over Villa four days earlier had been a real thriller and meant home fans were really up for this game against a United side desperate for their first title in 26 years. After a run of seven games in the autumn without a win, Alex Ferguson had reshaped his side and, with the arrival of Eric Cantona from Leeds, they now looked mean and hungry.

It promised to be tight and an early breakthrough would be crucial. But all the anticipation and excitement exploded into Norwich faces when United stormed into a three-goal lead within twenty minutes. With twelve minutes gone, a City penalty appeal was rejected, only for Ryan Giggs to race through at the other end and round Gunn to score, despite offside appeals. Six minutes later a slick move left City flat-footed again and winger Andrei Kanchelskis emulated Giggs by dancing round Gunn for the second.

The points were put beyond the reach of the shell-shocked Canaries after twenty minutes when Paul Ince powered through a tackle and fed Cantona. In typically composed style, the Frenchman swept the ball home, with the officials again ignoring City's offside protests.

It was a stunning and depressing scenario for the home side and even a headed goal on the hour by Robins failed to really lift them. Some of the frustration was vented when a two-footed tackle by Bryan Robson sent Crook spinning into the air and sparked an ugly melee. The win was the first of seven in a row for United, which ensured that the title finally returned to Old Trafford.

FA CARLING PREMIERSHIP	**1993-94**
Premiership	12th
Coca-Cola Cup	3rd round
FA Cup	4th round
UEFA Cup	3rd round

Another season of excitement and intrigue kicked off with the supporters again questioning the judgment of the board. Key midfielder David Phillips' contract dispute dragged on for weeks and he eventually left for Nottingham Forest. Then chairman Robert Chase revealed that Norwich wouldn't be signing up to football's new racial equality campaign, claiming they had no need to do so. Norwich were one of only two clubs not to back the initiative. It was a rather baffling move, particularly as some sections of the Barclay End were not averse to occasional racist outbursts against opposition players.

Mike Walker added centre-back Spencer Prior and goalkeeper Scott Howie to his squad, but the most prominent new face was Efan Ekoku, who had signed towards the end of the previous season. He won a regular place and looked lively in attack, bagging no fewer than four goals at Goodison Park to destroy Everton in a game that had visiting fans blinking in delighted disbelief. Ekoku became popularly known as The Chief, a reference to his father being a tribal chieftain in Nigeria, although Efan was actually born in Manchester.

The first half of the season saw Norwich chalk up a series of superb results away from home, but unable to reproduce that sort of success at Carrow Road. The back-to-front results were of great interest to the statisticians: By late November the club was third in the table, despite having only scored three goals in seven home games, but they had managed 21 in eight away trips. An extraordinary 4-0 win at Leeds was the highlight, featuring a memorable volleyed goal by Jeremy Goss.

That kind of form meant City tackled their first taste of European competition full of confidence. The UEFA Cup campaign commenced with a 3-0 aggregate win over Dutch side Vitesse Arnhem, achieved despite an intimidating atmosphere in the away leg and a very physical approach by the opposition. Marvellous performances followed in the autumn in Munich and Milan, which will live long in the memory and are covered in detail later in this chapter.

The first eight Premiership away games yielded five wins and three draws and helped City to reach the heady heights of second place for a spell. With the distractions of Europe perhaps playing a part, results began to suffer as Christmas approached and the away run came to an end at Oldham. Insufficient points were collected in home games for a serious title challenge. According to one tabloid newspaper, a Norwich game that should have resulted in a home victory was the 2-2 draw with Liverpool. The paper presented evidence that this fixture was part of a match-rigging scandal involving Reds goalkeeper Bruce Grobbelaar and others. It was alleged that Grobbelaar would have pocketed £80,000 had City won the game, but this did not happen because he made a late 'unintentional' save with his feet. This all emerged much later on, of course, with nothing having appeared amiss on the match-day itself.

With the club in the throes of UEFA Cup excitement, many City fans hardly noticed when manager Howard Kendall parted company with Everton, sparking rumours that Mike Walker could be a candidate for the vacancy. Walker had been linked with Atletico Madrid and even the England and Wales jobs, so the Everton gossip was not unexpected. Around the same time, Walker gave an interview in which he said investment was needed in the Norwich team while they were doing well, in order to build on the eighteen months of success achieved under his control. He was also unhappy over the terms of his own contract and it became clear that all was not well between him and the chairman.

Following a three-match Christmas holiday programme, involving fine away wins at Tottenham and Southampton, and a home defeat by Villa, Everton made a formal approach to Norwich to speak to Walker about their vacancy. To Walker's dismay, this was turned down. A few days later Walker walked out on the club without any prior announcement and within a short while was installed at Goodison. Now it was the chairman's turn to be angry and he complained about an illegal approach by Everton and referred the matter to the FA. Walker had left without speaking to his assistant Deehan or the players, and Jeremy Goss later said it had been a highly disappointing episode as the side 'had something good going' and now Walker had put a spanner in the works. But nobody blamed Walker for being ambitious and he clearly felt he'd been backed into a corner by his board's intransigence.

John Deehan was put in temporary charge of the side and had less than 24 hours to prepare for his first game, a tricky FA Cup-tie at Third Division Wycombe. It ended in a comfortable 2-0 win and Deehan was later confirmed as manager, with Gary Megson as his assistant. At 36 and 34 respectively, the pair were the youngest management team in the Premiership. Popular Walker was a hard act to follow and Deehan had the added difficulty of knowing that the board wanted healthy profits from the transfer market, which made team strengthening an almost impossible task. Deehan's contract stipulated that he must inform the board of any offers of £1 million or more for players. His fears became reality when Ruel Fox was sold to Newcastle for £2.5 million. Deehan was allocated around ten per cent of this fee to purchase replacement Neil Adams from Oldham.

A Premier League hearing was convened to consider the illegal approach allegation, in which Norwich claimed £226,000 for loss of league points and position. Norwich's dossier of evidence was compiled by a former local CID chief and included news film footage of Walker meeting an agent at Manchester airport. The tribunal decided Walker was 'indirectly induced' by Everton, as they had made it clear to him that if he presented himself to them, the job would be his. The Merseysiders were fined £75,000, with the tribunal accepting they had originally believed Robert Chase would be prepared to release Walker.

Deehan's first nine league games failed to yield a victory, but when Walker brought his Everton side to Carrow Road in March the atmosphere was hostile and City rose to the occasion and triumphed 3-0. Inevitably, Walker had to endure abuse from the crowd. He gently retaliated in the press by pointing out that he had built the team that won the match. This remark upset Deehan, but Walker later said he meant no offence by it. The whole unhappy saga meant the fans remained at loggerheads with their chairman, however, especially when transfer deadline day came and went with no further signings. One compensation was that highly rated Chris Sutton hadn't been sold, despite interest from Tottenham.

It had been a difficult baptism for Deehan. His first seven league games in charge were all drawn, but several ought to have been victories. In addition to losing the services of the dynamic Fox, injury deprived him of striker Robins, too. Apart from a freakish 4-5 home defeat by Southampton, goals were hard to come by in the final quarter of the campaign. From a high of second place prior to Christmas, City's final resting place was just below halfway.

Match of the Season 1993-94

Bayern Munich 1 Norwich 2

UEFA Cup, 2nd round, 1st leg, 20 October 1993

Victory over Vitesse Arnhem – Norwich's long-awaited debut in European competition – set up this mouth-watering tie against one of the biggest names in world football. And although City were in fine fettle in the Premiership, few expected the dramatic start they made in Germany, racing into a two-goal lead within 30 minutes.

DID YOU KNOW?

Newspapers reported that Norwich defender Tony Powell had 'disappeared' to the USA for sex-change surgery. In 2002 he was tracked down and denied it.

The breakthrough was another gem of a volley from Jeremy Goss, who blasted in the sweetest goal of his life after multi-capped Lothar Matthaus made a poor headed clearance. That was after just twelve minutes and the huge Olympic Stadium was shocked again seventeen minutes later when Crook's free-kick cleared a group of players and bounced awkwardly before Mark Bowen carefully headed it home.

Bayern pulled a goal back before the interval, but City looked in no mood to crumble after their dream start. The second-half involved some desperate defending and gallons of sweat and toil. Gunn produced several remarkable saves and the final whistle signalled lengthy celebrations by the travelling Canaries army.

The thrills continued in a dramatic second leg at Carrow Road with the Germans scoring early to level the tie and Norwich then having to defend superbly to keep the powerful visitors at bay. Goss popped up to net from close range early in the second-half and City hung on for an unforgettable triumph. The atmosphere inside Carrow Road that night was electric.

The third-round draw paired the club with mighty Inter Milan, who came to East Anglia and pinched a single-goal victory thanks to Dennis Bergkamp's late penalty. Goss hit the crossbar and three key City players picked up bookings. Which meant they had to miss the second leg. More than 3,000 City fans headed for Italy to witness a spirited display in the San Siro, but the makeshift Canaries couldn't get back on terms. Near the end Bergkamp popped up again to net a classy goal. The travelling army remained in place long after the final whistle, happily singing and chanting, to the bafflement of the *carabinieri*, who couldn't understand why defeated fans were in such good spirits.

FA CARLING PREMIERSHIP	**1994-95**
Premiership	20th (relegated)
Coca-Cola Cup	Quarter-finals
FA Cup	5th round

Big-spending Blackburn Rovers turned covetous eyes towards Norfolk in the summer of 1994 and, inevitably, the sight of their chequebook proved too attractive to resist. Chris Sutton was the target and Rovers were prepared to pay a £5 million fee, plus wages of £12,000 a week. Although City initially rejected approaches for their rangy striker, every man has his price and when the bidding reached British record levels, the time came to cave in. Weary of seeing their best players sold, many fans voiced the usual objections, but some were realistic enough to accept that the club couldn't possibly turn this sort of offer down. After all, the former Hellesdon High School pupil was a local product who had cost nothing.

The positive spin-off was that significant funds were now available to John Deehan to attempt to strengthen the squad. The rookie manager didn't hang around and splashed out in excess of £3 million on four 'quality' players. Burly Leeds central defender Jon Newsome arrived for a Norwich club record £1 million, Oldham midfielder Mike Milligan for £850,000, Manchester City striker Mike Sheron for £800,000, and Sheffield United defender Carl Bradshaw for £450,000. On paper, this quartet looked to have just the experience and quality needed. They would surely be adequate replacements for Ian Culverhouse, an ever-present last season now in contract dispute, and Ian Butterworth, victim of a serious waterskiing injury.

The season got off to a quiet start, with the new-look side needing a while to find its feet. The fireworks didn't begin until mid-September when City visited rain-soaked Ipswich. The dreadful conditions played havoc with pitch-markings and City supporters were convinced that a Newsome challenge on Ian Marshall took place outside the penalty area. With the white lines virtually invisible, the penalty decision appeared to be guesswork. Aggrieved Norwich fans didn't have long to wait for the pendulum to swing the other way. A few minutes into the second half, Crook was felled in an almost identical spot, again causing uncertainty among the poor officials. Initially, a free-kick was given, but the sheer weight of Norwich protests led to a linesman being consulted. To the astonishment of everyone, this lengthy chat led to the award of a penalty. Bradshaw netted what would prove to be a winner, but only after his first attempt had been parried.

DID YOU KNOW?

Full-back Kenny Brown played against his former club, Norwich, for three different teams in 1995-96 – Southend, Reading and Crystal Palace.

The scenes of Canary joy were repeated less than a fortnight later when new skipper Newsome thundered forward to score a dream goal against high-flying champions-elect Blackburn. The big defender ghosted past three opponents before netting a drive that dipped wildly before hitting the net. Along with his dominance in defence, this buccaneering goal would ensure Newsome's place among the Carrow Road legends.

One of Newsome's predecessors in defence, John O'Neill, was at this time negotiating a £70,000 settlement of his negligence and assault claim against John Fashanu, for the career-ending tackle back in 1987. O'Neill was now running a wine and sprits business in Londonderry.

Deehan's team climbed briefly into the top six during the autumn, but then sold striker Efan Ekoku to Wimbledon for £900,000. City were held to a goalless draw by Mike Walker's Everton – and there was genuine shock when news filtered through 48 hours later that the Merseyside club had sacked Walker just ten months after they prised him from Norwich. This came in the same week that Ossie Ardiles, Ron Atkinson and Brian Little all left managerial positions at top-flight clubs. Deehan could have been forgiven for fidgeting uncomfortably in his swivel chair.

Following Ekoku's departure, Deehan signed Ashley Ward from Crewe to boost his firepower and the Manchester-born target-man made an instant impact with a two-goal debut against Chelsea. Although City were by now well established in the top half, Deehan struggled to field a settled side and was willing to give youth its chance. Players like Jamie Cureton and Keith O'Neill were thrown into the fray and showed evidence of real quality.

The season's cruel turning point was a freak incident at Nottingham Forest, when goalkeeper Gunn fell awkwardly after saving an Ian Woan shot. With nobody near him, Gunn suffered a broken fibula and serious ankle damage. Young Andy Marshall came on for his goalkeeping debut and did well, although Lars Bohinen's swinging corner-kick eluded him and went straight in to win the game. Marshall followed this with a stunning home debut against Newcastle, which earned praise from Kevin Keegan and helped City to a 2-1 win. That game is still talked about as probably the most impressive home debut ever seen from a City player. Deehan later recruited Simon Tracey on loan to take pressure off Marshall, but

Tracey was not a success and Deehan would later rue the fact that he was never allowed to invest in a proper replacement.

After the turn of the year, a 0-4 hammering at Liverpool sparked a run of eleven league games without a win. Fears of relegation reinforced the unhappy atmosphere at Carrow Road generated by the anti-Robert Chase protests. The continued selling of players (Mark Robins to Leicester for £1 million was next) meant City fans were ever more convinced that their chairman must go. The campaign to oust him grew ever noisier. 'This is no longer a pleasant place to play football,' reflected the under-pressure Deehan.

A five-goal FA Cup hammering at Everton increased the gloom and the angry fans couldn't believe it when the transfer deadline came and went with no new recruits. It was rumoured that experienced Ray Houghton was available, but the board decided £300,000 was too much to pay. A week or two earlier, celebrity Norwich supporter Stephen Fry did his infamous vanishing act to Belgium. Poor Deehan must have considered joining him.

Typical of City's luck was the draw at West Ham, during which they tossed away a two-goal lead and had Andy Johnson sent off in a case of mistaken identity. The Hammers equaliser was a joke goal, ballooning slowly into the net off Tony Cottee's knee.

There was a brief respite from the misery when local rivals and fellow-strugglers Ipswich were beaten at Carrow Road (see below), but it was soon back to square one when depleted City were humbled 1-5 at Arsenal. This thrashing was topped in the last minute by a comical own-goal by Rob Newman. Four days later City lost to lowly Leicester, who scraped only their fifth win in 36 games. The downhill slide gathered pace and pressure mounted on Deehan. Some observers felt he only kept his job after the Leicester defeat because the squad was staying in the north for its next fixture.

With four clubs relegated this year, on account of league restructuring, prospects were bleak and some sort of result at high-flying Newcastle was imperative. However, a predicable 0-3 beating led to Deehan having a long chat with his wife and resigning on 9 April. An honest and likeable man, Deehan said he was not enjoying the game any more and stress was taking its toll. He headed to Tenerife to unwind and assistant Megson was put in temporary charge.

Megson's fire-and-brimstone approach was reflected in some spirited displays, but results and luck didn't improve. Against Forest, City hit the bar before being beaten by a late sucker-punch goal. Five days later Spurs squeezed a 1-0 win, thanks to a disputed Teddy Sheringham goal. City were now in the bottom four for the first time and the anti-Chase demos intensified. For the final two home games the management installed a new sound system, ostensibly to improve the atmosphere with 'motivational' rock music. This was laughed out of court, however, as most fans realised it was an attempt to drown the anti-Chase chanting.

After defeat by Liverpool, City's future in the top flight hung on the result of their trip to Leeds in the season's penultimate fixture. A Norwich victory would probably set up a 'winner takes all' situation in the final game with Villa, but anything less would surely mean curtains. City took the lead after a howler by keeper John Lukic and held on grimly until the later stages. With just eleven minutes left, a harsh penalty was awarded when Tony Yeboah hit the ground inside the Norwich box. Gary McAllister rolled the kick home and probable relegation soon became a certainty when Carlton Palmer netted in stoppage time. Nobody felt the misery more than skipper Newsome, playing against his former club, who crumpled to the ground in tears. Gunn admitted it was the second-worst day of his life, second only to the loss of his daughter Francesca. Norwich's anger was taken out on the referee, who was berated and jostled at the end. On reflection, relegation had actually not been caused by Mr Wilkie, but by a points haul of thirteen from a possible 66 over the latter half of the season.

Match of the Season 1994-95

Norwich 3 Ipswich 0

Premiership, 20 March 1995

Norwich went into this game with a great opportunity to end their lengthy winless run and hammer another nail in the coffin of relegation-bound local rivals Ipswich.

Their first derby 'double' for 43 years was also up for grabs and the prizes all came a little closer when City received a helping hand from referee Durkin near the end of the first half. He decided veteran John Wark's rash midfield challenge on speedy Darren Eadie was a sending-off offence. It mystified most observers, but paved the way for City to demolish the disheartened men from Suffolk.

Ten-man Town worked hard to keep the lively Canaries at bay, but it seemed clear that if anxious Norwich scored once they would go on to win comfortably. They were not going to emulate Manchester United – who'd hit nine past Ipswich sixteen days earlier – but they could surely grab their first win in twelve games.

The breakthrough came on 53 minutes when Newsome's through ball found Cureton racing clear to round keeper Craig Forrest and net from a tight angle. Five minutes later it was all over bar the shouting when Ward's turn and shot brought his seventh goal of the season. Twelve minutes from time Forrest made a hash of a Polston header and Eadie was on hand to do the rest.

A Bowen cross was deflected against the bar by Phil Whelan soon afterwards, while at the other end Ipswich's luck was summed up when an Alex Mathie header hit the woodwork. It was City's first victory since New Year's Eve and dramatically lifted the sagging morale of recent weeks.

LEAGUE DIVISION 1	**1995-96**
Endsleigh Division 1	16th
Coca-Cola Cup	Quarter-finals
FA Cup	3rd round

According to Norwich chairman Robert Chase, around 50 names were put forward for the manager's job in the early summer of 1995, but only one gained the unanimous approval of the board – Martin O'Neill.

The personable, up-and-coming young manager of Wycombe Wanderers had recently hoisted his club from non-league into Division Two and was still fondly remembered at Carrow Road for his two short but influential spells as a player with the Canaries. Two secret meetings at a hotel near Heathrow airport saw the details ironed out and O'Neill was unveiled to a surprised media, many of whom had been expecting Scotsman Jimmy Nicholl to get the job.

O'Neill brought with him a trio of coaches – John Robertson, Steve Walford and Paul Franklin – leaving erstwhile caretaker-manager Megson to head elsewhere to gain further managerial experience. Chairman Chase promised that O'Neill would get funds to buy new players and, for a while at least, some of the heat was off the unpopular chairman. Ominously, former boss John Deehan was quick to warn his successor that he might find it difficult to find money for new players, promises or otherwise.

City had to pay Wycombe £200,000 compensation for O'Neill. The only other pre-season acquisitions were midfielder Matthew Rush from West Ham and a plot of land adjacent to Carrow Road. Rush was injured early on and his career at Norwich never took off. The legendary Robert Fleck returned on loan from Chelsea at the end of August, and a month later signed permanently for £650,000. City fans welcomed this news, but were bemused by the failure to sign Dean Windass from Hull as Fleck's front-running partner. Windass might have turned a decent Division One side into genuine title challengers, but O'Neill was frustrated as negotiations kept stalling and his chairman employed what appeared to be delaying tactics. Hull were in dire financial trouble and were not happy with what went on. To the fury of O'Neill and the fans, Windass was eventually allowed to sign for Aberdeen, where his scarlet boots lit up Pittodrie on his better days.

Meanwhile, mischievous Fleck was soon up to his old tricks, getting sent from the dugout for abusing a linesman against Sheffield United, then, during the warm-up at Grimsby, scoring an apparently deliberate direct hit on a female Norwich supporter carrying a drink. Being clouted by a football was no joke for tearful Catherine Swallow, who was attending her very first game. Perhaps Fleck's boyish smile won her over, though, for she subsequently became a regular Canaries fan.

After a promising opening day, when Luton were beaten 3-1 at Kenilworth Road, results were mixed over the early weeks and O'Neill knew he must strengthen the side to have a chance of promotion. After the Windass saga, a much-publicised three-hour meeting took place between manager and chairman on this very topic. The pair emerged to present a united front to the media, but many sensed that O'Neill wasn't happy with life at Norwich. Fans were also bemused to hear the announcement that the club was in serious financial difficulties, despite all the player sales of recent years.

Nevertheless, by December Norwich had forced their way into the top six. As Christmas approached, speculation grew that First Division rivals Leicester wanted O'Neill as their manager. This was unwelcome news as the Canaries' decent league results had been accompanied by a run to the last eight of the Coca-Cola Cup, featuring a dramatic penalty shoot-out victory over Premiership Bolton. It was reported that O'Neill was on Leicester's short-list along with former Canaries boss Mike Walker. Many City fans feared the worst. The fact that O'Neill's family had never moved to East Anglia, giving him long and tiring car journeys to the ground, fuelled the rumours that he would soon be on his way.

The matter came to a head just before City's match at Leicester. According to contemporaneous accounts, O'Neill handed in his resignation in a ten-minute meeting at a hotel on the morning of the game – and Chase refused to accept it. Interviewed more recently for O'Neill's biography, Chase says O'Neill quit the day before the game in more amicable circumstances at the training ground, and 'no voices were raised'. Whatever the truth, it all came as a huge shock to the players, who were only told shortly before kick-off when coach Franklin suddenly took charge. The two teams thus took the field managerless, with fans speculating that O'Neill would join Leicester, whose second choice, Walker, might return to replace him at Norwich.

Events would prove them half right. O'Neill was soon installed at Leicester, but there was no chance of Walker returning to Norwich while his nemesis, Chase, was still in charge. Walker had left Norwich hurriedly and without farewells; the same happened with O'Neill. It led to more anger towards Chase from the fans, who didn't blame O'Neill for quitting a club where promises appeared to have been broken. Meanwhile, Walker found himself out on a limb.

He had turned down the chance to manage Luton because he was so confident of getting the Leicester job. Now he'd missed out on both. He had already suffered various setbacks in a relatively short managerial career but seemed able to accept this turn of events with equanimity. He explained the whole saga in illuminating detail via his new chat column in the *Eastern Daily Press*, called 'Walker's World'. It made fascinating reading.

The next Norwich home game, against Southend, was contested in an ugly atmosphere which had little to do with the opposition. There were arrests and outbreaks of violence among the demonstrating fans, and their mood was not helped by a Southend victory which their manager, Ronnie Whelan, attributed at least in part to the unusual atmosphere.

Chase ignored the renewed calls for his resignation and brought back Gary Megson from a coaching role at Bradford City to manage the Canaries, a decision far from popular with the bulk of supporters. Inevitably results were inconsistent during this stormy period and things reached another head in March when the club's two most valuable assets were sold. Jon Newsome went to Sheffield Wednesday for £1.65 million and Ashley Ward headed to Derby for £1 million. The Newsome news had been half-expected, but Ward's exit was a real shock and even the new manager was stunned by a deal that took place without his involvement. Megson was so livid he threw caution to the wind and criticised the board publicly, calling the sales ludicrous and presumably thus hastening the arrival of his own P45 in the process. 'I was not party to this,' he assured the angry fans.

Chase said it had been a painful decision to let Ward and Newsome leave, but the borrowing level from the bank simply had to be reduced by 50 per cent and he had no choice. As the season petered out and City drifted into mid-table mediocrity, the situation deteriorated further when former director Jimmy Jones made public a letter from Hull, written during the Windass saga. Its contents fuelled the anti-Chase flames yet further.

Match of the Season 1995-96

Crystal Palace 0 Norwich 1

Division 1, 5 May 1996

On the face of it, this was a meaningless end-of-season fixture between two clubs, neither of whom were in desperate need of points. City were clear of relegation danger and Palace were assured of a play-off place.

DID YOU KNOW?

Norwich fans refer to rivals Ipswich as 'Binmen', following a TV episode of Lovejoy in which a dustman finds a blue hat amongst the rubbish.

However, the occasion turned into an almighty party for Canaries fans, thanks to the momentous events of the preceding week. At a three-hour board meeting, discussions had taken place about a proposed purchase of Robert Chase's 34 per cent majority shareholding by popular former chairman Geoffrey Watling. The proposal was passed the following day and the 83-year old former jazz impresario took control of the club, with Chase resigning.

Norwich fans later described hearing the news as their own 'JFK moment'. Everybody could remember exactly where they were when they heard that Robert Chase had gone. The *Eastern Daily Press* devoted many pages to the event and reported that during Chase's ten-year reign some £26.4 million had been raised from player sales, while transfer-market spending only amounted to half that figure. And now the club was languishing in debt to the tune of £5 million. In the interests of balance, it should be pointed out that Chase did preside over successful periods in the club's history, with three top-five finishes, a First Division title, and two FA Cup semi-final appearances. However, few would dispute that his priorities always appeared to lie with the stadium and development issues rather than the team itself.

The momentous news from the boardroom saw supporters quickly planning a party for the final game of the season at Selhurst Park three days later. A massive travelling army, decked out with yellow and green balloons and banners, witnessed what was largely a scrappy game – yet they didn't seem to care a jot.

The fun on the terraces was far more entertaining than events on the pitch, and it was perhaps appropriate that a poor game should be decided by a bizarre own-goal. The ball flew past startled Palace keeper Nigel Martyn off the head of David Hopkin, who appeared to have forgotten which way his side was kicking. Only five minutes had passed and the goal gave City's experimental line-up the boost they needed to hang on grimly for the next 85 minutes. City fans weren't worried about the lack of quality on show – they were welcoming the dawn of a new era, heartened by the words of their new 83-year old leader, who said: 'Now let's cut the cackle and get on with the job.'

LEAGUE DIVISION 1	**1996-97**
Nationwide Division 1	13th
Coca-Cola Cup	1st round
FA Cup	4th round

Although the end of the Robert Chase regime heralded much celebrating among the Norwich faithful, it was clear there were still difficult times ahead for the club. Debts amounted to more than £5 million and a degree of reorganisation would be needed. The club's first chief executive was appointed to run things on a day-to-day basis, backroom staff were axed, and eleven professionals left the playing staff during the busy summer of 1996.

Manager Gary Megson was given the dreaded 'vote of confidence' and, sure enough, this was followed a mere ten days later by the sack. His right-hand man, Mick Wadsworth, had already left to manage Scarborough and Megson's departure for the second successive summer paved the way for the return of Mike Walker. Norwich fans were happy to overlook the circumstances of Walker's 1994 walk-out and his lack of success at Everton, as they had happy memories of what he had achieved at Carrow Road in his first stint. An end to all the demos and protests and a return to attractive passing football was on the cards.

Walker brought former Luton coach John Faulkner to the club as assistant manager and bolstered the coaching staff by recruiting his former Colchester United colleague Steve Foley. Two other well-known figures who had recently left the club – Duncan Forbes and Ian Crook – were hastily reappointed by Walker. Forbes was made chief scout while Crook was hauled from the clutches of local rivals Ipswich. Earlier in the summer Crook had been granted a free transfer and had signed for Ipswich, where he was unveiled at a Portman Road press conference on the very day that Walker arrived back at Norwich. Walker did not want to lose such a skilled performer and when a loophole in the paperwork was spotted, Norwich decided to exploit it. Crook's new contract with Ipswich was dated 26 June, but he was technically a Norwich player until 30 June, meaning he could be claimed back again. The player was happy to return under Walker, but did suffer censure from the FA for having signed overlapping contracts. It was a bizarre little episode and Crook would subsequently receive terrible stick from Ipswich fans when playing against them.

Walker's brand of pass-and-move football saw the season get off to a good start and the form of youngsters like Darren Eadie, Andy Johnson and Keith O'Neill was cause for hope. Superb back-to-back autumn victories over Grimsby and Ipswich took the Canaries to top place in the table and all seemed well with the world. Behind the scenes, important developments took place when a new-look board was created, accommodating the arrival of TV celebrity chef Delia Smith and her husband Michael Wynn Jones. The couple were among four new directors, and said to be injecting around £2 million of new capital into the club. Delia and husband, both long-standing Canaries supporters, would subsequently become majority shareholders with a stake of 58 per cent in the club.

Following all the departures and the restrictive financial circumstances, Walker found himself with a squad lacking in depth. Following the sale of Jamie Cureton to Bristol Rovers and a crop of injuries, the team lost its early-season consistency. As autumn turned into winter, so City's form cooled and they embarked on a run of ten games without a win. This reached its nadir just before Christmas with horrendous defeats at West Brom and Port Vale. The defence looked a shambles in a 1-5 hammering at The Hawthorns, and those fans hoping that this was a freak occurrence would soon be disappointed. Just three days later, at Vale Park, City leaked another six goals. The two results were greeted with horror and much gnashing of teeth, and instant action was demanded of the manager.

Walker went out and recruited Everton's Matt Jackson for £450,000 to bolster the shell-shocked defence. This upset Birmingham City, who had Jackson on loan and were expecting to secure his services permanently. Jackson's debut saw Norwich look in better shape, although a further three goals were conceded at QPR. Thanks to a generous piece of refereeing, Jackson survived being sent off after just a couple of minutes of this debut, after he rashly pulled back nippy John Spencer. The next four games were all won, which brought the dreadful run to an emphatic end. Walker brought in a trio of players on loan – former England midfielder David Rocastle, ex-Spurs and Newcastle defender Kevin Scott, and Swedish striker Ulf Ottossun. All three played their part as City remained in contention for a play-off place until the final weeks of the season.

A blot on the landscape was a row concerning talented midfielder Andy Johnson, who played well in the first half of the season, but then had what was described as a disagreement in training with assistant manager Faulkner, as a result of which he promptly submitted a written transfer request. To Walker's anger, this letter was mysteriously faxed to a local radio station before being handed to the club's management. The episode marked the beginning of the end of Johnson's career at Carrow Road and he subsequently joined Nottingham Forest.

DID YOU KNOW?

TV cookery doyenne and Norwich City director Delia Smith runs a catering business at Carrow Road with an annual turnover of £2.5 million.

The promotion dream ended at Portman Road, of all places – more of that below – and the season then petered out with City quickly tumbling from seventh in the table to a disappointing final resting place of thirteenth. Having exited the FA Cup at the hands of Martin O'Neill's Leicester City in the fourth round, this season looks on paper to have been something of a non-event, but that is far from the truth. Mike Walker had reversed a decline on the field, the new board had repaired much of the damage behind the scenes, the negative atmosphere at matches had largely disappeared, and highly promising youngsters like Craig Bellamy were breaking through.

Match of the Season 1996-97

Ipswich 2 Norwich 0

Division 1, 18 April 1997

With just three games left, Norwich found themselves travelling to Portman Road knowing that victory was essential if the play-offs were to stay within reach. They lay seventh in the table, one place and two points behind hosts Ipswich, but having played one game more. Defeat by the blue enemy would virtually ensure Ipswich's own place in the play-offs and condemn City to another season in the Nationwide League.

The tension of the situation helped create a terrific atmosphere, and the 2,300 Norwich fans contributed lustily to the incredible noise generated by a Friday night full-house of over 22,000. The match had been hyped-up in the local media as a do-or-die affair and this seemed to have more a positive effect on the home side. Norwich were never allowed to settle as George Burley's men poured forward in frantic style.

The all-important breakthrough came just after the half-hour, when Steve Sedgley slipped a pass through for Argentine full-back Mauricio Taricco to fire home. Portman Road erupted at this sickening blow for the Canaries. Had City survived until the break just one goal behind they might have been able to re-group and hit back – but it wasn't to be. A free-kick routine ten minutes later ended with Geraint Williams' overhead kick falling for veteran Paul Mason, who smashed the ball in off a post.

City continued to look second best after the break as hungry Ipswich refused to let their foot off the throttle. Crook, jeered mercilessly by the home fans, went close with a long-range shot, but the Ipswich defence were rarely put in serious difficulties. Walker seemed to accept that Ipswich would be unbeatable on this night and didn't make any obvious tactical switches.

Disappointed City fans couldn't even make a quick exit at the end, for they were locked inside the ground for fifteen minutes to abide by police and security procedures. Portman Road was the worst possible place to suffer such an important defeat. At least some consolation arrived a month later, when Sheffield United put Ipswich out of the play-offs by squeezing through on the away goals rule.

LEAGUE DIVISION 1	**1997-98**
Nationwide Division 1	15th
Coca-Cola Cup	1st round
FA Cup	3rd round

The sale of out-of-favour midfielder Andy Johnson to Nottingham Forest, plus a cut from Mike Sheron's move from Stoke to QPR, gave Mike Walker the funds he needed for a summer re-building programme. His shopping excursions yielded five new men – Oldham defender Craig Fleming, Wolves striker Iwan Roberts, Celtic midfielder Peter Grant and continental imports Erik Fugelstad and Victor Segura.

Despite the new faces, City got off to a poor start by losing their first three league games and departing from the Coca-Cola Cup in embarrassing fashion at humble Barnet. To add to the early-season atmosphere of discontent, supporters gave the thumbs-down to the club's new playing strip. Director Delia Smith had commissioned leading fashion designer Bruce Oldfield to create a new state-of-the-art kit, but his all-yellow effort didn't find favour among the fans and the garish change-strips also met with mixed reactions.

A single-goal win at Sunderland's Stadium of Light lifted the gloom a little, but Walker had to contend with a long list of injuries, a situation that persisted throughout the season. The manager was without the services of key performers Eadie, O'Neill, and Fleming for long periods and City were never able to field a settled combination throughout 1997-98. When Robert Fleck awoke on the morning of a match with Stockport and reported pain from a cricked neck, the *Eastern Football News* calculated that this was the 37th injury of the season, with 36 games gone. Injured players are an occupational hazard for a football manager, but Walker suffered far more than would normally be expected.

The inability to field a settled side inevitably led to mixed results and City spent most of the campaign disappointingly low in the table. Some fans even began calling for Walker's head. As if these struggles weren't enough to cope with, the manager suffered a tragic personal blow during the season when his wife Jackie died after illness.

The catalogue of injuries allowed some of the emerging talent in the youth and reserve ranks to emerge. Craig Bellamy, Adrian Forbes, Chris Llewellyn, Darren Kenton and Adrian Coote all made more appearances than might otherwise have been expected, but all five responded well and coped manfully. Indeed, the explosive Bellamy emerged as the season's leading scorer, with more than half his total of thirteen strikes coming in the final weeks of the season. This chirpy character was not known for his modesty and described himself as Norwich's answer to Juninho.

A wretched FA Cup third-round exit at Second Division Grimsby was followed by a five-goal thrashing in the league at Wolves. Erratic City promptly bounced back from this double blow by beating divisional leaders Nottingham Forest and then Sunderland – unbeaten in their previous seventeen – in the space of just twelve days. This topsy-turvy form was typical of the season overall, and the fans never knew quite what to expect. Another low point was reached in February when a depressing home defeat by Tranmere was followed by a 0-5 humbling at Ipswich. If the previous season's defeat at Portman Road had been hard to swallow, this one must have had the die-hards thinking about leaping into the River Wensum to end it all. In mitigation, Norwich had struggled to raise a side for the game due to the injury crisis, and conceded a morale-shattering opening goal after only 64 seconds.

Stalwart goalkeeper Bryan Gunn, having been replaced on a regular basis by Marshall, left the club mid-season to join Hibernian, after a marvellous stint extending to nearly twelve years and 477 games. Robert Fleck, another long-time favourite and high wage-earner, was also released, and the financial problems eased further when young full-back Danny Mills was sold to Premiership-bound Charlton.

A long run of games without victory after Christmas has been a regular trait of Norwich sides over the years and this bad habit manifested itself again in 1997-98. Between 29 January and 12 April, Canaries fans didn't have a single victory to celebrate. This plunged the club down to the lower reaches of the table and relegation became a real possibility. The miserable run was ended in style when Huddersfield were hammered 5-0 at Carrow Road. A relegation six-pointer followed at Stoke, but a 0-2 loss to Chris Kamara's team meant Norwich remained in danger. Remarkably, the next game saw a second successive 5-0 home win achieved, and everybody could breathe a huge sigh of relief as relegation was finally staved off.

In his programme notes for that final home game, against Swindon, Walker signed off by writing 'see you in August' to the fans. However, five days later, with one away game left to play, he had left the club. Mere survival in Division One was clearly not enough for the ambitious board and they decided the change was necessary. Vice-chairman Roger Munby paid tribute to Walker's work, particularly in bringing on the youngsters, and was sympathetic over his problems with injuries. He described Walker's departure as being a matter of 'mutual consent.'

DID YOU KNOW?

Norwich winger Terry Anderson drowned in mysterious circumstances in 1980 at Great Yarmouth. The coroner recorded an open verdict.

However, it seems the parting of the ways was first discussed back in early April, following a 2-3 home defeat by Bradford City. Walker earned a stay of execution that day and was able to lead the team to safety. The two 5-0 wins at the end of the season cheered up the fans no end, but weren't enough for the board. After Walker left on 30 April, director Michael Wynn Jones gave the players a stern pep-talk at the Colney training ground and put John Faulkner in charge for the final game.

Many supporters felt Walker had been unlucky during his second spell at Norwich, but were encouraged by the new board's impatience for success and awaited the arrival of a new manager with bated breath. On the season's final day, City beat already relegated Reading in the very last league game to be played at the 102-year-old Elm Park stadium. Norwich's travelling fans took the opportunity to bid an emotional farewell to former favourite Fleck, who was now playing for the Berkshire club.

Match of the Season 1997-98

Norwich 5 Swindon 0

Division 1, 25 April 1998

The final home game of the season saw Norwich still needing a victory to be mathematically certain of avoiding relegation to Division Two. Steve McMahon's Swindon had no such worries, even though they had only won once in their previous eleven outings. City were five points clear of the drop zone with two games to go, meaning in theory they could still be caught by Manchester City if they lost those final two matches.

The third-highest home crowd of the season, 18,443, turned up at Carrow Road, heartened by the 5-0 hammering handed out to Huddersfield twelve days earlier. A repeat of that score-line would be just the ticket to give them some happy memories to take into the summer break.

Things got off to a flying start when Welsh teenager Chris Llewellyn, enjoying his first spell in the Norwich first team, ghosted in to head Sutch's cross past Fraser Digby. A Craig Bellamy shot was then pushed against the goalpost before City doubled their lead before half-time. This time it was defender Jackson, newly crowned

Player of the Year, who rose high to head home another Sutch cross.

The match was finished as a contest shortly after the break when Iwan Roberts guided in a simple header from a Neil Adams free-kick. In his first season at Norwich, Roberts was still working hard to establish his form and this was only his fifth goal of the campaign. Ten minutes later he swapped passes with the ever-dangerous Bellamy and the youngster calmly stroked the ball in, with the Swindon camp waiting in vain for an offside flag.

Neale Fenn, who had joined City on loan from Tottenham just a few minutes before the transfer deadline, snatched the fifth goal that his hard work deserved. He turned superbly to fire home a fierce shot after a miskick from Llewellyn came his way. Eight minutes later, with the crowd calling for a sixth goal, Fenn smashed a twenty-yard drive against a post. Bellamy was substituted to a standing ovation, allowing a cameo appearance from departing defender Polston, who got the chance to wave farewell after eight years of fine service. Polston had totted up 263 first-team appearances and within a few weeks would follow Fleck to Reading.

Chapter Six

The Long Haul Back to the Top 1998-2003

LEAGUE DIVISION 1	**1998-99**
Nationwide Division 1	9th
Worthington Cup	3rd round
FA Cup	3rd round

For the first time since the arrival of John Bond 25 years earlier, Norwich City appointed a manager with no previous connections with the club. Bruce Rioch was given the role vacated by Mike Walker, and Rioch's brief was to work alongside a new Director of Football, the former Ipswich forward Bryan Hamilton.

These appeared to be far-sighted appointments by the board. Rioch had a fine playing career as an attacking midfielder with Luton, Aston Villa, Derby, Everton, and had won 24 Scotland caps. The son of an army officer, he then forged a reputation as a disciplinarian manager, enjoying spells at Torquay, Millwall, Middlesbrough, Bolton and Arsenal. A young-looking 50, Rioch brought a wealth of experience to Carrow Road, as did the new Director of Football. Hamilton had played at the top level with Ipswich and Everton and won 50 full caps for Northern Ireland. His managerial CV encompassed Leicester, Tranmere, Wigan and the Northern Ireland national side. Some fans has reservations about his Ipswich connections, but on the face of it, this new managerial duo looked like a real 'dream team.'

The new era at Norwich commenced with three straight wins, including a Carrow Road thriller with QPR which saw the home side surge into a 3-1 lead with just eight minutes on the clock. In the early weeks Rioch had the luxury of being able to call upon the services of fit and in-form Darren Eadie and Keith O'Neill – but, alas, this didn't last long. Both were struck down again and missed many games, O'Neill subsequently joining Premiership Middlesbrough for a seven-figure fee.

Another serious blow was the loss of Craig Bellamy, who had thirteen goals to his name when he was the victim of a dreadful challenge by Wolves' Kevin Muscat, which went unpunished. Although Bellamy only missed five games as a result of his injuries, the incident seemed to badly affect Norwich's momentum on a long-term basis. A two-goal lead at Molineux was frittered away after Bellamy was carried off, and results in subsequent weeks also suffered as the Canaries slipped out of the top six and down to halfway. The Wolves match marked the season's halfway point and up to that point a serious play-off challenge had been underway. From Bellamy's injury onwards, a promotion push never really looked on the cards.

The no-nonsense Rioch brought a degree of discipline and organisation to the City side, but still allowed flair and pace to flourish. His arrival seemed to galvanise Iwan Roberts in particular. Roberts' first season at Carrow Road had been highly disappointing, considering the size of his transfer fee, but now he seemed to have shed weight and regained an appetite for his task. Although his first league goal didn't arrive until the fifth game, he ended with 23 in all and won the Player of the Year award.

For the second season running, a sell-on clause in a contract handed City a windfall. Last season it came via Mike Sheron, now the transfer of Tim Sherwood from Blackburn to Tottenham yielded £500,000 for Norwich. Added to the huge O'Neill fee, it again meant that transfer income far outweighed transfer expenditure, a fact of life at Norwich these days. Rioch spent what little was made available to him wisely. He brought in Celtic defender Malky Mackay and Manchester United midfielder Phil Mulryne, who both looked the part right away. He also took French winger Cedric Anselin, Newcastle forward Paul Dalglish, and Chelsea midfielder Paul Hughes on loan. All three had mixed fortunes, but Anselin and Dalglish were subsequently offered contracts.

The serious decline in home form after the turn of the year was the main reason for the slipping away of promotion hopes. A last-minute wonder-goal by Hughes snatched victory over Swindon in the final home fixture, marking the end of a run of eleven home games with victory. This awful sequence included an extraordinary 3-4 home defeat by Port Vale, which ended the play-off hopes for good. In that match, City fought back from 1-3 down, only to throw it all away by leaving Ian Bogie unmarked to net the winner three minutes from the end. Most of the home fans were stunned into silence, but one particular character was prompted to stage a one-man pitch invasion, peeling off his Norwich shirt and attempting to hurl it at Rioch.

Unsurprisingly, the manager was prompted to make team changes after that calamitous defeat, and in the next home game – a lacklustre goalless draw with Portsmouth – City ended the match with seven players aged twenty or younger. One of them, 18-year-old Darel Russell, underlined his promise with a fantastic solo run that very nearly produced a winning goal.

DID YOU KNOW?

Bryan Gunn nearly missed a cup-tie at Bradford City in 1993 when a gate steward did not recognise him and refused him entry.

The way this season rather fizzled out was in direct contrast to some of the excitement of earlier on. A Bellamy header gave a sweet single-goal victory at Ipswich and the young Welshman enhanced his growing reputation further when he followed that with two excellent goals in a 4-1 humbling of Huddersfield. At Ipswich, City fans were only allocated 1,700 seats, but those who travelled into enemy territory had a Tuesday night to remember. In addition to Bellamy's goal, City created a host of chances against their over-confident opposition, and Roberts struck a post from 30 yards as well as missing a sitter.

On their travels, City had a fairly productive season, chalking up eight wins. The only real horror-shows came at Crystal Palace, where a poor defensive display led to a 1-5 crushing, and then at an extraordinary game with Crewe in January. At Gresty Road, City cruised into a two-goal lead well before half-time and rarely looked in any danger until a nightmare finish to the match. With just eight minutes left, Dario Gradi's men pulled a goal back and Norwich's nerve seemed to go completely. Five minutes later they were 2-3 down, with Rioch looking apoplectic. What made matters worse was that the opposition were generally having a poor season and hitherto had only four wins from 26 games to their name.

Considering their limited budget, Norwich were perhaps always outsiders for promotion this term, and in many ways ninth was a respectable finishing position in the circumstances. However, it was the fourth successive campaign in which the side had finished well short of the play-off places – a statistic made worse by the fact that local rivals Ipswich finished in the top five in three of those years. This time, City ended up fourteen points adrift of a play-off place and fifteen clear of relegation. Rioch and Hamilton knew they would probably have to improve on this next time, or the board would be getting twitchy again.

Match of the Season 1998-99

Norwich 4 QPR 2

Division 1, 22 August 1998

Impressive wins over Crewe and Stockport in the opening games of the season boosted optimism at Carrow Road, and this visit of QPR was seen as a chance to grab another three points and go top of the table.

Ray Harford's men had started the season poorly and their gloom deepened when Norwich got the match off to a rip-roaring start. In the second minute the fast-raiding Bellamy appeared to get the ball tangled between his feet, but recovered to finish superbly as keeper Lee Harper advanced. With the cheers still ringing around the ground, Rangers' Tony Scully went clear of the Norwich back four, only to tumble over the outstretched arm of the diving Andy Marshall. The keeper was yellow-carded and Gavin Peacock drove home the penalty.

Two minutes later Peter Grant nipped ahead of Harper, only to be impeded by Rangers' Norwegian defender Antti Heinola. The second penalty of the afternoon was tucked in smartly by Bellamy. It was breathless stuff and by the time the clock had ticked on to eight minutes a fourth goal had hit the net. A free-kick by Eadie struck a post and in the resulting melee O'Neill forced the ball to Jackson, who turned sharply and powered in a shot that caught a deflection on its way past Harper.

Things calmed down somewhat after this and the goalmouth action was less frequent over the next half-hour. After 37 minutes, however, former City striker Mike Sheron silenced the barrackers at the Barclay End by netting a fine shot from sixteen yards after a pull-back by Kevin Gallen. Minutes later and Sheron went within a whisker of equalising with a header.

After the break, City opened up a two-goal lead once again. Bellamy picked up a cross from Grant and twisted clear of one tackle, only for Steve Yates' outstretched leg to send him tumbling. Bellamy unerringly netted the game's third penalty and completed his hat-trick. Sheron forced a superb save from Marshall in the later stages, but Norwich clung onto their two-goal advantage and ended the afternoon proudly on top of Division One.

LEAGUE DIVISION 1	**1999-2000**
Nationwide Division 1	12th
Worthington Cup	2nd round
FA Cup	3rd round

When a football manager is unable to significantly strengthen his squad during a close season, the last thing he needs is a string of serious injuries soon after the new campaign starts. But that's exactly what happened to poor Bruce Rioch at the beginning of 1999-2000.

The only significant arrivals in the summer had been a couple of relatively unknown Frenchman in Jean-Yves de Blasiis from Bordeaux and Pape Diop, loaned from Racing Club de Paris, so Rioch could be forgiven for tearing his hair out with frustration when he lost no fewer than four key players in the early weeks. Bellamy damaged cruciate ligaments in a friendly at Southend in July, meaning he would be out for around nine months. Shortly afterwards, Eadie's old knee injury flared up again on the pre-season jaunt to Sweden. Then, in the first home league game Jackson landed badly and damaged his knee. In the following home game, Mulryne suffered a double fracture of his right leg in a bad tackle by Blackburn's Christian Dailly. When would the nightmare end?

Inevitably, the constantly re-jigged side got off to a poor start and could only draw two and lose three of the opening quintet of matches. But the injury-prone Eadie returned for the home game with Crewe and showed exactly what the side had been missing when he lashed home a spectacular winning goal seven minutes from the end. It lifted City off their miserable position at the bottom of Division One, and, slowly but surely, the side recovered some of its form and confidence. A fortunate win at Port Vale launched a run of eight games without defeat and relieved City fans could begin again to look at the league tables without wincing.

A quartet of 2-1 wins over December and the holiday period meant City established themselves in the top half of the table by the time the new millennium arrived. What many Canaries fans would really have liked, however, was a new face or two to strengthen the squad for a late promotion push. Rioch apparently felt the same way, but knew the board was battling with debts of around £7 million, following the announcement of an annual loss of £2.5 million. Even a windfall of almost £1 million, thanks to sell-on clauses relating to Danny Mills and Chris Sutton, failed to loosen those purse strings. Indeed, Rioch had to bite the bullet and accept that departures were probably more likely than arrivals. To the dismay, but not surprise, of City fans, Eadie was sold to Leicester for £3 million and none of this cash was directed into the manager's transfer budget.

Perhaps a cup run would have made money available, but there was nothing doing on that front. City departed from the FA Cup with little more than a whimper, with keeper Marshall making two uncharacteristic blunders to assist Coventry to a 3-1 win. Earlier on, Worthington Cup progress had been halted emphatically by Fulham, who were beginning to benefit from the Al Fayed patronage and chalked up an easy 6-0 aggregate victory.

To get Norwich anywhere near the play-off positions would have represented a fine achievement in the circumstances, and Rioch nearly managed it in late January. Only a late Craig Hignett equaliser for Barnsley prevented City from overtaking Stockport and moving into the top six. Sadly three of the next four matches were promptly lost and Norwich slid back into mid-table, never to rise again.

Although Rioch must have known from the start he would never have a fortune to spend on new players, the situation must have nagged away at him as the weeks went by. A play-off place might have been a possibility if only some new blood could have been injected in mid-January. When Crystal Palace visited Carrow Road in early March they outplayed the Canaries and should have won by more than Clinton Morrison's late goal. Rioch told the post-match press gathering that the game had left him 'with an empty feeling'. These were ominous words and two days later the former Arsenal supremo's resignation was formally announced. A stunned board of directors quickly placed Bryan Hamilton in charge of the team on a caretaker basis, ending his nine-month stint of concentrating on the blossoming Academy. Although Hamilton provided an experienced pair of hands, his strong Ipswich connections made many Norwich fans uneasy over the appointment. Hamilton was, of course, a respected professional who would give the job everything – but local rivalries are not trifling issues for the average supporter. In Suffolk and Norfolk you're either blue or you're yellow – there is no grey area.

It emerged that matters had come to a head with Rioch following a 1-1 draw at Nottingham Forest on 8 March, when he apparently made his unhappiness known to the directors. One of their number, Barry Skipper, visited Rioch's Norfolk Broads home the following day to see if there was room for negotiation, and to establish if another club was involved. These talks came to their conclusion a few days later, some 24 hours after the Palace home defeat. Skipper accepted that Rioch was an honourable man who was not inclined to act impulsively and there was genuine disappointment that he was not prepared to soldier on. Rioch, for his part, acknowledged that there was ambition within the club (many fans feared otherwise, as player after player was sold), but was convinced that money should have been made available to him after Christmas. It is believed the final straw was the board's inclination to invest more in the Academy instead of the first-team squad.

Defending the board's policy, chairman Bob Cooper said all possible funds had been made available to Rioch and a large budget had been in place to allow him a squad of 21 to 23 men, but this had been insufficient for Rioch's plans. Director Delia Smith used her *Eastern Football News* column to put a positive spin on the episode. She insisted it was 'total rubbish' to assume the club did not have the resources to make progress. She said she had ploughed her own cash into Norwich City and had even postponed a lucrative TV series in order to roll her sleeves up and generate some income herself to help pay the players' wages.

Once the dust had settled, Hamilton found himself needing to prepare the shell-shocked players for a trip to his former club, Ipswich, at Portman Road. Such a fixture was probably the last thing everyone needed at that point, but football's capacity to surprise and delight was never more apparent than when events unfolded in Suffolk later that week. Norwich's tremendous 2-0 derby win provided a Sunday afternoon that will live long in the memory of Norfolk folk.

Hamilton was able to bring in a couple of cheap imports and loan signings, but he could only inspire two more victories from the final nine games, and, predictably, the Canaries ended up halfway in the table. Hamilton was duly confirmed as full-time manager at the club and one welcome sight as the season fizzled out was the return from injury of the dynamic Craig Bellamy, who had been sorely missed.

Match of the Season 1999-2000

Ipswich 0 Norwich 2

Division 1, 19 March 2000

New caretaker-boss Bryan Hamilton's first job when he took charge of the Canaries was this tough-looking fixture at promotion-chasing Ipswich, the club where he had made his name 25 years earlier. Hamilton didn't make too many changes from the last side that Bruce Rioch had fielded. He brought in Lee Marshall in place of De Blasiis and called up forwards Anselin and Coote to warm the substitutes bench.

DID YOU KNOW?

Luton Town's Ashley Grimes was bizarrely sent off at Carrow Road in 1987 after he argued with a Luton team-mate and then spat at him.

The Portman Road faithful naturally found the Canaries' recent troubles vastly amusing, but they were certainly not laughing by time the half-time whistle sounded in this typically hard-fought local derby. Hero of the hour was leading scorer Iwan Roberts, well on his way to winning a second successive Player of the Year award. After nineteen minutes Roberts had cracked a shot goal-wards and his toothy grin looked a mile wide as the effort caught a deflection and flew past England Under-21 keeper Richard Wright. Just before the interval, Roberts netted an even sweeter effort, taking a pass from Dalglish and side-stepping a desperate challenge to curl a marvellous shot past the diving Wright.

Rarely have travelling Norwich fans enjoyed a half-time interval more as they chomped on their snacks that Sunday afternoon. The margin might have been even wider, for Llewellyn and Lee Marshall had both found themselves clear on goal but unable to hit the target. At the other end, Andy Marshall didn't have the difficult day he must have expected against George Burley's men. In the second half he was able to extend the run of clean sheets against Ipswich to four successive games without too much difficulty.

It was a truly wonderful start for the new boss Hamilton, who had given the sceptical City fans exactly what they wanted at the very first time of asking. He would be hard pushed to maintain anything like this level of performance and achievement in the coming weeks. Did this result signal the start of better times ahead, or was this merely a new manager's honeymoon period? Only time would tell.

LEAGUE DIVISION 1	**2000-01**
Nationwide Division 1	15th
Worthington Cup	3rd round
FA Cup	3rd round

You wait all summer for the football season to start – and then when it arrives it kicks you in the teeth. Those were the feelings of many a Norwich fan when their club not only got off to a bad start, but also sold its most valuable and popular player. When the news came that Craig Bellamy had moved to Coventry for £5 million, the fans could have been forgiven for thinking they were caught up in a Groundhog Day scenario. Haven't we been here before?

Hence, for the umpteenth time, the club came under heavy fire for selling its best players too cheaply. The board's acceptance of the Coventry bid was hardly surprising, though, for there were strong rumours that the transfer system was about to be dismantled. Clubs with a substantial overdraft are hardly likely to turn away seven-figure cash bids in such circumstances.

In addition to four players recruited cheaply by Bryan Hamilton at the tail-end of the previous season – Gaetano Giallanza, Fernando Derveld, Raymond De Waard and Paul McVeigh – the only other new face was 30-year-old Danish defender Steen Nedergaard. It was feared that Bellamy's departure during the first week of the season would leave Norwich woefully short of fire-power. And so it proved, for they failed to score in six of their opening eight league games and also drew a blank when Second Division Bournemouth came to Carrow Road in the Worthington Cup.

Hamilton had been in the game a long time and had to call upon all his experience and know-how to tackle this crisis. He turned to the loan system and borrowed Manchester City striker Jim Whitely and Newcastle midfielder Garry Brady. Then, delving into football's bargain bin, he captured Arsenal defender Brian McGovern and veteran striker Tony Cottee from Leicester. The latter proved a useful acquisition, despite being in his 36th year, and made a superb debut at Stockport, inspiring a 3-1 victory that started to turn the tide for anxious City. Unfortunately, Cottee was already thinking about his career after retirement and, after just seven weeks at Carrow Road, snapped up an offer to become player-manager of Barnet.

There was cause for celebration in the Worthington Cup when City found their shooting boots against Second Division Blackpool. After a 3-3 draw at home, City romped through the second leg to the tune of 5-0. With Italian striker Giallanza scoring twice and starting to look the genuine article, Hamilton could have been forgiven for thinking he had finally turned the corner. He dedicated the win to the loyal 300 fans who had trekked up to Bloomfield Road and his relief and pleasure was shared by chairman Bob Cooper, who ran on the pitch at the end to shake the players' hands. The win had come just a week after the season's low point, a depressing four-goal hammering in front of live TV cameras at Wolves.

Things started to look up after a two-goal deficit was overturned at home to Sheffield United, but this was something of false dawn, for the autumn was generally a miserable time. From a high of thirteenth in the table, City began to slip back towards the lower reaches again. After Cottee left, Hamilton persuaded the board to release funds for another desperately-needed forward and bought 20-year-old Scot Alex Notman, a player who had scored goals galore for Manchester United's reserves. Notman only managed one first team appearance at Old Trafford, but was a promising talent and cost City £250,000.

After four successive defeats, Notman made his debut at Fratton Park, Portsmouth, in what would prove to be Hamilton's last throw of the dice. Pompey won 2-0 and Hamilton decided the time had come to vacate the manager's chair. This didn't happen immediately after the game, for Hamilton emerged from the dressing room in angry mood, and was critical of the attitude of some of those wearing the Norwich shirt. A clear-the-air meeting took place on the following Monday between Hamilton and his players and, even then, there was no obvious signal that the manager was about to depart. A couple of hours later the air of confusion and anxiety was settled with the release of a press statement stating that Hamilton had resigned.

Chairman Cooper called this a tragedy, for his manager had proved to be dedicated and had worked under huge pressures, without having time on his side. Hamilton said that Norwich were close to being a good side, but the players were suffering a crisis of confidence and times had been tough since relegation from the Premiership in 1995. Hamilton had come under heavy fire from supporters and the local media, in particular for some of his signings. To add to the troubled waters, the club was experiencing planning difficulties concerning its indoor Academy arena at Colney, and several senior players were in contract disputes.

So, from the frying pan of coaching this troubled football club, Nigel Worthington was plunged into the fire of managing it. Hamilton's erstwhile assistant was asked to step into the caretaker-manager role and was quick to accept the challenge. A former Sheffield Wednesday and Northern Ireland full-back, Worthington had only been with Norwich for around six months, having shared the assistant manager role with Doug Livermore. He had previous managerial experience with Blackpool, and his first match in charge of the Canaries would bring back unwanted memories of that stint at Bloomfield Road. Norwich's opposition was Gillingham and some of the Kent club's fans decided to welcome Worthington to his new job by reminding him of the controversial 1999 meeting of Gillingham and Blackpool. They waved placards reading 'Still cheating Nigel?', referring to an incident when Blackpool were expected to throw the ball back to a Gillingham player after it had been kicked out to allow treatment to an injured player. Instead of sportingly doing this, Blackpool chose to keep the ball and scored a vital goal from the move. It led to ugly scenes and Worthington was accused of cheating.

If Gillingham were hoping for some sort of revenge they were disappointed, for Worthington's career as Norwich manager got off to a winning start thanks to a late Llewellyn goal. The City players showed renewed spirit and determination under their new boss. After an excellent win over QPR and good draws with high-flying Nottingham Forest and Blackburn, Worthington was offered the job on a full-time basis and settled down to the business of inching Norwich away from the relegation zone. His rebuilding programme was bolstered by the arrival of Zema Abbey from Cambridge United, Adam Drury from Peterborough, and Gary Holt from Kilmarnock, for a total outlay of around £1 million. Some of this was offset by the sale of Lee Marshall to Leicester.

Four successive defeats in March briefly re-ignited relegation worries, but generally there were indications that Worthington was doing things the right way and was building a squad that had the talent and spirit to go places in the future.

Match of the Season 2000-01

Norwich 4 Stockport 0

Division 1, 20 February 2001

Norwich went into this Tuesday night encounter in relatively buoyant mood. Nigel Worthington had been in charge for less than three months, during which time only three of twelve league games had been lost and the threat of relegation seemed to be diminishing. A healthy crowd of almost 20,000 enjoyed what turned into a one-sided game. Although City were not completely out of the relegation woods, they looked far more confident than they had before Christmas and attacked Stockport with verve and imagination.

DID YOU KNOW?

Rejected by Lincoln City and forced to work on a building site, Wayne 'Bertie' Biggins was rescued in 1984 and went on to score 21 goals for Norwich.

Former Tottenham forward Paul McVeigh, perhaps Bryan Hamilton's shrewdest signing, had an excellent game and was a real handful for Andy Kilner's struggling side, who had failed to win any of their previous five league games. The Edgeley Park club had sacked assistant manager David Moss just days before this game and all was not well within their ranks.

Barely fifteen minutes into the game, McVeigh sent the ball down the line to Lee Marshall, who drilled a cross into the Stockport box and Llewellyn turned the ball past Lee Jones. Twenty minutes later the inevitable second goal arrived when former Canary Ali Gibb attempted to chest a Sutch cross back towards his keeper, but could only direct it into the path of a grateful Roberts.

Within three minutes Roberts grabbed his second to kill the match as a contest. Mackay sent over a deep free-kick and Abbey floated a cushioned header across to the waiting Roberts, who curved a header neatly over Jones. After the interval, Roberts completed his hat-trick and registered his fifteenth goal of the season when he headed home a teasing cross from the effervescent McVeigh.

Thanks to the brave efforts of keeper Jones, no further goals were added, but it was a chastening day for the visitors, who were utterly outplayed. It was a rare occasion when Norwich's front-three of Roberts, Abbey and McVeigh had really clicked as a unit and had run rings around the opposing defence. This game marked the day that 23-year-old McVeigh came of age at Carrow Road and established himself as a fans' favourite. His first City goal would come four days later when he fired the winner against Wolves.

LEAGUE DIVISION 1	**2001-02**
Nationwide Division 1	6th (play-offs)
Worthington Cup	1st round
FA Cup	3rd round

As Norwich's 100th season dawned, Nigel Worthington, the club's 21st manager since the war, prepared for his first full campaign by making five intriguing-looking signings. He'd only lost the services of one regular player in the summer – goalkeeper Andy Marshall, who joined Ipswich – and his new recruits therefore boosted the squad into a unit of some depth and quality.

The air of optimism at Carrow Road was well founded, but it certainly wasn't to be plain-sailing on the opening day. Nothing went right for Worthington during the visit to Millwall's New Den. For starters he was deprived of two of his new boys – midfielder Mark Rivers from Crewe was injured and striker Marc Libbra from Toulouse had returned to France following a family bereavement. Then, once the game got underway, newly appointed skipper Neil Emblen – signed from Wolves – damaged a hamstring so badly he wouldn't start another game all season. Oh, and to cap it all, Norwich lost the match 0-4.

Luckily, this tale of woe did not set the pattern for the season. The following Saturday saw a packed Carrow Road enjoy the sunshine and a visit from Kevin Keegan's attack-minded Manchester City. The direction of the match – and perhaps the entire season – turned on an incident after 75 minutes of goalless action. Libbra was summoned from the bench to make his debut in place of the tiring Roberts. It took the 29-year-old Frenchman just nineteen seconds to write his name in Canaries folklore. Has any other Norwich player achieved hero status in such a short time?

Libbra tossed aside his tracksuit and jogged to his position in attack. A Mulryne free-kick was chipped forward and headed on by Abbey. Libbra collected the ball, turned one way and then the other before flipping the ball over the head of defender Steve Howey. As it came down he smashed it first time into the City net and Carrow Road exploded. It was a goal from Heaven. Perhaps even better than Justin Fashanu's classic from 1980. With his first touches of the ball as a Norwich player, Libbra had created a little piece of magic that was to prove pivotal to the club's progress over subsequent months. Suddenly there was a spring in the players' steps, the fans had something they could talk about for years to come, and the belief and confidence that deserted the club in the mid-1990s came flooding back. Whatever Libbra did after this game, he could rest assured that he had certainly made his mark.

DID YOU KNOW?

Following the death of his daughter, goalkeeper Bryan Gunn launched his own leukaemia charity appeal in 1993 and within 12 months had raised £160,000.

Before the game ended, McVeigh clouted a second goal and even a broken foot for unlucky Llewellyn could not spoil the frenzied atmosphere of delight. The next three league games were all won without a goal being conceded and City were on their way. Progress was only hampered in the early weeks by a 0-4 humbling at Preston, where Mackay's absence from the defence proved decisive. With Mulryne playing the best football of his life and Roberts consistent in front of goal, City reached second place in the table on a couple of occasions and were rarely out of the top four until the end of January. Cup-ties did not prove a distraction from the important league business. After the embarrassing Worthington Cup exit at Brentford, City were outclassed 4-0 in the FA Cup third round by Gianfranco Zola and Chelsea. When the little Italian flicked home one of the sweetest goals of this or any other season, even City fans had to applaud.

Excellent away wins in tough games at Gillingham and Grimsby emphasised that this Norwich side was up for a serious tilt at the play-offs. The occasional slip-up did occur and twice in a six-day period in November the side threw away the chance to go top of the table, losing games that, on paper, looked to be there for the taking. Bradford City came to Carrow Road and were flattered to win 4-1 in an open game, and then bottom-of-the-table Stockport beat City 2-1, thanks to an inspiring debut by their new player-manger Carlton Palmer.

Lowly Stockport may have surprised Norwich, but the Canaries were more ruthless when visiting 23rd-placed Sheffield Wednesday a few weeks later. A 5-0 thumping represented City's best away win in many a year and was particularly satisfying for Worthington, who had spent more than ten years of his playing career at Hillsborough. Results were mixed after this and it became touch and go whether a top-six place, and entry into the play-offs, would be achieved. When Holt missed a penalty and Steve Bruce's Birmingham sneaked a 1-0 win at Carrow Road in mid-March, prospects looked bleak. This was the fifth successive game without a victory and it dropped City to tenth. The table showed they would probably need five or six wins from their final seven games to make the top six – requiring a level of consistency not sustained thus far.

But the team passed its test with flying colours. A late McVeigh winner in a scrappy Easter game at Bradford City paved the way for an exciting run-in. More than 20,000 packed into Carrow Road and saw Grimsby snatch a draw, leaving City with two games left and two wins required. The pressure was really on at Barnsley, but the superb support of around 4,000 travelling fans undoubtedly helped the team. The club had shrewdly offered cut-price travel to the game as a gesture of goodwill and this boosted numbers and had the desired effect on the players. The 2-0 success at Oakwell came on a day when main rivals Burnley were losing 1-3 at Grimsby.

After pocket calculators came out, it was deduced that Norwich's task on the final day of the season was straightforward. At home to already relegated Stockport, they simply had to produce a better result than Burnley did in their home match with Coventry. The two clubs had the same number of points and an identical goal difference. On paper, Norwich had the easier-looking fixture, but nothing could be taken for granted. City's hopes were boosted in the very first minute of their match when Stockport keeper Andy Dibble handled outside his area and was sent off. He was replaced by rookie James Spencer, who had celebrated his seventeenth birthday just ten days earlier, and had only one first-team game under his belt. The youngster was only beaten twice, however, but that proved sufficient as Burnley could only win by a single goal. Norwich's game finished several minutes earlier and there was a short and agonising wait before the fans with radios could confirm the good news.

Reaching the play-offs naturally sparked celebrations. The club's new chairman, Roger Munby, called it 'a point of take-off following the financial and reputational wreckage of the mid-1990s'. Worthington, assisted by lieutenants Livermore and Foley, had moved the club forward, instilled team spirit and used limited resources well. He had created a squad good enough for promotion to the Premiership, but the issue would subsequently rest on one shortcoming in Norwich's make-up ... they were not good at penalties!

Match of the Season 2001-02

Birmingham 1 Norwich 1 (4-2 on penalties)

Division 1, play-off final, 12 May 2002

Norwich overcame Wolves in two exciting legs of the play-off semifinal to reach the final at Cardiff's Millennium Stadium. A three-goal second-half salvo at Carrow Road had given them a 3-1 lead to take to Molineux and, despite a sensational second-half strike by Wolves' Kevin Cooper, they held their nerve and squeezed through 3-2 on aggregate.

Led by former Canaries legend Steve Bruce, Birmingham would prove tough opposition and had the psychological advantage of having doubled Norwich in the league, without the Canaries managing a single goal. But the stadium, ablaze with colour and noise, generated a real cup final atmosphere, which meant league form was of little relevance. With the sliding roof closed, the noise was intense and the early exchanges frantic.

Sitting a few feet apart in the VIPs area, Norwich director Delia Smith and Birmingham managing director Karren Brady attracted lingering attention from the cameras. Viewers were treated to a series of agonised close-ups as two of football's leading ladies got caught up in the drama. No doubt the media pack were hoping to witness a cat-fight but, perhaps to their disappointment, both women acted with perfect dignity when microphones were thrust before them.

For the first ten minutes Birmingham dominated without making a breakthrough. Then Dane David Nielsen almost capped his successful first few months at the club by nearly giving Norwich the lead, and Clint Easton, another Worthington signing who was coming good at the right time, also went agonisingly close. Holt, a workaholic in midfield, gave another fine display and Rivers also provided Birmingham with some anxious moments. Green had one superb save to make, and the Blues also hit a post, but the 90 minutes ended in stalemate.

Just 40 seconds into the first period of extra-time substitute Roberts did the trick. Still not fully fit after injury, the big striker leaped to head home a cross by fellow sub Notman and Norwich had one foot in the Premiership. The joy lasted only eleven minutes before Geoff Horsfield beat Green to get the blue half of the stadium dancing and screaming.

So it all came down to the dreaded drama of a penalty shoot-out. Norwich minds must have relived the traumas of missed spot-kicks earlier in the season. Birmingham won the toss to take the kicks in front of their fans and the psychological advantage swung a little further in their favour. Roberts netted the first Norwich kick, but Mulryne and Sutch both missed theirs. With Birmingham scoring four from four, the Canaries' promotion dream died in dramatic and tearful fashion. It had been a wonderful day for the 32,500 City fans present, but the manner of defeat was a bitter pill to swallow.

LEAGUE DIVISION 1	**2002-03**
Nationwide Division 1	8th
Worthington Cup	1st round
FA Cup	5th round

Just when Norwich City finally looked like getting their finances and long-term security plans into reasonable shape, along came the collapse of ITV digital and associated problems. The implications were serious for the Nationwide League clubs and the subsequent lack of promised TV money caused most clubs to cut back drastically on their transfer spending.

Nigel Worthington was eager at the very least to equal his side's top-six finish of the previous season, and added one new name to the squad – Darlington defender Paul Heckingbottom. In addition, the in-form Mulryne agreed a new three-year contract. A cracking opening day saw Grimsby pounded into submission by four goals. Mulryne's ferocious long-range opener would prove to be one of the goals of the season. A couple of days later – not for the first time – the team lacked motivation for the traditional Worthington Cup opener against inferior opponents. Little Cheltenham scored an unlikely 3-0 victory at Carrow Road, but it was a hiccup that was soon forgotten. League form remained excellent and after ten games the Canaries were proudly perched in the top three and had only lost one game – at home to Sheffield Untied.

An impressive 2-0 win at Reading's Madejski Stadium was another early-season highlight, with the quality of football impressive up to the end of October. At this point, the onset of cooler weather seemed to bring with it a chilling loss of form and, ever so gradually, City's confidence ebbed away. The dip was hard to explain – even for Worthington – and after totting up 29 points from the first fourteen games, City went on a bad run that yielded just fifteen from the next fourteen encounters, which translated as relegation form. This falling away had not happened the previous season and it was a depressing turn of events for the fans after such a promising start.

Away form in particular was dire during the mid-season period, while home displays were edgy, anxious and lacking in conviction. Given the shortage of cash, Worthington knew that any new blood would have to come via loans or from the youth and reserve ranks. The team – and the forward line in particular – seemed badly in need of inspiration and Worthington hoped he'd found the right man when he captured Preston striker David Healy on loan. The former Manchester United striker made his City debut in early February, by which time the team were seventh in the table and clinging on to fading play-off hopes. Healy pepped up the attack for a while, but overall he didn't make a huge difference and City still found goals hard to come by.

To cover for suspensions and injuries, Worthington was allowed to spend £65,000 on Stockport defender Keith Briggs and also borrowed Sheffield Wednesday's Leigh Bromby. Academy products Dean Sinclair, Jason Shackell and Ryan Jarvis also got their chances at first-team level. It was the first time that true home-grown talent had burst into the first team in around four years. Jarvis, a local lad from Fakenham, made history by becoming the club's youngest ever first-team player, at the age of sixteen years and 282 days. It was valuable experience for the young lads, but none of the new faces could help inspire a genuine turnaround in the team's form.

Particularly disappointing, for obvious reasons, was the 0-2 home reverse at the hands of Ipswich, who by this time were neck-and-neck with Norwich on the outer fringes of the play-off zone. The only difference between the clubs was that Town had appointed Joe Royle in place of manager George Burley and were on an excellent run of form after a poor start. The Carrow Road derby was played out in the usual red-hot atmosphere and decided by two late Town goals, both created by 16-year-old super-kid Dean Bowditch.

The FA Cup produced a little cheer at last. After four successive seasons of falling at the first hurdle, City made it into the last sixteen – the first time they'd reached the fifth round in eight years. A routine win over Brighton was followed by a dramatically narrow 1-0 success over brave non-League outfit Dagenham & Redbridge. Garry Hill's Daggers made life difficult at Carrow Road and with most of the nation willing the underdogs to another giant-killing, Norwich's Zema Abbey poked home a last-minute winner that caused tears and heartbreak among the men from Essex. City's fifth round tie at Premiership Southampton ended in a predictable 0-2 defeat at the new St Mary's Stadium.

Meanwhile, a depressing spell of just one win in eleven league games was turned around in early March. Strangely enough, the game that instigated the upturn was a defeat at leaders Portsmouth. City put up a plucky performance that night and were unlucky to lose 2-3. It seemed to put them in good heart for the final run-in and they subsequently won four of the next five games. It was enough to push them right back into the play-off chase. For a few hopeful weeks, optimistic Canaries fans were dreaming of a repeat of the 2002 excitement, but defeat at struggling Derby soon brought them back down to earth. The final resting place was eighth, five points short of the final play-off place.

DID YOU KNOW?

For the 2002-03 season, ex-Norwich winger Keith O'Neill sponsored non-league Abingdon Town, who wore his name on their shirts.

The season ended with a heartening 2-0 win over Preston and within a day or two major work on the stadium began, with the old South Stand being demolished to make way for a brand new state-of-the-art edifice. Major developments were being planned for the club-owned land adjacent to the ground which also abuts the River Wensum. In the 2003 close season, Worthington made two significant additions to his squad in Canadian defender Jim Brennan from Nottingham Forest and attacking midfielder Damien Francis from crisis club Wimbledon. After eight successive seasons in Division One, the success-starved Carrow Road faithful will be hoping this pair can help hoist City back up there with football's big boys.

Match of the Season 2002-03

Norwich 4 Grimsby 0

Division 1, 10 August 2002

A near full-house shirt-sleeved crowd assembled at Carrow Road to usher in the start of another football season. After the play-off drama of three months earlier, they were hungry for more excitement and eager to see City maintain the momentum achieved over the past eighteen months or so.

For once, City didn't disappoint and turned in an opening day performance to rank alongside those of 1993 and 1995, at Arsenal and Luton, respectively. It took half an hour to come, but the season's first goal was a gem and well worth the wait. Clint Easton squared the ball neatly for Phil Mulryne and the Northern Ireland international crashed in a stunning shot from outside the area that dipped and swerved on its way past keeper Danny Coyne.

Before the interval, City doubled their lead when Easton's low, skimming cross saw experienced defender Steve Chettle intervene, but fail to gain proper control, and the ball fell nicely for a jubilant McVeigh to sweep home from ten yards. The Mariners battled on gamely, but were never in the hunt against a rampant Norwich. The third goal came just before the hour mark when Nedergaard's chip forward saw the visitors' player-manager, Paul Groves, make a complete hash of an attempted header back to his goalkeeper. The ball dropped to leave Mulryne with the easiest of chances to grab his second goal.

The scoring was completed twenty minutes before the end when Gary Holt's persistence led to McVeigh and Roberts calmly swapping passes before the former gently lobbed the ball over the advancing Coyne. It had been a perfect start so far as the home fans were concerned, for if Norwich could produce this level of performance before they'd even hit their full stride, who knew what they could achieve over the season as a whole?

Duncan Forbes had 33 years with City, as player, backroom employee, and chief scout

Kevin Keelan – 673 first-team appearances

Ted MacDougall – 66 Norwich goals in three years

John Faulkner – Norwich City coach during Mike Walker's second spell in charge

Player of the Year for 2002-03 went to Adam Drury (second right)

City's FA Youth Cup victors 1983. Goss (front, second left); Donowa (second right)

Wayne 'Bertie' Biggins' football career was rescued from a building site

Bryan Gunn, later Sheriff of Norwich

Popular striker Robert Fleck prepares for kick-off

Defensive stalwarts Ian Butterworth, No 4, and Andy Linighan, right

Kevin Keelan fists away from team-mate Tony Powell's boot

Mick Harford fires in at Bryan Gunn, who is wearing tights on Luton's plastic pitch

Iwan Roberts celebrates a goal with his trademark toothy grin

Local rivals Ipswich won both legs by 2-1

Mike Phelan impressed Alex Ferguson, who bought him for Manchester United

Phil Boyer in action against Birmingham City

Bruce Rioch in his younger days. He managed Norwich in the late-1990s

Doug Livermore, who has played for and coached the Canaries

Tottenham go close in the 1973 League Cup final, which Norwich lost 0-1

Midfielder Neil Adams played 200+ games

Martin O'Neill had two spells as a Norwich player and one as manager

Paul Haylock, near left, and Greg Downs, No 3, on defensive duty

Flying winger Ruel Fox goes stride for stride

Goalkeeper Chris Woods won the first 4 of his 43 England caps while with Norwich

John Ryan top-scored from midfield in 1977-78

Jeremy Goss memorably scored
twice against Bayern Munich in 1993

This locomotive name-plate hangs over the players' tunnel at Carrow Road

Spencer Prior, left, John Polston, No 5, and goalkeeper Gunn in the thick of it

Mel Machin, coach of Norwich who became manager of Manchester City

Zema Abbey signed from Cambridge in 2000

Dave Stringer's squad of 1989-90. The manager is front, middle

Andy Townsend played in two World Cup finals for the Republic of Ireland

Norwich's first-team squad of 1985-86

Norwich overcame Ipswich to reach Wembley

An example of Norwich's programme 2002-03

Skipper Martin O'Neill leads out the team in 1983

Steve Walford lunges for the ball ahead of Dave Watson and Peter Mendham

Local lad Danny Mills climbs highest. He played for England in the 2002 World Cup

Self-styled Canary Fairy – Sean Yallop

Andy Johnson played 75 games for Norwich

Dale Gordon entertains at the club's 2003 Open Day

John Bond, far right, lines up with his Norwich squad for the 1979-80 season

Kevin Drinkell, centre, was Norwich's leading scorer between 1986-88

Willie Young, far right, had a short and unhappy spell at Carrow Road in 1983

Norwich won this thriller 5-3

Inside the inner sanctum. The Home dressing room in 2003

Dale Gordon, former Norwich hero, signs autographs at the Open Day in 2003

2003 Player of the Year Adam Drury, right, with runner-up, keeper Robert Green

Mike Sheron – 38 Norwich appearances
but only 7 goals

Keith Bertschin looks on as Greg Downs challenges

Bryan Gunn fists clear with Ian Butterworth, No 4, in attendance

Martin O'Neill locks legs with Luton's Steve White in a 1982 promotion battle

GUIDE TO SEASONAL SUMMARIES

Col 1: Match number (for league fixtures); Round (for cup-ties).
e.g. 2:1 means 'Second round; first leg.'
e.g. 4R means 'Fourth round replay.'

Col 2: Date of the fixture and whether Home (H), Away (A), or Neutral (N).

Col 3: Opposition.

Col 4: Attendances. Home gates appear in roman; Away gates in *italics*.
Figures in **bold** indicate the largest and smallest gates, at home and away.
Average home and away attendances appear after the final league match.
N.B. Home attendances are those registered with the Football League and should be taken as accurate.

Col 5: Respective league positions of Norwich and their opponents after the match.
Norwich's position appears on the top line in roman.
Their opponents' position appears on the second line in *italics*.
For cup-ties, the division and position of opponents is provided.
e.g. *2:12* means the opposition are twelfth in Division 2.

Col 6: The top line shows the result: W(in), D(raw), or L(ose).
The second line shows Norwich's cumulative points total.

Col 7: The match score, Norwich's given first.
Scores in **bold** indicate Norwich's biggest league win and heaviest defeat.

Col 8: The half-time score, Norwich's given first.

Col 9: The top line shows Norwich's scorers and times of goals in roman.
The second line shows opponents' scorers and times of goals in *italics*.
A 'p' after the time of a goal denotes a penalty; 'og' an own-goal.
The third line gives the name of the match referee.

Team line-ups: Norwich line-ups appear on the top line, irrespective of whether they are home or away. Opposition teams appear on the second line in *italics*.
Players of either side who are sent off are marked !
Norwich players making their league debuts are displayed in **bold**.
In the era of squad numbers, players' names are positioned as far as possible as if they were still wearing shirts 1 to 11.

Substitutes: Names of substitutes appear only if they actually took the field.
A player substituted is marked *
A second player substituted is marked ^
A third player substituted is marked "
These marks indicate the sequence of substitutions.

N.B. For clarity, all information appearing in *italics* relates to opposing teams.

No	Date	Att	Pos	Pt	F-A	H-T	Scorers, Times, and Referees	1	2	3	4	5	6	7	8	9	10	11	12 sub used
1	H EVERTON			D	1-1	1-0	Bone 39	Keelan	Payne	Butler	Stringer	Forbes	Briggs	Livermore*	Bone	Cross	Paddon	Anderson	O'Donnell
	12/8	28,851		1			*Royle 79*	*Lawson*	*Newton*	*McLoughlan*	*Kendall*	*Kenyon*	*Lyons*	*Husband*	*Bernard*	*Royle*	*Harvey*	*Connolly*	
							Ref: B Homewood	The First Division adventure kicks off and Keelan saves spectacularly from Jim Husband. Against the run of play Bone takes Livermore's pass and speeds through for a fine solo goal. Joe Royle heads John Connolly's cross firmly in to level. Cross has a late penalty appeal waved away.											
2	A IPSWICH			W	2-1	1-1	Anderson 13, Bone 72	Keelan	Payne	Butler	Stringer	Forbes	Briggs	Livermore	Bone	Cross	Paddon	Anderson	
	15/8	*29,544*		3			*Hamilton 24*	*Best*	*Mills*	*Beattie*	*Collard*	*Hunter*	*Jefferson*	*Hamilton*	*Viljoen*	*Belfitt*	*Whymark*	*Lambert*	
							Ref: R Kirkpatrick	A tense but marvellous night against the old enemy. Paddon splits the Town defence and Anderson skips through to lob David Best. Forbes' clearance falls conveniently for Bryan Hamilton to equalise. The travelling fans are singing again when Cross sets up Bone for a sweet winner.											
3	A MANCHESTER C		11	L	0-3	0-1		Keelan	Payne	Butler	Stringer	Forbes	Briggs	Livermore	Bone	Cross	Paddon	Anderson*	Hubbard
	19/8	*30,920*	*12*	3			*Lee 14, 78, Bell 74*	*Corrigan*	*Barrett*	*Donachie*	*Doyle*	*Booth*	*Towers*	*Summerbee*	*Bell*	*Davies**	*Lee*	*Jeffries*	*Mellor*
							Ref: V James	Keelan palms away Mike Summerbee's lob, but Francis Lee is on hand to shoot in. After the break Paddon touches a free-kick to Stringer who nets a scorcher, but the linesman spots an infringement. Keelan can't hold a Summberbee corner and Colin Bell nets. Lee slots in a smart third.											
4	H SOUTHAMPTON		13	D	0-0	0-0		Keelan	Payne	Butler	Stringer	Forbes	Briggs	Livermore*	Bone	Cross	Paddon	Anderson	Foggo
	23/8	25,434	*6*	4				*Martin*	*McCarthy*	*Burns*	*Fisher*	*McGrath*	*Steele*	*Stokes*	*Channon*	*Davies*	*O'Neill*	*Jenkins*	
							Ref: B Daniels	Stringer is booked for a heavy challenge on the dangerous Mick Channon. Forbes keeps a tight rein on Ron Davies, the former City centre-forward. Ref Daniels struggles to control a frenetic game. Paddon goes close with a thundering free-kick which clears Eric Martin's crossbar.											
5	H DERBY		9	W	1-0	0-0	Gemmill 54(og)	Keelan	Payne	Butler	Stringer*	Forbes	Briggs	Livermore	Bone	Cross	Paddon	Anderson	Self
	26/8	29,487	*15*	6				*Boulton*	*Powell*	*Nish*	*Hennessey**	*McFarland*	*Todd*	*McGovern*	*Gemmill*	*O'Hare*	*Hector*	*Walker*	*Durban*
							Ref: T Oliver	The reigning champions parade David Nish, who, at £225,000, recently became the UK's most expensive player. Bone goes close early and then Keelan does well to prevent a Jim Walker corner going in. City celebrate after Archie Gemmill hooks a Paddon drive into his own net.											
6	H STOKE		9	W	**2-0**	2-0	Paddon 32, Stringer 43	Keelan	Payne	Butler	Stringer	Forbes	Briggs	Livermore	Bone	Cross	Paddon	Anderson	
	30/8	30,269	*19*	8				*Banks*	*Pejic*	*Marsh*	*Lees*	*Smith*	*Skeels*	*Robertson*	*Greenhoff*	*Ritchie*	*Hurst**	*Dobing*	*Conroy*
							Ref: A Hart	Struggling Stoke put up little resistance. Paddon and Stringer beat Gordon Banks with drives from outside the area within a ten-minute spell. The goals come either side of Terry Lees having an effort disallowed for the visitors. Tony Waddington's experienced outfit looks dispirited.											
7	A LEEDS		11	L	0-2	0-2		Keelan	Payne	Butler	Stringer	Forbes	Briggs	Livermore	Bone	Cross	Paddon	Anderson*	Hubbard
	2/9	*34,261*	*4*	8			*Jordan 6, Charlton 26*	*Harvey*	*Reaney*	*Cherry*	*Bremner*	*Charlton*	*Hunter*	*Lorimer*	*Clarke*	*Jordan*	*Giles*	*Gray*	
							Ref: W Castle	Joe Jordan glances in a Jack Charlton free-kick. Charlton nets a rare goal with his feet after Jordan's effort is blocked on the goal-line. Trevor Cherry hits the bar from 30 yards. Bone is the main threat as Canaries improve after the break. Forbes is booked for the third successive game.											
8	H SHEFFIELD UTD		10	D	1-1	0-0	*Goulding 78(og)*	Keelan	Payne	Butler	Stringer	Forbes	Briggs	Livermore	Bone	Cross	Paddon	Anderson*	O'Donnell
	9/9	22,228	*8*	9			Dearden 60	*McAllister*	*Goulding*	*Hemsley*	*Flynn*	*McKenzie*	*Hockey*	*Woodward*	*Badger*	*Dearden*	*Currie*	*Scullion*	
							Ref: H New	Johnny Harris's men start without skipper Eddie Colquhoun who is taken ill at their hotel. A mad motorway dash sees Ian McKenzie arrive in the nick of time. Billy Dearden's opener is cancelled out as Steve Goulding deflects a Bone shot in. Late City pressure fails to yield a winner.											
9	A WEST HAM		12	L	**0-4**	0-3	*[Taylor 41]*	Keelan	Payne	Butler	Anderson	Forbes	Briggs	Livermore	Bone	Cross	Paddon	O'Donnell	
	16/9	*27,780*	*9*	9			*Brooking 31, Robson 37, 78p,*	*Grotier*	*McDowell*	*Lampard*	*Bonds*	*Taylor*	*Moore*	*Tyler*	*Best*	*Holland*	*Brooking*	*Robson*	
							Ref: A Jones	Ron Saunders is away spying on a player and City use Anderson as makeshift defender. Ron Greenwood's men run riot, with Trevor Brooking and Bryan Robson heading in Bobby Moore crosses and Tommy Taylor stabbing in after a corner. Briggs pulls down Brooking for a penalty.											
10	H ARSENAL		11	W	3-2	2-1	Anderson 2, 82, Cross 30	Keelan	Payne	Butler	Govier	Forbes	Briggs	Livermore	Bone	Cross*	Paddon	Anderson	O'Donnell
	23/9	32,170	*6*	11			*Storey 29, Radford 63*	*Barnett*	*Rice*	*McNab*	*Storey*	*McLintock*	*Roberts*	*Marinello*	*Ball*	*Radford*	*Kennedy*	*Graham*	
							Ref: D Turner	A storming game sees ex-Gunner Anderson convert Bone's pass after John Roberts dithers. Peter Storey hammers a leveller but Cross's head regains the lead from Paddon's cross. John Radford fires in, but Anderson wins it with a superbly directed header from Neil O'Donnell's chip.											

11	A	CRYSTAL PALACE	10	W	**2-0**	2-0	Bone 12, Paddon 26	Keelan	Payne	Butler	Govier	Forbes	Briggs	Livermore	Bone*	Cross	Paddon	Anderson	**Blair**
	30/9	*21,255*	19	13				*Jackson*	*Payne D*	*Roffey*	*Kellard*	*Phillip*	*McCormick*	*Pinkney*	*Craven*	*Jenkins*	*Hinshelwood*	*Hughes*	
							Ref: K Styles	Ross Jenkins clears off the line from Govier, but Anderson returns the ball and Bone fires home. Paddon heads over the stranded John Jackson for another. Expensive signing Iain Phillip has an unhappy debut for a mediocre Palace, for whom Paul Hinshelwood is the only bright spark.											
12	A	NEWCASTLE	12	L	1-3	1-1	Cross 24	Keelan	Payne	Butler*	Govier	Forbes	Briggs	Livermore	Bone	Cross	Paddon	Anderson	Blair
	7/10	*18,080*	*11*	13			*Tudor 29, 53, Guthrie 73*	*McFaul*	*Craig*	*Guthrie*	*Gibb*	*Howard*	*Moncur*	*Barrowlough*	*Smith*	*Tudor*	*Hodgson*	*Hibbitt*	
							Ref: R Capey	Bone's low cross is slid in by Cross, but John Tudor quickly levels by lobbing Keelan. Butler departs in the first half with a gashed leg. Tudor lashes in Terry Hibbitt's cross. City are polished off by Joe Harvey's outfit when Ron Guthrie thunders the ball in after a free-kick is teed up.											
13	H	TOTTENHAM	10	W	2-1	1-1	Cross 3, 77	Keelan	Payne	Black	Stringer	Forbes	Briggs	Livermore	Bone	Cross	Paddon	Anderson	
	14/10	34,445	*5*	15			*Chivers 31*	*Jennings*	*Kinnear*	*Knowles*	*Naylor*	*England*	*Beal*	*Gilzean*	*Perryman*	*Chivers*	*Coates*	*Peters**	*Pearce*
							Ref: P Partridge	A big crowd is enthralled by a vibrant game. Cross gets City off to a dream start after Anderson's sprint and cross. Martin Chivers glances in a deft header from Alan Gilzean's cross. Bad defending allows Cross to net the winner from a corner. Skilful Spurs are sunk by City's work-rate.											
14	A	LEICESTER	6	W	2-1	0-0	Cross 73, Paddon 89	Keelan	Payne	Black	Stringer	Forbes	Briggs	Livermore	Bone	Cross	Paddon	Anderson	
	21/10	*19,787*	*18*	17			*Weller 76*	*Shilton*	*Whitworth*	*Roife*	*Sammels*	*Sjoberg*	*Woollett*	*Farrington*	*Birchenall*	*Weller*	*Worthington*	*Glover*	
							Ref: R Lee	Bone has a shot superbly saved by Peter Shilton. Less than 20 minutes from the end Cross beats John Sjoberg and fires home in his 50th game. Keith Weller's fierce shot squeezes through Keelan's hands. A free-kick is touched to Paddon in the final minute and his 35-yarder flies in.											
15	H	LIVERPOOL	7	D	1-1	0-1	Anderson 70	Keelan	Payne*	Butler	Stringer	Forbes	Briggs	Livermore	Bone	Cross	Paddon	Anderson	Howard
	28/10	36,500	*1*	18			*Cormack 18*	*Clemence*	*Lawler*	*Lindsay*	*Smith*	*Lloyd*	*Thompson*	*Keegan*	*Cormack*	*Heighway*	*Boersma*	*Callaghan*	
							Ref: N Paget	The second-highest league gate in City's history see the fast-breaking Reds threaten to end Norwich's 28-match unbeaten home run. Peter Cormack heads home Alec Lindsay's cross. Bill Shankly's side is pegged back as Anderson flicks the ball in after Payne's cross caused havoc.											
16	A	SOUTHAMPTON	10	L	0-1	0-1		Keelan	Payne*	Butler	Stringer	Forbes	Briggs	Livermore	Bone	Cross	Paddon	Anderson	Howard
	4/11	***17,775***	12	18			*McCarthy 33*	*Martin*	*McCarthy*	*Kirkup*	*Fisher*	*Bennett*	*Steele*	*Paine*	*O'Neill*	*Channon**	*Davies*	*Stokes*	*Byrne*
							Ref: W Gow	Payne is carried off for the second week running, this time with a broken ankle. A corner drifts over a decoy man to the feet of Rob McCarthy, who has plenty of time to pick his spot. Ted Bates' side rarely threaten again but City fail to maintain their midfield dominance of the first half.											
17	H	IPSWICH	8	D	0-0	0-0		Keelan	Butler	Black	Stringer	Forbes	Briggs	Livermore	Bone	Cross	Paddon	Anderson	
	11/11	34,640	*7*	19				*Best*	*Mills*	*Harper*	*Morris*	*Hunter*	*Beattie*	*Hamilton*	*Viljoen*	*Johnson*	*Whymark*	*Lambert*	
							Ref: H Hackney	The first top-flight derby at Carrow Road is, predictably, tight and tense. This is a poor spectacle and it's Ipswich who look the more likely scorers, but Keelan is in top form. New signing David Johnson gives City problems. Kevin Beattie has an effort cleared off the line by Butler.											
18	H	WEST BROM	6	W	**2-0**	1-0	Stringer 9, Paddon 47	Keelan	Butler	Black	Stringer	Forbes	Briggs	Livermore	Bone	Cross	Paddon	Anderson	
	18/11	21,607	*19*	21				*Latchford*	*Nisbet*	*Wilson*	*Cantello*	*Robertson*	*Merrick*	*Suggett*	*Brown T*	*Gould*	*Brown A*	*Hartford*	
							Ref: R Tinkler	Albion strike the woodwork, but City go ahead when Butler's dipping free-kick is met by Stringer and the ball flies in off his shins. Forbes picks up a fifth booking of the season. Seconds after Len Cantello hits the bar, Paddon nets another piledriver free-kick after a foul on Bone.											
19	A	BIRMINGHAM	7	L	1-4	1-1	Black 22 *[Hatton 85]*	Keelan	Butler	Black	Stringer*	Govier	Briggs	Livermore	Bone	Cross	Paddon	Anderson	O'Donnell
	25/11	*32,890*	*16*	21			*Pendrey 36, Hope 73, Want 75,*	*Latchford D*	*Martin*	*Want*	*Pendrey*	*Hynd*	*Harland*	*Hope*	*Calderwood*	*Latchford B*	*Hatton*	*Taylor*	
							Ref: G Kew	Black's first league goal is a freak as his 40-yard lob somehow drifts in. After Gary Pendrey levels, City go down to ten men when Stringer exits clutching his ribs and then sub O'Donnell is knocked unconscious. The disruption is too much and Fred Goodwin's men hit three more.											
20	H	MANCHESTER U	11	L	0-2	0-1		Keelan	Butler	Black	Stringer	Govier	Briggs	Livermore	**Cheesley**	Cross	Paddon	Anderson*	Howard
	2/12	35,770	*17*	21			*Moore 15, MacDougall 89*	*Stepney*	*O'Neill*	*Dunne*	*Morgan*	*Sadler*	*Buchan*	*Young*	*MacDougall*	*Charlton*	*Davies*	*Moore*	
							Ref: D Smith	To many fans' dismay, popular Bone is dropped and replaced by debutant Cheesley. Ian Moore nets a rising drive from 18 yards after good work by £200,000 signing Ted MacDougall. The Scot then strikes a post and, near the end, ensures Norwich's first home defeat in 32 matches.											
21	A	CHELSEA	13	L	1-3	0-0	Bone 76	Keelan	Butler	Black	Stringer	Govier	Briggs*	Livermore	Bone	Cross	Paddon	Anderson	Howard
	9/12	*29,998*	*5*	21			*Garner 47, Hutchinson 57, 78*	*Phillips*	*Harris*	*McCreadie*	*Hollins*	*Droy*	*Webb*	*Garner*	*Hudson*	*Osgood*	*Hutchinson*	*Houseman*	
							Ref: C Fallon	After a quiet first half at the Bridge, Alan Hudson squares to big Bill Garner, who beats Keelan. Ian Hutchinson volleys a second. The recalled Bone then nets a brilliant solo goal, dribbling round John Phillips. The City revival is quickly crushed as Hutchinson slides in his second goal.											

No	Date		Att	Pos	Pt	F-A	H-T	Scorers, Times, and Referees	1	2	3	4	5	6	7	8	9	10	11	12 sub used
22	A	COVENTRY		13	L	1-3	0-1	Howard 63	Keelan	Butler	Black	Stringer	Govier	Briggs	Livermore	Bone	Cross	Paddon	Anderson*	Howard
	16/12		*19,819*	*10*	21			*Stein 13, 71, Alderson 47*	*Ramsbottom*	*Coop*	*Cattlin*	*Smith*	*Dugdale*	*Parker*	*Mortimer*	*Alderson*	*Stein*	*Carr*	*Hutchison*	
								Ref: R Crabb	Colin Stein heads in Brian Alderson's corner and Alderson thunders in a second. The Sky Blues look lively under the control of Joe Mercer and Gordon Milne. Howard pulls a goal back, but Mortimer hits the post, Alderson has one ruled out and Stein converts a rebound off Keelan.											
23	H	WOLVERHAMPTON		13	D	1-1	1-0	Bone 21	Keelan	Butler	Black	Stringer	Govier	Briggs	Livermore	Bone	Cross	Paddon	Anderson	
	23/12		**19,320**	*9*	22			*Dougan 71*	*Parkes*	*Taylor*	*Shaw*	*Bailey*	*McAlle*	*Jefferson*	*Sunderland**	*Richards*	*Hibbitt*	*Hegan*	*Kindon*	*Dougan*
								Ref: R Toseland	City are on top through the first half, with Anderson making his 250th appearance. Briggs' corner is headed on by Govier for Bone to nod in. Failure to add a second is costly. Defensive hesitation leaves Keelan stranded and Bernard Shaw finds Derek Dougan, who heads the equaliser.											
24	A	ARSENAL		14	L	0-2	0-0		Keelan	Butler	Black	Stringer	Govier	Briggs*	Livermore	Bone	Cheesley	Paddon	Anderson	Howard
	26/12		*39,038*	*2*	22			*Radford 60, Ball 75*	*Wilson*	*Nelson**	*McNab*	*Storey*	*Blockley*	*Simpson*	*Armstrong*	*Ball*	*Radford*	*Kennedy*	*Kelly*	*George*
								Ref: J Taylor	Norwich play some neat football early on, but after a deadlocked first half, Charlie George comes on for the injured Sammy Nelson and livens up Bertie Mee's men. George Armstrong crosses to John Radford and he chips in the first. Alan Ball fires in from 12 yards to end the contest.											
25	H	MANCHESTER C		14	D	1-1	1-0	Paddon 22	Keelan	Butler	Black	Stringer*	Govier	Briggs	Livermore	Bone	Cheesley	Paddon	Anderson	Foggo
	30/12		23,900	*11*	23			*Towers 74*	*Corrigan*	*Jeffries*	*Pardoe*	*Doyle*	*Booth*	*Barrett*	*Summerbee*	*Hill*	*Marsh*	*Mellor*	*Towers*	
								Ref: J Hunting	Tommy Booth impedes young Cheesley, and Paddon thrashes home the free-kick in characteristic style. Keelan keeps the scores level with an astonishing acrobatic save from Rodney Marsh. Both defences look uneasy and Norwich's is punished when Tony Towers powers in a shot.											
26	A	DERBY		15	L	0-1	0-1		Keelan	Butler	Black	Stringer	Govier	Briggs	Livermore	Cheesley*	Cross	Paddon	Anderson	O'Donnell
	6/1		*27,850*	*5*	23			*Hinton 35p*	*Boulton*	*Nish*	*Daniel*	*O'Hare*	*McFarland*	*Todd*	*McGovern*	*Gemmill*	*Davies*	*Hector*	*Hinton*	
								Ref: W Hall	Butler's tackle on Kevin Hector is harshly deemed worthy of a penalty, which Alan Hinton cracks past Keelan. Near the end, Roy McFarland's high tackle on Anderson in the area goes unpunished, leaving City feeling hard done by. Derby boss Brian Clough scoffs at Norwich's moans.											
27	H	LEEDS		15	L	1-2	0-2	Cross 84	Keelan	Payne	Butler	Stringer	Forbes	Briggs*	Livermore	Howard	Cross	Paddon	Anderson	O'Donnell
	20/1		27,236	*3*	23			*Jordan 21, Clarke 35*	*Harvey*	*Reaney*	*Cherry*	*Bremner*	*Madeley*	*Hunter*	*Lorimer*	*Clarke*	*Jordan*	*Giles*	*Bates*	
								Ref: E Wallace	Paul Reaney lobs the ball forward and City stand like statues as Joe Jordan cashes in. Jordan fluffs a sitter soon after. Peter Lorimer's drive is blocked on the line by Butler, but Allan Clarke snaps up the rebound. Cross' slick finish bags a consolation in this fifth meeting of the season.											
28	A	SHEFFIELD UTD		17	L	0-2	0-2		Keelan	Payne	Butler	Stringer	Forbes	Briggs*	Livermore	Bone	Cross	Paddon	Anderson	Howard
	27/1		*20,459*	*15*	23			*Dearden 29, Woodward 35*	*McAlister*	*Badger*	*Hemsley*	*Flynn*	*Colquhoun*	*Eddy*	*Woodward*	*Salmons*	*Dearden*	*Currie*	*Scullion**	*Speight*
								Ref: B Homewood	City are relieved as the ref fails to spot a Butler handball and later gives a goal-kick when Forbes heads a United chance behind. Bill Dearden sidefoots Alan Woodward's flag-kick into the net. Woodward then curls another corner straight in with Keelan distracted by a hefty challenge.											
29	H	WEST HAM		17	L	0-1	0-1		Keelan	Payne	Butler	Stringer	Anderson	Briggs	Livermore	Bone*	Cross	Paddon	Howard	O'Donnell
	10/2		32,286	*7*	23			*Robson 32*	*Ferguson*	*McDowell*	*Lampard*	*Bonds*	*Taylor*	*Moore*	*Ayris*	*Best*	*Lutton*	*Brooking*	*Robson*	
								Ref: B Castle	City are desperate for points after ten winless league games and it shows. It's a disappointing display against Ron Greenwood's men. Trevor Brooking's corner is backheeled by Billy Bonds for Bryan 'Pop' Robson to net. Hammers field debutant Bertie Lutton, on loan from Brighton.											
30	H	NEWCASTLE		20	L	0-1	0-1		Keelan	Payne	Butler	Stringer	Govier*	**Hockey**	Livermore	Blair	Cross	Paddon	**Suggett**	Anderson
	24/2		26,411	*5*	23			*Macdonald 23*	*McFaul*	*Craig*	*Clark*	*Nattrass*	*Howard*	*Moncur*	*Barrowcl'gh*	*Reid*	*Macdonald*	*Tudor*	*Hibbitt*	
								Ref: M Sinclair	New faces Hockey and Suggett provide much-needed new blood, but some players have next week's Wembley date on their minds. Malcolm Macdonald outpaces Govier to hammer the winner. The ref refuses to allow Paddon to receive treatment and a hail of cushions comes his way.											
31	H	COVENTRY		20	D	1-1	1-0	Cross 44	Keelan	Payne	Butler	Stringer	Forbes	Hockey	Livermore	Blair	Cross	Paddon	Anderson	
	7/3		28,829	*11*	24			*Carr 80*	*Glazier*	*Coop*	*Cattlin*	*Smith*	*Barry*	*Parker*	*McGuire*	*Alderson**	*Stein*	*Carr*	*Hutchison*	*Dugdale*
								Ref: T Oliver	Tommy Hutchison is in fine form and gives Payne a torrid time, the full-back being booked for one challenge on him. Forgetting the Wembley misery of four days ago, Cross nets after Livermore cashes in on a Willie Carr blunder. Carr equalises after Keelan blocks a Hutchison effort.											

No	Venue	Opponent	Pos	Res	F-A	H-T	Scorers, Times, and Referees	1	2	3	4	5	6	7	8	9	10	11	12 sub used
32	A	TOTTENHAM	21	L	0-3	0-1		Keelan	Payne	Butler	Stringer	Forbes	Hockey	Livermore	Howard*	Cross	Paddon	**Mellor**	Blair
	10/3	*25,081*	*9*	24			*Pearce 3, Chivers 77p, 87*	*Jennings*	*Kinnear*	*Knowles*	*Coates*	*Collins*	*Beal*	*Neighbour*	*Perryman*	*Chivers*	*Peters*	*Pearce*	
							Ref: R Matthewson	Cyril Knowles' free-kick eludes the Norwich defence and Jimmy Pearce shows a cool finish. Payne brings down Pearce for Martin Chivers to shoot home from the spot. Relegation worries deepen as Chivers finishes things off by nodding in Pearce's excellent chip over Keelan's head.											
33	H	LEICESTER	21	D	1-1	1-1	Paddon 23p	Keelan	Butler	Black	Stringer	Forbes	Hockey	Howard	Suggett	Cheesley	Paddon	Mellor	
	17/3	25,299	*14*	25			*Glover 39*	*Shilton*	*Whitworth*	*Rofe*	*Sammels*	*Manley*	*Cross*	*Farrington*	*Birchenall*	*Weller*	*Worthington*	*Glover*	
							Ref: G Tew	City look anxious and disjointed, even after Mellor, in his first home game, wins a penalty when pulled back by Steve Whitworth. Paddon puts away the spot-kick, and Cheesley goes close to a second but Peter Shilton saves well. Len Glover gallops clear to equalise with a brilliant goal.											
34	A	LIVERPOOL	21	L	1-3	0-0	Mellor 77	Keelan	Butler	Black	Stringer	Forbes	Hockey	Howard*	Suggett	Briggs	Paddon	Mellor	Cheesley
	24/3	*42,995*	*1*	25			*Lawler 50, Hughes 54, Hall 87*	*Clemence*	*Lawler*	*Lindsay*	*Smith*	*Lloyd*	*Hughes*	*Keegan*	*Cormack*	*Hall*	*Heighway*	*Callaghan*	
							Ref: H New	A dogged display against the leaders, but City crumble to two goals in four minutes. Chris Lawler bursts through to chest over the line. Steve Heighway's shot is blocked and falls to Emlyn Hughes, who cracks home from 18 yards. Black's cross finds Mellor who gives City late hope.											
35	H	BIRMINGHAM	21	L	1-2	0-2	Stringer 61	Keelan	Butler	Black	Stringer	Forbes	Briggs*	Hockey	Anderson	Suggett	Paddon	Mellor	Cross
	31/3	23,899	*15*	25			*Latchford R 15, 30*	*Latchford D*	*Martin*	*Paget*	*Pendrey*	*Hynd*	*Roberts*	*Campbell*	*Francis*	*Latchford R*	*Hatton*	*Taylor*	
							Ref: V James	Bob Hatton hits the bar, but Bob Latchford is on hand to convert the rebound. Forbes is given a roasting by Latchford, who strides away from his marker to shoot the second, deflected in off Butler. Stringer powers home a header from Suggett's corner, but late pressure yields nothing.											
36	A	EVERTON	22	D	2-2	2-0	Cross 43, 44	Keelan	Butler	Black	Stringer	Forbes	Hockey*	Anderson	Suggett	Cross	Paddon	Mellor	O'Donnell
	3/4	*21,806*	*15*	26			*Belfitt 48, Kendall 53p*	*Lawson*	*Wright*	*McLaughlan*	*Kendall*	*Kenyon*	*Hurst*	*Husband*	*Bernard*	*Belfitt*	*Harper*	*Connolly*	
							Ref: C Howell	The run without a win looks set to end as Cross converts a cool lob over Dave Lawson and then beats him with a looping header. But it all goes pear-shaped as Joe Harper's backheel sets up Rod Belfitt, and then Stringer is harshly penalised when the ball appears to strike his shoulder.											
37	A	MANCHESTER U	22	L	0-1	0-0		Keelan	Butler	Black	Stringer	Forbes	Hockey	Anderson	Suggett	Cross	Paddon	Mellor	
	7/4	***48,593***	*19*	26			*Martin 82*	*Stepney*	*Young*	*James*	*Graham*	*Holton*	*Buchan*	*Morgan*	*Kidd**	*Charlton*	*Law*	*Martin*	*Anderson*
							Ref: H Hackney	It's a relegation 'four-pointer' against Frank O'Farrell's side, and City fight hard to keep them at bay. Second-half United pressure is relentless and the winner comes late when Mick Martin, standing in for the AWOL George Best, heads a fine goal after Willie Morgan jinked past Black.											
38	H	CHELSEA	22	W	1-0	1-0	Cross 38	Keelan	Payne	Black	Stringer	Forbes	Hockey	Livermore	Suggett*	Cross	Paddon	Mellor	Cheesley
	14/4	24,425	*15*	28				*Bonetti*	*Harris*	*McCreadie*	*Hollins*	*Hinton*	*Droy*	*Britton*	*Baldwin*	*Osgood*	*Boyle*	*Brolly*	
							Ref: B Raby	After 19 league games without a win, roars of relief greet Cross's 14th goal of the season. Mellor and Suggett are involved in a move which Cross finishes with a venomous shot. Man-of-the-match Suggett has too much guile for Dave Sexton's side. Survival hopes are given a boost.											
39	A	WEST BROM	20	W	1-0	0-0	Cross 84	Keelan	Payne	Black	Stringer	Forbes	Hockey	Livermore	Suggett	Cross	Paddon*	Mellor	Cheesley
	21/4	*23,431*	*22*	30				*Osborne*	*Minton*	*Wilson*	*Cantello*	*Wile*	*Merrick**	*Brown A*	*Shaw*	*Astle*	*Hartford*	*Johnston*	*Robertson*
							Ref: W Johnson	Still on a high after the Chelsea win, City look determined not to lose this 'four-pointer'. Paddon goes off injured during a rugged affair littered with fouls. Mellor surges down the right and miscues his shot, but Roger Minton allows it to reach Cross, who scores. Cue wild celebrations!											
40	A	WOLVERHAMPTON	20	L	0-3	0-0		Keelan	Payne	Black	Stringer	Forbes	Hockey*	Livermore	Suggett	Cheesley	Paddon	Mellor	Howard
	23/4	*20,222*	*8*	30			*Sunderland 55, 84, Richards 77*	*Parkes*	*Taylor*	*Parkin*	*Bailey*	*Jefferson*	*McAlle*	*Powell*	*Sunderland*	*Richards*	*Dougan*	*Wagstaffe*	
							Ref: D Nippard	Another gruelling 90 minutes in the mud and rain. The conditions are so bad that two players change their shirts during the first half. The Alan Sunderland/John Richards partnership is in great form. Richards' goal is his 34th this season. City now need two more points to ensure safety.											
41	H	CRYSTAL PALACE	20	W	2-1	1-1	Suggett 35, Stringer 90	Keelan	Payne	Black	Stringer	Forbes	Hockey	Livermore	Suggett	Cross	Paddon	Mellor	
	24/4	**36,688**	*21*	32			*Rogers 27p*	*Jackson*	*Mulligan*	*Taylor*	*Roffey*	*Blyth*	*Phillip*	*Possee*	*Payne*	*Craven*	*Cooke*	*Rogers*	
							Ref: H Williams	A huge crowd generates a great atmosphere. Two points will preserve top-flight football, but there are glum faces when Forbes impedes Derek Possee and Don Rogers does the rest. Suggett's first City goal soon cancels this out. Stringer's dramatic injury-time header sparks joyful scenes.											
42	A	STOKE	20	L	0-2	0-1		Keelan	Payne	Black	Stringer	Forbes	Hockey	Livermore	Suggett	Cross	Briggs	Mellor	
	28/4	*19,350*	*14*	32			*Greenhoff 25, Ritchie 58*	*Farmer*	*Marsh*	*Pejic*	*Mahoney*	*Smith*	*Bloor*	*Robertson*	*Greenhoff*	*Ritchie*	*Hurst*	*Eastham**	*Burrows*
	Home	Away					Ref: J Wrennall	With relegation avoided, the lack of tension allows a flowing game. Geoff Hurst and Jimmy Greenhoff combine cleverly for the first goal. John Ritchie stabs home a cross from Mike Pejic to clinch the two points and a place in the next Watney Cup for Tony Waddington's high-scorers.											
Average	28,557	27,187																	

League Cup			Att			F-A	H-T	Scorers, Times, and Referees	1	2	3	4	5	6	7	8	9	10	11	12 sub used
2	H	LEICESTER		11	W	2-1	1-0	Bone 37, 72	Keelan	Payne	Butler	Stringer	Forbes	Briggs	Livermore	Bone	Cross	Paddon	Anderson	
		6/9	22,498	*17*				*Sammels 75*	*Shilton*	*Whitworth*	*Sjoberg*	*Woollett*	*Manley*	*Cross*	*Weller*	*Sammels*	*Worthington*	*Stringfellow*	*Farrington*	
								Ref: R Challis	Bone nets a handsome overhead kick. Paddon can make the tie safe but hits a penalty wide. Soon afterwards Bone's fan club is in ecstasy again following a neat dummy and backheel. Jon Sammels puts Jimmy Bloomfield's men back in with a chance. Paddon is booked for time-wasting.											
3	A	HULL		10	W	2-1	1-0	Paddon 7, 48	Keelan	Payne	Butler	Govier	Forbes	Briggs	Livermore	Bone*	Cross	Paddon	Anderson	Blair
		3/10	*11,524*	*2:15*				*Holme 74*	*Wealands*	*Banks*	*DeVries*	*Wilkinson*	*Neill*	*McGill*	*Knighton*	*Houghton*	*Pearson*	*Wagstaff**	*Butler*	*Holme*
								Ref: D Laing	Briggs touches a free-kick aside and Paddon powers it into the net. The bearded midfielder repeats the trick with a 30-yarder after the interval. Bone storms off angrily when subbed. Phil Holme nets for Terry Neill's side two minutes after he comes on. Keelan makes two fine late saves.											
4	A	STOCKPORT		7	W	5-1	2-0	Cross 11, 64, Stringer 24, Bone 47,	Keelan	Payne	Butler	Stringer	Forbes	Briggs	Howard	Bone	Cross	Paddon	Anderson	
		1/11	*16,533*	*4:13*				*Lawther 61* [Howard 84]	*Ogley*	*Ingle*	*Ormrod*	*Spratt*	*Hart*	*Ashworth*	*Garbett*	*Lawther*	*Griffiths*	*Davidson*	*Bingham*	
								Ref: C Thomas	Brian Doyle's side beat West Ham and C Palace in earlier rounds, but have no use for star fan Mike Yarwood's Champagne tonight. Cross heads in early; Stringer nets from a corner. The final goal is the best, Howard netting after a slick move. Saunders wins manager of the month.											
5	A	ARSENAL		6	W	3-0	2-0	Paddon 17, 28, 50	Keelan	Butler	Black	Stringer	Forbes*	Briggs	Livermore	Bone	Cross	Paddon	Anderson	Howard
		21/11	*37,671*	*2*					*Barnett*	*Rice*	*McNab*	*Storey*	*McLintock*	*Simpson*	*Marinello*	*Ball*	*Radford*	*George*	*Kelly*	
								Ref: R Matthewson	Paddon squeezes in a shot through the hands of Geoff Barnett and fires a second home from a tight angle. After an aerial collision, big Forbes is in pain and unable to breathe properly. He is taken to hospital with a punctured lung. Paddon's fine hat-trick is completed by a left-foot drive.											
SF 1	A	CHELSEA		13	W	2-0	2-0	Bone 11, Cross 12	Keelan	Butler	Black	Stringer	Govier	Briggs	Livermore	Bone	Cross	Paddon	Anderson*	Howard
		13/12	*31,775*	*5*					*Phillips*	*Locke*	*McCreadie*	*Hollins*	*Webb*	*Harris*	*Garland*	*Hudson*	*Osgood*	*Hutchinson*	*Houseman*	
								Ref: H New	City break the deadlock with two in a minute. An error by Peter Houseman lets in Cross, whose pass sets up Bone for a fine finish. Bone returns the compliment, feeding Cross, whose lob over John Phillips goes in via the bar. Briggs hits a post. Wembley Stadium is looming large!											
SF 2	H	CHELSEA		14	W	1-0	0-0	Govier 50	Keelan	Butler	Black	Stringer	Govier	Briggs	Livermore	Cheesley	Cross	Paddon	Anderson	
		3/1	34,265	*8*					*Bonetti*	*Locke*	*Harris*	*Hollins*	*Webb*	*Dempsey*	*Baldwin*	*Hudson*	*Osgood*	*Kember*	*Garland*	
								Ref: G Hill (Norwich win 3-0 on aggregate)	The original second leg was abandoned due to thick fog with City leading 3-2 and only five minutes remaining. City have to do it all over again and Govier heads in Stringer's corner to clinch the Wembley place. The fans are in great voice and 'On The Ball City' never sounded so good.											
F	N	TOTTENHAM		20	L	0-1	0-0		Keelan	Payne	Butler	Stringer	Forbes	Briggs	Livermore	Blair*	Cross	Paddon	Anderson	Howard
		3/3	*100,000*	*9*				*Coates 73*	*Jennings*	*Kinnear*	*Knowles*	*Pratt**	*England*	*Beal*	*Gilzean*	*Perryman*	*Chivers*	*Peters*	*Pearce*	*Coates*
		(Rec: £132,000)						Ref: D Smith (At Wembley Stadium)	The club's first trip to Wembley sees the players looking surprisingly relaxed, but the game is no classic. Ralph Coates comes on early for the injured John Pratt and breaks the deadlock with a low drive after Mike England's effort fell to him. Forbes heads a half-chance over the bar.											

FA Cup																				
3	H	LEEDS		15	D	1-1	1-1	Cross 42	Keelan	Butler	Black	Stringer	Forbes	Briggs	Howard	Bone	Cross	Paddon	Anderson	
		13/1	32,310	*3*				*Lorimer 18*	*Harvey*	*Reaney*	*Cherry*	*Bremner*	*Madeley*	*Hunter*	*Lorimer*	*Clarke*	*Jones*	*Giles*	*Bates*	
								Ref: G Hill	Don Revie's celebrated side dominate early, full of poise and accurate passing. Peter Lorimer powers them into an early lead. City battle hard and come back into the game. Cross's header is knocked away by Paul Reaney after David Harvey missed it but Mr Hill says it crossed the line.											
3R	A	LEEDS		15	D	1-1	1-0	Cross 40	Keelan	Butler	Black	Stringer	Forbes	Briggs	Howard	Bone*	Cross	Paddon	Anderson	Cheesley
		17/1	*36,087*	*3*		*aet*		*Giles 69*	*Harvey*	*Reaney*	*Cherry*	*Bremner*	*Madeley*	*Hunter*	*Lorimer*	*Clarke*	*Jones*	*Giles*	*Bates*	
								Ref: G Hill	Keelan puts on a marvellous 120-minute display to keep Leeds at bay. He is only beaten once, by Johnny Giles' bobbling left-foot shot. Earlier Bone had flicked on a Briggs centre for Cross to net a fine header. City survive extra-time and Revie moans that his side should have had six.											
3 2R	N	LEEDS		17	L	0-5	0-4		Keelan	Payne	Butler	Stringer	Forbes	Howard	Livermore	Bone	Cross	Paddon	Anderson	
		29/1	*33,275*	*3*				*Clarke 2, 14, 20, Jones 37, Lorimer 71*	*Harvey*	*Reaney*	*Cherry*	*Bremner*	*Madeley*	*Hunter*	*Lorimer*	*Clarke**	*Jones*	*Giles*	*Bates*	*Yorath*
		(at Villa Park)						Ref: R Matthewson	Norwich's resistance finally crumbles when Allan 'Sniffer' Clarke bags a slick hat-trick in the first 20 minutes. Peter Lorimer's punt swerves viciously to make it five. Don Revie urges City not to fret and says he is sure they'll survive the drop. Over 100,000 watched the three ties.											

		Home					Away					
	P	W	D	L	F	A	W	D	L	F	A	Pts
1 Liverpool	42	17	3	1	45	19	8	7	6	27	23	60
2 Arsenal	42	14	5	2	31	14	9	6	6	26	29	57
3 Leeds	42	15	4	2	45	13	6	7	8	26	32	53
4 Ipswich	42	10	7	4	34	20	7	7	7	21	25	48
5 Wolves	42	13	3	5	43	23	5	8	8	23	31	47
6 West Ham	42	12	5	4	45	25	5	7	9	22	28	46
7 Derby	42	15	3	3	43	18	4	5	12	13	36	46
8 Tottenham	42	10	5	6	33	23	6	8	7	25	25	45
9 Newcastle	42	12	6	3	35	19	4	7	10	25	32	45
10 Birmingham	42	11	7	3	39	22	4	5	12	14	32	42
11 Manchester C	42	12	4	5	36	20	3	7	11	21	40	41
12 Chelsea	42	9	6	6	30	22	4	8	9	19	29	40
13 Southampton	42	8	11	2	26	17	3	7	11	21	35	40
14 Sheffield U	42	11	4	6	28	18	4	6	11	23	41	40
15 Stoke	42	11	8	2	38	17	3	2	16	23	39	38
16 Leicester	42	7	9	5	23	18	3	8	10	17	28	37
17 Everton	42	9	5	7	27	21	4	6	11	14	28	37
18 Manchester U	42	9	7	5	24	19	3	6	12	20	41	37
19 Coventry	42	9	5	7	27	24	4	4	13	13	31	35
20 NORWICH	42	7	9	5	22	19	4	1	16	14	44	32
21 Crys Palace	42	7	7	7	25	21	2	5	14	16	37	30
22 West Brom	42	8	7	6	25	24	1	3	17	13	38	28
	924	236	130	96	724	436	96	130	236	436	724	924

Odds & ends

Double wins: (2) Crystal Palace, West Brom.
Double losses: (5) Birmingham, Leeds, Man U, Newcastle, West Ham.

Won from behind: (1) Crystal Palace (h).
Lost from in front: (2) Newcastle (a), Birmingham (a).

High spots: Seven straight League Cup wins to reach Wembley.
Escaping relegation, despite the distraction of 18 cup-ties.
Attracting 30,000-plus to eleven home matches (one abandoned).
Victory in the first-ever East Anglian derby in Division One.
Dave Stringer's late winner on 24 April 24, which confirmed survival.
Hugely enjoyable home wins against Arsenal and Tottenham.

Low spots: The run of 19 league games without a win.
The narrow loss at Wembley in a disappointing League Cup final.
Defeat by Ipswich in the Texaco Cup final.
Losing skipper Duncan Forbes for seven weeks due to a punctured lung.
The League Cup semi-final abandonment, only 5 minutes from Wembley.
By far the club's lowest-ever tally of league goals (36).

Player of the Year: Kevin Keelan.
Ever-presents: (1) Kevin Keelan.
Hat-tricks: (1) Graham Paddon (LC) v Arsenal.
Opposing hat-tricks: (1) Allan Clarke (Leeds) (LC).
Leading scorer: (16) David Cross.

	Appearances						Goals			
	Lge	*Sub*	LC	*Sub*	FAC	*Sub*	**Lge**	LC	FAC	**Tot**
Anderson, Terry	**33**	*1*	7		3		**4**			**4**
Black, Alan	**22**		3		2		**1**			**1**
Blair, Jim	**2**	*3*	1	*1*						
Bone, Jimmy	**26**		5		3		**5**	4		**9**
Briggs, Max	**34**		7		2					
Butler, Geoff	**35**		7		3					
Cheesley, Paul	**6**	*3*	1			*1*				
Cross, David	**36**	*1*	7		3		**11**	3	2	**16**
Foggo, Ken		*2*								
Forbes, Duncan	**32**		5		3					
Govier, Steve	**12**		3					1		**1**
Hockey, Trevor	**13**									
Howard, Trevor	**6**	*8*	1	*3*	3		**1**	1		**2**
Hubbard, Phil		*2*								
Keelan, Kevin	**42**		7		3					
Livermore, Doug	**37**		6		1					
Mellor, Ian	**11**						**1**			**1**
O'Donnell, Neil	**1**	*8*								
Paddon, Graham	**38**		7		3		**7**	5		**12**
Payne, Clive	**27**		4		1					
Self, Glen		*1*								
Stringer, Dave	**38**		6		3		**4**	1		**5**
Suggett, Colin	**11**						**1**			**1**
(own-goals)							**1**			**1**
23 players used	**462**	*29*	**77**	*4*	**33**	*1*	**36**	**15**	**2**	**53**

No	Date		Att	Pos	Pt	F-A	H-T	Scorers, Times, and Referees	1	2	3	4	5	6	7	8	9	10	11	12 sub used
1	A	WOLVERHAMPTON			L	1-3	1-1	Suggett 12	Keelan	**Prophett**	Black	Stringer	Govier	Briggs	Anderson	Suggett	Cross	Paddon	Mellor	
	25/8		*22,744*		0			*Dougan 8, 60, McCalliog 84*	*Parkes*	*Taylor*	*Parkin*	*Hegan*	*Jefferson*	*McAlle*	*McCalliog*	*Sunderland*	*Richards*	*Dougan*	*Wagstaffe*	
								Ref: V James	Derek Dougan's glancing header is cancelled out by Suggett. In attempting to keep out Dougan's second, Keelan ends up tangled in the netting and brings down the frame of the goal. He is carried off but returns after repairs to him and to the goal. Jim McCalliog's rasping drive seals it.											
2	H	QP RANGERS			D	0-0	0-0		Keelan	Prophett	Black	Stringer	**Rollings**	Briggs	Anderson*	Suggett	Cross	Paddon	Mellor	O'Donnell
	29/8		24,285		1				*Parkes*	*Clement*	*Watson*	*Vena*	*Mancini*	*Hazell*	*Thomas*	*Delve*	*Leach*	*Bowles*	*Givens*	
								Ref: P Reeves	An entertaining affair, but both defences hold firm. Cross heads home, but Mr Reeves spots a push and rules it out. In the later stages, Suggett tumbles under a Terry Mancini challenge but penalty appeals are waved away. Teenager Andy Rollings fills in for suspended skipper Forbes.											
3	H	WEST HAM		16	D	2-2	1-1	Mellor 36, Paddon 80p	Keelan	Prophett	Black	Stringer	Rollings	Briggs	Anderson	Suggett	Cross	Paddon	Mellor	
	1/9		25,378	*14*	2			*Best 12, Robson 71*	*Ferguson*	*Lampard*	*Lock*	*Bonds*	*Taylor*	*Moore*	*Best*	*Holland*	*MacDougall*	*Brooking*	*Robson*	
								Ref: J Hunting	Kevin Lock's free-kick is headed in by Clyde Best. Ian Mellor swivels to net a brilliant equaliser on the volley. Ron Greenwood's men regain the lead when Bryan Robson backheels Trevor Brooking's corner past Keelan. Billy Bonds hauls down Paddon, who picks himself up to level.											
4	A	SOUTHAMPTON		16	D	2-2	2-1	Steele 16 (og), Cross 42	Keelan	Prophett	Black	Stringer	Rollings	Briggs	Anderson	Suggett	Cross	Paddon*	Mellor	**Kellock**
	4/9		*17,658*	*10*	3			*Gilchrist 2, 88*	*Martin*	*McCarthy*	*Steele*	*Fisher*	*Bennett*	*Byrne*	*Paine*	*Channon*	*Gilchrist*	*O'Neill*	*Stokes*	
								Ref: P Walters	Paul Gilchrist converts Hugh Fisher's cross but Jim Steele blunders by deflecting Suggett's shot past his keeper. Cross fires in Mellor's centre. Mick Channon is held but has his penalty saved. Paddon goes off with torn shoulder ligaments. Gilchrist saves a point from Tery Paine's cross.											
5	A	MANCHESTER C		18	L	1-2	0-2	Suggett 60	Keelan	Prophett	Black	Stringer	Forbes	Briggs	Anderson	Suggett	Cross	Grapes*	Mellor	Howard
	8/9		*31,209*	*6*	3			*Lee 42, Bell 44*	*Corrigan*	*Pardoe*	*Donachie*	*Doyle*	*Booth*	*Towers*	*Summerbee*	*Bell*	*Law**	*Lee*	*Marsh*	*Carrodus*
								Ref: P Baldwin	Skipper Forbes returns from his ban, but Stringer's defensive header goes astray and Francis Lee blasts past Keelan. Denis Law's astute pass sends Colin Bell gliding through to score. Suggett's smart volley gives Joe Corrigan no chance. A first win of the season remains out of reach.											
6	H	SOUTHAMPTON		16	W	2-0	0-0	Stringer 58, Cross 67	Keelan	Prophett	Black	Stringer	Forbes	Briggs	Anderson	Suggett	Cross	Howard	Mellor	
	12/9		24,747	*10*	5				*Martin*	*McCarthy*	*Kirkup**	*Fisher*	*Bennett*	*Byrne*	*Paine*	*Channon*	*Gilchrist*	*O'Neill*	*Stokes*	*Mills*
								Ref: J Bent	Stringer heads in a Suggett cross to break the deadlock. Forbes nearly increases the lead but heads against a post. The points are made safe when Suggett's spectacular overhead kick is netted by Cross. The crossbar saves Lawrie McMenemy's men further humiliation after a Cross header.											
7	H	ARSENAL		17	L	**0-4**	0-3	*[Kennedy 85]*	Keelan	Prophett*	Black	Stringer	Forbes	Briggs	Livermore	Suggett	Cross	Anderson	Mellor	Howard
	15/9		29,076	*11*	5			*George 14, McNab 34, Ball 44p,*	*Wilson*	*Rice*	*McNab*	*Storey*	*Blockley*	*George*	*Armstrong*	*Ball*	*Radford*	*Kennedy*	*Kelly*	
								Ref: J Yates	Shortly after a City penalty appeal was ignored, Charlie George beats Keelan with a low drive. A rare goal for Bob McNab, from close range after George hit a post. John Radford is bundled over and Alan Ball converts from the spot. Ray Kennedy swivels to crack home a real beauty.											
8	A	SHEFFIELD UTD		19	L	0-1	0-1		Keelan	**Wilson**	Black	Stringer	Forbes	Briggs*	Livermore	Suggett	Cross	Paddon	Mellor	O'Donnell
	22/9		*19,974*	*9*	5			*Flynn 20*	*McAlister*	*Goulding*	*Hemsley*	*Flynn*	*Colquhoun*	*Eddy*	*Woodward*	*Salmons*	*Dearden*	*Currie*	*Bone*	
								Ref: R Toseland	A debut for experienced full-back Les Wilson, Saunders' new signing from Bristol City. John Flynn nets a firm header from Alan Woodward's cross. Paddon hits the net but the whistle goes for a foul on Tom McAlister. Forbes makes several buccaneering surges upfield, but to no avail.											
9	H	LEEDS		20	L	0-1	0-1		Keelan	Prophett	Wilson*	Stringer	Forbes	Briggs	Livermore	Suggett	Cross	Paddon	Mellor	Payne
	29/9		**31,798**	*1*	5			*Giles 14*	*Harvey*	*Reaney*	*Cherry*	*Bremner*	*McQueen*	*Hunter*	*Jordan*	*Clarke*	*Jones*	*Giles*	*Madeley*	
								Ref: B Daniels	Johnny Giles spearheads a break upfield and his 35-yard piledriver ends in the net after being half-saved by Keelan. Norwich refuse to cave in to Don Revie's table-toppers and launch a series of attacks. Suggett is unlucky as his fine shot flashes just wide. This is not Leeds at their best.											
10	A	DERBY		20	D	1-1	1-1	Suggett 21	Keelan	Prophett	Payne	Stringer	Forbes	Briggs	Livermore	Suggett	Cross	Paddon	Mellor	
	6/10		*25,984*	*4*	6			*Davies 31*	*Boulton*	*Webster*	*Nish*	*Powell*	*Daniel*	*Todd*	*Newton*	*Gemmill*	*Davies*	*Hector*	*Hinton*	
								Ref: R Capey	Building on the good display at Leeds, City shock Derby as Suggett stabs in from close range. Big Roger Davies nets a first-timer after sloppy defensive work. Stringer impedes Kevin Hector, but Alan Hinton lashes the penalty wide. £100,000 signing Henry Newton makes his debut.											

No	Venue / Date	Opponent	Att	Pos	Res / Pts	F-A	H-T	Scorers, Times, Referees	1	2	3	4	5	6	7	8	9	10	11	12 sub used
11	H	COVENTRY		20	D	0-0	0-0		Keelan	Prophett	Payne	Stringer	Forbes	Briggs	Livermore	Suggett	Cross	Paddon	Mellor	
	13/10		22,841	4	7				*Glazier*	*Coop*	*Holmes*	*Mortimer*	*Craven*	*Dugdale*	*Smith*	*Alderson*	*Stein*	*Green*	*Hutchison*	
								Ref: I Smith	Gordon Milne's men have made a fine start to the season, but Norwich attack them hard and a second win of the season looks on the cards. Cross gives John Craven and Alan Dugdale a tricky afternoon, but can't find a way through. Coventry go close late on but don't deserve a win.											
12	H	TOTTENHAM		20	D	1-1	0-1	Livermore 85	Keelan	Prophett	Black	Stringer	Forbes	Briggs	Livermore	Cheesley*	Cross	Paddon	Mellor	Suggett
	20/10		24,819	*15*	8			*Gilzean 45*	*Daines*	*Evans*	*Knowles*	*Pratt*	*England*	*Naylor*	*Gilzean*	*Perryman*	*Chivers*	*Peters*	*Coates*	
								Ref: W Castle	Bill Nicholson's side have long spells on top and City look uneasy at the back. Veteran Alan Gilzean, 35 two days later, steals in to convert a John Pratt corner. Mike England has an effort stopped on the line. Doug Livermore saves Norwich late on, netting after Cross hits the crossbar.											
13	A	CHELSEA		20	L	0-3	0-2		Keelan	Prophett	Black	Stringer	Forbes	Briggs	Livermore*	Suggett	Cross	Paddon	Mellor	Howard
	26/10		*21,953*	*17*	8			*Baldwin 7, 60, Kember 33*	*Bonetti*	*Hollins*	*Wilkins G*	*Kember*	*Webb**	*Harris*	*Garland*	*Hudson*	*Osgood*	*Baldwin*	*Houseman*	*Wilkins R*
								Ref: T Oliver	Friday-night action at Stamford Bridge gets off to a bad start when Peter Houseman pulls the ball back for Tommy Baldwin to score. Steve Kember goes clear to fire past Keelan. City's chances disappear entirely when Alan Hudson's 25-yarder is parried by Keelan and Baldwin nets.											
14	H	LEICESTER		19	W	1-0	1-0	Rofe 25 (og)	Keelan	Payne*	Wilson	Stringer	Forbes	Briggs	Howard	Suggett	Cross	Paddon	O'Donnell	Anderson
	3/11		20,565	*13*	10				*Shilton*	*Whitworth*	*Rofe*	*Stringfellow*	*Munro*	*Cross**	*Weller*	*Sammels*	*Worthington*	*Birchenall*	*Glover*	*Graham*
								Ref: M Sinclair	Frustrated Saunders wields the axe and makes four changes. His new-look side has a midweek cup win and today faces Jimmy Bloomfield's outfit. Dennis Rofe wins the ball from Suggett but his back-pass eludes Peter Shilton. Keith Weller and Len Glover are booked for arguing.											
15	A	STOKE		19	L	0-2	0-1		Keelan	Prophett	Black	Stringer	Forbes	Briggs*	Livermore	Suggett	Cross	Paddon	Howard	Mellor
	10/11		*15,563*	*17*	10			*Ritchie 33, Goodwin 87*	*Farmer*	*Marsh*	*Pejic*	*Dodd*	*Smith**	*Mahoney*	*Robertson*	*Greenhoff*	*Hurst*	*Haslegrave*	*Ritchie*	*Goodwin*
								Ref: G Kew	Tony Waddington's men are always on top. Geoff Hurst is foiled by Keelan at close range. Greenhoff nets but Stoke are furious as Mr Kew rules it out for offside. Mike Pejic's free-kick is converted by John Ritchie for his first home goal since City's last visit. Dave Goodwin seals it.											
16	H	EVERTON		20	L	1-3	0-0	McLaughlin 50(og) *[Forbes 88(og)]*	Keelan	Prophett	Wilson	Stringer	Forbes	Howard	Livermore	Suggett	Cheesley*	Paddon	Mellor	Payne
	17/11		19,825	*4*	10			*Clements 52, Bernard 69,*	*Lawson*	*Darracott*	*McLaughlin*	*Clements*	*Kenyon*	*Hurst*	*Bernard*	*Buckley*	*Lyons*	*Harper*	*Connolly*	
								Ref: T Bosi	John McLaughlin misjudges a header, which sails past his own keeper. Everton hit back and after Pat Buckley's centre deflects in off Forbes, the jeers ring out and cushions are hurled on the pitch. After the match, an explosive row in the boardroom sees Saunders resign on the spot.											
17	A	MANCHESTER U		20	D	0-0	0-0		Keelan	Butler	Wilson	Stringer	Forbes	Briggs	Howard	Suggett	Mellor	Paddon	O'Donnell	
	24/11		*36,338*	*18*	11				*Stepney*	*Buchan*	*Young*	*Greenhoff*	*Holton*	*James*	*Morgan**	*Macari*	*Kidd*	*Graham*	*Best*	*Fletcher*
								Ref: K Styles	Managerless City put on a brave display against Tommy Docherty's men. George Best's recent indiscretions are forgiven as he shows some of his old magic. Brian Kidd hits the bar. Bournemouth's John Bond is favourite for the manager's job and is to be interviewed after this match.											
18	A	BURNLEY		22	L	0-1	0-0		Keelan	Butler	Wilson	Stringer	Forbes	Prophett	Briggs	O'Donnell	**MacDougall**	Suggett	Mellor*	Howard
	8/12		*13,231*	*3*	11			*Ingham 62*	*Stevenson*	*Noble*	*Newton*	*Dobson*	*Waldron*	*Thomson*	*Nulty*	*Ingham*	*Fletcher*	*Collins*	*James*	
								Ref: G Hill	New boss Bond gives a debut to Ted MacDougall, signed from West Ham in a swap deal involving Paddon. But star of this show is Leighton James, who creates Billy Ingham's headed winner. Alan Stevenson saves superbly from lively sub Trevor Howard. City drop to bottom place.											
19	H	LIVERPOOL		21	D	1-1	1-1	Cheesley 1	Keelan	**Machin**	**Benson***	Stringer	Forbes	Prophett	Anderson	MacDougall	Suggett	Cheesley	Briggs	Howard
	15/12		20,184	*2*	12			*Cormack 18*	*Clemence*	*Smith*	*Lindsay*	*Thompson*	*Lloyd*	*Hughes*	*Keegan*	*Cormack*	*Waddle*	*Heighway*	*Callaghan*	
								Ref: D Nippard	Bond's first home game gets off to a rip-roaring start as young Paul Cheesley skates clear across a snow-covered pitch to beat Ray Clemence in the first minute. It's his first goal in 23 senior games. Peter Cormack levels from Ian Callaghan's corner. Debutant John Benson goes off hurt.											
20	A	LEEDS		21	L	0-1	0-0		Keelan	Machin	Prophett	Stringer	Forbes	Howard	Grapes	MacDougall	Suggett	Cheesley*	Briggs	O'Donnell
	22/12		*34,747*	*1*	12			*Yorath 55*	*Harvey*	*Reaney*	*Cherry*	*Bremner*	*McQueen*	*Hunter*	*Lorimer*	*Jordan*	*Jones*	*Yorath*	*Madeley*	
								Ref: D Turner	The runaway league leaders are given a tough afternoon. Terry Yorath nets with a fine diving header from Peter Lorimer's pass, to silence the barracking from home fans. Young Grapes has a fine game on the wing and Howard goes close to grabbing a late reward for Norwich's efforts.											
21	H	IPSWICH		22	L	1-2	1-0	McDougall 26	Keelan	Butler	Prophett	Stringer	Forbes	**Steele**	Grapes	MacDougall	Suggett	Briggs	Howard	
	26/12		29,637	*6*	12			*Johnson 63p, Lambert 78*	*Best*	*Hammond**	*Mills*	*Morris*	*Hunter*	*Beattie*	*Hamilton*	*Osborne*	*Johnson*	*Whymark*	*Lambert*	*Woods*
								Ref: V James	David Best punches a high ball to the feet of debutant Steele, whose shot hits the bar. MacDougall swoops to net the rebound. City hold on grimly until Forbes impedes David Johnson, who tucks in the penalty. Pacy Johnson does the damage again, setting up Mick Lambert's winner.											

No	Date	Att	Pos	Pt	F-A	H-T	Scorers, Times, and Referees	1	2	3	4	5	6	7	8	9	10	11	12 sub used
22 H	MANCHESTER C		22	D	1-1	1-1	MacDougall 7	Keelan	Prophett	Benson	Stringer	Govier	Bridge	Grapes	MacDougall*	Suggett	Blair	Steele	Howard
	29/12	23,978	*14*	13			*Law 39*	*MacRae*	*Barrett*	*Donachie*	*Doyle*	*Booth*	*Towers*	*Carrodus*	*Bell*	*Marsh*	*Law*	*Leman*	
							Ref: J Homewood	MacDougall opens the scoring courtesy of a Grapes cross to give Blues manager Ron Saunders an uncomfortable return to Norfolk. Colin Bell's goalbound header is unwittingly blocked by Dennis Leman. Undaunted, Bell then sets up Denis Law, who darts in to poach a neat goal.											
23 A	WEST HAM		22	L	2-4	0-2	MacDougall 49, 88	Keelan	Howard	Govier	Stringer	Rollings	Prophett*	Grapes	MacDougall	Suggett	Briggs	**Sissons**	Silvester
	1/1	*32,259*	*12*	13			*Gould 24, Paddon 45, 54, Brooking 60*	*Day*	*McDowell*	*Lampard*	*Bonds*	*Taylor*	*Moore*	*McGiven*	*Paddon*	*Gould*	*Brooking**	*Best*	*Coleman*
							Ref: K Burns	Bobby Gould despatches a rebound and ex-City man Graham Paddon hits two cracking drives, either side of a MacDougall strike. Trevor Brooking nets a clever shot to leave Norwich further marooned at the bottom. Winger John Sissons has a quiet debut against his former team.											
24 A	ARSENAL		22	L	0-2	0-1		Keelan	Machin	Benson	Stringer	Forbes	Briggs	Grapes	MacDougall	Suggett	Mellor	Sissons	
	12/1	*22,084*	*11*	13			*Ball 4, 46*	*Wilson*	*Rice*	*Storey*	*Kelly*	*Blockley*	*Simpson*	*Armstrong*	*Ball*	*Radford*	*Kennedy*	*Brady*	
							Ref: W Gow	Alan Ball pounces after a Ray Kennedy effort is blocked. Ball makes things safe immediately after the interval with a fine diving header at the near post from Geordie Armstrong's cross. City always look to go forward, but rarely test Bob Wilson. Liam Brady, just 17, looks a real find.											
25 H	WOLVERHAMPTON		22	D	1-1	1-0	MacDougall 44	Keelan	Machin	Benson	Stringer	Forbes	Howard*	Grapes	MacDougall	Suggett	Silvester	Sissons	Prophett
	19/1	19,404	*14*	14			*Dougan 67*	*Parkes*	*Palmer*	*Parkin*	*Bailey*	*Munro*	*McAlle*	*Powell*	*Sunderland*	*Richards*	*Dougan*	*Wagstaffe*	*Hibbitt*
							Ref: E Wallace	John Richards misses two great chances early on. Benson sends over a cross and MacDougall thunders in to net a glorious diving header. Injury victim Peter Silvester plays his first 90 minutes for over two years. Party-pooper Derek Dougan loops a header over the stranded Keelan.											
26 A	LIVERPOOL		22	L	0-1	0-0		Keelan	Machin	Benson	Stringer	Prophett	Howard	Steele	MacDougall	Suggett	Silvester	Sissons	
	2/2	*31,742*	*2*	14			*Cormack 89*	*Clemence*	*Smith*	*Lindsay*	*Thompson*	*Lloyd**	*Hughes*	*Keegan*	*Hall*	*Boersma*	*Toshack*	*Callaghan*	*Cormack*
							Ref: R Tinkler	MacDougall nets but is called offside. When sub Peter Cormack comes on, Kevin Keegan departs in error and has to be called back! Norwich frustrate Bill Shankly and the Kop and MacDougall goes close near the end. Disaster in the last minute as Cormack heads in Callaghan's cross.											
27 A	QP RANGERS		22	W	2-1	2-0	Howard 23, Benson 25	Keelan	Machin	Benson	Stringer	Prophett	Howard	Steele	MacDougall	Suggett	Briggs	Sissons	
	5/2	***12,427***	*6*	16			*Bowles 63*	*Parkes*	*Clement*	*Gillard*	*Venables*	*Mancini*	*McLintock*	*Thomas*	*Francis*	*Leach*	*Bowles*	*Givens*	
							Ref: K Baker	Skilful Stan Bowles twice strikes a post, but City storm ahead with two in two minutes. Howard nets a stylish near-post header, then Benson lets loose a real screamer from 25 yards. Keelan saves a Gerry Francis penalty, shortly before Bowles converts a Francis cross. Points at last!											
28 H	SHEFFIELD UTD		21	W	2-1	2-0	MacDougall 25, Stringer 40	Keelan	Machin	Benson	Stringer	Prophett	Howard	Steele	MacDougall	Suggett	**Boyer**	Grapes	
	9/2	21,651	*10*	18			*Hemsley 86*	*Hope*	*Badger*	*Hemsley*	*Flynn*	*Colquhoun*	*Eddy*	*Woodward*	*Speight*	*Staniforth*	*Bone*	*Garbett*	
							Ref: D Smith	Record signing Phil Boyer, £145,000 from Bournemouth, helps inspire a lively first half. Poor defensive work lets in MacDougall for a simple first, then Steele's corner is guided in at the near post by Stringer. Ted Hemsley's lob is inexplicably fumbled by Keelan to provide a late scare.											
29 H	DERBY		22	L	2-4	1-3	Howard 38, Stringer 65	Keelan	Machin	Benson	Stringer	Prophett	Howard	Steele	MacDougall	Suggett	Boyer	Sissons	
	23/2	25,175	*3*	18			*Hector 4, Bourne 11, 64, Davies 17*	*Boulton*	*Webster*	*Nish*	*Rioch*	*McFarland*	*Todd*	*Powell*	*Gemmill*	*Davies*	*Hector*	*Bourne*	
							Ref: H Hackney	City are Ram-raided as Derby quickly go three up. Roger Davies sets up Kevin Hector, Jeff Bourne is left unmarked to net Archie Gemmill's cross, and Roger Davies glances in the third. A rare Colin Todd error lets in Howard, but Bourne restores the advantage with a fierce drive.											
30 A	COVENTRY		22	L	0-1	0-1		Keelan	Machin	Benson	Stringer	Forbes	Howard	Prophett	MacDougall	Suggett	Boyer	Sissons	
	26/2	*16,420*	*14*	18			*Mortimer 20*	*Glazier*	*Coop*	*Holmes*	*Mortimer*	*Craven*	*Dugdale*	*Green**	*Alderson*	*Cross*	*Carr*	*Hutchison*	*McGuire*
							Ref: R Capey	David Cross, who left Norwich for Coventry for £150,000 in November, gets jeered by both sets of fans. He hasn't scored since New Year's Day. Dennis Mortimer nets after a run and cross by Tommy Hutchison. Mortimer also hits the post and the home side miss further chances.											
31 A	IPSWICH		22	D	1-1	0-0	Boyer 81	Keelan	Machin	Benson*	Stringer	Forbes	Howard	Prophett	MacDougall	Suggett	Boyer	Sissons	Kellock
	2/3	*24,988*	*5*	19			*Hamilton 49*	*Sivell*	*Burley*	*Mills*	*Morris*	*Hunter*	*Beattie*	*Hamilton*	*Talbot*	*Johnson*	*Whymark*	*Woods*	
							Ref: A Hart	City's local rivals are having a good season, but a gritty display holds them at bay in the first half. David Johnson and Peter Morris set up a neat goal by Bryan Hamilton. Norwich heads don't drop and Suggett crosses for Boyer to net a late equaliser. Norwich-born Clive Woods stars.											

No	Date	Venue	Opponent	Att		Res	F-A	H-T	Scorers, Times, Referees	1	2	3	4	5	6	7	8	9	10	11	12
32		H	CHELSEA		22	D	2-2	0-1	Stringer 60, MacDougall 75	Keelan	Machin	Benson	Stringer	Forbes	Howard	Prophett	MacDougall	Suggett	Boyer	Sissons	
	9/3			19,357	*19*	20			*Houseman 1, Kember 50*	*Phillips*	*Locke*	*Harris*	*Hollins*	*Droy*	*Webb*	*Cooke*	*Garland*	*Kember*	*Garner*	*Houseman*	
									Ref: M Lowe	Peter Houseman stuns City, heading in Charlie Cooke's cross in less than 60 seconds. Steve Kember lashes a second after Bill Garner miscues. Stringer heads City back into the game at the far post. Suggett's corner is headed home by MacDougall to cap a highly entertaining afternoon.											
33		A	TOTTENHAM		22	D	0-0	0-0		Keelan	Machin	Benson	Stringer	Forbes	Howard	Prophett	MacDougall	Suggett	Boyer	Sissons	
	16/3			*18,466*	*16*	21				*Jennings*	*Evans*	*Naylor*	*Pratt*	*England*	*Beal*	*McGrath**	*Perryman*	*Chivers*	*Peters*	*Coates*	*Dillon*
									Ref: J Williams	In complete contrast to last week's thriller, this proves to be dull fare. MacDougall brings a fine save out of Pat Jennings. Martin Chivers goes close with two fine first-half efforts for Bill Nicholson's side. Bond fails in a bid to sign Bobby Moore and Don Masson before the deadline.											
34		H	BIRMINGHAM		21	W	2-1	1-0	Boyer 41, Suggett 52	Keelan	Machin	Benson	Stringer	Forbes	Prophett	Howard	MacDougall	Suggett	Boyer	Sissons	
	20/3			18,309	*22*	23			*Styles 62*	*Latchford*	*Pendrey*	*Styles*	*Kendall*	*Hynd*	*Roberts*	*Campbell*	*Francis*	*Burns*	*Hatton*	*Taylor**	*Gallagher*
									Ref: H Davey	Howard, in his 150th game, does well to set up a Boyer strike. Howard also assists in the second as Suggett hooks home. Archie Styles cuts the deficit, then Prophett impedes Trevor Francis to concede a penalty. Keelan saves Francis's effort, meaning City rise off the bottom at long last.											
35		H	STOKE		21	W	**4-0**	0-0	Sissons 56, 75, MacDougall 59, [Suggett 87]	Keelan	Machin	Benson	Stringer	Forbes	Howard*	Prophett	MacDougall	Suggett	Boyer	Sissons	Grapes
	23/3			19,824	*15*	25				*Farmer*	*Marsh*	*Pejic*	*Dodd*	*Smith*	*Mahoney*	*Robertson*	*Greenhoff*	*Hurst*	*Hudson*	*Ritchie*	
									Ref: R Challis	In an open game, it is surprising that it takes so long for a first goal. Sissons breaks the deadlock by hammering a cracker past Tony Farmer. MacDougall snaps up a second straight away and the contest is over. Suggett flicks a neat fourth over Farmer and survival hopes remain alive.											
36		H	MANCHESTER U		22	L	0-2	0-0		Keelan	Machin*	Prophett	Stringer	Forbes	Howard	Grapes	MacDougall	Suggett	Boyer	Sissons	**Kent**
	6/4			27,899	*21*	25			*Macari 65, Greenhoff 86*	*Stepney*	*Forsyth*	*Houston*	*Greenhoff*	*Holton*	*Buchan*	*Morgan*	*Macari*	*McIlroy*	*McCalliog*	*Daly*	
									Ref: D Biddle	A relegation crunch game. Bond predicts the losers will almost certainly be relegated. MacDougall forces Stepney to save well early on. Lou Macari breaks clear to lob Keelan with defenders waiting for an offside flag. Brian Greenhoff races through for a second. City look doomed.											
37		A	EVERTON		22	L	1-4	0-0	MacDougall 47 *[Lyons 67]*	Keelan	Prophett	Benson	Stringer	Forbes	Howard	Grapes	MacDougall	Suggett	Boyer	Kellock	
	13/4			*27,967*	*7*	25			*Buckley 54, Telfer 62, Latchford 65,*	*Lawson*	*Darracott*	*Sargeant*	*Clements*	*Kenyon*	*Hurst*	*Bernard*	*Buckley*	*Latchford*	*Lyons*	*Telfer*	
									Ref: H New	Supermac's far-post header raises spirits, but before long Mick Buckley calmly steers Everton level. The floodgates open and George Telfer slots in a nicely-taken effort. Bob Latchford nets a powerful downward header and Mike Lyons gets in on the act with City calling for offside.											
38		A	NEWCASTLE		22	D	0-0	0-0		Keelan	Butler	Benson	Stringer	Forbes	Howard*	Steele	MacDougall	Suggett	Boyer	Kent	Grapes
	15/4			*29,202*	*18*	26				*McFaul*	*Crossan*	*Kennedy*	*McDermott*	*Howard*	*Moncur*	*Barrowcl'gh**	*Cassidy*	*Macdonald*	*Tudor*	*Hibbitt*	*Bruce*
									Ref: R Lee	Ravaged by injury and preoccupied over the forthcoming FA Cup final, Joe Harvey's men are kept at bay by City. Malcolm Macdonald is well shackled by Forbes, although he does have two late efforts well saved by Keelan. Home-produced Paul Kent is given his first full 90 minutes.											
39		H	NEWCASTLE		22	D	1-1	0-0	MacDougall 74	Keelan	Benson	Prophett	Stringer	Forbes	Steele	Grapes	MacDougall	Suggett*	Boyer	Sissons	Kent
	17/4			**17,673**	*18*	27			*Cassidy 54*	*McFaul*	*Crossan*	*Kennedy*	*McDermott*	*Howard*	*Moncur*	*Robson*	*Cassidy*	*Macdonald*	*Tudor*	*Laughton*	
									Ref: B Daniels	Tommy Cassidy breaks the deadlock, beating Keelan easily from Malcolm Macdonald's pass. Boyer goes close on three occasions. Benson's cross is nodded in by MacDougall and the inevitable relegation axe is staved off a bit longer. Ron Saunders, sacked by Man C, is in the crowd.											
40		H	BURNLEY		22	W	1-0	1-0	MacDougall 2p	Keelan	Butler	Benson	Stringer	Forbes	Grapes	Steele	MacDougall	Suggett	Boyer	Sissons	
	20/4			17,782	*5*	29				*Stevenson*	*Noble*	*Thomson*	*Dobson*	*Waldron*	*Rodaway*	*Nulty*	*Hankin*	*Fletcher*	*Ingham*	*James*	
									Ref: J Yates	Boyer is hauled down and MacDougall sends Alan Stevenson the wrong way from the spot. Spirited City go close as Billy Steele clips the bar from 30 yards. Keelan makes two astounding saves after the interval. With Southampton drawing elsewhere, City are now definitely relegated.											
41		A	BIRMINGHAM		22	L	1-2	1-2	Stringer 3	Keelan	Butler	Benson	Stringer	Forbes	Grapes*	Steele	MacDougall	Suggett	Boyer	Sissons	**Davies**
	27/4			***44,182***	*19*	29			*Hatton 40, Burns 42*	*Latchford*	*Martin*	*Pendrey*	*Kendall*	*Hynd*	*Roberts*	*Campbell*	*Francis*	*Burns*	*Hatton*	*Taylor*	
									Ref: W Johnson	The Blues need a win to stay up, hence the enormous crowd. Stringer heads in Suggett's free-kick to a stunned silence. Bob Hatton's drive and Kenny Burns' header ensure safety for Fred Goodwin's men. At 17 years and 29 days, Ian Davies becomes the youngest-ever City first-teamer.											
42		A	LEICESTER		22	L	0-3	0-0		Keelan	Prophett	Benson	Stringer	Forbes	Steele	Grapes	MacDougall	Suggett	Boyer	Sissons	
	29/4			*16,786*	*9*	29			*Worthington 47, 88, Earle 80*	*Shilton*	*Whitworth*	*Rofe*	*Earle*	*Kruse*	*Cross*	*Weller*	*Sammels*	*Worthington*	*Birchenall*	*Tomlin*	
		Home		Away					Ref: J Rice	Frank Worthington rams in a loose ball. Steve Earle pokes home a rebound off Keelan and Worthington rounds things off from Jon Sammels' pass. City attack boldly, but have nothing to show for it. John Bond gives free transfers to Kellock, Anderson, Wilson, O'Donnell and Jacobs.											
Average		23,057		24,568																	

League Cup	Att		F-A	H-T	Scorers, Times, and Referees	1	2	3	4	5	6	7	8	9	10	11	12 sub used
2 H WREXHAM	20	W	6-2	3-0	Cross 4, 6, Mellor 25, 57, Kellock 85,	Keelan	Prophett	Payne	Stringer	Forbes	Briggs	Livermore	Kellock	Cross	Paddon	Mellor	
10/10	10,937 *3:8*				*Smallm' 78, Ashcroft 86* [Liverm' 82]	*Lloyd*	*Jones*	*Fogg*	*Davis*	*May*	*Whittle*	*Moir**	*Sutton*	*Smallman*	*Tinnion*	*Thomas*	*Ashcroft*
					Ref: A Hart	Early on, Brian Lloyd twice fails to hold on to the ball and Cross pounces. Mellor nets a splendid solo goal and then fires in off a post to finish off John Neal's men. Livermore's 30-yarder and Kellock's tap-in increase their misery. Dave Smallman and sub Billy Ashcroft net late headers.											
3 A EVERTON	20	W	1-0	1-0	Cross 1	Keelan	Payne	Wilson	Stringer	Forbes	Briggs*	Howard	Suggett	Cross	Paddon	O'Donnell	Mellor
30/10	*22,046 2*					*Lawson*	*Darracott*	*McLaughlin*	*Clements*	*Kenyon*	*Hurst*	*Bernard*	*Buckley*	*Royle*	*Harper*	*Husband**	*Harvey*
					Ref: J Williams	The fastest goal ever seen in a senior game at Goodison arrives on 15 seconds. Cross beats Dave Lawson after a miscued shot by Howard falls for him. City look brighter after the four team changes made in the wake of a miserable display at Chelsea. Joe Harper hits the bar for Everton.											
4 A SOUTHAMPTON	20	W	2-0	1-0	Suggett 21, Mellor 89	Keelan	Butler	Wilson	Stringer	Forbes	Briggs	Howard	Suggett	Mellor	Livermore*	O'Donnell	Anderson
21/11	*14,415 8*					*Martin*	*McCarthy*	*Mills*	*Fisher*	*Bennett**	*Steele*	*Paine*	*Channon*	*Gilchrist*	*O'Neill*	*Stokes*	*O'Brien*
					Ref: T Spencer	Without a manager, Norwich fight hard at The Dell and are rewarded when Suggett races clear to convert Mellor's pass. Paul Bennett hits the bar and misses a sitter for Saints. Wilson clears another effort off the line. Suggett slips the ball to Mellor, who streaks clear to clinch the win.											
5 A MILLWALL	21	D	1-1	1-0	Howard 35	Keelan	Butler	Prophett*	Stringer	Forbes	O'Donnell	Grapes	Suggett	Cheesley	Briggs	Howard	Anderson
16/1	*10,708 2:16*				*Wood 48*	*King*	*Donaldson*	*Jones*	*Dorney*	*Kitchener*	*Allder*	*Bolland*	*Clark*	*Wood*	*Saul*	*Hill*	
					Ref: H New	A real backs-to-the-wall fight at the inhospitable Den. Doug Allder hits the post and makes a mess of the rebound. The lively Howard volleys past Bryan King after his initial header wasn't cleared. Alf Wood levels from Frank Saul's cross. The Lions have a late penalty appeal ignored.											
5R H MILLWALL	22	W	2-1	1-0	Suggett 6, Sissons 83p	Keelan	Butler	Prophett	Stringer	Forbes	O'Donnell	Grapes	Silvester	Suggett	Mellor	Sissons	
16/1	7,737 *2:17*				*Smethurst 72*	*King*	*Donaldson*	*Jones*	*Dorney*	*Kitchener*	*Allder*	*Bolland*	*Clark*	*Wood*	*Smethurst*	*Hill*	
					Ref: R Kirkpatrick	The energy crisis means a midweek afternoon kick-off. Silvester, in his first full game for two years after injury, tees up Suggett for the opener. Derek Smethurst's well-placed drive equalises for Benny Fenton's men. Silvester is hauled down by Alan Dorney and Sissons slots a winner.											
SF H WOLVERHAMPTON	22	D	1-1	0-0	Mellor 58	Keelan	Butler	Prophett	Stringer	Forbes	Howard	Steele	Silvester	Suggett	Mellor	Sissons	
1 23/1	20,517 *14*				*Richards 72*	*Parkes*	*Palmer*	*Parkin**	*Bailey*	*Munro*	*McAlle*	*Powell*	*Sunderland*	*Richards*	*Dougan*	*Wagstaffe*	*Hibbitt*
					Ref: G Kew	Wembley beckons as Mellor's shot squeezes in under the dive of Phil Parkes. Mike Bailey's shot is blocked by Keelan, but John Richards nets the rebound. Mellor shoots wide and Geoff Palmer's lob is blocked on the line in the closing stages. All is not lost, says a disappointed Bond.											
SF A WOLVERHAMPTON	22	L	0-1	0-0		Keelan	Butler	Prophett	Stringer	Forbes	Howard	Steele	Silvester	Suggett	Mellor	Sissons	
2 26/1	*32,605 14*				*Richards 48*	*Parkes*	*Palmer*	*Hibbitt*	*Bailey*	*Munro*	*McAlle*	*Powell*	*Sunderland*	*Richards*	*Dougan*	*Wagstaffe*	
					Ref: P Partridge (Norwich lose 1-2 on aggregate)	At the height of a tense battle, skipper Forbes is booked for the sixth time this term. John Richards evades Stringer and slips the ball wide of the advancing Keelan. City have now failed to beat Wolves in 12 meetings all told. The victors invite City to share their champagne afterwards.											

FA Cup																	
3 H ARSENAL	22	L	0-1	0-1		Keelan	Butler	Prophett	Stringer	Forbes	Briggs	Grapes	MacDougall	Suggett	Howard	Mellor	
5/1	21,500 *12*				*Kelly 31*	*Wilson*	*Rice*	*McNab*	*Storey*	*Blockley*	*Simpson*	*Kelly*	*Ball*	*Radford*	*Kennedy*	*Armstrong*	
					Ref: R Tinkler	With Bond away on a spying mission, Stringer goes close with a diving header that is cleared off the line by Bob McNab. Geordie Armstrong's corner is not cleared properly and Eddie Kelly volleys home the loose ball. Battling City are constantly frustrated by well-organised visitors.											

		Home					Away					
	P	W	D	L	F	A	W	D	L	F	A	Pts
1 Leeds	42	12	8	1	38	18	12	6	3	28	13	62
2 Liverpool	42	18	2	1	34	11	4	11	6	18	20	57
3 Derby	42	13	7	1	40	16	4	7	10	12	26	48
4 Ipswich	42	10	7	4	38	21	8	4	9	29	37	47
5 Stoke	42	13	6	2	39	15	2	10	9	15	27	46
6 Burnley	42	10	9	2	29	16	6	5	10	27	37	46
7 Everton	42	12	7	2	29	14	4	5	12	21	34	44
8 QP Rangers	42	8	10	3	30	17	5	7	9	26	35	43
9 Leicester	42	10	7	4	35	17	3	9	9	16	24	42
10 Arsenal	42	9	7	5	23	16	5	7	9	26	35	42
11 Tottenham	42	9	4	8	26	27	5	10	6	19	23	42
12 Wolves	42	11	6	4	30	18	2	9	10	19	31	41
13 Sheffield U	42	7	7	7	25	22	7	5	9	19	27	40
14 Manchester C	42	10	7	4	25	17	4	5	12	14	29	40
15 Newcastle	42	9	6	6	28	21	4	6	11	21	27	38
16 Coventry	42	10	5	6	25	18	4	5	12	18	36	38
17 Chelsea	42	9	4	8	36	29	3	9	9	20	31	37
18 West Ham	42	7	7	7	36	32	4	8	9	19	28	37
19 Birmingham	42	10	7	4	30	21	2	6	13	22	43	37
20 Southampton	42	8	10	3	30	20	3	4	14	17	48	36
21 Manchester U	42	7	7	7	23	20	3	5	13	15	28	32
22 NORWICH	42	6	9	6	25	27	1	6	14	12	35	29
	924	218	149	95	674	433	95	149	218	433	674	924

Odds & ends

Double wins: (0).
Double losses: (3) Arsenal, Everton, Leeds.

Won from behind: (0).
Lost from in front: (4) Everton (h), Ipswich (h), Everton (a), Birm'ham (a).

High spots: Reaching the last four of both League and Texaco Cups.
The arrival of dynamic duo Ted MacDougall and Phil Boyer.
The unbeaten run in March, which raised outside hopes of survival.

Low spots: Relegation appeared inevitable as early as October.
Ron Saunders quitting after a row with new chairman Arthur South.
Woeful away form in the league – just 12 goals and one win.
Geoffrey Watling's resignation as long-serving chairman in August.

Player of the Year: Kevin Keelan.
Ever-presents: (2) Kevin Keelan, Dave Stringer.
Hat-tricks: (0).
Opposing hat-tricks: (0).
Leading scorer: (11) Ted MacDougall.

	Appearances						Goals			
	Lge	*Sub*	LC	*Sub*	FAC	*Sub*	**Lge**	LC	FAC	**Tot**
Anderson, Terry	**8**	*1*		*2*						
Benson, John	**20**						**1**			**1**
Black, Alan	**11**									
Blair, Jim	**1**									
Boyer, Phil	**15**						**2**			**2**
Briggs, Max	**24**		4		1					
Butler, Geoff	**6**		5		1					
Cheesley, Paul	**4**		1				**1**			**1**
Cross, David	**15**		2				**2**	3		**5**
Davies, Ian		*1*								
Forbes, Duncan	**32**		7		1					
Govier, Steve	**3**									
Grapes, Steve	**14**	*2*	2		1					
Howard, Trevor	**22**	*6*	5		1		**2**	1		**3**
Keelan, Kevin	**42**		7		1					
Kellock, Billy	**1**	*2*	1					1		**1**
Kent, Paul	**1**	*2*								
Livermore, Doug	**9**		2				**1**	1		**2**
Machin, Mel	**15**									
MacDougall, Ted	**25**				1		**11**			**11**
Mellor, Ian	**17**	*1*	5	*1*	1		**1**	4		**5**
O'Donnell, Neil	**3**	*3*	4							
Paddon, Graham	**14**		2				**1**			**1**
Payne, Clive	**3**	*2*	2							
Prophett, Colin	**34**	*1*	5		1					
Rollings, Andy	**4**									
Silvester, Paul	**2**	*1*	3							
Sissons, John	**17**		3				**2**	1		**3**
Steele, Billy	**11**		2							
Stringer, Dave	**42**		7		1		**5**			**5**
Suggett, Colin	**41**	*1*	6		1		**5**	2		**7**
Wilson, Les	**6**		2							
(own-goals)							**3**			**3**
32 players used	**462**	*23*	**77**	*3*	**11**		**37**	**13**		**50**

No	Date	Att	Pos	Pt	F-A	H-T	Scorers, Times, and Referees	1	2	3	4	5	6	7	8	9	10	11	12 sub used
1	H BLACKPOOL			W	2-1	0-0	Powell 48, MacDougall 63	Keelan	Machin	**Sullivan**	**Morris**	Forbes	Stringer	Grapes	MacDougall	Boyer	Suggett	**Powell**	
	17/8	18,551		2			*Bentley 86*	*Burridge*	*Hatton*	*Bentley*	*Alcock*	*James*	*Suddaby*	*Tong**	*Suddick*	*Dyson*	*Evanson*	*Walsh*	*Curtis*
							Ref: K Baker	Morris (ex-Ipswich) and Powell (Bond's sixth capture from Bournemouth) take a bow. Powell's is a scoring debut after a clearance flies in off his chest. After MacDougall's header clinches the win, City begin to look a little ragged and Bill Bentley gets forward to head in a consolation.											
2	H SOUTHAMPTON			W	1-0	0-0	Grapes 48	Keelan	Machin	Sullivan	Morris	Forbes	Stringer	Grapes*	MacDougall	Boyer	Suggett	Powell	Benson
	21/8	22,251		4				*Martin*	*McCarthy*	*Peach*	*Fisher**	*Bennett*	*Steele*	*Gilchrist*	*Channon*	*Osgood*	*O'Neil*	*Chatterley*	*Stokes*
							Ref: B Daniels	Morris feeds Grapes with a through ball, and he steers home his first senior goal. It goes sour for Grapes as the goal hero limps off injured. Boyer puts on a great display as City outwit a side relegated alongside them. The third victims, Manchester U, have also started with two wins.											
3	A ASTON VILLA		2	D	1-1	0-0	Suggett 76	Keelan	Machin	Sullivan	Morris	Forbes	Stringer	Grapes	MacDougall	Boyer	Suggett	Powell	
	24/8	*23,297*	*8*	5			*Graydon 52*	*Cumbes*	*Gidman*	*Aitken*	*Ross*	*Nicholls*	*Robson*	*Graydon*	*Little B*	*Morgan*	*Brown*	*Hamilton*	
							Ref: K McNally	Brian Little's cross is headed in by the diving figure of Ray Graydon. City equalise completely out of the blue when MacDougall and Stringer set up Suggett, who lashes an amazing 30-yard shot past Jim Cumbes. Villa's new boss, former City hero Ron Saunders, is not a happy man.											
4	A SOUTHAMPTON		2	D	1-1	0-0	Suggett 79	Keelan	Machin	Sullivan	Morris	Forbes	Stringer	Grapes	MacDougall	Boyer	Suggett	Powell	
	27/8	*16,367*	*18*	6			*Fisher 49*	*Turner*	*Mills*	*Peach*	*Fisher*	*Earls*	*Steele*	*Gilchrist*	*Channon*	*Osgood*	*O'Neil*	*Stokes*	
							Ref: C White	A superb long-range drive by little Hugh Fisher puts Saints in the driving seat. Suggett takes a return pass from Morris to save City a point. Four more cautions take City's tally to nine in four games. Forbes escapes punishment, despite a long-running feud with Peter Osgood, though.											
5	H SHEFFIELD WED		3	D	1-1	0-1	Grapes 50	Keelan	Machin	Sullivan	Morris	Forbes	Stringer	Grapes	MacDougall	Boyer	Suggett	Powell	
	31/8	20,714	*19*	7			*Craig 36*	*Springett*	*Rodrigues*	*Shaw*	*Dowd*	*Holsgrove*	*Eustace*	*Potts*	*McIver*	*Joicey*	*Craig*	*Prudham*	
							Ref: A Turvey	After MacDougall hits a post, Tommy Craig puts Steve Burtenshaw's struggling side ahead after a well-worked free-kick routine involving Peter Rodrigues. Norwich hit back after the break as a cross by Powell is missed by MacDougall, but falls to Grapes who beats Peter Springett.											
6	A HULL		3	D	0-0	0-0		Keelan	Machin	Sullivan	Morris	Forbes	Stringer	Benson	MacDougall	Boyer	Suggett	Powell	
	7/9	***5,436***	*10*	8				*Wealands*	*Blampey*	*DeVries*	*Burnett*	*Deere*	*Galvin*	*Grimes*	*McGill*	*Fletcher*	*Wagstaff*	*Greenwood*	
							Ref: J Rice	A small Boothferry Park crowd shivers as Humberside is hit by fierce gales. Keelan saves superbly from Jimmy McGill and then rather luckily from veteran Ken Wagstaff. Lanky Peter Fletcher, a new signing by the Tigers from Manchester U, gives skipper Forbes a testing afternoon.											
7	H NOTTS COUNTY		2	W	**3-0**	1-0	Sullivan 2, MacDougall 76, Boyer 83	Keelan	Benson	Sullivan	Morris	Forbes	Stringer	Machin	MacDougall	Boyer	Suggett	Powell	
	14/9	17,948	*8*	10				*Brown*	*Brindley*	*O'Brien*	*Masson*	*Needham*	*Stubbs*	*Randall*	*Probert*	*Bradd*	*Mann**	*Scanlon*	*Bolton*
							Ref: R Challis	Morris catches County cold as he intercepts a pass and puts Sullivan through, the full-back coolly drawing keeper Roy Brown before scoring. Jimmy Sirrell's men remain in the game until late when MacDougall heads in Machin's cross, and Boyer goes clear to converts Suggett's pass.											
8	A FULHAM		3	L	**0-4**	0-2	*[Lacy 71]*	**Hansbury**	Benson	Sullivan	Morris	Forbes	Stringer	Grapes	MacDougall	Boyer	Suggett	Powell	
	21/9	*9,414*	*2*	10			*Busby 18, Fraser 43, Barrett 48,*	*Mellor*	*Fraser*	*Strong*	*Mullery*	*Lacy*	*Moore*	*Conway,Jm*	*Slough*	*Busby*	*Lloyd*	*Barrett*	
							Ref: H Powell	Unbeaten City are rocked by first-half strikes by Viv Busby and John Fraser. The contest is as good as over when Les Barrett's intended cross drifts over poor league debutant Hansbury. Big John Lacy heads in a free-kick for the fourth. Alec Stock's side leapfrog City into second spot.											
9	A SUNDERLAND		2	D	0-0	0-0		Keelan	Benson	Sullivan	Morris	Forbes	Stringer	Butler*	MacDougall	Boyer	Suggett	Powell	Steele
	24/9	*27,737*	*3*	11				*Montgomery*	*Malone*	*Bolton*	*Moncur*	*Ashurst*	*Porterfield*	*Kerr*	*Hughes*	*Belfitt*	*Robson*	*Towers*	
							Ref: J Goggins	After the nightmare at Craven Cottage, the defence looks resolute tonight and the Stringer-Forbes partnership gives Rod Belfitt and Bryan Robson little leeway. Keelan saves a Tony Towers curling shot and Powell knocks a late effort off the line. Boyer works tirelessly in attack.											
10	H MANCHESTER U		2	W	2-0	1-0	MacDougall 23p, 57	Keelan	Butler	Sullivan	Morris	Forbes	Stringer	Machin	MacDougall	Boyer	Suggett	Powell	
	28/9	25,056	*1*	13				*Stepney*	*Forsyth*	*Houston*	*Greenhoff*	*Sidebottom*	*Buchan*	*Morgan**	*McIlroy*	*Macari*	*McCalliog*	*Daly*	*Young*
							Ref: J Hunting	The table-toppers, unbeaten thus far, are put under intense pressure. Boyer is brought down by Arnold Sidebottom and ex-Red MacDougall converts from the spot. Jubilation greets his second, on the volley from Machin's free-kick. United followers cause mayhem in the city centre.											

No		Opponent	Pos		F-A	H-T	Scorers, Times, and Referees	1	2	3	4	5	6	7	8	9	10	11	subs used
11	H	MILLWALL	2	W	2-0	1-0	Powell 37, MacDougall 73p	Keelan	Butler	Sullivan	Morris	Benson	Stringer	Machin*	MacDougall	Boyer	Suggett	Powell	Livermore
5/10		19,216	*20*	15				*King*	*Brown B*	*Jones*	*Donaldson*	*Kitchener*	*Dorney*	*Saul*	*Bolland*	*Wood*	*Allder*	*Hill*	
							Ref: M Lowe	Barry Kitchener handles and the flag goes up, but Powell is allowed to step in and score. Eddie Jones handles (and is booked, unlike Kitchener) and MacDougall knocks in the penalty. The Lions look lethargic. Bond is named divisional manager of the month. Prophett moves to Swindon.											
12	A	NOTT'M FOR	2	W	3-1	0-1	Machin 50, 64, 89	Keelan	Butler	Sullivan	Morris	Forbes	Stringer	Machin	MacDougall	Boyer	Suggett	Powell	
12/10		*13,613*	*12*	17			*Butlin 30*	*Peacock*	*O'Kane*	*Jones*	*Chapman!*	*Greenwood*	*Richardson*	*Dennehy*	*Bowyer*	*Martin**	*Butlin*	*Jackson*	*Lyall*
							Ref: A Morrissey	Miah Dennehy's clever dribble sets up a Barry Butlin goal. Machin coolly nets his first City goal in 51 games. Seizing on a clearance, Machin rifles a second past Dennis Peacock. He completes a stunning hat-trick direct from a free-kick. Sammy Chapman is sent off after two cautions.											
13	H	PORTSMOUTH	3	W	2-0	1-0	Stringer 15, Boyer 58	Keelan	Butler	Sullivan	Morris	Forbes	Stringer	Machin	MacDougall	Boyer	Suggett	Powell	
19/10		20,899	*20*	19				*Best*	*Ellis**	*Wilson*	*Piper*	*Went*	*Stephenson*	*Foggo*	*Kellard*	*Davies*	*Hand*	*Marinello*	*Roberts*
							Ref: H Hackney	Stringer is virtually unchallenged as he rises to head in a Machin corner. Pompey, without a win in six, know they are beaten again after Boyer conjures up a solo effort. After a long run forward he stumbles, then regains composure, before lobbing over the head of keeper David Best.											
14	A	ORIENT	2	W	**3-0**	3-0	Boyer 25, 38, MacDougall 26p	Keelan	Butler	Sullivan	Morris	Forbes	Stringer	**Miller**	MacDougall	Boyer	Suggett	Powell	
26/10		*8,708*	*17*	21				*Jackson*	*Fisher*	*Downing*	*Allen*	*Hoadley*	*Boyle*	*Cunningham*	*Brisley*	*Bullock*	*Walley*	*Possee*	
							Ref: H Davey	Miller debuts after signing from Ipswich for £45,000. Morris makes an interception and then slips Boyer through for the first. Tom Walley brings down MacDougall to concede a penalty, duly converted. City are well on top and Boyer nets after John Jackson lets Miller's volley slip.											
15	A	WEST BROM	2	D	1-1	0-1	MacDougall 54	Keelan	Benson	Sullivan	Morris	Forbes	Stringer	Miller	MacDougall	Boyer	Suggett	Powell	
2/11		*12,177*	*5*	22			*Shaw 34*	*Osborne*	*Nisbet*	*Wilson*	*Hughes*	*Wile*	*Rushbury*	*Glover*	*Brown T*	*Shaw**	*Merrick*	*Johnston*	*Mayo*
							Ref: G Flint	City defenders hesitate fatally and David Shaw takes advantage to slide the ball home. Stringer forces a corner and the flag-kick leads to MacDougall's equaliser. City show great determination to stay on terms with Don Howe's men. There is little of the flair seen last Saturday.											
16	H	BRISTOL ROV	2	L	0-1	0-1		Keelan	Benson	Sullivan	Morris	Forbes	Stringer	Miller	MacDougall	Boyer	Suggett	Powell	
9/11		21,172	*10*	22			*Bannister 30*	*Eadie*	*Bater*	*Parsons**	*Aitken*	*Taylor*	*Prince*	*Stephens*	*Stanton*	*Warboys*	*Bannister*	*Fearnley*	*Rudge*
							Ref: J Homewood	City fluff their lines on BBC's Match of the Day. Bruce Bannister snaps his 122nd league goal. Jim Eadie tips away Forbes' drive and late on MacDougall hits a post. Benson is barracked, prompting Bond to announce that he will never substitute a player because of crowd pressure.											
17	A	OLDHAM	3	D	2-2	1-0	Boyer 25, 57	Keelan	Machin	Sullivan	Morris	Forbes	Stringer*	Miller	MacDougall	Boyer	Suggett	Powell	Butler
16/11		*12,004*	*17*	23			*Jones 62, Robins 85*	*Ogden*	*Wood*	*Whittle*	*McNeil*	*Hicks*	*Bailey*	*Bell*	*Blair*	*Jones*	*Young*	*Robins*	
							Ref: P Willis	A Suggett drive is parried by Chris Ogden and Boyer swoops. He grabs a second as MacDougall tees up a Butler cross for him. George Jones pulls one back with a shot in off the bar and City lose their composure. Keelan is booked for squaring up to Jones before Ian Robins levels.											
18	H	BOLTON	3	W	2-0	1-0	Miller 40, 87	Hansbury	Machin	Sullivan	Morris	Forbes	Stringer	Miller	MacDougall	**Goodwin**	Suggett	Powell	
23/11		18,649	*10*	25				*Siddall*	*McAllister*	*Dunne*	*Nicholson*	*Jones P*	*Allardyce*	*Byrom*	*Curran*	*Lee*	*Greaves*	*Thompson*	
							Ref: K Burns	Veteran ex-England winger Peter Thompson is in splendid form and gives Norwich constant trouble. Suggett clips the ball forward for Miller to net his first City goal. Near the end Suggett intercepts a pass and sets up Miller, who cracks in a fine shot. Unlucky Bolton are left pointless.											
19	A	YORK	3	L	0-1	0-1		Hansbury	Benson	Sullivan	Morris	Forbes	Stringer	Miller	MacDougall	Goodwin	Suggett	Machin	
30/11		*7,456*	*14*	25			*Seal 32*	*Crawford*	*Hunter*	*Coop*	*Holmes*	*Swallow*	*Topping*	*Lyons*	*Cave*	*Seal*	*Jones*	*Woodward*	
							Ref: D Richardson	Ian Holmes' path is blocked by Sullivan, but somehow the midfielder still gets a cross in and Barry Swallow gets a crucial touch before Jimmy Seal beats Hansbury. Tom Johnston's men keep City in check and they look well below par – although a poor game improves after the interval.											
20	H	CARDIFF	3	D	1-1	1-0	Miller 1	Hansbury	Machin	Sullivan	Morris	Forbes	Stringer	Miller	MacDougall	Boyer	Suggett	Powell*	Grapes
7/12		17,685	*20*	26			*Reece 54*	*Irwin*	*Dwyer*	*Pethard*	*Buchanan*	*Morgan*	*Larmour*	*Reece*	*Smith*	*Showers*	*Finnieston*	*Anderson*	
							Ref: R Clay	Directly from the kick-off Sullivan finds MacDougall, who swings over a cross that is tucked away by Miller. In a breakaway raid, a cross by Willie Anderson is only parried away by Hansbury and Gil Reece knocks in the equaliser. Billy Irwin makes good saves to frustrate Norwich.											
21	A	BLACKPOOL	3	L	1-2	0-2	Boyer 53	Keelan	Machin	Sullivan	Morris	Forbes	Stringer	Miller	MacDougall	Boyer	Suggett	Powell	
14/12		*6,683*	*9*	26			*Hart 24, Walsh 34*	*Burridge*	*Curtis*	*Bentley*	*Alcock*	*Hart*	*Hatton*	*Tong*	*Ainscow*	*Walsh*	*Evanson*	*Dyson**	*Davies*
							Ref: J Hough	Machin clears off the line, but the ball falls to Paul Hart to poke the opener. Ten minutes later Harry Potts' side celebrate again when Mickey Walsh's spectacular shot swirls into the net from the edge of the box. Second-best City pull one back when John Burridge drops a corner-kick.											

No	Date	Att	Pos	Pt	F-A	H-T	Scorers, Times, and Referees	1	2	3	4	5	6	7	8	9	10	11	12 sub used
22 H	BRISTOL CITY		3	W	3-2	1-2	Suggett 17, Boyer 65, 66	Keelan	Machin	Sullivan	Morris	Forbes	Stringer	Miller	MacDougall	Boyer	Suggett	Powell*	Steele
	21/12	**17,439**	*8*	28			*Ritchie 41, Mann 42*	*Cashley*	*Collier*	*Drysdale*	*Sweeney*	*Rodgers*	*Merrick*	*Tainton*	*Ritchie*	*Cheesley*	*Griffin**	*Mann*	*Durrell*
							Ref: A Porter	City lead after Suggett's corner swerves straight in. Tom Ritchie scrambles an equaliser for Alan Dicks' men and Jimmy Mann goes on a solo run and beats Keelan. Two inside a minute from Boyer win the points in this topsy-turvy contest. Ray Cashley spills a free-kick for the winner.											
23 A	NOTTS COUNTY		3	D	1-1	0-0	MacDougall 90	Keelan	Machin	Sullivan	Morris	Forbes	Stringer	Miller	MacDougall	Boyer	Suggett	Steele	
	26/12	*13,977*	*10*	29			*Mann 63*	*McManus*	*Brindley*	*Richards*	*Bolton*	*Needham*	*Stubbs*	*Carterl*	*Probert*	*Bradd*	*Randall*	*Mann*	
							Ref: D Turner	Les Bradd heads a Kevin Randall cross against a post and Arthur Mann nets the rebound. Boyer sets up a far-post header for MacDougall's late leveller. Bond speaks out against Keith Weller, who walked out on Leicester during a game, calling for managers to get tough on the 'rebels'.											
24 H	OXFORD		3	W	1-0	1-0	Boyer 39	Keelan	Machin	Sullivan	Morris	Forbes	Stringer	Miller	MacDougall	Boyer	Suggett	Powell	
	28/12	23,617	*6*	31				*Burton*	*Light*	*Shuker*	*Roberts*	*Clarke C*	*Briggs*	*Aylott*	*Duncan*	*Bray*	*Gough*	*Heron*	
							Ref: L Hayes	Gerry Summers' outfit knock the ball about well and Norwich look rather disjointed and anxious. The pressure eases after Miller rides a tackle and tucks the ball to Boyer, who beats the advancing Roy Burton. A fierce long-range drive by Morris rocks the Oxford bar after the interval.											
25 A	CARDIFF		3	L	1-2	0-2	MacDougall 64	Keelan	Benson	Sullivan	Morris	Forbes	Stringer	Machin	MacDougall	Boyer	Suggett	Powell	
	11/1	*11,637*	*18*	31			*Reece 10, 43*	*Irwin*	*Dwyer*	*Pethard*	*Buchanan*	*Morgan*	*Larmour*	*Villars*	*Smith*	*Showers*	*Reece*	*Anderson*	
							Ref: D Nippard	MacDougall's header back to Keelan is a little too powerful and is parried by the keeper to Gil Reece, who accepts the gift. The Welshman nets again after a Tony Villars wing-raid. It looks bleak for City, but hopes flicker after MacDougall gets away and beats the advancing Billy Irwin.											
26 H	YORK		3	L	2-3	0-2	Suggett 63, Stringer 84	Keelan	Machin	Sullivan	Morris	Forbes	Stringer	**McGuire**	MacDougall	Boyer	Suggett	Powell	
	18/1	23,382	*15*	31			*Seal 1, Jones 2, 75*	*Crawford*	*Calvert*	*Coop*	*Holmes*	*Swallow*	*Topping*	*Lyons*	*Cave*	*Seal*	*Jones*	*Butler**	*Woodward*
							Ref: J Taylor	City are rocked by an amazing York start - two goals in 95 seconds! A low cross is jabbed in by Jimmy Seal on 38 seconds, then Chris Jones sweeps past an exposed Keelan. Suggett's 30-yarder is cancelled out after Jones gets clear. New signing Mick McGuire sets up Stringer's goal.											
27 A	OXFORD		3	L	1-2	1-1	MacDougall 36	Keelan	Machin	Sullivan	Morris	Forbes	Stringer	Miller	MacDougall	Boyer	McGuire	Powell	
	25/1	*8,410*	*8*	31			*Shuker 5p, Heron 80*	*Burton*	*Light*	*Shuker*	*Roberts*	*Clarke C*	*Aylott*	*Duncan*	*Jeffrey*	*Clarke D*	*McCulloch*	*Heron*	
							Ref: T Bosi	Derek Clarke is bundled over by Stringer and McGuire for John Shuker's early penalty. MacDougall bangs in Miller's cross. An entertaining affair is decided when Brian Heron lets fly from distance. The promotion bid looks shaky. John Benson joins Bournemouth as player-manager.											
28 A	BRISTOL ROV		3	W	2-0	1-0	Suggett 30, MacDougall 48	Keelan	Machin	Sullivan	Livermore	Powell	Stringer	Steele	MacDougall	Boyer	McGuire	Suggett*	Grapes
	1/2	*12,730*	*18*	33				*Eadie*	*Bater*	*Parsons*	*Aitken*	*Taylor*	*Prince*	*Stephens*	*Coombes*	*Warboys**	*Bannister*	*Fearnley*	*Staniforth*
							Ref: B Gow	Suggett buries a free header from MacDougall's pass. With Jim Eadie stranded out of goal, Suggett plays in a deep cross for MacDougall to tap in the second. City are nicely back on course after three losses, but this was not a game to remember. Don Megson's side are having a bad run.											
29 H	WEST BROM		3	W	3-2	1-1	MacDougall 28p, 70, McGuire 58	Keelan	Machin !	Sullivan	Livermore*	Powell	Stringer	Miller	MacDougall	Boyer	Suggett	McGuire	Steele
	8/2	34,509	*8*	35			*Mayo 6, Hughes 57*	*Osborne*	*Nisbet**	*Thompson*	*Cantello*	*Wile*	*Rushbury*	*Brown T*	*Hughes*	*Mayo*	*Glover*	*Johnston*	*Shaw*
							Ref: G Kew	A bumper crowd sees a thriller. Joe Mayo stabs in Willie Johnston's pass. MacDougall converts after John Wile impedes him. Lyndon Hughes fires the Baggies ahead again. McGuire's levels after a fine solo run and MacDougall tucks in the winner. Machin departs for violent conduct.											
30 A	BOLTON		3	D	0-0	0-0		Keelan	Morris	Sullivan	McGuire	Forbes	Stringer	Steele	MacDougall	Boyer	Suggett	Powell	
	15/2	*15,506*	*8*	36				*Siddall*	*Ritson*	*Dunne*	*Reid*	*Jones P*	*Allardyce*	*Byrom*	*Greaves*	*Curran*	*Lee*	*Thompson*	
							Ref: M Lowe	In Machin's absence, Morris is asked to curtail the dangerous Peter Thompson. He does the job well and City soak up plenty of pressure from Jimmy Armfield's side. Keelan's late save foils Peter Reid and, at the other end, MacDougall goes close to punishing a Sam Allardyce error.											
31 H	OLDHAM		3	W	1-0	0-0	Boyer 84	Keelan	Morris	Sullivan	McGuire	Forbes	Stringer	Miller*	MacDougall	Boyer	Suggett	Powell	Steele
	22/2	20,872	*17*	38				*Ogden*	*Wood*	*Whittle*	*Robins*	*Hicks*	*Holt*	*McVitie*	*Bell*	*Chapman*	*Young*	*Groves*	
							Ref: P Reeves	Jimmy Frizzell's side are battling to get away from the drop zone and very nearly leave Norfolk with a point. Boyer does the trick in the closing stages with his first goal in nine games – a far-post header from a Morris cross. He then limps off for treatment, returning to clear off the line.											

No	Venue / Date	Opponent / Att	Pos	Res / Pts	F-A	H-T	Scorers, Times, and Referees	1	2	3	4	5	6	7	8	9	10	11	12 sub used
32	H	SUNDERLAND	4	D	0-0	0-0		Keelan	Butler	Powell	Morris	Forbes	Stringer	Steele	MacDougall	Boyer !	Suggett	McGuire	
	8/3	29,285	2	39				Montgomery	Malone	Guthrie!	Moncur	Watson	Longhorn*	Kerr	Hughes	Halom	Robson	Towers	Bolton
							Ref: C White	A bad-tempered contest between promotion chasers. Keelan tips over a thundering free-kick from Tony Towers. Ron Guthrie and Boyer are sent off for a flare-up when things boil over in the latter stages. A high number of bookings means suspensions are bound to impede the run-in.											
33	A	MANCHESTER U	4	D	1-1	0-0	MacDougall 68	Keelan	Butler	Powell	Morris	Forbes	Stringer	McGuire	MacDougall	Boyer	Suggett	**Peters**	
	15/3	**56,202**	1	40			Pearson 51	Stepney	Forsyth	Houston	Greenhoff	James	Buchan	Coppell*	McIlroy	Macari	Pearson	Daly	Young
							Ref: T Reynolds	The vastly experienced Martin Peters (£50,000 from Spurs) has a useful debut at the home of the leaders. Stuart Pearson converts Steve Coppell's cross from close-range. A weak kick by Alex Stepney gifts an equaliser to MacDougall, who has another effort cleared off the line.											
34	H	HULL	4	W	1-0	0-0	MacDougall 87p	Keelan	Butler	Powell	Morris	Forbes	Stringer	McGuire	MacDougall	Boyer	Suggett	Peters	
	22/3	20,990	14	42				Wealands	Banks	Daniel	Grimes	Croft	Roberts	Lord	McGill	Wood	Hemmerm'n*	Greenwood	DeVries
							Ref: R Toseland	After two good away points a win is vital, but City fade after a bright start. Several chances are missed as the Tigers hang on grimly. Near the end Dave Roberts handles a rebound off keeper Jeff Wealands and MacDougall nets from the spot. Malcolm Lord goes close with a fine shot.											
35	A	BRISTOL CITY	4	W	1-0	1-0	Suggett 17	Keelan	Butler	Powell	Morris	Forbes	Stringer	McGuire	MacDougall	Boyer	Suggett	Peters	
	29/3	22,204	5	44				Cashley	Sweeney	Drysdale	Emanuel*	Collier	Merrick	Tainton	Mann	Gillies	Fear	Brolly	Gow
							Ref: J Hunting	MacDougall hooks the ball into the danger area and it is only partially cleared, allowing Suggett to lash a low shot past Ray Cashley. Keith Fear and Jimmy Mann miss good chances and it takes a gritty Norwich display to hang on. It's a killer blow for the home side's promotion bid.											
36	H	FULHAM	5	L	1-2	1-1	Forbes 42	Keelan	Butler*	Powell	Morris	Forbes	Stringer	McGuire	MacDougall	Boyer	Suggett	Peters	Steele
	31/3	29,909	9	44			Mitchell 20, 60	Mellor	Fraser	Strong	Mullery	Lacy	Moore	Dowie	Mitchell	Busby	Slough	Barrett	
							Ref: A Robinson	Alec Stock's in-form outfit ease ahead through John Mitchell's rasping shot. Forbes goes upfield to head in the equaliser from a corner-kick. McGuire is dispossessed by Alan Mullery, who feeds Mitchell to knock in the winner. Fulham have only lost once in their last ten away games.											
37	H	ORIENT	5	W	2-0	1-0	Boyer 44, MacDougall 82p	Keelan	Butler	Powell	Morris	Forbes	Stringer	McGuire	MacDougall	Boyer	Suggett	Peters	
	5/4	18,116	14	46				Jackson	Fisher	Downing	Allen*	Hoadley	Walley	Cunningham	Grealish	Bullock	Heppolette	Possee	Roeder
							Ref: T Glasson	The lively Boyer bursts through and Orient's offside claims are ignored as he forces the ball past John Jackson at the second attempt. His all-action displays are a crucial part of City's game-plan these days. When his shot is handled by Tom Walley, MacDougall scores from the spot.											
38	A	SHEFFIELD WED		W	1-0	0-0	Stringer 68	Keelan	Butler	Powell*	Morris	Forbes	Stringer	McGuire	MacDougall	Boyer	Suggett	Peters	Sullivan
	8/4	7,483	22	48				Fox	Cameron	Knighton	Mullen	Thompson	Shaw	Potts	Harvey	Thompson	Henson	Joicey	
							Ref: G Trevett	Doomed Wednesday haven't scored at home for nearly 700 minutes. Their line-up shows ten changes from the one at Carrow Road earlier on. Stringer clears off the line and Brian Joicey's header is flicked against the bar by Keelan. MacDougall heads the winner from a Peters flick-on.											
39	A	MILLWALL	4	D	1-1	0-1	Butler 90	Keelan	Butler	Sullivan	Morris	Forbes	Stringer	Powell	MacDougall	Boyer	Suggett	Peters	
	12/4	10,565	21	49			Kitchener 27	King	Evans	Moore	Dorney	Kitchener	Saul	Burnett	Bolland	Clark	Allder	Hazell	
							Ref: P Walters	Boyer appeals against a ban to an independent tribunal, thus making himself available for vital promotion games. Barry Kitchener heads in Doug Allder's corner kick. A limp display by City is largely forgotten when Butler heads home Sullivan's cross in the game's dying seconds.											
40	H	NOTT'M FOR	4	W	**3-0**	1-0	Peters 44, Boyer 74, 85	Keelan	Butler	Sullivan	Morris	Forbes	Powell	McGuire	MacDougall	Boyer	Suggett	Peters	
	19/4	24,552	17	51				Middleton	O'Kane	Jones	Chapman	Cottam	Robertson	Dennehy*	Lyall	O'Hare	Butlin	McGovern	Anderson
							Ref: J Yates	Points are essential and City's nerve holds with Peters heading them ahead at a vital time. The best home performance for some time sees Boyer knock in a Peters nod-down and then crash a brilliant goal past John Middleton. Stringer is out due to his first ban in 11 years as a pro.											
41	H	PORTSMOUTH	3	W	**3-0**	1-0	McGuire 25, Peters 79, Boyer 88	Keelan	Butler	Sullivan	Morris	Forbes	Powell	McGuire	MacDougall	Boyer	Suggett	Peters	
	26/4	18,977	17	53				Figgins	Piper	Went	Kane	Hand	Cahill	Marinello	Foggo	Graham	Stewart	Mellows	
							Ref: C Newsome	To clinch promotion today, City need to win and Villa must beat Sunderland. McGuire, having a great game, buries a diving header. Peters makes it safe with a header and then Suggett sends Boyer through to finish Pompey off. Villa win 2-0, meaning the celebrations can begin.											
42	H	ASTON VILLA	3	L	1-4	1-2	Boyer 26 [Carrodus 86]	Keelan	Butler	Sullivan	Morris	Forbes	Powell	McGuire	MacDougall	Boyer	Suggett	Peters	
	30/4	**35,999**	2	53			Leonard 10, Gidman 20, McDonald 75,	Cumbes	Robson	Aitken	Ross	Nicholls	Gidman	McDonald	Pimblett	Leonard	Hamilton	Carrodus	
	Home	Away					Ref: R Tinkler	The result is academic, but a huge crowd gathers to celebrate promotion. Villa can't catch Man U, but Ron Saunders still gets them motivated against his old club. Keith Leonard heads home and John Gidman scores in his first game since a firework accident put him out for six months.											
Average	23,799	14,362																	

League Cup	Att			F-A	H-T	Scorers, Times, and Referees	1	2	3	4	5	6	7	8	9	10	11	12 sub used
2 A BOLTON		3	D	0-0	0-0		Keelan	Machin	Sullivan	Morris	Forbes	Stringer	Benson	MacDougall	Boyer	Suggett	Powell	
10/9	*11,205*	*11*					*Siddall*	*Ritson*	*Dunne*	*Nicholson*	*Jones P*	*McAllister*	*Byrom*	*Jones G*	*Greaves*	*Whatmore**	*Thompson*	*Phillips*
						Ref: J Williams	Boyer hits a post early on with Barry Siddall beaten. Ex-England flanker Peter Thompson, who passed a late fitness test, proves a big threat every time the ball reaches him. The match is held up for spell when the referee has to go off for treatment after an almighty goalmouth melee.											
2R H BOLTON		2	W	3-1	1-1	Stringer 30, MacDougall 70, Boyer 80	Hansbury	Machin	Sullivan	Morris	Forbes	Stringer	Benson	MacDougall	Boyer	Suggett	Powell	
17/9	14,417	*19*				*Jones P 7p*	*Siddall*	*Ritson*	*Dunne*	*Nicholson*	*Jones P*	*Rimmer*	*Byrom*	*Whatmore*	*Greaves*	*Phillips*	*Thompson*	
						Ref: L Hayes	Stringer handles to give Paul Jones an early chance to score from the spot against debutant Hansbury. Stringer makes amends when he heads home a Suggett corner-kick. MacDougall conjures up a smart finish and Boyer makes it safe, scoring after falling and then quickly recovering.											
3 A WEST BROM		2	D	1-1	1-1	Boyer 15	Keelan	Butler	Sullivan	Morris	Benson	Stringer	Grapes	MacDougall	Boyer	Suggett	Powell	
9/10	*11,631*	*5*				*Stringer 20 (og)*	*Latchford*	*Nisbet*	*Wilson*	*Cantello*	*Wile*	*Robertson*	*Glover*	*Brown*	*Mayo*	*Merrick*	*Johnston*	
						Ref: A Hart	Morris sends over a dipping cross and Boyer nods it past Dave Latchford. Don Howe's men quickly get back on terms when a Willie Johnston corner rather fortunately rebounds into the net off Stringer. Johnston has a fine game and Len Cantello nearly wins the tie with a sizzling shot.											
3R H WEST BROM		2	W	2-0	0-0	MacDougall 103, Boyer 119	Keelan	Butler	Sullivan	Morris	Forbes	Stringer	Machin	MacDougall	Boyer	Suggett	Powell	
16/10	18,235	*5*		*aet*			*Latchford*	*Nisbet*	*Wilson*	*Cantello*	*Wile*	*Robertson*	*Glover*	*Shaw*	*Mayo**	*Hughes*	*Johnston*	*Donaghy*
						Ref: A Hart	The Baggies put up a brave rearguard action and the tie goes into extra-time. The deadlock is finally broken when Machin knocks a pass over the head of Ally Robertson and MacDougall dribbles round Latchford. The keeper then drops Sullivan's cross and Boyer makes the result safe.											
4 A SHEFFIELD UTD		2	D	2-2	1-1	MacDougall 30, 54	Keelan	Butler*	Sullivan	Morris	Forbes	Stringer	Miller	MacDougall	Boyer !	Suggett	Powell	Machin
12/11	*17,091*	*1:6*				*Woodward 45, Eddy 70p*	*Brown*	*Badger*	*Hemsley*	*Garbett*	*Colquhoun !*	*Eddy*	*Woodward*	*Speight**	*Dearden*	*Currie*	*Field*	*Flynn*
						Ref: D Wallace	MacDougall finds himself in space to slot home. Alan Woodward nets a fierce shot after a great run by Tony Field. Morris's shot is deflected to MacDougall who regains the lead. A push by Morris allows the Blades to level it again. Boyer and Eddie Colquhoun are sent off for fighting.											
4R H SHEFFIELD UTD		3	W	2-1	0-0	Goodwin 85, 116	Hansbury	Butler*	Sullivan	Morris	Forbes	Stringer	Miller	MacDougall	Goodwin	Suggett	Machin	Benson
27/11	19,507	*1:5*		*aet*		*Dearden 67*	*Brown*	*Badger*	*Hemsley*	*Garbett*	*Colquhoun*	*Flynn*	*Woodward*	*Bradford*	*Dearden*	*Currie*	*Field**	*Cammack*
						Ref: D Wallace	A simple tap-in by Billy Dearden puts Ken Furphy's men ahead. Five minutes from time City are saved by Steve Goodwin's career-first goal – set up by MacDougall's knockdown. With extra-time almost over, Goodwin does it again, taking his chance after a devastating run by Suggett.											
QF H IPSWICH		3	D	1-1	1-1	Suggett 17	Keelan	Machin	Sullivan	Morris	Forbes	Stringer	Miller	MacDougall	Boyer	Suggett	Powell	
4/12	34,802	*1:2*				*Whymark 40*	*Sivell*	*Mills*	*Harper*	*Talbot*	*Hunter*	*Beattie*	*Hamilton*	*Viljoen*	*Johnson*	*Whymark*	*Woods*	
						Ref: J Taylor	In an electric atmosphere, City are pressed back during the early exchanges. Against the run of play Suggett gives Norwich the lead. A Trevor Whymark header is desperately scooped away by Keelan, but Mr Taylor rules it had crossed the line. Seconds later Bryan Hamilton hits a post.											
QF A IPSWICH		3	W	2-1	1-1	Miller 34, 47	Keelan	Machin	Sullivan	Morris	Forbes	Stringer	Miller	MacDougall	Boyer	Suggett	Powell	
R 10/12	*29,241*	*1:6*				*Johnson 30*	*Sivell*	*Burley*	*Mills*	*Talbot*	*Hunter*	*Beattie*	*Hamilton**	*Viljoen*	*Johnson*	*Whymark*	*Woods*	*Lambert*
						Ref: J Taylor	Hot favourites Ipswich go ahead through David Johnson after a goalmouth scramble. Miller, signed from Ipswich six weeks earlier, equalises by converting MacDougall's cross. Portman Road is stunned when Miller collects Boyer's pass and takes it round Laurie Sivell for the winner.											
SF A MANCHESTER U		3	D	2-2	1-0	Powell 23, MacDougall 88	Keelan	Machin	Sullivan	Morris	Forbes	Stringer	Benson	MacDougall	Boyer	Suggett	Powell	
1 15/1	*58,010*	*1*				*Macari 51, 52*	*Stepney*	*Forsyth*	*Houston*	*Greenhoff*	*James*	*Buchan*	*Morgan*	*McIlroy*	*Macari*	*Daly**	*McCalliog*	*Young*
						Ref: H New	Powell shoots City ahead after going round Steve James. Lou Macari flicks an equaliser after Keelan flaps at a corner. Macari steers in Stewart Houston's pass. United old-boy MacDougall stuns Old Trafford right at the death, pouncing when Houston's back-pass gets stuck in the mud.											
SF H MANCHESTER U		3	W	1-0	0-0	Suggett 54	Keelan	Machin	Sullivan	Morris	Forbes	Stringer	Benson	MacDougall	Boyer	Suggett	Powell	
2 22/1	31,672	*1*					*Stepney*	*Forsyth*	*Houston*	*Greenhoff*	*James**	*Buchan*	*Morgan*	*McIlroy*	*Macari*	*Daly*	*McCalliog*	*Young*
						Ref: K Burns (Norwich win 3-2 on aggregate)	Resolute United keep City at bay until a Powell corner leads to chaos in the area and Suggett flings himself forward to bury a brave header. Keelan ensures a Wembley date with two sensational saves from Alex Forsyth and Sammy McIlroy. Forbes gets an eighth booking this season.											

League Cup (cont)

F	N	ASTON VILLA	3	L	0-1	0-0		Keelan	Machin	Sullivan	Morris	Forbes	Stringer	Miller	MacDougall	Boyer	Suggett	Powell
	1/3	*100,000*	*4*				*Graydon 80*	*Cumbes*	*Robson*	*Aitken*	*Ross*	*Nicholl*	*McDonald*	*Graydon*	*Little*	*Leonard*	*Hamilton*	*Carrodus*
		Rec: £196,000					Ref: G Hill											
		(At Wembley)																

An all-Second Division affair pulls in 100,000 and competition record receipts but the game is a disappointing spectacle. Ray Graydon nets the rebound after Keelan saved his penalty, given for handball on the line by Machin. It's Ron Saunders' third successive LC final as a manager.

FA Cup

3	A	COVENTRY	3	L	0-2	0-2		Keelan	Machin	Sullivan	Morris	Forbes	Stringer	Benson	MacDougall	Boyer	Suggett	Livermore	
	4/1	*19,265*	*1:15*				*Alderson 25, Lloyd 39*	*Ramsbottom*	*Oakey*	*Cattlin*	*Craven*	*Lloyd*	*Dugdale*	*Carr*	*Alderson**	*Stein*	*Cross*	*Hutchison*	*Holmes*
							Ref: R Matthewson												

Brian Alderson cracks in a first-time shot for his first goal in four months. Gordon Milne's men look the livelier side and are rarely troubled after Larry Lloyd belts the ball forward from near the halfway line and it sails straight in. It's Norwich's seventh successive third round exit.

			Home					Away					
	P	W	D	L	F	A	W	D	L	F	A	Pts
1 Manchester U	42	17	3	1	45	12	9	6	6	21	18	61
2 Aston Villa	42	16	4	1	47	6	9	4	8	32	26	58
3 NORWICH	42	14	3	4	34	17	6	10	5	24	20	53
4 Sunderland	42	14	6	1	41	8	5	7	9	24	27	51
5 Bristol City	42	14	5	2	31	10	7	3	11	16	23	50
6 West Brom	42	13	4	4	33	15	5	5	11	21	27	45
7 Blackpool	42	12	6	3	31	17	2	11	8	7	16	45
8 Hull	42	12	8	1	25	10	3	6	12	15	43	44
9 Fulham	42	9	8	4	29	17	4	8	9	15	22	42
10 Bolton	42	9	7	5	27	16	6	5	10	18	25	42
11 Oxford	42	14	3	4	30	19	1	9	11	11	32	42
12 Orient	42	8	9	4	17	16	3	11	7	11	23	42
13 Southampton	42	10	6	5	29	20	5	5	11	24	34	41
14 Notts County	42	7	11	3	34	26	5	5	11	15	33	40
15 York	42	9	7	5	28	18	5	3	13	23	37	38
16 Nott'm For	42	7	7	7	24	23	5	7	9	19	32	38
17 Portsmouth	42	9	7	5	28	20	3	6	12	16	34	37
18 Oldham	42	10	7	4	28	16	0	8	13	12	32	35
19 Bristol Rov	42	10	4	7	25	23	2	7	12	17	41	35
20 Millwall	42	8	9	4	31	19	2	3	16	13	37	32
21 Cardiff	42	7	8	6	24	21	2	6	13	12	41	32
22 Sheffield Wed	42	3	7	11	17	29	2	4	15	12	35	21
	924	232	139	91	658	378	91	139	232	378	658	924

Odds & ends

Double wins: (3) Nott'm For, Orient, Bristol City.
Double losses: (2) Fulham, York.

Won from behind: (6) Nott'm For (a), Bristol City (h), West Brom (h), Sheffield U (h) (LC), Bolton (h) (LC), Ipswich (a) (LC).
Lost from in front: (0).

High spots: Promotion back to Division One at the first attempt.
The away displays in the League Cup final, especially at Portman Road.
The cut-price signing and contribution of World Cup star Martin Peters.
Machin's hat-trick at Forest, his only goals in 51 games to May 1975.
Phil Boyer named in the PFA's divisional team of the season.
A settled side: Nine men played 35 or more league games.

Low spots: A highly disappointing second Wembley defeat in two years.
Defeat at Fulham: The only loss in the first 19 league and LC games.
The BBC-televised home defeat by Bristol Rov: the first in eight months.

Player of the Year: Colin Suggett.
Ever-presents: (1) Ted McDougall.
Hat-tricks: (1) Mel Machin v Nott'm For (a).
Opposing hat-tricks: (0).
Leading scorer: (22) Ted McDougall (+2 in Texaco Cup).

	Appearances						Goals			
	Lge	*Sub*	LC	*Sub*	FAC	*Sub*	Lge	LC	FAC	Tot
Benson, John	**9**	*1*	4	*1*	1					
Boyer, Phil	**40**		10		1		**16**	3		**19**
Butler, Geoff	**17**	*1*	4				**1**			**1**
Forbes, Duncan	**39**		10		1		**1**			**1**
Goodwin, Steve	**2**		1					2		**2**
Grapes, Steve	**6**	*2*	1	*2*			**2**			**2**
Hansbury, Roger	**4**		2							
Keelan, Kevin	**38**		9		1					
Livermore, Doug	**2**	*1*			1					
Machin, Mel	**24**		9	*1*	1		**3**			**3**
MacDougall, Ted	**42**		11		1		**17**	5		**22**
McGuire, Mick	**16**						**2**			**2**
Miller, Johnny	**14**		6				**3**	2		**5**
Morris, Peter	**40**		11		1					
Peters, Martin	**10**						**2**			**2**
Powell, Tony	**40**		10				**2**	1		**3**
Steele, Billy	**4**	*5*								
Stringer, Dave	**39**		11		1		**2**	1		**3**
Suggett, Colin	**41**		11		1		**6**	2		**8**
Sullivan, Colin	**35**	*1*	11		1		**1**			**1**
20 players used	**462**	*11*	**121**	*4*	**11**		**58**	**16**		**74**

No	Date		Att	Pos	Pt	F-A	H-T	Scorers, Times, and Referees	1	2	3	4	5	6	7	8	9	10	11	12 sub used
1	A	MANCHESTER C			L	0-3	0-0		Keelan	Machin	Sullivan	Morris	Forbes	Powell	Grapes	MacDougall	Peters	Suggett	McGuire	
	16/8		*29,103*		0			*Bell 60, Tueart 80, 83*	*Corrigan*	*Hammond*	*Donachie*	*Doyle*	*Watson*	*Oakes*	*Hartford*	*Bell*	*Marsh*	*Royle*	*Tueart*	
								Ref: D Turner	An evenly balanced contest is crying out for a goal when Colin Bell obliges with a fierce shot, at the end of a slick move. Dennis Tueart seals the win with two quick goals, including a spectacular overhead kick. Doug Livermore moves on after five years, joining Cardiff for £20,000.											
2	H	LEEDS			D	1-1	0-0	Madeley 50(og)	Keelan	Machin	Sullivan	Morris	Forbes	Powell	Grapes	MacDougall	Suggett	Peters	McGuire	
	20/8		25,686		1			*Cherry 70*	*Harvey*	*Reaney*	*Gray*	*Bremner*	*McQueen*	*Cherry*	*Lorimer*	*Clarke*	*McKenzie*	*Yorath*	*Madeley*	
								Ref: J Yates	It's nip and tuck until a freak goal gives City the lead. Suggett's cross eludes MacDougall but flies in off Paul Madeley. Jimmy Armfield's men hit back when Trevor Cherry blasts home a shot on the turn. Before the game, Leeds' Mick Jones announces he is quitting due to a knee injury.											
3	H	ASTON VILLA		12	W	5-3	4-1	MacDougall 24p, 45, 81, Forbes 42,	Keelan	Machin	Sullivan	Morris	Forbes	Powell	Grapes	MacDougall	Suggett	Peters	McGuire	
	23/8		21,797	*18*	3			*Graydon 26p, 76, Aitken 59* [Grapes 44]	*Cumbes*	*Gidman*	*Aitken*	*Ross*	*Nicholl*	*Phillips*	*Graydon*	*Little*	*Leonard*	*Hamilton*	*Carrodus*	
								Ref: M Taylor	Sweet revenge for the mauling in April and the drab Wembley final a few weeks earlier. Chris Nicholl handles and Forbes pushes Graydon for the early penalties. Forbes ignores a bloody nose to head City ahead. MacDougall completes his hat-trick with a solo goal of sheer arrogance.											
4	A	ARSENAL		16	L	1-2	1-1	Peters 30	Keelan	Machin	Sullivan	Morris	Forbes	Powell	Grapes	MacDougall	Peters	Suggett	Boyer	
	26/8		*22,613*	*7*	3			*Ball 18p, Kelly 87*	*Rimmer*	*Rice*	*Storey*	*Kelly*	*Mancini*	*O'Leary*	*Armstrong*	*Cropley*	*Ball*	*Kidd*	*Brady*	
								Ref: R Capey	McGuire is missing due to tonsilitis. Forbes, playing with a broken nose, fouls Brian Kidd and Alan Ball converts from the spot. Peters avoids David O'Leary's challenge to tuck in a fine equaliser. City hearts are broken near the end when Eddie Kelly nets a 35-yarder out of the blue.											
5	A	TOTTENHAM		16	D	2-2	0-1	Boyer 52, MacDougall 82	Keelan	Machin	Sullivan	Morris	Forbes	Powell	Grapes	MacDougall	Boyer	Suggett	Peters	
	30/8		*23,145*	*14*	4			*Pratt 42, Duncan 62*	*Jennings*	*Smith*	*Knowles**	*Pratt*	*McAllister*	*Osgood*	*McNab*	*Naylor*	*Duncan*	*Jones*	*Neighbour*	*Hoddle*
								Ref: P Reeves	John Pratt nets a long-range screamer. Boyer deflects a Sullivan shot past Pat Jennings to level. John Duncan restores the Spurs lead with a drive in off the post. A point is saved when Grapes' cross is headed home by MacDougall. Glenn Hoddle, 17, comes on for his senior debut.											
6	H	EVERTON		11	W	4-2	3-0	MacDougall 16, 32, 40, Suggett 48	Keelan	Machin	Sullivan	Morris	Forbes	Powell	Grapes	Suggett	Boyer	MacDougall	Peters	
	6/9		20,407	*10*	6			*Latchford 63, Pearson 67*	*Lawson*	*Bernard*	*Clements*	*Pearson*	*Kenyon*	*Lyons*	*Buckley*	*Dobson*	*Latchford*	*Smallman*	*Jones*	
								Ref: R Challis	MacDougall powers in another brilliant hat-trick. A near-post header is followed by a fine first-time shot and a perfect finish past on-rushing Dave Lawson. Suggett's rasping shot has the fans in raptures. Bob Latchford scores one and makes one to briefly rouse Billy Bingham's outfit.											
7	A	BURNLEY		13	D	4-4	1-3	MacDougall 30p, 68, Peters 76,	Keelan	Machin	Butler	Morris	Forbes	Powell	McGuire	MacDougall	Boyer	Suggett*	Peters	Stringer
	13/9		*15,496*	*16*	7			*Noble 1, 27p, 44p, 88* [Boyer 90]	*Stevenson*	*Brennan*	*Newton*	*Noble*	*Waldron*	*Thomson*	*Flynn*	*Hankin*	*Summerbee*	*Collins*	*James*	
								Ref: K McNally	Another thriller. Peter Noble outpaces Powell for the first, then tucks home a penalty after a Suggett foul. Peters is pushed for City's penalty, but Noble despatches another after Butler handles. Noble's late glancing header looks a winner until Boyer dramatically converts Peters' cross.											
8	H	LEICESTER		10	W	2-0	1-0	MacDougall 4p, 90	Keelan	Machin	Butler	Morris	Forbes	Powell	McGuire	MacDougall	Boyer	Suggett	Peters	
	20/9		22,799	*18*	9				*Wallington*	*Whitworth*	*Rofe*	*Kember*	*Sims*	*Woollett*	*Weller*	*Sammels*	*Worthington*	*Lee**	*Garland*	*Alderson*
								Ref: D Nippard	Steve Sims' blatant push gives City an early penalty. The fifth spot-kick in City's last 150 minutes of play arrives as Powell handles but Keelan saves Frank Worthington's effort. Mark Wallington tries to fly-kick clear in the last minute but the ball hits MacDougall and he nets a real gift.											
9	A	IPSWICH		10	L	0-2	0-0		Keelan	Machin	Butler	Morris	Forbes	Powell	McGuire	MacDougall*	Boyer	Suggett	Peters	Stringer
	23/9		*34,825*	*15*	9			*Beattie 55, Hamilton 65*	*Cooper*	*Burley*	*Mills*	*Osborne*	*Hunter*	*Beattie*	*Hamilton*	*Viljoen*	*Lambert**	*Whymark*	*Woods*	*Gates*
								Ref: K Baker	Powell makes an astonishing goal-line clearance to keep out an effort by tricky Clive Woods. City's front men rarely get a look-in against the Allan Hunter-Kevin Beattie partnership. Beattie nets the opener, is also booked and departs injured. It's Ipswich's second-biggest crowd ever.											
10	A	SHEFFIELD UTD		10	W	1-0	0-0	MacDougall 57	Keelan	Machin	Butler	Morris	Forbes	Powell	Steele*	MacDougall	Boyer	Suggett	Peters	McGuire
	27/9		*20,624*	*22*	11				*Brown*	*Badger*	*Hemsley*	*Eddy*	*Colquhoun*	*Flynn*	*Woodward*	*Field*	*Cammack*	*Currie*	*Bradford*	
								Ref: P Partridge	The struggling Blades are injury-hit but look in positive mood. Keelan rides his luck on more than one occasion. MacDougall's looping header proves the winner. Ted Hemsley hits a post late on to cap a miserable afternoon for Ken Furphy's men. Nine days later Furphy will be sacked.											

No	Date	Venue	Opponent	Att	Pos	Res	F-A	H-T	Scorers, Times, and Referees	1	2	3	4	5	6	7	8	9	10	11	12 sub used
11	4/10	H	STOKE	22,318	12	L	0-1	0-0		Keelan	Machin	Sullivan	McGuire	Forbes	Powell	Miller*	MacDougall	Boyer	Suggett	Peters	Steele
					10	11			Haslegrave 73	Shilton	Marsh	Pejic	Mahoney	Dodd	Bloor	Haslegrave	Greenhoff	Moores	Hudson	Salmons	
									Ref: B Homewood	Tony Waddington's outfit prove a tough nut to crack. More emphatic finishing would have left Norwich totally embarrassed. Alan Hudson, Sean Haslegrave and Jimmy Greenhoff all have efforts knocked off the line. Haslegrave knocks in an Ian Moores cross to decide the contest.											
12	11/10	H	DERBY	23,022	10	D	0-0	0-0		Keelan	Machin	Butler	McGuire	Forbes	Powell	Grapes	MacDougall	Boyer	Steele	Peters	
					5	12				Boulton	Thomas	Nish	Rioch	McFarland	Todd	Powell	Gemmill	Lee*	Hector	George	Davies
									Ref: G Kew	The reigning champs are a shade lucky to stay on terms under heavy City pressure. Colin Boulton saves superbly from McGuire. Bruce Rioch and Peters get involved in a jostling match. Sub Roger Davies nearly steals it for Dave Mackay's men, but Keelan saves at point-blank range.											
13	18/10	A	NEWCASTLE	31,868	12	L	2-5	1-1	McGuire 43, MacD' 86 [Jones 90(og)]	Keelan	Machin	Jones	McGuire	Forbes	Powell	Grapes	MacDougall	Boyer	Suggett*	Peters	Butler
					11	12			Macdonald 5, 72 Gowling 47, 70,	Mahoney	Nattrass	Kennedy	Nulty	Craig D	Howard	Burns	Barrowcl'gh	Macdonald	Gowling	Craig T	
									Ref: M Lowe	Malcolm Macdonald pounces to net from a free-kick, but McGuire darts in to level. Alan Gowling nets from a tight angle, misses a real sitter and then heads his second. Debutant David Jones, City's new recruit from Nottingham Forest, stretches and diverts the ball into his own goal.											
14	25/10	H	BIRMINGHAM	20,178	11	W	1-0	1-0	Boyer 22	Keelan	Butler	Sullivan	McGuire	Forbes	Powell	Grapes	MacDougall	Boyer	Machin	Peters	
					19	14				Latchford	Martin	Pendrey	Kendall	Gallagher	Roberts	Campbell	Burns	Hibbitt	Hatton	Taylor	
									Ref: J Wrenall	McGuire sets off on a great run, beating two men before shooting, and sees his effort parried by Dave Latchford straight to a grateful Boyer. Despite the absence of Trevor Francis, Brum's Gordon Taylor is a constant threat on the wing and Norwich's defence often looks ill at ease.											
15	1/11	A	MANCHESTER U	50,587	13	L	0-1	0-0		Keelan	Butler	Sullivan	McGuire	Forbes	Powell	Steele	MacDougall	Boyer	Machin	Peters	
					1	14			Pearson 79	Roche	Nicholl	Houston	Jackson	Greenhoff	Buchan	Coppell	McIlroy	Pearson	Macari	Daly	
									Ref: H Hackney	Boyer hits the bar with a chip, shortly before Stuart Pearson nets a Lou Macari pass. United boss Tommy Docherty lashes out at City's tactics, calling them a 'parasitic' team which lives off others' mistakes. Leading scorer MacDougall is recalled by Scotland for a midweek international.											
16	8/11	H	MIDDLESBROUGH	19,795	15	L	0-1	0-0		Keelan	Butler*	Sullivan	Machin	Forbes	Powell	Grapes	MacDougall	Boyer	McGuire	Peters	Steele
					9	14			Souness 51	Platt	Craggs	Spraggon	Souness	Boam	Maddren	Brine	Mills	Hickton	Cooper	Armstrong	
									Ref: J Bent	A misdirected header by McGuire puts City's defence in trouble and spiky Scot Graeme Souness steps in to shoot Jack Charlton's outfit ahead. The goal bonanzas of earlier this season now seem a distant memory and the disgruntled home fans seem resigned to a long, hard winter ahead.											
17	15/11	A	COVENTRY	14,897	16	L	0-1	0-1		Keelan	Jones	Sullivan	Morris	Forbes	Powell	Miller	MacDougall	Boyer	Suggett	Peters	
					12	14			Mortimer 18	King	Coop	Brogan	Dugdale	Lloyd	Holmes	Powell	Mortimer	Cross	Murphy	Hutchison	
									Ref: W Johnson	Norwich tackle their bogey side in torrential rain and on a mudbath of a pitch. Boyer and Forbes go close, but Gordon Milne's men take the honours when Denis Mortimer drives home a left-foot shot. It's the home side's first home win in three months, but 16th in a row against City!											
18	22/11	H	NEWCASTLE	19,700	18	L	1-2	1-1	Sullivan 8	Keelan	Jones	Sullivan	Morris	Forbes	Powell*	Miller	MacDougall	Boyer	Suggett	Peters	Wilson
					11	14			Nulty 6, 73	Mahoney	Nattrass	Kennedy	Nulty	Craig D	Howard	Burns	Barrowcl'gh	Macdonald	Gowling	Craig T	
									Ref: M Lowe	Sullivan punishes hesitation by Stewart Barrowclough to thrash in a splendid goal. Geoff Nulty levels with a diving header from a David Craig cross. Keelan can't hold an Alan Gowling header and Nulty swoops again. A late City penalty claim is refused and cushions come raining on.											
19	29/11	A	LIVERPOOL	34,780	16	W	3-1	0-0	Suggett 68, Peters 77, MacDougall 89	Keelan	Jones	Sullivan	Morris	Forbes	Stringer	Machin	MacDougall	Boyer	Suggett	Peters	
					6	16			Hughes 87	Clemence	Smith	Neal	Thompson	Kennedy	Hughes	Keegan	Hall	Heighway	Toshack	Callaghan	
									Ref: A Morrissey	After four losses, City shock the Reds with their determination. Suggett's finish is deadly from 25 yards. Then Peters knocks in Sullivan's pass after a perfectly timed run. Emlyn Hughes prods in a John Toshack head-down, but MacDougall caps a great day by swooping on a rebound.											
20	6/12	H	WEST HAM	27,020	16	W	1-0	0-0	MacDougall 78	Keelan	Jones	Sullivan	Morris	Forbes	Stringer	Machin	MacDougall	Boyer	Suggett	Peters	
					6	18				Day	Coleman	Lampard	McDowell	Taylor T	Lock	Taylor A	Paddon	Robson	Brooking	Holland	
									Ref: H Harvey	West Ham are third in the table at kick-off, but City control proceedings for long spells and look confident in the wake of the Anfield victory. Ex-Hammers Peters and MacDougall combine for the latter to head past Mervyn Day. Fighting fans spill on the pitch after the final whistle.											
21	13/12	A	ASTON VILLA	30,478	17	L	2-3	1-2	Peters 2, MacDougall 55	Keelan	Jones	Sullivan	Morris	Forbes	Stringer	Machin	MacDougall	Boyer	Suggett	Peters	
					12	18			Graydon 17, Deehan 23, 57	Burridge	Gidman	Robson	Ross	Nicholl	Phillips	Graydon	Deehan	Gray	Hamilton	Carrodus	
									Ref: B Daniels	On a rock-hard pitch, Peters fires a shot in off the post, and soon after hits the bar. Ray Graydon levels, finishing off a move he started himself. John Deehan, 18, scores the second and third goals of his career, one from close range and the winner a very tidy finish from a Graydon cross.											

No	Date		Att	Pos	Pt	F-A	H-T	Scorers, Times, and Referees	1	2	3	4	5	6	7	8	9	10	11	12 sub used
22	H	MANCHESTER C		16	D	2-2	0-2	Boyer 61, 66	Keelan	Jones	Sullivan	Morris	Forbes	Stringer	Machin	MacDougall	Boyer	Suggett	Peters	
	20/12		19,692	*7*	19			*Tueart 13, Royle 37*	*Corrigan*	*Clements*	*Donachie*	*Doyle*	*Watson*	*Oakes*	*Barnes*	*Booth*	*Royle*	*Hartford*	*Tueart*	
								Ref: M Sinclair	Dennis Tueart surges forward almost unchallenged to fire past Keelan. Alan Oakes' chip forward causes defensive chaos and Joe Royle nets the second. Morris's low drive into the area is converted by Boyer. A Sullivan cross is flicked on by MacDougall for jubilant Boyer to equalise.											
23	A	QP RANGERS		17	L	0-2	0-1		Keelan	Jones	Sullivan	Morris	Forbes	Stringer	Machin	MacDougall	Boyer	Suggett	Peters	
	26/12		*21,774*	*3*	19			*Masson 31, Bowles 89*	*Parkes*	*Clement*	*Gillard*	*Leach*	*McLintock*	*Webb*	*Thomas*	*Francis*	*Masson*	*Bowles*	*Givens*	
								Ref: R Lees	Gerry Francis's clever through ball is netted by Don Masson from a narrow angle. Both goalkeepers make a series of fine saves during an open game. Stan Bowles drives in the second from a Don Givens cross. Disappointed Bond says the match was a good advert for attacking football.											
24	H	WOLVERHAMPTON		18	D	1-1	0-1	Peters 68	Keelan	Jones	Sullivan	Morris	Forbes	Stringer	Machin	MacDougall	Boyer	Suggett	Peters	
	27/12		25,115	*21*	20			*Bell 24*	*Parkes*	*Sunderland*	*Parkin*	*Bailey*	*Daley*	*McAlle*	*Hibbitt*	*Carr*	*Bell*	*Daly**	*Farley*	*Kindon*
								Ref: R Toseland	Norman Bell, 20, grabs the first senior goal of his career, heading past Keelan after a fine run by Alan Sunderland. City look well below par against Bill McGarry's men. They get back on terms when a Suggett corner reaches Peters who sends an impressive overhead kick into the net.											
25	H	BURNLEY		17	W	3-1	2-0	Peters 34, Forbes 40, Boyer 59	Keelan	Jones	Sullivan	Morris	Forbes	Stringer	Machin	MacDougall	Boyer	Suggett	Peters	
	10/1		**18,059**	*21*	22			*Newton 64*	*Stevenson*	*Docherty*	*Newton*	*Ingham*	*Waldron*	*Thomson*	*Bradshaw*	*Flynn*	*Kennerley*	*Loggie*	*Casper*	
								Ref: K Burns	Joe Brown's side is ravaged by injury and suspension. Peters flicks a header past Alan Stevenson to gain the lead. A Jones free-kick is headed home by Forbes. City are in the comfort zone when Boyer's glancing header goes in. Minutes later, however, Keith Newton nets a fierce drive.											
26	A	EVERTON		17	D	1-1	0-0	Boyer 64	Keelan	Jones	Sullivan	McGuire	Forbes	Stringer	Machin	MacDougall	Boyer	Suggett	Peters	
	17/1		*23,164*	*11*	23			*Dobson 55*	*Lawson*	*Bernard*	*Darracott*	*Buckley*	*Kenyon*	*Lyons*	*Hamilton*	*Dobson*	*Latchford*	*Pearson**	*Jones G*	*Jones D*
								Ref: T Spencer	Martin Dobson's raking left-foot shot is seen late by Keelan and finds the net. City hit back quickly and Boyer beats Dave Lawson with a well-placed header from Jones's cross. A scrappy affair but a deserved point. Before the game John Bond's car was broken into at the team's hotel.											
27	A	LEEDS		15	W	**3-0**	1-0	MacDougall 10, 87, McGuire 65	Keelan	Jones	Sullivan	McGuire	Forbes	Stringer	Machin	MacDougall	Boyer	Suggett	Peters	
	31/1		*27,254*	*4*	25				*Harvey*	*Reaney*	*Gray F*	*Cherry*	*Madeley*	*Hunter*	*Lorimer**	*Clarke*	*McKenzie*	*Yorath*	*Gray E*	*Jordan*
								Ref: D Wallace	City get off to a great start as Peters robs Paul Madeley and sets in motion a move that ends with MacDougall sliding in. Despite all Leeds' huff and puff, they are caught again when McGuire's shot is deflected in. With home fans flocking for the exits, MacDougall powers in a header.											
28	H	ARSENAL		14	W	3-1	2-1	Peters 2, 73, MacDougall 19	Keelan	Jones	Sullivan	McGuire	Forbes	Stringer	Machin	MacDougall	Boyer	Suggett	Peters	
	7/2		23,038	*18*	27			*Kidd 7*	*Rimmer*	*Rice*	*Storey*	*Ross*	*Mancini*	*Powling*	*Armstrong*	*Ball*	*Stapleton*	*Kidd*	*Brady*	
								Ref: R Capey	Terry Mancini fouls MacDougall and the free-kick is curled straight in by Peters. Bertie Mee's men level when Brian Kidd converts Alan Ball's cross with a crisp shot. Machin's glorious through-pass is netted by MacDougall. Peters caps a thrilling victory with a typical near-post header.											
29	H	COVENTRY		16	L	0-3	0-1		Keelan	Jones	Sullivan	McGuire	Forbes	Stringer	Machin	MacDougall	Boyer	Suggett	Peters	
	21/2		20,798	*10*	27			*Ferguson 29, Craven 50, Cross 78*	*Blyth*	*Oakley*	*Cattlin*	*Craven*	*Dugdale*	*Coop*	*Cartwright**	*Powell*	*Cross*	*Ferguson*	*Hutchison*	*Holmes*
								Ref: A Robinson	City are brought back to earth with a bump. The unbeaten run is shattered as Mick Ferguson heads in Tommy Hutchison's cross, John Craven nets after David Cross hits the post and Cross converts Hutchison's pass. Ex-Sky Blue McGuire admits his old teammates could have had six.											
30	A	BIRMINGHAM		18	D	1-1	0-1	Peters 50	Keelan	Powell	Sullivan	McGuire	Forbes	Stringer	Steele	MacDougall	Boyer	Suggett	Peters	
	28/2		*22,359*	*19*	28			*Francis 33p*	*Latchford*	*Page*	*Styles*	*Kendall*	*Gallagher*	*Burns*	*Emmanuel*	*Francis*	*Withe*	*Hatton*	*Calderwood*	
								Ref: A Turvey	Returning after a long injury-absence, Powell brings down Trevor Francis, who atones for two earlier misses by netting from the spot. When McGuire is tripped by Malcolm Page, Peters – on defensive duties this afternoon – strolls forward to blast the free-kick into the roof of the net.											
31	H	TOTTENHAM		13	W	3-1	0-0	Suggett 66, MacDougall 74p, Boyer 88	Keelan	Jones	Sullivan	McGuire	Forbes	Powell	Steele	MacDougall	Boyer	Suggett	Peters	
	6/3		21,220	*15*	30			*Chivers 55*	*Jennings*	*Naylor**	*McAllister*	*Pratt*	*Young*	*Osgood*	*Coates*	*Perrryman*	*Duncan*	*Chivers*	*Neighbour*	*Jones*
								Ref: M Lowe	Ralph Coates stumbles and wins a disputed free-kick, which gentle giant Martin Chivers fires home off a post. Suggett nips in to equalise after a scramble. Keith Osgood punches a Jones effort off the line and MacDougall nets the penalty. Boyer buries a real beauty from Suggett's pass.											

No	H/A	Opponent	Att	Pos	Res	F-A	H-T	Scorers, Times, and Referees	1	2	3	4	5	6	7	8	9	10	11	subs used
32	A	DERBY		16	L	1-3	1-0	Forbes 23	Keelan	Jones	Sullivan	McGuire	Forbes	Powell	Steele	MacDougall	Boyer	Suggett	Peters	
	13/3		*27,005*	*4*	30			*Gemmill 47, Rioch 71, James 75*	*Moseley*	*Webster*	*Nish*	*Rioch*	*McFarland*	*Todd*	*Powell*	*Gemmill*	*Hector*	*Davies*	*James*	
								Ref: R Challis	A corner causes havoc in the home box and Forbes heads past Graham Moseley. Archie Gemmill rifles Dave Mackay's men level with a fine shot. Bruce Rioch scores a sensational solo goal, beating several men before rounding Keelan. Leighton James squeezes a shot inside the post.											
33	H	MANCHESTER U		15	D	1-1	0-1	Boyer 63	Keelan	Jones	Sullivan	McGuire	Forbes	Powell	Steele*	MacDougall	Boyer	Suggett	Peters	Miller
	17/3		28,178	*2*	31			*Hill 9*	*Stepney*	*Forsyth*	*Houston*	*Daly*	*Greenhoff*	*Buchan*	*Coppell*	*McIlroy*	*Pearson*	*McCreery*	*Hill*	
								Ref: T Glasson	Alex Forsyth's up-and-under is flicked on by Stuart Pearson for Gordon Hill to race through and shoot past Keelan. The long-awaited equaliser comes as MacDougall chases a 'lost cause' and forces the ball across for partner Boyer to net his 100th league goal. Boyer then hits a post.											
34	H	LIVERPOOL		17	L	0-1	0-0		Keelan	Jones	Sullivan	McGuire	Forbes	Powell	Miller	MacDougall	Boyer	Suggett	Peters	
	20/3		29,013	*3*	31			*Fairclough 59*	*Clemence*	*Smith*	*Neal*	*Thompson*	*Kennedy*	*Hughes*	*Keegan*	*Hall*	*Heighway*	*Fairclough*	*Callaghan*	
								Ref: D Nippard	Boyer, called up for his England debut in midweek, hits the bar and misses two sitters. David Fairclough, standing in for John Toshack, nips in to score after Jones' back-pass fails to reach Keelan. Dunlop Tyres sponsor the match, the first commercial venture of this sort at Norwich City.											
35	A	WEST HAM		15	W	1-0	1-0	MacDougall 16	Keelan	Jones	Sullivan	McGuire	Forbes	Powell	Miller	MacDougall	Boyer	Suggett	Peters	
	27/3		*20,628*	*12*	33				*Day*	*Coleman*	*Lampard*	*Bonds*	*Taylor T*	*Lock*	*Holland*	*Curbishley*	*Jennings*	*McDowell*	*Robson*	
								Ref: R Matthewson	Suggett's fine through-ball is volleyed in for MacDougall's 26th of the season. He is always fired up when meeting his former clubs and a fierce challenge on Mervyn Day and flare-up with Billy Bonds sees the crowd pelt him with missiles. Hammers have won just once in 17 matches.											
36	H	IPSWICH		12	W	1-0	1-0	Peters 39	Keelan	Morris	Sullivan	McGuire	**Davids**	Powell	Miller	MacDougall*	Boyer	Suggett	Peters	Steele
	31/3		31,024	*7*	35				*Cooper*	*Burley*	*Mills*	*Sharkey*	*Hunter*	*Peddelty*	*Osborne**	*Talbot*	*Johnson*	*Whymark*	*Lambert*	*Woods*
								Ref: J Taylor	City seize the initiative and MacDougall brings a fine save from Paul Cooper and Boyer strikes the post. Young defender John Peddelty is dispossessed by Peters, who makes himself space and fires a winner past Cooper. Neil Davids, 20, copes well with such a high-profile debut.											
37	H	SHEFFIELD UTD		12	L	1-3	1-3	Boyer 44	Keelan	Morris	Sullivan	McGuire	Davids	Powell	Miller	MacDougall	Boyer	Suggett	Peters	
	3/4		19,937	*22*	35			*Guthrie 5, Stainrod 22, Currie 43*	*Brown*	*Franks*	*Goulding**	*Speight*	*Colquhoun*	*Kenworthy*	*Woodward*	*Stainrod*	*Guthrie*	*Currie*	*Bradford*	*Flynn*
								Ref: J Homewood	The Blades are several points adrift at the bottom with just three wins from 39 league and cup games. However, a Chris Guthrie volley and a Simon Stainrod tap-in sees them surge ahead. It gets worse as Tony Currie's cross eludes everyone to drift in. Jim Brown stars after the break.											
38	A	MIDDLESBROUGH		11	W	1-0	0-0	Steele 54	Keelan	Morris	Steele	McGuire	Jones	Powell	Miller	MacDougall	Boyer	Suggett	Peters	
	6/4		*16,000*	*9*	37				*Platt*	*Craggs*	*Cooper*	*Souness*	*Boam*	*McAndrew*	*Boersma*	*Mills*	*Smith*	*Maddren**	*Armstrong*	*Foggon*
								Ref: G Flint	Boss Jack Charlton can't believe it as David Armstrong and Graeme Souness both hit the woodwork and then a Terry Cooper penalty is saved comfortably by Keelan. Steele has an industrious game and pops up in attack to find the net when John Craggs lingers over a Suggett cross.											
39	A	LEICESTER		11	D	0-0	0-0		Keelan	Jones	Morris	McGuire	Forbes	Powell	Steele*	MacDougall	Boyer	Suggett	Peters	**Bond**
	10/4		*19,856*	*9*	38				*Wallington*	*Whitworth*	*Rofe*	*Kember*	*Blockley*	*Woollett*	*Weller*	*Lee*	*Worthington*	*Alderson**	*Sammels*	*Glover*
								Ref: R Lee	Forbes heads a Leicester clearance back down the pitch to put MacDougall clear, but he is crudely hauled down by Jeff Blockley. The defender accepts a booking with a rueful smile, having cynically done his duty. Bond's son Kevin comes on for a brief debut, but doesn't touch the ball!											
40	H	QP RANGERS		11	W	3-2	1-1	MacDougall 27, Morris 67, Boyer 77	Keelan	Jones	Steele	Morris	Forbes	Powell	McGuire	MacDougall	Boyer	Suggett	Peters	
	17/4		**31,231**	*2*	40			*Thomas 43, Powell 87 (og)*	*Parkes*	*Clement*	*Gillard*	*Hollins*	*McLintock*	*Webb*	*Thomas*	*Francis*	*Masson*	*Bowles*	*Givens*	
								Ref: K Styles	Going full-tilt for the title, QPR have won 11 and drawn one of their last 12 games. An opportunist MacDougall strike is cancelled out by a super Dave Thomas goal. Morris hammers his first in 84 City games and Boyer nods a third. Powell blunders under pressure from Don Givens.											
41	A	WOLVERHAMPTON		11	L	0-1	0-1		Keelan	Machin	Morris	McGuire	Forbes	Powell	Steele*	MacDougall	Boyer	Suggett	Peters	Grapes
	19/4		*16,168*	*20*	40			*Richards 40*	*Pierce*	*Sunderland*	*Parkin*	*Patching*	*Palmer*	*McAlle**	*Carr*	*Hibbitt*	*Bell*	*Richards*	*Kelly*	*Daley*
								Ref: K Styles	After the magnificent effort against high-riding QPR 48 hours earlier, City buckle against a side battling to avoid the drop. John Richards rises to head Martin Patching's cross over Keelan, and then runs around him to prod the ball into the net. Gary Pierce tips over a Peters bicycle kick.											
42	A	STOKE		10	W	2-0	0-0	MacDougall 47, Suggett 65	Keelan	Jones	Morris	McGuire	Forbes	Powell	Steele	MacDougall	Boyer	Suggett	Peters	
	24/4		*15,598*	*12*	42				*Shilton*	*Lumsden*	*Pejic*	*Dodd*	*Smith**	*Bloor*	*Sheldon*	*Greenhoff*	*Conroy*	*Haslegrave*	*Salmons*	*Bowers*
		Home	Away					Ref: E Read	A rather meaningless end-of-season contest, with the home side bidding farewell to long-serving defender Eric Skeels after almost 600 games. Alan Dodd slips up to allow MacDougall a run on goal and he beats Peter Shilton. Suggett makes it a happy end of term with a 25-yard strike.											
Average		23,335	24,677																	

LEAGUE DIVISION 1 (CUP-TIES) Manager: John Bond SEASON 1975-76

League Cup	Att	Pos	Res	F-A	H-T	Scorers, Times, and Referees	1	2	3	4	5	6	7	8	9	10	11	12 sub used
2 H MANCHESTER C		11	D	1-1	0-0	MacDougall 78	Keelan	Machin	Butler	Morris	Forbes	Powell	Grapes	MacDougall	Boyer	Suggett	Peters	
10/9	18,328	*13*				*Watson 84*	*Corrigan*	*Clements*	*Donachie*	*Doyle*	*Watson*	*Oakes*	*Hartford*	*Bell*	*Royle*	*Marsh*	*Tueart*	
						Ref: B Daniels	Dave Watson concedes a free-kick and, when it is flicked towards him, hesitates to allow MacDougall an opening goal. The big England man makes amends by charging through to volley an equaliser from Kenny Clements cross. Bond is furious over the visitors' dull, defensive tactics.											
2 A MANCHESTER C		13	D	2-2	1-2	MacDougall 44, 87	Keelan	Machin	Butler	Morris	Forbes	Powell	McGuire	MacDougall	Boyer	Suggett	Peters	
R 17/9	*29,667*	*9*		*aet*		*Tueart 29p, Royle 42*	*Corrigan*	*Clements*	*Donachie*	*Doyle*	*Watson*	*Oakes*	*Hartford*	*Bell*	*Royle**	*Marsh*	*Tueart*	*Barnes*
						Ref: H Davey	Powell's foul on Dennis Tueart gives City a penalty, duly despatched. Joe Royle glances in a Tueart cross, but even this doesn't save him from barracking by some home fans. MacDougall nods in a Butler centre and then rises high to head a last-ditch equaliser from Suggett's deep cross.											
2 N MANCHESTER C		10	L	1-6	1-3	Peters 6 *[Butler 50 (og), Doyle 60]*	Keelan	Machin	Butler	Morris	Forbes	Powell	Steele	MacDougall	Boyer	Suggett	Peters	
RR 29/9	*6,238*	*11*				*Tueart 1, 8p, 55p, Royle 20,*	*Corrigan*	*Clements*	*Donachie*	*Doyle*	*Watson*	*Oakes*	*Hartford*	*Bell*	*Royle*	*Marsh*	*Tueart*	
(At Chelsea)						Ref: J Hunting	A rain-soaked night sees battle resume with the lowest-ever crowd for a senior match at Chelsea. Dennis Tueart's solo goal on 45 seconds is followed by Peters' clever lob. Powell trips Colin Bell for a penalty and things get steadily worse. It's these sides' fourth meeting in 44 days.											

FA Cup	Att	Pos	Res	F-A	H-T	Scorers, Times, and Referees	1	2	3	4	5	6	7	8	9	10	11	12 sub used
3 H ROCHDALE		18	D	1-1	1-1	MacDougall 4p	Keelan	Jones	Powell	Morris	Forbes	Stringer	Machin	MacDougall	Boyer	Suggett	Peters	
3/1	14,187	*4:16*				*Mullington 33*	*Poole*	*Hallows*	*Lacey*	*Sum'rscales*	*Mulvaney*	*Hanvey*	*Ferguson*	*Mountford*	*Cooper*	*Whelan*	*Mullington*	
						Ref: T Bune	MacDougall is tripped by Gary Cooper and picks himself up to net his 20th of the season. The expected goal-rush fails to materialise and Phil Mullington shoots in off a post after Suggett loses control in the home area. Keeper Mike Poole does well, but Norwich look rather slipshod.											
3R A ROCHDALE		18	D	0-0	0-0		Keelan	Powell	Sullivan	Morris	Forbes	Stringer	Machin	MacDougall	Boyer	Suggett	Peters	
6/1	*8,284*	*4:16*		*aet*			*Poole*	*Hallows*	*Lacey*	*Sumr'scales*	*Mulvaney*	*Hanvey*	*Ferguson*	*Mountford*	*Cooper**	*Whelan*	*Mullington*	*Murty*
						Ref: J Hunting	Boyer nets a powerful shot but is ruled offside. City are outfought by Walter Joyce's Fourth Division outfit. They go agonisingly close when Tony Whelan's header hits the bar and Bob Mountford's follow-up hits exactly the same spot. Later, unlucky Mountford heads against a post.											
3 H ROCHDALE		17	W	2-1	1-0	MacDougall 34p, Suggett 68	Keelan	Jones	Sullivan	McGuire	Forbes	Stringer	Machin	MacDougall	Boyer	Suggett	Peters	
RR 13/1	18,868	*4:16*				*Mountford 53*	*Poole*	*Hallows*	*Lacey*	*Sumr'scales*	*Mulvaney*	*Hanvey*	*Ferguson*	*Mountford*	*Fielding*	*Whelan*	*Mullington*	
						Ref: J Hunting	Dick Mulvaney handles a MacDougall overhead kick to concede a penalty. Bob Mountford equalises with a smart header from Tony Whelan's cross. Brave Rochdale finally succumb when Suggett lashes home Sullivan's cross, with referee Hunting ignoring their desperate offside pleas.											
4 H LUTON		17	W	2-0	1-0	Peters 24, Jones 53	Keelan	Jones	Sullivan	McGuire	Forbes	Stringer	Machin	MacDougall	Boyer	Suggett	Peters	
24/1	24,328	*2:8*					*Barber*	*Ryan John*	*Buckley*	*Anderson*	*Faulkner*	*Futcher P*	*King**	*Spiring*	*Futcher R*	*Chambers*	*Aston*	*Ryan Jim*
						Ref: J Yates	Harry Haslam's men are upset when Sullivan crosses after the ball appeared to go out, but Mr Yates allows Peters to carry on and head in. City ease through with little difficulty, particularly after Jones heads home a corner. Shortly after the final whistle, a snowstorm engulfs Norfolk.											
5 H BRADFORD CITY		16	L	1-2	1-1	Peters 39	Keelan	Jones	Sullivan	McGuire	Forbes	Stringer	Machin	MacDougall	Boyer	Suggett	Peters	
23/2	27,047	*4:19*				*Hutchins 38, McGinley 87*	*Downsboro'*	*Podd*	*Cooper*	*Johnson*	*Middleton*	*Fretwell*	*McGinley*	*Ingram*	*Cooke*	*Hall*	*Hutchins*	
						Ref: J Homewood	A tie twice postponed due to flu at Bradford. Don Hutchins beats Jones to fire home, but Peters quickly nets a near-post header. Jones has one disallowed and McGuire and Forbes both strike wood – all within 60 seconds. A late clearance hits Billy McGinley, who accepts a shock goal.											

		Home						Away					
	P	W	D	L	F	A	W	D	L	F	A	Pts
1 Liverpool	42	14	5	2	41	21	9	9	3	25	10	60
2 QP Rangers	42	17	4	0	42	13	7	7	7	25	20	59
3 Manchester U	42	16	4	1	40	13	7	6	8	28	29	56
4 Derby	42	15	3	3	45	30	6	8	7	30	28	53
5 Leeds	42	13	3	5	37	19	8	6	7	28	27	51
6 Ipswich	42	11	6	4	36	23	5	8	8	18	25	46
7 Leicester	42	9	9	3	29	24	4	10	7	19	27	45
8 Manchester C	42	14	5	2	46	18	2	6	13	18	28	43
9 Tottenham	42	6	10	5	33	32	8	5	8	30	31	43
10 NORWICH	42	10	5	6	33	26	6	5	10	25	32	42
11 Everton	42	10	7	4	37	24	5	5	11	23	42	42
12 Stoke	42	8	5	8	25	24	7	6	8	23	26	41
13 Middlesbro	42	9	7	5	23	11	6	3	12	23	34	40
14 Coventry	42	6	9	6	22	22	7	5	9	25	35	40
15 Newcastle	42	11	4	6	51	26	4	5	12	20	36	39
16 Aston Villa	42	11	8	2	32	17	0	9	12	19	42	39
17 Arsenal	42	11	4	6	33	19	2	6	13	14	34	36
18 West Ham	42	10	5	6	26	23	3	5	13	22	48	36
19 Birmingham	42	11	5	5	36	26	2	2	17	21	49	33
20 Wolves	42	7	6	8	27	25	3	4	14	24	43	30
21 Burnley	42	6	6	9	23	26	3	4	14	20	40	28
22 Sheffield Utd	42	4	7	10	19	32	2	3	16	14	50	22
	924	229	127	106	736	494	106	127	229	494	736	924

Odds & ends

Double wins: (1) West Ham.
Double losses: (2) Coventry, Newcastle.

Won from behind: (1) Tottenham (h).
Lost from in front: (2) Aston Villa (a), Derby (a).

High spots: Excellent away wins at Leeds and Liverpool.
Five wins in the last four weeks, to finish in the top half of the table.
The thrilling 3-2 victory over in-form title-chasers QPR.
Consistent top-class finishing by Ted MacDougall.
A dramatic improvement in the side's disciplinary record.

Low spots: The FA Cup exit at home to lowly Fourth Division Bradford C.
Crowd violence at the end of the West Ham home game.

Player of the Year: Martin Peters.
Ever-presents: (3) Kevin Keelan, Ted MacDougall, Martin Peters.
Hat-tricks: (2) Ted MacDougall, v Aston Villa (h), Everton (h).
Opposing hat-tricks: (2) Peter Noble (Burnley) Dennis Tueart (Man C LC).
Leading scorer: (28) Ted MacDougall.

	Appearances						Goals			
	Lge	*Sub*	LC	*Sub*	FAC	*Sub*	**Lge**	LC	FAC	**Tot**
Bond, Kevin		*1*								
Boyer, Phil	**39**		3		5		**11**			**11**
Butler, Geoff	**8**	*1*	3							
Davids, Neil	**2**									
Forbes, Duncan	**39**		3		5		**3**			**3**
Grapes, Steve	**10**	*1*	1				**1**			**1**
Jones, David	**23**				4				1	**1**
Keelan, Kevin	**42**		3		5					
Machin, Mel	**28**		3		4					
MacDougall, Ted	**42**		3		5		**23**	3	2	**28**
McGuire, Mick	**29**	*1*	1		3		**2**			**2**
Miller, Johnny	**8**	*1*								
Morris, Peter	**26**		3		2		**1**			**1**
Peters, Martin	**42**		3		5		**10**	1	2	**13**
Powell, Tony	**31**		3		3					
Steele, Billy	**12**	*3*	1				**1**			**1**
Stringer, Dave	**12**	*2*			5					
Suggett, Colin	**38**		3		5		**4**		1	**5**
Sullivan, Colin	**31**				4		**1**			**1**
Wilson, Paul		*1*								
(own-goals)							**1**			**1**
20 players used	**462**	***9***	**33**		**55**		**58**	**4**	**6**	**68**

LEAGUE DIVISION 1 — Manager: John Bond — SEASON 1976-77

No	Date		Att	Pos	Pt	F-A	H-T	Scorers, Times, and Referees	1	2	3	4	5	6	7	8	9	10	11	12 sub used
1	A	LIVERPOOL			L	0-1	0-0		Keelan	**Ryan**	Stringer	Jones	Forbes	Powell	Machin	Steele	Boyer	Suggett	Peters	
	21/8		*49,753*		0			*Heighway 55*	*Clemence*	*Neal*	*Jones*	*Thompson*	*Kennedy*	*Hughes*	*Keegan*	*Johnson*	*Heighway*	*Toshack*	*Callaghan*	
								Ref: J Taylor	After a sending off in a friendly in Norway, MacDougall is banned for the opening two games. He is badly missed. John Ryan, £40,000 from Luton, makes his debut. Powell's weak header fails to clear a corner and Bob Paisley's men take the lead as Steve Heighway exploits the error.											
2	H	ARSENAL			L	1-3	0-1	Peters 80p	Keelan	Ryan	Jones	Machin*	Forbes	Powell	Steele	**Gibbins**	Boyer	Suggett	Peters	Sullivan
	25/8		26,769		0			*Nelson 8, Macdonald 70, Stapleton 82*	*Rimmer*	*Rice*	*Nelson*	*Ross*	*O'Leary*	*Simpson*	*Ball*	*Armstrong*	*Macdonald*	*Stapleton*	*Brady*	
								Ref: K Baker	Sammy Nelson pounces on a rebound to head home. Gibbins has a shot cleared off the line by Pat Rice. Malcolm Macdonald nets his first Arsenal goal with a glancing header. Frank Stapleton tucks in the clincher. Forbes, who tries a shot from 40 yards, is booked for a rugby tackle.											
3	A	WEST BROM		22	L	0-2	0-1		Keelan	Ryan	Jones	Davies	Forbes	Powell	Steele	MacDougall	Boyer	Suggett	Peters	
	28/8		*17,045*	*12*	0			*Brown A 41, Brown T 47p*	*Osborne*	*Mulligan*	*Cantello*	*Brown T*	*Wile*	*Robertson*	*Martin*	*Brown A*	*Mayo*	*Giles*	*Johnston*	
								Ref: M Sinclair	Ally Brown tries his luck with a volley and it skids past Keelan. Steele bundles Tony Brown over and the same player knocks in the penalty. Browned-off City drop to bottom of the table. More than two years after his debut as a substitute, Ian Davies at last gets another opportunity.											
4	H	BIRMINGHAM		22	W	1-0	1-0	Boyer 9	Keelan	Ryan	Sullivan	Powell	Forbes	Steele	Grapes	MacDougall	Boyer	Suggett	Peters	
	4/9		19,271	*11*	2				*Latchford*	*Page*	*Styles*	*Kendall*	*Gallagher*	*Want*	*Pendrey*	*Francis*	*Withe*	*Burns*	*Hibbitt*	
								Ref: K Salmon	Boyer nets a fine header in the opening stages from a Steele cross, but is flagged offside. Peters is booked for arguing about it. Minutes later Boyer swoops to score after Dave Latchford parries Ryan's free-kick. Steele stars in midfield. Willie Bell's men suffer a first loss in five games.											
5	A	COVENTRY		22	L	0-2	0-1		Keelan	Ryan	Sullivan	Powell	Forbes	Steele	Grapes	MacDougall	Boyer	Suggett	Peters	
	11/9		***12,948***	*16*	2			*Ferguson 30, Forbes 67(og)*	*Blyth*	*Coop*	*McDonald*	*Powell B*	*Holmes*	*Dugdale*	*Cartwright*	*Yorath*	*Ferguson*	*Beck*	*Green*	
								Ref: J Hough	Barry Powell crosses for the in-form Mick Ferguson to head firmly home. A rather drab affair is settled when John Beck's cross is headed past Keelan by Forbes. The crowd is Coventry's lowest since arriving in the top flight. Bobby McDonald and Terry Yorath make their home debuts.											
6	H	DERBY		21	D	0-0	0-0		Keelan	Ryan*	Sullivan	Powell	Jones	Steele	Grapes	**Busby**	Boyer	Suggett	Peters	Machin
	18/9		23,020	*19*	3				*Moseley*	*Nish*	*Thomas*	*Rioch*	*McFarland*	*Todd*	*Newton*	*Gemmill*	*Hector*	*George*	*James*	
								Ref: B Daniels	A jolt for the fans as goal legend MacDougall joins Southampton for £50,000. Recently unhappy at City, he wants to be nearer his business interests in the south. Replacement is Viv Busby, £50,000 from Fulham. Ryan nets a free-kick, but it is mysteriously ruled out by the referee.											
7	A	TOTTENHAM		21	D	1-1	0-1	Osgood 64(og)	Keelan	Ryan	Sullivan	Steele	Jones	Powell	Machin*	Busby	Boyer	Suggett	Peters	**Proudlove**
	25/9		*22,240*	*17*	4			*Hoddle 29*	*Jennings*	*Naylor*	*Stead*	*Pratt*	*Hoddle*	*Osgood*	*Conn*	*Perryman*	*Moores*	*Jones*	*Neighbour*	
								Ref: P Reeves	Teenager Glenn Hoddle shoots Spurs ahead, aided by a deflection. City fight back heroically, carrying a dazed Jones and limping Ryan. The latter's cross misses Boyer, but flies in off Keith Osgood. Two more heroes depart: Forbes to Torquay on loan and Stringer to Cambridge Utd.											
8	H	NEWCASTLE		17	W	3-2	3-0	Peters 3, 35p, Busby 14	Keelan	Machin	Sullivan	Steele	Jones	Powell	**Neighbour**	Busby	Boyer	Suggett	Peters	
	2/10		21,417	*13*	6			*Craig T 52p, Gowling 69*	*Mahoney*	*Nattrass*	*Kennedy*	*Cassidy*	*McCaffrey*	*Nulty*	*Barrowcl'gh*	*Cannell*	*Burns*	*Gowling*	*Craig T*	
								Ref: B James	Jimmy Neighbour has a splendid debut. Peters lets fly to net a beauty before Busby swoops on a Geoff Nulty error. Irving Nattrass pulls Boyer for Peters to do the rest from the spot. Peters fouls Micky Burns for Tommy Craig's successful penalty, then Alan Gowling hooks in as he falls.											
9	A	QP RANGERS		15	W	3-2	1-1	Sullivan 14, Busby 55, Peters 87p	Keelan	Machin	Sullivan	Steele	Jones	Powell	Neighbour	Busby	Boyer	Suggett	Peters	
	5/10		*16,086*	*16*	8			*Masson 35p, Webb 77*	*Parkes*	*Clement*	*Gillard*	*Hollins*	*McLintock*	*Webb*	*Thomas*	*Kelly*	*Masson*	*Bowles*	*Givens*	
								Ref: T Bune	An indirect free-kick inside the box is nudged to Sullivan to fire home. Eddie Kelly hits the bar before Don Masson levels from the spot after a foul on Stan Bowles. Busby and David Webb chip in with headers. Busby is hauled down by Dave Clement for Peters' dramatic late winner.											
10	A	MIDDLESBROUGH		16	L	0-1	0-0		Keelan	Machin	Sullivan	Steele	Jones	Powell	Neighbour	Gibbins	Boyer	Suggett	Peters	
	9/10		*22,000*	*1*	8			*Souness 84*	*Platt*	*Craggs*	*Cooper*	*Souness*	*Boam*	*Maddren*	*McAndrew*	*Mills*	*Willey**	*Boersma*	*Armstrong*	*Brine*
								Ref: J Butcher	The weekend's only Div 1 game (due to internationals) is won by Graeme Souness forcing the ball home late on. Boyer, now off the transfer list, hits a post. Low-scoring Boro go top of the league for the first time in 26 years, but it won't last: within a few weeks they're down to 14th.											

No	H/A	Opponent / Date	Att	Pos	Res / Pts	F-A	H-T	Scorers, Times, and Referees	1	2	3	4	5	6	7	8	9	10	11	12
11	H	LEEDS		17	L	1-2	0-0	Gibbins 78	Keelan	Machin	Sullivan	Steele	Jones	Powell	Neighbour	Gibbins	Boyer	Suggett	Peters	
		16/10	25,217	14	8			*Gray F 51, Gray E 77*	*Harvey*	*Reaney*	*Hampton*	*Madeley*	*McQueen*	*Gray F*	*Cherry*	*Lorimer*	*Jordan*	*Currie*	*Gray E*	
								Ref: J Homewood	Against the run of play, Frank Gray rifles home a low drive at the end of a swift raid. His brother Eddie runs on to Tony Currie's pass to net a demoralising second. But unlucky City hit back within seconds as Gibbins gets on the end of a Jones' free-kick to nod in his first senior goal.											
12	A	MANCHESTER U		17	D	2-2	0-2	Ryan 71, Boyer 85	Keelan	Machin	Sullivan	Steele*	Jones	Powell	Neighbour	Gibbins	Boyer	Suggett	Peters	Ryan
		23/10	***54,356***	*9*	9			*Daly 39p, Hill 43*	*Stepney*	*Nicholl*	*Houston*	*Daly*	*Greenhoff B*	*Waldron*	*Coppell*	*McIlroy**	*Pearson*	*Macari*	*Hill*	*McGrath*
								Ref: K McNally	Suggett's challenge on Gordon Hill concedes a disputed penalty. Four minutes later United are two up when Hill curls in a 20-yard free-kick. Moments after coming on as sub, Ryan's shot-cum-centre loops over Alex Stepney. Boyer stuns Old Trafford by heading in Neighbour's cross.											
13	H	MANCHESTER C		18	L	0-2	0-0		Keelan	Ryan	Sullivan	Steele	Jones	Powell	Neighbour	Gibbins	Boyer	Suggett	Peters	
		30/10	22,861	*2*	9			*Kidd 86, Royle 88*	*Corrigan*	*Clements*	*Donachie*	*Doyle*	*Watson*	*Power*	*Owen*	*Kidd*	*Royle*	*Hartford*	*Tueart*	
								Ref: J Bent	Tony Book's outfit annoy the Carrow Road faithful with a stream of backpasses, but overall they look the better side. The breakthrough comes late in the day when Brian Kidd heads home a corner-kick. Set up by Dennis Tueart, Joe Royle cracks in a second off the underside of the bar.											
14	A	LEICESTER		18	D	1-1	0-0	Boyer 64	Keelan	Ryan	Sullivan	Machin	Jones	Powell	Neighbour	Steele	Boyer	Suggett	Peters	
		6/11	*17,781*	*6*	10			*Worthington 80*	*Wallington*	*Whitworth*	*Rofe*	*Kember*	*Sims*	*Wooller*	*Weller*	*Sammels*	*Worthington*	*Alderson*	*Garland*	
								Ref: B Perkin	Suggett dribbles round Mark Wallington and, when his shot is blocked on the line, Boyer nips in to do the honours. Jimmy Bloomfield's side are draw specialists, so it's no surprise when an equaliser arrives near the end. Frank Worthington skims a low drive over the mud past Keelan.											
15	H	WEST HAM		17	W	1-0	1-0	Peters 17	Keelan	Ryan	Sullivan	Steele*	Jones	Powell	Neighbour	**Osgood**	Boyer	Suggett	Peters	Machin
		10/11	24,762	*21*	12				*Day*	*Bonds*	*Lampard*	*Curbishley*	*Lock**	*Taylor T*	*Devonshire*	*Pike*	*Jennings*	*Brooking*	*Robson B*	*Coleman*
								Ref: C Maskell	City fans welcome ex-England man Peter Osgood, on loan from Southampton. Ex-Hammer Peters loops a header over Mervyn Day for the only goal. John Lyall's side respond as Bryan Robson brings a fine save out of Keelan. The next day Graham Paddon rejoins from West Ham.											
16	A	BRISTOL CITY		18	L	1-3	0-2	Boyer 80	Keelan	Ryan	Sullivan	Paddon	Jones	Powell	Neighbour	Osgood	Boyer	Suggett	Peters	
		20/11	*19,641*	*17*	12			*Ritchie 34, Cormack 39, Sweeney 46p*	*Shaw*	*Gillies*	*Merrick**	*Sweeney*	*Collier*	*Hunter*	*Tainton*	*Ritchie*	*Fear*	*Cormack*	*Whitehead*	*Mann*
								Ref: A Robinson	Tom Ritchie heads Alan Dicks' men ahead after a corner, with Keelan stranded. Minutes later Keelan parries a Clive Whitehead effort only for Peter Cormack to pounce at close range. Ryan pulls Ritchie's shirt and Gerry Sweeney nets from the spot. Peters' fine pass is buried by Boyer.											
17	H	ASTON VILLA		17	D	1-1	1-1	Boyer 33	Keelan	Ryan	Sullivan	Suggett	Jones	Powell	Neighbour	Osgood	Boyer	Paddon	Peters	
		27/11	22,554	*4*	13			*Little 36*	*Findlay*	*Gidman*	*Smith*	*Phillips*	*Nicholl*	*Mortimer*	*Robson*	*Little*	*Gray*	*Cropley*	*Carrodus*	
								Ref: D Reeves	Paddon is welcomed back to Carrow Road for a lively contest of full-blooded challenges. Osgood and Paddon engineer an opening for Boyer to beat Jake Findlay. Ron Saunders' men respond quickly and Brian Little fires home with City handball claims being ignored by Mr Reeves.											
18	A	SUNDERLAND		15	W	1-0	1-0	Busby 25	Keelan	Ryan	Sullivan	Suggett*	Jones	Powell	Neighbour	Busby	Boyer	Paddon	Peters	Machin
		18/12	*23,468*	*22*	15				*Siddall*	*Malone*	*Bolton*	*Towers*	*Clarke*	*Holton*	*Kerr*	*Hughes*	*Lee*	*Brown*	*Foggon**	*Rowell*
								Ref: D Richardson	Unmarked Busby rises to head in Ryan's cross to give Bond a 44th birthday present. City go down to ten men when Jim Holton's challenge leaves Paddon with a broken leg. Bond comes on and has words with Holton, but the big defender is as upset as anyone by the appalling injury.											
19	H	QP RANGERS		13	W	2-0	1-0	Machin 36, Busby 87	Keelan	Ryan	Sullivan	Machin	Jones	Powell	Neighbour	Busby	Boyer	Steele	Peters	
		27/12	27,343	*18*	17				*Parkes*	*Clement*	*Gillard*	*Kelly*	*Hollins*	*Webb**	*Thomas*	*Leach*	*Masson*	*Bowles*	*Givens*	*Eastoe*
								Ref: P Richardson	Machin gets forward to deflect a volley into Rangers' net for his first goal in the top flight. Sullivan sends a ball down the middle and Busby fastens onto it and cracks an absolute picture of a goal past the stunned Phil Parkes. In two months, Busby has yet to feature on a losing side.											
20	H	LEICESTER		12	W	3-2	2-2	Busby 4, 38, 87	Keelan	Ryan	Sullivan	Machin	Jones	Powell	Neighbour	Busby	Boyer	Steele*	Peters	Suggett
		1/1	22,046	*9*	19			*Sammels 34, Earle 39*	*Wallington*	*Whitworth*	*Rofe*	*Kember*	*Blockley*	*Sims*	*Weller*	*Sammels*	*Worthington*	*Alderson*	*Earle*	
								Ref: T Bune	The rampant Busby knocks in Neighbour's cross. Jon Sammels levels, making the most of defensive hesitancy. Busby regains the lead after a cavalier charge by Ryan. Steve Earle hits back immediately, but Busby has the last laugh, coolly slotting the winner after Neighbour's assist.											
21	A	ARSENAL		14	L	0-1	0-1		Keelan	Ryan	Sullivan	Machin	Jones	Powell	Neighbour	Busby	**Reeves***	Suggett	Peters	Steele
		15/1	*30,537*	*4*	19			*Rice 39*	*Rimmer*	*Rice*	*Nelson*	*Ross*	*O'Leary*	*Simpson*	*Hudson*	*Brady*	*Macdonald*	*Stapleton*	*Armstrong*	
								Ref: W Gow	The Gunners are on top early on, but don't look sharp in front of goal. Pat Rice's long ball from the flank looks like an intended cross, but Keelan fumbles it into the net at his near post. City work hard to level and go close in the later stages. 19-year-old loanee Kevin Reeves debuts.											

No	Date		Att	Pos	Pt	F-A	H-T	Scorers, Times, and Referees	1	2	3	4	5	6	7	8	9	10	11	12 sub used
22	H	LIVERPOOL		14	W	2-1	1-0	Peters 14p, Neighbour 46	Keelan	Ryan	Sullivan	Machin	Jones	Powell	Neighbour	Gibbins	Busby*	Suggett	Peters	Steele
	22/1		25,913	*1*	21			*Neal 52p*	*Clemence*	*Neal*	*Kettle*	*Thompson*	*Kennedy*	*Hughes*	*Keegan*	*Case*	*Heighway*	*Fairclough*	*Callaghan*	
								Ref: R Challis	Inexperienced Brian Kettle brings down Neighbour for Peters to net from the spot. Shortly after the break Neighbour nets wonder goal, beating three men before placing a careful shot past Ray Clemence. Ryan hauls down Kevin Keegan for a penalty and City are hanging on by the end.											
23	H	STOKE		13	D	1-1	1-0	Reeves 2	Keelan	Ryan	Sullivan	Machin	Forbes	Powell	Neighbour	Reeves	Gibbins	Suggett	Peters	
	29/1		18,408	*15*	22			*Salmons 48*	*Shilton*	*Marsh*	*Pejic*	*Mahoney*	*Smith*	*Dodd*	*Bloor*	*Suddick*	*Tudor*	*Conroy*	*Salmons*	
								Ref: R Lewis	Reeves dispossesses Alan Bloor to bang in his first goal for the club in the early stages. Stoke have gone six games without scoring and it takes a freak goal to end the run. Forbes, returning after nearly five months out, hits a clearance against Geoff Salmons and the ball ricochets home.											
24	H	WEST BROM		11	W	1-0	1-0	Gibbins 45	Keelan	Ryan	Sullivan	Machin	Jones	Powell	Neighbour	Reeves	Gibbins	Suggett*	Peters	Steele
	5/2		19,613	*13*	24				*Osborne*	*Mulligan*	*Robson*	*Brown T*	*Wile*	*Robertson*	*Cantello*	*Treacy*	*Cross*	*Giles*	*Johnston**	*Trewick*
								Ref: B James	Gibbins connects with Neighbour's cross with a diving header to give John Osborne no chance. Soon afterwards, Gibbins goes close with a curling shot. More problems for Bond as Suggett departs with another injury. Reeves' loan from Bournemouth becomes a fully-fledged move.											
25	A	BIRMINGHAM		12	L	2-3	2-1	Steele 4, Reeves 25	Keelan	Ryan	Sullivan	Steele	Jones	Powell	Neighbour	Reeves	Gibbins	**Evans**	Peters	
	12/2		*21,809*	*11*	24			*Burns 2, 49, Broadhurst 70*	*Latchford*	*Page*	*Styles*	*Kendall*	*Gallagher*	*Want*	*Broadhurst*	*Francis*	*Hibbitt*	*Burns*	*Connolly*	
								Ref: H Hackney	Kenny Burns slots in after a Ken Hibbitt corner. Steele is quick to level, despatching Ryan's pass with a minimum of fuss. Reeves finishes calmly after good work by Evans. Burns buries a header after the break to end the home fans' booing. Kevan Broadhurst fires a debut winner.											
26	A	IPSWICH		12	L	**0-5**	0-2	*[Mariner 68]*	Keelan	Ryan	Sullivan	Machin*	Forbes	Powell	Neighbour	Reeves	Gibbins	Steele	Peters	Evans
	15/2		*34,735*	*2*	24			*Wark 12p, Whymark 39, 75, 84,*	*Cooper*	*Burley*	*Mills*	*Talbot*	*Hunter*	*Beattie*	*Osborne*	*Wark*	*Mariner**	*Whymark*	*Woods*	*Gates*
								Ref: R Capey	Peters fouls Woods and, to City's dismay, Mr Capey rules that it was inside the area. Norfolk-born Trevor Whymark is a thorn in City's side. He sweeps home George Burley's cross before the break. Forbes and Powell have an utterly miserable day against the title-chasing local rivals.											
27	H	COVENTRY		11	W	**3-0**	2-0	Busby 20, 77, Reeves 22	Keelan	Ryan	Sullivan	Machin*	Jones	Powell	Neighbour	Reeves	Busby	Steele	Peters	Evans
	19/2		17,900	*14*	26				*Blyth*	*Coop*	*McDonald*	*Yorath*	*Roberts*	*Dugdale*	*Beck*	*Wallace**	*Ferguon*	*Powell*	*Hutchison*	*Holmes*
								Ref: M Sinclair	Ian Wallace goes to hospital with an eye injury in the early stages. City take advantage of a fragile-looking defence with two in two minutes. Busby returns in triumph to improve his superb goals-per-game ratio. The misery of the local derby defeat is forgotten as Reeves bags a third.											
28	A	MANCHESTER C		11	L	0-2	0-0		Keelan	Ryan	Sullivan	Evans*	Jones	Powell	Neighbour	Reeves	Busby	Steele	Peters	Bond
	1/3		*36,021*	*3*	26			*Tueart 60p, 64p*	*Corrigan*	*Clements*	*Donachie*	*Doyle*	*Watson*	*Power*	*Owen*	*Kidd*	*Royle*	*Hartford*	*Tueart*	
								Ref: R Kirkpatrick	With Norwich pointing out an upraised flag, Dennis Tueart is brought down by Evans. After consultations a penalty is given. Twice it has to be retaken for encroachment. Minutes later Ryan brings down Brian Kidd for another. All four spot-kicks are stroked expertly to Keelan's right.											
29	H	TOTTENHAM		13	L	1-3	1-0	Neighbour 25	Keelan	Ryan	Sullivan	Davies	Jones	Powell	Neighbour	Reeves	Busby	Steele	Peters	
	5/3		23,554	*19*	26			*Taylor 58, Pratt 80, Armstrong 84*	*Daines*	*Naylor*	*Gorman*	*Pratt*	*Hoddle*	*Osgood*	*Perryman*	*Armstrong*	*Coates*	*Jones*	*Taylor*	
								Ref: D Richardson	Neighbour stabs in Peters' back-header against their former club. Spurs hit back to climb off the bottom of the table. Peter Taylor hooks home after a corner and sparks a City collapse. Gerry Armstrong tees up the second for John Pratt and then nets himself after his first shot is blocked.											
30	H	MIDDLESBROUGH		12	W	1-0	0-0	Ryan 53	Keelan	Ryan	Sullivan	Forbes	Jones	Powell	Neighbour	Reeves	Busby	Suggett	Peters	
	9/3		**17,629**	*8*	28				*Cuff*	*Craggs*	*Cooper*	*Souness*	*Boam*	*Maddren*	*McAndrew*	*Mills*	*Brine*	*Wood**	*Armstrong*	*Boersma*
								Ref: A Turvey	Reeves head narrowly wide in a forgettable first half. Reeves and Peters pave the way for Ryan to unleash a typically fierce 25-yarder which hits the net and leaves Pat Cuff in a tangled heap. A late David Armstrong effort nearly saves Jack Charlton's side a point, but Keelan is alert.											
31	A	NEWCASTLE		12	L	1-5	1-2	Reeves 13 *[Craig T 62]*	Keelan	Ryan	Sullivan	Forbes	Jones	Powell	Neighbour*	Reeves	Busby	Suggett	Peters	**Fleeting**
	12/3		*26,216*	*5*	28			*Oates 8, McCaffery 30,73,Gowling 55,*	*Mahoney*	*Blackhall*	*Kennedy*	*Nattrass*	*McCaffrey*	*Nulty*	*Barrowcl'gh*	*Oates*	*Burns*	*Gowling*	*Craig T*	
								Ref: M Lowe	Graham Oates' well-struck opener is cancelled out by Reeves' far-post header. City are a shambles at the back and Keelan looks unusually shaky. Defender Aiden McCaffery grabs two as Richard Dinnis' outfit cruise to their best win in ages. Tommy Craig nets a glorious 30-yarder.											

No	Venue	Opponent	Att	Pos	Res	F-A	H-T	Scorers, Times, and Referees	1	2	3	4	5	6	7	8	9	10	11	12
32	A	LEEDS		13	L	2-3	2-1	Neighbour 10, Gibbins 45	Keelan	Ryan	Sullivan	Machin*	Jones	Powell	Neighbour	Reeves	Gibbins	Steele	Peters	Evans
	23/3		*18,700*	*9*	28			*Reaney 40, Hampton 47, Jordan 90*	*Harvey*	*Reaney*	*Hampton*	*Madeley*	*McQueen*	*Gray F*	*Cherry*	*Lorimer*	*Jordan*	*Currie*	*Gray E*	
								Ref: C Steel	Neighbour converts at the far post from Steele's pass. Peter Lorimer hits the wall with a free-kick, but Paul Reaney is on hand to score. His full-back partner Peter Hampton gets in on the scoring act after the break. City hang on till the final minute when Joe Jordan dives to head in.											
33	H	MANCHESTER U		12	W	2-1	2-0	Suggett 7, Reeves 33	Keelan	Ryan	Sullivan	Machin	Jones	Powell	Neighbour	Reeves	Gibbins	Suggett*	Peters	Steele
	2/4		26,125	*6*	30			*Powell 57 (og)*	*Stepney*	*Nicholl*	*Houston*	*McIlroy*	*Greenhoff B*	*Buchan*	*Coppell*	*Greenhoff J*	*McCreery*	*Macari*	*Hill**	*McGrath*
								Ref: J Homewood	Tommy Docherty's side arrive on a 12-match unbeaten run. Suggett sets a thriller in motion by netting a splendid drive. Reeves dances round Buchan and coolly beats Alex Stepney to delight home fans. Keelan advances too far and confuses Powell, who heads into the unguarded net.											
34	A	DERBY		12	D	2-2	2-1	Gibbins 3, 45	Keelan	Ryan	Evans	Machin	Jones	Powell	Neighbour	Reeves	Gibbins	Steele	Peters	
	6/4		*21,342*	*19*	31			*James 33, Powell 49*	*Boulton*	*Langan*	*Webster*	*Daly*	*McFarland*	*Todd*	*Powell*	*Gemmill*	*Hector**	*George*	*James*	*Hales*
								Ref: E Garner	Gibbins buries a brave diving header, but the troubled Rams get back on terms when Leighton James curls in a free-kick. On the stroke of half-time Reeves' cross is headed home by Gibbins. Steve Powell equalises with a ferocious drive. Near the end Peters hits the post with a free-kick.											
35	H	IPSWICH		13	L	0-1	0-1		Keelan	Ryan	Sullivan	Machin*	Jones	Powell	Neighbour	Reeves	Gibbins	Steele	Peters	Boyer
	9/4		**31,088**	*1*	31			*Whymark 24*	*Cooper*	*Burley*	*Mills*	*Talbot*	*Hunter*	*Beattie*	*Osborne*	*Wark*	*Mariner**	*Whymark*	*Woods*	*Lambert*
								Ref: K Styles	City show scant respect for the league leaders and open in lively fashion. But Ipswich hold firm and stun the home fans when Brian Talbot's free-kick is nodded down by Kevin Beattie and Trevor Whymark nips ahead of Machin and Keelan to score. Boyer returns after 14 weeks out.											
36	A	WEST HAM		13	L	0-1	0-0		Keelan	Ryan	Sullivan	Machin	Jones	Powell	Neighbour	Reeves	Boyer	Steele	Peters	
	11/4		*27,084*	*20*	31			*Pike 72*	*Day*	*Bonds*	*Lampard*	*Pike*	*McGiven*	*Taylor T*	*Radford*	*Robson B*	*Devonshire*	*Brooking*	*Taylor A*	
								Ref: P Reeves	A mediocre game comes to life as Geoff Pike hits the net with a fine volley from outside the box, after Alan Devonshire's cross is headed out to him. Keelan turns over a Billy Bonds effort and Bryan Robson misses a great chance. The points ease John Lyall's side's relegation worries.											
37	H	BRISTOL CITY		13	W	2-1	1-1	Peters 11, Reeves 84	Keelan	Ryan	Sullivan	Suggett	Jones	Powell	Neighbour*	Reeves	Gibbins	Steele	Peters	Evans
	16/4		18,434	*22*	33			*Cormack 40*	*Shaw*	*Sweeney*	*Merrick*	*Gow*	*Collier*	*Hunter*	*Tainton*	*Ritchie*	*Gillies**	*Cormack*	*Whitehead*	*Mann*
								Ref: L Hayes	Alan Dicks' men are showing signs of getting out of the relegation mire, but Peters puts them in their place with a fine volley. Peter Cormack darts in to equalise from Clive Whitehead's cross. Late excitement for the restless fans as Reeves bustles in to score from Sullivan's deep cross.											
38	A	EVERTON		14	L	1-3	0-1	Steele 54	Keelan	Ryan	Sullivan	Suggett	Jones	Powell	Evans	Reeves	Gibbins	Steele	Peters	
	19/4		*26,644*	*13*	33			*McNaught 11, King 60, Pearson 84*	*Davies*	*Robinson*	*Pejic*	*Lyons*	*McNaught*	*King**	*Rioch*	*Dobson*	*McKenzie*	*Pearson*	*Goodlass*	*Buckley*
								Ref: J Sewell	Ronnie Goodlass's corner is headed in by Ken McNaught. A Reeves header is blocked on the line but Steele follows up to score. Ryan's tackle on Duncan McKenzie produces a penalty that Keelan saves, but Andy King nets the rebound. Jim Pearson robs Peters before grabbing a third.											
39	A	ASTON VILLA		14	L	0-1	0-1		Hansbury	Bond	Sullivan	Suggett	Forbes	Powell	Machin	Reeves	Gibbins	Steele*	Peters	Jones
	23/4		*35,899*	*5*	33			*Little 31*	*Burridge*	*Smith*	*Robson*	*Phillips*	*Young*	*Mortimer**	*Graydon*	*Little*	*Deehan*	*Cropley*	*Cowans*	*Hughes*
								Ref: K Hackett	Keelan is dropped for the first time in 13 years at Norwich. Ryan, Jones and Evans are also rested. Powell obstructs Brian Little and from the free-kick by Ray Graydon, Little heads past Hansbury. Machin nearly wins an unexpected point when he hits the crossbar in the late stages.											
40	H	EVERTON		12	W	2-1	2-0	Reeves 27, Busby 36	Hansbury	Ryan	Sullivan	Suggett	Jones*	Powell	Neighbour	Reeves	Gibbins	Busby	Peters	Bond
	30/4		19,725	*14*	35			*Pearson 46*	*Davies*	*Darracott*	*Pejic*	*Lyons*	*McNaught*	*King*	*Buckley*	*Rioch*	*McKenzie*	*Pearson*	*Goodlass**	*Hamilton*
								Ref: J Bent	Neighbour's cross is laid back for Reeves to thump home. Nine minutes later, Reeves' chip is headed in by the returning Busby. Jim Pearson pulls one back with a looping header over Hansbury. Any lingering fears that City might be dragged into the relegation fight are now banished.											
41	A	STOKE		12	D	0-0	0-0		Hansbury	Ryan	Sullivan	Suggett	Forbes	Powell	Neighbour	Reeves	Gibbins	Busby	Peters	
	7/5		*13,202*	*18*	36				*Shilton*	*Dodd*	*Marsh**	*Mahoney*	*Smith*	*Bloor*	*Ruggiero*	*Salmons*	*Conroy*	*Crooks*	*Goodin*	*Bithell*
								Ref: W Gow	Low-scoring Stoke are in disarray, teetering on the brink of relegation and with George Eastham just named as new manager to replace long-serving Tony Waddington. Hansbury has a superb game, frustrating the Potters with fine saves. John Ruggiero goes close with a 30-yarder.											
42	H	SUNDERLAND		15	D	2-2	0-0	Reeves 47, Busby 75	Hansbury	Ryan	Sullivan	Suggett*	Forbes	Powell	Neighbour	Reeves	Gibbins	Busby	Peters	Jones
	14/5		27,787	*16*	37			*Rowell 83, Kerr 84*	*Siddall*	*Docherty*	*Bolton*	*Arnott*	*Waldron*	*Ashurst*	*Towers**	*Elliott*	*Holden*	*Lee*	*Rowell*	*Kerr*
		Home	Away					Ref: B Martin	Reeves beats Barry Siddall with a far-post header from a Suggett corner. Peters' through ball is neatly converted by Busby. Jimmy Adamson's men could still be relegated, but launch an amazing late fightback. Gary Rowell heads in and, a minute later, sub Bobby Kerr races in to level.											
Average		22,925	26,072																	

League Cup			Att			F-A	H-T	Scorers, Times, and Referees	1	2	3	4	5	6	7	8	9	10	11	12 sub used
2	A	EXETER		22	W	3-1	2-1	MacDougall 6p, Grapes 33, Boyer 83	Keelan	Ryan	Sullivan	Powell	Forbes	Steele	Grapes	MacDougall	Boyer	Suggett	Peters	
31/8			*9,449*	*3:14*				*Kellow 40*	*Key*	*Templeman*	*Hooker*	*Hore*	*Saxton**	*Hatch*	*Hodge*	*Kellow*	*Morrin*	*Beer*	*Jordan*	*Clapham*
									Alan Hooker saves spectacularly with his hands to give MacDougall his chance from the spot. Grapes lashes in a second before Tony Kellow buries an opportunist effort from a tight angle. Johnny Newman's men are finished off when Boyer fires home under the body of Richard Key.											
3	A	ASTON VILLA		21	L	1-2	0-1	Suggett 49	Keelan	Ryan	Sullivan	Steele	Jones	Powell	Machin	Gibbins	Boyer	Suggett*	Peters	Proudlove
21/9			*31,295*	*8*				*Gray 39, 64*	*Burridge*	*Gidman*	*Smith*	*Phillips*	*Nicholl*	*Mortimer*	*Graydon*	*Little*	*Gray*	*Cowans*	*Carrodus*	
								Ref: J Hunting	Ray Graydon's high cross is sent looping into the net by the head of Andy Gray. Gordon Smith's misdirected clearance is punished by Suggett, who nets a real sizzler past helpless John Burridge. Gray calmly tucks in Villa's second. It's the two clubs' sixth meeting in just over two years.											

FA Cup																				
3	A	LEEDS		12	L	2-5	1-5	Suggett 34, Peters 52 *[Hampton 44]*	Keelan	Ryan	Sullivan	Machin	Jones	Powell	Neighbour	Busby	Steele	Suggett	Peters	
8/1			*28,130*	*13*				*Clarke 13, Rean' 19, Jor' 30, McQ' 41,*	*Harvey*	*Reaney*	*Hampton*	*Gray F*	*McQueen*	*Madeley*	*Lorimer*	*Clarke*	*Jordan*	*Currie*	*Gray E*	
								Ref: J Taylor	Sloppy first-half defending spells disaster for City and Leeds are ruthless. Allan Clarke stabs the first, Paul Reaney nets a diving header and Joe Jordan lofts home the third. Then it's Gordon McQueen's turn with a close-range header, followed by full-back Peter Hampton's solo effort.											

		P	W	D	L	F	A	W	D	L	F	A	Pts
			Home					Away					
1	Liverpool	42	18	3	0	47	11	5	8	8	15	22	57
2	Manchester C	42	15	5	1	38	13	6	9	6	22	21	56
3	Ipswich	42	15	4	2	41	11	7	4	10	25	28	52
4	Aston Villa	42	17	3	1	55	17	5	4	12	21	33	51
5	Newcastle	42	14	6	1	40	15	4	7	10	24	34	49
6	Manchester U	42	12	6	3	41	22	6	5	10	30	40	47
7	West Brom	42	10	6	5	38	22	6	7	8	24	34	45
8	Arsenal	42	11	6	4	37	20	5	5	11	27	39	43
9	Everton	42	9	7	5	35	24	5	7	9	27	40	42
10	Leeds	42	8	8	5	28	26	7	4	10	20	25	42
11	Leicester	42	8	9	4	30	28	4	9	8	17	32	42
12	Middlesbro	42	11	6	4	25	14	3	7	11	15	31	41
13	Birmingham	42	10	6	5	38	25	3	6	12	25	36	38
14	QP Rangers	42	10	7	4	31	21	3	5	13	16	31	38
15	Derby	42	9	9	3	36	18	0	10	11	14	37	37
16	NORWICH	42	12	4	5	30	23	2	5	14	17	41	37
17	West Ham	42	9	6	6	28	23	2	8	11	18	42	36
18	Bristol City	42	8	7	6	25	19	3	6	12	13	29	35
19	Coventry	42	7	9	5	34	26	3	6	12	14	33	35
20	Sunderland	42	9	5	7	29	16	2	7	12	17	38	34
21	Stoke	42	9	8	4	21	16	1	6	14	7	35	34
22	Tottenham	42	9	7	5	26	20	3	2	16	22	52	33
		924	240	137	85	753	430	85	137	240	430	753	924

Odds & ends

Double wins: (1) QP Rangers.
Double losses: (4) Arsenal, Leeds, Ipswich, Manchester C.

Won from behind: (0).
Lost from in front: (3) Leeds (a), Tottenham (h), Birmingham (a).

High spots: Ending Manchester United's long unbeaten run in April.
Viv Busby's wonderful 'route one' goal against QPR in December.

Low spots: Losing Mick McGuire for the entire season due to injury.
Graham Paddon's broken leg, shortly after his return to the club.
The departure of goal-machine Ted MacDougall.
The disastrous first-half performance in the Leeds FA Cup-tie.
The behaviour of Manchester U followers on 2 April.

Player of the Year: Martin Peters
Ever-presents: (2) Martin Peters, Tony Powell.
Hat-tricks: (1) Viv Busby v Leicester (h).
Opposing hat-tricks: (1) Trevor Whymark v Ipswich (a).
Leading scorer (11): Viv Busby.

	Appearances Lge	*Sub*	LC	*Sub*	FAC	*Sub*	Goals Lge	LC	FAC	Tot
Bond, Kevin	1	*2*								
Boyer, Phil	21	*1*	2				5	1		6
Busby, Viv	17				1		11			11
Davies, Ian	2									
Evans, Doug	4	*4*								
Fleeting, Jim		*1*								
Forbes, Duncan	12		1							
Gibbins, Roger	20		1				5			5
Grapes, Steve	3		1					1		1
Hansbury, Roger	4									
Jones, David	35	*2*	1		1					
Keelan, Kevin	38		2		1					
Machin, Mel	23	*3*	1		1		1			1
MacDougall, Ted	3		1					1		1
Neighbour, Jimmy	33				1		3			3
Osgood, Peter	3									
Paddon, Graham	3									
Peters, Martin	42		2		1		7		1	8
Powell, Tony	42		2		1					
Proudlove, Andy		*1*				*1*				
Reeves, Kevin	21						8			8
Ryan, John	36	*1*	2		1		2			2
Steele, Billy	29	*4*	2		1		2			2
Stringer, Dave	1									
Suggett, Colin	31	*1*	2		1		1	1	1	3
Sullivan, Colin	38	*1*	2		1		1			1
(own-goals)							1			1
26 players used	462	*21*	22		11	*1*	47	4	2	53

No	Date		Att	Pos	Pt	F-A	H-T	Scorers, Times, and Referees	1	2	3	4	5	6	7	8	9	10	11	12 sub used
1	A	WEST HAM			W	3-1	1-0	Ryan 32, Jones 58, 73	Keelan	Ryan	Sullivan	Evans	Jones	Powell	Neighbour	Busby	Reeves	Suggett	Gibbins	
	20/8		*28.178*		2			*Robson B 70p*	*Day*	*Lampard*	*Brush*	*Pike*	*Taylor T*	*Lock*	*Taylor A*	*Robson B*	*Radford*	*Brooking*	*Devonshire*	
								Ref: K Baker	Boyer has left for Southampton, but City look in good shape without him. Ryan nets a low 25-yarder. Jones exchanges passes with Gibbins and fires in a beauty. Jones brings down Alan Taylor for a home penalty, but quickly makes amends with a superb 30-yard drive past Mervyn Day.											
2	H	MIDDLESBROUGH			D	1-1	1-1	Gibbins 36	Keelan	Ryan	Sullivan	Evans	Jones	Powell	Neighbour	Reeves	Busby	Suggett	Gibbins	
	24/8		15,102		3			*Souness 25*	*Platt*	*Craggs*	*Cooper*	*Souness**	*Boam*	*Maddren*	*Mahoney*	*Mills*	*Woof*	*McAndrew*	*Armstrong*	*Hickton*
								Ref: D Smith	Graeme Souness' free-kick is deflected slowly into the net off City's defensive wall. Gibbins equalises by leaping to head in a Neighbour cross. Boro look a dour outfit and this rugged game features five bookings. Neighbour tangles with Jim Platt late on, but penalty claims are rejected.											
3	H	QP RANGERS		7	D	1-1	1-0	Gibbins 27	Keelan	Ryan	Sullivan	Evans	Jones	Powell	Neighbour	Reeves*	Busby	Suggett	Gibbins	Davies
	27/8		17,914	*19*	4			*Needham 86*	*Parkes*	*Clement*	*Gillard*	*Hollins*	*Needham*	*Webb*	*Eastoe*	*Leach*	*Masson*	*Bowles*	*Givens**	*Williams*
								Ref: B Martin	City are on top for the first half and Gibbins stabs home Neighbour's centre. New manager Frank Sibley galvanises his men after the interval and they silence the home fans when Dave Needham rises high to head a late equaliser. Three days later Bond puts Busby on the transfer list.											
4	A	MANCHESTER C		12	L	**0-4**	0-2		Keelan	Ryan	Forbes	Evans*	Jones	Powell	Neighbour	Busby	Gibbins	Suggett	Machin	Sullivan
	3/9		*41,269*	*1*	4			*Channon 8, 48, Power 39, Hartford 63*	*Corrigan*	*Clements*	*Donachie*	*Owen*	*Watson*	*Booth*	*Barnes*	*Channon*	*Kidd*	*Hartford*	*Power*	
								Ref: A Hamil	Mick Channon bags his first goal for his new club from a Peter Barnes cross. Paul Power cracks home Channon's pass to increase Norwich's misery. Channon puts the result beyond doubt with a fine finish after he had collected a misplaced pass. Asa Hartford powers home the fourth.											
5	H	BRISTOL CITY		9	W	1-0	0-0	Gibbins 87	Keelan	Ryan	Sullivan	Machin	Jones	Powell	Neighbour	Busby*	Reeves	Suggett	Davies	Gibbins
	10/9		**13,940**	*19*	6				*Shaw*	*Gillies*	*Sweeney*	*Gow*	*Collier*	*Hunter*	*Tainton*	*Ritchie*	*Mabbutt*	*Cormack*	*Whitehead*	
								Ref: P Richardson	Unrest at Carrow Road among the club's smallest top-flight crowd. City's inability to break down Alan Dicks' side prompts jeering at John Bond when he walks from the directors' box to the dug-out. Sub Gibbins is cheered when brought on, and he obliges with a late diving header.											
6	A	EVERTON		12	L	0-3	0-1		Hansbury	Ryan	Sullivan	Machin*	Jones	Powell	Neighbour	Reeves	Gibbins	Suggett	Peters	Bond
	17/9		*34,405*	*5*	6			*Rioch 44, McKenzie 49, Dobson 88*	*Wood*	*Darracott*	*Pejic*	*Lyons*	*Higgins*	*Rioch**	*King*	*Dobson*	*Latchford*	*McKenzie*	*Thomas*	*Jones*
								Ref: W Johnson	Everton win 13 corners and hit the bar in a one-sided first half. Their breakthrough is controversial when a Bruce Rioch effort is ruled to have crossed the line, Hansbury disagreeing furiously. Duncan McKenzie nets a header and Bob Latchford's backheel is fired in by Martin Dobson.											
7	H	ARSENAL		10	W	1-0	1-0	Ryan 9	Keelan	Bond	Sullivan	Ryan	Jones	Powell	Neighbour	Reeves	Gibbins	Suggett	Peters	
	24/9		19,312	*11*	8				*Jennings*	*Rice*	*Nelson*	*Price*	*O'Leary*	*Simpson*	*Matthews**	*Ross*	*Macdonald*	*Stapleton*	*Rix*	*Walford*
								Ref: R Toseland	Bond switches Ryan – with quick success. Ryan picks the ball up in the centre-circle and charges forward on a splendid run that ends with him unleashing a great drive past a helpless Pat Jennings. Terry Neill's side step up a gear after the break but find the returning Keelan in top form.											
8	A	NOTT'M FOR		12	D	1-1	0-0	Peters 78	Keelan	Bond	Sullivan	Ryan	Jones	Powell	Neighbour	Reeves	Gibbins	Suggett	Peters	
	1/10		*23,741*	*2*	9			*Burns 74*	*Shilton*	*Anderson*	*Barrett*	*Bowyer*	*Lloyd*	*Burns*	*O'Neill*	*Gemmill*	*Withe*	*Woodcock*	*Robertson*	
								Ref: M Baker	After soaking up much pressure from Brian Clough's side, City finally crack when Kenny Burns rises to head his first goal for the club. Colin Barrett is booked for fouling Neighbour and, from Sullivan's free-kick, Peters loops in a header. Forest had won six out of seven before today.											
9	H	NEWCASTLE		8	W	2-1	1-1	Peters 22, Reeves 66	Keelan	Bond	Sullivan	Ryan	Jones	Powell	Neighbour	Reeves	Gibbins	Suggett	Peters	
	5/10		16,630	*22*	11			*Craig T 9*	*Mahoney*	*Blackhall*	*Kennedy*	*McLean*	*McCaffrey*	*Nattrass*	*Barrowcl'gh*	*Callaghan**	*Burns*	*Gowling*	*Craig T*	*Oates*
								Ref: J Bent	Keelan is presented with a crystal decanter and glasses to mark his 600th senior game. Tommy Craig beats him early with a bending 25-yarder. Neighbour's corner is headed on by Gibbins for Peters to steal in and equalise. Reeves produces a majestic header to beat Richard Dinnis' side.											
10	H	WOLVERHAMPTON		6	W	2-1	1-0	Peters 31, 50	Keelan	Bond	Sullivan	Ryan	Jones	Powell	Neighbour	Reeves	Gibbins	Suggett*	Peters	**Nightingale**
	8/10		18,474	*13*	13			*Sunderland 61*	*Bradshaw*	*Palmer*	*Daly**	*Daley*	*Brazier*	*Parkin*	*Hibbitt*	*Carr*	*Richards*	*Patching*	*Sunderland*	*Kindon*
								Ref: D Reeves	Peters glides forward in typical fashion to head in Neigbour's centre. His left-foot shot after the break beats Paul Bradshaw for another classic piece of crafty poaching. Subdued Wolves get one back as Willie Carr's shot is blocked, but cannons against Alan Sunderland, who runs it in.											

No	Venue / Date	Opponent	Att / Pos	Pts	Res	F-A	H-T	Scorers, Times, and Referees	1	2	3	4	5	6	7	8	9	10	11	subs used
11	A	ASTON VILLA	7		L	0-3	0-1		Keelan	Bond	Sullivan	Ryan	Jones	Powell	Neighbour	Reeves	Gibbins	Evans	Peters	
	15/10		*32,978* 10	13				*Gray 18, Cowans 62, Little 77*	*Rimmer*	*Gidman*	*Smith*	*Phillips*	*McNaught*	*Mortimer*	*Deehan**	*Little*	*Gray*	*Cropley*	*Carrodus*	*Cowans*
								Ref: T Morrissey	Andy Gray is left unmarked to put Villa in front. City look lively in midfield, but are undone by moments of madness in defence. Between games, Peters is despatched by Bond to Switzerland in a bid to persuade his old Spurs pal Martin Chivers to return to the UK to join Norwich.											
12	H	LEICESTER	7		W	2-0	1-0	Gibbins 28, Ryan 52p	Keelan	Bond	Sullivan	Ryan*	Jones	Powell	Neighbour	Reeves	Gibbins	Suggett	Peters	McGuire
	22/10		18,122 *21*	15					*Wallington*	*Whitworth*	*Rofe*	*Kember*	*Webb*	*Williams*	*Weller*	*Salmons*	*Waddle*	*Sammels*	*Armstrong*	
								Ref: K Salmon	A superb display of wing-play by Neighbour underpins this welcome win. His first-time cross is headed in at the near post by Gibbins. David Webb fells Reeves for Ryan's penalty. McGuire is welcomed back for his first senior game in 18 months following major Achilles problems.											
13	A	DERBY	7		D	2-2	0-2	Reeves 68, 86	Keelan	Bond	Sullivan	Ryan	Jones	Powell	Neighbour	Reeves	Gibbins*	Suggett	Peters	McGuire
	29/10		*21,957 16*	16				*Daly 9, Hughes 36*	*Middleton*	*Langan*	*Nish*	*Daly*	*Daniel*	*Todd*	*Powell*	*Hector*	*Hughes*	*Masson*	*Ryan*	
								Ref: C Newsome	Kevin Hector's cross-shot is parried into the path of Gerry Daly, who hits the target. Billy Hughes' firm header doubles the lead. Reeves makes amends for missing a sitter by netting from close range. Ignoring offside appeals, Neighbour crosses and Reeves rises to head a fine equaliser.											
14	A	LEEDS	9		D	2-2	2-1	Gibbins 30, Ryan 37	Keelan	Bond	Sullivan	Ryan	Jones	Powell	Neighbour	Reeves	Gibbins	Suggett	Peters	
	5/11		*24,345 12*	17				*Lorimer 33, 50*	*Harvey*	*Cherry*	*Gray F*	*Lorimer*	*McQueen*	*Madeley*	*Gray E**	*Hankin*	*Jordan*	*Flynn*	*Graham*	*Harris*
								Ref: A Hughes	Gibbins glances in a cross, whipped in first time by Jones. Peter Lorimer equalises by rifling in a fierce angled shot. Suggett pushes an indirect free-kick into the path of Ryan, who powers City ahead with a fine drive. Lorimer hits back again, beating Keelan after Joe Jordan sets him up.											
15	H	CHELSEA	7		D	0-0	0-0		Keelan	Bond	Sullivan	Ryan	Jones	Powell	Neighbour	Reeves	Gibbins	Suggett	Peters	
	12/11		19,566 *15*	18					*Bonetti*	*Wilkins G*	*Sparrow*	*Britton*	*Droy*	*Wicks*	*Aylott*	*Wilkins R*	*Langley*	*Swain*	*Cooke*	
								Ref: C Maskell	Peter Bonetti's brilliant display keeps City at bay, particularly after the break when they swarm all over Ken Shellito's side. Steve Wicks and Micky Droy are commanding. Police broadcast an appeal for witnesses to trouble in the Barclay Stand when two fans are slashed with a razor.											
16	A	MANCHESTER U	9		L	0-1	0-0		Keelan	Bond	Sullivan	Ryan	Jones	Powell	Neighbour	Reeves	Gibbins	Suggett	Peters	
	19/11		***48,129*** *15*	18				*Pearson 73*	*Roche*	*Nicholl*	*Houston*	*McIlroy**	*Greenhoff B*	*Buchan*	*Coppell*	*Greenhoff J*	*Pearson*	*Macari*	*Hill*	*McCreery*
								Ref: T Mills	Keelan is kept busy and only beaten once, when Stuart Pearson picks up the pieces after Steve Coppell's drive bounces off the keeper. City are told that Carrow Road should hold a maximum of 19,000 until safety work is done. Bond is looking at strikers Kevin Hector and Tony Kellow.											
17	H	BIRMINGHAM	8		W	1-0	0-0	Gibbins 90	Keelan	Bond	Sullivan	Ryan	Jones	Powell	Neighbour	Reeves	Gibbins	Paddon	Peters	
	26/11		17,161 *16*	20					*Montgomery*	*Calderwood*	*Pendrey*	*Dillon*	*Howard*	*Want*	*Page*	*Francis*	*Bertschin*	*Hibbitt*	*Emmanuel*	
								Ref: R Challis	Paddon returns to action after nearly a year out with a broken leg. Trevor Francis, who hits the bar, and 17-year-old Kevin Dillon prove a real handful for City's defence. Reeves misses a good chance near the end and a goalless draw looks inevitable until Gibbins cracks in Reeves' pass.											
18	A	WEST BROM	8		D	0-0	0-0		Keelan	Bond	Sullivan	Ryan	Jones	Powell	Neighbour	Suggett	Gibbins	Paddon	Peters	
	3/12		*19,264 3*	21					*Godden*	*Mulligan*	*Statham*	*Brown T*	*Wile*	*Robertson*	*Martin*	*Regis*	*Cross*	*Robson*	*Cunningham*	
								Ref: S Bates	The high-flying Baggies dominate after the break, but hard-working Jones and Powell ensure they end up with their third successive goalless draw. Bond denies he had a big-money offer to manage Tampa Bay Rowdies and the speculation ends when Gordon Jago joins the US club.											
19	H	LIVERPOOL	7		W	2-1	1-0	Suggett 17, Peters 67	Keelan	Bond	Sullivan	Ryan	Jones	Powell	Neighbour	Suggett	Gibbins	Paddon	Peters	
	10/12		24,983 *3*	23				*Thompson 81*	*Clemence*	*Neal*	*Smith**	*Thompson*	*Kennedy*	*Hughes*	*Dalglish*	*Fairclough*	*Heighway*	*McDermott*	*Case*	*Johnson*
								Ref: D Smith	Suggett, who asked to be rested a fortnight ago at Birmingham, looks happier now. He is on hand to rifle in after Paddon's clever backheel. A famous victory looks assured as Peters volleys in a fine goal. There is late anxiety, however, after a superb diving header from Phil Thompson.											
20	A	CHELSEA	7		D	1-1	0-1	Suggett 74	Keelan	Bond	Sullivan	Ryan	Jones	Powell	Neighbour	Suggett	Gibbins	Paddon	Peters	
	17/12		*22,751 15*	24				*Wilkins R 39*	*Bonetti*	*Harris*	*Sparrow*	*Britton*	*Droy*	*Wicks*	*Aylott*	*Wilkins R*	*Langley*	*Swain*	*Walker*	
								Ref: A Gunn	The ever-reliable Peters celebrates his 600th senior appearance. A cross by Clive Walker sails over Keelan's head, hits the post and is netted by Ray Wilkins. Suggett saves a point for City as he stoops to head in a cross from Peters. Relief all round and a nice 45th birthday gift for Bond.											
21	H	IPSWICH	6		W	1-0	1-0	Ryan 17	Keelan	Bond	Sullivan	Ryan	Jones	Powell	Neighbour	Suggett	Gibbins	Paddon*	Peters	Reeves
	26/12		27,887 *7*	26					*Cooper*	*Burley*	*Tibbott*	*Talbot*	*Hunter*	*Osman*	*Mills*	*Viljoen*	*Mariner*	*Whymark**	*Woods*	*Gates*
								Ref: P Reeves	Russell Osman handles but Ryan's spot-kick is pushed against the bar by penalty-specialist Paul Cooper, only for Ryan to net the rebound. To City's relief, Mr Reeves misses a handball at the other end. Trevor Whymark picks up a knee injury that effectively ends his top-flight career.											

No	Date		Att	Pos	Pt	F-A	H-T	Scorers, Times, and Referees	1	2	3	4	5	6	7	8	9	10	11	12 sub used
22	A	COVENTRY		8	L	4-5	3-2	Ryan 32p, Reeves 36, 44, Peters 75	Keelan	Bond	Sullivan	Ryan	Jones	Powell	Neighbour	Suggett	Gibbins	Reeves	Peters	
	27/12		*21,578*	*7*	26			*P'12p, Wal'26, Go'56, McD'67, Gr' 82*	*Blyth*	*Beck*	*McDonald*	*Yorath*	*Roberts*	*Gooding*	*Graydon*	*Wallace*	*Ferguson*	*Powell*	*Hutchison*	
								Ref: L Shapter	Barry Powell's penalty kick-starts a goal rush and one of the most remarkable games seen at Highfield Road. Ian Wallace nets a magnficent overhead kick. City go agonisingly close to making it 5-5 in the dying moments as Peters hits a post and Ryan's penalty is saved by Jim Blyth.											
23	A	MIDDLESBROUGH		8	D	2-2	1-1	Suggett 19, Ryan 50	Keelan	Bond	Sullivan	Ryan	Jones	Powell	Neighbour	Reeves	Gibbins	Suggett	Peters	
	31/12		*15,646*	*15*	27			*Cummins 30, Armstrong 89*	*Cuff*	*Craggs*	*Bailey*	*Souness*	*Hickton*	*Ramage*	*McAndrew*	*Cummins*	*Ashcroft*	*Mills*	*Armstrong*	
								Ref: G Nolan	Suggett goes clear and beats Pat Cuff. Stan Cummins levels, netting a rebound after Keelan's stunning save. Ryan sets off on a charge from halfway and, as defenders back off, lashes home a 20-yarder. Keelan punches a David Mills' cross to the feet of David Armstrong, who fires in.											
24	H	WEST HAM		8	D	2-2	0-1	Ryan 64p, Peters 75	Keelan	Bond	Sullivan	Ryan	Jones	Powell	Neighbour	Suggett	Gibbins	Reeves	Peters	
	2/1		**29,480**	*19*	28			*Devonshire 7, Hales 84*	*Ferguson*	*Brush*	*Lampard*	*Bonds*	*Taylor T*	*Curbishley*	*Devonshire*	*Robson B*	*Cross*	*Brooking*	*Hales*	
								Ref: K Baker	The stylish Alan Devonshire makes scoring look easy to give Hammers an early lead. Billy Bonds pushes Peters to win a spot-kick that Ryan crashes in off the bar. Peters nets a left-foot volley to stun his former club but Derek Hales rescues a point, heading in Trevor Brooking's cross.											
25	A	QP RANGERS		9	L	1-2	0-2	Reeves 57	Keelan	Bond	Sullivan	Ryan	Forbes	Powell	Neighbour	Reeves	Gibbins	Suggett	Peters	
	14/1		*14,247*	*20*	28			*Eastoe 2, Cunningham 23*	*Parkes*	*Shanks*	*Gillard*	*Hollins*	*Howe*	*Cunningham*	*Eastoe*	*Francis*	*James**	*Bowles*	*Givens*	*Wallace*
								Ref: J Bent	After just 90 seconds, Peter Eastoe is left unmarked to head in Leighton James' free-kick. With City appealing in vain for offside, Tommy Cunningham rounds Keelan to add a second. Reeves' shot is fumbled over the line by Phil Parkes. Rangers deserve their first win in ten games.											
26	H	MANCHESTER C		9	L	1-3	0-1	Gibbins 64	Keelan	Bond	Sullivan	Ryan	Jones	Powell	**Lythgoe**	Suggett	Gibbins	Reeves	Peters	
	21/1		20,397	*2*	28			*Kidd 20, 55, Owen 76*	*Corrigan*	*Clements*	*Donachie*	*Booth*	*Watson*	*Owen*	*Barnes*	*Bell*	*Kidd*	*Hartford*	*Tueart*	
								Ref: J Sewell	Brian Kidd puts Tony Book's side two ahead with a couple of far-post headers. Roger Gibbins gets clear of the defence to crack in a left-foot shot. Gary Owen collects a Powell clearance and nets to ensure the home side's seventh successive win. Norwich play their part in a fine game.											
27	A	BRISTOL CITY		10	L	0-3	0-3		Keelan	Bond	Sullivan	Ryan	Jones	Powell	McGuire	Suggett	Gibbins	Reeves*	Peters	Neighbour
	4/2		*16,929*	*17*	28			*Ritchie 10, Royle 13, Whitehead 15*	*Shaw*	*Sweeney*	*Merrick*	*Gow*	*Collier*	*Hunter*	*Mann*	*Ritchie*	*Royle*	*Cormack*	*Whitehead*	
								Ref: R Crabb	Keelan breaks his right hand after five minutes, but refuses to come off and only uses his left hand for the rest of the game! The Robins make the most of this with three quick goals and then ease up. Keith Robson is signed from Cardiff, where he had been transfer-listed for fighting.											
28	H	NOTT'M FOR		9	D	3-3	1-3	Ryan 44p, Suggett 68, Robson 70	Hansbury	Ryan	Sullivan	McGuire	Jones	Powell	**Robson**	Paddon	Gibbins	Suggett	Peters	
	25/2		26,004	*1*	29			*Withe 15, Barrett 20, O'Neill 23*	*Shilton*	*Anderson*	*Barrett*	*McGovern*	*Needham*	*Burns*	*O'Neill*	*Gemmill*	*Withe*	*Woodcock*	*Robertson*	
								Ref: T Bune	Peter Withe sidefoots in a Tony Woodcock pass and Colin Barrett exploits a Powell error. Martin O'Neill nets and again City are three-down early. Barrett handles in the area to signal a fightback. Suggett lobs in a real beauty and then debutant Robson cracks home a joyful equaliser.											
29	A	ARSENAL		9	D	0-0	0-0		Hansbury	Ryan	Sullivan	McGuire	Jones	Powell	Robson	Suggett	Paddon	Reeves	Peters	
	28/2		*23,506*	*5*	30				*Jennings*	*Rice*	*Nelson*	*Price*	*O'Leary*	*Young*	*Brady*	*Sunderland*	*Macdonald**	*Stapleton*	*Hudson*	*Heeley*
								Ref: A Turvey	What appear to be unnecessary bookings cause anger in both camps. Suggett and Robson both hit shots narrowly wide and Reeves lobs over an open goal. Sir Alf Ramsey's reign as Birmingham consultant/manager is coming to an end, but their bid to replace him with John Bond fails.											
30	A	WOLVERHAMPTON		9	D	3-3	2-2	Ryan 39, Reeves 45, 46	Hansbury	Ryan	Sullivan	McGuire	Jones	Powell	Suggett	Robson	Paddon	Reeves	Peters	
	4/3		*16,813*	*17*	31			*Daley 15, 29, Hibbitt 58*	*Bradshaw*	*Palmer*	*Parkin*	*Daley*	*Hazell*	*McAlle*	*Hibbitt**	*Carr*	*Farley*	*Rafferty*	*Patching*	*Daly*
								Ref: S Bates	Steve Daley nets from long range and then hooks in while flat on the floor. City hit back as Ryan nearly breaks the net with a free-kick. Reeves converts an easy chance and then gains the lead with a great turn of speed and fine finish. Ryan's misplaced pass leads to Hibbitt's equaliser.											
31	H	ASTON VILLA		8	W	2-1	1-0	Reeves 30, Ryan 84p	Hansbury	Ryan	Sullivan	McGuire	Jones	Powell	Robson	Suggett	Reeves	Paddon	Peters	
	11/3		19,031	*11*	33			*Gregory 88*	*Rimmer*	*Gidman*	*Smith*	*Phillips*	*McNaught*	*Mortimer*	*Craig*	*Little*	*Deehan*	*Evans A**	*Carrodus*	*Gregory*
								Ref: K Salmon	Robson beats Jimmy Rimmer in the air and Reeves is on hand to score. John Gregory pushes Peters and Ryan beats Rimmer from the spot. Gregory heads in a Gordon Smith free-kick and then John Gidman goes agonisingly close to an equaliser. What a relief after 11 without a win.											

No	Venue / Date	Opponent	Att	Pos	Res / Pts	F-A	H-T	Scorers, Times, Referees	1	2	3	4	5	6	7	8	9	10	11	12 sub used
32	H	EVERTON		8	D	0-0	0-0		Hansbury	Ryan	Sullivan	McGuire	Jones	Powell	Robson	Suggett	Reeves	Paddon	Peters	
	15/3		19,502	2	34				Wood	Jones	Pejic	Lyons	Darracott	Ross	King	Dobson	Latchford	McKenzie	Thomas	
								Ref: M Sinclair	Hansbury makes a fine save from Bob Latchford at point-blank range. Robson goes close to a winner with a rising shot. John Bond obstinately refuses to bow to the crowd's calls for the introduction of sub Neighbour. Gibbins departs for New England Teamen in the USA for £25,000.											
33	A	LEICESTER		8	D	2-2	1-1	Ryan 10, 69	Hansbury	Ryan	Sullivan	McGuire	Jones	Powell	Robson	Suggett	Reeves	Paddon	Peters	
	18/3		13,077	22	35			Williams 38, Davies 57	Wallington	Whitworth	Rofe	Kelly	Williams	Webb	Weller	Hughes*	Davies	Salmons	Smith	Kember
								Ref: R Lewis	Ryan curls in a fine 20-yarder. Tommy Williams heads in Keith Weller's cross to bring Frank McLintock's strugglers level. Roger Davies nets a bizarre goal, connecting with the ball at the third attempt. The Foxes are demoralised as Ryan's cross-shot is palmed in by Mark Wallington.											
34	H	COVENTRY		9	L	1-2	1-0	Reeves 4	Hansbury	Ryan	Sullivan	McGuire	Jones	Powell	Paddon	Reeves	Robson	Suggett	Peters*	Bond
	25/3		20,732	6	35			Powell 66p, Wallace 89	Blyth	Roberts	McDonald	Yorath	Holton	Osgood	Beck	Wallace	Thompson	Powell	Hutchison	
								Ref: M Peck	Reeves' early headed goal raises hopes the 27 December thriller may be repeated. Gordon Milne's men level as Ryan fouls Tommy Hutchison and Barry Powell scores from the spot. Ian Wallace, not fully fit, is on hand to net a late winner and inflict the season's second home defeat.											
35	A	IPSWICH		9	L	**0-4**	0-2		Hansbury	Ryan	Sullivan	McGuire*	Jones	Powell	Neighbour	**Downs**	Paddon	Reeves	Robson	Suggett
	27/3		29,930	16	35			Talbot 12, 32, Geddis 62, Mills 79	Cooper	Burley	Mills	Talbot	Hunter	Beattie	Osborne*	Wark	Mariner	Geddis	Woods	Lambert
								Ref: K Styles	Bobby Robson's men have reached the FA Cup semi-finals, but badly need league points to keep them clear of the lower reaches. Industrious local lad Brian Talbot destroys City in the first half. Paul Mariner gives Jones a torrid time all afternoon, but his own best effort strikes the bar.											
36	H	DERBY		9	D	0-0	0-0		Hansbury	Bond	Sullivan	Ryan	Jones	Powell	Neighbour	Suggett	Paddon	Reeves	Lythgoe	
	29/3		18,349	12	36				Middleton	Langan	Buckley	Rioch	McFarland	Todd	Curran	Daly	Powell*	George	Ryan	Daniel
								Ref: D Richardson	After the disastrous Easter weekend, a little pride is restored by a good display against Tommy Docherty's side but City are out of luck in front of goal. Reeves is called up for England Under-21s, which means City must pay Bournemouth another £5,000 as part of the transfer agreement.											
37	H	LEEDS		9	W	**3-0**	1-0	Ryan 24, Jones 60, Hart 81(og)	Hansbury	Bond	Sullivan	Ryan	Jones	Powell	Neighbour	Suggett	Paddon	Reeves	Lythgoe	
	1/4		19,615	7	38				Harvey	Reaney	Hampton	Flynn*	Hart	Cherry	Harris	Gray E	Lorimer	Gray F	Graham	Thomas
								Ref: C Downey	This is more like it. A fine run and fierce drive by Ryan is the platform for a fine win. Suggett's flick gives Jones a close-range chance and he rams the ball high into David Harvey's net. Lythgoe's low cross is turned into his own goal by big Paul Hart, Leeds' new club-record signing.											
38	A	BIRMINGHAM		9	L	1-2	0-0	Reeves 57	Hansbury	Peters	Sullivan	Ryan	Jones	Powell	Neighbour	Suggett	Paddon	Reeves	Lythgoe	
	8/4		20,858	12	38			Gallagher 46, Francis 86	Montgomery	Calderwood	Pendrey	Towers	Gallagher	Howard	Page	Francis	Bertschin	Hibbitt*	Fox	Connolly
								Ref: C Maskell	Unbeaten since manager Jim Smith arrived, the Blues lead through Joe Gallagher's power header. Reeves levels, knocking in a Suggett cross. Jones misjudges a cross by John Connolly and Trevor Francis slides in the winner. City drop out of the top ten for the first time in six months.											
39	H	MANCHESTER U		13	L	1-3	1-0	Lythgoe 24	Hansbury	Peters	Sullivan	Ryan	Jones	Powell	Neighbour	Suggett	Paddon	Reeves	Lythgoe	
	15/4		20,373	11	38			Jordan 67, McIlroy 69, Coppell 78	Stepney	Albiston	Houston	McIlroy	McQueen	Buchan	Coppell	Jordan	Pearson	Greenhoff B	McCreery*	McGrath
								Ref: B Martin	Local lad Lythgoe's first senior goal is well-taken after Neighbour's cross is deflected to him by Alex Stepney. The visitors are lively in attack, but their success comes surprisingly late. City crack after Joe Jordan's venomous effort. Sammy McIlroy and Steve Coppell poach two more.											
40	A	LIVERPOOL		14	L	0-3	0-2		Hansbury	Bond	Ryan	Paddon	Jones	Powell	Neighbour	Reeves	Lythgoe	Suggett	Peters	
	22/4		44,857	4	38			Ryan 5(og), Fairclough 32, 46	Clemence	Neal	Smith	Thompson	Hughes	Kennedy	Case	McDermott	Souness	Dalglish	Fairclough	
								Ref: R Kirkpatrick	Ryan blunders when his swerving back-pass goes well out of the reach of a startled Hansbury. Powell is beaten by a bouncing ball and David Fairclough nets a simple goal. Just after half-time the game slips completely out of reach as Terry McDermott sets up Fairclough's fierce shot.											
41	A	NEWCASTLE		12	D	2-2	0-1	Ryan 57, Reeves 81	**Baker**	Bond	Sullivan	**Halsey !**	Jones	Powell	Neighbour	Reeves	Robson*	Ryan	Peters	Lythgoe
	26/4		**7,600**	21	39			Kennedy 21, Burns 71	Carr	Kelly	Kennedy	McGhee	Blackley	Callaghan	Barrowcl'gh	Burns	McGhee	Larnach	Walker	
								Ref: D Shaw	United's lowest crowd in more than 50 years turn up to see their already relegated side. They get four fine goals for their trouble. Mark Halsey, 18, gets two yellow cards and is sent off on his Norwich debut. Ryan's super-cool chip and Reeves' excellent 20-yard volley save City a point.											
42	H	WEST BROM		12	D	1-1	0-1	Forbes 90	Baker	Bond	Sullivan	Ryan	Forbes	Powell*	Neighbour	Reeves	Robson	Suggett	Peters	Lythgoe
	29/4		18,317	6	40			Regis 23	Godden	Batson	Statham	Brown T	Wile	Robertson	Cantello	Robson	Regis	Hughes	Cunningham	
		Home	Away					Ref: R Challis	A typically dull end-of-season affair looks like being settled by Cyrille Regis's early strike. He turns and beats Baker after collecting a punt from Tony Godden. Veteran Forbes, recalled shortly after his testimonial, stabs an equaliser in the dying seconds and brings the house down.											
Average		20,042	24,860																	

League Cup	Att	Pos	Res	F-A	H-T	Scorers, Times, and Referees	1	2	3	4	5	6	7	8	9	10	11	12 sub used
2 A BURNLEY		7	L	1-3	0-2	Ryan 57p	Keelan	Ryan	Sullivan	Evans	Jones	Powell	Neighbour	**Night'gale***	**Downs**	Suggett	Gibbins	Forbes
30/8	*6,477*	*2:22*				*Morley 24, Noble 29, Ingham 88*	*Stevenson*	*Scott*	*Brennan*	*Burke*	*Robinson*	*Rodaway*	*Cochrane*	*Ingham*	*Noble*	*Flynn*	*Morley*	
						Ref: T Moris												

Tony Morley snaps Harry Potts strugglers ahead and then crosses for Peter Noble to double the lead. Eighteen-year-old Greg Downs misses a decent chance to register a debut goal for City. Ian Brennan trips Neighbour for Ryan's spot-kick goal. Billy Ingham embarrasses City further.

FA Cup	Att	Pos	Res	F-A	H-T	Scorers, Times, and Referees	1	2	3	4	5	6	7	8	9	10	11	12 sub used
3 A ORIENT		8	D	1-1	0-1	Gibbins 90	Keelan	Bond	Sullivan	Ryan	Jones	Powell	Neighbour	Suggett	Gibbins	Reeves	Peters	
6/1	*14.538*	*2:15*				*Kitchen 27*	*Jackson*	*Fisher*	*Roffey*	*Grealish*	*Hoadley*	*Roeder*	*Chiedozie*	*Gray*	*Mayo*	*Kitchen*	*Bennett*	
						Ref: T Morris												
3R H ORIENT		9	L	0-1	0-0		Keelan	Bond	Sullivan	Ryan	Fleeting	Powell	Neighbour	Suggett	Gibbins	Reeves	Peters	
16/1	20,421	*2:14*				*Kitchen 88*	*Jackson*	*Fisher*	*Roffey*	*Grealish*	*Hoadley*	*Roeder*	*Chiedozie*	*Gray*	*Mayo*	*Kitchen*	*Bennett*	
						Ref: C Maskell												

3 (6/1): O's sweeper Glenn Roeder strolls forward and goes close with a 30-yarder. Keelan saves an effort by Joe Mayo, but new recruit Peter Kitchen converts the rebound. A minute into injury-time City finally get a deserved equaliser when Suggett's cross is headed firmly home by Gibbins.

3R (16/1): The Londoners prove a tough nut to crack. Peter Kitchen races through in the dying minutes to stab in John Chiedozie's cross. City desperately push forward and Reeves' header is brilliantly saved by John Jackson. For the ninth time in ten years, City fail to get beyond the first hurdle.

		Home					Away					
	P	W	D	L	F	A	W	D	L	F	A	Pts
1 Nott'm For	42	15	6	0	37	8	10	8	3	32	16	64
2 Liverpool	42	15	4	2	37	11	9	5	7	28	23	57
3 Everton	42	14	4	3	47	22	8	7	6	29	23	55
4 Manchester C	42	14	4	3	46	21	6	8	7	28	30	52
5 Arsenal	42	14	5	2	38	12	7	5	9	22	25	52
6 West Brom	42	13	5	3	35	18	5	9	7	27	35	50
7 Coventry	42	13	5	3	48	23	5	7	9	27	39	48
8 Aston Villa	42	11	4	6	33	18	7	6	8	24	24	46
9 Leeds	42	12	4	5	39	21	6	6	9	24	32	46
10 Manchester U	42	9	6	6	32	23	7	4	10	35	40	42
11 Birmingham	42	8	5	8	32	30	8	4	9	23	30	41
12 Derby	42	10	7	4	37	24	4	6	11	17	35	41
13 NORWICH	42	10	8	3	28	20	1	10	10	24	46	40
14 Middlesbro	42	8	8	5	25	19	4	7	10	17	35	39
15 Wolves	42	7	8	6	30	27	5	4	12	21	37	36
16 Chelsea	42	7	11	3	28	20	4	3	14	18	49	36
17 Bristol City	42	9	6	6	37	26	2	7	12	12	27	35
18 Ipswich	42	10	5	6	32	24	1	8	12	15	37	35
19 QP Rangers	42	8	8	5	27	26	1	7	13	20	38	33
20 West Ham	42	8	6	7	31	28	4	2	15	21	41	32
21 Newcastle	42	4	6	11	26	37	2	4	15	16	41	22
22 Leicester	42	4	7	10	16	32	1	5	15	10	38	22
	924	223	132	107	741	490	107	132	223	490	741	924

Odds & ends

Double wins: (0).
Double losses: (3) Coventry, Manchester C, Manchester U.

Won from behind: (1) Newcastle (h).
Lost from in front: (3) Coventry (a), Coventry (h), Manchester U (h).

High spots: Holding a top-ten place from August till early April.
Sixteen goals from midfielder Ryan – mostly spectacular efforts.
Coming back from 0-3 to hold champions-elect Nott'm For to a draw.
The astonishing 4-5 see-saw thriller at Coventry in December.
The final goal of the season coming from recalled 'warhorse' Forbes.
The excellent win over Liverpool in December.
Finishing above local rivals Ipswich for the first time in 12 seasons.

Low spots: The run of 23 away trips without a win (in all competitions).
Being watched by Newcastle's lowest crowd since World War I.
The four-goal Easter Monday hammering at Portman Road.
Being dumped out of both cups by Second Division clubs.
An average drop in home crowds of nearly 3,000 per match.

Player of the Year: John Ryan.
Ever-presents: (2) Tony Powell, John Ryan.
Hat-tricks: (0).
Opposing hat-tricks: (0).
Leading scorer: (16) John Ryan.

	Appearances						Goals			
	Lge	*Sub*	LC	*Sub*	FAC	*Sub*	Lge	LC	FAC	Tot
Baker, Clive	**2**									
Bond, Kevin	**26**	*2*			2					
Busby, Viv	**5**									
Davies, Ian	**1**	*1*								
Downs, Greg	**1**		1							
Evans, Doug	**5**		1							
Fleeting, Jim					1					
Forbes, Duncan	**3**			*1*			**1**			**1**
Gibbins, Roger	**27**	*1*	1		2		**7**		1	**8**
Halsey, Mark	**1**									
Hansbury, Roger	**14**									
Jones, David	**40**		1		1		**3**			**3**
Keelan, Kevin	**26**		1		2					
Lythgoe, Phil	**6**	*2*					**1**			**1**
Machin, Mel	**3**									
McGuire, Mick	**9**	*2*								
Neighbour, Jimmy	**33**	*1*	1		2					
Nightingale, Mark		*1*	1							
Paddon, Graham	**18**									
Peters, Martin	**34**				2		**7**			**7**
Powell, Tony	**42**		1		2					
Reeves, Kevin	**36**	*1*			2		**12**			**12**
Robson, Keith	**10**						**1**			**1**
Ryan, John	**42**		1		2		**15**	1		**16**
Suggett, Colin	**38**	*1*	1		2		**4**			**4**
Sullivan, Colin	**40**	*1*	1		2					
(own-goals)							**1**			**1**
26 players used	**462**	***13***	**11**	***1***	**22**		**52**	**1**	**1**	**54**

No	Date		Att	Pos	Pt	F-A	H-T	Scorers, Times, and Referees	1	2	3	4	5	6	7	8	9	10	11	12 sub used
1	H	SOUTHAMPTON			W	3-1	1-0	Reeves 38, Ryan 60, Chivers 70	Keelan	Bond	Sullivan	Ryan	**Hoadley**	Powell	Neighbour	Reeves	**Chivers**	Robson	Peters	
	19/8		21,123		2			*MacDougall 83*	*Wells*	*Waldron*	*Peach*	*Williams*	*Nicholl*	*Pickering*	*Ball*	*Boyer*	*MacDougall*	*Baker**	*Curran*	*Hebberd*
								Ref: B Homewood	Reeves flicks a back-header over Peter Wells for the lead. Reeves and Wells collide and the ball falls for Ryan to bury a second goal. Former England man Martin Chivers, recruited from Switzerland, nets a fine debut header. Ex-Orient defender Phil Hoadley also enjoys a happy debut.											
2	A	BRISTOL CITY		4	D	1-1	1-0	Ryan 45p	Keelan	Bond	Sullivan	Ryan	Hoadley	Powell	Neighbour	Reeves	Chivers	Robson	Peters	
	22/8		*19,274*	*5*	3			*Cormack 65p*	*Shaw*	*Sweeney*	*Cooper*	*Mann*	*Rodgers*	*Hunter*	*Tainton*	*Ritchie*	*Royle*	*Cormack*	*Garland**	*Whitehead*
								Ref: M Baker	Norman Hunter is booked for a foul on Reeves and then hauls down Neighbour for Ryan to score from the spot. Reeves intercepts a back pass, but sweeps his shot wide. The linesman spots a handball by Hoadley, which is hotly disputed, but gives Peter Cormack the chance to equalise.											
3	A	COVENTRY		11	L	1-4	0-2	Peters 86 *[Ferguson 77]*	Keelan	Bond	Sullivan	Ryan	Hoadley	Powell	Neighbour	Reeves	Chivers	Robson	Peters	
	26/8		*20,452*	*4*	3			*Beck 12, Powell 45, Wallace 51,*	*Sealey*	*Osgood*	*McDonald*	*Beck*	*Holton*	*Gillespie*	*Nardiello**	*Wallace*	*Ferguson*	*Powell*	*Hutchison*	*Bannister*
								Ref: J Hough	An off-colour display and Keelan's alertness saves City from a worse hammering. Ian Wallace's header soon after the interval kills the contest. Teenager Gary Bannister debuts for Gordon Milne's side and goes close twice. Colin Suggett (200-plus games) signs for Newcastle for £60k.											
4	H	MANCHESTER C		11	D	1-1	1-0	Chivers 45	Keelan	Bond	Sullivan	Ryan	Hoadley	Powell	Neighbour	Reeves	Chivers	Robson	Peters	
	2/9		18,607	*15*	4			*Channon 60*	*Corrigan*	*Clements*	*Donachie*	*Power*	*Booth*	*Futcher P*	*Channon*	*Hartford*	*Futcher R*	*Owen*	*Barnes*	
								Ref: K Salmon	A lively first-half display by the Canaries is capped by Chivers nodding in after Joe Corrigan can only palm away a fierce shot by Reeves. In a game of six bookings, Norwich are frustrated to be pegged back as Mick Channon's cross-shot eludes Keelan's grasp and squeezes into the net.											
5	A	WEST BROM		11	D	2-2	2-1	Chivers 39, Ryan 45	Keelan	Bond	Sullivan	Ryan	Hoadley	Powell	Neighbour	Reeves	Chivers	Robson	Peters*	McGuire
	9/9		*21,947*	*4*	5			*Cunningham 15, Robson 90*	*Godden*	*Batson*	*Statham*	*Cantello*	*Wile*	*Robertson*	*Robson*	*Brown A*	*Cunningham*	*Regis*	*Johnston*	
								Ref: S Bates	Albion pressure pays off as Laurie Cunningham swoops after Keelan blocked an Ally Brown header. Tony Godden and John Wile collide to allow Chivers in. Ryan's powerful shot delights the travelling fans. Another point slips away as Bryan Robson nods home in the dying seconds.											
6	H	BIRMINGHAM		6	W	**4-0**	1-0	Robson 2, Ryan 48p, Chivers 61, [Reeves 87]	Baker	Bond	Sullivan	Ryan	Hoadley	Powell	Neighbour	Reeves	Chivers	Robson	Peters	
	16/9		16,407	*22*	7				*Freeman*	*Dillon**	*Rathbone*	*Dennis*	*Gallagher*	*Broadhurst*	*Ainscow*	*Towers*	*Givens*	*Emmanuel*	*Fox*	*Barrowcl'gh*
								Ref: T Mills	Jim Smith's side look woeful after Robson accepts an early gift. Youngster Mark Dennis, making his debut, fouls Reeves to hand Ryan his penalty. Chivers glances in a classy header from a Neighbour cross. The rout is completed when Reeves dives to head in a centre from Robson.											
7	A	BOLTON		11	L	2-3	2-1	Robson 34, Reeves 44	Baker	Bond	Sullivan	Ryan	Hoadley	Powell*	Neighbour	Reeves	Chivers	Robson	Peters	Paddon
	23/9		*19,901*	*16*	7			*Worthington 20, 53, Whatmore 47*	*McDonagh*	*Nicholson*	*Burke*	*Greaves*	*Walsh**	*Jones P*	*Morgan*	*Whatmore*	*Gowling*	*Worthington*	*Smith*	*Allardyce*
								Ref: M Lowe	Robson rises to head in off the bar, equalising Frank Worthington's fierce shot. Reeves tucks the ball in at the far post to shock Ian Greaves' outfit. Neil Whatmore slips his shot under Baker's body to level matters. Worthington shows great skill to control the ball and rifle the winner.											
8	H	DERBY		8	W	3-0	2-0	Ryan 12, Reeves 36, Robb 60	Keelan	Bond	Sullivan	Ryan	Hoadley	Powell	Neighbour	Reeves	**Robb**	Robson*	Peters	**Mendham**
	30/9		16,585	*17*	9				*Middleton*	*Langan*	*Buckley*	*Daly*	*McFarland*	*McCaffery*	*Powell*	*Rioch*	*Caskey*	*Clarke*	*Nish*	
								Ref: P Reeves	Peters nods down a Bond free-kick and Ryan nets a magnificent shot from 25 yards. Hoadley sends over a good cross and Reeves heads home. Scot Davie Robb, recruited from Tampa Bay Rowdies to replace injury victim Chivers, heads Neighbour's cross firmly past John Middleton.											
9	H	LIVERPOOL		11	L	1-4	0-3	Ryan 79p	Keelan	Bond	Sullivan	Ryan	Hoadley	Powell	Neighbour	Reeves	Robb*	Robson	Peters	Davies
	7/10		**25,632**	*1*	9			*Heighway 6, 10, Johnson 36, Case 48*	*Clemence*	*Neal*	*Kennedy A*	*Thompson*	*Kennedy R*	*Hansen*	*Dalglish*	*Case*	*Heighway*	*Johnson*	*Souness*	
								Ref: C Downey	Bob Paisley's men are going great guns at the top. Steve Heighway nets a low drive in off a post and then volleys a second. Neighbour hits the woodwork, but David Johnson pick his spot for the Reds' third. Jimmy Case powers in a free-kick. Robson is brought down for a City penalty.											
10	A	MIDDLESBROUGH		12	L	0-2	0-1		Keelan	Bond	Sullivan	Ryan	Hoadley	Powell	Neighbour	Reeves	Robb*	Paddon	Peters	Downs
	14/10		*18,203*	*19*	9			*Peters 24 (og), Mills 62*	*Stewart*	*Craggs*	*Bailey*	*Mahoney*	*Boam*	*McAndrew*	*Cochrane*	*Mills*	*Ashcroft*	*Burns*	*Armstrong*	
								Ref: M Peck	The miserable run of away form continues. Ian Bailey's centre is inadvertently knocked past Keelan by Peters. City's depression deepens when Terry Cochrane's back-heel sets up David Mills. A few days later a testimonial for Martin Peters sees Norwich beat the England 1966 side 4-2.											

No	Venue	Opponent / Date	Att	Pos	Res / Pts	F-A	H-T	Scorers, Times, and Referees	1	2	3	4	5	6	7	8	9	10	11	12 sub used
11	H	LEEDS		12	D	2-2	0-1	Ryan 53, Peters 72	Keelan	Bond	Davies	Ryan	Hoadley	Powell	Neighbour	Reeves	Downs	Mendham	Peters	
		21/10	19,981	14	10			*Gray F 29, Hawley 68*	*Harvey*	*Cherry*	*Gray F*	*Flynn*	*Hart*	*Madeley*	*Gray E*	*Hankin*	*Hawley*	*Currie*	*Graham*	
								Ref: P Richardson	Managerless Leeds net a bizarre goal: Keelan, angry over a challenge the ref ignored, hurls the ball down and stomps towards the official. This leaves John Hawley the simple task of rolling the ball in. The other players can't believe it. Peters does keep his cool minutes later, however.											
12	A	CHELSEA		13	D	3-3	0-1	Peters 59, 78, Ryan 75	Keelan	Bond	Davies	Ryan	Hoadley	Powell	Neighbour	Reeves	**Symonds**	Mendham	Peters	
		28/10	*23,941*	*20*	11			*Swain 31, Walker 68, Stanley 71p*	*Phillips*	*Wilkins G*	*Stride*	*Stanley*	*Wicks*	*Harris*	*McKenzie*	*Wilkins R*	*Langley*	*Swain*	*Walker*	
								Ref: A McDonald	Kenny Swain's header is cancelled out by one from skipper Peters. Clive Walker's intended cross deceives Keelan and goes in off a post. When Hoadley fells Walker, the points looks out of reach, but a great comeback sees Ryan chip in a beauty and then Peters heads powerfully home.											
13	H	TOTTENHAM		13	D	2-2	1-2	Ryan 43p, Peters 90	Keelan	Bond	Davies	Ryan	Hoadley	Powell	Neighbour	Reeves	Symonds	Mendham*	Peters	Downs
		4/11	25,695	*9*	12			*Lee 6, Taylor 31*	*Kendall*	*Naylor*	*McAllister*	*Holmes*	*Lacy*	*Perryman*	*Pratt*	*Ardiles**	*Lee*	*Hoddle*	*Taylor*	*Villa*
								Ref: B Hill	Colin Lee sidefoots Keith Burkinshaw's men into an early lead and Peter Taylor makes it two in a swift break forward. Ryan reduces the arrears following Don McAllister's handball. An equaliser is joyfully received in the dying seconds when Peters curls in an exquisite free-kick.											
14	A	SOUTHAMPTON		12	D	2-2	1-1	Neighbour 41, Powell 86	Keelan	Bond	Davies	Ryan	Hoadley	Powell	Neighbour	Reeves	Symonds	Mendham	Peters	
		11/11	*21,183*	*16*	13			*Holmes 32, Nicholl 58*	*Gennoe*	*Golac*	*Peach*	*Williams*	*Nicholl*	*Waldron*	*Ball*	*Boyer*	*Funnell*	*Holmes*	*Curran*	
								Ref: R Challis	Nick Holmes slams a 25-yarder in off the bar, but Neighbour levels, his shot flying in off a post. Chris Nicholl rams home a downward header from a David Peach free-kick. Powell repeats last week's Houdini act with a late diving header. Bond signs an astonishing nine-year contract.											
15	H	COVENTRY		11	W	1-0	0-0	Bond 73	Keelan	Bond	Davies	Ryan	Hoadley	Powell	Neighbour	Peters	Reeves	Symonds	Mendham	
		18/11	17,696	*8*	15				*Sealey*	*Coop*	*McDonald*	*Blair*	*Osgood*	*Gillespie*	*Bannister*	*Wallace*	*Thompson*	*Powell*	*Hutchison*	
								Ref: B Homewood	Coventry, fielding four teenagers, are in attacking mood, but lack bite in the final third. In his 52nd City appearance, Kevin Bond gets on the scoresheet for the first time, snapping up a rebound. It's the first win in seven – perhaps the swapping around of shirt numbers did the trick?											
16	H	EVERTON		14	L	0-1	0-0		Keelan	Bond	Davies*	Ryan	Hoadley	Powell	Neighbour	Reeves	Symonds	Mendham	Peters	Robson
		25/11	19,383	*2*	15			*Lyons 84*	*Wood*	*Todd*	*Pejic*	*Lyons*	*Wright*	*Ross*	*King*	*Dobson*	*Latchford*	*Kenyon*	*Thomas*	
								Ref: R Lewis	Keepers George Wood and Keelan are both kept on their toes, but this is generally a rather dour affair. Mike Lyons breaks the deadlock, rifling a shot home late on, to leave City feeling hard done by on the balance of play. It is announced that skipper Peters has been awarded an MBE.											
17	H	ARSENAL		15	D	0-0	0-0		Keelan	Bond	Davies	Ryan	Hoadley	Powell	Neighbour	Reeves	Chivers*	Symonds	Peters	Robson
		9/12	20,165	*4*	16				*Jennings*	*Rice*	*Nelson**	*Price*	*O'Leary*	*Young*	*Brady*	*Sunderland*	*Stapleton*	*Gatting*	*Rix*	*Walford*
								Ref: P Reeves	The squad has a Majorcan break to re-charge batteries, but Peters doesn't travel due to family illness. Pat Rice pushes Peters to hand City a late penalty, but Ryan's kick is well saved by Pat Jennings. Moments later Reeves nets but is given offside and some angry fans storm the pitch.											
18	A	ASTON VILLA		13	D	1-1	0-0	Reeves 68	Keelan	Bond	Davies	Ryan	Hoadley	Powell	McGuire	Reeves	Chivers	Symonds	Peters	
		16/12	*26,228*	*10*	17			*McGuire 80 (og)*	*Rimmer*	*Gidman*	*Williams*	*Evans A*	*McNaught*	*Mortimer*	*Craig*	*Deehan*	*Swain*	*Cowans*	*Gregory*	
								Ref: R Kirkup	After spells of heavy Villa pressure, City take a surprise lead, Reeves running in Davies' deep cross. Returning from injury, unlucky McGuire deflects the ball in when trying to keep it away from Villa debutant Kenny Swain. The blunder means it's now 28 away games without victory.											
19	A	IPSWICH		14	D	1-1	1-0	Davies 25	Keelan	Bond	Davies	Ryan	Hoadley	Powell	McGuire	Reeves	Chivers*	Robson	Symonds	Neighbour
		26/12	*26,336*	*16*	18			*Mills 46*	*Cooper*	*Burley*	*Mills*	*Talbot*	*Osman*	*Butcher*	*Wark*	*Muhren*	*Mariner*	*Gates*	*Woods*	
								Ref: M Taylor	Taking his cue from Kevin Bond last month, Davies nets his career-first goal. City's man-for-man marking system keeps Town at bay despite heavy pressure. Mick Mills heads an equaliser from close range 30 seconds after the break, but City hold firm after this in an absorbing contest.											
20	H	WEST BROM		14	D	1-1	0-1	Peters 51	Keelan	Bond	Davies	McGuire	Hoadley	Powell	Neighbour	Reeves	**Fashanu**	Symonds	Peters	
		13/1	20,972	*1*	19			*Regis 11*	*Godden*	*Batson*	*Statham*	*Brown T*	*Wile*	*Robertson*	*Robson*	*Brown A*	*Regis*	*Trewick*	*Johnston*	
								Ref: D Richardson	Justin Fashanu, 17, comes in to replace Chivers and a fine team display shows the FA Cup debacle has been forgotten. Cyrille Regis fires in a crisp shot from 18 yards. Peters ghosts in for a far-post equaliser. Fash goes close and Regis hits the bar. The point means Albion hit top spot.											
21	H	QP RANGERS		13	D	1-1	1-0	Davies 7	Keelan	Bond	Davies	McGuire	Hoadley	Powell	Neighbour	Reeves	Fashanu	Symonds	Peters	
		31/1	14,203	*19*	20			*Francis 87*	*Parkes*	*Clement*	*Gillard*	*Hollins*	*Howe*	*Roeder*	*Shanks**	*Francis*	*Hamilton*	*Bowles*	*Goddard*	*Busby*
								Ref: J Sewell	Peters' cross finds Davies, who nets a fierce drive in the early stages. But City fail to build on this and ex-England skipper Gerry Francis saves a point for Steve Burtenshaw's side, rifling in a fine shot. The game was a disgrace to Division One, says Bond. Sullivan joins Cardiff for £60k.											

No	Date		Att	Pos	Pt	F-A	H-T	Scorers, Times, and Referees	1	2	3	4	5	6	7	8	9	10	11	12 sub used
22	H	BOLTON		13	D	0-0	0-0		Keelan	Bond	Davies	Ryan	Hoadley	Powell	Lythgoe	Reeves	Fashanu*	McGuire	Peters	Robb
	3/2		15,369	*17*	21				*McDonagh*	*Nicholson*	*Dunne*	*Greaves*	*Jones P*	*Walsh*	*Morgan*	*Burke*	*Whatmore*	*Worthington*	*McNab*	
								Ref: J Bray	Ryan, dropped after the FA Cup debacle at Leicester, is recalled, but has a quiet game. Lythgoe, loaned out to Bristol Rovers earlier in the season, is called up and works hard in midfield. A small and impatient crowd sees another game of little quality and the run of draws goes on.											
23	A	DERBY		12	D	1-1	0-0	Peters 85	Keelan	Bond	Davies	Ryan	Forbes	Powell	Neighbour	Reeves*	Robb	Robson	Peters	**Bennett**
	10/2		*20.837*	*14*	22			*Buckley 75*	*McKeller*	*Langan*	*Buckley*	*Rioch*	*McFarland*	*Wicks*	*Carter*	*Powell*	*Duncan*	*Clarke*	*Greenwood*	
								Ref: K Baker	Shortly after Robb misses a good chance, Steve Buckley curves a 25-yarder past Keelan and in off a post. Peters saves the day with a powerful header from Neighbour's fine cross. City reflect on missed chances, but they have equalled the League record of drawing seven times in a row.											
24	A	LIVERPOOL		14	L	**0-6**	0-1	*[Kennedy A 80, Kennedy R 90]*	Keelan	Bond	Forbes	Ryan	Hoadley	Powell	Neighbour	Symonds	Chivers	Lythgoe	Peters	
	21/2		***35,754***	*1*	22			*Dalglish 3, 48, Johnson 46, 50,*	*Clemence*	*Neal*	*Hughes*	*Kennedy A*	*Kennedy R*	*Hansen*	*Dalglish*	*Johnson*	*Heighway*	*McDermott*	*Souness*	
								Ref: B Martin	Kenny Dalglish heads in early on from close-range and the Reds take complete command. David Johnson shoots home after the interval and Dalglish flicks a third. Keelan, later found to have broken a thumb, blunders to allow Johnson a tap-in. Alan Kennedy hits the pick of the goals.											
25	H	MIDDLESBROUGH		14	W	1-0	0-0	Peters 65	Hansbury	Bond	Davies	Ryan	Forbes	Powell	Neighbour*	Robson	Fashanu	Paddon	Peters	McGuire
	24/2		**13,896**	*19*	24				*Stewart*	*Craggs*	*Johnson*	*Mahoney*	*Boam*	*McAndrew**	*Burns*	*Proctor*	*Ashcroft*	*Cummins*	*Armstrong*	*Hodgson*
								Ref: D Hutchinson	Jim Stewart mishandles a cross and Peters nods the winner in a drab game. Boro look the better of two uninspired sides. Chivers, a flop after his good start at the club, joins Brighton. Ex-Canary John Benson returns as a coach. Kevin Bond is called up for the England Under-21 squad.											
26	A	MANCHESTER C		13	D	2-2	1-1	Robson 8, Peters 80	Hansbury	Bond	Symonds	Ryan	Hoadley	Powell	McGuire	Fashanu	Robson	Paddon	Peters	
	27/2		*30,012*	*14*	25			*Owen 17, 59p*	*Corrigan*	*Clements*	*Donachie*	*Power*	*Booth*	*Futcher P*	*Channon*	*Hartford*	*Futcher R*	*Owen*	*Barnes*	
								Ref: R Newsome	Robson cashes in on an error by Paul Futcher. Gary Owen levels with a fine header. Peter Barnes is a constant threat and when Symonds brings him down, Owen nets from the spot. Peters comes to the rescue again with a delightful poacher's goal. McGuire clears off the line near the end.											
27	A	LEEDS		15	D	2-2	0-1	Bond 56, Fashanu 61	Hansbury	Bond	Symonds	Ryan	Hoadley	Powell	McGuire	Fashanu	Robson	Paddon	Peters	
	3/3		*23,038*	*5*	26			*Hawley 19, 64*	*Harvey*	*Cherry*	*Gray F*	*Flynn*	*Parkinson*	*Madeley*	*Harris*	*Hird*	*Hawley*	*Currie*	*Graham*	
								Ref: J Butcher	John Hawley nearly bursts the net from a pass by new signing Kevin Hird. Ryan, saying farewell before moving to the USA, charges down a clearance for Bond to let fly and net a wonder goal. Fashanu heads his first senior goal, but Hawley's tap-in prevents a long-awaited away win.											
28	H	WOLVERHAMPTON		14	D	0-0	0-0		Hansbury	Bond	Symonds	McGuire	Reeves	Powell	Neighbour	Fashanu	Robson	Paddon	Peters	
	7/3		15,427	*19*	27				*Bradshaw*	*Palmer*	*Parkin*	*Daniel*	*McAlle*	*Berry*	*Hibbitt*	*Daley*	*Rafferty*	*Richards**	*Carr*	*Patching*
								Ref: C Maskell	Bond makes a rallying call for a display that will bring back the missing fans. Sadly it doesn't happen and we get yet another draw. George Berry has a fine game, but colleagues John Richards and Willie Carr miss chances. City sign young forwards Alan Cordice and Greg Shepherd.											
29	H	CHELSEA		10	W	2-0	1-0	Fashanu 10, Peters 72	Hansbury	Bond	Symonds	McGuire	Hoadley	Powell	Neighbour	Reeves	Fashanu	Paddon*	Peters	Robson
	10/3		19,071	*21*	29				*Borota**	*Wilkins G*	*Stride*	*Bannon*	*Sitton*	*Nutton*	*Aylott*	*Wilkins R*	*Harris*	*Langley*	*Walker*	*Bumstead*
								Ref: R Kirkpatrick	Fashanu nets a near-post header, but soon after collides with Blues' new keeper Petar Borota. Cut and concussed, the Yugolsav is half-led and half-hauled off. Tommy Langley goes in goal and keeps City out until Peters head in a Reeves cross. Danny Blanchflower's men look doomed.											
30	A	NOTT'M FOR		11	L	1-2	0-0	Fashanu 66	Hansbury	Bond	Evans	McGuire	Hoadley	Powell	Neighbour	Reeves	Fashanu	Robson	Peters	
	14/3		*24,046*	*6*	29			*Woodcock 52, 60*	*Shilton*	*Barrett*	*Clark*	*McGovern*	*Lloyd*	*Needham*	*Francis*	*Gemmill*	*Birtles*	*Woodcock*	*Robertson*	
								Ref: N Ashley	Bond puts Peters in defence and brings in Evans to mark John Robertson. Forest are three days away from a Wembley League Cup final. Tony Woodcock strikes twice and the Bond plan is abandoned. Peters moves up and immediately Neighbour's cross is flicked in by Fashanu's head.											
31	A	TOTTENHAM		10	D	0-0	0-0		Hansbury	Bond	Davies	McGuire	Hoadley	Powell	Neighbour	Reeves	Robson	Evans	Peters*	Forbes
	17/3		*24,982*	*11*	30				*Kendall*	*Naylor*	*McAllister*	*Holmes*	*Lacy*	*Perryman*	*Pratt*	*Ardiles**	*Lee*	*Hoddle*	*Villa*	*Taylor*
								Ref: M Taylor	Bond is frustrated to lose Fashanu, who is banned for two matches after a series of 'silly' bookings. Evans stalks Ossie Ardiles to such good effect that the Argentine gets subbed. Hansbury performs heroics in goal to keep Tottenham at bay. Draw specialists City have done it again.											

32	H	BRISTOL CITY	9	W	3-0	3-0	Neighbour 10, Evans 26, Reeves 31	Hansbury	Bond	Davies*	McGuire	Hoadley	Powell	Neighbour	Reeves	Robson	Paddon	Evans	Downs
24/3		14,507	14	32				Shaw	Sweeney	Gillies	Gow	Rodgers	Hunter	Tainton	Ritchie	Royle*	Mabbutt	Whitehead	Cormack
							Ref: A Cox	Neighbour rides a fierce tackle from Gerry Sweeney and cracks home a fine 20-yarder. Bond's low cross is sidefooted home by Evans for his first senior goal. The points are in the bag early as Reeves pounces to crack the ball high into the net after Robson's header hit the woodwork.											
33	A	BIRMINGHAM	9	L	0-1	0-1		Hansbury	Bond	Davies	McGuire	Hoadley	Powell	Neighbour*	Reeves	Robson	Paddon	Evans !	Peters
27/3		12,168	21	32			Givens 20	Freeman	Page	Dennis	Towers	Gallagher	Pendrey	Ainscow	Buckley*	Givens	Barrowcl'gh	Dillon	Broadhurst
							Ref: C White	Reeves and Robson go close in the opening minutes, but the relegation-haunted Blues go ahead as Don Givens nods in an Alan Ainscow chip. Evans is sent off for a late tackle on Ainscow. In the final minute Bond fouls Mark Dennis in the area, but Hansbury saves Tony Towers' kick.											
34	A	EVERTON	9	D	2-2	1-0	Reeves 26, 53	Hansbury	Symonds	Davies	Bond	Hoadley	Powell	Neighbour	Reeves	Robson	Paddon	McGuire	
30/3		28,825	2	33			Lyons 64, 86	Wood	Todd	Heard	Lyons	Wright	Ross	Higgins*	Dobson	King	Telfer	Thomas	Barton
							Ref: R Banks	Two up with over an hour gone, City unbelievably let slip that elusive away win again. Reeves and Neighbour combine at speed for the first and Reeves is left in space to fire another. Mick Lyons knocks in two rebounds, the second after George Telfer hit a post during an onslaught.											
35	H	MANCHESTER U	11	D	2-2	0-0	Paddon 62, Robson 71	Hansbury	Bond	Davies	McGuire	Hoadley	Powell	Neighbour*	Reeves	Robson	Paddon	Peters	Symonds
7/4		20,077	8	34			McQueen 74, Macari 83	Bailey	Albiston	Houston	McIlroy	McQueen	Buchan	Coppell	Greenhoff J	Jordan	Macari	Thomas	
							Ref: B Daniels	Paddon shoots his first of the season. Gary Bailey can't hold Bond's shot and Robson pounces. Micky Thomas' free-kick is headed fiercely in by Gordon McQueen and another lead is surrendered as Lou Macari exploits Neighbour's blunder. This 20th draw is a new Division 1 record.											
36	A	QP RANGERS	10	D	0-0	0-0		Hansbury	Bond	Davies	McGuire*	Hoadley	Powell	Symonds	Reeves	Robson	Paddon	Peters	Fashanu
13/4		14,654	20	35				Richardson	Clement	Wallace*	Hollins	Howe	Roeder	McGee	Shanks	Walsh	Busby	Goddard	Allen
							Ref: T Glasson	A real bore draw for those who venture to Loftus Road on Good Friday. Hard-working John Hollins is man-of-the-match, but even he can't inspire a goal from his relegation-bound side. Bond says the only real winner was the pitch, which cut up badly and prevented flowing football.											
37	H	IPSWICH	12	L	0-1	0-0		Hansbury	Bond*	Davies	McGuire	Hoadley	Powell	Robson	Reeves	Symonds	Paddon	Peters	Fashanu
14/4		25,061	9	35			Thijssen 63	Sivell	Burley	Mills	Thijssen	Osman	Beattie*	Wark	Muhren	Mariner	Gates	Woods	Geddis
							Ref: M Sinclair	Lowestoft-born Laurie Sivell keeps City's best efforts out in his first game in 15 months. Dutchman Frans Thijssen wins a tight derby with his first goal in GB football. Although he hasn't played in months, David Jones is booked for dissent – the ref heard his abuse from the sidelines.											
38	A	WOLVERHAMPTON	14	L	0-1	0-1		Hansbury	Bond	Davies	McGuire	Hoadley	Powell	Lythgoe*	Reeves	Robson	Paddon	Peters	Fashanu
16/4		18,457	19	35			Hibbitt 29	Bradshaw	Palmer	Parkin	Daniel	McAlle	Berry	Hibbitt	Daley	Rafferty	Richards	Carr*	Patching
							Ref: D Clarke	City have a dreadful first half and it is no surprise when Kenny Hibbitt lashes the ball past Hansbury after a run and cross from Willie Carr. The visitors improve significantly after the interval and go close to an equaliser. The win is a real lifeline for John Barnwell's struggling outfit.											
39	H	ASTON VILLA	15	L	1-2	1-1	Fashanu 31	Hansbury	Bond	Davies	McGuire	Hoadley	Powell	Mendham	Reeves	Fashanu	Paddon	Peters	
21/4		15,061	10	35			Shelton 13, Cropley 74	Rimmer	Gidman	Gibson	Gregory	McNaught*	Mortimer	Shelton	Cowans	Deehan	Cropley	Swain	Linton
							Ref: R Toseland	City welcome back Peter Mendham after a pelvic injury. Gary Shelton tucks the ball in after a scramble. Fashanu levels from close range. Big Ken McNaught is carried off after a Fash clash. Ivor Linton speeds past Hoadley and finds Alex Cropley, who smashes in a fine winning goal.											
40	A	MANCHESTER U	15	L	0-1	0-0		Hansbury	Bond	Davies	McGuire	Hoadley	Powell	Neighbour	Reeves	Robson	Fashanu	Peters	
25/4		33,678	10	35			Macari 88	Bailey	Nicholl	Albiston	McIlroy	McQueen	Buchan*	Coppell	McCreery	Jordan	Macari	Thomas	Grimes
							Ref: M Scott	FA Cup finalists United look ordinary for much of the game. Peters hits a post, but Fashanu was offside anyway. Peters shoots a good chance wide. Lou Macari scrambles a late winner from Ashley Grimes' free-kick. This week work commences on Carrow Road's new-look River End.											
41	A	ARSENAL	14	D	1-1	0-0	Fashanu 72	Hansbury	Bond	Davies	McGuire	Hoadley	Powell	Neighbour	Reeves	Fashanu	Paddon	Peters	
28/4		28,885	6	36			Walford 58	Jennings	Devine	Nelson	Talbot	Gatting	Walford	Brady	Sunderland	Stapleton	Price	Rix	
							Ref: A Gunn	Stunning saves by Pat Jennings, plus the woodwork, save Terry Neill's men from going behind. Frank Stapleton beats Hansbury in the air and Steve Walford does the rest. City grab a deserved equaliser when Paddon's corner is powered in off the underside of the bar by Fashanu's head.											
42	H	NOTT'M FOR	15	D	1-1	1-0	Reeves 27	Hansbury	Bond	Davies	McGuire	Hoadley	Powell	Neighbour	Reeves	Fashanu	Paddon	Peters	
5/5		17,651	3	37			Woodcock 56	Shilton	Anderson	Clark	McGovern	Lloyd	Burns	Francis	Bowyer	Birtles	Woodcock	Robertson	
	Home	Away					Ref: C Downey	In a whirlwind first half, City look in positive mood and take the lead when Bond speeds past Larry Lloyd and crosses for Reeves to rise above Viv Anderson and head in. Tony Woodcock levels from a Trevor Francis cross. This 23rd draw of the season beats Tranmere's old FL record.											
Average	17,874	23,178																	

League Cup

No	Venue	Opponent	Pos	Res	F-A	H-T	Scorers, Times, and Referees	1	2	3	4	5	6	7	8	9	10	11	12 sub used
2	A	WREXHAM	11	W	3-1	2-1	Roberts 6(og), Ryan 13, 87	Keelan	Bond	Sullivan	Ryan	Hoadley	Powell	Neighbour	Reeves	Chivers	Robson	Peters	
29/8		12,428	2:3				*McNeill 38p*	*Davies*	*Hill*	*Dwyer**	*Davis*	*Roberts*	*Thomas*	*Shinton*	*Sutton*	*McNeill*	*Whittle*	*Cartwright*	*Williams*
							Ref: R Chadwick	A Reeves effort is deflected in by John Roberts to give City a great start. Ryan runs on to a long ball and shoots past Dai Davies. The ball hits Neighbour's arm and Dixie McNeill converts the penalty. A far more clear-cut penalty near the end sees Keelan save brilliantly from McNeill.											
3	A	CHESTER	8	W	2-0	0-0	Peters 51, Reeves 74	Keelan	Bond	Sullivan	Ryan	Hoadley	Powell	Neighbour	Reeves	Robb	Robson	Peters	
4/10		8,749	3:5					*Lloyd*	*Nickeas*	*Raynor*	*Storton*	*Jeffries*	*Oakes*	*Delgado**	*Livermore*	*Edwards*	*Mellor*	*Walker*	*Phillips*
							Ref: D Civil	Ciy have to withstand spells of intense pressure from Alan Oakes' outfit. Ex-Canary Ian Mellor dribbles past Keelan but then miskicks in front of a gaping net. Brian Lloyd fumbles a cross and Peters takes full advantage. Reeves makes the tie safe when he glances in a Peters free-kick.											
4	H	MANCHESTER C	13	L	1-3	1-0	Peters 30	Keelan	Bond	Davies	Ryan	Hoadley	Powell	Neighbour	Reeves	Symonds	Mendham	Peters	
8/11		19,423	6				*Barnes 55, Channon 80, 86*	*Corrigan*	*Clements*	*Donachie*	*Booth*	*Watson*	*Viljoen**	*Channon*	*Owen*	*Kidd*	*Hartford*	*Barnes*	*Futcher P*
							Ref: R Toseland	Peters celebrates his 35th birthday by shooting City ahead. Tony Book's men pull level when Peter Barnes, usually noted for his skills on the deck, heads a fine goal. Mick Channon makes up for a bad miss with two late goals against the run of play. Bond calls the result a real travesty.											

FA Cup

No	Venue	Opponent	Pos	Res	F-A	H-T	Scorers, Times, and Referees	1	2	3	4	5	6	7	8	9	10	11	12 sub used
3	A	LEICESTER	14	L	0-3	0-2		Keelan	Bond	Davies	Ryan	Hoadley	Powell	Neighbour	Reeves	Chivers	McGuire	Peters	
6/1		19,680	2:16				*May 15, Weller 24, Henderson 75*	*Wallington*	*Whitworth*	*Williams*	*Ridley*	*May*	*O'Neill*	*Weller*	*Peake*	*Henderson*	*Goodwin*	*Buchanan*	
							Ref: N Ashley	Clad in his trade-mark black tights, Keith Weller orchestrates an easy win for Jock Wallace's young side (six players under 21). Bond blames the result on a lack of effort and promptly transfer-lists Chivers, Ryan and Paddon. Letting Chivers live in London hasn't worked out, he fumes.											

		Home						Away					
		P	W	D	L	F	A	W	D	L	F	A	Pts
1	Liverpool	42	19	2	0	51	4	11	6	4	34	12	68
2	Nott'm For	42	11	10	0	34	10	10	8	3	27	16	60
3	West Brom	42	13	5	3	38	15	11	6	4	34	20	59
4	Everton	42	12	7	2	32	17	5	10	6	20	23	51
5	Leeds	42	11	4	6	41	25	7	10	4	29	27	50
6	Ipswich	42	11	4	6	34	21	9	5	7	29	28	49
7	Arsenal	42	11	8	2	37	18	6	6	9	24	30	48
8	Aston Villa	42	8	9	4	37	26	7	7	7	22	23	46
9	Manchester U	42	9	7	5	29	25	6	8	7	31	38	45
10	Coventry	42	11	7	3	41	29	3	9	9	17	39	44
11	Tottenham	42	7	8	6	19	25	6	7	8	29	36	41
12	Middlesbro	42	10	5	6	33	21	5	5	11	24	29	40
13	Bristol City	42	11	6	4	34	19	4	4	13	13	32	40
14	Southampton	42	9	10	2	35	20	3	6	12	12	33	40
15	Manchester C	42	9	5	7	34	28	4	8	9	24	28	39
16	NORWICH	42	7	10	4	29	19	0	13	8	22	38	37
17	Bolton	42	10	5	6	36	28	2	6	13	18	47	35
18	Wolves	42	10	4	7	26	26	3	4	14	18	42	34
19	Derby	42	8	5	8	25	25	2	6	13	19	46	31
20	QP Rangers	42	4	9	8	24	33	2	4	15	21	40	25
21	Birmingham	42	5	9	7	24	25	1	1	19	13	39	22
22	Chelsea	42	3	5	13	23	42	2	5	14	21	50	20
		924	209	144	109	716	501	109	144	209	501	716	924

Odds & ends

Double wins: (0).
Double losses: (1) Liverpool.

Won from behind: (0).
Lost from in front: (2) Bolton (a), Manchester C (h), (LC).

High spots: Steering clear of the drop zone, despite the lack of wins.
The emergence of powerful young striker Justin Fasha u.
Exciting goalscoring debuts by Martin Chivers and Davie Robb.

Low spots: Only seven wins from the 42 league games
Not a single away win (the only club of the 92 in this position).
The Anfield nightmare: Keeper Keelan injured and six conceded.
FA Cup defeat at Leicester: the transfer-listing of three senior players.
Another drop in attendances – now 25% down on four years earlier.
The mediocre form of big-name signing Chivers, after a promising start.

City drew 23 of their 42 League games – a new Football League record.
Seven draws in a row equalled the previous League record.

Player of the Year: Tony Powell.
Ever-presents: (2) Kevin Bond, Tony Powell.
Hat-tricks: (0).
Hat-tricks against: (0).
Leading scorer: (12) Martin Peters.

	Appearances						Goals			
	Lge	*Sub*	LC	*Sub*	FAC	*Sub*	**Lge**	LC	FAC	**Tot**
Baker, Clive	**2**									
Bennett, Dave		*1*								
Bond, Kevin	**42**		3		1		**2**			**2**
Chivers, Martin	**11**		1		1		**4**			**4**
Davies, Ian	**26**	*1*	1		1		**2**			**2**
Downs, Greg	**1**	*2*								
Evans, Doug	**4**						**1**			**1**
Fashanu, Justin	**13**	*3*					**5**			**5**
Forbes, Duncan	**3**	*1*								
Hansbury, Roger	**18**									
Hoadley., Phil	**39**		3		1					
Keelan, Kevin	**22**		3		1					
Lythgoe, Phil	**3**									
McGuire, Mick	**22**	*2*			1					
Mendham, Peter	**7**	*1*	1							
Neighbour, Jimmy	**33**	*1*	3		1		**2**			**2**
Paddon, Graham	**16**	*1*					**1**			**1**
Peters, Martin	**38**	*1*	3		1		**10**	2		**12**
Powell, Tony	**42**		3		1		**1**			**1**
Reeves, Kevin	**38**		3		1		**9**	1		**10**
Robb, Davie	**4**	*1*	1				**1**			**1**
Robson, Keith	**26**	*3*	2				**4**			**4**
Ryan, John	**25**		3		1		**9**	2		**11**
Sullivan, Colin	**10**		2							
Symonds, Richard	**17**	*2*	1							
(own-goals)								1		**1**
25 players used	**462**	*20*	**33**		**11**		**51**	**6**		**57**

No	Date		Att	Pos	Pt	F-A	H-T	Scorers, Times, and Referees	1	2	3	4	5	6	7	8	9	10	11	12 sub used
1	A	EVERTON			W	4-2	3-2	McGuire 10, Fashanu 36, 64, Peters 41	Keelan	Bond	**McDowell**	McGuire	Hoadley	Powell	Neighbour	Reeves	Fashanu*	Paddon	Peters	**Taylor**
	18/8		*26,539*		2			*Ross 13p, Nulty 40*	*Wood*	*Barton*	*Bailey*	*Lyons*	*Wright*	*Ross*	*Nulty*	*Todd*	*King*	*Kidd*	*Heard**	*Eastoe*
								Ref: C Seal	A thrilling start to the new season. McGuire calmly heads over stranded George Wood to spark a goal rush. It's not all smiles, though, as Bond gets protective when son Kevin tangles with Brian Kidd. All City goals are headers. After 41 winless away games, the celebrations are joyous.											
2	H	TOTTENHAM			W	**4-0**	0-0	Reeves 48, 59, Peters 51, Fashanu 88	Keelan	Bond	McDowell	McGuire	Hoadley	Nightingale	Neighbour	Reeves	Fashanu	Paddon	Peters	
	22/8		17,670		4				*Daines*	*Lee*	*Smith*	*Yorath*	*Lacy*	*Perryman*	*Falco*	*Ardiles*	*Jones*	*Hoddle*	*Villa*	
								Ref: B Martin	Spurs play neat football, but City move up a gear in the second period. After Reeves heads the opener, Peters tucks in a corner. Reeves turns and fires the clincher and Fashanu finishes the job, converting Peters' low cross. McDowell looks a useful signing at £90,000 from West Ham.											
3	H	LEEDS		1	W	2-1	2-1	Bond 16p, 37	Keelan	Bond	McDowell	McGuire	Hoadley	Powell	Neighbour	Reeves	Fashanu*	Paddon	Peters	Taylor
	25/8		18,444	*10*	6			*Hart 17*	*Harvey*	*Hird*	*Hampton**	*Flynn*	*Hart*	*Stevenson*	*Harris*	*Cherry*	*Hankin*	*Curtis*	*Graham*	*Parkinson*
								Ref: C Downes	Paul Hart handles and Bond tucks home the penalty. Within a minute, Hart makes amends by burying a bullet header from Arthur Graham's corner. Neighbour jinks past defenders and lays the ball off for Bond to rifle in from 30 yards. City are top of the League for the first time ever.											
4	A	COVENTRY		2	L	0-2	0-0		Keelan	Bond	McDowell*	McGuire	Hoadley	**Brown**	Neighbour	Reeves	Fashanu	Paddon	Peters	Ryan
	1/9		*18,181*	*10*	6			*McDonald 50, Ferguson 63*	*Murcott*	*Roberts*	*McDonald*	*Blair*	*Holton*	*Gillespie*	*Hutchison*	*English**	*Ferguson*	*Powell*	*Hunt*	*Hateley*
								Ref: D Reeves	Jim Blyth hurts his back warming up, so youth keeper Steve Murcott is called from the stands. He keeps a clean sheet in the only senior game of his career, to help end City's great start. The first half is uneventful but Gordon Milne's men spark into life after Bobby McDonald's opener.											
5	A	MIDDLESBROUGH		4	L	0-1	0-1		Keelan	Bond	Symonds	Nightingale*	Hoadley	Powell	Neighbour	Reeves	Fashanu	Paddon	Taylor	Ryan
	8/9		*19,575*	*3*	6			*Proctor 20*	*Platt*	*Craggs*	*Bailey*	*Johnston*	*Ashcroft*	*McAndrew*	*Hodgson*	*Proctor*	*Jankovic*	*Cummins*	*Armstrong*	
								Ref: T Mills	Yugolsav Bosco Jankovic is in lively form and he goes on a thrusting run to set up Mark Proctor, whose fierce shot beats Keelan. The sprinkler system suddenly comes on mid-match and gives spectators a soaking. Bond amuses everyone by going over and attempting to stem the flow!											
6	H	NOTTINGHAM F		3	W	3-1	2-0	Reeves 39, Fashanu 43, Robson 57	Keelan	Bond	Symonds	McDowell	Hoadley	Powell	Taylor	Reeves	Fashanu	Paddon	Robson	
	15/9		18,621	*2*	8			*Woodcock 83*	*Shilton*	*Anderson*	*Gray*	*McGovern*	*Lloyd*	*Burns*	*O'Neill*	*Bowyer*	*Birtles*	*Woodcock*	*Robertson*	
								Ref: D Richardson	Neighbour moves to West Ham for £135k, but City look sharp without him. European Cup holders Forest's 12-match unbeaten run is ended in emphatic fashion. Reeves and Fash beat Peter Shilton with towering headers. Robson glances in another before Tony Woodcock's consolation.											
7	A	LIVERPOOL		4	D	0-0	0-0		Keelan	Bond	McDowell	Taylor*	Hoadley	Powell	Robson	Reeves	Fashanu	Paddon	Peters	Symonds
	22/9		*44,120*	*7*	9				*Clemence*	*Neal*	*Kennedy A*	*Thompson*	*Fairclough*	*Irwin*	*Dalglish*	*Case*	*Johnson**	*McDermott*	*Souness*	*Heighway*
								Ref: P Willis	City pass another stern test with flying colours. Hoadley does a fine marking job on Kenny Dalglish. As expected, it's one-way traffic towards Keelan, but City work hard to keep a clean sheet. After a challenge involving Graeme Souness, Taylor falls awkwardly and is stretchered off.											
8	H	BOLTON		5	W	2-1	0-0	Fashanu 47, Peters 58	Keelan	Bond	Ryan	Bennett	Hoadley	Powell	Robson	Reeves	Fashanu	Paddon	Peters	
	29/9		16,500	*18*	11			*Whatmore 59*	*McDonagh*	*Clement*	*Burke*	*Greaves*	*Allardyce*	*Walsh*	*Morgan*	*Whatmore*	*Gowling*	*Cantello*	*Worthington*	
								Ref: R Lewis	Fashanu bravely beats Sam Allardyce in a near-post challenge to head past Jim McDonagh. Paddon's corner is flicked on by Reeves for Peters to knock in the second. A minute later Neil Whatmore raises the hopes of Ian Greaves' outfit by getting in ahead of Powell to pull a goal back.											
9	H	STOKE		4	D	2-2	0-1	Bond 58p, Reeves 76	Keelan	Bond	McDowell	Bennett	Hoadley	Powell	Robson*	Reeves	Fashanu	Paddon	Peters	McGuire
	6/10		17,060	*21*	12			*Irvine 13, Richardson 73p*	*Jones*	*Evans*	*Scott*	*Irvine*	*Smith*	*Dodd*	*Johnson PA*	*Heath*	*O'Callaghan*	*Crooks*	*Richardson*	
								Ref: C Maskell	Sammy Irvine fires home a loose ball from 15 yards to boost Alan Durban's struggling outfit. Two reckless tackles yield successful penalties and bookings for the offenders. Paul Richardson's spot-kick leaves Norwich trailing but Reeves nets a handsome diving header to save a point.											
10	A	TOTTENHAM		5	L	2-3	2-2	Peters 7, Reeves 20	Keelan	Bond	McDowell	McGuire	Hoadley	Powell	Robson	Reeves	Fashanu	Bennett	Peters	
	10/10		*26,488*	*14*	12			*Hoddle 1, 77, Villa 34*	*Daines*	*Hughton*	*McAllister*	*Yorath**	*Miller*	*Perryman*	*Ardiles*	*Armstrong*	*Jones*	*Hoddle*	*Villa*	*Pratt*
								Ref: L Shapter	After 20 seconds Terry Yorath feeds Glenn Hoddle, who shoots high into the net. Peters levels from a Bond free-kick. Reeves puts City ahead with a fine header from McDowell's cross. Ricky Villa beats Bennett twice in a solo run and fires an equaliser. Hoddle glances in the winner.											

11	A	WOLVERHAMPTON	7	L	0-1	0-1		Keelan	Bond	McDowell	Symonds	Hoadley	Powell	Taylor	McGuire	Fashanu	Bennett	Peters	
13/10		28,060	3	12			Carr 9	Bradshaw	Palmer	Parkin	Daniel	Berry	Hughes	Hibbitt	Carr	Gray	Richards	Thomas	
							Ref: D Richardson	One again City fail to come up with the goods in front of BBC's Match of the Day cameras. Willie Carr knocks in a scrappy goal after a Kenny Hibbitt corner. City recruit Justin Fashanu's younger brother John. Billy Steele is advised to retire following the knee injury of 30 months ago.											
12	H	MANCHESTER C	6	D	2-2	0-1	Peters 50, Bond 64p	Keelan	Bond	McDowell	Taylor	Hoadley	Powell	**Goble**	Reeves	Fashanu*	Paddon	Peters	McGuire
20/10		18,000	9	13			Bennett 20, 80	Corrigan	Ranson	Power	Reid	Caton	Futcher	McKenzie*	Viljoen	Robinson	Bennett	Deyna	Stepanovic
							Ref: T Bune	Dave Bennett hooks in after Keelan parries a shot. Peters is on hand to level at the far post and Bond converts a penalty after Fashanu is pushed by Ray Ranson. Malcolm Allison's side level with a fluke when Bennett's intended cross sails straight in. Their point was deserved, however.											
13	A	BRIGHTON	4	W	4-2	1-1	Goble 9, Paddon 49, Taylor 67,	Keelan	Bond	Downs	Taylor	Brown	Powell	Goble	Reeves	Fashanu	Paddon	Peters	
27/10		23,180	22	15			Foster 19, Ryan 46 [Reeves 80]	Moseley	Rollings !	Williams	Horton	Foster	Stevens	Ryan	Ward	Chivers*	Sayer	O'Sullivan	Clark
							Ref: B Daniels	In his second game, young Goble coolly shoots over Graham Moseley. Steve Foster's equaliser is his first Albion goal. Gerry Ryan's volley is quickly cancelled out by Paddon from close range and City move up a gear. Ex-Canary Andy Rollings is sent off for a left-hook on Fashanu.											
14	H	EVERTON	5	D	0-0	0-0		Keelan	Bond	Downs	McGuire	Brown	Powell	Goble	Evans*	Fashanu	Paddon	Peters	Nightingale
3/11		18,349	18	16				Wood	Gidman	Bailey	Lyons	Higgins	Ross	Nulty	Wright	Latchford	Kidd	King	
							Ref: K Salmon	City are without Hoadley, suspended for reaching the 20-points mark, and are also missing the energetic front-running of the absent Taylor and Reeves. Evans sends both Fashanu and Peters clear with through passes but both fail to hit the target. Gordon Lee's side hang on determinedly.											
15	A	WEST BROM	7	L	1-2	1-1	Peters 5	Keelan	Bond	Downs	Ryan	Brown	Powell	McGuire	Reeves	Fashanu*	Paddon	Peters	Jones
10/11		19,341	11	16			Wile 27, Robson 70	Godden	Trewick	Pendrey	Mills	Wile	Robertson	Robson	Brown A	Deehan	Owen	Barnes	
							Ref: B Stevens	Keelan punches straight to John Wile, who heads home. Bryan Robson combines with John Deehan and nets a stunning winner. Albion enjoy revenge for the cup defeat of three days ago. Bond hits out at Tommy Docherty, who this week said football management involves dishonesty.											
16	H	SOUTHAMPTON	6	W	2-1	0-1	Fashanu 79, McGuire 88	Keelan	Bond	Downs	McGuire	Brown	Powell	Goble	Reeves	Fashanu	Paddon	Peters	
17/11		18,215	13	18			Andruszewski 26	Wells	Golac	Holmes	Williams S	Watson	Waldron	Ball	Boyer	Channon	Andrusz'ski	Hebberd	
							Ref: G Napthine	Manny Andruszewski produces a clinical finish from a Nick Holmes pass. Late drama as Fashanu nets a real 'route one' goal and then paves the way for McGuire to shoot a winner. Reeves makes his full England debut against Bulgaria, replacing Kevin Keegan in Ron Greenwood's side.											
17	A	MANCHESTER U	8	L	**0-5**	0-3	[Jordan 54, 77]	Keelan	Bond	Downs	Taylor	Brown	Powell	McGuire	Reeves	Fashanu*	Paddon	Peters	**Barham**
24/11		**46,540**	1	18			Macari 17, Moran 22, Coppell 43,	Bailey	Nicholl	Grimes	McIlroy	Moran	Buchan	Coppell	Wilkins	Jordan	Macari	Thomas	
							Ref: K Redfern	Dave Sexton's side return to the top of the league with a powerful display. City's heads drop after Kevin Moran powers home the second goal with his head. Steve Coppell's strike is a superb solo effort. Joe Jordan completes the demolition job despite the attentions of three defenders.											
18	H	ASTON VILLA	8	D	1-1	0-1	Bond 88p	Keelan	Bond	Downs	Mendham	Brown	Powell	Robson	Reeves	Fashanu !	Paddon	Peters	
1/12		15,885	9	19			Evans 22	Rimmer	Swain	Pejic	Evans	McNaught	Mortimer !	Bremner	Little	Geddis	Cowans	Shaw	
							Ref: A Cox	Allan Evans' header is scrambled away but ruled to have crossed the line. Fashanu is dismissed for pole-axing Evans. Angry fans hurl coins and both managers appeal for calm. A linesman spots an infringement and Bond levels from the spot. Denis Mortimer is sent off for arguing.											
19	A	DERBY	8	D	0-0	0-0		Keelan	Ryan	Downs	Mendham	Brown	Jones	Robson	Reeves*	Fashanu	Paddon	Peters	McGuire
8/12		15,381	20	20				McKellar	Langan	Buckley	Daly	Webb	Osgood	Emery	Powell B	Duncan	Davies	Rioch	
							Ref: P Tyldesley	City grind out their fourth draw in a row at Derby. Reeves exits with a pulled hamstring. Jones gets through his first full game since injury 18 months ago. Not so lucky is Steele, whose knee trouble has forced him to quit and his testimonial this week sees an England X1 beat City 5-0.											
20	H	BRISTOL CITY	5	W	2-0	1-0	Taylor 25, Robson 46	Keelan	Bond	Downs	Ryan	Brown	Jones	Mendham*	Taylor	Robson	Paddon	Peters	Lythgoe
15/12		**12,473**	19	22				Shaw	Sweeney	Whitehead	Gow	Rodgers*	Merrick	Fitzpatrick	Tainton	Royle	Ritchie	Garland	Cormack
							Ref: G Flint	City are without Fashanu and Reeves, but both replacements score. Taylor drives the first past John Shaw with help from Robson. After the break, newly arrived sub Peter Cormack tries to play his way out of trouble, but is robbed by Robson, who shoots past the advancing Shaw.											
21	A	ARSENAL	6	D	1-1	0-0	Bond 68	Keelan	Bond	Downs	Ryan	Brown	Jones	Mendham	Taylor	Robson	Paddon	Peters	
21/12		18,869	3	23			Stapleton 53	Jennings	Devine	Nelson*	Talbot	O'Leary	Walford	Brady	Sunderland	Stapleton	Hollins	Rix	McDermott
							Ref: J Martin	On a snow-covered pitch, Alan Sunderland's shot is half-cleared and Frank Stapleton swoops to nod in. Steve Walford misjudges Peters' astute pass and Bond strides in to crash the ball home. City stage a rousing finale against Terry Neill's highly placed side, but have to share the spoils.											

LEAGUE DIVISION 1 — Manager: John Bond — SEASON 1979-80

No	Date	Opponent	Att	Pos	Pt	F-A	H-T	Scorers, Times, and Referees	1	2	3	4	5	6	7	8	9	10	11	12 sub used
22	H	IPSWICH		5	D	3-3	2-1	Mendham 23, Taylor 43, Robson 89	Keelan	Bond	Downs	Ryan	Brown*	Jones	Mendham	Taylor	Robson	Paddon	Peters	Fashanu
	26/12		24,335	*14*	24			*Gates 15, Muhren 54, Wark 71*	*Cooper*	*Burley*	*Butcher*	*Thijssen*	*Hunter*	*Osman*	*Wark*	*Muhren*	*Mills*	*Brazil*	*Gates*	
								Ref: D Hutchinson	Magnificent Boxing Day entertainment in front of a newly opened River End Stand. The lead swaps hands a couple of times in a breathtaking contest. John Wark thinks he's won it, until Robson deflects the ball home in the dying moments and sends most of Carrow Road into a frenzy.											
23	A	LEEDS		7	D	2-2	1-2	Mendham 12, Taylor 74	Keelan	Bond	Downs	Mendham*	Brown	Jones	Ryan	Taylor	Fashanu	Paddon	Peters	Nightingale
	29/12		*23,493*	*11*	25			*Hird 22, Hankin 45*	*Lukic*	*Cherry*	*Stevenson*	*Hamson*	*Hart*	*Madeley*	*Gray*	*Hird*	*Hankin*	*Connor*	*Harris*	
								Ref: J Sewell	Taylor's low cross eludes John Lukic, presenting Mendham with an easy second career goal in three days. Kevin Hird nets a thundering drive from 20 yards. Ray Hankin's mis-hit shot flies off Keelan's knee into goal. Taylor has two attempts parried by Lukic but his third effort goes in.											
24	A	CRYSTAL PALACE		5	D	0-0	0-0		Keelan	Bond	Downs	Ryan	Brown	Powell	Taylor*	Mendham	Fashanu	Paddon	Peters	Nightingale
	1/1		*30,254*	*11*	26				*Burridge*	*Hinshelwood*	*Fenwick*	*Nicholas*	*Cannon*	*Gilbert*	*Murphy**	*Francis*	*Flanagan*	*Walsh*	*Hilaire*	*Kember*
								Ref: D Reeves	Bond urges the game be called off after seeing the icy state of the pitch, but Mr Reeves disagrees. Taylor collides with Jim Cannon shortly after the interval and is carried off with a serious knee injury. Both sets of defenders do well to keep clean sheets in the tricky conditions.											
25	H	COVENTRY		4	W	1-0	1-0	Robson 45	Keelan	Bond	Downs	Ryan	Brown	Powell	Mendham	Reeves	Robson*	Paddon	Peters	Fashanu
	12/1		16,467	*13*	28				*Blyth*	*Coop*	*McDonald*	*Gooding*	*Dyson*	*Gillespie*	*Nardiello**	*English*	*Hateley*	*Blair*	*Hutchison*	*Whitton*
								Ref: D Vickers	Gordon Milne fields seven Sky Blues under the age of 21, but they pay for missed opportunities, particularly via Mark Hateley. The recalled Robson whips home an angled shot on the stroke of half-time to take City to fourth. Robson is later injured and will be out for several weeks.											
26	H	LIVERPOOL		10	L	3-5	2-2	Peters 2, Reeves 33, Fashanu 81	Keelan	Bond	Downs	Ryan	Brown	Jones	Mendham*	Reeves	Fashanu	Paddon	Peters	McGuire
	9/2		**25,624**	*1*	28			*Faircl' 4, 18, 75, Dalglish 88, Case 89*	*Clemence*	*Neal*	*Kennedy A*	*Thompson*	*Kennedy R*	*Hansen*	*Dalglish*	*Case*	*Fairclough*	*McDermott*	*Lee*	
								Ref: M Scott	Peters gets the ball rolling with his first in three months, but City are stunned by a smart David Fairclough hat-trick. Fashanu juggles, turns and smashes in an amazing swerving shot. The last of Keelan's 673 senior games ends in misery as the Reds strike twice to win a remarkable game.											
27	H	WOLVERHAMPTON		13	L	0-4	0-2		Hansbury	Bond	Downs	Mendham	Brown	Jones	Goble	Reeves	Fashanu	Paddon	Peters	
	23/2		17,063	*10*	28			*Hibbitt 15p, 48p, Eves 40, Richards 46*	*Bradshaw*	*Palmer*	*Parkin*	*Daniel*	*Berry*	*Hughes*	*Hibbitt*	*Carr*	*Gray*	*Richards*	*Eves*	
								Ref: P Reeves	After the Liverpool classic, City put in their worst home performance for a long time. The defence looks all at sea against moderate opposition. Brown chops down John Richards and Jones fouls Peter Daniel for the crucial spot-kicks. Mel Eves and Richards chip in with simple goals.											
28	H	MIDDLESBROUGH		12	D	0-0	0-0		Hansbury	Bond	Symonds	Mendham	Jones	McDowell	Halsey	Reeves	Fashanu*	Paddon	Peters	McGuire
	27/2		14,631	*9*	29				*Platt*	*Craggs*	*Johnson*	*Hedley*	*Ashcroft*	*McAndrew*	*Cochrane*	*Nattrass*	*Hodgson*	*Burns*	*Armstrong*	
								Ref: J Hunting	Inevitably, Bond makes changes in defence. Halsey also gets another chance, two years after his debut-day sending off. Jones is looking good again after his long injury absence. After a defensive mix-up, Fashanu gets the game's clearest opportunity, but Jim Platt saves with his legs.											
29	A	MANCHESTER C		12	D	0-0	0-0		Hansbury	Bond	Symonds	Mendham	Jones	McDowell	Halsey	Reeves	Taylor*	Paddon	Peters	Fashanu
	1/3		*32,248*	*16*	30				*Corrigan*	*Ranson*	*Daley*	*Reid*	*Caton*	*Booth**	*Henry*	*Robinson*	*Bennett*	*Power*	*Tueart*	*Deyna*
								Ref: M Robinson	Hansbury's second successive clean sheet is timely as Keelan now seems certain to be leaving. City have a long injury-list and Taylor plays despite being less than fully fit. The home club gets the chance to take a close look at Reeves, for whom they have already had bids rejected.											
30	H	BRIGHTON		12	D	2-2	0-2	Reeves 46, Taylor 54	Hansbury	Bond	Symonds	Mendham	Jones	McDowell	McGuire	Reeves	Taylor	Paddon	Peters	
	8/3		15,640	*16*	31			*Horton 12, Lawrenson 22*	*Moseley*	*Gregory*	*Williams*	*Horton*	*Foster*	*Suddaby*	*McNab*	*Ward*	*Clarke*	*Lawrenson*	*O'Sullivan**	*Stevens*
								Ref: R Toseland	Reeves, all set to join Man City for £1m, is cheered every time he touches the ball. Brian Horton cracks in a low drive and before City recover, Mark Lawrenson strides through to clip a second. Reeves heads a 'farewell' goal and then Taylor equalises after a fumble by Graham Moseley.											
31	A	BOLTON		12	L	0-1	0-0		Hansbury	Bond	Symonds	McGuire	Jones	Powell	Mendham	Taylor	Robson	Paddon*	Peters	McDowell
	11/3		***10,442***	*22*	31			*Whatmore 87*	*McDonagh*	*Clement*	*Nicholson*	*Cantello*	*Jones*	*Walsh*	*Nowak*	*Whatmore*	*Thompson*	*Wilson*	*Reid*	
								Ref: P Partridge	Sub McDowell comes on and is immediately clattered by Dave Clement. Not wearing pads, he sustains a dreadful 9-inch gash that will need 40 stitches. Bond dashes on but the ref advises him not to look. Lowly Bolton get reward for their pressure when Peter Reid sets up Neil Wharton.											

No	Date	Opponent	Att	Pos	Pts	Res	F-A	H-T	Scorers, Times, and Referees	1	2	3	4	5	6	7	8	9	10	11	12
32	A	STOKE		13		L	1-2	0-2	Bond 51p	Hansbury	Nightingale	Bond	McGuire*	Jones	Powell	**Woods**	Taylor	Robson	Paddon	Peters	Mendham
	15/3		*14,123*	*16*	31				*Heath 22, Bond 35(og)*	*Fox*	*Evans*	*Doyle*	*Heath*	*Smith*	*Dodd*	*Johnson P*	*Richardson*	*Chapman*	*Crooks*	*Cook*	
									Ref: A Porter	Woods, 32, locally born and a lifelong supporter is recruited from Ipswich for £120k. Lively Adrian Heath nets a close-range goal just before Paul Richardson misses from the spot. Heath pressurises Bond into stabbing past Hansbury. Mike Doyle impedes Robson for a Bond penalty.											
33	H	WEST BROM		13		D	1-1	0-1	Bond 64p	Hansbury	Bond	Nightingale	Taylor	Jones	Powell*	Woods	Reeves	Robson	Paddon	Peters	Mendham
	22/3		14,811	*12*	32				*Bond 45(og)*	*Godden*	*Batson*	*Cowdrill*	*Moses*	*Wile*	*Robertson*	*Robson*	*Brown A*	*Deehan*	*Owen*	*Barnes*	
									Ref: D Letts	Bond scores for both sides for the second game running – a Football League first? He prods Peter Barnes' cross into his own net when dashing back to cover. Taylor crosses and Brendan Batson pushes Fashanu, to hand City their penalty. Barry Cowdrill debuts for Ron Atkinson's outfit.											
34	A	ASTON VILLA		14		L	0-2	0-0		Hansbury	Bond	Downs	Nightingale*	Jones	Hoadley	Woods	Fashanu	Taylor	Robson	Peters	Paddon
	26/3		*17,956*	*6*	32				*Cowans 73p, Hopkins 90*	*Rimmer*	*Linton**	*Gibson*	*Ormsby*	*McNaught*	*Heard*	*Bremner*	*Swain*	*Evans*	*Cowans*	*Morley*	*Hopkins*
									Ref: K Walmsley	Fashanu goes agonisingly close to breaking the deadlock, striking the crossbar with a header. Seven minutes later Hoadley holds back Kenny Swain for Gordon Cowans to score from the spot. Robert Hopkins, 17, comes on for his debut and nets at the far post with his very first touch.											
35	A	SOUTHAMPTON		15		L	0-2	0-0		Hansbury	Bond	Downs	McGuire	Mendham	Jones	Woods	Taylor	Robson	Paddon	Peters	
	29/3		*18,921*	*5*	32				*Nicholl 72, Baker 82*	*Katalinic*	*Golac*	*Andrusz'ski*	*Baker*	*Watson*	*Nicholl*	*Williams S*	*Boyer*	*Channon*	*Holmes*	*George*	
									Ref: K Baker	Mick Channon is left unattended at a corner and picks out Chris Nicholl, who powers home a header. Bond is booked for fouling ex-Canary Phil Boyer. Charlie George's firm drive is blocked by Hansbury, but Graham Baker is on hand to net. City's plunge down the table continues.											
36	H	ARSENAL		13		W	2-1	1-1	Jones 32, Fashanu 66	Hansbury	Bond	Symonds	McDowell*	Hoadley	Jones	Woods	Fashanu	Robson	Paddon	Peters	Downs
	2/4		16,923	*4*	34				*Rix 9*	*Jennings*	*Devine*	*Nelson**	*Talbot*	*O'Leary*	*Young*	*Brady*	*Sunderland*	*Stapleton*	*Price*	*Rix*	*Vaessen*
									Ref: J Sewell	Symonds misses a great chance but Graham Rix demonstrates exactly how it should be done. Jones crashes home an equaliser after a corner. Brian Talbot is brought down by Hansbury, who then brilliantly saves Liam Brady's penalty. Good work by Paddon sets up Fashanu's winner.											
37	A	IPSWICH		15		L	2-4	0-1	Bond 82, Robson 90	Hansbury	Bond	Symonds	McDowell	Hoadley	Jones	Woods	Taylor	Robson	Paddon	Peters	
	5/4		*28,968*	*3*	34				*Wark 21, 71p, 90p, Mariner 85*	*Cooper*	*Burley*	*Mills*	*Thijssen*	*Hunter*	*Osman*	*Wark*	*Muhren*	*Mariner*	*Brazil*	*Gates**	*McCall*
									Ref: R Lewis	City have sunk down the table and Town gone the other way since the classic on Boxing Day. This contest is disjointed until springing to life with five goals in the last 20 minutes. John Wark slips decisive penalties either side of Hansbury. Woods feels odd lining up against old mates.											
38	H	CRYSTAL PALACE		13		W	2-1	1-1	Fashanu 28, 57	Hansbury	Bond	Symonds	Mendham	McDowell	Jones	Woods	Fashanu	Robson*	Paddon	Peters	Taylor
	7/4		17,562	*11*	36				*Francis 10*	*Burridge*	*Hinshelwood*	*Sansom*	*Nicholas*	*Cannon*	*Gilbert*	*Murphy**	*Francis*	*Smillie*	*Flanagan*	*Hilaire*	*Fenwick*
									Ref: B Hill	A superb volley by Gerry Francis gains the lead, but Fashanu nets a simple response. With Taylor warming up to come on, Fashanu gains a reprieve by netting from close range. It is announced that Norwich will take part in a 'no offsides' experiment in next season's Willhire Cup.											
39	H	MANCHESTER U		15		L	0-2	0-0		Hansbury	Symonds	McDowell	Mendham	Nightingale*	Jones	Woods	Fashanu	Robson	Paddon	Peters	Taylor
	19/4		24,697	*2*	36				*Jordan 58, 90*	*Bailey*	*Nicholl*	*Albiston*	*McIlroy*	*Moran*	*Buchan*	*Coppell*	*Wilkins*	*Jordan*	*Ritchie*	*Thomas*	
									Ref: C Downey	The clash with Dave Sexton's all-star side is a big disappointment. Fashanu heads City's best opportunity wide of the target. Andy Ritchie's ferocious shot is parried by Hansbury and Joe Jordan nets from 10 yards. Arthur Albiston's cross in the dying seconds is touched in by Jordan.											
40	A	BRISTOL CITY		15		W	3-2	1-0	Robson 25, 74, Peters 46	Hansbury	Bond	Symonds	Barham	McDowell	Jones	Woods	Fashanu	Robson	Paddon	Peters	
	26/4		*16,123*	*21*	38				*Rodgers 65, Ritchie 88*	*Cashley*	*Sweeney*	*Whitehead*	*Gow*	*Rodgers*	*Merrick**	*Fitzpatrick*	*Ritchie*	*Royle*	*Mann*	*Pritchard*	*Tainton*
									Ref: A Seville	Fashanu butts David Rodgers in the face, reducing Bristol to ten men. Fashanu goes unpunished but later apologises. Norwich says he will be disciplined. John Ritchie missed a penalty after 25 seconds, but makes amends with a late tap-in winner. The Robins are doomed to relegation.											
41	A	NOTT'M FOR		16		L	0-2	0-1		Hansbury	Bond	McDowell	Barham	Jones	Symonds	Woods*	**Shepherd**	Robson	Paddon	Peters	Mendham
	30/4		*21,242*	*5*	38				*Bond 5 (og), Francis 55*	*Shilton*	*Anderson*	*Gray*	*McGovern*	*Lloyd*	*Burns*	*Mills*	*Bowles*	*Birtles*	*Francis*	*Robertson*	
									Ref: J Hough	Fashanu, fined and dropped for the Bristol incident, is replaced by energetic Scottish debutant Shepherd. Kevin Bond deflects Frank Gray's low drive past Hansbury. Brian Clough's men clinch the victory when Trevor Francis seizes on Gray's pass and provides a lesson in slick finishing.											
42	H	DERBY		12		W	4-2	1-0	R'son 29, Fash' 56, Pad' 60, Woods 64	Hansbury	Bond	Symonds	Barham	Jones	McDowell	Woods	Fashanu	Robson	Paddon	Peters	
	3/5		16,194	*21*	40				*McCaffery 59, Swindlehurst 70*	*Cherry*	*Langan*	*Buckley*	*Daly*	*McFarland**	*McCaffery*	*Powell S*	*Powell B*	*Biley*	*Swindlehurst*	*Wilson*	*Richards*
		Home	Away						Ref: B Daniels	The game springs to life with five goals in 14 minutes. Fashanu returns and celebrates with a far-post goal. Paddon rifles in after a razor-sharp move. Woods' first Norwich goal rounds off the season. Already-doomed Derby win a big ovation from their fans after this entertaining game.											
Average		17,225	23,984																		

League Cup			Att			F-A	H-T	Scorers, Times, and Referees	1	2	3	4	5	6	7	8	9	10	11	12 sub used
2:1	A	GILLINGHAM		1	D	1-1	0-1	Taylor 69	Keelan	Bond	McDowell	McGuire	Hoadley	Nightingale	Neighbour	Reeves	Taylor	Paddon	Peters	
		28/8	*10,594*	*3:23*				*Overton 42*	*Hillyard*	*Sharpe*	*Barker*	*Overton*	*Weatherly*	*Crabbe*	*NIcholl*	*Bruce*	*Price*	*Funnell*	*Richardson*	
								Ref: T Glasson	Steve Bruce heads on a corner for Gills skipper John Overton to net and set up a potential giant-killing. Gerry Summers' men are well on top, but City escape when McDowell's pass is deflected for Taylor to net his first City goal. It comes just in time to save him from being taken off!											
2:2	H	GILLINGHAM		2	W	4-2	1-2	Taylor 28, Paddon 55, 88, Reeves 78	Keelan	Bond	Symonds	McGuire	Hoadley	Nightingale	Ryan	Reeves	Fashanu	Paddon	Taylor	
		5/9	10,406	*3:15*				*Bruce 26, 35*	*Hillyard*	*Sharpe*	*Barker**	*Overton*	*Weatherly*	*Crabbe*	*NIcholl*	*Bruce*	*Price*	*Funnell*	*Richardson*	*Westwood*
								Ref: A Seville (Norwich win 5-3 on aggregate)	Two pieces of slipshod defending allow Steve Bruce to give the Kent side the lead twice in the first half. Stand-in skipper Paddon fires in the second equaliser. Reeves, the subject of a recent £1m bid from Manchester C, grabs the lead with a cool finish. Paddon swerves in the fourth.											
3	H	MANCHESTER U		4	W	4-1	2-1	Nicholl 24(og), Hoadley 27, Bennett 56, [Fashanu 76]	Keelan	Bond	McDowell*	Bennett	Hoadley	Powell	Robson	Reeves	Fashanu	Paddon	Taylor	Ryan
		26/9	18,312	*3*				*Wilkins 22*	*Bailey*	*Nicholl*	*Albiston*	*McIlroy**	*McQueen*	*Buchan*	*Grimes*	*Wilkins*	*Coppell*	*Macari*	*Thomas*	*Ritchie*
								Ref: R Toseland	Ray Wilkins snaps his first goal since leaving Chelsea, but Jimmy Nicholl's ugly slice cancels it out after a Peters effort came back off a post. The referee diverts the ball to Robson, who sets up a goal for Hoadley. Skilful Bennett's career-first goal precedes Fashanu's clinching header.											
4	A	WEST BROM		4	D	0-0	0-0		Keelan	Bond	Downs	Taylor*	Brown	Powell	Goble	Reeves	Fashanu	Paddon	Peters	Jones
		31/10	*24,062*	*9*					*Godden*	*Batson*	*Statham*	*Mills*	*Wile*	*Robertson*	*Robson*	*Brown A*	*Regis*	*Owen*	*Brown T*	
								Ref: P Reeves	Keelan puts in a tremendous display on his 663rd appearance, which breaks Ron Ashman's club record. The rugged Brown is another star in defence. Jones' enjoys his first game back in 18 months after his knee injury. Ron Atkinson's side have conceded just one goal in five games.											
4R	H	WEST BROM		5	W	3-0	2-0	Reeves 19, 75, McGuire 28	Keelan	Ryan	Downs	McGuire	Brown	Powell	Goble	Reeves	Fashanu	Paddon	Peters	
		7/11	19,676	*12*					*Godden*	*Trewick*	*Statham*	*Mills*	*Wile*	*Robertson*	*Robson*	*Brown A*	*Regis*	*Owen**	*Brown T*	*Barnes*
								Ref: M Taylor	Kevin Bond cries off ill and Reeves is an injury doubt till the last minute. Reeves shakes off his problem and strikes early when his header is deflected in. McGuire slides a shot past Tony Godden. The tie is beyond Albion when Reeves' applies a stylish finish 15 minutes from time.											
5	H	LIVERPOOL		8	L	1-3	1-3	Reeves 42	Keelan	Bond	Downs	Mendham	Hoadley	Powell	McGuire*	Reeves	Robson	Paddon	Peters	Taylor
		5/12	23,278	*2*				*Johnson 10, 30, Dalglish 35*	*Clemence*	*Neal*	*Kennedy A*	*Thompson*	*Kennedy R*	*Hansen*	*Dalglish*	*Case*	*Johnson*	*McDermott*	*Souness*	
								Ref: C White	City start brightly but are caught cold at the back as Hoadley is robbed and David Johnson finds the net. Peters goes close to levelling. Johnson drills a fine shot around Keelan. Kenny Dalglish piles on the agony, jinking into the box and netting a cracker. Reeves converts a Bonds cross.											

FA Cup																				
3	A	YEOVIL		5	W	3-0	1-0	Paddon 22, Robson 86, Fashanu 87	Keelan	Bond	Downs	Ryan	Brown	Powell	Mendham	Paddon	Fashanu	Robson	Peters	
		5/1	*8,523*	*NL*					*Parker*	*Battams*	*Payne*	*Harmison*	*Broom*	*Gold**	*Morrall*	*Jones*	*Green*	*Scott*	*Finnigan*	*Williams*
								Ref: R Challis	Up against The Huish's notorious slope, Paddon shows a clinical finish to settle City nerves. The setback only spurs the non-leaguers on and their hopes stay alive until near the end. Robson heads the second and a minute later Fashanu beats Parker in a race for the ball to nick another.											
4	A	WOLVERHAMPTON		7	D	1-1	1-0	Bond 39	Keelan	Bond	Downs	Ryan	Brown	Powell	Mendham	Reeves	Fashanu*	Paddon	Peters	**Shepherd**
		26/1	*25,516*	*14*				*Gray 62*	*Bradshaw*	*Palmer*	*Parkin*	*Daniel*	*Hughes*	*Berry*	*Hibbitt*	*Carr*	*Gray*	*Richards*	*Thomas*	
								Ref: D Richardson	Bond swoops on George Berry's lazy square pass and chips a clever goal over the head of Paul Bradshaw. John Richards nods on an Emlyn Hughes free-kick and Andy Gray rams the ball high into the net. The limping figure of Keelan makes fine saves. The injury list is lengthening.											
4R	H	WOLVERHAMPTON		7	L	2-3	1-3	Bond 20, Mendham 53	Keelan	Bond	Downs	Ryan	Brown	Powell	Mendham	Reeves	Fashanu	Paddon	Peters	
		30/1	23,101	*14*				*Eves 6, Richards 23, Berry 45*	*Bradshaw*	*Palmer*	*Parkin*	*Daniel*	*Hughes*	*Berry*	*Hibbitt*	*Carr*	*Gray*	*Richards*	*Eves*	
								Ref: D Richardson	Defensive disasters give City a mountain to climb. Mel Eves finishes nicely after a Bond and Mendham's mix-up. Bond's header equalises, but John Richards nets after Keelan flaps at a lob. Brown's poor header leads to Wolves' third goal. Mendham is on hand after Paddon hits a post.											

		Home					Away					
	P	W	D	L	F	A	W	D	L	F	A	Pts
1 Liverpool	42	15	6	0	46	8	10	4	7	35	22	60
2 Manchester U	42	17	3	1	43	8	7	7	7	22	27	58
3 Ipswich	42	14	4	3	43	13	8	5	8	25	26	53
4 Arsenal	42	8	10	3	24	12	10	6	5	28	24	52
5 Nott'm For	42	16	4	1	44	11	4	4	13	19	32	48
6 Wolves	42	9	6	6	29	20	10	3	8	29	27	47
7 Aston Villa	42	11	5	5	29	22	5	9	7	22	28	46
8 Southampton	42	14	2	5	53	24	4	7	10	12	29	45
9 Middlesbro	42	11	7	3	31	14	5	5	11	19	30	44
10 West Brom	42	9	8	4	37	23	2	11	8	17	27	41
11 Leeds	42	10	7	4	30	17	3	7	11	16	33	40
12 NORWICH	42	10	8	3	38	30	3	6	12	20	36	40
13 Crys Palace	42	9	9	3	26	13	3	7	11	15	37	40
14 Tottenham	42	11	5	5	30	22	4	5	12	22	40	40
15 Coventry	42	12	2	7	34	24	4	5	12	22	42	39
16 Brighton	42	8	8	5	25	20	3	7	11	22	37	37
17 Manchester C	42	8	8	5	28	25	4	5	12	15	41	37
18 Stoke	42	9	4	8	27	26	4	6	11	17	32	36
19 Everton	42	7	7	7	28	25	2	10	9	15	26	35
20 Bristol City	42	6	6	9	22	30	3	7	11	15	36	31
21 Derby	42	9	4	8	36	29	2	4	15	11	38	30
22 Bolton	42	5	11	5	19	21	0	4	17	19	52	25
	924	228	134	100	722	437	100	134	228	437	722	924

Odds & ends

Double wins: (1) Bristol City.
Double losses: (2) Manchester U, Wolverhampton.

Won from behind: (6) Brighton (a), Southampton (h), Arsenal (h), Crystal Palace (h), Gillingham (h) (LC), Manchester U (h) (LC).
Lost from in front: (3) Tottenham (a), West Brom (a), Liverpool (h).

High spots: Topping the Football League (for one week in late August).
Kevin Keelan breaking the club appearances record and later being awarded an MBE in the Queen's birthday honours list.
Justin Fashanu's goal against Liverpool (BBC TV's 'Goal of the Season').
Kevin Reeves winning his first full England cap.
John Bond winning 'Manager of the Month' for August.

Low spots: The coin-throwing episode in the Aston Villa home game.
Goalkeeper Keelan saying farewell after 17 fabulous years.
The slide from 4th to 15th position shortly after Christmas 1979.
McDowell's shocking injury in the match at Bolton.
The shambolic performance at home to Wolves in February.
The death of 36-year-old ex-City favourite Terry Anderson, who drowned after going on a seaside training run.

Kevin Bond scored goals for both sides – two games running!

Player of the Year: Kevin Bond.
Ever-presents: (0).
Hat-tricks: (0).
Hat-tricks against: (2) David Fairclough (Liverp'l), John Wark (Ipswich).
Leading scorer: (13) Justin Fashanu.

	Appearances						Goals			
	Lge	*Sub*	LC	*Sub*	FAC	*Sub*	**Lge**	LC	FAC	**Tot**
Barham, Mark	**3**	*1*								
Bennett, Dave	**4**		1					1		**1**
Bond, Kevin	**40**		5		3		**9**		2	**11**
Brown, Roger	**16**		2		3					
Downs, Greg	**17**	*1*	3		3					
Evans, Doug	**1**									
Fashanu, Justin	**31**	*3*	4		3		**11**	1	1	**13**
Goble, Steve	**5**		2				**1**			**1**
Halsey, Mark	**2**									
Hansbury, Roger	**16**									
Hoadley, Phil	**15**		4					1		**1**
Jones, David	**22**	*1*		*1*			**1**			**1**
Keelan, Kevin	**26**		6		3					
Lythgoe, Phil		*1*								
McDowell, John	**20**	*1*	2							
McGuire, Mick	**14**	*5*	4				**2**	1		**3**
Mendham, Peter	**17**	*3*	1		3		**2**		1	**3**
Neighbour, Jimmy	**5**		1							
Nightingale, Mark	**6**	*3*	2							
Paddon, Graham	**39**	*1*	6		3		**2**	2	1	**5**
Peters, Martin	**40**		5		3		**8**			**8**
Powell, Tony	**21**		4		3					
Reeves, Kevin	**23**		6		2		**8**	**4**		**12**
Robson, Keith	**23**		2		1		**8**		**1**	**9**
Ryan, John	**10**	*2*	2	*1*	3					
Shepherd, Greig	**1**					*1*				
Symonds, Richard	**14**	*1*	1							
Taylor, Alan	**20**	*4*	3	*1*			**5**	**2**		**7**
Woods, Clive	**11**						**1**			**1**
(own-goals)								**1**		**1**
29 players used	**462**	***27***	**66**	***3***	**33**	***1***	**58**	**13**	**6**	**77**

LEAGUE DIVISION 1 — Manager: John Bond ⇨ Ken Brown — SEASON 1980-81

No	Date		Att	Pos	Pt	F-A	H-T	Scorers, Times, and Referees	1	2	3	4	5	6	7	8	9	10	11	12 sub used
1	H	STOKE			W	5-1	4-1	Downs 7, Fashanu 32, 45, 51,	Hansbury	McDowell	Downs	Mendham	Bond	Powell	Woods Cl	Fashanu	**Royle**	Paddon	Goble	
	16/8		14,616		2			*Heath 44* [Woods 43]	*Fox*	*Evans*	*Hampton*	*Doyle*	*Dodd*	*Richardson*	*Ursem*	*Heath**	*Chapman*	*Cook*	*Bracewell*	*Johnson PA*
								Ref: R Challis	A tremendous opening half delights a disappointing crowd. Fashanu's first strike is a 25-yard gem which gives beleagured Peter Fox no chance. Fashanu completes the first City hat-trick in nearly four years. Peter Hampton debuts but Alan Durban's outfit miss the departed Garth Crooks.											
2	A	ASTON VILLA		8	L	0-1	0-0		Hansbury	McDowell	Downs	Mendham	Bond	Powell	Woods Cl	Fashanu	Royle	Paddon	Goble*	Nightingale
	20/8		*25,970*	*4*	2			*Shaw 76*	*Rimmer*	*Swain*	*Gibson*	*Evans*	*McNaught*	*Mortimer*	*Bremner*	*Shaw*	*Withe*	*Cowans*	*Morley*	
								Ref: S Bates	Home keeper Jimmy Rimmer is rarely troubled by a very defensive-looking City line-up. Gordon Cowans misses an open goal to let City off the hook. The deadlock is eventually broken when Gary Shaw is set up by speedy winger Tony Morley, and his crisp shot flies past Hansbury.											
3	H	LEEDS		14	L	2-3	0-1	Fashanu 70, Woods 84	Hansbury	McDowell*	Downs	Mendham	Bond	Powell	Woods Cl	Fashanu	Royle	Paddon	Goble	Barham
	23/8		17,890	*19*	2			*Hart 6, Graham 53, Connor 82*	*Lukic*	*Cherry*	*Greenhoff*	*Flynn*	*Hart*	*Madeley*	*Chandler*	*Hamson**	*Connor*	*Sabella*	*Graham*	*Thomas*
								Ref: R Toseland	Trevor Cherry's free-kick is parried by Hansbury and Paul Hart is on hand to net. Arthur Graham makes it two from close range. Fashanu pulls one back with a header in off John Lukic, but Terry Connor turns in a low cross to foil the comeback bid. Clive Woods heads in a late corner.											
4	A	LIVERPOOL		18	L	1-4	0-1	Bennett 79 *[Johnson 87]*	Hansbury	Bond	Downs	Barham	Forbes	Powell	Woods Cl	Fashanu	Royle	Paddon	Bennett	
	30/8		*35,315*	*5*	2			*Hansen 44, McDer' 65, Kennedy A 72,*	*Clemence*	*Neal*	*Kennedy A*	*Thompson*	*Kennedy R*	*Hansen*	*Dalglish*	*Case*	*Johnson*	*McDermott*	*Souness*	
								Ref: P Partridge	Alan Hansen lets fly from 25 yards and his shot dips into the net. City look beaten when Terry McDermott's shot is deflected in. Alan Kennedy converts a simple header. Bennett nets his first league goal from a corner, but the Reds are in the comfort zone as Dave Johnson cracks another.											
5	A	WEST BROM		20	L	0-3	0-1		Hansbury	Bond	Symonds	Barham	Forbes*	Powell	Woods Cl	Fashanu	Royle	Paddon	Bennett	Downs
	6/9		*15,414*	*6*	2			*Barnes 45p, Owen 46, A Brown 66*	*Godden*	*Trewick*	*Statham*	*Moses*	*Wile*	*Robertson*	*Robson**	*Brown A*	*Regis*	*Owen*	*Barnes*	*Deehan*
								Ref: L Burden	Veteran Forbes has a nightmare game against Cyrille Regis. He wrestles him to the floor to give Albion a penalty, which Peter Barnes bravely converts, having missed his previous three attempts. After Gary Owen's fine superb header, Forbes is subbed. Ally Brown cracks in a low shot.											
6	H	SOUTHAMPTON		18	W	1-0	1-0	Fashanu 12	Hansbury	Bond	Nightingale	Barham*	Hoadley	Powell	Woods Cl	Fashanu	**Muzinic**	Paddon	Goble	Mendham
	13/9		18,158	*2*	4				*Wells*	*Golac*	*McCartney**	*Williams*	*Watson*	*Nicholl*	*Boyer*	*Channon*	*George*	*Holmes*	*Baker G*	*Hebberd*
								Ref: D Vickers	Goble goes on a fine run, ending with a low cross that is netted by Fashanu. Yugolsav international Muzinic, £300,000 from Hadjuk Split, shows nice touches on his debut. A local student is brought in to interpret for him. Speculation mounts that John Bond is on his way to Man C.											
7	A	BRIGHTON		18	L	0-2	0-0		Hansbury	Bond	Nightingale	Barham	Hoadley	Powell	Woods Cl*	Fashanu	Muzinic	Paddon	Goble	Royle
	20/9		*14,877*	*14*	4			*Robinson 55, Stevens 60*	*Moseley*	*Gregory*	*Williams*	*Horton*	*Foster*	*Lawrenson*	*Stevens*	*Ward*	*Robinson*	*Smith*	*McNab !*	
								Ref: E Read	John Gregory's free-kick is forced in by Michael Robinson after a goalless first half. Suffolk-born Gary Stevens polishes City off, poking in a Steve Foster flick-on. When Mark Lawrenson is booked, Neil McNab pushes the ref and is sent off, leaving Alan Mullery's team a man short.											
8	H	BIRMINGHAM		18	D	2-2	2-1	Paddon 15, Fashanu 40	Hansbury	Bond	Downs	Barham	Jack	Powell	Woods Cl*	Fashanu	Muzinic	Paddon	Goble	Hoadley
	27/9		13,801	*14*	5			*Ainscow 24, Worthington 69*	*Wealands*	*Langan*	*Dennis*	*Curbishley*	*Gallagher*	*Todd*	*Ainscow*	*Givens**	*Worthington*	*Gemmill*	*Dillon*	*Lynex*
								Ref: C White	Shortly after Barham hits the bar, Paddon tries a pot-shot which flies in off Jeff Wealands' hands. Alan Ainscow levels with a far-post header, but Fashanu hits back, netting a fine header from Goble's cross. Frank Worthington punishes City for missing further chances with a neat goal.											
9	A	MIDDLESBROUGH		19	L	1-6	0-2	Fashanu 72 *[Johnston 75]*	Hansbury	Bond	Symonds	Barham	Jack*	Powell	Woods Cl	Fashanu	Muzinic	Paddon	Goble	Royle
	4/10		*12,837*	*11*	5			*McAnd' 7,50, Jan' 31,80, W'ds 71(og),*	*Platt*	*Craggs*	*Bailey*	*Johnston*	*Angus*	*McAndrew*	*Hodgson*	*Proctor*	*Shearer*	*Jankovic*	*Armstrong*	
								Ref: R Banks	The curse of the Match of the Day cameras strikes again, City putting on a dreadful defensive display. Hansbury looks unhappy throughout, not least when Woods turns David Hodgson's header past him. The final goal, by Bosco Jankovic, is a thundering drive, and pick of the bunch.											
10	H	WOLVERHAMPTON		20	D	1-1	0-1	Fashanu 80	Hansbury	Bond	Downs*	Barham	Forbes	Nightingale	Muzinic	Fashanu	Royle	Paddon	Goble	Mendham
	11/10		12,995	*17*	6			*Hibbitt 1*	*Bradshaw*	*Humphrey*	*Brazier*	*Daniel*	*Hughes*	*Villazan*	*Hibbitt*	*Carr*	*Gray*	*Richards*	*Eves*	
								Ref: M Bidmead	Manchester C make a formal approach for John Bond prior to kick-off and the boss apparently stays away from Carrow Road during the game. After 58 seconds Hansbury and Downs have a horrendous mix-up and Kenny Hibbitt nets. Fashanu's power header goes in via a Forbes touch.											

11	A	COVENTRY	19	W	1-0	1-0	Downs 25	Hansbury	Bond	Downs	McGuire	Hoadley	Nightingale	Barham	Fashanu	Royle	Paddon	Goble	
18/10		*12,235*	15	8				*Sealey*	*Coop*	*Roberts**	*Gooding*	*Dyson*	*Gillespie*	*Van Gool*	*Daly*	*Thompson*	*English*	*Hunt*	*Bannister*
							Ref: K McNally	John Benson follows Bond to City, so Ken Brown is made caretaker, to be assisted by Mel Machin. The upheaval inspires the first away points after six straight defeats. Downs cracks in a 25-yard volleyed winner. The next day Brown and Machin are offered the positions permanently.											
12	A	ARSENAL	19	L	1-3	0-1	Barham 48	Hansbury	Bond	Downs	McGuire	Hoadley	Nightingale	Barham	Fashanu	Royle	Paddon	Goble	
21/10		*21,839*	*5*	8			*Talbot 40, McDermott 84, Sansom 89*	*Wood*	*Devine*	*Sansom*	*Talbot*	*Walford*	*Young*	*Hollins**	*Sunderland*	*Stapleton*	*Gattting*	*Rix*	*McDermott*
							Ref: M Taylor	Brown is confirmed as the club's 26th manager since it turned pro 75 years ago. Graham Rix's cross is rifled in by Brian Talbot, but Barham equalises with his first City goal – a superb volley. Terry Neill's side win it late as shots by Brian McDermott and Ken Sansom beat Hansbury.											
13	H	NOTT'M FOR	18	D	1-1	0-0	Royle 53	Hansbury	Bond	Downs	McGuire	Hoadley	Nightingale	Barham	Fashanu	Royle	Paddon	Goble	
25/10		17,849	*4*	9			*Robertson 49*	*Sutton*	*Gunn*	*Gray F*	*McGovern*	*Lloyd*	*Burns*	*O'Neill*	*Bowyer*	*Ward*	*Wallace*	*Robertson*	
							Ref: R Lewis	It's one-way traffic towards debutant Steve Sutton early on, but City fail to turn this into goals, Goble the chief culprit. John Robertson shoots in via the bar from close range, against the run of play. Royle grabs his first league goal for Norwich, smashing home Paddon's pass on the run.											
14	H	CRYSTAL PALACE	18	D	1-1	1-1	Fashanu 16	Hansbury	Bond	Downs	McGuire	Hoadley	Nightingale	Barham	Fashanu	Royle	Paddon	Goble	
29/10		15,782	*22*	10			*Francis 10*	*Barron*	*Hinshelwood*	*Fenwick*	*Nicholas*	*Cannon*	*Gilbert*	*Lovell*	*Francis*	*Walsh*	*Flanagan*	*Smillie**	*Sealy*
							Ref: C Maskell	Leeds pull out of a deal to buy Fashanu. Unsettled Kevin Bond is told to 'play up and shut up' by Brown. Ernie Walley, caretaker-boss of crisis club Palace, drops stars Allen and Hilaire. Gerry Francis curls a fine goal. Royle wins a free-kick that finds Fashanu, and he nets from close in.											
15	A	MANCHESTER C	18	L	0-1	0-0		Hansbury	Bond	Downs	McGuire	Hoadley*	Nightingale	Barham	Fashanu	Royle	Paddon	Goble	Powell
1/11		*33,056*	*21*	10			*Power 61*	*Corrigan*	*Ranson*	*McDonald*	*Reid*	*Caton*	*Power*	*Tueart*	*MacKenzie*	*Gow*	*Hutchison**	*Bennett*	*Daley*
							Ref: G Tyson	John Bond is reviving the home side and they get their third win in ten days. Kevin Bond has a fine game, despite his outburst in the press about the way chairman South treated his departing dad. Paul Power nets a superb 20-yarder. Hoadley is carried off after a goal-saving tackle.											
16	H	EVERTON	17	W	2-1	0-0	Fashanu 70, Royle 85	Hansbury	Bond	Downs	McGuire	Hoadley	Nightingale	Barham	Fashanu	Royle	Paddon	Goble	
8/11		14,557	*8*	12			*Latchford 86*	*McDonagh*	*Gidman*	*Bailey*	*Wright*	*Lyons**	*Stanley*	*McMahon*	*Eastoe*	*Latchford*	*Hartford*	*McBride*	*O'Keefe*
							Ref: D Reeves	Two points, but it's a long and tortuous wait. City are starting to look bereft of ideas when Fashanu finally lashes the ball home, after he and Royle had efforts blocked. Gary Stanley's poor back-pass is lobbed over Jim McDonagh by ex-Evertonian Royle. Bob Latchford nets a tap-in.											
17	H	ASTON VILLA	19	L	1-3	1-0	Paddon 25	Hansbury	Bond	Downs	McGuire	Hoadley	Nightingale	Barham	Fashanu	Royle	Paddon	Goble*	Jack
12/11		17,050	*1*	12			*Shaw 61, 84, Evans 86*	*Rimmer*	*Swain*	*Williams*	*Evans*	*McNaught*	*Mortimer*	*Bremner*	*Shaw*	*Withe*	*Cowans*	*Morley*	
							Ref: T Bune	Paddon shocks the champions-elect with a blockbuster. Gary Shaw punishes slackness in defence. Ex-City boss Ron Saunders has clearly got Villa fit, for they come on strong in the final stages. Shaw is given acres of space to head in Peter Withe's cross and then sets up Allan Evans.											
18	A	STOKE	20	L	1-3	0-1	Royle 87	Hansbury	Bond	Downs	McGuire	McDowell	Nightingale	Barham	Fashanu	Royle	Paddon	Woods Cl*	Bennett
15/11		*11,207*	*12*	12			*Chapman 7, 51, 58*	*Fox*	*Evans*	*Hampton*	*Dodd*	*O'Callaghan*	*Doyle*	*Bracewell*	*Heath*	*Chapman*	*Richardson*	*Munro*	
							Ref: G Nolan	The events of the opening day are but a distant memory after this flop. Big Lee Chapman collects the first threesome of his career. He rises to head in a Ray Evans free-kick, slots home a Paul Richardson cross and then pounces when Adrian Heath's shot escapes from Hansbury's grasp.											
19	H	SUNDERLAND	18	W	1-0	1-0	Goble 12	Baker	Bond	Downs	McGuire*	McDowell	Powell	Barham	Fashanu	Royle	Paddon	Goble	Jack
22/11		15,024	*14*	14				*Turner*	*Whitworth*	*Bolton*	*Allardyce*	*Hindmarch*	*Buckley*	*Arnott*	*Robson**	*Hawley*	*Chisholm*	*Cummins*	*Brown*
							Ref: J Bray	Goble finishes coolly from McGuire's pass, despite heated calls for offside. The points are welcome, but this is no classic. Bond is set to sign for Man City, but they are struggling to raise the fee. A farewell friendly is staged for Kevin Keelan to mark his record of 681 first-team games.											
20	A	LEICESTER	18	W	2-1	2-1	Fashanu 12, Royle 25	Baker	Bond	Powell	McGuire	Hoadley	Nightingale	Barham*	Fashanu	Royle	Paddon	Goble	Muzinic
29/11		*13,958*	*22*	16			*Young 23*	*Wallington*	*Williams*	*Gibson*	*Peake*	*Scott*	*O'Neill*	*Hamill**	*Melrose*	*Young*	*Wilson*	*Smith*	*MacDonald*
							Ref: M Heath	Unmarked Fashanu heads in, but Alan Young races in to volley an equaliser. Moments later Royle slots in a neat goal. Barham is carried off injured in the closing minutes. Dave Watson (£50k now, plus £50k after 25 games) arrives from Liverpool and debuts for the reserves today.											
21	H	MANCHESTER U	19	D	2-2	0-2	Jovanovic 58(og), Fashanu 73	Baker	Nightingale	Bond	McGuire*	Hoadley	Powell	Barham	Fashanu	Royle	Paddon	Goble	Muzinic
6/12		19,228	*6*	17			*Bond 10(og), Coppell 33*	*Bailey*	*Nicholl*	*Albiston*	*McIlroy*	*Jovanovic*	*Buchan*	*Coppell*	*Greenhoff*	*Jordan*	*Macari*	*Duxbury*	
							Ref: B Daniels	Joe Jordan's shot rebounds off Baker and into the net off Bond. Steve Coppell thrashes in a fine 25-yarder. Undaunted, the home fans generate an electric atmosphere after the break. Nikola Jovanovic heads Goble's chip into his own net and Fashanu tucks in the equaliser after a corner.											

No	Date		Att	Pos	Pt	F-A	H-T	Scorers, Times, and Referees	1	2	3	4	5	6	7	8	9	10	11	12 sub used
22	A	CRYSTAL PALACE		19	L	1-4	1-3	Royle 25	Baker	Bond	Downs	Muzinic	Hoadley	Nightingale	Barham	Fashanu	Royle	Paddon	Goble	
	13/12		*15,257*	*22*	17			*Allen 19, 42, Murphy 21, Francis 72*	*Barron*	*Hinshelwood*	*Boyle*	*Nicholas*	*Cannon*	*Gilbert*	*Murphy**	*Francis*	*Allen*	*Sealy*	*Hilaire*	*Walsh*
								Ref: L Shapter	City are unlucky to be first opponents after the triumphant return to Selhurst of popular Malcom Allison. Clive Allen outjumps Baker to nod the first. Jerry Murphy shoots in off a post before Royle scores with a firm header. Allen nets a Sealy cross and Francis cracks in a picture goal.											
23	H	COVENTRY		19	W	2-0	2-0	Royle 22, Paddon 34	Baker	Bond	Muzinic*	McGuire	Powell	McDowell	Mendham	Fashanu	Royle	Paddon	Goble	Powell
	20/12		12,630	*16*	19				*Sealey*	*Thomas*	*Roberts*	*Blair*	*Dyson*	*Gillespie*	*Bodak*	*Gooding**	*Thompson*	*Hateley*	*Hunt*	*Jones*
								Ref: D Hutchinson	Five team-changes have the desired effect after the Selhurst Park nightmare. Fashanu finds himself closely policed by rugged Gary Gillespie and Paul Dyson, but Royle and Paddon put away their chances well. Gordon Milne's side improve after the break, but miss several chances.											
24	A	IPSWICH		19	L	0-2	0-1		Baker	Bond	Powell	McGuire*	Hoadley	**Watson**	Mendham	Fashanu	Royle	Paddon	Goble	Woods Cl
	26/12		*27,890*	*3*	19			*Brazil 43, Wark 49*	*Cooper*	*Burley*	*McCall*	*Thijssen*	*Osman*	*Butcher*	*Wark*	*Muhren*	*Mariner*	*Brazil*	*Gates**	*O'Callaghan*
								Ref: P Reeves	A tough baptism for Dave Watson, plucked from Liverpool reserves. Town haven't lost at home in over 14 months. Alan Brazil jinks into the City box and dummies Baker before firing in. After the interval Arnold Muhren crosses from the left and John Wark fires home a first-timer.											
25	H	TOTTENHAM		20	D	2-2	1-1	Fashanu 33, Bond 82p	Baker	Bond	Downs*	McGuire	Hoadley	McDowell	Mendham	Fashanu	Royle	Fashanu	Goble	Woods Cl
	27/12		23,898	*10*	20			*Archibald 18, Hoddle 48*	*Aleksic*	*Roberts*	*O'Reilly*	*Yorath*	*Lacy*	*Perryman*	*Brooke*	*Archibald*	*Villa**	*Hoddle*	*Crooks*	*Miller*
								Ref: B Martin	Steve Archibald nets a fine shot, but Fashanu lashes an equaliser. Royle hits a post before Glenn Hoddle nets a wonderful curling shot. Milija Aleksic collides with a post and is taken off with a gashed leg. Hoddle goes in goal and is beaten from the spot after John Lacy fouled Fashanu.											
26	A	SUNDERLAND		20	L	0-3	0-2		Baker	McDowell	Symonds	McGuire	Hoadley*	Watson	Mendham	Fashanu	Royle	Paddon	Jack	Bennett
	10/1		*17,749*	*17*	20			*Rowell 24, 67, Cummins 31*	*Turner*	*Whitworth*	*Bolton*	*Elliott*	*Hindmarch*	*Rowell*	*Arnott*	*Brown*	*Hawley*	*Chisholm*	*Cummins*	
								Ref: N Midgley	Gary Rowell has an easy task to open the scoring from six yards. Little Stan Cummins doubles the lead when he capitalises on a poor back-pass by Hoadley. Rowell hooks in his second after a corner. On this form Ken Knighton's side look more likely to survive the drop than City.											
27	H	LIVERPOOL		20	L	0-1	0-1		Baker	Bond	Barham	McGuire*	Hoadley	Watson	Robson	Royle	Paddon	Bennett	Woods Cl	Jack
	17/1		23,829	*3*	20			*McDermott 23*	*Clemence*	*Neal*	*Kennedy A*	*Thompson*	*Kennedy R*	*Irwin*	*Dalglish*	*Lee*	*Fariclough**	*McDermott*	*Souness*	*Case*
								Ref: C Downey	Paddon replaces the transfer-listed Bond as skipper as Brown shuffles his pack. City look a much-improved side this afternoon, with Watson in outstanding form against his ex-team. Baker gets to a Kenny Dalglish shot, but can only parry it to Terry McDermott, who sweeps it into goal.											
28	A	LEEDS		20	L	0-1	0-0		Baker	Bond	Barham	Jack	McDowell	Watson	Mendham	Fashanu	Royle	Paddon	Bennett	
	31/1		*15,836*	*14*	20			*Harris 80*	*Lukic*	*Greenhoff*	*Gray*	*Flynn*	*Hart*	*Cherry*	*Harris*	*Hird*	*Connor*	*Sabella*	*Graham*	
								Ref: K Redfern	Battling City look all set to take a vital point back to Norfolk when Carl Harris strikes. He collects the ball just inside the area and hammers a superb rising drive past the helpless Baker. Allan Clarke's dour Leeds side have only hit 23 goals in 28 games, but this is their 11th clean sheet.											
29	A	SOUTHAMPTON		20	L	1-2	0-0	Watson 73	Hansbury	McDowell	Powell*	Barham	Hoadley	Watson	Mendham	Fashanu	Royle	Paddon	Goble	Muzinic
	7/2		*20,454*	*4*	20			*Williams 58, George 63*	*Wells*	*Golac*	*Holmes*	*Williams*	*Waldron*	*Nicholl*	*Keegan*	*Channon*	*George*	*Moran*	*Baker G*	
								Ref: C White	Enigmatic Steve Williams bursts into life with a magnificent solo run, beating four men before shooting home. City were fortified by a trip to Marbella this week, but the gloom returns as Charlie George nets a rebound off Baker. Watson's first senior goal comes after a Goble corner.											
30	H	WEST BROM		20	L	0-2	0-1		Hansbury	McDowell	Powell	Barham	Muzinic	Watson	Jack	Robson	Royle*	Paddon	Goble	Woods Cl
	14/2		15,218	*5*	20			*Regis 17, Owen 89p*	*Godden*	*Batson*	*Statham*	*Moses*	*Wile*	*Bennett*	*Robson*	*Deehan*	*Regis*	*Owen*	*Barnes*	
								Ref: A Challinor	Relegation worries intensify. Fashanu and Hoadley are absent with a stomach complaint. Peter Barnes' floated cross is headed in by Cyrille Regis. Owen falls over Hansbury and Mr Challinor waves away City appeals that he dived. Owen's spot-kick squirms under the keeper's body.											
31	A	BIRMINGHAM		20	L	0-4	0-0		Hansbury	Bond	Muzinic*	McGuire	Mendham	Watson	Barham	Fashanu	Royle	Paddon	Goble	Jack
	20/2		*14,686*	*10*	20			*Ainscow 74, Evans 77, 87 Gemmill 85*	*Wealands*	*Langan*	*Broadhurst*	*Dillon*	*Gallagher*	*Todd*	*Ainscow*	*Evans*	*Worthington*	*Gemmill*	*Handysides*	
									Colin Todd fouls McGuire in the early stages, but Bond misses a penalty for the very first time – in probably his final City game! Jim Smith's outfit strike with four late goals to inflict Norwich's sixth loss in a row. Alan Ainscow's header with barely 15 minutes left sparks the goal-rush.											

32	H	BRIGHTON		20	W	3-1	2-0	McGuire 9, Watson 31, Fashanu 50	Hansbury	McDowell	Downs	McGuire	Hoadley	Watson	**O'Neill**	Fashanu	Royle	Paddon	Barham	
	28/2		16,199	19	22			Robinson 82	Digweed	Stevens	Williams	Clark	Foster	Lawrenson	McNab	Stille	Robinson	Smith	O'Sullivan*	Ryan
								Ref: M Dimblebee	Martin O'Neill, £350k from Nott'm Forest, debuts and helps turn the tide. McGuire combines with Royle before netting a 25-yarder. Watson deflects a McGuire shot past Perry Digweed. Fashanu makes the points safe, converting from close in. Michael Robinson heads a consolation.											
33	A	WOLVERHAMPTON		21	L	0-3	0-1	[McDowell 63 (og)]	**Woods Ch**	McDowell	Downs	McGuire	**Walford**	Watson	O'Neill	Fashanu	Royle	Paddon	Barham	
	14/3		21,605	18	22			Palmer 31, Richards 50,	Bradshaw	Palmer	Parkin	Clarke	McAlle	Berry	Hibbitt	Carr	Gray	Richards	Eves	
								Ref: D Webb	Two more signings come in for this 'four-pointer'. Chris Woods is on loan from QPR and Steve Walford cost £175k from Arsenal. The latter has an unhappy start, but Woods saves a Wayne Clarke penalty. Geoff Palmer's half-volley is followed by two scrappy and fortunate goals.											
34	H	MIDDLESBROUGH		20	W	2-0	2-0	Royle 26, 45	Woods Ch	McDowell	Downs	McGuire	Walford	Watson	O'Neill	Fashanu	Royle	Paddon	Barham	
	17/3		14,549	13	24				Platt	Nattrass	Bailey	Johnston	Ashcroft	McAndrew*	Cochrane	Proctor	Hodgson	Shearer	Armstrong	Angus
								Ref: G Napthine	He may have 17 goals to his name so far this season, but when Fashanu misses a couple of chances, the home fans are quick to get on his back. Royle restores sanity by volleying the first and then bravely diving to head another after Watson hits the post. It's a gritty display by Norwich.											
35	H	ARSENAL		20	D	1-1	1-0	Fashanu 30	Woods Ch	McDowell	Downs	McGuire	Walford	Watson	O'Neill	Fashanu	Royle*	Paddon	Barham	Robson
	21/3		19,569	7	25			Talbot 82	Jennings	Devine	Sansom	Talbot	O'Leary	Young	Nicholas	Sunderland	Stapleton	McDermott	Rix	
								Ref: M Scott	After a good run by O'Neill, Fashanu converts at the near post. Victory is snatched away near the end when a mistake by Woods – otherwise excellent today – allows Brian Talbot to net at close range. Bond and Powell have departed for the USA, but defensively City look more solid.											
36	A	NOTT'M FOR		20	L	1-2	1-0	Fashanu 45	Woods Ch	McDowell	Downs	McGuire	Walford	Watson	O'Neill*	Fashanu	Royle	Paddon	Barham	Symonds
	28/3		22,353	6	25			Francis 53, 55	Shilton	Anderson	Gray F	Gray S	Needham*	Burns	Ponte	Wallace	Francis	Walsh	Robertson	Aas
								Ref: A Saunders	With his marker Dave Needham grounded by a head injury, Fashanu swoops to volley City ahead. Trevor Francis responds with two goals in 90 seconds. First he strikes home a 25-yarder on the turn, then – looking offside a – gets clear to tuck the ball past former Forest keeper Woods.											
37	H	MANCHESTER C		20	W	2-0	2-0	McGuire 13, McDowell 33p	Woods Ch	McDowell	Downs	McGuire	Walford	Watson	O'Neill*	Fashanu	Royle	Paddon	Barham	Bennett
	4/4		17,957	12	27				Corrigan	Ranson	McDonald	Reid	Booth	Power	Bennett	MacKenzie	Henry	Hutchison	Reeves	
								Ref: R Lewis	After a 50-yard surge by Paddon, Barham's shot is followed into the net by McGuire. When the speedy Barham is bundled over in the area, McDowell converts from the spot. Victory is sweet over John Bond & Co, but the points are the vital thing. Hansbury joins the USA exodus.											
38	A	EVERTON		19	W	2-0	1-0	Royle 24, Fashanu 82	Woods Ch	McDowell	Downs	McGuire	Walford	Watson	O'Neill	Fashanu	Royle	Paddon	Barham	
	11/4		16,254	15	29				McDonagh	Gidman	Ratcliffe	Wright	Lyons	Stanley	Ross	Eastoe*	Varadi	Hartford	Lodge	Megson
								Ref: K Baker	An enjoyable return to Goodison Park for Royle as he draws Jim McDonagh out and sidefoots past him expertly. The referee allows play to continue after Billy Wright and Fashanu start wrestling, and the latter is able to power through and clinch what could prove two crucial points.											
39	A	TOTTENHAM		19	W	3-2	2-2	O'Neill 8, Watson 27, Roberts 61(og)	Woods Ch	McDowell*	Downs	McGuire	Walford	Watson	O'Neill	Fashanu	Royle	Paddon	Barham	Hoadley
	18/4		34,413	9	31			Hoddle 23p, Miller 35	Aleksic	Hughton	Miller	Roberts	Brooke*	Perryman	Ardiles	Archibald	Galvin	Hoddle	Crooks	Hazard
								Ref:M Robinson	O'Neill shocks the FA Cup finalists, darting through to score. Watson fouls Garth Crooks for Glenn Hoddle to convert a penalty. Watson heads City in front, but Paul Miller levels from close range Graham Roberts slices in under pressure from Royle and the survival hopes remain alive.											
40	H	IPSWICH		17	W	1-0	0-0	Fashanu 62	Woods Ch	Symonds	Downs	McGuire	Walford	Watson	O'Neill	Fashanu	Royle	Paddon	Barham*	Jack
	20/4		26,083	2	33				Cooper	Steggles*	Mills	Parkin	Osman	Butcher	Wark	Muhren	Turner	Brazil	McCall	D'Avray
								Ref: R Challis	A tense derby with both sides desperate for points for different reasons. Town are chasing the League title, but their hopes are seriously dented when Fashanu, shaping to cross, belts the ball past surprised Paul Cooper. Stand-in Robin Turner fails to equalise with only the keeper to beat.											
41	A	MANCHESTER U		19	L	0-1	0-0		Woods Ch	Symonds	Downs	McGuire	Walford	Watson	O'Neill	Fashanu*	Royle	Paddon	Bennett	Nightingale
	25/4		40,165	7	33			Jordan 57	Bailey	Duxbury	Albiston	Moran	McQueen	Buchan	Coppell	Birtles	Jordan	Macari	Wilkins	
								Ref: R Bridges	Joe Jordan, who spends much of the game 'roughing up' Woods, nets a freak winner. Facing the wrong way, he flicks a heel at a cross and the ball slithers under Woods. Despite City's eight-point April, their relegation rivals are also winning and things will be decided on the final day.											
42	H	LEICESTER		20	L	2-3	1-2	McGuire 25, Fashanu 61	Woods Ch	McDowell*	Downs	McGuire	Walford	Watson	O'Neill	Fashanu	Royle	Paddon	Barham	Jack
	2/5		25,307	21	33			Melrose 20, 22, 78	Wallington	Williams	Leet*	Ramsey	May	O'Neill	Lynex	Melrose	Young	Wilson	MacDonald	Henderson
		Home	Away					Ref: B Daniels	Jock Wallace's men are already doomed and he fields a young side. Jim Melrose's early goals shock Norwich, but the fightback is tremendous, with wave after wave of attacks. Melrose'e cruel late winner condemns City to the drop, as their three main rivals all pick up points elsewhere.											
Average		17,140	21,113																	

League Cup	Att		F-A	H-T	Scorers, Times, and Referees	1	2	3	4	5	6	7	8	9	10	11	12 sub used
2:1 A SHREWSBURY	14	D	1-1	1-0	Fashanu 30	Hansbury	Bond	Downs	Barham	Forbes	Powell	Woods Cl	Fashanu	Royle	Paddon	Bennett	
26/8	*5,536 2:16*				*Biggins 80*	*Wardle*	*King*	*Leonard*	*Turner*	*Griffin*	*Keay*	*Tong*	*Lindsay*	*Biggins*	*Dungworth*	*Petts*	
					Ref: J Hunting	John Bond is away spying on West Brom. After several close shaves, Bob Wardle is beaten by a header from unmarked Fashanu, from a cross by Bennett. Graham Turner's men deserve their late equaliser, when Paul Petts' cross is not cleared properly and Steve Biggins rifles the ball in.											
2:2 H SHREWSBURY	18	W	2-0	0-0	Fashanu 113, Royle 119	Hansbury	Bond	Downs	Barham	Forbes	Powell	Woods Cl	Fashanu	Royle	Paddon	Bennett	
3/9	9,185 *2:22*		*aet*			*Wardle*	*King*	*Larkin*	*Turner*	*Griffin*	*Keay*	*Tong*	*Atkins*	*Biggins**	*Dungworth*	*Petts*	*Lindsay*
					Ref: K Salmon (Norwich win 3-1 on aggregate)	The Shrews put up stout resistance, but this was unconvincing fare from City. Many observers are mystified when Fashanu's early strike is ruled out. In extra time, Fashanu converts a superb header. Forbes gets a slight touch to Royle's clincher and jokingly claims the goal later on.											
3 A IPSWICH	19	D	1-1	0-1	Fashanu 84	Hansbury	Bond	Muzinic	Barham	Hoadley	Powell	Woods Cl	Fashanu	Jack*	Paddon	Goble	Royle
23/9	*26,462 1*				*Osman 14*	*Cooper*	*Burley*	*Mills*	*Thijssen*	*Osman*	*Butcher*	*Wark*	*Muhren*	*Mariner*	*Brazil**	*Gates*	*O'Callaghan*
					Ref: P Richardson	Russell Osman gets forward to beat Hansbury with a towering header. The City keeper has a fine game to prevent further goals. The home fans are in good voice after being publicly criticised by manager Bobby Robson. Fashanu silences them with an equaliser against the run of play.											
3R H IPSWICH	19	L	1-3	0-1	Powell 49	Hansbury	Bond	Hoadley	Barham	Jack*	Powell	Woods Cl	Fashanu	Muzinic	Paddon	Goble	Symonds
8/10	24,523 *1*				*Mariner 26, 79, Muhren 76*	*Cooper*	*Burley*	*Mills*	*Thijssen*	*Osman*	*Butcher*	*Wark*	*Muhren*	*Mariner*	*Brazil*	*Gates*	
					Ref: P Richardson	Four days after the Ayresome Park debacle, Paul Mariner puts City behind and the heads drop again. Powell restores hope, but a well-worked goal involving Town's Dutch duo is the turning point. Another loss and speculation mounts that boss Bond may be on his way to Maine Road.											

FA Cup	Att		F-A	H-T	Scorers, Times, and Referees	1	2	3	4	5	6	7	8	9	10	11	12 sub used
3 H CAMBRIDGE U	20	W	1-0	0-0	Downs 53	Baker	McDowell	Downs	McGuire	Hoadley	Watson	Mendham	Fashanu	Royle	Paddon	Goble	
3/1	18,420 *2:10*					*Key*	*Donaldson*	*Murray*	*Smith*	*Fallon*	*Finney*	*Streete*	*Spriggs*	*Reilly*	*Taylor*	*Christie**	*Gibbins*
					Ref: G Napthine	John Docherty's men push City all the way in this first-ever competitive local derby between the sides. Downs lets fly from distance and the shot swirls past a floundering Richard Key. Ex-City striker Roger Gibbins joins the end-to-end action, but the lively visitors are kept in check.											
4 A MANCHESTER C	20	L	0-6	0-2	*[Bennett 79, Power 82, McDonald 90]*	Baker	Bond	Barham	Powell	McDowell	Watson	Mendham*	Fashanu	Royle	Paddon	Bennett	Robson
24/1	*38,919 11*				*Reeves 20, Gow 25, McKenzie 74,*	*Corrigan*	*Henry*	*McDonald*	*Booth*	*Power*	*Caton*	*Boyer**	*Gow*	*MacKenzie*	*Hutchison*	*Reeves*	*Bennett*
					Ref: R Toseland	Ex-City hero Kevin Reeves nets a breathtaking volley and shortly afterwards Gerry Gow curls another past Baker. City collapse in the final 16 minutes and four further goals fly in. It means great satisfaction for home manager Bond, following the circumstances of his Carrow Road exit.											

		Home					Away					
	P	W	D	L	F	A	W	D	L	F	A	Pts
1 Aston Villa	42	16	3	2	40	13	10	5	6	32	27	60
2 Ipswich	42	15	4	2	45	14	8	6	7	32	29	56
3 Arsenal	42	13	8	0	36	17	6	7	8	25	28	53
4 West Brom	42	15	4	2	40	15	5	8	8	20	27	52
5 Liverpool	42	13	5	3	38	15	4	12	5	24	27	51
6 Southampton	42	15	4	2	47	22	5	6	10	29	34	50
7 Nott'm For	42	15	3	3	44	20	4	9	8	18	24	50
8 Manchester U	42	9	11	1	30	14	6	7	8	21	22	48
9 Leeds	42	10	5	6	19	19	7	5	9	20	28	44
10 Tottenham	42	9	9	3	44	31	5	6	10	26	37	43
11 Stoke	42	8	9	4	31	23	4	9	8	20	37	42
12 Manchester C	42	10	7	4	35	25	4	4	13	21	34	39
13 Birmingham	42	11	5	5	32	23	2	7	12	18	38	38
14 Middlesbro	42	14	4	3	38	16	2	1	18	15	45	37
15 Everton	42	8	6	7	32	25	5	4	12	23	33	36
16 Coventry	42	9	6	6	31	30	4	4	13	17	38	36
17 Sunderland	42	10	4	7	32	19	4	3	14	20	34	35
18 Wolves	42	11	2	8	26	20	2	7	12	17	35	35
19 Brighton	42	10	3	8	30	26	4	4	13	24	41	35
20 NORWICH	42	9	7	5	34	25	4	0	17	15	48	33
21 Leicester	42	7	5	9	20	23	6	1	14	20	44	32
22 Crys Palace	42	6	4	11	32	37	0	3	18	15	46	19
	924	243	118	101	756	472	101	118	243	472	756	924

Odds & ends

Double wins: (2) Everton, Tottenham.
Double losses: (5) Aston Villa, Coventry, Leeds, Liverpool, West Brom.

Won from behind: (0).
Lost from in front: (2) Aston Villa (h), Nott'm For (a).

High spots: Four good signings: Watson, O'Neill, Walford and Woods.
Four successive wins in April – but not enough to escape the drop.
A fine comeback at home to Manchester U – helped by the crowd!
The fine against Stoke – despite the summer outgoings (e.g. Peters).

Low spots: Relegation after six seasons in the top flight.
The acrimony surrounding John Bond's autumn departure.
Six-goal hammerings at Manchester City and Middlesbrough.

Player of the Year: Joe Royle.
Ever-presents: (1) Graham Paddon.
Hat-tricks: (1) Justin Fashanu (Stoke, h).
Hat-tricks against: (2) Lee Chapman (Stoke, a), Jim Melrose (Leicester, h).
Leading scorer: (22) Justin Fashanu.

	Appearances						Goals			
	Lge	*Sub*	LC	*Sub*	FAC	*Sub*	**Lge**	LC	FAC	**Tot**
Baker, Clive	**10**				2					
Barham, Mark	**34**	*1*	4		1		**1**			**1**
Bennett, Dave	**5**	*4*	2		1		**1**			**1**
Bond, Kevin	**28**		4		1		**1**			**1**
Downs, Greg	**28**	*1*	2		1		**2**		1	**3**
Fashanu, Justin	**40**		4		2		**19**	3		**22**
Forbes, Duncan	**3**		2							
Goble, Steve	**25**		2		1		**1**			**1**
Hansbury, Roger	**22**		4							
Hoadley, Phil	**17**	*2*	2		1					
Jack, Ross	**5**	*6*	2							
McDowell, John	**20**				2		**1**			**1**
McGuire, Mick	**28**				1		**3**			**3**
Mendham, Peter	**11**	*2*			2					
Muzinic, Drazen	**9**	*3*	2							
Nightingale, Mark	**14**	*2*								
O'Neill, Martin	**11**						**1**			**1**
Paddon, Graham	**42**		4		2		**3**			**3**
Powell, Tony	**17**	*2*	4		1			1		**1**
Robson, Keith	**2**	*1*				*1*				
Royle, Joe	**38**	*2*	2	*1*	2		**9**	1		**10**
Symonds, Richard	**5**	*1*		*1*						
Walford, Steve	**10**									
Watson, Dave	**18**				2		**3**			**3**
Woods, Chris	**10**									
Woods, Clive	**10**	*3*	4				**2**			**2**
(own-goals)							**2**			**2**
26 players used	**462**	*30*	**44**	*2*	**22**	*1*	**49**	**5**	**1**	**55**

No	Date		Att	Pos	Pt	F-A	H-T	Scorers, Times, and Referees	1	2	3	4	5	6	7	8	9	10	11	12 sub used
1	A	ROTHERHAM			L	**1-4**	1-2	Shepherd 7	Woods Ch	Barham	Muzinic*	McGuire	Walford	Watson	Mendham	Shepherd	**Bertschin**	Paddon	Bennett	Nightingale
	29/8		*8.919*		0			*Fern 8, 90, Seasman 27, Moore 48*	*Mountford*	*Forrest*	*Taylor*	*Green*	*Stancliffe*	*Mullen*	*Towner*	*Seasman*	*Moore**	*Fern*	*Henson*	*Gooding*
								Ref: V Callow	Three points for a win from today, but City end up with zero as Tony Towner inspires the Millers. Rod Fern levels 45 seconds after Shepherd's early strike. O'Neill and Fashanu have departed and Bertschin makes his debut. The club has announced a crippling annual loss of £327,000.											
2	H	CRYSTAL PALACE			W	1-0	1-0	Cannon 7(og)	Woods Ch	Nightingale	Downs	McGuire	Walford	Watson	Barham	Shepherd	Bertschin	Paddon*	Jack	Mendham
	2/9		14,434		3				*Barron*	*Hinshelwood*	*Dare*	*Price*	*Cannon*	*Gilbert*	*Smillie*	*Bason*	*Walsh*	*Langley*	*Brooks**	*Lovell*
								Ref: J Deakin	A good attacking display erases some of the Millmoor misery. Nightingale sends Barham away and his cross sees Jim Cannon, under pressure from Bertschin, divert the ball past Paul Barron. Woods, who has joined for £225,000 form QPR following his loan spell, keeps a clean sheet.											
3	H	BARNSLEY		9	D	1-1	1-1	Jack 42	Woods Ch	Nightingale	Downs	McGuire	Walford	Watson	Barham	Shepherd	Bertschin	Paddon*	Jack	Mendham
	5/9		13,677	*6*	4			*Parker 26*	*Horn*	*Joyce*	*Chambers*	*Glavin*	*Banks*	*McCarthy*	*Evans*	*Parker*	*Aylott*	*McHale*	*Barrowcl'gh*	
								Ref: K Salmon	The newly promoted Tykes are full of fight and energy. Ronnie Glavin's probing run into the City area sets up Derrick Parker for a simple opening goal. Nightingale goes on the overlap and sends over a cross that is headed superbly past Bobby Horn by Jack for his first league goal.											
4	A	WREXHAM		7	W	3-2	1-0	Shepherd 24, Jack 48, Barham 69	Woods Ch	Nightingale	Symonds	McGuire	Walford	Watson	Barham	Shepherd	Woods Cl	Paddon	Jack*	Hoadley
	12/9		*4,007*	*22*	7			*Vinter 52, McNeil 66p*	*Niedzwiecki*	*Jones J*	*Bater*	*Dowman*	*Ciegelski*	*Hill**	*Fox*	*McNeil*	*Edwards*	*Vinter*	*Carrodus*	*Hunt*
								Ref: K Salmon	Shepherd gets clear of the back four to tuck in the first and Jack despatches a loose ball to make it two. Mick Vinter knocks in a rebound and Dixie McNeil levels with a controversial spot-kick, apparently given for pushing. Barham wins the points when he rifles in a cross by Paddon.											
5	H	NEWCASTLE		5	W	2-1	1-1	Watson 18, Jack 80	Woods Ch	Nightingale*	Downs	McGuire	Walford	Watson	Barham	Shepherd	Woods Cl	Paddon	Jack	**Hart**
	19/9		14,384	*18*	10			*Waddle 12*	*Carr*	*Brownlie*	*Davies*	*Trewick*	*Barton**	*Halliday*	*Walker*	*Martin*	*Varadi*	*Wharton*	*Waddle*	*Carney*
								Ref: C White	Chris Waddle slips the ball into an empty net, but Watson rises to equalise with a fine header. Steve Carney handles, but McGuire misses from the spot on 50 minutes. Jack misses an easy chance, heading over an open goal, but makes amends with a fine header ten minutes from the end.											
6	A	GRIMSBY		3	W	2-1	2-0	Jack 28p, Woods Cl 41	Woods Ch	Nightingale	Downs	McGuire	Walford	Watson	Barham	Shepherd	Woods Cl	Paddon	Jack	
	22/9		*10,185*	*6*	13			*Whymark 67*	*Batch*	*Stone*	*Crombie**	*Waters*	*Wigginton*	*Moore K*	*Brolly*	*Whymark*	*Drinkell*	*Mitchell*	*Cumming*	*Kilmore*
								Ref: A Challinor	City's best display of the season so far. Shepherd hits a post early on. Clive Wigginton fouls Jack, who tucks in the penalty himself. Woods cuts in and arrows home an excellent goal. George Kerr's side pull one back when Norfolk-born Trevor Whymark nods in a Mike Brolly cross.											
7	A	CHELSEA		3	L	1-2	1-1	Jack 42	Woods Ch	Nightingale	Downs	McGuire	Walford	Watson*	Barham	Shepherd	Woods Cl	Paddon	Jack	Bertschin
	26/9		*14,509*	*9*	13			*Bumstead 40p, Driver 46*	*Borota*	*Locke*	*Hutchings*	*Rh'-Brown*	*Pates*	*Chivers*	*Driver*	*Bumstead*	*Lee*	*Mayes*	*Fillery*	
								Ref: J Martin	Downs prevents a goal by handling on the goalline and John Bumstead drives in the penalty. Barham collects a Watson free-kick and sets up Jack, who produces an elegant turn and shot. In a breakaway raid, Phil Driver nets a fine header from Chris Hutchings' cross to win the points.											
8	H	OLDHAM		8	L	1-2	1-1	Jack 34p	Woods Ch	Nightingale	**Donachie**	McGuire	Walford	Hoadley	Barham	Jack	Bertschin	Paddon*	Woods Cl	Shepherd
	3/10		13,710	*4*	13			*McDonough 32, Heaton 60*	*McDonnell*	*Sinclair*	*Ryan*	*Keegan*	*Hoolickin*	*Futcher*	*Wylde*	*Heaton*	*Steel*	*Palmer*	*McDonough*	
								Ref: R Lewis	Willie Donachie, signed from Portland Timbers, debuts after a minute's silence for the late Bill Shankly. Jimmy Frizzell's men score via Darren McDonough's long-distance header, in off the bar. Jack nets for the sixth game in a row after Bertschin was held. Paul Heaton buries a fine shot.											
9	A	QP RANGERS		13	L	0-2	0-0		Woods Ch	Nightingale	Donachie	Mendham	Walford	Watson	Barham	Jack	Bertschin	Shepherd	Woods Cl*	Muzinic
	10/10		*11,806*	*8*	13			*Gregory 71, Stainrod 79*	*Burridge*	*Gregory*	*Fenwick*	*Waddle*	*Hazell*	*Roeder*	*Mickl'white**	*Stainrod*	*Allen*	*Currie*	*Gillard*	*Burke*
								Ref: G Napthine	The plastic pitch is a bit slippery, but for the first 70 minutes Woods does superbly against his former team. Then he is beaten by a neat chip from John Gregory. Defeat is confirmed when Simon Stainrod stabs home after Steve Burke's cross somehow slips under the keeper's body.											
10	H	SHREWSBURY		9	W	2-1	1-1	Bertschin 42, Mendham 88	Woods Ch	Symonds	Donachie	McGuire	Walford	Hoadley	Barham	Jack	Bertschin	Mendham	Woods Cl*	**Fashanu**
	17/10		**11,979**	*12*	16			*Petts 24*	*Wardle*	*Leonard*	*Johnson*	*Petts*	*Keay*	*MacLaren*	*Tong*	*McNally*	*Atkins**	*Bates*	*Biggins*	*Cross*
								Ref: T Ward	The recent slump is reflected by the attendance, and the grumbling starts when Carleton Leonard's long ball sets up Paul Petts. Bertschin halts the slow-handclapping by slipping in his first City goal. Sub John Fashanu enjoys a lively introduction before Mendham's half-volley wins it.											

No / Date	Venue	Opponent	Att	Pos	Res / Pts	F-A	H-T	Scorers, Times, and Referees	1	2	3	4	5	6	7	8	9	10	11	12
11	A	WATFORD		13	L	0-3	0-2		Woods Ch	Symonds	Donachie	McGuire	Walford	Hoadley	Barham	Fashanu	Bertschin*	Mendham	Woods Cl	Jack
24/10			*14,463*	2	16			*Bolton 38, Barnes 43, Blissett 84*	*Sherwood*	*Rice*	*Pritchett*	*Taylor*	*Terry*	*Bolton*	*Callaghan*	*Blissett*	*Jenkins**	*Jackett*	*Barnes*	*Rostron*
								Ref: A Hamil	The Canaries are swept aside on a dismal afternoon in Hertfordshire. Ian Bolton's intended cross somehow squeezes in at the near post. John Barnes is left unmarked to head a second for Graham Taylor's men. A Bolton free-kick bounces off the post and Luther Blissett heads another.											
12	H	BOLTON		12	D	0-0	0-0		Woods Ch	Symonds	Donachie	McGuire	Walford	Watson	Barham*	**Haylock**	Jack	Mendham	Bennett	Shepherd
31/10			12,991	*21*	17				*McDonagh*	*Whitworth*	*Bennett*	*Henry*	*Jones*	*Gowling*	*Chandler*	*Kidd*	*Hoggan*	*Cantello*	*Thompson*	
								Ref: J Bray	Local boy Paul Haylock debuts in a match dominated by City. Inspired goalkeeping by Eire international Jim McDonagh keeps Bolton on terms, but they are constantly torn apart and lucky not to be well behind by half-time. As one-sided a goalless draw as you could wish to see!											
13	A	CARDIFF		13	L	0-1	0-0		Woods Ch	Symonds	Donachie	McGuire	Walford	Watson	Shepherd	Haylock	Jack	Mendham	Bennett	
7/11			*5,704*	*12*	17			*Bennett D 66*	*Grotier*	*Jones*	*Gilbert*	*Maddy*	*Thomas*	*Bennett G*	*Bennett D*	*Micallef*	*Stevens*	*Hughes*	*Lewis*	
								Ref: D Hedges	Richie Morgan's Cardiff look a disjointed outfit and this is a poor contest, especially in the first half. The home side should have been punished for some slipshod work. Major frustration for manager Brown as Walford fails to make an interception and Dave Bennett nets a sweet effort.											
14	H	CAMBRIDGE		11	W	2-1	1-0	Walford 27, McGuire 86	Woods Ch	Haylock	Donachie	McGuire	Walford	Watson	Symonds	Muzinic	Jack	Royle	Bennett*	Shepherd
14/11			13,467	*7*	20			*Fallon 88*	*Webster*	*Streete*	*Murray*	*Taylor*	*Fallon*	*O'Neill*	*Finney*	*Spriggs*	*Mayo*	*Reilly*	*Gibbins*	
								Ref: K Hackett	The first league meeting between the clubs ends in a rather lucky City win – just like last year's cup-tie, Brown admits. John Docherty's side prove a handful and Steve Fallon's late goal gets alarm bells ringing. United's lanky striker George Reilly does well as an emergency defender.											
15	H	DERBY		7	W	4-1	2-0	Barham 1, Bertschin 26, Fashanu 49,	Woods Ch	Symonds	Donachie	McGuire	Walford	Watson	Barham*	Muzinic	Bertschin	Fashanu	Mendham	Jack
21/11			13,457	*17*	23			*Osgood 59* [Mendham 60]	*Jones*	*Coop*	*Buckley*	*Powell S**	*Sheridan*	*Powell B*	*Emery*	*Hector*	*Clayton*	*Swindlehurst*	*Emson*	*Osgood*
								Ref: J Moules	This is more like it! Fit-again Barham buries a 20-yarder after just 48 seconds. Muzinic's corner is headed home by Bertschin and City look confident. Fashanu nets his first senior goal from a Barham pass, but gets in the way of Woods, allowing Keith Osgood to score a consolation.											
16	A	CRYSTAL PALACE		7	L	1-2	0-0	Mendham 62	Woods Ch	Symonds	Donachie	McGuire	Walford	Watson	Barham	Muzinic	Bertschin	Fashanu	Mendham*	Jack
24/11			*9,010*	*15*	23			*Mabbutt 58, 88*	*Barron*	*Bason*	*Boulter*	*Murphy*	*Cannon*	*Lovell*	*Price**	*Smillie*	*Langley*	*Mabbutt*	*Hilaire*	*Galliers*
								Ref: A Seville	Palace's new caretaker-boss Steve Kember gets a boost in his first home game when Kevin Mabbutt nets a dipping shot. Mendham levels with a fine left-foot volley. To City's horror, both points are lost near the end as a Walford clearance cannons into the net off the back of Mabbutt.											
17	A	BLACKBURN		8	L	0-3	0-1		Woods Ch	Symonds	Donachie	McGuire	Walford	Watson	Haylock*	Bennett	Bertschin	Fashanu	Mendham	Jack
28/11			*8,153*	*10*	23			*Garner 44, 60, Miller 83*	*Gennoe*	*Branagan*	*Rathbone*	*Arnott*	*Keeley*	*Fazackerley*	*Miller*	*Stonehouse*	*Bell*	*Garner*	*Brotherston*	
								Ref: F Roberts	Fashanu, eager but gauche, is booked for a crude challenge on Glenn Keeley. Simon Garner pounces to net two clinical efforts either side of the break. Dwindling City hopes are dead and buried when Ian Miller leaves Watson in his wake and beats Woods with a fine shot on the run.											
18	H	LEICESTER		12	D	0-0	0-0		Woods Ch	Symonds	Donachie	McGuire	Walford	Watson	Jack	Muzinic	Royle*	Bertschin	Bennett	Mendham
5/12			13,367	*9*	24				*Wallington*	*Williams*	*Leet*	*Peake*	*May*	*O'Neill*	*Lynex*	*Hebberd*	*Lineker*	*Wilson*	*Kelly*	
								Ref: C Downey	Three are axed after the Ewood Park fiasco. The home side welcomes back Eddie Kelly for a second spell with them. Gary Lineker goes close twice near the end. City are booed by unhappy home fans. Sir Arthur South has announced cutbacks and seven backroom staff get redundancy.											
19	H	LUTON		12	L	1-3	1-3	Deehan 43	Woods Ch	Symonds	Downs	McGuire	Walford	Watson	Barham	Muzinic*	**Deehan**	Bertschin	Bennett	Mendham
28/12			**19,348**	*1*	24			*Antic 3, White 10, Stein 14*	*Findlay*	*Stephens*	*Aizlewood*	*Antic*	*Goodyear*	*Donaghy*	*Hill*	*Stein*	*White*	*Fuccillo*	*Moss*	
								Ref: M Dimblebee	Raddy Antic fires David Pleat's table-toppers ahead and stunned City concede two more before recovering composure. John Deehan, signed on loan from West Brom, taps home a simple debut goal and sets up a much less one-sided second half. The Hatters twice strike the Norwich bar.											
20	A	CHARLTON		11	D	0-0	0-0		Woods Ch	Symonds	Downs	McGuire	Walford	Watson	Mendham	Jack	Deehan	Bertschin	Bennett	
30/12			*6,277*	*10*	25				*Johns*	*Naylor**	*Ferns*	*Gritt*	*McAllister*	*Phillips L*	*Lansdowne*	*Walsh*	*Hales*	*Berry*	*Robinson*	*Elliott*
								Ref: M James	Paul Walsh hits the City bar, Martin Robinson misses a sitter, but Bertschin also goes close with a lob. It's City's first away draw in 36 league games. A big 'clear the air' meeting involving directors, coaching staff and players sees the manager and his coach given a vote of confidence.											
21	H	ROTHERHAM		10	W	2-0	1-0	Deehan 17, Bertschin 51	Woods Ch	Symonds	Downs	McGuire	Walford	Watson	Mendham	Jack	Deehan	Bertschin	Bennett	
16/1			12,750	*18*	28				*Mountford*	*Forrest*	*Taylor*	*Rhodes*	*Stancliffe*	*Green*	*Towner*	*Gooding*	*Moore*	*Fern**	*Henson*	*Alexander*
								Ref: D Axcell	Deehan signs for £175,000 after one month on loan. He opens the scoring on a very tricky surface after Watson heads a corner in his direction. Bertschin chests the ball down and cracks in a magnificent drive. The win comes as a big relief, but this was certainly not a memorable match.											

No	Date		Att	Pos	Pt	F-A	H-T	Scorers, Times, and Referees	1	2	3	4	5	6	7	8	9	10	11	12 sub used
22	A	NEWCASTLE		11	L	1-2	0-0	Downs 58	Woods Ch	Symonds	Downs	McGuire	Walford	Watson	Mendham	Jack	Deehan	Bertschin	Barham	
	30/1		*14,447*	*10*	28			*Mills 50, Varadi 72*	*Carr*	*Brownlie*	*Saunders*	*Trewick*	*Carney*	*Haddock*	*Mills*	*Martin*	*Varadi*	*Wharton*	*Waddle*	
								Ref: D Scott	Debutant David Mills applies a sweet finish after a through ball from Imre Varadi. Downs decides to go it alone and after a lengthy run, clips home a fine equaliser. Varadi, who was a City target in the summer, beats Woods from close range. Arthur Cox's outfit deserve the victory.											
23	H	SHEFFIELD WED		11	L	2-3	1-1	O'Neill 29, Barham 70	Woods Ch	Symonds	Downs	McGuire	Walford	Watson	Mendham*	O'Neill	Deehan	Bertschin	Bennett	Barham
	3/2		15,767	*6*	28			*Bannister 41, 86, Shirtliff Pe 75*	*Bolder*	*Sterland*	*Williamson*	*Pickering*	*Shirtliff Pe*	*Smith*	*Megson*	*Shirtliff Pa**	*Bannister*	*Pearson*	*Mellor*	*Owen*
								Ref: M Dimblebee	Bargain buy Martin O'Neill returns for a second spell and raps in a scorcher. City go in level after a superb first half, but are then undone by two horrendous errors. Woods drops a corner at the feet of Peter Shirtliff and then Watson's dreadful back-pass lets in grateful Gary Bannister.											
24	H	WREXHAM		11	W	4-0	2-0	Bertschin 28, O'Neill 43, Watson 54, [Bennett 56]	Woods Ch	Symonds	Downs*	McGuire	Walford	Watson	Barham	O'Neill	Deehan	Bertschin	Bennett	Jack
	6/2		12,300	*21*	31				*Niedzwiecki*	*Jones J*	*Bater*	*Dowman*	*Ciegelski*	*Ronson*	*Fox*	*McNeil*	*Edwards**	*Buxton !*	*Hunt*	*Jones S*
								Ref: D Vickers	Bertschin buries a 10-yard header and O'Neill converts a rebound to leave City cruising by the break. McGuire's free-kick is headed home by Watson and the demoralised Robins concede again as Bennett taps in Bertschin's cross. Steve Buxton departs for fouling Downs and arguing.											
25	A	OLDHAM		12	L	0-2	0-1		Woods Ch	Symonds	Downs	McGuire	Walford	Watson	Jack	O'Neill	Deehan	Bertschin	Mendham	
	16/2		*5,283*	*3*	31			*Wylde 26, Keegan 48*	*McDonnell*	*Hoolickin**	*Ryan*	*Keegan*	*Clements*	*Futcher*	*Wylde*	*Heaton*	*Atkinson*	*Palmer*	*McDonough*	*Steel*
								Ref: G Tyson	Rodger Wylde applies a clever finish after outpacing Symonds. Ged Keegan pokes in John Ryan's cross. Spells of City pressure go unrewarded in a game of six bookings. The Latics are chasing promotion, but after this game their hopes collapse due to a run of ten games without victory.											
26	H	CHELSEA		12	W	2-1	2-1	Mendham 3, Jack 35	Woods Ch	Haylock	Downs	McGuire	Walford	Watson	Jack	O'Neill	Shepherd*	Bertschin	Mendham	Mountford
	20/2		16,018	*9*	34			*Walker 26*	*Francis*	*Locke*	*Hutchings*	*Nutton*	*Droy**	*Pates*	*Rh'-Brown*	*Hales*	*Lee*	*Walker*	*Fillery*	*Mayes*
								Ref: M Lowe	Mendham flashes in an early drive and sparks a good City display. Big Micky Droy surprises everyone by popping up on the flank and his low cross is netted by Clive Walker. An O'Neill cross is headed back by Bertschin for Jack to touch home. Peter Mountford comes on for his debut.											
27	A	BARNSLEY		12	W	1-0	1-0	Bertschin 42	Woods Ch	Haylock	Downs	McGuire	Walford	Watson	Jack	O'Neill	Shepherd	Bertschin	Mendham	
	24/2		*15,360*	*10*	37				*Horn*	*Law*	*Chambers*	*Cooper*	*Banks*	*McCarthy*	*Evans*	*Parker**	*Aylott*	*McHale*	*Birch*	*Glavin*
								Ref: K Barratt	O'Neill is playing well and his arrival has made City look far more effective. His low cross is turned past Bobby Horn by in-rushing Bertschin. O'Neill says afterwards he thinks there's still time to join the promotion race. Hoadley, Paddon and Hansbury all leave the club for Hong Kong.											
28	H	QP RANGERS		12	L	0-1	0-1		Woods Ch	Haylock	Downs	McGuire	Walford	Watson	Jack	O'Neill	Deehan	Bertschin	Mendham*	**Mountford**
	27/2		15,928	*7*	37			*Roeder 40*	*Hucker*	*Howe*	*Gillard*	*Neill*	*Hazell*	*Roeder*	*Currie*	*Flanagan*	*Allen*	*Stainrod*	*Gregory*	
								Ref: B Hill	Terry Venables urges Glenn Roeder to go up for a corner and he duly volleys it straight past Woods. The referee is felled by a cigarette lighter, thrown from the Barclay end. Donachie returns to the USA. City complain that part of the huge Kevin Reeves fee is still unpaid by Man City.											
29	H	WATFORD		12	W	4-2	1-2	O'Neill 38, Watson 60, Deehan 65p,	Woods Ch	Haylock	Downs	McGuire	Walford	Watson	Jack	O'Neill	Deehan	Bertschin	Mendham	
	13/3		15,534	*2*	40			*Barnes 5, Taylor 41* [Bertschin 74]	*Sherwood*	*Rice*	*Rostron*	*Taylor*	*Terry*	*Bolton*	*Callaghan**	*Blissett*	*Jenkins*	*Lohman*	*Barnes*	*Armstrong*
								Ref: H Taylor	High-flying Hornets surge ahead as John Barnes nets a low cross. O'Neill cracks in McGuire's pass, but Les Taylor's rasping drive restores the lead. A great fightback sees Watson, nursing a cut head, bravely equalise. Jan Lohman concedes a penalty, and later Bertschin seals a fine win.											
30	A	ORIENT		11	D	1-1	1-1	Jack 32	Woods Ch	Haylock*	Downs	McGuire	Walford	Watson	Jack	O'Neill	Deehan	Bertschin	Mendham	Bennett
	16/3		*2,933*	*21*	41			*Jennings 10*	*Day*	*Hughton*	*Roffey*	*Fisher*	*Gray*	*Foster*	*Margerrison**	*Silkman*	*Godfrey*	*Moores*	*Jennings*	*Hallybone*
								Ref: R Milford	Billy Jennings rifles the relegation-haunted Londoners into an early lead. Mervyn Day, who has a fine game, blocks a Deehan effort but Jack nods in the loose ball. John Margerrison is stretchered off after a crude challenge by Bertschin. A sub-3,000 crowd generates little atmosphere.											
31	A	BOLTON		11	W	1-0	0-0	O'Neill 85	Woods Ch	Haylock	Downs	Mendham	Walford	Watson	Jack	O'Neill	Deehan	Bertschin	Mendham	
	20/3		*6,199*	*18*	44				*McDonagh*	*Whitworth*	*Bennett*	*Henry*	*Jones*	*McElhinney*	*Chandler*	*Foster*	*Gowling*	*Hoggan*	*Langley*	
								Ref: P Willis	After playing well for just a point at Orient, City look below-par at Burnden Park but snatch all three! Jack brings down John Chandler, but Paul Jones' penalty is brilliantly saved by Woods. O'Neill jubilantly snaps up a late winner as his shot deflects into the net off unlucky Jones.											

32	H	CARDIFF	11	W	2-1	0-0	Jack 60, Bertschin 80	Woods Ch	Haylock	Downs	McGuire	Walford	Watson	Jack	O'Neill	Mendham	Bertschin	Bennett	
27/3		12,720	21	47			*Gilbert 79*	*Healey*	*Jones*	*Gilbert*	*Pontin*	*Hughes**	*Mullen*	*Grapes*	*Henderson*	*Kitchen*	*Bennett D*	*Stevens*	*Micallef*
							Ref: D Reeves	Struggling Cardiff hit five last week and are in 'revival' mode. After Jack's close-range goal, they battle back and Tim Gilbert cracks a cross high into the net. Straight from the re-start O'Neill finds Bertschin, who nets. Two days earlier, Norwich gave nine of their squad free transfers.											
33	A	CAMBRIDGE	10	W	2-1	0-0	Mendham 58, Deehan 65	Woods Ch	Haylock	Downs	McGuire	Walford	Watson	Bennett	O'Neill	Deehan	Bertschin	Mendham	
3/4		*7,035*	14	50			*Fallon 85*	*Key*	*Donaldson*	*Murray*	*Smith*	*Fallon*	*O'Neill*	*Cartwright*	*Spriggs**	*Gibbins*	*Finney*	*Goldsmith*	*Turner*
							Ref: T Bune	The U's have a long injury list and ex-Canary Roger Gibbins teams up with teenager Martin Goldsmith in attack. Deehan gets the all-important second after seizing on a poor 40-yard back-pass by Lindsay Smith. Steve Fallon nets a late consolation, but City hang on to notch a 'double.'											
34	H	CHARLTON	9	W	**5-0**	2-0	O'Neill 5, Deehan 23, 60, 71, Jack 70	Woods Ch	Haylock	Downs	Barham	Walford	Watson	Bennett*	O'Neill	Deehan	Bertschin	Mendham	Jack
10/4		14,908	14	53				*Johns*	*Naylor*	*Elliott*	*Mehmet*	*Gritt*	*Phillips L*	*Ambrose**	*Walsh*	*Hales*	*Berry*	*Robinson*	*Lansdowne*
							Ref: J Hunting	O'Neill scrambles an early goal and Alan Mullery's men crumble. Deehan nets after an O'Neill miskick and then heads a picture goal. Crosses by Barham set up Jack and Deehan's hat-trick goal. City are now just five points adrift of the top three. Royle's knee injury forces him to retire.											
35	A	LUTON	9	L	0-2	0-0		Woods Ch	Haylock*	Downs	McGuire	Walford	Watson	Barham	O'Neill	Deehan	Bertschin	Mendham	Jack
12/4		*15,061*	1	53			*Stein 54, Jennings 57*	*Findlay*	*Stephens*	*Money*	*Horton*	*Goodyear*	*Donaghy*	*Hill*	*Stein*	*White*	*Fuccillo*	*Moss**	*Jennings*
							Ref: B Martin	City boldly attack the leaders at fortress Kenilworth Road. Dave Watson scoops a good chance over the bar, and Downs strikes Jake Findlay's post. Brian Stein achieves the breakthrough for relieved Luton and shortly afterwards sub Billy Jennings pounces to net his first Hatters goal.											
36	A	DERBY	10	W	2-0	1-0	O'Neill 43, Bennett 90	Woods Ch	Haylock	Downs	McGuire	Walford	Bennett	Barham	O'Neill	Deehan	Bertschin	Mendham	
17/4		*12,508*	14	56				*Banovic*	*Barton*	*Buckley*	*Skivington*	*Sheridan*	*McAlle*	*George*	*Attley*	*Wilson**	*Swindlehurst*	*Emson*	*Hector*
							Ref: D Allison	Many feel the Luton defeat ended the promotion dream, but City aren't finished yet. A Woods drop-kick is headed on and O'Neill volleys in. In the last minute Dave Swindlehurst misses a chance after Bennett's bad back-pass. Moments later Bennett makes amends with a cracking shot.											
37	A	SHREWSBURY	6	W	2-0	2-0	Deehan 3, Mendham 24	Woods Ch	Haylock	Downs	McGuire	Walford	Watson	Bennett	O'Neill	Deehan	Bertschin	Mendham*	Barham
20/4		*3,590*	20	59				*Wardle*	*Griffin*	*Johnson*	*Cross*	*Blake*	*MacLaren*	*Petts*	*McNally*	*Tong*	*Bates*	*Dungworth*	
							Ref: N Midgley	Deehan heads home an inswinging corner. A Bertschin shot is cleared off the line, but Mendham is on hand to score. Later on, Mendham has a toe broken. Shrews' manager Graham Turner is full of praise for City's first-half display. Norwich rise into the top six and the tension mounts.											
38	H	BLACKBURN	5	W	2-0	2-0	Bertschin 10, McGuire 36	Woods Ch	Haylock	Downs	McGuire	Walford	Watson	Barham	O'Neill	Deehan	Bertschin*	Bennett	Jack
24/4		16,309	10	62				*Butcher*	*Branagan*	*Rathbone*	*Speight*	*Keeley*	*Fazackerley*	*Miller*	*Stonehouse*	*Lowey**	*Garner*	*Hamilton*	*Murphy*
							Ref: G Napthine	City's biggest crowd in four months enjoys a splendid first-half display. Bertschin's downward header gets the ball rolling. Deehan hits the bar before Bennett and Bertschin set up McGuire, who drills in a fierce shot. Jack goes close with an overhead kick. O'Neill is superb in midfield.											
39	A	LEICESTER	4	W	4-1	1-0	Deehan 22, Barham 47, Bertschin 53,	Woods Ch	Haylock	Symonds	McGuire	Walford	Watson	Barham	O'Neill	Deehan	Bertschin	Bennett	
1/5		*19,630*	8	65			*May 88* [Leet 61(og)]	*Wallington*	*Friar*	*Leet*	*Peake*	*May*	*O'Neill*	*Lynex*	*Lineker*	*Melrose*	*Welsh*	*Kelly*	
							Ref: J Worrall	Rampant City maintain the momentum and force the Foxes on to the back foot. Deehan rifles the first, Barham nets a half-volley and Bertschin finishes off a clever move with a volley. Youngster Norman Leet lobs into his own goal to make it four. Larry May's late header is academic.											
40	H	GRIMSBY	3	W	2-1	0-0	Deehan 56, Bertschin 67	Woods Ch	Haylock	Downs	McGuire	Walford	Watson	Barham	O'Neill	Deehan*	Bertschin	Bennett	Jack
5/5		18,360	19	68			*Whymark 90*	*Batch*	*Stone*	*O'Dell*	*Waters*	*Cooper*	*Crombie*	*Ford*	*Kilmore*	*Whymark*	*Moore K**	*Brolly*	*Beacock*
							Ref: C Maskell	On a tense evening Grimsby make life tough for Norwich. But nearly an hour of frustration is forgotten when two close-range goals hit Nigel Blatch's net. Carrow Road roars its relief. It's so tight at the top that Trevor Whymark's late strike might be crucial in terms of goal-difference.											
41	H	ORIENT	3	W	2-0	0-0	Bertschin 48p, Bennett 86	Woods Ch	Haylock	Downs	McGuire	Walford	Watson	Barham	O'Neill	Deehan*	Bertschin	Bennett	Jack
8/5		19,197	22	71				*Day*	*Foster*	*Peach*	*Cornwell*	*Gray*	*Cunningham*	*Godfrey*	*Sussex*	*Houchen*	*McNeil*	*Margerrison*	
							Ref: M Scott	The prize is within grasp, but after all the great displays of recent weeks, the Canaries have now got the jitters! Six are booked as the home fans urge their men on. Nigel Gray fells Deehan and Bertschin nets a viciously struck penalty. Bennett skilfully shoots a second past Mervyn Day.											
42	A	SHEFFIELD W	3	L	1-2	0-0	Bertschin 86	Woods Ch	Haylock	Downs	McGuire	Walford	Watson	Barham*	O'Neill	Deehan	Bertschin	Bennett	Jack
15/5		***24,687***	4	71			*McCulloch 60, Bannister 86*	*Bolder*	*Sterland*	*Williamson*	*Smith*	*Shirtliff Pe*	*Taylor*	*Megson*	*Shelton**	*Bannister*	*McCulloch*	*Curran*	*Simmons*
	Home	Away					Ref: A Hamil	One point will clinch promotion. Andy McCulloch heads in to stun the big away following. Bertschin nets Bennett's cross, but Gary Bannister restores the lead within seconds. A pitch invasion holds the game up. News that Leicester have only drawn means City are going up anyway!											
Average	14,184	10,465																	

League Cup	Att		F-A	H-T	Scorers, Times, and Referees	1	2	3	4	5	6	7	8	9	10	11	12 sub used
2:1 H CHARLTON	8	W	1-0	1-0	Jack 2	Woods	Nightingale	Donachie	McGuire	Walford	Hoadley	Barham	Jack	Bertschin	Shepherd*	Woods Cl	Muzinic
7/10	9,729 *15*					*Johns*	*Naylor*	*Ferns*	*Gritt*	*McAllister*	*Phillips L*	*Elliott*	*Walsh*	*Hales*	*Landsowne*	*Robinson*	
					Ref: G Flint	After just 64 seconds a perfectly weighted Donachie cross is headed home by Jack from six yards. A rather dour game only springs to life when tricky youngster Paul Walsh hits the bar and forces Woods into a fine save from a header. Only Jack and Barham give decent displays.											
2:2 A CHARLTON	13	W	1-0	0-0	Jack 89	Woods	Symonds	Donachie	McGuire	Walford	Watson	Barham	Haylock	Jack	Mendham	Bennett	
28/10	*7,366* *6*					*Johns*	*Naylor*	*Dickenson*	*Gritt*	*McAllister*	*Phillips L*	*Elliott*	*Walsh*	*Hales*	*Landsowne**	*Robinson*	*Madden*
					Ref: D Letts (Norwich win 2-0 on aggregate)	Brown makes changes for the second leg, with Walford playing sweeper and young Paul Haylock coming in for his senior debut to do a man-marking job on Martin Robinson. After a Terry Naylor handball, Jack misses a penalty, but makes amends near the end with a far-post header.											
3 A ARSENAL	13	L	0-1	0-1		Woods	Symonds	Donachie*	McGuire	Walford	Watson	Shepherd	Haylock	Jack	Mendham	Bennett	Muzinic
10/11	*19,899* *1:14*				*Nicholas 6*	*Jennings*	*Hollins*	*Sansom*	*Talbot*	*O'Leary*	*Whyte*	*McDermott*	*Sunderland**	*Davis*	*Nicholas*	*Rix*	*Meade*
					Ref: E Read	Peter Nicholas lobs over Woods to register his first Gunners' goal. Woods stars, ending the game battered and bruised, but unbeaten over the last 84 minutes. Home boss Neill generously says he was relieved to hear the final whistle, but in truth Pat Jennings was never really troubled.											

FA Cup						1	2	3	4	5	6	7	8	9	10	11	12 sub used
3 A STOKE	11	W	1-0	1-0	Jack 10	Woods Ch	Symonds	Downs	McGuire	Walford	Watson	Mendham	Jack	Deehan	Bertschin	Bennett	
2/1	*12,805* *1:15*					*Fox*	*Evans*	*Hampton**	*Dodd*	*O'Callaghan*	*Doyle*	*Griffiths*	*Heath*	*Chapman*	*Bracewell*	*Ursem*	*Johnson PA*
					Ref: G Flint	Deehan's corner is scrambled in at close range by Jack to give City a great start. Richie Barker's side look nervy and disjointed and ideal giant-killing material. Chants of 'Barker out' can be heard as the home side struggle to break Norwich down. Peter Fox foils a good Deehan attempt.											
4 H DONCASTER	10	W	2-1	1-1	Jack 20, Watson 57	Woods Ch	Symonds	Downs	McGuire	Walford	Watson	Mendham	Jack	Deehan	Bertschin	Barham	
23/1	17,311 *3:19*				*Dawson 18*	*Humphries*	*Lally*	*Cooper*	*Russell*	*Lister*	*Dowd*	*Pugh*	*Dawson*	*Douglas*	*Snodin G*	*Little**	*Snodin I*
					Ref: B Daniels	Plucky Rovers come out fighting and strike the post in the early stages. Then a piledriver from Richard Dawson deflects off Walford and flies in. City level quickly when Mendham's shot from a narrow angle falls for Jack. Watson heads home a Barham corner to put City in the last 16.											
5 A WEST BROM	11	L	0-1	0-1		Woods Ch	Symonds	Downs	McGuire	Walford	Watson	Barham*	O'Neill	Deehan	Bertschin	Mendham	Jack
13/2	*18,867* *1:14*				*Regis 24*	*Grew*	*Bennett*	*Statham*	*Lewis*	*Wile*	*Robertson*	*Cross*	*King*	*Regis*	*Owen*	*MacKenzie*	
					Ref: J Worrell	Cyrille Regis accelerates away from Watson and thrashes home a marvellous goal. It's a spectacular effort that will subsequently be shown countless times on TV. It pushes his claims for the England 1982 World Cup squad. City push forward in response, but fail to beat Mark Grew.											

		Home					Away					
	P	W	D	L	F	A	W	D	L	F	A	Pts
1 Luton	42	16	3	2	48	19	9	10	2	38	27	88
2 Watford	42	13	6	2	46	16	10	5	6	30	26	80
3 NORWICH	42	14	3	4	41	19	8	2	11	23	31	71
4 Sheffield W	42	10	8	3	31	23	10	2	9	24	28	70
5 QP Rangers	42	15	4	2	40	9	6	2	13	25	34	69
6 Barnsley	42	13	4	4	33	14	6	6	9	26	27	67
7 Rotherham	42	13	5	3	42	19	7	2	12	24	35	67
8 Leicester	42	12	5	4	31	19	6	7	8	25	29	66
9 Newcastle	42	14	4	3	30	14	4	4	13	22	36	62
10 Blackburn	42	11	4	6	26	15	5	7	9	21	28	59
11 Oldham	42	9	9	3	28	23	6	5	10	22	28	59
12 Chelsea	42	10	5	6	37	30	5	7	9	23	30	57
13 Charlton	42	11	5	5	33	22	2	7	12	17	43	51
14 Cambridge	42	11	4	6	31	19	2	5	14	17	34	48
15 Crystal Pal	42	9	2	10	25	26	4	7	10	9	19	48
16 Derby	42	9	8	4	32	23	3	4	14	21	45	48
17 Grimsby	42	5	8	8	29	30	6	5	10	24	35	46
18 Shrewsbury	42	10	6	5	26	19	1	7	13	11	38	46
19 Bolton	42	10	4	7	28	24	3	3	15	11	37	46
20 Cardiff	42	9	2	10	28	32	3	6	12	17	29	44
21 Wrexham	42	9	4	8	22	22	2	7	12	18	34	44
22 Orient	42	6	8	7	23	24	4	1	16	13	37	39
	924	239	111	112	710	461	112	111	239	461	710	1275

Odds & ends

Double wins: (5) Cambridge, Derby, Grimsby, Shrewsbury, Wrexham.
Double losses: (4) Luton, Oldham, Sheffield W.

Won from behind: (4) Newcastle (h), Shrewsbury (h), Watford (h), Doncaster (h) (FAC).
Lost from in front: (2) Rotherham (a), Sheffield W (h).

High spots: Achieving promotion – thanks to a remarkable late run.
The return of the influential Martin O'Neill – at a bargain price.
A superb fight-back to crush high-flying Watford in March.
The fine 4-1 win at Leicester in May, crucial to the promotion bid.
Bertschin defying his early barrackers with a 12-goal tally.

Low spots: The severe financial problems behind the scenes.
The referee being felled by a missile in the QPR home match.
Joe Royle having to retire because of knee trouble.
Losing Justin Fashanu – subsequently a £1million flop at Forest.

Player of the Year: Greg Downs.
Ever-presents: (2) Steve Walford, Chris Woods.
Hat-tricks: (1) John Deehan, v Charlton (h).
Hat-tricks against: (0).
Leading scorer: (14) Ross Jack.

	Appearances						Goals			
	Lge	*Sub*	LC	*Sub*	FAC	*Sub*	Lge	LC	FAC	Tot
Barham, Mark	**25**	*2*	2		2		**4**			**4**
Bennett, Dave	**21**	*1*	2		1		**3**			**3**
Bertschin, Keith	**35**	*1*	1		3		**12**			**12**
Deehan, John	**22**				3		**10**			**10**
Donachie, Willie	**11**		3							
Downs, Greg	**28**				3		**1**			**1**
Fashanu, John	**4**	*1*					**1**			**1**
Hart, Andrew		*1*								
Haylock, Paul	**21**		2							
Hoadley, Phil	**3**	*1*	1							
Jack, Ross	**24**	*11*	3		2	*1*	**10**	2	2	**14**
McGuire, Mick	**39**		3		3		**2**			**2**
Mendham, Peter	**25**	*4*	2		3		**6**			**6**
Mountford, Peter		*2*								
Muzinic, Drazen	**6**	*1*		*2*						
Nightingale, Mark	**8**	*1*	1							
O'Neill, Martin	**20**				1		**6**			**6**
Paddon, Graham	**8**									
Royle, Joe	**2**									
Shepherd, Greig	**12**	*3*	2				**2**			**2**
Symonds, Richard	**18**		2		3					
Walford, Steve	**42**		3		3		**1**			**1**
Watson, Dave	**38**		2		3		**3**		1	**4**
Woods, Chris	**42**		3		3		**1**			**1**
Woods, Clive	**8**		1							
(own-goals)							**2**			**2**
25 players used	**462**	***29***	**33**	***2***	**33**	***1***	**64**	**2**	**3**	**69**

No	Date	Opponent	Att	Pos	Pt	F-A	H-T	Scorers, Times, and Referees	1	2	3	4	5	6	7	8	9	10	11	12 sub used
1	H	MANCHESTER C			L	1-2	0-2	Deehan 58	Woods	Haylock	Downs	McGuire	Walford	Watson	Barham	O'Neill	Deehan	Bertschin	Mendham*	Jack
	28/8		22,638		0			*Cross 3, Power 45*	*Corrigan*	*Ranson*	*McDonald*	*Baker*	*Bond*	*Caton*	*Hareide*	*Reeves*	*Cross*	*Hartford*	*Power*	
								Ref: B Daniels	Ex-Canary David Cross heads his first Blues goal. Ray Ranson's low cross is turned in neatly by Paul Power. Deehan bundles in a consolation. The long-running feud between Ken Brown and Blues' boss John Bond is stoked up by Anglia TV but the men bury the hatchet after the match.											
2	A	ARSENAL			D	1-1	0-0	Deehan 73	Woods	Haylock	**Smith**	McGuire	Walford	Watson	Barham	O'Neill	Deehan	Bertschin	Mendham*	Mountford
	31/8		*22,652*		1			*Woodcock 72*	*Wood*	*Hollins*	*Sansom**	*Talbot*	*Davis*	*Whyte*	*Robson*	*Sunderland*	*Woodcock*	*Chapman*	*Rix*	*Devine*
								Ref: L Burden	Tony Woodcock's lightning pace gets him into position to open the scoring for Terry Neill's side. Within 60 seconds, Deehan rises to send in a downward header past keeper George Wood. Ex-Forest defender Colin Smith has been rescued from the dole queue to make his City debut.											
3	A	SWANSEA		19	L	**0-4**	0-3		Woods	Haylock	Smith	McGuire	Walford	Watson	Barham	O'Neill	Deehan	Bertschin	Mendham	
	4/9		*11,694*	*2*	1			*Latchford 12, 29, 81, James R 40*	*Davies*	*Marustik*	*Hadziabdic*	*Irwin*	*Stevenson*	*Rajkovic*	*Curtis*	*James R**	*James L*	*Charles*	*Latchford*	*Stanley*
								Ref: B Stevens	Bob Latchford heads in Chris Marustik's cross and is unmarked to nod home Leighton James's free-kick. Robbie James kills off any lingering Norwich hopes, converting after Latchford hits the bar. John Toshack's men rise to second in the table after Latchford completes his hat-trick.											
4	H	BIRMINGHAM		17	W	**5-1**	3-1	Bertschin 9, 80, O'Neill 26, 29,	Woods	Haylock	Downs	McGuire	Walford	Watson	Barham	O'Neill	Deehan	Bertschin*	Mendham	Smith
	8/9		13,860	*21*	4			*Broadhurst 37* [Barham 57]	*Blyth*	*Langan*	*Dennis*	*Scott**	*V d Hauwe*	*Broadhurst*	*Summerfield*	*Dillon*	*Harford*	*Curbishley*	*Carrodus*	*Hagan*
								Ref: J Martin	A miserable return to Carrow Road for manager Ron Saunders. Norwich's finishing is lethal and O'Neill's second goal a real classic. He cuts into the area and crashes a swerving shot past Jim Blyth. Bertschin collides with Blyth as he nets the fifth, and sustains back and ankle injuries.											
5	H	SOUTHAMPTON		17	D	1-1	0-0	Deehan 59p	Woods	Haylock	Downs	McGuire	Walford	Watson	Barham	O'Neill	Deehan	Bertschin*	Mendham	Smith
	11/9		16,492	*20*	5			*Armstrong 71*	*Shilton*	*Baker*	*Rofe*	*Williams*	*Nicholl*	*Wright*	*Ball*	*Agboola*	*Fashanu*	*Armstrong*	*Cassells*	
								Ref: J Deakin	Chris Nicholl clatters into Deehan, who makes no mistake from the spot. Lawrie McMenemy's outfit get a deserved equaliser when David Armstrong's shot is deflected in by Watson, following a fine run by Keith Cassells. Bertschin departs early again - this time with a head wound.											
6	A	EVERTON		19	D	1-1	0-0	Haylock 58	Woods	Haylock	Downs	McGuire	Walford	Watson*	Barham	O'Neill	Deehan	Fashanu	Mendham	**Van Wijk**
	18/9		*20,281*	*13*	6			*Irvine 54*	*Southall*	*Borrows*	*Walsh*	*Ratcliffe*	*Wright*	*McMahon*	*Irvine**	*Heath*	*Sharp*	*King*	*Sheedy*	*Ross*
								Ref: C Newsome	Everton make several team changes after losing to Notts County. Alan Irvine tries a pot-shot from 25 yards and the ball flies past a surprised Woods. City respond quickly and when Barham's cross eludes everybody in the danger area, Haylock collects and fires in his first senior goal.											
7	H	WEST BROM		19	L	1-3	1-1	Deehan 45	Woods	Haylock	Downs	McGuire	Walford	Deehan	Barham	O'Neill	Fashanu*	Bertschin	Mendham	**Alexander**
	25/9		15,130	*7*	6			*Regis 40, 64, 87*	*Grew*	*Batson*	*Whitehead*	*Zondervan*	*Bennett*	*Robertson*	*Jol*	*Brown*	*Regis*	*Owen*	*Eastoe*	
								Ref: J Moules	Cyrille Regis gives Woods no chance with a scorching header from Clive Whitehead's cross. Deehan levels, soaring high to head home. Regis' second is a drive that flies in off a post. The big man displays his skills on the deck, completing a fine hat-trick by dancing around the keeper.											
8	A	SUNDERLAND		21	L	1-4	0-0	Bennett 88	Woods	Haylock	Downs	McGuire	Walford	**Walsh**	Barham	O'Neill	Deehan	Bertschin	Bennett	
	2/10		*13,144*	*15*	6			*Rowell 50, 73, McCoist 69, Cooke 80*	*Turner*	*Nicholl*	*Munro*	*Venison*	*Hindmarch*	*Elliott*	*Buckley*	*Rowell*	*McCoist*	*Pickering*	*Cooke*	
								Ref: A Challinor	The deadlock is broken as Gary Rowell dummies past City debutant Mick Walsh (loaned from Everton) and buries a fine shot. Ally McCoist rifles in a second and Barry Venison sets up another for Rowell. John Cooke taps in the fourth. Bennett's curling free-kick is too late to matter.											
9	A	WATFORD		21	D	2-2	1-2	Deehan 12, Bertschin 61	Woods	Haylock	Van Wijk	McGuire	Walford	Walsh	Barham	O'Neill	Deehan	Bertschin	Bennett	
	9/10		*18,597*	*4*	7			*Jackett 19, Terry 44*	*Sherwood*	*Patching*	*Rostron*	*Taylor**	*Terry*	*Bolton*	*Callaghan*	*Blissett*	*Jenkins*	*Jackett*	*Barnes*	*Armstrong*
								Ref: D Civil	The fans are depressed after one win in eight league games and a poor display against Preston in the Milk Cup. Brown reshuffles and Deehan drops into defence, but still manages a superb 30-yard opening goal. The Hornets hit back, but Bertschin saves a point with a powerful header.											
10	H	TOTTENHAM		21	D	0-0	0-0		Woods	Haylock	Van Wijk	McGuire	Walford	Walsh	Barham	O'Neill	Deehan	Bertschin	Bennett	
	16/10		22,628	*6*	8				*Clemence*	*Price*	*Lacy*	*Miller*	*Brooke*	*O'Reilly*	*Mabbutt*	*Archibald*	*Hazard*	*Villa*	*Crooks*	
								Ref: K Hackett	Deehan again looks good as a sweeper but, for all City's neat football, they rarely trouble Ray Clemence. New Dutch signing Dennis Van Wijk looks impressive. He admits he only came over from Ajax to get fit and learn English, and never really expected to play First Division football.											

No	Venue	Opponent / Date	Att	Pos	Pts	F-A	H-T	Scorers, Times, and Referees	1	2	3	4	5	6	7	8	9	10	11	12 sub used
11	H	ASTON VILLA		19	W	1-0	0-0	Deehan 50p	Woods	Haylock	Walsh	McGuire	Walford	Watson	Van Wijk	O'Neill	Deehan	Bertschin !	Bennett	
		23/10	15,761	11	11				Rimmer	Jones	Gibson !	Evans*	McNaught	Mortimer	Bremner	Shaw	Geddis	Cowans	Morley	Williams
								Ref: K Salmon	Ken McNaught brings Deehan down and the ex-Villa man picks himself up to score from the spot. In the latter stages Bertschin and Colin Gibson clash near the halfway line and both are sent off. It's a largely undistinguished affair, but three points lifts City out of the bottom three.											
12	A	COVENTRY		21	L	0-2	0-0		Woods	Haylock	Walsh	Barham	Walford	Watson	Van Wijk	O'Neill	Deehan	Bertschin	Bennett	
		30/10	8,305	12	11			Hateley 75, Thompson G 85	Sealey	Thomas	Roberts	Butterworth	Dyson	Gillespie	Hendrie*	Jacobs	Hateley	Thompson G	Hunt	Whitton
								Ref: L Shapter	Not a great advert for First Division football, this game is heading for a goalless finish and home fans begin slow-handclapping. Then it springs to life as Mark Hateley heads his first of the season. Garry Thompson, shortly to begin an odyssey featuring eight more clubs, bags the second.											
13	H	NOTTS CO		21	L	1-2	0-0	Deehan 70	Woods	Haylock	**Hareide**	McGuire*	Walford	Watson	Barham	O'Neill	Deehan	Van Wijk	Bennett	Mendham
		6/11	**13,472**	15	11			Mair 52, Christie 87	Avramovic	Goodwin	Worthington	Hooks	Kilcline	Richards	Chiedozie	Christie	McCulloch	Clarke	Mair	
								Ref: D Reeves	Gordon Mair taps in a scrappy goal, but Deehan's brave diving header puts City on terms. John Chiedozie's cross is netted from close range by Trevor Christie. It's frustrating for home fans and one unwisely hurls a missile at Raddy Avramovic. Ken Brown comes on to appeal for order.											
14	A	WEST HAM		22	L	0-1	0-0		Woods	Haylock	Hareide	Van Wijk	Walford	Watson	Barham*	O'Neill	Deehan	Bertschin	Bennett	**Metcalf**
		13/11	22,463	2	11			Clark 53	Parkes	Stewart	Lampard	Bonds	Martin	Devonshire	Van der Elst	Goddard	Clark	Allen	Pike	
								Ref: B Hill	The Hammers' superb start to the season was halted by a thrashing at Stoke last week. City enjoy lots of possession but go down to a sloppy goal. Sandy Clark taps in after shots strike a defender and then a post. Barham mishits a clearance, which very nearly screams into his own net.											
15	H	STOKE		20	W	4-2	0-1	D'han 48p, 57p, B'ham 55, B'schin 77	Woods	Haylock	Hareide*	Van Wijk	Walford	Watson	Barham	O'Neill	Deehan	Bertschin	Bennett	Jack
		20/11	13,658	10	14			McIlroy 21, O'Callaghan 76	Harrison	Parkin D	Hampton	Bracewell	Watson	McAughtrie	Maguire*	McIlroy	O'Callaghan	Thomas	Chamb'lain M	Berry
								Ref: M Dimblebee	Sammy McIlroy taps in the opener, but City turn things around in a big way after bringing on Jack. Deehan nets two spot-kicks given for handballs and Barham and Bertschin both beat Mark Harrison with headers. Brendan O'Callaghan's fierce header is but a momentary setback.											
16	A	MANCHESTER U		21	L	0-3	0-2		Woods	Haylock	Hareide	Van Wijk	Walford	Watson	Barham	O'Neill	Deehan	Bertschin	Bennett*	Jack
		27/11	34,579	4	14			Muhren 36, Robson 44, 56	Bailey	Duxbury	Albiston	Moses	Moran	McQueen	Robson	Muhren	Stapleton	Whiteside*	Coppell	McGarvey
								Ref: J Key	Hareide keeps his place at No 3 and this prompts Downs to slap in a transfer request. A clear Norwich throw-in is given United's way and the move ends with Arnold Muhren scoring with a lovely chip. Bryan Robson rounds Woods for the second and converts another at the back post.											
17	H	LIVERPOOL		20	W	1-0	0-0	Deehan 75	Woods	Haylock	Hareide	McGuire	Walford	Watson	Barham*	O'Neill	Deehan	Bertschin	Van Wijk	Jack
		4/12	22,909	1	17				Grobbelaar	Neal	Kennedy	Thompson	Johnston	Hansen	Dalglish	Lee	Rush	Lawrenson	Souness	
								Ref: J Hunting	Bob Paisley wins his 19th Manager of the Month award, but his team - runaway league leaders - are stopped in their tracks by determined City. On a thrilling afternoon for the home fans, Van Wijk's corner kick sneaks across the face of the goal for a jubilant Deehan to do the honours.											
18	A	BRIGHTON		20	L	0-3	0-1		Woods	Haylock	Hareide	Van Wijk	Walford*	McGuire	Jack	O'Neill	Deehan	Bertschin	Mountford	**Crowe**
		11/12	9,994	18	17			Case 34, Ritchie 75, Robinson 78	Digweed	Ramsey	Nelson	Grealish	Foster	Stevens	Case	Ritchie	Robinson	Ward	Gatting	
								Ref: M Taylor	After the Lord Mayor's show Jimmy Case cuts in and lets fly in characteristic fashion. After an eight-match absence, Andy Ritchie curls in a fine free-kick to kill City's hopes. Michael Robinson steers in another for Jimmy Melia's men. The depressing run of away results continues.											
19	H	NOTT'M FOREST		21	L	0-1	0-1		Woods	Haylock	Hareide	McGuire	Walford	Watson	Jack*	O'Neill	Deehan	Bertschin	Van Wijk	**Donowa**
		18/12	14,151	3	17			Hodge 1	Sutton	Swain	Bowyer	Gunn	Young	Walsh	Proctor	Wallace	Birtles	Hodge	Robertson	
								Ref: D Vickers	The points are decided by one of the fastest goals ever seen in a City match. After 22 seconds Colin Walsh and Ian Wallace combine to set up Steve Hodge, who steers past Woods. No Norwich player had touched the ball at this point. Bertschin and Hareide miss decent opportunities.											
20	A	IPSWICH		20	W	3-2	1-1	Mendham 24, 65, O'Neill 88	Woods	Haylock	Hareide	Mendham	Walford	Watson	Barham	O'Neill	**Channon**	Bertschin	Van Wijk	
		27/12	29,596	11	20			Osman 39, Mariner 68	Cooper	Steggles	McCall	Thijssen	Osman	Butcher	Wark	McCall	Mariner	Brazil	Gates	Putney
								Ref: A Gunn	Mendham shocks Bobby Ferguson's side with a header, but Russell Osman heads Town on terms. Mendham crashes a second in off the bar, but Paul Mariner nets Eric Gates' cross. Near the end, O'Neill curls in a beauty and this time Town can't respond. A Boxing Day to remember!											
21	H	LUTON		20	W	1-0	1-0	Channon 11	Woods	Haylock	Downs	Mendham	Walford	Watson	Barham	O'Neill	Channon	Bertschin	Van Wijk	
		28/12	21,367	17	23				Findlay	Stephens	Money	Horton	Goodyear	Donaghy	Hill	Geddis	Walsh	Fuccillo*	Moss	Antic
								Ref: T Mills	Veteran Channon marks his first home appearance by pouncing on an early chance. He is looking a good capture and the previous day's victory seems to have inspired City. Manager David Pleat reports City coach Machin for a late incident in which he deliberately delays a Luton throw.											

No	Date		Att	Pos	Pt	F-A	H-T	Scorers, Times, and Referees	1	2	3	4	5	6	7	8	9	10	11	12 sub used
22	A	STOKE		19	L	0-1	0-1		Woods	Haylock	Deehan	Mendham	Walford	Watson	Barham	O'Neill	Channon	Bertschin	Van Wijk*	Downs
	1/1		*15,669*	*13*	23			*McIlroy 32*	*Fox*	*Parkin D*	*Hampton*	*Bracewell*	*Watson*	*Berry*	*Painter*	*McIlroy*	*O'Callaghan*	*Thomas**	*Chamb'lain M*	*Maskery*
								Ref: K Walmsley	Richie Barker's side get a dreadful display at Notts County out of their systems and deserve the New Year's Day points. Deehan, wearing the unfamiliar No.3, makes a rare slip to allow in Sammy McIlroy. Brendan O'Callaghan heads just over and Deehan makes a goalline clearance.											
23	H	SWANSEA		17	W	1-0	0-0	Channon 58	Woods	Haylock	Downs	Mendham	Walford	Watson	Barham	O'Neill	Channon	Bertschin	Deehan	
	3/1		16,296	*19*	26				*Davies*	*Robinson**	*Hadziabdic*	*Lewis*	*Evans*	*Rajkovic*	*Curtis*	*James R*	*Mahoney*	*Stevenson*	*Latchford*	*Stanley*
								Ref: C Downey	Dai Davies fumbles Deehan's deflected drive and Channon converts the rebound expertly. After a glorious 18 months or so, John Toshack's side is sliding back down the table again. They take a real pounding after the break, but keep City out. Robbie James hits a post on a rare raid.											
24	A	MANCHESTER C		20	L	1-4	1-3	O'Neill 35	Woods	Haylock*	Downs	Mendham	Walford	Hareide	Barham	O'Neill	Deehan	Bertschin	Van Wijk	Channon
	15/1		*22,000*	*8*	26			*Cross 8, 31, Bond 14, Hartford 84*	*Corrigan*	*Ranson*	*Bond*	*Reid*	*Power*	*Kinsey*	*Tueart*	*Reeves*	*Cross*	*Hartford*	*Bodak*	
								Ref: R Bridges	Ex-Canary David Cross bags a couple, both simple close-range chances. Another old pal, Kevin Bond, heads in Asa Hartford's corner. O'Neill provides a glimmer of hope, hammering in a 30-yard free-kick. This will prove to be John Bond's last home game as Manchester City manager.											
25	H	EVERTON		20	L	0-1	0-1		Woods	Haylock	Downs	Mendham	Walford	Hareide	Barham	O'Neill	Deehan	Channon	Van Wijk*	Bertschin
	22/1		14,180	*7*	26			*Ratcliffe 20*	*Arnold*	*Stevens*	*Bailey*	*Ratcliffe*	*Higgins*	*McMahon*	*King*	*Heath*	*Sharp*	*Reid*	*Sheedy*	
								Ref: H Taylor	Adrian Heath's crossfield pass is expertly slotted home by defender Kevin Ratcliffe. City struggle to respond and feel hard done by when a loud penalty appeal is turned down. The arrival as sub of Bertschin is greeted warmly by the home fans, but they are jeering loudly by the end.											
26	A	SOUTHAMPTON		21	L	**0-4**	0-1	*[Moran 73]*	Woods	Haylock	Hareide	Mendham	Walford	Watson*	Barham	Bertschin	Deehan	Channon	Van Wijk	Downs
	5/2		*17,244*	*17*	26			*Williams 35, Holmes 46, Wallace 51,*	*Shilton*	*Agboola*	*Mills**	*Williams*	*Nicholl*	*Wright*	*Holmes*	*Puckett*	*Moran*	*Armstrong*	*Wallace*	*Cassells*
								Ref: M Bodenham	Watson goes off in the first half with a head injury and City suffer the consequences. Steve Williams rifles in with the team a man short and still disorganised. Nick Holmes' cross drifts over Woods and Danny Wallace gets clear and chips home. Steve Moran lashes in a fierce fourth.											
27	A	TOTTENHAM		21	D	0-0	0-0		Woods	Haylock	Hareide	Mendham	Walford	Watson	Barham	Van Wijk	Deehan	Bertschin	Downs	
	26/2		*23,342*	*8*	27				*Clemence*	*Hughton*	*Lacy*	*Price*	*Hazard**	*Perryman*	*Galvin*	*Mabbutt*	*Gibson*	*Villa*	*Crooks*	*Roberts*
								Ref: E Read	A clean sheet away from home is a rare event, but City have little trouble holding lack-lustre Spurs. Watson and Walford are superb in central defence. Deehan goes to ground in the Spurs area, but penalty appeals are ignored. Pat Jennings keeps a clean sheet in his 1,000th senior match.											
28	H	WATFORD		19	W	3-0	1-0	Watson 19, Van Wijk 76, Deehan 88	Woods	Haylock	Downs	Mendham	Walford	Watson	Barham	Bennett	Deehan	Bertschin	Van Wijk	
	2/3		16,662	*2*	30				*Sherwood*	*Rice*	*Rostron*	*Taylor*	*Sims*	*Bolton*	*Callaghan**	*Blissett*	*Barnes*	*Jackett*	*Jobson*	*Armstrong*
								Ref: G Napthine	Van Wijk was to be dropped today, but is reprieved when Hareide fractures a cheekbone colliding with coach Stringer in training, hours before kick-off. Inevitably, Van Wijk plays a key role in the game, netting his first City goal after Deehan's shot was blocked. Watford are well beaten.											
29	A	ASTON VILLA		19	L	2-3	1-1	Barham 18, Van Wijck 49	Woods	Haylock	Downs	Mendham	Symonds	Watson	Barham	Bennett*	Deehan	Bertschin	Van Wijk	Channon
	5/3		*18,624*	*5*	30			*Withe 23, Deacy 53, Shaw 79*	*Spink*	*Deacy*	*Gibson*	*Evans*	*McNaught*	*Mortimer*	*Bremner*	*Shaw*	*Withe*	*Cowans*	*Walters*	
								Ref: J Worrall	Barham races through to score at the end of a fine move. Five minutes later Peter Withe cancels it out with a firm header from Gordon Cowans' free-kick. Van Wijk fires a shot past Nigel Spink, but Villa aren't finished and Eamonn Deacy and Gary Shaw display excellent finishing skills.											
30	A	NOTTS CO		20	D	2-2	2-1	Deehan 2p, Bertschin 35	Woods	Haylock	Downs	Mendham	Walford	Watson	Barham	Bennett	Deehan	Bertschin	Van Wijk*	Jack
	19/3		***8,064***	*15*	31			*Worthington 45, Christie 86p*	*Leonard*	*Benjamin*	*Worthington*	*Hunt*	*Kilcline*	*Richards*	*Chiedozie*	*Fashanu*	*McCulloch*	*Christie*	*Clarke**	*Harkouk*
								Ref: K Cooper	Pedro Richards' handball gives Deehan a dream start. Bertschin nets a close-range header, but future Canaries boss Nigel Worthington drills County back into the game. Another lead disappears when Bennett loses possession and then brings down John Chiedozie in the closing stages.											
31	H	COVENTRY		20	D	1-1	0-0	Walford 79	Woods	Haylock	Downs	Mendham	Walford	Watson	Barham	O'Neill*	Deehan	Bertschin	Bennett	Channon
	23/3		13,944	*12*	32			*Whitton 68*	*Sealey*	*Thomas*	*Roberts*	*Jacobs*	*Dyson*	*Gillespie*	*Whitton*	*Francis*	*Hunt*	*Hateley*	*Hendrie*	
								Ref: J Scales	Points are desperately needed and the pressure increases when Steve Whitton nets from the far post. Less than ten minutes later Carrow Road roars with relief as Walford hammers in from 20 yards. It's only his second goal in 97 senior games for City and it lights up a cold, damp night.											

32	H	WEST HAM		21	D	1-1	0-1	Deehan 67p	Woods	Haylock	Downs	Mendham	Walford	Watson	Barham	O'Neill	Deehan	Bertschin*	Channon	Jack
26/3			18,582	*13*	33			*Dickens 25*	*Parkes*	*Stewart*	*Lampard*	*Bonds*	*Martin*	*Devonshire*	*Orr*	*Goddard*	*Swindlehurst*	*Dickens*	*Pike*	
								Ref: J Bray	Alan Dickens reacts quicker than Mendham to gain possession and send a great shot into the top corner. City rarely threaten and get a lifeline from the ref when he rules that Alvin Martin pushed Channon inside the area. McGuire, who started the season as skipper, leaves for Barnsley.											
33	A	LUTON		19	W	1-0	1-0	Bennett 26	Woods	Haylock	Downs	Mendham	Walford	Watson	O'Neill	Channon*	Deehan	Bertschin	Bennett	Jack
2/4			*11,211*	*21*	36				*Godden*	*Stephens*	*Thomas**	*Horton*	*Goodyear*	*Elliott*	*Hill*	*Aylott*	*Walsh*	*Donaghy*	*Moss*	*Daniel*
								Ref: M James	Two emphatic defeats have dropped Luton into the bottom three and they look an anxious outfit. Bennett's smart volley beats Tony Godden. City fight a largely rearguard action after this, but hold firm. David Moss goes close to a last-minute leveller but Woods makes a superb stop.											
34	H	IPSWICH		19	D	0-0	0-0		Woods	Haylock	Downs	Mendham	Walford	Watson	O'Neill	Channon	Deehan	Bertschin	Van Wijk*	Barham
4/4			**23,476**	*8*	37				*Cooper*	*Burley*	*Gernon*	*Thijssen*	*Osman*	*Butcher*	*Wark*	*McCall*	*Mariner*	*Kinsella*	*O'Callaghan*	
								Ref: B Hill	Feisty derby fare again, but this time no goals. City look to have far more urgency about them, with several Ipswich stars appearing short of motivation since manager Bobby Robson's departure. Frans Thijssen makes his farewell appearance and Tony Kinsella debuts for the visitors.											
35	A	BIRMINGHAM		18	W	4-0	2-0	Bertschin 24, 56, Deehan 40, 72	Woods	Haylock	Downs	Mendham	Walford	Watson	Barham	Channon	Deehan	Bertschin	Bennett	
9/4			*11,733*	*22*	40				*Coton*	*Broadhurst*	*Hagan*	*Stevenson*	*Blake*	*V d Hauwe*	*Handysides**	*Ferguson*	*Harford*	*Halsall*	*Hopkins*	*Phillips*
								Ref: J Moules	City 's relegation worries are eased and Brum drop to bottom after this comfortable win. Ex-Blue Bertschin is jeered but nets a fine solo goal. Deehan rises to head home before half-time. Bertschin beats Tony Coton after another run. Deehan adds a fourth, heading in Bennett's cross.											
36	H	SUNDERLAND		18	W	2-0	0-0	Deehan 48, 63	Woods	Haylock	Downs	Mendham	Walford	Watson	Barham	Channon	Deehan	Bertschin	Bennett	
16/4			15,883	*16*	43				*Turner**	*Whitfield*	*Munro*	*Atkins*	*Chisholm*	*Pickering*	*Venison*	*Rowell*	*West*	*James*	*McCoist*	*Buckley*
								Ref: B Daniels	Chris Turner fractures his skull in a sickening aerial collision with Bertschin. After the lengthy stoppage, Nick Pickering dons the green jersey. He survives for 23 minutes until Deehan hammers in a Channon cross. The decider is a cute backheel that completely wrong-foots Pickering.											
37	H	ARSENAL		15	W	3-1	1-1	Deehan 30, 86, Bertschin 79	Woods	Haylock	Downs	Mendham*	Walford	Watson	Barham	Channon	Deehan	Bertschin	Bennett	O'Neill
20/4			16,858	*12*	46			*Davis 29*	*Wood*	*Kay*	*Sansom*	*Talbot*	*O'Leary*	*Whyte*	*McDermott*	*Hill*	*Davis*	*Chapman*	*Rix**	*Hollins*
								Ref: D Axcell	Paul Davis nets the first goal City have conceded in 420 minutes' play. Deehan then makes the most of a deflection off debutant Colin Hill just 44 seconds after the re-start. Bertschin fires City into the lead and the Gunners fail to clear a Watson cross, allowing Deehan to rifle in a third.											
38	A	LIVERPOOL		13	W	2-0	0-0	Lawrenson 52(og), O'Neill 73	Woods	Haylock	Downs	O'Neill	Walford	Watson	Barham	Channon	Deehan	Bertschin	Bennett	
23/4			***37,022***	*1*	49				*Grobbelaar*	*Neal*	*Kennedy*	*Lawrenson*	*Whelan*	*Hansen*	*Dalglish*	*Lee*	*Hodgson*	*Johnston*	*Souness*	
								Ref: D Lloyd	Bob Paisley's men have already clinched the title, but City show scant respect and tear into them. It's an outstanding display and the opening goal comes as Mark Lawrenson and Bertschin stretch together for a cross. O'Neill stuns Anfield, picking up a loose ball and burying a beauty.											
39	H	MANCHESTER U		14	D	1-1	0-0	Barham 59	Woods	Haylock	Downs	O'Neill	Walford	Watson	Barham	Channon	Deehan	Bertschin	Bennett	
30/4			22,986	*4*	50			*Whiteside 49*	*Bailey*	*Duxbury*	*Grimes*	*Moses*	*Moran*	*McQueen*	*Robson*	*Wilkins*	*Stapleton*	*Whiteside*	*Cunningham*	
								Ref: D Reeves	City look good going forward and this turns into the best home display of the season. Ron Atkinson's men are lucky to be level at the interval. Norman Whiteside nets from close range after a Frank Stapleton run. O'Neill squares to Barham, who thunders in a well-deserved equaliser.											
40	A	WEST BROM		14	L	0-1	0-1		Woods	Haylock	Downs	O'Neill	Walford	Watson*	Barham	Channon	Deehan	Bertschin	Bennett	Jack
2/5			*9,221*		50			*Thompson 29*	*Barron*	*Webb*	*Statham*	*Zondervan*	*Wile*	*Robertson*	*Lewis**	*Perry*	*Thompson*	*Owen*	*Cross*	*Luke*
								Ref: A Crickmore	Brown is named April's Manager of the Month. In front of Albion's lowest top-flight crowd for 26 years, City suffer a bad blow when Watson departs early with a head injury. Deehan switches to a defensive role against his old club. Nicky Cross' centre is headed in by Garry Thompson.											
41	A	NOTT'M FOREST		14	D	2-2	2-1	Bennett 15, 45	Woods	Haylock	Downs	O'Neill	Walford	Watson	Barham	Channon	Deehan	Bertschin	Bennett	
7/5			*16,308*	*4*	51			*Walsh 35, Bowyer 59*	*V Breukelen*	*Anderson*	*Swain*	*Gunn*	*Young*	*Bowyer*	*Hodge*	*Wallace*	*Davenport*	*Walsh*	*Robertson*	
								Ref: A Hamil	The remote mathematical possibility of relegation is removed by this point from the City Ground. A thoroughly entertaining game features two stunning strikes by Bennett. The first is a clever overhead kick and the other a curling shot. Ian Bowyer saves a point with a shot in off the bar.											
42	H	BRIGHTON		14	W	2-1	1-0	Channon 41, Deehan 73	Woods	Haylock	Downs	O'Neill	Walford	Watson	Barham	Channon	Deehan	Bertschin	Bennett	
14/5			20,306	*22*	54			*Smith 66*	*Moseley*	*O'Reagan*	*Pearce*	*Grealish*	*Stevens*	*Gatting*	*Case*	*Howlett*	*Ryan*	*Smith**	*Smillie*	*Rodon*
		Home	Away					Ref: A Ward	City fans celebrate a wonderful last quarter of the season and create a carnival atmosphere. Channon produces a clinical finish from a Deehan lay-off. Gordon Smith's well-taken effort equalises for already-doomed Brighton. Deehan's 25-yarder flies past the surprised Graham Moseley.											
Average		17,678	18,178																	

LEAGUE DIVISION 1 (CUP-TIES)

Manager: Ken Brown

SEASON 1982-83

Milk Cup	Att			F-A	H-T	Scorers, Times, and Referees	1	2	3	4	5	6	7	8	9	10	11	12 sub used
2:1 H PRESTON		21	W	2-1	1-1	Bertschin 16, O'Neill 88	Woods	Haylock	Downs	McGuire*	Walford	Smith	Barham	O'Neill	Deehan	Bertschin	Bennett	Mendham
6/10	7,273	*3:13*				*Bruce 9*	*Litchfield*	*Walsh*	*McAteer*	*Coleman*	*Westwell*	*Gowling*	*Kelly*	*Bell*	*Elliott*	*Naughton*	*Bruce*	
						Ref: A Ward	City's lowest crowd for a competitive match since the mid-1950s see a dreadful performance by their favourites. Even O'Neill's late winner - a toe-poke from a Bertschin pass - doesn't disguise the horror. Bertschin's volley cancels out Alex Bruce's early success with a close-range flick.											
2:2 A PRESTON		19	W	2-1	1-0	Bertschin 21, Bennett 80	Woods	Haylock	Van Wijk	Mendham*	Walford	Watson	Barham	O'Neill	Deehan	Bertschin	Bennett	Jack
26/10	6,082	*3:17*				*Elliott 56*	*Litchfield*	*Walsh*	*McAteer*	*Clark*	*Westwell*	*Gowling*	*Kelly*	*Bell*	*Elliott*	*Naughton*	*Bruce*	
						Ref: K Redfern (Norwich win 4-2 on aggregate)	O'Neill sets up Bertschin to increase the aggregate lead. Steve Elliott reduces the arrears with his 12th goal from 16 games so far this season. Gordon Lee's side are sunk when Bennett cracks in Barham's cross ten minutes from time. Relieved Norwich get an easier ride than expected.											
3 A SUNDERLAND		21	D	0-0	0-0		Woods	Haylock	Hareide	McGuire	Walford	Watson	Barham	O'Neill	Deehan	Van Wijk	Bennett	
10/11	10,934	*20*					*Turner*	*Nicholl*	*Munro*	*Atkins*	*Elliott*	*Pickering*	*Buckley**	*Rowell*	*McCoist*	*West*	*Venison*	*Chisholm*
						Ref: N Glover	City regain some pride following the league defeat at this venue last month. Alan Durban's men find Woods in good form. Deehan goes close but Iain Munro heads off the line. Roker Park lacks its usual atmosphere. Top athlete Steve Cram is spotted among the disappointed home fans.											
3R H SUNDERLAND		20	W	3-1	1-1	Watson 41, 61, Deehan 77	Woods	Haylock	Van Wijk	McGuire	Walford	Watson	Barham	O'Neill	Deehan	Bertschin*	Jack	**Donowa**
24/11	19,776	*21*				*Cummins 15*	*Turner*	*Venison*	*Munro*	*Atkins*	*Elliott*	*Nicholl*	*Buckley**	*Rowell*	*McCoist*	*West*	*Cummins*	*Hindmarch*
						Ref: M Scott	Little Stan Cummins puts the visitors ahead with a far-post strike. Watson rams in a loose ball to equalise and puts City ahead after Barham's free-kick hits the bar. Deehan makes it safe with a clinical finish from a Walford cross. Young winger Louie Donowa makes his senior debut.											
4 A LIVERPOOL		21	L	0-2	0-1	Lawrenson 42, Fairclough 80	Woods	Haylock	Van Wijk	McGuire	Walford	Watson	Barham	O'Neill	Deehan	Bertschin	Hareide	
30/11	13,235	*1*					*Grobbelaar*	*Neal*	*Kennedy*	*Thompson*	*Johnson*	*Hansen*	*Dalglish*	*Lee*	*Rush*	*Lawrenson**	*Souness*	*Fairclough*
						Ref: D Shaw	Deehan finds the net early on with a header but, to City's dismay, it's ruled out. The league leaders surge ahead when Mark Lawrenson coolly converts a Phil Neal centre. Norwich remain in the match until near the end when David Fairclough races on to Graeme Souness' pass to score.											

FA Cup																		
3 H SWANSEA		17	W	2-1	2-1	Bertschin 24, 40	Woods	Haylock	Downs	Mendham	Walford	Watson	Barham	O'Neill	Deehan	Bertschin	Van Wijk	
8/1	13,222	*19*				*Gale 14*	*Davies*	*Richards*	*Hadziabdic*	*Rajkovic*	*Charles*	*Lewis*	*Curtis*	*James R**	*Gale*	*Marustik*	*Latchford*	*Mahoney*
						Ref: L Robinson	Teenager Darren Gale raps in the first goal of his career. Bertschin puts City on terms with a first-time shot and then thunders home a superb header from Barham's cross. Deehan allows Bertschin to take a 42nd-minute penalty, but Dai Davies prevents a hat-trick with an excellent stop.											
4 A COVENTRY		20	D	2-2	0-1	Hareide 70, Barham 87	Woods	Hareide	Downs	Mendham	Walford	Watson	Barham	O'Neill	Deehan	Bertschin	Van Wijk	
29/1	13,083	*5*				*Thompson G 40, Roberts 65*	*Sealey*	*Thomas*	*Roberts*	*Hormantsc'k*	*Dyson*	*Gillespie*	*Whitton*	*Francis*	*Hunt*	*Hateley*	*Thompson G*	
						Ref: B Hill	Dave Sexton's men are flying high in the league and it's no surprise when they surge ahead. Steve Whitton's cross is netted by Garry Thompson and a rare Brian Roberts goal looks decisive. But City storm back and Hareide nets a disputed goal. Barham pounces on Gerry Francis' slip-up.											
4R H COVENTRY		20	W	2-1	0-1	Bertschin 50, Roberts 98 (og)	Woods	Hareide	Downs	Mendham	Walford	Watson	Barham	O'Neill	Deehan	Bertschin	Van Wijk	
2/2	18,625	*5*		*aet*		*Hateley 3*	*Sealey*	*Thomas*	*Roberts*	*Hormantsc'k*	*Dyson*	*Gillespie*	*Whitton*	*Francis*	*Hunt*	*Hateley*	*Thomps'n G !*	
						Ref: B Hill	Mark Hateley stuns Carrow Road early on and City face an uphill battle again. Hareide's effort is spilled by Les Sealey and Bertschin pounces to equalise. In extra-time Brian Roberts is pressurised into an own-goal - three minutes after Garry Thompson is red-carded for two bad fouls.											
5 H IPSWICH		21	W	1-0	1-0	Bertschin 6	Woods	Haylock	Hareide	Mendham	Walford	Watson	Barham	Van Wijk	Deehan	Bertschin	Downs	
19/2	28,001	*13*					*Cooper*	*Putney*	*Gernon*	*Thijssen*	*Osman*	*Butcher*	*Wark*	*McCall**	*Mariner*	*Brazil*	*O'Callaghan*	*Turner*
						Ref: R Lewis	A lively encounter gets off to a great start as ex-Ipswich man Bertschin evades Terry Butcher's rash tackle and finds space to force his shot through Paul Cooper. Town battle hard to even things up, but Alan Brazil hits the bar and a Butcher goalbound effort is knocked off the line.											
QF A BRIGHTON		19	A	0-1	0-0		Woods	Haylock	Downs	Mendham	Symonds	Watson	Barham	Bennett	Deehan	Bertschin	Van Wijk*	McGuire
12/3	28,800	*21*				*Case 67*	*Moseley*	*Ramsey*	*Gatting*	*Grealish*	*Foster*	*Stevens*	*Case*	*Ritchie*	*Robinson*	*Ryan*	*Smillie*	
						Ref: A Robinson	Norwich's first FA Cup QF since 1959, and this is a fast and furious affair, played in a great atmosphere. There is anger over Jimmy Case's decisive goal. The linesman flagged for a handball and then a push by Case before he netted, but after consultations, the ref allows it to stand.											

		Home					Away					
	P	W	D	L	F	A	W	D	L	F	A	Pts
1 Liverpool	42	16	4	1	55	16	8	6	7	32	21	82
2 Watford	42	16	2	3	49	20	6	3	12	25	37	71
3 Manchester U	42	14	7	0	39	10	5	6	10	17	28	70
4 Tottenham	42	15	4	2	50	15	5	5	11	15	35	69
5 Nottingham F	42	12	5	4	34	18	8	4	9	28	32	69
6 Aston Villa	42	17	2	2	47	15	4	3	14	15	35	68
7 Everton	42	13	6	2	43	19	5	4	12	23	29	64
8 West Ham	42	13	3	5	41	23	7	1	13	27	39	64
9 Ipswich	42	11	3	7	39	23	4	10	7	25	27	58
10 Arsenal	42	11	6	4	36	19	5	4	12	22	37	58
11 West Brom	42	11	5	5	35	20	4	7	10	16	29	57
12 Southampton	42	11	5	5	36	22	4	7	10	18	36	57
13 Stoke	42	13	4	4	34	21	3	5	13	19	43	57
14 NORWICH	42	10	6	5	30	18	4	6	11	22	40	54
15 Notts County	42	12	4	5	37	25	3	3	15	18	46	52
16 Sunderland	42	7	10	4	30	22	5	4	12	18	39	50
17 Birmingham	42	9	7	5	29	24	3	7	11	11	31	50
18 Luton	42	7	7	7	34	33	5	6	10	31	51	49
19 Coventry	42	10	5	6	29	17	3	4	14	19	42	48
20 Manchester C	42	9	5	7	26	23	4	3	14	21	47	47
21 Swansea	42	10	4	7	32	29	0	7	14	19	40	41
22 Brighton	42	8	7	6	25	22	1	6	14	13	46	40
	924	255	111	96	810	454	96	111	255	454	810	1275

Odds & ends

Double wins: (3) Birmingham, Luton, Liverpool.
Double losses: (2) Manchester C, West Brom.

Won from behind: (6) Stoke (h), Arsenal (h), Preston (h) (LC), Sunderland (h) (LC), Swansea (h) (FAC), Coventry (h) (FAC).
Lost from in front: (1) Aston Villa (A).

High spots: A tremendous late run to steer clear of the drop.
The superb win away to champions Liverpool in April.
Memorable wins over Ipswich in both League and FA Cup.
Ken Brown's Manager of the Month award for April.
Dave Bennett's cracking double strike at Nottingham Forest.

Low spots: Brighton's controversial winner in the FA Cup quarter-final.
The 0-4 defeat at Southampton in February, which indicated relegation was on the horizon.
A bad incident involving a missile from the Barclay End (v Notts Co).
Sunderland keeper Chris Turner's nasty head injury at Carrow Road.

Player of the Year: Dave Watson.
Ever-presents: Paul Haylock (League only), Chris Woods.
Hat-tricks: (0).
Hat-tricks against: (2) Latchford (Swansea a), Cyrille Regis (WBA h).
Leading scorer: (21) John Deehan.

	Appearances						Goals			
	Lge	*Sub*	LC	*Sub*	FAC	*Sub*	Lge	LC	FAC	Tot
Alexander, Phil		*1*								
Barham, Mark	**37**	*1*	5		5		**4**		1	**5**
Bennett, Dave	**22**		3		1		**4**	1		**5**
Bertschin, Keith	**39**	*1*	4		5		**8**	2	4	**14**
Channon, Mick	**17**	*3*					**3**			**3**
Crowe, Mark		*1*								
Deehan, John	**40**		5		5		**20**	1		**21**
Donowa, Louie		*1*		*1*						
Downs, Greg	**26**	*2*	1		5					
Fashanu, John	**2**									
Hareide, Aage	**12**		2		3				1	**1**
Haylock, Paul	**42**		5		3	*1*	**1**			**1**
Jack, Ross	**2**	*8*	1	*2*						
McGuire, Mick	**15**		4			*1*				
Mendham, Peter	**25**	*1*	1	*1*	5		**2**			**2**
Metcalf, Mark		*1*								
Mountford, Peter	**1**	*1*								
O'Neill, Martin	**34**	*1*	5		3		**5**	1		**6**
Smith, Colin	**2**	*2*	1							
Symonds, Richard	**1**				1					
Van Wijk, Dennis	**22**	*1*	4		5		**2**			**2**
Walford, Steve	**41**		5		4		**1**			**1**
Walsh, Mick	**5**									
Watson, Dave	**35**		4		5		**1**	2		**3**
Woods, Chris	**42**		5		5					
(own-goals)							**1**		1	**2**
25 players used	**462**	***25***	**55**	***4***	**55**	***2***	**52**	**7**	**7**	**66**

No	Date	Att	Pos	Pt	F-A	H-T	Scorers, Times, and Referees	1	2	3	4	5	6	7	8	9	10	11	12 sub used
1	A SUNDERLAND			D	1-1	0-0	Bertschin 56	Woods	**Devine**	Downs	Mendham	**Young**	Watson	Barham	Van Wijk	Deehan	Bertschin	Bennett	
	27/8	*17,057*		1			*West 61*	*Turner*	*Venison*	*Munro*	*Atkins*	*Chisholm*	*Proctor*	*Bracewell*	*Rowell*	*West*	*Pickering*	*Atkinson*	
							Ref: A Banks	Bad feeling from the two clubs' last meeting seems to spill over into this game and five men are yellow-carded before the interval. Bertschin's soaring header puts City ahead. Ex-Arsenal veteran Willie Young has replaced the departed Walford, but he slips to allow Colin West to level.											
2	H LIVERPOOL			L	0-1	0-1		Woods	Haylock	Downs	Mendham	Young	Watson	Barham	Channon	Deehan	Bertschin	Bennett	
	31/8	23,859		1			*Souness 30*	*Grobbelaar*	*Neal*	*Kennedy*	*Lawrenson*	*Johnston*	*Hansen*	*Dalglish*	*Lee*	*Rush*	*Robinson*	*Souness*	
							Ref: D Axcell	Michael Robinson intercepts a Barham pass, switches the ball to Sammy Lee and he finds Graeme Souness, who nets an excellent chip. Mark Lawrenson clears Bertschin's lob off the line and Lee manages the same from a Young effort. Channon scores near the end, but it's disallowed.											
3	H WOLVERHAMPTON		11	W	3-0	2-0	Bertschin 4, Deehan 9, 89	Woods	Haylock	Downs	Mendham	Young	Watson	Barham	Channon	Deehan	Bertschin	Van Wijk	
	4/9	13,713	*21*	4				*Burridge*	*Humphrey*	*Palmer*	*Smith*	*Pender*	*Dodd*	*Towner*	*Daniel*	*Eves*	*Livingstone*	*Kellock**	*Clarke*
							Ref: D Vickers	Graham Hawkins' newly promoted side are having a tough time. Bertschin heads home an early corner and their heads drop. Channon does the spadework for Deehan's second with less than ten minutes gone. Deehan lashes in a late drive to give the scoreline a more realistic appearance.											
4	A LUTON		12	D	2-2	2-0	Channon 9, Mendham 19	Woods	Haylock	Downs	Mendham	Young	Watson	Barham	Channon	Deehan	Bertschin	Van Wijk	
	6/9	*11,095*	*6*	5			*Elliott 58, Stein 89*	*Sealey*	*Stephens*	*Turner*	*Horton*	*Elliott*	*Donaghy*	*Hill*	*Stein B*	*Walsh*	*Bunn**	*Moss*	*Antic*
							Ref: A Gunn	David Pleat's men have the bulk of the possession, but look vulnerable to fast breaks. City hit them twice in the first 20 minutes, but when a David Moss corner is only partially cleared, Paul Elliott brings the Hatters back into the game. Brian Stein levels late with a fine 25-yard drive.											
5	A ASTON VILLA		13	L	0-1	0-1		Woods	Haylock*	Downs	Mendham	Young	Watson	Barham	Channon	Deehan	Bertschin	Van Wijk	Devine
	10/9	*18,887*	*6*	5			*Mortimer 12*	*Spink*	*Williams*	*Gibson*	*Evans*	*Ormsby*	*Mortimer*	*Curbishley*	*Rideout*	*Withe*	*McMahon*	*Walters*	
							Ref: N Midgley	Peter Withe lobs a hopeful ball forward and Dennis Mortimer, looking well offside, chips the ball over Woods with the City defence standing still and waiting for a whistle. However, this was a mediocre display by Norwich and they can have few complaints about the final outcome.											
6	H NOTT'M FOREST		17	L	2-3	2-2	Bertschin 4, Deehan 38p	Woods	Haylock*	Downs	Mendham	Hareide	Watson	Devine	Channon	Deehan	Bertschin	Van Wijk	Donowa
	17/9	15,017	*9*	5			*Walsh 23p 44, 66*	*V Breukelen*	*Anderson*	*Swain*	*Todd*	*Fairclough*	*Bowyer*	*Walsh**	*Wallace*	*Davenport*	*Hodge*	*Wigley*	*Smalley*
							Ref: E Scales	Bertschin's downward header beats Hans Van Breukelen, but Colin Walsh levels after Woods brought down Steve Hodge. Chris Fairclough fouls Deehan for a City penalty. Walsh strikes with two headers, the second of which sees him badly hurt and carried off with a neck injury.											
7	A ARSENAL		19	L	**0-3**	0-1		Woods	Devine	Downs	Mendham	Hareide	Watson	Bennett	Channon	Deehan	Bertschin	Van Wijk*	Young
	24/9	*24,438*	*8*	5			*Chapman 38, Sunderland 70, 83*	*Jennings*	*Robson*	*Sansom*	*Whyte*	*O'Leary*	*Hill*	*Sunderland*	*Davis*	*Chapman*	*Nicholas**	*Rix*	*McDermott*
							Ref: H Taylor	Woods flaps at a Graham Rix corner and Lee Chapman swoops to head his first of the season. Chapman has otherwise had a miserable time with the Gunners, unlike his newly arrived colleague, Charlie Nicholas, who is stirring up great interest. Alan Sunderland bags a smart brace.											
8	H MANCHESTER U		19	D	3-3	0-1	Bennett 64, Channon 78, Donowa 89	Woods	Haylock	Downs	Mendham	Hareide	Watson*	Devine	Channon	Donowa	Bertschin	Bennett	**Pickering**
	1/10	19,680	*4*	6			*Whiteside 44, 56, Stapleton 53*	*Bailey*	*Duxbury*	*Albiston*	*Wilkins*	*Moran*	*McGrath*	*Robson*	*Muhren**	*Stapleton*	*Whiteside*	*Graham*	*Moses*
							Ref: R Lewis	A breathtaking game. Norman Whiteside nets a 15-yarder. Frank Stapleton buries a fine header and Whiteside tucks in his second at the near post. Bennett loops a header over Gary Bailey, Channon converts Mendham's free-kick and Donowa equalises on his full debut, near the end.											
9	A WATFORD		19	W	3-1	0-0	Rostron 73 (og), Devine 78, Donowa 80	Woods	Haylock	Downs	Mendham	Hareide	Watson	Donowa	Channon	Devine	Bertschin	Bennett	
	15/10	*12,745*	*18*	9			*Terry 90*	*Steele*	*Rice*	*Sinnott*	*Jobson*	*Terry*	*Jackett*	*Callaghan*	*Barnes*	*Reilly*	*Rostron*	*Johnson**	*Bolton*
							Ref: M Bodenham	On a miserable and wet afternoon, a goalless draw looks likely until City grab three in seven minutes. Wilf Rostron steers the ball past his own keeper after Donowa's flick. Man-of-the-match Devine combines with Bertschin for the second, then Donowa nets a real beauty from 30 yards.											
10	H LEICESTER		16	W	3-1	1-1	Donowa 45, B'tschin 61, Channon 82p	Woods	Haylock	Downs	Mendham	Hareide	Watson	Donowa	Channon	Devine	Bertschin	Bennett	
	19/10	14,586	*22*	12			*Eastoe 31*	*Wallington*	*Williams*	*Wilson*	*MacDonald*	*Hazell*	*Banks*	*Lynex*	*Lineker*	*Eastoe*	*Ramsey*	*English*	
							Ref: A Ward	Gordon Milne's side go ahead through Peter Eastoe's excellent shot from distance. Tom English fluffs an easy chance soon afterwards. Donowa levels with a header and, in his 100th City game, Bertschin gains the lead. Bertschin is impeded when seeking another - Channon does the rest.											

No	Venue	Opponent / Date	Att	Pos	Res	Pts	F-A	H-T	Scorers, Times, and Referees	1	2	3	4	5	6	7	8	9	10	11	12
11	A	WEST HAM		16	D		0-0	0-0		Woods	Haylock	Downs	Mendham	Hareide	Watson	Donowa	Channon	Devine	Bertschin	Bennett	
		22/10	*18,958*	4		13				*Parkes*	*Stewart*	*Walford*	*Bonds*	*Martin*	*Devonshire*	*Whitton**	*Cottee*	*Swindlehurst*	*Brooking*	*Pike*	*Dickens*
									Ref: D Brazier	Hareide and Haylock have outstanding games in defence as City fight hard to subdue John Lyall's high-flying Hammers - who just three weeks ago were top of the league. The club announces that the Poll-Withey double glazing firm is paying £150,000 to be the new club shirt sponsors.											
12	H	QP RANGERS		16	L		**0-3**	0-2		Woods	Haylock	Downs	Mendham	Hareide	Watson	Donowa	Channon !	Devine	Bertschin	Bennett*	Barham
		29/10	16,532	*3*		13			*Fenwick 11p, 19, Stainrod 76*	*Hucker*	*Neill*	*Dawes*	*Waddock*	*Wicks*	*Fenwick*	*Micklewhite*	*Stewart*	*Allen**	*Stainrod*	*Gregory*	*Fereday*
									Ref: V Callow	Under little pressure, Devine inexplicably handles to give Rangers a dream start. Terry Fenwick then nets a stunning header from Ian Stewart's corner. Before the break, Channon's late tackle on Gary Waddock gets him sent off. After a free-kick routine, Simon Stainrod shoots the third.											
13	H	SOUTHAMPTON		15	W		1-0	0-0	Bertschin 62	Woods	Haylock	Downs	Mendham	Hareide	Watson	Donowa	Channon*	Devine	Bertschin	Barham	Van Wijk
		5/11	14,303	*8*		16				*Shilton*	*Rofe*	*Baker*	*Williams*	*Whitlock*	*Foyle*	*Holmes*	*Moran*	*Worthington*	*Armstrong*	*D Wallace*	
									Ref: K Hackett	The Saints look a tight and efficient outfit. They subdue City and a rather dour first hour ensues. Then Bertschin breaks the deadlock with a spectacular header from a Donowa cross. Channon has a generally unhappy game against his former team, but City hang on grimly to the lead.											
14	A	NOTTS CO		17	D		1-1	1-1	Barham 19	Woods	Haylock	Downs	Mendham	Hareide	Watson	Donowa	Deehan	Devine	Bertschin	Barham	
		12/11	***7,882***	*20*		17			*Fashanu 21*	*McDonagh*	*Goodwin*	*Worthington*	*Richards*	*Hunt*	*Roeder*	*O'Neill*	*Fashanu*	*Christie*	*Harkouk*	*Chiedozie*	
									Ref: A Robinson	Relief as City survive a loud penalty appeal in the first minute. Barham calmly chips a goal, but within two minutes ex-Canary Justin Fashanu powerfully heads in a John Chiedozie cross. City look a little shaky at the back. Talks over signing Paul Futcher of Derby seem to have failed.											
15	H	WEST BROM		13	W		2-0	0-0	Downs 54, Barham 64	Woods	Haylock	Downs	Mendham	Hareide*	Watson	Donowa	Deehan	Devine	Bertschin	Barham	Van Wijk
		19/11	13,368	*14*		20				*Barron*	*Whitehead*	*Cowdrill*	*Zondervan*	*McNaught*	*Robertson*	*Jol*	*Thompson*	*Perry**	*Owen*	*Luke*	*Cross*
									Ref: C Downey	Hareide departs at half-time with a suspected broken collar-bone. Mendham's short free-kick is thundered home by Greg Downs' trusty left foot. Barham get the all-important second when he coolly shoots wide of Paul Barron. Ron Wylie's team never look likely to stage a comeback.											
16	A	EVERTON		11	W		2-0	0-0	Donowa 46, Bailey 77(og)	Woods	Haylock	Downs	Mendham	Deehan	Watson	Donowa	Channon	Van Wijk	Bertschin	Barham	
		26/11	*14,106*	*17*		23				*Southall*	*Harper*	*Bailey*	*Ratcliffe*	*Mountfield*	*Reid*	*Irvine*	*Heath**	*Gray*	*King*	*Sheedy*	*Stevens*
									Ref: M Heath	Less than 60 seconds after the break, Barham beats three men before crossing for Donowa to head home. John Bailey is jeered by home fans as he opts to pass back instead of going forward, and the jeers turns to howls of misery as the ball somehow eludes Neville Southall and goes in.											
17	H	TOTTENHAM		9	W		2-1	1-1	Bertschin 3, Channon 83	Woods	Devine	Downs	Mendham	Deehan	Watson	Donowa	Channon	Van Wijk	Bertschin	Barham*	**Godbold**
		3/12	22,148	*4*		26			*Dick 4*	*Clemence*	*Hughton*	*Thomas*	*Roberts*	*Stevens*	*Perryman*	*Cooke**	*Archibald*	*Falco*	*Hoddle*	*Dick*	*O'Reilly*
									Ref: G Napthine	City are in confident form and in the early stages Bertschin strikes a magnificent shot past Ray Clemence. Straight from the kick-off Ally Dick goes on a super solo run and beats Woods. An entertaining game is decided when Devine supplies Channon, who strides into the box to fire in.											
18	A	BIRMINGHAM		6	W		1-0	1-0	Downs 15	Woods	Haylock	Downs	Mendham	Deehan	Watson	Donowa	Channon	Van Wijk	Bertschin	Hareide	
		10/12	*9,971*	*17*		29				*Coton*	*Hagan*	*V d Hauwe*	*Blake*	*Wright*	*Stevenson*	*Gayle*	*Phillips*	*Harford*	*Halsall*	*Kuhl*	
									Ref: J Hough	Downs bursts forward to steer the ball past Tony Coton. Bertschin gets round Coton but takes the ball too far and can't find the net from a tight angle. Ron Saunders' side is kept at bay and Woods makes several good saves. It's now clear Barham's knee injury last week was a serious one.											
19	H	COVENTRY		9	D		0-0	0-0		Woods	Haylock	Downs	Mendham	Deehan	Watson	Donowa	Channon	Hareide*	Bertschin	Van Wijk	**Clayton**
		17/12	16,646	*5*		30				*Avramovic*	*Roberts*	*Pearce*	*Daly*	*Peake*	*Allardyce*	*Bennett*	*Gynn*	*Bamber*	*Gibson*	*Platnauer*	
									Ref: M James	Brown receives Manager of the Month for November. Bobby Gould's men are fresh from an amazing 4-0 win over leaders Liverpool. The match is deadlocked and both sides maintain unbeaten runs. Watson hits the bar with a header and brings a fine save from Raddy Avramovic.											
20	A	STOKE		10	L		0-2	0-1		Woods	Haylock	Downs	Mendham	Deehan	Watson	Donowa	Channon	Devine	Bertschin	Van Wijk	
		26/12	*12,049*	*21*		30			*Maguire 23, James 82*	*Fox*	*Bould*	*Hampton*	*James*	*Dyson*	*McAughtrie*	*Painter*	*McIlroy*	*O'Callaghan*	*Maguire*	*Chamb'l'n M*	
									Ref: F Roberts	New Stoke boss Bill Asprey inspires his men to their first win in ten league games, against a Norwich side unbeaten in ten. Paul Maguire converts Brendan O'Callaghan's flick-on. City fail to break down a stubborn defence. Robbie James makes it safe with a fine long-range effort.											
21	H	IPSWICH		10	D		0-0	0-0		Woods	Haylock	Downs	Mendham*	Deehan	Watson	Donowa	Channon	Devine	Bertschin	Van Wijk	Hareide
		27/12	**25,679**	*14*		31				*Sivell*	*Parkin*	*Gernon*	*Kinsella*	*Osman*	*Butcher*	*Wark*	*McCall*	*Mariner*	*Gates*	*O'Callaghan*	
									Ref: J Hunting	Ipswich regain some pride after their poor display against City in the Milk Cup last month. Woods is kept on his toes and does well to keep a clean sheet. Paul Mariner is booked for one over-physical challenge on him. Inevitably the tempo is high and Mr Hunting gives 43 free-kicks.											

No	Date		Att	Pos	Pt	F-A	H-T	Scorers, Times, and Referees	1	2	3	4	5	6	7	8	9	10	11	12 sub used
22	A	WOLVERHAMPTON		10	L	0-2	0-0		Woods	Haylock	Downs	Mendham	Deehan	Watson	Donowa	Channon*	Devine	Bertschin	Van Wijk	Hareide
	31/12		*10,725*	*22*	31			*Troughton 51, Towner 76*	*Burridge*	*Humphrey*	*Palmer*	*Cartwright*	*Pender*	*Dodd*	*Towner*	*Clarke*	*Troughton**	*Eves*	*Crainie*	*Butler*
								Ref: K Cooper	Norwich look the better side in the first half, but events after the break make it a disappointing end to 1983. The lowly Wolves - just two wins in 22 games - take the lead as lively Danny Crainie sets up Sammy Troughton to blast in. Tony Towner then heads in Crainie's floated cross.											
23	H	ARSENAL		10	D	1-1	0-0	Deehan 81	Woods	Haylock	Downs	Mendham	Hareide	Watson	Donowa*	Channon	Deehan	Bertschin	Van Wijk	Clayton
	2/1		20,482	*11*	32			*Woodcock 49*	*Jennings*	*Hill*	*Sansom*	*Cork*	*O'Leary*	*Caton*	*Meade*	*Davis*	*Woodcock*	*Nicholas*	*Allinson*	
								Ref: T Holbrook	A Tony Woodcock shot looks to be going wide when it deflects off Hareide and beats Woods. It's a cruel blow but City hit back with less than ten minutes left. Deehan - who has a header pushed onto the post by Pat Jennings - dives to head home City's first goal in 516 minutes of play.											
24	H	SUNDERLAND		10	W	3-0	3-0	Downs 10, Bertschin 23, Hareide 29	Woods	Haylock	Downs	Mendham	Hareide	Watson	Devine	Channon*	Donowa	Bertschin	Van Wijk	Clayton
	14/1		**13,204**	*14*	35				*Turner*	*Venison*	*Pickering*	*Atkins*	*Hindmarch*	*Elliott*	*Bracewell*	*Rowell*	*West*	*Proctor*	*James*	
								Ref: D Letts	Carrow Road enjoys a vintage display by the ageing Channon. Downs nets a wind-assisted drive. Bertschin increases the lead with a header from Haylock's cross. Hareide nets a far-post header with less than 30 minutes on the clock and City cruise home against Alan Durban's side.											
25	A	NOTT'M FOREST		10	L	**0-3**	0-3		Woods	Haylock	Downs	Mendham	Hareide	Clayton	Devine	Channon	Deehan	Bertschin	Van Wijk*	Godbold
	21/1		*13,993*	*4*	35			*Thijssen 5, Hodge 16, Anderson 29*	*V Breukelen*	*Anderson*	*Swain*	*Fairclough*	*Hart*	*Bowyer*	*Thijssen*	*Wallace*	*Birtles**	*Hodge*	*Walsh*	*Wigley*
								Ref: R Guy	On a frost-bound pitch, Gary Birtles and Frans Thijssen combine to produce a neat opening goal. Steve Hodge nets another from close range. Colin Walsh's corner-kick is touched home by Viv Anderson. Three down after 29 minutes is a complete reversal of last Saturday's situation.											
26	A	MANCHESTER U		10	D	0-0	0-0		Woods	Haylock	Downs	Mendham	Hareide	Watson	Devine	Channon	Deehan	Bertschin	Van Wijk	
	4/2		*36,851*	*2*	36				*Bailey*	*Moss*	*Albiston*	*Wilkins*	*Moran*	*Duxbury*	*Robson*	*Muhren*	*Stapleton*	*Whiteside*	*Graham*	
								Ref: G Peck	Devine gives an outstanding performance as gritty Norwich hold Ron Atkinson's title-chasing side at bay for 90 minutes. Several City players' contracts are about to expire, but chairman Sir Arthur South promises: 'I'll move heaven and earth to keep our current crop of stars at the club.'											
27	H	ASTON VILLA		9	W	3-1	0-0	Deehan 72, 85, Channon 81	Woods	Haylock	Downs	Mendham	Devine	Watson	Clayton*	Channon	Deehan	Bertschin	Van Wijk	Bennett
	11/2		14,392	*12*	39			*Shaw 90*	*Day*	*Williams*	*Deacy*	*Evans*	*Bremner*	*Mortimer*	*Curbishley*	*Shaw*	*Rideout*	*Walker*	*Gibson*	
								Ref: E Scales	After the cup battles, the two clubs meet for the fourth time in 35 days. A sadly tame affair bursts into life in the last 20 minutes. Deehan buries a fine shot to get things moving. Channon scores from close range from a corner and Deehan fires a sweet goal after Bertschin's square pass.											
28	A	QP RANGERS		9	L	0-2	0-0		Woods	Haylock	Downs	Mendham	Devine	Watson	Clayton	Channon*	Deehan	Bertschin	Van Wijk	**Rigby**
	14/2		*12,901*	*5*	39			*Dawes 71, Waddock 78*	*Hucker*	*Neill*	*Dawes*	*Waddock*	*Wicks*	*Fenwick*	*Fillery*	*Stewart*	*Burke*	*Stainrod*	*Gregory*	
								Ref: H King	Deehan forces a great save from Peter Hucker, but within seconds Terry Venables' side take the lead. They break upfield and Ian Dawes ends the move with a curling shot in off a post. Clayton slips on the plastic allowing Steve Burke to cross for Gary Waddock to fire the second goal.											
29	H	WEST HAM		7	W	1-0	0-0	Deehan 77	Woods	Haylock	Downs	Mendham	Hareide	Watson	Devine	Channon	Deehan	Bertschin	Van Wijk	
	25/2		16,294	*4*	42				*Parkes*	*Stewart*	*Lampard*	*Bonds*	*Walford*	*Hilton*	*Barnes*	*Cottee*	*Swindlehurst*	*Allen*	*Dickens*	
								Ref: J Ashworth	This game features some neat football, but is short of genuine excitement. Home fans are roused with 13 minutes left when Channon's flicked header is swooped upon by Deehan, who steers it past Phil Parkes as he falls. The chance came after an error by former Canary Steve Walford.											
30	A	SOUTHAMPTON		8	L	1-2	0-1	Deehan 60	Woods	Haylock	Downs	Mendham	Hareide	Watson	Bennett	Channon	Deehan	Rigby	Van Wijk	
	3/3		*17,456*	*5*	42			*Armstrong D 12, Puckett 84*	*Shilton*	*Mills*	*Dennis*	*Williams*	*Armstrong K*	*Agboola*	*Holmes*	*Curtis**	*Worthington*	*Armstrong D*	*Wallace*	*Puckett*
								Ref: K Baker	A low cross squirms out of Woods' grasp and David Armstrong takes advantage. Peter Shilton makes a sensational save from Bennett, but Deehan brings City level when left unmarked at a corner. Sub David Puckett's first involvement is to hammer home a pass from Armstrong.											
31	H	NOTTS CO		11	L	0-1	0-0		Woods	Haylock	Downs*	Mendham	Hareide	Watson	Bennett	Channon	Deehan	Rigby	Van Wijk	Donowa
	14/3		13,230	*21*	42			*O'Neill 55*	*Leonard*	*Hodson*	*Clarke*	*Richards*	*Kilcline*	*Hunt*	*O'Neill*	*McCulloch*	*Christie*	*Mair*	*Chiedozie*	
								Ref: J Moules	A dreadful game from City's point of view, with precious few efforts on Mick Leonard's goal. Ex-Norwich hero Martin O'Neill is taunted over his controversial departure last summer, but his reply is to blast the winner after a blunder by Downs. The Canaries are jeered off at the whistle.											

No / Date		Opponent / Att			F-A	H-T	Scorers, Times, and Referees	1	2	3	4	5	6	7	8	9	10	11	12
32	H	LUTON	11	D	0-0	0-0		Woods	Haylock	Downs	Mendham	Watson	Hareide	Bennett	Channon	Deehan	Rigby	Van Wijk	
17/3		14,181	*7*	43				*Sealey*	*Stephens*	*Thomas*	*Antic*	*Elliott*	*Goodyear*	*Donaghy*	*Stein B*	*Walsh*	*Aylott*	*Bunn*	
							Ref: M Scott	The liveliness of this game is not reflected by the scoreline. Luton enjoy the better of the first period, but City are more positive after the break. Mitchell Thomas, 19, keeps a tight rein on Channon, 16 years his senior. City have few problems from the new England cap Paul Walsh.											
33	A	LEICESTER	15	L	1-2	0-2	Deehan 50	Woods	Haylock	Downs	Mendham	Hareide	Watson	Devine	Channon	Deehan	Bennett*	Donowa	Rigby
31/3		*11,278*	*14*	43			*Smith A 11, 21*	*Wallington*	*Smith R*	*Williams*	*MacDonald*	*Hazell*	*O'Neill*	*Lynex*	*Lineker*	*Smith A*	*Ramsey*	*Peake*	
							Ref: P Tyldesley	In their first real attack, Steve Lynex's corner falls for Alan Smith to smash past Woods. Smith then nets Paul Ramsey's driven cross. Deehan brings Norwich back into the game with a near-post header from Donowa's cross. Leicester now look safe after an awful start to the campaign.											
34	H	WATFORD	13	W	**6-1**	3-1	Deehan 8, 37, 74p, 83p, Downs 26,	Woods	Haylock	Downs	Mendham	Hareide	Watson	Devine	Channon	Deehan	**Rosario**	Donowa	
7/4		14,451	*10*	46			*Johnston 40* [Devine 87]	*Sherwood*	*Bardsley*	*Jackett*	*Taylor*	*Terry*	*Sinnott*	*Callaghan*	*Johnston*	*Reilly*	*Barnes*	*Atkinson**	*Richardson*
							Ref: J Bray	Rosario, a young 'A' level student, debuts and City stroll to their biggest top-flight win. Deehan nets a foursome, including two late penalties after Steve Terry holds Rosario and Steve Sherwood hauls down Donowa. Earlier Deehan netted a looping header and a well-taken snap-shot.											
35	A	WEST BROM	13	D	0-0	0-0		Woods	Haylock	Downs	Mendham	Hareide	Watson	Devine	Channon	Rosario	Van Wijk	Donowa	
14/4		*11,572*	*16*	47				*Barron*	*Ewbanks*	*Statham*	*Hunt*	*McNaught*	*Bennett*	*Grealish*	*Thompson*	*Cross*	*Mackenzie*	*Morley*	
							Ref: K Walmsley	The run of successive away defeats comes to an end, largely thanks to the continuing good form of keeper Woods. Nicky Cross, stepping into the side for Cyrille Regis, could have won it for Albion but misses a sitter near the end. Without Deehan, Norwich look unlikely to score today.											
36	H	STOKE	12	D	2-2	0-1	Rosario 54, Deehan 72	Woods	Devine	Downs	Mendham	Hareide*	Watson	Rosario	Channon	Deehan	Van Wijk	Donowa	Haylock
21/4		16,084	*19*	48			*McIlroy 5, Chamberlain M 70*	*Fox*	*Bould*	*Hampton*	*James*	*Dyson*	*McAughtrie*	*Painter*	*McIlroy*	*O'Callaghan*	*Maguire*	*Chamb'lain M*	
							Ref: A Buksh	Woods blocks Ian Painter's shot but Sammy McIlroy knocks in the rebound. Rosario rises to head his first senior goal. Mark Chamberlain converts a Painter cross, but City bounce back again with Deehan netting a fine goal from 15 yards. Woods keeps out a swirling Painter corner.											
37	A	IPSWICH	12	L	0-2	0-1		Woods	Haylock	Downs	Van Wijk*	Hareide	Watson	Devine	Deehan	Bertschin	Rosario	Donowa	Clayton
23/4		*22,135*	*19*	48			*Zondervan 27, Sunderland 74*	*Cooper*	*Putney*	*Barnes*	*Zondervan*	*Osman*	*Cranson*	*Sunderland*	*Brennan*	*D'Avray*	*McCall*	*Gates*	
							Ref: A Challinor	City's local rivals now seem in better shape to fight relegation after their miserable winter. Steve McCall's cross is netted by Romeo Zondervan and Alan Sunderland makes the points safe after being set up by Russell Osman. Deehan handles, but Eric Gates' penalty is saved by Woods.											
38	H	EVERTON	13	D	1-1	0-1	Hareide 84	Woods	Haylock	Downs	Mendham	Hareide	Watson	Devine	Channon	Deehan	Bertschin*	Van Wijk	Rosario
28/4		13,624	*11*	49			*Gray 44*	*Southall*	*Stevens*	*Bailey*	*Ratcliffe*	*Mountfield*	*Reid*	*Curran**	*Heath*	*Gray*	*Steven*	*Richardson*	*Sharp*
							Ref: D Vickers	Andy Gray rises high to nod in a hanging cross from Adrian Heath. Howard Kendall's side are mostly on top and rue not getting a second when Norwich conjure up a surprise late leveller. A corner-kick finds Hareide and he touches home the second and final goal of his English sojourn.											
39	A	TOTTENHAM	14	L	0-2	0-1		Woods	Haylock	**Spearing**	Mendham	Downs	Watson	Devine	Channon	Deehan	Bertschin	Van Wijk*	Rosario
5/5		*18,874*	*7*	49			*Falco 42, Spearing 78(og)*	*Parks*	*Thomas*	*Hughton*	*Stevens*	*Miller*	*Perryman*	*Cooke*	*Archibald*	*Falco**	*Mabbutt*	*Galvin*	*Crooks*
							Ref: A Robinson	City are in little trouble for most of the first half, despite a reorganised defence. The turning point is when Mark Falco curls a shot over Woods who is caught off his line. Ex-England youth skipper Spearing debuts at full-back and unluckily deflects a Steve Archibald drive past Woods.											
40	H	BIRMINGHAM	17	D	1-1	0-0	Watson 47	Woods	Haylock	Spearing	Mendham	Downs	Watson	Devine	Channon	Deehan	Rosario	Van Wijk	
7/5		13,601	*20*	50			*Gayle 87*	*Coton*	*Hagan*	*V d Hauwe*	*Blake*	*Wright*	*Roberts*	*Gayle*	*Kuhl**	*Harford*	*Rogers*	*Hopkins*	*Rees*
							Ref: M Dimblebee	One point will ensure safety, and it looks a formality after Watson heads home Van Wijk's corner. Mick Harford heads on a late free-kick and Howard Gayle buries a surprise equaliser. Hareide quits Carrow Road after 18 months to pursue a business opportunity in his native Norway.											
41	A	COVENTRY	17	L	1-2	1-1	Deehan 35p	Woods	Haylock	Spearing	Mendham	Downs	Watson	Devine	**Farrington**	Deehan*	Rosario	Van Wijk	**Goss**
12/5		*14,007*	*19*	50			*Ferguson 37, Bennett 70*	*Suckling*	*Butterworth*	*Pearce*	*Daly**	*Jacobs*	*Allardyce*	*Bennett*	*Gynn*	*Ferguson*	*Gibson*	*Platnauer*	*Grimes*
							Ref: N Ashley	The final weekend and Coventry will go down unless they win. They've conceded 19 in the last four games. Dave Bennett curls a corner-kick directly into goal to put them ahead. Rosario hits the post and Birmingham fail to score elsewhere, so Coventry have saved themselves again!											
42	A	LIVERPOOL	14	D	1-1	1-1	Devine 24	Woods	Haylock	Spearing*	Mendham	Downs	Devine	Donowa	Channon	Deehan	Bertschin	Van Wijk	Farrington
15/5		***38,837***	*1*	51			*Rush 30*	*Grobbelaar*	*Neal*	*Kennedy*	*Lawrenson*	*Whelan*	*Hansen*	*Dalglish*	*Lee*	*Rush*	*Lawrenson*	*Souness*	
	Home	Away					Ref: V Callow	Joe Fagan has won the title in his first year as boss and the trophy is paraded before the kick-off. The form-book indicates a big home win, but Devine silences the Kop with a superb shot. Ian Rush levels with his 47th of the season. A good day is spoiled by Spearing breaking his ankle.											
Average	16,432	16,944																	

Milk Cup			Att			F-A	H-T	Scorers, Times, and Referees	1	2	3	4	5	6	7	8	9	10	11	12 sub used
2:1	A	CARDIFF		19	D	0-0	0-0		Woods	Haylock	Downs	Mendham	Hareide	Young	Devine	Channon	Donowa	Bertschin	Bennett	
	4/10		4,425	*2:18*					*Dibble*	*Smith*	*Bodin*	*Dwyer*	*Mullen*	*Tong*	*Owen*	*Gibbins*	*Townsend*	*Crawford*	*Matthews*	
								Ref: K Baker	Len Ashurst's outfit press forward for more than an hour, but with no success. Woods is given some anxious moments by the ex-Canary Roger Gibbins and Chris Townsend, a 17-year-old on Work Experience. City look stronger late on, but in the last minute Gibbins' shot shaves a post.											
2:2	H	CARDIFF		16	W	3-0	1-0	Channon 23, 49, 63	Woods	Haylock	Downs	Mendham	Hareide	Watson	Devine	Channon	Donowa	Bertschin	Bennett*	Barham
	26/10		9,887	*2:17*					*Dibble*	*Smith*	*Bodin*	*Dwyer*	*Mullen*	*Tong**	*Owen*	*Gibbins*	*Heycock*	*Bennett*	*Matthews*	*Townsend*
								Ref: B Hill (Norwich win 3-0 on aggregate)	A very one-sided return match with the visitors hampered by having three first-choice players cup-tied. Youngster Russell Heycock gets a debut. Andy Dibble is beaten three times by experienced Channon, whose memorable hat-trick is witnessed by his nine-year-old son Michael.											
3	H	SUNDERLAND		15	D	0-0	0-0		Woods	Haylock	Downs	Mendham	Hareide	Watson	Devine	Channon	Deehan	Donowa	Barham	
	9/11		12,406	*17*					*Turner*	*Venison*	*Pickering*	*Atkins*	*Chisholm*	*Elliott*	*Bracewell*	*Rowell*	*West*	*Proctor*	*James*	
								Ref: D Reeves	Stalemate at a fog-shrouded Carrow Road. It worsens near the end but Mr Reeves resists the temptation to call the game off. Gary Rowell gets through and beats Woods, but Downs clears off the line. Six minutes from time Chris Turner makes a brilliant save from a Channon effort.											
3R	A	SUNDERLAND		13	W	2-1	1-0	Bertschin 29, 65	Woods	Haylock	Downs	Mendham	Deehan	Watson	Donowa	Channon	Bertschin	Van Wijk	Barham	
	22/11		*14,149*	*16*				*West 89*	*Turner*	*Venison*	*Pickering*	*Atkins*	*Chisholm*	*Hindmarch**	*Bracewell*	*Rowell*	*West*	*Proctor*	*James*	*Robson*
								Ref: N Wilson	City know beforehand that a local derby with Ipswich awaits the winners. Bertschin silences the famous Roker roar with a shot from the edge of the box. Turner saves another Bertschin effort from Donowa's cross, but he hooks in the rebound. Colin West scrambles a late consolation.											
4	A	IPSWICH		11	W	1-0	0-0	Channon 54	Woods	Haylock	Downs	Mendham	Deehan	Watson	Donowa	Channon	Bertschin	Van Wijk	Barham	
	30/11		*25,570*	*12*					*Cooper*	*Burley*	*McCall*	*Putney*	*Steggles*	*Butcher*	*Wark*	*Brennan**	*Mariner*	*Gates*	*O'Callaghan*	*D'Avray*
								Ref: M Taylor	Channon celebrates his recent 35th birthday by tucking the ball home as Donowa heads Barham's cross to him. Bertschin strikes a post as City push forward against a disappointing home side. Jubilation for the travelling fans, but home boss Bobby Ferguson publicly berates his players.											
QF	H	ASTON VILLA		10	L	0-2	0-2		Woods	Haylock	Downs	Mendham	Hareide	Watson*	Devine	Channon	Deehan	Bertschin	Van Wijk	Donowa
	17/1		21,568	*7*				*Shaw 21, Rideout 33*	*Spink*	*Williams*	*Gibson**	*Evans*	*Bremner*	*Mortimer*	*Curbishley*	*Shaw*	*Withe*	*McMahon*	*Rideout*	*Deacy*
								Ref: T Mills	Watson is carried off and taken to hospital after clashing heads with Peter Withe after just four minutes. Gary Shaw scores after his first effort is saved by Woods. Paul Rideout cracks in a low drive. 'That keeps me in work for another week,' says under-pressure Villa boss Tony Barton.											

FA Cup																				
3	A	ASTON VILLA		10	D	1-1	1-1	Deehan 26	Woods	Haylock	Downs	Mendham	Hareide	Watson	Devine	Channon	Deehan	Bertschin	Van Wijk	
	7/1		*21,454*	*7*				*Withe 35*	*Spink*	*Bremner*	*Walker*	*Evans*	*Ormsby*	*Mortimer*	*Birch*	*Shaw*	*Withe*	*McMahon*	*Walters*	
								Ref: R Bridges	Channon's low cross is touched past Nigel Spink by ex-Villain Deehan. The good start is spoiled by slack defending and Peter Withe scores after a Dennis Mortimer free-kick. City tighten up after this and fight hard for a replay. It will be one of three Villa visits in a five-week spell.											
3R	H	ASTON VILLA		10	W	3-0	1-0	Channon 7, Mendh'm 65, Bertschin 71	Woods	Haylock	Downs	Mendham	Hareide	Watson	Devine	Channon*	Deehan	Bertschin	Van Wijk	Donowa
	11/1		16,420	*7*					*Spink*	*Bremner*	*Walker*	*Evans*	*Glover*	*Mortimer*	*Birch*	*Shaw**	*Withe*	*McMahon*	*Walters*	*Rideout*
								Ref: D Brazier	A surprisingly comfortable win at chilly Carrow Road. Mendham ends Villa's resistance after a sparkling interchange of passes between Channon and Deehan. The icing on the cake is Bertschin's spectacular third - a great shot from an acute angle after he was put in by Mendham.											
4	A	TOTTENHAM		10	D	0-0	0-0		Woods	Haylock	Downs	Mendham	Hareide	Watson	Devine	Channon	Deehan	Bertschin	Van Wijk	
	28/1		*37,792*	*12*					*Parks*	*Stevens*	*Bowen*	*Roberts*	*Miller*	*Perryman*	*Mabbutt*	*Archibald*	*Falco**	*Hoddle*	*Galvin*	*Hazard*
								Ref: J Worrall	Keith Burkinshaw's outfit has a very good home record in recent years in this competition, but Norwich keep a tight rein on their highly skilled forward line. Steve Archibald's finishing is uncharacteristically wayward when two good chances come his way. Tony Parks is rarely troubled.											
4R	H	TOTTENHAM		10	W	2-1	2-0	Van Wijk 37, Channon 41	Woods	Haylock	Downs	Mendham	Hareide	Watson	Devine	Channon	Deehan	Bertschin	Van Wijk	
	1/2		26,811	*12*				*Falco 47*	*Parks*	*Stevens*	*Hughton*	*Roberts*	*Miller*	*Perryman*	*Mabbutt*	*Archibald*	*Falco**	*Ardiles*	*Galvin*	*Hazard*
								Ref: J Worrall	A great night for Norwich amid a frenzied atmosphere. Van Wijk beats Tony Parks with a blockbuster to delight home fans. It gets even better when Channon steers in the rebound after his first effort struck Chris Hughton. Mark Falco's clever scissors-kick ensures a tight second half.											
5	A	DERBY		15	L	1-2	0-0	Deehan 85	Woods	Haylock	Downs*	Mendham	Hareide	Watson	Devine	Channon	Deehan	Bertschin	Van Wijk	Bennett
	18/2		*25,793*	*2:20*				*Gemmill 54p, Davison 75*	*Cherry*	*Barton*	*Buckley*	*Gemmill*	*Watson*	*Powell*	*Futcher*	*Davison*	*Wilson*	*Garner**	*Robertson*	*Plummer*
								Ref: A Saunders	Derby are a Division Two club in crisis, but they show aggression and passion. Archie Gemmill nets from the spot after Haylock impedes John Robertson. Haylock's sliced clearance is netted by Bob Davison. Deehan sweeps in Bennett's cross and Watson goes very close with a header.											

		Home						Away					
		P	W	D	L	F	A	W	D	L	F	A	Pts
1	Liverpool	42	14	5	2	50	12	8	9	4	23	20	80
2	Southampton	42	15	4	2	44	17	7	7	7	22	21	77
3	Nott'm For	42	14	4	3	47	17	8	4	9	29	28	74
4	Manchester U	42	14	3	4	43	18	6	11	4	28	23	74
5	QP Rangers	42	14	4	3	37	12	8	3	10	30	25	73
6	Arsenal	42	10	5	6	41	29	8	4	9	33	31	63
7	Everton	42	9	9	3	21	12	7	5	9	23	30	62
8	Tottenham	42	11	4	6	31	24	6	6	9	33	41	61
9	West Ham	42	10	4	7	39	24	7	5	9	21	31	60
10	Aston Villa	42	14	3	4	34	22	3	6	12	25	39	60
11	Watford	42	9	7	5	36	31	7	2	12	32	46	57
12	Ipswich	42	11	4	6	34	23	4	4	13	21	34	53
13	Sunderland	42	8	9	4	26	18	5	4	12	16	35	52
14	NORWICH	42	9	8	4	34	20	3	7	11	14	29	51
15	Leicester	42	11	5	5	40	30	2	7	12	25	38	51
16	Luton	42	7	5	9	30	33	7	4	10	23	33	51
17	West Brom	42	10	4	7	30	25	4	5	12	18	37	51
18	Stoke	42	11	4	6	30	23	2	7	12	14	40	50
19	Coventry	42	8	5	8	33	33	5	6	10	24	44	50
20	Birmingham	42	7	7	7	19	18	5	5	11	20	32	48
21	Notts Co	42	6	7	8	31	36	4	4	13	19	36	41
22	Wolves	42	4	8	9	15	28	2	3	16	12	52	29
		924	226	118	118	745	505	118	118	226	505	745	1268

Odds & ends

Double wins: (1) Watford.
Double losses: (2) Nott'm For and QPR.

Won from behind: (1) Leicester (h).
Lost from in front: (2) Nott'm For (h) and Coventry (a).

High spots: The amazing fightback from 0-3 down v Manchester U.
Reaching the heady heights of the top six in December.
Hammering six goals past Watford in April.
Beating Ipswich to reach the last eight of the Milk Cup.
Spoiling the championship 'party' at Liverpool on the final day.
England call-ups for Dave Watson and Chris Woods.

Low spots: Losing the services of wages rebel Martin O'Neill.
The replacement of Steve Walford with Willie Young.
A 0-3 hammering and Mick Channon sent off at home to QPR.
Serious injuries to Mark Barham and Tony Spearing.

Player of the Year: Chris Woods.
Ever-presents: (2) Greg Downs and Chris Woods.
Hat-tricks: (2) Deehan (v Watford, h), Channon (v Cardiff, h, LC).
Hat-tricks against: (1) Colin Walsh (Nott'm For, h).
Leading scorer: (17) John Deehan.

	Appearances						Goals			
	Lge	*Sub*	LC	*Sub*	FAC	*Sub*	**Lge**	LC	FAC	**Tot**
Barham, Mark	**10**	*1*	3	*1*			**2**			**2**
Bennett, Dave	**12**	*1*	2			*1*	**1**			**1**
Bertschin, Keith	**33**		6		5		**7**	2	1	**10**
Channon, Mick	**37**		6		5		**5**	4	2	**11**
Clayton, Paul	**3**	*4*								
Deehan, John	**34**		4		5		**15**		2	**17**
Devine, John	**31**	*1*	4		5		**3**			**3**
Donowa, Louie	**23**	*2*	5	*1*		*1*	**4**			**4**
Downs, Greg	**42**		6		5		**4**			**4**
Farrington, Mark	**1**	*1*								
Godbold, Daryl		*2*								
Goss, Jeremy		*1*								
Hareide, Aage	**26**	*2*	4		5		**2**			**2**
Haylock, Paul	**38**	*1*	6		5					
Mendham, Peter	**41**		6		5		**1**		1	**2**
Pickering, Mike		*1*								
Rigby, Jon	**3**	*2*								
Rosario, Robert	**6**	*2*					**1**			**1**
Spearing, Tony	**4**									
Van Wijk, Dennis	**31**	*2*	3		5				1	**1**
Watson, Dave	**40**		4		5		**1**			**1**
Woods, Chris	**42**		6		5					
Young, Willie	5	*1*	1							
(own-goals)							**2**			**2**
23 players used	**462**	***24***	**66**	***2***	**55**	***2***	**48**	**6**	**7**	**61**

No	Date		Att	Pos	Pt	F-A	H-T	Scorers, Times, and Referees	1	2	3	4	5	6	7	8	9	10	11	12 sub used
1	H	LIVERPOOL			D	3-3	1-2	Mend'm 29, Berts'n 48, Chan'n 89p,	Woods	Haylock	Van Wijk	Mendham	**Bruce**	Watson	Devine	Channon	Deehan	Bertschin	**Gordon**	
	25/8		**22,005**		1			*Bruce 2(og), Dalglish 25, Neal 68p*	*Grobbelaar*	*Neal*	*Kennedy*	*Lawrenson*	*Whelan*	*Hansen*	*Dalglish**	*Lee*	*Walsh*	*Wark*	*Molby*	*Robinson*
								Ref: R Lewis	Steve Bruce, £135k from Gillingham, has a nightmare start, heading Jan Molby's cross into his own net. The game develops into a real thriller, City surging back from 0-2 down. It ends with an iffy penalty for each side - Paul Walsh and Channon apparently both 'conning' the referee.											
2	A	COVENTRY			D	0-0	0-0		Woods	Haylock	Van Wijk	Mendham	Bruce	Watson	Devine	Channon	Deehan	Bertschin	Gordon	
	28/8		*10,632*		2				*Ogrizovic*	*Stephens*	*Pearce*	*Jol*	*Kilcline*	*Peake*	*Bennett*	*Gynn*	*Latchford*	*Gibson*	*Platnauer*	
								Ref: R Nixon	Woods does brilliantly well to keep Bobby Gould's side at bay. The home side have clear opportunities but fail to hit the target even with goal-machine Bob Latchford making his debut. Norwich winger Dave Bennett, 24, announces he is quitting the full-time game due to knee trouble.											
3	A	TOTTENHAM		20	L	1-3	0-1	Bertschin 84	Woods	Haylock	Van Wijk	Mendham	Watson	Bruce	Devine*	Channon	Deehan	Bertschin	Gordon	**Goss**
	1/9		*24,947*	*2*	2			*Galvin 26, Chiedozie 52, Falco 65*	*Clemence*	*Stevens*	*Hughton*	*Roberts*	*Miller*	*Perryman*	*Chiedozie**	*Falco*	*Allen*	*Hazard*	*Galvin*	*Mabbutt*
								Ref: H King	The Canaries are outclassed from the start by Peter Shreeves' in-form side. Tony Galvin lobs over a stranded Woods and Nigerian winger John Chiedozie doubles the lead with a header. Mark Falco fires in a spectacular shot. Bertschin converts a rebound to give City a late consolation.											
4	H	WEST BROM		13	W	2-1	0-0	Farrington 48, Mendham 63	Woods	Haylock	Devine	Mendham	Bruce	Watson	Gordon*	Farrington	Deehan	Bertschin	Van Wijk	Goss
	5/9		14,234	*7*	5			*Grealish 55*	*Godden*	*Whitehead*	*Statham*	*Hunt*	*Bennett*	*Robertson*	*Grealish*	*Thompson*	*Regis*	*Mackenzie*	*Morley*	
								Ref: T Ward	Farrington, recently warned that his days at City might be numbered, knuckles down and has a fine game. He fires a 20-yard volley past Tony Godden. Steve Mackenzie sets up a close-range equaliser for Tony Grealish. Farrington whips over a cross for Mendham to head the winner.											
5	A	SOUTHAMPTON		15	L	1-2	0-1	Donowa 75	Woods	Haylock	Devine*	Mendham	Watson	Bruce	Gordon	Farrington	Deehan	Bertschin	Van Wijk	Donowa
	15/9		*16,431*	*20*	5			*Jordan 1, Watson 66 (og)*	*Shilton*	*Mills*	*Dennis*	*Williams*	*Agboola*	*Wright*	*Holmes*	*Curtis*	*Jordan*	*Armstrong*	*Wallace**	*Puckett*
								Ref: R Milford	A dreadful start as Joe Jordan is left unmarked to head in Danny Wallace's free-kick after just 43 seconds. Woods struggles with a knee injury and is beaten again when Watson, under pressure from Alan Curtis, steers a header into his own net. Donowa bursts through to hit a fine reply.											
6	H	STOKE		17	D	0-0	0-0		Woods	Haylock	Van Wijk	Mendham*	Watson	Bruce	Gordon	Farrington	Deehan	Devine	Donowa	Goss
	19/9		13,591	*18*	6				*Fox*	*Bould*	*Hemming*	*James*	*Berry*	*O'Callaghan*	*Painter*	*Ebanks*	*Saunders*	*Hudson*	*Chamberlain*	
								Ref: J Moules	City line up with two wingers, but relegation-favourites Stoke somehow keep their goal intact. A Deehan shot is cleared off the line by Mark Chamberlain. Even the skilful Alan Hudson, in his second spell at Stoke, will surely not save Bill Asprey's outfit from the trapdoor this season?											
7	H	WATFORD		15	W	3-2	1-1	Deehan 6p, 71, 76	Woods	Haylock	Van Wijk	Mendham	Watson	Bruce	Gordon	Farrington	Deehan	Devine	Donowa	
	22/9		14,896	*22*	9			*Johnston 41, Terry 50*	*Sherwood*	*Bardsley*	*Jackett*	*Taylor*	*Terry*	*Sinnott*	*Callaghan*	*Reilly*	*Johnston*	*Blissett*	*Barnes*	
								Ref: J Ashworth	After hitting four against Watford last term, Deehan is at it again. Steve Terry handles to concede an early penalty. Graham Taylor's men hit back as Mo Johnston scrambles one in and Terry heads a corner. Deehan levels after a corner and then slams home a great drive on the run.											
8	A	NOTT'M FOREST		16	L	1-3	0-1	Mendham 86	**Corrigan**	Haylock	Van Wijk	Mendham	Watson	Bruce	Gordon	Farrington	Deehan	Devine	Donowa	
	29/9		*15,166*	*2*	9			*Watson 22(og), Hodge 87, Christie 90*	*Sutton*	*McInally*	*Swain*	*Gunn*	*Fairclough*	*Bowyer*	*Wigley**	*Metgod*	*Christie*	*Davenport*	*Hodge*	*Mills*
								Ref: P Tyldesley	Joe Corrigan, 35, on loan from Brighton, replaces injured Woods, whose run of 171 consecutive games ends. Watson heads a spectacular own goal. A drab game bursts into life late on, with Mendham rifling in from 30 yards. Steve Hodge and Trevor Christie both net from close range.											
9	H	CHELSEA		15	D	0-0	0-0		Corrigan	Haylock	Van Wijk*	Bruce	Mendham	Watson	Gordon	Farrington	Deehan	Devine	Donowa	Channon
	6/10		18,272	*9*	10				*Niedzwiecki*	*Wood*	*Rougvie*	*Pates*	*McLaughlin*	*Bumstead*	*Nevin*	*Spackman**	*Dixon*	*Speedie*	*Canoville*	*Jones K*
								Ref: J Bray	Chelsea's travelling army of fans give the game a cup-tie atmosphere. Uncompromising full-back Doug Rougvie gets stuck in, to the ire of the home fans. A hectic and over-physical game remains deadlocked. City recruit Asa Hartford, 33, initially on trial, after a spell playing in USA.											
10	A	SUNDERLAND		17	L	1-2	0-1	Channon 82	Corrigan	Haylock	Devine*	Bruce	Mendham	Watson	Gordon	Channon	Deehan	**Hartford**	Donowa	Farrington
	13/10		*15,155*	*9*	10			*Gayle 8, Berry 90*	*Turner*	*Venison*	*Pickering*	*Bennett*	*Chisholm*	*Elliott*	*Daniel*	*Gayle*	*Wylde**	*Berry*	*Walker*	*West*
								Ref: A Robinson	A long punt forward by Chris Turner ends at Howard Gayle's feet and he fires past Corrigan. Channon gallops past three men on a superb run before blasting the equaliser. Sub Colin West crosses for Steve Berry to grab a near-post winner. A harsh outcome after a brave performance.											

11 A	ASTON VILLA		17	D	2-2	2-1	Deehan 9, Donowa 45	Woods	Haylock	Downs	Bruce	Mendham	Watson	Devine	Channon	Deehan	Hartford	Donowa	
20/10		*14,149*	12	11			*Withe 17, 67*	*Day*	*Williams*	*Gibson*	*Evans*	*Ormsby*	*McMahon**	*Birch*	*Rideout*	*Withe*	*Cowans*	*Six*	*Mortimer*
							Ref: L Shapter	Deehan buries a low shot, but Peter Withe soon responds with a typical far-post header. Channon crosses and Donowa nets a powerful header just before the interval. A Haylock clearance holds up in the wind and falls to Withe, who curls in a beauty, despite Didier Six looking offside.											
12 H	QP RANGERS		16	W	2-0	1-0	Channon 9, Deehan 57	Woods	Haylock	Downs	Bruce	Mendham	Watson	Devine	Channon	Deehan	Hartford	Donowa	
27/10		14,731	*13*	14				*Hucker*	*Neill*	*Dawes*	*Fereday*	*MacDonald*	*Fenwick*	*Micklewhite*	*Fillery*	*Bannister*	*Stainrod*	*Gregory*	
							Ref: M Scott	The game goes ahead despite the major fire two days earlier which destroyed the Main Stand. Channon, playing his 850th senior game, finishes well after a Devine pass. City overcome Rangers' annoying offside tactics and keep Peter Hucker busy. Channon sets up the Deehan clincher.											
13 A	SHEFFIELD WED		13	W	2-1	1-0	Deehan 22, Donowa 80	Woods	Haylock	Downs	Bruce	Mendham	Watson	Devine*	Channon	Deehan	Hartford	Donowa	Van Wijk
3/11		*21,847*	*6*	17			*Sterland 85*	*Hodge*	*Sterland*	*Shirtliff*	*Smith*	*Lyons*	*Worthingt'n**	*Marwood*	*Blair*	*Varadi*	*Chapman*	*Shelton*	*Pearson*
							Ref: V Callow	Persistent Deehan forces his way into the box to score. Haylock's foul provides Andy Blair with a penalty, but Woods dives to save it. Donowa nets after his first attempt is blocked. Mel Sterland blasts a fine goal, but Norwich hang on for their first away win in the league for 11 months.											
14 H	LUTON		10	W	**3-0**	2-0	Mendham 18, Hartford 26, Gordon 46	Woods	Haylock	Downs	Bruce	Mendham*	Watson	Donowa	Channon	Deehan	Hartford	Gordon	Van Wijk
10/11		14,395	*19*	20				*Dibble*	*Breacker*	*Turner*	*Todd*	*North S*	*Donaghy*	*Hill*	*Stein*	*Bunn*	*Parker*	*Moss**	*Nwajiobi*
							Ref: G Napthine	Norwich dominate the first half and the result is never in doubt after Hartford's first league goal for City. Experienced Hartford and Channon run the game and David Pleat's men only threaten when already three down. They look fragile despite fielding the on-loan veteran Colin Todd.											
15 A	LEICESTER		13	L	0-2	0-1		Woods	Haylock	Downs	Bruce	Mendham	Watson	Donowa	Channon	Deehan	Hartford	Gordon	
17/11		*9,693*	*18*	20			*Banks 13, Lynex 88p*	*Andrews*	*Feeley*	*Wilson*	*Smith R*	*Hazell !*	*O'Neill*	*Lynex*	*Lineker*	*Eastoe**	*Ramsey*	*Banks*	*Smith A*
							Ref: D Scott	Ian Banks' deflected shot beats Woods. Big Bob Hazell gets a red card after horrendous tackles on Mendham and Gordon. An equaliser eludes City and Gordon Milne's men clinch the win with a Steve Lynex penalty. The referee didn't see Watson handle Banks' shot but a linesman did.											
16 H	EVERTON		12	W	4-2	3-1	Deehan 15, 65, Gordon 17, Donowa 26	Woods	Haylock	Downs	Bruce	Mendham	Watson	Donowa	Channon	Deehan	Hartford	Gordon	
24/11		16,925	*1*	23			*Sharp 27, Sheedy 50*	*Southall*	*Stevens*	*V d Hauwe**	*Ratcliffe*	*Mountfield*	*Reid*	*Steven*	*Heath*	*Sharp*	*Bracewell*	*Sheedy*	*Gray*
							Ref: H Taylor	Everton's record of five clean sheets in a row is wiped out in a cracking first half. Deehan slips one past Neville Southall, then Gordon rams in a rebound. Donowa converts a low cross before Graeme Sharp nods in. Kevin Sheedy nets soon after hitting the bar, but Deehan fires another.											
17 A	MANCHESTER U		14	L	0-2	0-2		Woods	Haylock	Downs	Bruce	Mendham	Watson	Donowa	Channon	Deehan*	Hartford	Gordon	Goss
1/12		***36,635***	*2*	23			*Robson 14, Hughes 32*	*Bailey*	*Gidman*	*Duxbury*	*Moses*	*McQueen*	*McGrath*	*Robson*	*Strachan*	*Hughes*	*Whiteside*	*Olsen*	
							Ref: F Roberts	Mark Hughes crosses for Bryan Robson to head home. Minutes later City lose the injured Deehan. Hughes collects Jesper Olsen's pass and calmly beats Woods. More Norwich woe as Watson goes off with concussion. leaving them a man short and intent on mere damage limitation.											
18 H	WEST HAM		11	W	1-0	1-0	Farrington 30	Woods	Haylock	Downs	Bruce	Mendham	Watson	Donowa	Channon	Farrington	Hartford	Gordon	
8/12		13,908	*12*	26				*McAlister*	*Stewart*	*Walford*	*Allen*	*Martin*	*Gale*	*Whitton*	*Goddard*	*Cottee*	*Dickens*	*Pike**	*Hilton*
							Ref: D Hedges	A drab game is lifted by a great goal from Farrington. He takes Donowa's pass, turns Ray Stewart and cracks home a fierce drive. It's a happy return after a seven-match absence for the Liverpudlian. Brown will soon have another option as Barham is nearly fit again after a year out.											
19 A	NEWCASTLE		10	D	1-1	1-0	Donowa 21	Woods	Haylock	Downs	Bruce	Mendham	Watson	Donowa	Channon	Deehan	Hartford	Gordon*	Van Wijk
15/12		*20,030*	*14*	27			*Waddle 58*	*Carr*	*Brown*	*Saunders*	*Heard*	*Anderson*	*Roeder*	*Megson*	*Wharton*	*Waddle*	*Beardsley*	*McCreery*	
							Ref: R Dilkes	Donowa turns and shoots and a deflection helps it travel beyond Kevin Carr. The Geordies' danger-man, Chris Waddle, is largely subdued until the second half when he seizes on defender Wes Saunders' through-ball and races clear to beat Woods expertly. It's his 11th goal of the season.											
20 H	TOTTENHAM		11	L	1-2	0-1	Deehan 71p	Woods	Haylock	Downs*	Bruce	Mendham	Watson	Donowa	Channon	Deehan	Hartford	Gordon	Van Wijk
22/12		17,682	*1*	27			*Crooks 35, Galvin 62*	*Clemence*	*Stevens*	*Hughton*	*Roberts*	*Miller*	*Perryman*	*Chiedozie*	*Falco*	*Galvin*	*Mabbutt*	*Crooks**	*Hazard*
							Ref: K Hackett	Peter Shreeves' skilful Spurs surge ahead when Garth Crooks nets a glorious header from John Chiedozie's cross. Tony Galvin increases the lead with a fine curling shot from 25 yards. Deehan, whose poor pass set up the Galvin goal, nets a penalty after Mark Falco handled a cross.											
21 H	ARSENAL		11	W	1-0	1-0	Deehan 43	Woods	Haylock	Van Wijk	Bruce	Mendham	Watson	Donowa	Channon	Deehan	Hartford	Gordon	
26/12		17,702	*4*	30				*Lukic*	*Anderson*	*Sansom*	*Talbot*	*O'Leary*	*Adams*	*Robson*	*Caton*	*Mariner*	*Woodcock*	*Allinson**	*NIcholas*
							Ref: B Hill	A tight and tense first half ends with Deehan pouncing to put the Canaries ahead. After this, Don Howe's men enjoy plenty of possession but are held at bay. Woods makes a great save from Viv Anderson's close-range header. Hartford has a superb game, despite a minor calf problem.											

No	Date		Att	Pos	Pt	F-A	H-T	Scorers, Times, and Referees	1	2	3	4	5	6	7	8	9	10	11	12 sub used
22	A	WEST BROM		10	W	1-0	1-0	Channon 30	Woods	Haylock	Van Wijk*	Bruce	Mendham	Watson	Devine	Channon	Deehan	Farrington	Donowa	Gordon
	29/12		*13,403*	*8*	33				*Godden*	*Nicholl*	*Statham*	*Hunt*	*Bennett*	*Robertson*	*Grealish**	*Thompson*	*Cross*	*Mackenzie*	*Valentine*	*Whitehead*
								Ref: D Brazier	John Devine makes a fine return to action after eight weeks out and plays a vital role against Johnny Giles' physical side. Farrington hits a first-time shot which flashes across the goalmouth and Channon pounces on it to drill home. It's a great end to 1984 and keeps City in the top ten.											
23	A	IPSWICH		11	L	0-2	0-1		Woods	Haylock	Downs	Bruce	Mendham	Watson	Devine	Channon	Deehan	Farrington*	Donowa	Gordon
	1/1		*21,710*	*20*	33			*Gates 3, Dozzell 65*	*Cooper*	*Yallop*	*Butcher*	*Zondervan*	*Osman*	*Cranson*	*Putney*	*Brennan*	*Dozzell*	*McCall*	*Gates*	
								Ref: T Bune	Ipswich have gone 558 minutes without a home league goal, but Eric Gates capitalises early on a chance created by Terry Butcher and Jason Dozzell. The latter, who was 17 three weeks ago, turns expertly and fires a second goal when Romeo Zondervan nods on Trevor Putney's pass.											
24	H	SOUTHAMPTON		10	W	1-0	0-0	Deehan 52	Woods	Haylock	Downs	Bruce	Mendham	Watson*	Barham	Channon	Deehan	Goss	Donowa	Farrington
	12/1		13,735	*8*	36				*Shilton*	*Mills*	*Dennis*	*Curtis*	*Wright*	*Bond*	*Holmes**	*Moran*	*Jordan*	*Armstrong*	*Wallace*	*Baker*
								Ref: D Reees	Huge efforts are made to clear the pitch of snow, but sadly the game is far from a classic. After a challenge by Joe Jordan, Watson is left in agony and needs lengthy treatment before being stretchered off. Deehan snaps a winner after his first shot is parried and rebounds back to him.											
25	A	LIVERPOOL		10	L	**0-4**	0-1		Woods	Haylock	Downs	Bruce	Mendham	Van Wijk	Barham	Channon	Deehan	Hartford	Donowa*	Devine
	19/1		*30,627*	*7*	36			*Wark 36, Rush 56, 90, Dalglish 86*	*Grobbelaar*	*Neal*	*Kennedy*	*Gillespie*	*Nicol*	*Hansen*	*Dalglish*	*Whelan*	*Rush*	*MacDonald*	*Wark*	
								Ref: L Robinson	A low first-time shot by John Wark puts City behind. Ian Rush swoops to head in Steve Nicol's cross and Kenny Dalglish makes it three with a clever lob. A bad day is capped in the last minute when Rush converts Dalglish's pass. It's The Reds' best win of an indifferent season thus far.											
26	H	NOTT'M FOREST		11	L	0-1	0-0		Woods	Haylock	Van Wijk	Bruce	Mendham	Watson	Barham	Farrington	Deehan	Hartford	Devine	
	2/2		14,669	*6*	36			*Davenport 87*	*Segers*	*McInally*	*Swain*	*Fairclough*	*Hart*	*Walsh*	*Wigley*	*Metgod*	*Clough*	*Davenport*	*Hodge*	
								Ref: M Dimblebee	Devine works hard despite the barracking he is getting from certain sections of Carrow Road. Haylock comes to the rescue by clearing Johnny Metgod's effort off the line. Nigel Clough is booked for dissent and then sets up the winner as his shot is parried to the feet of Peter Davenport.											
27	A	QP RANGERS		10	D	2-2	2-2	Channon 28, Deehan 39	Woods	Haylock	Downs	Bruce	Mendham	Van Wijk	Barham	Channon	Deehan	Hartford	Donowa	
	2/3		*12,975*	*16*	37			*Wicks 1, Fereday 27*	*Hucker*	*Fereday*	*Dawes*	*Waddock*	*Wicks*	*Fenwick*	*Robinson*	*Cooper**	*Bannister*	*Byrne*	*Gregory*	*James*
								Ref: E Read	Frank Sibley's side look sharp in the first half. Steve Wicks heads home a corner before some fans have taken their seats. John Byrne's deep cross is superbly headed in by Wayne Fereday. City hit back late with a splendid Channon volley, followed by Deehan netting Donowa's pass.											
28	H	ASTON VILLA		10	D	2-2	0-0	Haylock 59, Rowell 85	Woods	Haylock	Van Wijk	Bruce	Mendham	Watson	Barham	Channon	Clayton	Hartford	Donowa*	**Rowell**
	9/3		21,853	*11*	38			*Evans 58p, 71p*	*Spink*	*Williams*	*Dorigo*	*Evans*	*Ormsby*	*McMahon**	*Gibson*	*Kerr*	*Withe*	*Cowans*	*Walters*	*Bradley*
								Ref: J Moules	City appear to have a Milk Cup hangover in the early stages. Barham brings down Paul Kerr for Allan Evans to slot home a penalty. Haylock responds with a fine curling shot. Channon's foul brings another penalty, but debutant Rowell pounces on a poor Evans back-pass to equalise.											
29	H	SUNDERLAND		11	L	1-3	1-2	Deehan 43	Woods	Haylock	Downs	Van Wijk	Mendham	Watson	Barham	Channon	Deehan	Hartford	Donowa*	Rowell
	16/3		**13,389**	*18*	38			*Wallace 11, Downs 33(og), Hodgson 90*	*Turner*	*Venison*	*Pickering*	*Corner*	*Chisholm*	*Elliott*	*Wallace**	*Lemon*	*Hodgson*	*Berry*	*Walker*	*Gayle*
								Ref: J Ball	A 'rehearsal' for the Milk Cup final. Ian Wallace holds off Downs to fire his first goal for Len Ashurst's men. Downs misdirects a clearance into his own net. Deehan's bullet header lifts City, but as they toil hard for an equaliser Howard Gayle breaks out and tees up David Hodgson.											
30	H	COVENTRY		10	W	2-1	2-1	Channon 28, 39	Woods	Haylock	Van Wijk	Bruce	Mendham	Watson	Barham	Channon	Deehan	Hartford	Donowa	
	30/3		14,067	*19*	41			*Gynn 45*	*Ogrizovic*	*Stephens*	*Pearce*	*Hibbitt*	*Kilcline*	*McGrath*	*Bennett*	*Gynn*	*Regis**	*Gibson*	*Adams*	*Peake*
								Ref: N Butler	The newly won Milk Cup is paraded before the home fans and Norwich turn in an attacking display. Channon makes the most of slip-ups by Lloyd McGrath and Kenny Hibbitt. After Micky Gynn pulls one back, the visitors fail to really test Woods, who is hampered by a hip injury.											
31	H	SHEFFIELD WED		11	D	1-1	1-1	Barham 5	Woods	Haylock	Van Wijk	Bruce	Mendham*	Watson	Barham	Channon	Deehan	Hartford	Donowa	Rowell
	3/4		15,138	*5*	42			*Haylock 30(og)*	*Hodge*	*Shirtliff*	*Morris*	*Smith*	*Lyons*	*Worthingon*	*Marwood**	*Blair*	*Varadi*	*Chapman*	*Shelton*	*Stainrod*
								Ref: K Miller	Barham gets the crowd on its feet by netting an early near-post header. Minutes later Deehan is on target, but a baffling offside decision foils him. Brian Marwood's cross is accidentally turned past Woods by Haylock. City have a let-off when Andy Blair blasts a penalty over the bar.											

No	Venue / Date	Opponent	Att	Pos	Pts	Res	F-A	H-T	Scorers, Times, and Referees	1	2	3	4	5	6	7	8	9	10	11	12
32	A	ARSENAL		11		L	0-2	0-0		**Benstead**	Haylock	Van Wijk	Bruce	Devine	Watson	Barham	**Fairclough**	Deehan	Hartford	Clayton	
	6/4		*19,597*	*7*	42				*Nicholas 80, Robson 86*	*Lukic*	*Anderson*	*Sansom*	*Williams*	*O'Leary*	*Caton*	*Robson*	*Rix*	*Mariner**	*Talbot*	*Nicholas*	*Allinson*
									Ref: T Holbrook	Graham Benstead, on loan from QPR, makes his debut and remains unbeaten until the last ten minutes. Deehan misses a sitter and moments later Charlie Nicholas elbows Barham, but escapes with a booking. Nicholas and Stewart Robson stun City with two late 25-yard blockbusters.											
33	H	IPSWICH		11		L	0-2	0-1		Woods	Haylock	Van Wijk	Bruce	Devine	Watson	Barham	Channon	Deehan	Hartford !	Donowa	
	8/4		18,227	*18*	42				*Butcher 5, D'Avray 47*	*Cooper*	*Burley*	*Gernon*	*Zondervan*	*Sunderland*	*Butcher*	*McCall*	*Brennan*	*D'Avray*	*Wilson*	*Gates*	
									Ref: C Downey	Town avenge their Milk Cup reverse here a month ago. Terry Butcher, who ended that game in tears of despair, powers in Eric Gates' free-kick with his head. Hartford, who upset Ipswich in the cup-tie, is sent off for fouling Mark Brennan. Mich D'Avray nets a Steve McCall free-kick.											
34	A	WATFORD		11		L	0-2	0-0		Woods	Haylock	Van Wijk	Bruce	Devine	Watson	Barham*	Channon	Deehan	Hartford	Rowell	Fairclough
	13/4		*15,327*	*17*	42				*Barnes 84, Rostron 87*	*Coton*	*Gibbs*	*Rostron*	*Taylor*	*Terry*	*McClelland*	*Callaghan*	*Blissett*	*West*	*Jackett*	*Barnes*	
									Ref: D Axcell	Brown wins Manager of the Month for March, but April is proving tricky. Barham departs with a hamstring injury. Watford have two strong penalty claims rejected. With time running out, John Barnes fires home after a corner. Wilf Rostron ensures the victory with a diving header.											
35	A	LUTON		15		L	1-3	1-0	Channon 14	Woods	Haylock	Van Wijk	Bruce	Devine	Watson	Donowa	Channon	Deehan	Hartford	Rowell	
	16/4		*8,794*	*20*	42				*Nwajiobi 53, 89, Moss 64*	*Sealey*	*Breacker*	*Thomas*	*Nicholas*	*Foster*	*Donaghy*	*Hill*	*Stein B*	*Moss*	*Nwajiobi*	*Preece*	
									Ref: M Cotton	Channon tucks in an early goal, but Luton ease relegation worries with a fine second-half display. Unluckily beaten in the FA Cup semi-final three days earlier, Meka Nwajiobi cheers up David Pleat with a smart double. A push by Bruce on Brian Stein leads to David Moss's penalty.											
36	H	LEICESTER		16		L	1-3	1-1	Donowa 10	Woods	Haylock	Van Wijk	Bruce	Mendham	Watson	Donowa	Channon	Deehan	Hartford*	Gordon	Rowell
	20/4		13,395	*18*	42				*Smith A 45, 90*	*Andrews*	*Feeley*	*Wilson*	*Smith R*	*Williams*	*O'Neill*	*Lynex*	*Lineker*	*Smith A*	*Peake*	*Banks*	
									Ref: A Gunn	A fifth successive defeat by a two-goal margin raises serious relegation fears. Donowa pops up in the six-yard box to shoot home, but the good start comes to nothing. Alan Smith poaches goals at the end of each half, fastening on to rebounds from Gary Lineker shots on both occasions.											
37	A	STOKE		15		W	3-2	2-1	Rosario 4, Gordon 33, Donowa 78	Woods	Haylock	Van Wijk	Rigby	Mendham	Downs	Donowa	Rosario	Deehan	Clayton	Gordon	
	24/4		***4,597***	*22*	45				*Bertschin 10, Saunders 90*	*Fox*	*Bould*	*Maskery*	*Dodd*	*Berry*	*Dyson*	*Painter*	*McIlroy*	*Bertschin*	*Hudson**	*Heath*	*Saunders*
									Ref: G Tyson	Already relegated and managerless, Stoke provide weak opposition for a much-changed City line-up. Rosario races clear to beat Barry Siddall, but ex-Canary Keith Bertschin hits his first Stoke goal in 23 games to level. Close-range goals by Gordon and Donowa make sure of the points.											
38	A	EVERTON		16		L	0-3	0-1		Woods	Haylock	Van Wijk	Bruce	Downs*	Watson	Donowa	Rosario	Deehan	Rigby	Gordon	Clayton
	27/4		*32,085*	*1*	45				*Mountf'ld 43, Steven 49, Bracewell 57*	*Southall*	*Stevens*	*V d Hauwe*	*Ratcliffe*	*Mountfield*	*Richardson*	*Steven*	*Sharp*	*Gray*	*Bracewell*	*Harper*	
									Ref: G Courtney	Howard Kendall's champions-elect cruise home after Derek Mountfield breaks Norwich resistance with a simple header. Trevor Steven nets from close range and Paul Bracewell bangs in a third after Bruce is caught in possession. Canaries are plunged back into the relegation battle.											
39	H	MANCHESTER U		19		L	0-1	0-1		Woods	Rigby	Van Wijk	Downs	Mendham	Watson	Donowa	Channon	Deehan	Hartford	Clayton	
	4/5		16,006	*4*	45				*Moran 34*	*Bailey*	*Gidman*	*Albiston*	*Whiteside*	*Moran*	*McGrath*	*Robson*	*Strachan*	*Hughes*	*Stapleton*	*Olsen*	
									Ref: T Ward	Four games without a win has seen Ron Atkinson's men slip right out of the title race, but they go ahead at Carrow Road when Jesper Olsen's corner is flicked on and Kevin Moran steams in to net a bullet header. Norwich toil manfully for the next hour or so, but cannot fashion a goal.											
40	A	WEST HAM		19		L	0-1	0-0		Woods	Haylock	Van Wijk	Bruce	Rigby	Watson	Barham !	Channon*	Deehan	Hartford	Donowa	Downs
	6/5		*16,233*	*13*	45				*Barnes 86*	*Parkes*	*Stewart*	*Brush*	*Orr*	*Martin*	*Gale*	*Allen*	*Bonds*	*Cottee*	*Goddard*	*Dickens**	*Barnes*
									Ref: L Shapter	It's a Bank Holiday deadlock until the dying minutes when Tony Cottee's goalbound effort rebounds off Woods and is netted by Bobby Barnes. Moments later Barnes clearly pulls down Watson, but, to City's horror, no penalty is given. Barham is red-carded for arguing with the referee.											
41	H	NEWCASTLE		20		D	0-0	0-0		Woods	Haylock	Van Wijk	Bruce	Mendham	Watson	Barham	Rosario	Deehan	Hartford*	Donowa	Rigby
	11/5		18,399	*14*	46					*Thomas*	*Anderson*	*Wharton*	*McCreery*	*Clarke*	*Roeder*	*McDonald*	*Cunningham*	*Waddle*	*Beardsley*	*Heard*	
									Ref: A Buksch	Despite the dreadful run of results, home fans are sympathetic over Monday's injustice and turn up in good numbers for this vital game. City dominate but find Martin Thomas in great form. In a rare late raid, Peter Beardsley hits the post. City's top-flight future is hanging by a thread.											
42	A	CHELSEA		20		W	2-1	1-1	Hartford 16, Bruce 82	Woods	Haylock	Van Wijk	Bruce	Mendham	Watson	Barham	Rosario	Deehan	Hartford	Downs	
	14/5		*22,882*	*6*	49				*Thomas 43*	*Niedzwiecki*	*Lee*	*Jones J*	*Pates*	*McLaughlin*	*Bumstead*	*Nevin*	*Spackman*	*Dixon*	*Speedie*	*Thomas**	*Canoville*
Average	Home 16,058		Away 18,234						Ref: L Burden	City hearts miss a beat as a Deehan penalty is saved, but Hartford is quick to bury the rebound. Micky Thomas heads over Woods, but Bruce drives in a dramatic late winner. The three points will ensure safety - unless Coventry manage a victory in all three of their remaining matches!											

Milk Cup			Att			F-A	H-T	Scorers, Times, and Referees	1	2	3	4	5	6	7	8	9	10	11	12 sub used
2:1	A	PRESTON		15	D	3-3	2-1	Deehan 10, Bruce 32, Watson 46	Woods	Haylock	Van Wijk	Bruce	Mendham	Watson	Gordon	Farrington	Deehan	Devine	Donowa	
		25/9	5,265	3:7				Houghton 43, 90, Wilkins 85	Litchfield	Jones M	Farrelly	Twentyman	Booth	Clark	Kelly	Murphy*	Houghton	Naughton	Houston	Wilkins
								Ref: T Hobrook	Deehan cracks in a 25-yarder and emphatic headers by Bruce and Watson give City a commanding lead just after the break. Alan Kelly's side refuse to give up and a late flurry sees them draw level again. Peter Houghton and Paul Wilkins score from close range to keep this tie alive.											
2:2	H	PRESTON		15	W	6-1	2-0	Hartford 30, 70, Donowa 45, 81,	Corrigan	Haylock	Devine	Bruce	Mendham	Watson	Gordon	Channon	Deehan	**Hartford**	Donowa	
		10/10	13,506	3:12				Twentyman 63 [Chan'n 48, Bruce 61]	Litchfield	Jones M	Rudge	Jones D	Twentyman	Clark	Kelly	Farrelly*	Houghton	Naughton	Greenwood	Houston
								Ref: D Axcell (Norwich win 9-4 on aggregate)	Preston have shipped 14 goals and lost their last four league games, so City are brimming with confidence. Hartford, on his debut, gets the party going with a clever lob. Bruce's header puts the tie well beyond Preston's reach on the hour. Cut-price admissions help boost the crowd.											
3	H	ALDERSHOT		16	D	0-0	0-0		Woods	Haylock*	Downs	Bruce	Mendham	Watson	Devine	Channon	Deehan	Hartford	Donowa	Van Wijk
		31/10	12,137	4:19					Coles	Day	Shrubb	Massey	Peters	Mazzon	Burvill	Banton	Foyle	McDonald	Staff	
								Ref: K Barrett	A rare meeting with the Shots, and their boss Len Walker promises his struggling outfit won't hump the ball forward and use spoiling tactics. He is proved right and City are given a good fight. Channon has a header cleared off the line. Paul Staff misses an open goal at the other end.											
3R	A	ALDERSHOT		13	W	4-0	2-0	Peters 14(og), Deehan 21, Channon 61,	Woods	Haylock	Downs	Bruce	Mendham	Watson	Gordon	Channon	Deehan	Hartford	Donowa	
		6/11	9,773	4:20				[Mendham 89]	Coles	Day	Souter	Massey	Peters	Mazzon	Burvill	Banton	Foyle	McDonald	Staff*	Foley
								Ref: M James	Thick fog gives the three-sided Recreation Ground an eerie look, and an abandonment is a possibility for long periods. The visitors' nerves are settled somewhat by Gary Peters heading past his own keeper. Deehan sweeps in a second and a Channon special silences the noisy home fans.											
4	H	NOTTS CO		13	W	3-0	1-0	Channon 45, Deehan 72, Donowa 77	Woods	Haylock	Downs	Bruce	Mendham	Watson	Gordon	Channon	Deehan	Hartford	Donowa	
		21/11	14,540	2:22					McDonagh	Benjamin	Lahtinen	Richards	Watson	Goodwin	O'Neill	Fashanu	Young	Harkouk	Burke	
								Ref: A Buksch	Struggling County work hard, but Channon's close-range header on the stroke of half-time is a mortal blow. It is the ex-England man's 300th career goal. Deehan heads in Donowa's cross and returns the compliment. Ex-Canaries Martin O'Neill and Justin Fashanu have a quiet return.											
QF	A	GRIMSBY		10	W	1-0	1-0	Deehan 28	Woods	Haylock	Downs	Bruce	Mendham	Van Wijk	Barham	Channon	Deehan	Hartford	Donowa	
		16/1	15,050	2:7					Batch	Seagraves	Agnew	Foley	Crombie	Moore	Ford	Wilkinson	Lund	Bonnyman	Emson	
								Ref: J Worrall	A perfectly weighted cross by Barham is headed past Nigel Batch by Deehan. David Booth's outfit are under constant pressure, but somehow remain in contention. Bruce hits the crossbar and Barham twice fails to score after getting clean through. Two City penalty appeals are ignored.											
SF	A	IPSWICH		11	L	0-1	0-1		Woods	Devine	Van Wijk	Bruce	Mendham	Watson	Barham	Channon	Deehan	Hartford	Clayton	
1		23/2	27,404	20				D'Avray 6	Cooper	Burley	McCall	Zondervan	Cranson	Butcher	Putney	Brennan	D'Avray	Dozzell	Gates	
								Ref: D Hutchinson	Van Wijk is pulled up for an early foul and George Burley's floated free-kick is headed past Woods by an unmarked Mich D'Avray. Romeo Zondervan looks to have grabbed a second, but the referee rules it never crossed the line. City are relieved to end a tense game just one behind.											
SF	H	IPSWICH		10	W	2-0	1-0	Deehan 35, Bruce 87	Woods	Haylock	Van Wijk	Bruce	Mendham	Watson	Barham	Channon	Deehan	Hartford	Donowa	
2		6/3	23,545	20					Cooper	Burley	McCall	Zondervan	Cranson	Butcher	Putney	Brennan	D'Avray*	Dozzell	Gates	Sunderland
								Ref: G Courtney (Norwich win 2-1 on aggregate)	Ipswich, playing their third big game in five days, are forced onto the back foot by determined City. Deehan's shot deflects in off Ian Cranson's knee. With extra-time looming, Bruce books a Wembley place and sends Carrow Road into a frenzy with a glorious and powerful late header.											
F	N	SUNDERLAND		11	W	1-0	0-0	Chisholm 46 (og)	Woods	Haylock	Van Wijk	Bruce	Mendham	Watson	Barham	Channon	Deehan	Hartford	Donowa	
		24/3	100,000	18					Turner	Venison	Pickering	Bennett	Chisholm	Corner*	Daniel	Wallace	Hodgson	Berry	Walker	Gayle
		Rec: £860,935						Ref: N Midgley (At Wembley Stadium)	Third time lucky at Wembley as Hartford's powerful shot from an angle cannons past Chris Turner off Gordon Chisholm. City are much the better side and the opposition look tentative - just like City did on previous visits here. It's a great day for the veterans Channon and Hartford.											

FA Cup																				
3	A	BIRMINGHAM		11	D	0-0	0-0		Woods	Haylock	Downs	Bruce	Mendham	Watson	Barham	Channon	Deehan	Farrington	Goss	
		5/1	12,941	2:3					Seaman	Ranson	Roberts	Wright	Hagan	Daly	Platnauer	Clarke	Bremner	Geddis	Hopkins	
								Ref: J Moules	Ex-manager Ron Saunders is keen to put one over his old club, but Norwich shut down all avenues to goal effectively. Barham makes a quiet return after a year out with injury. Jeremy Goss, who joined City on a work experience scheme, gives a workmanlike display on his full debut.											

3R	H	BIRMINGHAM	10	D	1-1	0-0	Haylock 77	Woods	Haylock	Spearing	Bruce	Mendham	Van Wijk	Barham	Channon	Deehan	Hartford	Devine	
	23/1	11,883	*2:3*		*aet*		*Wright 75*	*Seaman*	*Ranson*	*Roberts*	*Wright*	*Armstrong*	*Daly**	*Platnauer*	*Clarke*	*Bremner*	*Geddis*	*Hopkins*	*Fagan*
							Ref: J Moules												

With three hours of goalless football fast approaching, defender Billy Wright hammers in an unstoppable 30-yarder. City quickly respond and from Hartford's through ball, Haylock steers his shot in. In extra-time, David Seaman saves a Deehan penalty after Channon was brought down.

3	A	BIRMINGHAM	10	D	1-1	0-0	Mendham94	Woods	Haylock	Downs	Bruce	Mendham	Van Wijk	Barham	Channon	Farrington*	Hartford	Devine	Donowa
2R	26/1	*11,755*	*2:3*		*aet*		*Geddis 108*	*Seaman*	*Ranson*	*Roberts*	*Wright*	*Armstrong*	*Daly**	*Platnauer*	*Clarke*	*Bremner*	*Geddis*	*Hopkins*	*Fagan*
							Ref: L Shapter												

These two sides just can't be separated. Woods saves a late Billy Wright penalty after Bruce handled a Ray Ranson cross. In extra-time Mendham latches on to Channon's pass and shoots past David Seaman. David Geddis brings it level again. Audible groans greet the whistle.

3	H	BIRMINGHAM	10	W	1-0	1-0	Bruce 10	Woods	Haylock	Downs	Bruce	Mendham	Van Wijk	Barham	Channon	Farrington	Hartford	Devine
3R	28/1	12,396	*2:3*					*Seaman*	*Ranson*	*Roberts*	*Wright*	*Armstrong*	*Daly*	*Platnauer*	*Clarke*	*Bremner*	*Geddis*	*Hopkins*
							Ref: L Shapter											

Here we go again! This is City's 100th home tie in the FA Cup and the third replay represents a new club record. Perhaps inevitably, the four-match marathon is settled by a scrappy goal. Bruce is the scorer, bundling it in with David Geddis getting the final touch as he tries to clear it.

4	A	WEST HAM	11	L	1-2	1-0	Donowa 26	Woods	Haylock	Van Wijk	Bruce	Mendham	Watson	Barham	Channon	Deehan	Hartford	Donowa
	4/2	*20,098*	*15*				*Pike 60, Stewart 62p*	*McAlister*	*Stewart*	*Brush*	*Dickens*	*Martin*	*Walford*	*Allen*	*Barnes*	*Goddard*	*Cottee*	*Pike*
							Ref: R Milford											

City's fifth FA Cup tie in 30 days. Donowa rams a fierce shot past Tom McAlister before half-time. John Lyall's men gain the upper hand after the interval and Geoff Pike cracks home a tremendous volley. Van Wijk clashes with Paul Allen and Ray Stewart settles the tie from the spot.

			Home						Away					
		P	W	D	L	F	A	W	D	L	F	A	Pts
1	Everton	42	16	3	2	58	17	12	3	6	30	26	90
2	Liverpool	42	12	4	5	36	19	10	7	4	32	16	77
3	Tottenham	42	11	3	7	46	31	12	5	4	32	20	77
4	Manchester U	42	13	6	2	47	13	9	4	8	30	34	76
5	Southampton	42	13	4	4	29	18	6	7	8	27	29	68
6	Chelsea	42	13	3	5	38	20	5	9	7	25	28	66
7	Arsenal	42	14	5	2	37	14	5	4	12	24	35	66
8	Sheffield Wed	42	12	7	2	39	21	5	7	9	19	24	65
9	Nott'm For	42	13	4	4	35	18	6	3	12	21	30	64
10	Aston Villa	42	10	7	4	34	20	5	4	12	26	40	56
11	Watford	42	10	5	6	48	30	4	8	9	33	41	55
12	West Brom	42	11	4	6	36	23	5	3	13	22	39	55
13	Luton	42	12	5	4	40	22	3	4	14	17	39	54
14	Newcastle	42	11	4	6	33	26	2	9	10	22	44	52
15	Leicester	42	10	4	7	39	25	5	2	14	26	48	51
16	West Ham	42	7	8	6	27	23	6	4	11	24	45	51
17	Ipswich	42	8	7	6	27	20	5	4	12	19	37	50
18	Coventry	42	11	3	7	29	22	4	2	15	18	42	50
19	QP Rangers	42	11	6	4	41	30	2	5	14	12	42	50
20	NORWICH	42	9	6	6	28	24	4	4	13	18	40	49
21	Sunderland	42	7	6	8	20	26	3	4	14	20	36	40
22	Stoke	42	3	3	15	18	41	0	5	16	6	50	17
		924	237	107	118	785	503	118	107	237	503	785	1279

Odds & ends

Double wins: (2) Sheffield W and West Brom.
Double losses: (6) Manchester U, Tottenham, Nott'm For, Leicester, Ipswich, Sunderland.
Won from behind: (1) Watford (H).
Lost from in front: (3) Luton (a), Leicester (h), West Ham (a)(FAC).

High spots: Winning the Milk Cup at Wembley.
The glorious late winner in the Milk Cup semi-final with Ipswich.
Smashing four past defensive experts Everton in November.
The superb form of new signing Steve Bruce.

Low spots: Plummeting from the top half to relegation in six weeks.
The ban on English clubs – post-Heysel disaster – meaning Norwich won't play in Europe next term.
Three defeats inflicted in a 14-week period by local rivals Ipswich.
The serious fire in the Main Stand at Carrow Road in November.

Player of the Year: Steve Bruce.
Ever-presents: (0).
Hat-tricks: (1) John Deehan (v Watford, h).
Hat-tricks against: (0).
Leading scorer: (18) John Deehan.

	Appearances						Goals			
	Lge	*Sub*	LC	*Sub*	FAC	*Sub*	Lge	LC	FAC	Tot
Barham, Mark	**14**		4		5		**1**			**1**
Benstead, Graham	**1**									
Bertschin, Keith	**5**						**2**			**2**
Bruce, Steve	**39**		9		5		**1**	3	1	**5**
Channon, Mick	**30**	*1*	8		5		**8**	3		**11**
Clayton, Paul	**4**	*1*	1							
Corrigan, Joe	**3**		1							
Deehan, John	**40**		9		3		**13**	5		**18**
Devine, John	**20**	*1*	4		3					
Donowa, Louie	**33**	*1*	8		1	*1*	**7**	3	1	**11**
Downs, Greg	**19**	*1*	4		3					
Fairclough, David	**1**	*1*								
Farrington, Mark	**10**	*2*	1		3		**2**			**2**
Gordon, Dale	**21**	*2*	4				**3**			**3**
Goss, Jeremy	**1**	*4*			1					
Hartford, Asa	**28**		8		4		**2**	3		**5**
Haylock, Paul	**41**		8		5		**1**		1	**2**
Mendham, Peter	**36**		9		5		**4**	1	1	**6**
Rigby, Jon	**4**	*1*								
Rosario, Robert	**4**						**1**			**1**
Rowell, Gary	**2**	*4*					**1**			**1**
Spearing, Tony					1					
Van Wijk, Dennis	**29**	*4*	5	*1*	4					
Watson, Dave	**39**		8		2			1		**1**
Woods, Chris	**38**		8		5					
(own-goals)								1		**1**
25 players used	**462**	***23***	**99**	***1***	**55**	***1***	**46**	**20**	**4**	**70**

CANON DIVISION 2 — Manager: Ken Brown — SEASON 1985-86

No	Date		Att	Pos	Pt	F-A	H-T	Scorers, Times, and Referees	1	2	3	4	5	6	7	8	9	10	11	12 sub used
1	H	OLDHAM			W	1-0	1-0	Mendham 26	Woods	Haylock	Van Wijk	Bruce	**Phelan**	Watson	Mendham	**Drinkell**	Deehan	**Brooke**	**Williams**	
	17/8		12,508		3				*Goram*	*Donachie*	*Barlow*	*McDonough*	*O'Callaghan**	*McGuire*	*Palmer*	*Henry*	*Quinn*	*Futcher*	*Atkinson*	*Fairclough*
								Ref: J Bray	A new-look City side presses forward from the start and, when Watson's header leaves Andy Goram stranded, Mendham nips in to score with a simple header. Ex-Canary Mick McGuire handles, but debutant Brooke hits a post with his penalty. City strike wood on two other occasions.											
2	A	BLACKBURN			L	1-2	1-0	Bruce 30	Woods	Haylock	Van Wijk	Bruce	Phelan	Watson	Mendham	Drinkell	Deehan	Brooke	Williams	
	20/8		*6,567*		3			*Fazackerley 63p, Garner 87*	*Gennoe*	*Hamilton*	*Rathbone*	*Barker*	*Mail*	*Fazackerley*	*Miller*	*Patterson*	*Quinn*	*Garner*	*Brotherston*	
								Ref: M Scott	Bruce heads home a Brooke free-kick to silence the Ewood faithful. When Watson handles, big defender Derek Fazackerley strides forward to convert the penalty. City bow to pressure from Bobby Saxton's men as local favourite Simon Garner grabs a late winner, his 100th league goal.											
3	A	MILLWALL		15	L	**2-4**	1-1	Brooke 22, Deehan 90p *[Hinsh'w'd 76]*	Woods	Haylock	Van Wijk	Bruce	Phelan	Watson	Mendham	Drinkell	Deehan	Brooke	Williams*	Donowa
	24/8		*7,100*	*11*	3			*Kinsella 5, Lovell 47p, Wilson 68,*	*Sansome*	*Hinshelwood*	*Roffey*	*Briley*	*McLeary*	*Nutton*	*Lowndes*	*Wilson*	*Fashanu*	*Lovell*	*Kinsella*	
								Ref: A Robinson	Tony Kinsella fires an early goal, but Brooke's first City goal cancels it out. Brooke collides with Paul Hinshelwood and Steve Lovell converts the penalty. Robert Wilson's header and Hinshelwood's close-range goal kill the contest. Wilson handles Bruce's header for a late City penalty.											
4	H	BARNSLEY		14	D	1-1	0-0	Bruce 90	Woods	Haylock	Van Wijk	Bruce	Phelan	Watson	Barham	Drinkell	Deehan	Mendham	Brooke	
	26/8		13,510	*9*	4			*Owen 55*	*Baker*	*Joyce*	*Goodison*	*Glavin*	*Burns*	*Futcher*	*Owen*	*Thomas*	*Walsh*	*Jeffels*	*Campbell*	
								Ref: E Scales	Ex-Canary keeper Clive Baker has a fine game on his return. The poor start to the season continues as Gordon Owen gives The Tykes the lead. Two loud penalty claims by City are rejected. Bruce saves a point in the third minute of injury-time, powerfully heading in a Barham corner.											
5	A	PORTSMOUTH		14	L	0-2	0-1		Woods	Haylock*	Spearing	Bruce	Phelan	Watson	Barham	Drinkell	Deehan	Mendham	Williams	Donowa
	31/8		*15,504*	*1*	4			*Morgan 24, 82*	*Knight*	*Swain*	*Hardyman*	*Dillon*	*Blake*	*Ball*	*O'Callaghan*	*Kennedy*	*Morgan*	*Channon**	*Hilaire*	*Wood*
								Ref: D Reeves	Inevitably, the old warhorse and ex-Norwich favourite Mick Channon plays a key role. He sets up Nicky Morgan, who lashes home a rising right-foot drive. City lack punch and Morgan wraps things up for the leaders by scoring from close in when Woods fails to cling on to a corner.											
6	H	SHEFFIELD UTD		12	W	4-0	1-0	Bruce 41, Drinkell 61, 78, Haylock 89	Woods	Haylock	Spearing	Bruce	Phelan	Watson	Barham	Drinkell	Deehan	Mendham	Williams	
	7/9		12,899	*10*	7				*Burridge*	*Eckhardt*	*Kenworthy*	*Thompson*	*Stancliffe*	*McNaught*	*Morris*	*Cockerill*	*Withe*	*Foley**	*Bolton*	*Edwards*
								Ref: R Lewis	Keeper John Burridge has an unhappy afternoon, despite his nickname 'Budgie' suggesting he'd be at home against the Canaries. Bruce and Drinkell both take advantage of rebounds off the little keeper. Haylock nets a rare goal, when he cuts inside and seals the win with a great shot.											
7	A	MIDDLESBROUGH		13	D	1-1	0-1	Drinkell 60	Woods	Haylock	Spearing	Bruce	Phelan	Watson	Barham	Drinkell	Rosario*	Mendham	Williams	Van Wijk
	14/9		*5,475*	*18*	8			*Rowell 1p*	*Pears*	*Laws*	*Heard*	*McAndrew*	*Mowbray*	*Nattrass*	*Gill**	*O'Riordan*	*Stephens*	*Rowell*	*Beagrie*	*Cook*
								Ref: J McAuley	Former colleagues repeatedly come back to haunt the Canaries, and Gary Rowell is no exception. He is hauled down by Bruce in the match's first attack and gets up to convert from the spot. Drinkell grabs a richly deserved equaliser when he jinks into the box and crashes in a beauty.											
8	H	CRYSTAL PALACE		10	W	4-3	2-2	Watson 24, Drinkell 44, Phelan 55,	Woods	Haylock	Spearing	Bruce	Phelan	Watson	Barham	Drinkell	Rosario	Mendham	Williams	
	18/9		13,475	*15*	11			*Gray 21, 26p, Droy 90* [Barham 78]	*Wood*	*Locke*	*Sparrow*	*Finnigan*	*Droy*	*Cannon*	*Irvine*	*Ketteridge*	*Barber*	*Gray*	*Higginbot'm**	*Wright*
								Ref: J Ball	Andy Gray shocks Norwich with a well-taken goal, but Watson swoops to equalise at the near post. Spearing's handball gives Palace a penalty. Phelan's effort is the pick of the goals as City go ahead for the first time in this thriller. Ian Wright is making the third appearance of his career.											
9	A	HUDDERSFIELD		10	D	0-0	0-0		Woods	Haylock	Spearing	Bruce	Phelan	Watson	Barham	Drinkell	Rosario	Mendham	Williams	
	21/9		*7,225*	*7*	12				*Cox*	*Jones J*	*Bray*	*Doyle*	*Webster*	*Jones P*	*Curran*	*Cork*	*Tempest*	*Wilson Phil*	*Cowling**	*Raynor*
								Ref: J Worrall	Two top-ten sides meet at Leeds Road, but it's generally a dull affair. Phelan goes close for Norwich with a free-kick. Mick Buxton's outfit nearly grab the winner ten minutes from the end when Dale Tempest produces an overhead kick that strikes the bar with Woods well beaten.											
10	H	HULL		8	W	2-0	1-0	Rosario 9, Mendham 61	Woods	Haylock	Spearing	Bruce	Phelan	Watson	Barham	Drinkell	Rosario	Mendham	Williams	
	28/9		12,639	*14*	15				*Norman*	*Jobson*	*Pearson*	*Doyle*	*Skipper !*	*McEwan*	*Swann**	*Bunn*	*Whitehead*	*Horton*	*Roberts*	*Brentano*
								Ref: M Cotton	Rosario, deputising for Deehan, nets a well-taken effort. Watson strikes a post, but Mendham produces a cool finish to score the all-important second. Twelve minutes from the end Peter Skipper is sent off for dissent. Talks with Reading striker Trevor Senior appear to have collapsed.											

11	H	WIMBLEDON	9	L	1-2	1-2	Drinkell 5	Woods	Haylock	Spearing*	Bruce	Phelan	Watson	Barham	Drinkell	Rosario	Mendham	Van Wijk	Brooke
5/10		12,707	6	15			Martin 16p, Cork 19	Beasant	Gage	Winterburn*	Galliers	Gayle	Martin	Evans	Cork	Holloway	Sanchez	Hodges	Thorn
							Ref: H Taylor	Drinkell heads City into an early lead, but Dave Bassett's muscular side bounce back and Alan Cork's effort is handled by Bruce. Dave Martin despatches the penalty, before Cork puts the Dons ahead. Brian Gayle's push gives City a penalty, but Bruce's effort is saved by Dave Beasant.											
12	A	CARLISLE	7	W	4-0	1-0	Rosario 20, Phelan 54, Drinkell 88, [Brooke 90]	Woods	Culverh'se	Van Wijk	Bruce	Phelan	Watson	Barham	Drinkell	Rosario	Mendham	Brooke	
12/10		2,907	22	18				Carr	Haigh	McCartney	Ashurst	Saunders	Halsall	Halpin	Gorman*	Wakenshaw	Cooke	Gavin	Entwistle
							Ref: G Courtney	Culverhouse arrives from Spurs and is nearly joined in the side by rookie Harvey Lim, but Woods recovers. Rosario drives in Brooke's pull-back and sets up Phelan. Drinkell glances a third and Brooke nets a fine Phelan pass. Bryan 'Pop' Robson quits as Carlisle boss after the game.											
13	H	SHREWSBURY	6	W	3-1	2-1	Mendham 28, Drinkell 35, Barham 83	Woods	Culverhouse	Van Wijk	Bruce	Phelan	Watson	Barham	Drinkell	Rosario*	Mendham	Brooke	Williams
19/10		11,732	21	21			Van Wijk 27 (og)	Perks	Kerr	Hughes	Cross	Pearson !	Stevens	McNally	Hackett	Nardiello	Robinson	Daly	
							Ref: N Butler	Van Wijk pokes an unlucky own goal past Woods, but Mendham's rocket is the immediate response. The in-form Drinkell forces City ahead. Nigel Pearson is sent off for chopping Barham down when he was looking certain to score. Five minutes later Barham does net a simple goal.											
14	A	SUNDERLAND	5	W	2-0	0-0	Williams 61, Mendham 87	Woods	Culverhouse	Van Wijk	Bruce	Phelan	Watson	Barham	Drinkell	Biggins	Mendham	Williams	
26/10		17,908	17	24				Bolder	Burley	Kennedy	Pickering*	Bennett	Elliott	Gray	Venison	Swindlehurst	Gates	Gayle	Atkinson
							Ref: R Banks	Ex-King's Lynn striker Wayne Biggins signs from Burnley and replaces Rosario. David Williams fires his first Norwich goal. Woods makes a tremendous flying save from a header by ex-Ipswich favourite Eric Gates. Roker is silenced when Biggins' cross is headed home by Mendham.											
15	A	BRIGHTON	6	D	1-1	0-0	Biggins 63	Woods	Culverhouse	Van Wijk	Bruce	Phelan	Watson	Barham	Rosario	Biggins	Mendham	Williams	
2/11		10,423	8	25			Saunders 54	Moseley	Oliver	Pearce	Wilson	Young	O'Reilly	Saunders	Hutchings	Fashanu	Biley*	Mortimer	Keown
							Ref: D Axcell	Chris Cattlin's team lead after Dean Saunders swivels to shoot in off a post. Minutes later 'Bertie' Biggins celebrates his first Norwich goal, converting Rosario's lay-off after a run by Phelan. After five victories from six games in October, Ken Brown is named Manager of the Month.											
16	H	BRADFORD C	6	D	0-0	0-0		Woods	Culverhouse	Van Wijk	Bruce	Phelan	Watson	Barham	Drinkell	Biggins	Mendham	Williams*	Brooke
9/11		13,939	15	26				Litchfield	Clegg	Withe	McCall	Jackson	Evans	Hendrie	Abbott	Campbell	Singleton	Graham	
							Ref: K Miller	Trevor Cherry's Bantams bring a noisy army of fans to Carrow Road. Newly promoted, they are enjoying their club's first season at this level after a period of 48 years in the lower divisions. Norwich are generally off-colour, although they force Peter Litchfield into a number of saves.											
17	A	STOKE	5	D	1-1	0-0	Drinkell 70	Woods	Culverhouse	Van Wijk	Bruce	Phelan	Watson	Barham	Drinkell	Biggins	Mendham	Williams*	Gordon
16/11		6,469	18	27			Bertschin 53p	Fox	Bould	Mills	Williams	Dyson	Berry	Adams	Maskery	Bertschin	Shaw	Heath	
							Ref: G Ashby	Adrian Heath is brought down for a penalty, rammed home by ex-Canary Keith Bertschin, but Norwich are convinced the offence was outside the box. Gordon galvanises City's attack and Drinkell's header skids off the wet pitch past Peter Fox. George Berry skims the bar with a header.											
18	H	GRIMSBY	5	W	3-2	1-0	Watson 43, Biggins 51, Lyons 54 (og)	Woods	Culverhouse	Van Wijk	Bruce	Phelan	Watson	Barham	Drinkell	Biggins	Mendham	Williams	
23/11		12,108	14	30			Culverhouse 69 (og), Emson 84	Batch	Barratt	Agnew	Peake	Lyons	Moore K	Ford	Gilligan*	Hobson	Bonnyman	Emson	Moore A
							Ref: C Downey	Three goals in 11 minutes for City. Watson's power header is followed by Biggins stealing in at the near post, and player-manager Mike Lyons slicing into his own net. Culverhouse follows suit with an over-hit lobbed back-pass. Paul Emson side-steps Woods to set up a nervous finale.											
19	A	LEEDS	4	W	2-0	1-0	Drinkell 38, Bruce 57	Woods	Culverhouse	Van Wijk	Bruce	Phelan	Watson	Barham*	Drinkell	Biggins	Mendham	Williams	Brooke
30/11		11,480	15	33				Swinburne	Caswell	Robinson*	Snodin	McGregor	Linighan	Ritchie	Sheridan	McCluskey	Hamson	Dickinson	Simmonds
							Ref: C Thrussell	The club is in crisis as the entire board of directors resigns in a row over construction of the new Main Stand. New Leeds boss Billy Bremner is unhappy as Drinkell nets a fine header at the far post and Bruce adds a finishing touch to a Williams corner. Drinkell goes close to a third goal.											
20	H	BLACKBURN	3	W	3-0	2-0	Bruce 22, Van Wijk 29, Barham 54	Woods	Culverhouse	Van Wijk	Bruce	Phelan	Watson	Barham	Drinkell	Biggins*	Mendham	Williams	Gordon
7/12		12,820	10	36				Gennoe	Branagan	Rathbone	Barker	Keeley*	Mail	Miller	Lowey	Quinn	Thompson	Hamilton	Brotherston
							Ref: M Dimblebee	Bruce rushes forward to crack a rasping drive past Terry Gennoe. Van Wijk plays a neat wall pass with Phelan and fires in the second. Gennoe dashes out of goal, only for the ball to fall to Mendham who crosses for Barham to head a third. Big Glenn Keeley is carried off with an injury.											
21	A	OLDHAM	1	W	3-1	0-0	Drinkell 51, Barlow 69(og), Barham 84	Woods	Culverhouse	Van Wijk	Bruce	Phelan	Watson	Barham	Drinkell	Biggins*	Mendham	Williams	Deehan
14/12		3,949	12	39			Phelan 75(og)	Goram	Donachie*	Barlow	McDonough	Hoolickin	McGuire	Palmer	Henry	Quinn	Futcher	Atkinson	Bullock
							Ref: R Nixon	A meagre crowd sees Drinkell net an acrobatic header. Andy Barlow misjudges a cross and rockets a header past Andy Goram. Joe Royle's men benefit as Phelan steers into his own net. Barham ensures City go top with a superb solo goal, slipping the ball home after a lengthy run.											

No	Date			Att	Pos	Pt		F-A	H-T	Scorers, Times, and Referees	1	2	3	4	5	6	7	8	9	10	11	12 sub used
22		H	MILLWALL		1		W	**6-1**	4-0	Mend'm 4, Williams 9, 33, Barh'm 20,	Woods	Culverhouse	Van Wijk	Bruce	Phelan	Watson*	Barham	Drinkell	Biggins	Mendham	Williams	Deehan
	21/12			12,349	*19*	42				*Sher'gham 83* [Drinkell 58, Phelan 77]	*Granville*	*Stevens*	*Hinshelwood*	*Briley*	*Walker*	*Lowndes*	*McLeary*	*Chatterton**	*Sheringham*	*Lovell*	*Otulakowski*	*Leslie*
										Ref: V Callow	A standing ovation after a magnificent first half. Four great goals in the first 33 minutes, including another Barham solo effort, and blistering shots by Drinkell and Williams. Drinkell's header and Phelan's powerful drive make it six. Teddy Sheringham nets a consolation dipping shot.											
23		H	CHARLTON		1		W	3-1	0-0	Drinkell 67, 84, Deehan 88	Woods	Culverhouse	Van Wijk	Bruce	Phelan	Watson	Barham	Drinkell	Biggins	Mendham	Williams*	Deehan
	26/12			17,984	*3*	45				*Flanagan 64*	*Johns*	*Humphrey*	*Reid*	*Curbishley*	*Thompson*	*Pender*	*Gritt*	*Stuart*	*Pearson*	*Aizlewood*	*Flanagan*	
										Ref: J Ball	Biggins hits the crossbar, but after an hour's stalemate Mick Flanagan drives in a Steve Gritt cross. City respond in style. Drinkell nets after a hectic scramble, and gains the lead with a downward header at the far post. Sub Deehan curls a right-foot shot into the roof of Nicky Johns' net.											
24		A	FULHAM		1		W	1-0	0-0	Drinkell 90	Woods	Culverhouse	Van Wijk	Bruce	Phelan	Watson	Barham	Drinkell	Biggins*	Mendham	Williams	Deehan
	1/1			*7,463*	*21*	48					*Peyton*	*Cottington*	*Elkins**	*Scott*	*Hopkins*	*Parker*	*Marshall*	*Achampong*	*Fishenden*	*Carr*	*Donnellan*	*Barnett*
										Ref: M James	Ray Harford's side has slipped into the relegation zone, but they give leaders Norwich a tough time. Woods saves well from Brian Cottington and beats out a shot by debutant Paul Fishenden, on loan from Wimbledon. Van Wijk's free-kick finds Drinkell, who nets a last-minute winner.											
25		H	MIDDLESBROUGH		1		W	2-0	1-0	Williams 44p, Bruce 84	Woods	Culverhouse	Van Wijk	Bruce	Phelan	Watson	Barham	Drinkell	Biggins	Mendham	Williams	
	11/1			13,730	*20*	51					*Pears*	*Laws*	*O'Riordan*	*McAndrew*	*Mowbray*	*Pallister*	*Hamilton*	*Heard*	*Stephens*	*Rowell*	*Slaven*	
										Ref: I Hemley	Tony Mowbray pushes Biggins in the back and Williams slots in the penalty. Bruce makes sure of the points by planting a firm header past Stephen Pears. The cross comes from man-of-the-match Williams. City stay top, but appear to be feeling the pressure in this stuttering display.											
26		H	PORTSMOUTH		1		W	2-0	0-0	Barham 77, Drinkell 86	Woods	Culverhouse	Van Wijk	Bruce	Phelan	Watson	Barham	Drinkell	Biggins	Mendham	Williams	
	18/1			**20,129**	*2*	54					*Gosney*	*Swain*	*Sandford*	*Dillon*	*Blake*	*Tait*	*O'Callaghan*	*Kennedy*	*Channon*	*Wood*	*Hilaire*	
										Ref: N Butler	The top two meet with City seeking a club record ninth successive win. It's a pulsating affair that is decided late on when Barham volleys home Van Wijk's deep cross. Phelan has an effort blocked by Andy Gosney, but Drinkell pounces at close range. Pompey boss Alan Ball looks livid.											
27		A	CRYSTAL PALACE		1		W	2-1	2-0	Mendham 13, Biggins 38	Woods	Culverhouse	Deehan	Bruce	Phelan	Watson	Barham	Drinkell	Biggins	Mendham	Williams	
	25/1			*8,369*	*8*	57				*Barber 46*	*Wood*	*Howard*	*Hughton*	*Taylor*	*Nebbeling*	*Cannon*	*Finnigan*	*Wright*	*Barber*	*Gray*	*Sparrow*	
										Ref: R Milford	City arrive at Selhurst late due to heavy traffic. In the warm-up, Van Wijk pulls a hamstring and Deehan steps in. Mendham ends a smart move with a hefty volley. The lead is doubled by Biggins from a Williams corner. Another club record falls as this is the tenth away game unbeaten.											
28		A	BARNSLEY		1		D	2-2	2-1	Deehan 39, Mendham 43	Woods	Culverhouse	Deehan	Bruce	Phelan	Watson	Barham	Drinkell	Biggins	Mendham	Williams	
	1/2			*5,608*	*10*	58				*Hirst 26, Thomas 86*	*Baker*	*Burns*	*Gray*	*Thomas*	*May*	*Futcher*	*Owen*	*Jonsson*	*Walsh*	*Hirst*	*Cross*	
										Ref: I Hendrick	David Hirst buries a 15-yarder, but Deehan levels with a fine header. Mendham's well-timed run brings him a close-range goal. The run of straight wins ends in dramatic style as Gwyn Thomas' shot hits the underside of the bar, then a post, and a linesman decides it crossed the line.											
29		A	SHREWSBURY		1		W	3-0	2-0	Drinkell 3, 64, Barham 20	Woods	Culverhouse	Deehan	Bruce	Phelan	Watson	Barham	Drinkell	Biggins	Mendham	Williams	
	8/2			*5,157*	*14*	61					*Perks*	*Williams*	*Hughes*	*Cross*	*Pearson*	*Stevens*	*McNally*	*Hackett*	*Nardiello**	*Robinson*	*Daly*	*Leonard*
										Ref: J Worrall	Barham's cross is headed in by Drinkell. Barham scores after Williams puts him in the clear. Drinkell drills in a third goal after a corner. Now it's 18 matches without defeat and full-back Culverhouse still hasn't tasted defeat in the league since arriving from Tottenham five months ago.											
30		A	WIMBLEDON		1		L	1-2	1-0	Barham 22	Woods	Culverhouse	Deehan	Bruce	Phelan	Watson	Barham	Drinkell	Biggins	Mendham	Williams	
	8/3			*5,827*	*4*	61				*Evans 61, Cork 64*	*Beasant*	*Gage*	*Winterburn*	*Galliers*	*Morris*	*Smith*	*Evans*	*Cork*	*Fishenden*	*Sanchez*	*Fairweather*	
										Ref: G Ashby	City look distinctly uneasy about their Plough Lane surroundings and the notoriously tricky opposition. Barham's opening goal eases those worries, but the inevitable aerial bombardment yields an equaliser through Stewart Evans. The Dons inflict the first league loss since October.											
31		H	HUDDERSFIELD		1		W	4-1	1-1	Drinkell 4, Biggins 60, 85, Bruce 72	Woods	Culverhouse	Deehan	Bruce	Phelan	Watson	Barham	Drinkell	Biggins	Mendham	Williams	
	12/3			12,772	*18*	64				*Curran 38*	*Mason*	*Brown*	*Bray*	*Doyle*	*Webster*	*Jones J*	*Curran*	*Cork*	*Raynor*	*Winter*	*Cowling*	
										Ref: D Hedges	Stand-in keeper Keith Mason blunders, allowing Drinkell's early effort through his legs. Well-travelled Terry Curran levels, but Joey Jones slips to allow Biggins to end his goal drought. Bruce's close-range header means City are cruising and Biggins' tap-in is the icing on the cake.											

No	Ven	Opponent / Date	Att	Pos	Res / Pts	FT	HT	Scorers, Times, Referees	1	2	3	4	5	6	7	8	9	10	11	12
32	H	CARLISLE		1	W	2-1	1-0	Williams 32p, 55	Woods	Culverhouse	Deehan	Bruce	Phelan	Watson	Barham	Drinkell	Biggins	Mendham	Williams	
		15/3	13,852	*22*	67			*McGarvey 66*	*Endersby*	*Lomax**	*McCartney*	*Baker*	*Saunders*	*Halsall*	*Hill*	*Cooke*	*McGarvey*	*Bishop*	*Halpin*	*Haigh*
								Ref: H Taylor	A shot from Bruce strikes the hand of Wes Saunders and Williams converts the penalty. Drinkell unselfishly sets up Williams after collecting a Barham cross. Scott McGarvey, on loan from Portsmouth, flicks in a consolation goal for veteran manager Bob Stokoe's relegation-bound side.											
33	A	SHEFFIELD UTD		1	W	5-2	2-1	Smith 6(og), Drinkell 41, Mendh'm 65,	Woods	Culverhouse	Deehan	Bruce	Phelan	Watson	Barham	Drinkell	Biggins	Mendham	Williams	
		22/3	*11,894*	*7*	70			*Edwards 34, 80* [Barh'm 89, Big'ns 90]	*Burridge*	*Smith P*	*Bolton*	*Lewington*	*Stancliffe*	*McNaught*	*Morris*	*Edwards*	*Withe**	*Eves*	*Foley*	*Arnott*
								Ref: K Redfern	Deehan's teasing cross is headed into his own net by Paul Smith. Keith Edwards levels from close range, but Drinkell regains the lead with a header. Mendham lashes a third before Edwards gets clear to bag his second. Barham's calm finish and Biggins' looping shot climax a fine win.											
34	H	FULHAM		1	W	2-1	2-1	Barham 22, Deehan 40	Woods	Culverhouse	Deehan	Bruce	Phelan	Watson	Barham	Drinkell	Biggins	Mendham	Williams	
		29/3	17,320	*22*	73			*Coney 30*	*Peyton*	*Cottington*	*Carr*	*Scott*	*Marshall*	*Parker**	*Donnellan*	*Achampong*	*Coney*	*Dreyer*	*Barnett*	*Pike*
								Ref: T Holbrook	Barham's well-struck goal livens up the big crowd. Ray Harford's struggling side play some good football and fully deserve their equaliser by Dean Coney after Peter Scott beats City's offside trap. A spot of head-tennis ends with Deehan ramming Norwich's second past Gerry Peyton.											
35	A	CHARLTON		1	L	0-1	0-0		Woods	Culverh'se*	Deehan	Bruce	Phelan	Watson	Barham	Drinkell	Biggins	Mendham	Williams	Van Wijk
		31/3	*8,458*	*3*	73			*Pearson 49*	*Lange*	*Humphrey*	*Reid*	*Curbishley*	*Thompson*	*Pender*	*Shipley*	*Melrose*	*Pearson*	*Aizlewood*	*Flanagan**	*Stuart*
								Ref: D Axcell	Lennie Lawrence's men are the better side in the first period at Selhurst Park, and take the lead just after the break. Mark Reid's fierce cross rebounds into the net off the head of John Pearson. Norwich exert plenty of pressure, but Charlton hang on and move back into the top three.											
36	H	BRIGHTON		1	W	3-0	0-0	Connor 50(og), Drink'l 71, Williams 81p	Woods	Culverhouse	Van Wijk	Bruce	Phelan	Watson	Barham*	Drinkell	Biggins	Deehan	Williams	Gordon
		5/4	15,155	*8*	76				*Digweed*	*Htuchings*	*Pearce*	*Jacobs*	*Young*	*Gatting*	*Saunders*	*Penney*	*Biley**	*Connor*	*Mortimer*	*O'Regan*
								Ref: K Baker	The deadlock is broken by a spectacular own goal as Terry Connor dives to head a cross past Perry Digweed under no pressure at all. Drinkell converts Gordon's cross, then Williams nets from the spot after Graham Pearce fells Biggins. Six games left and promotion is nearly clinched.											
37	H	SUNDERLAND		1	D	0-0	0-0		Woods	Culverhouse	Van Wijk	Bruce	Phelan	Watson	Barham	Drinkell	Biggins	Deehan	Gordon	
		9/4	17,752	*19*	77				*Dibble*	*Venison*	*Kennedy*	*Gray*	*Hetzke*	*Elliott**	*Ford*	*Gayle*	*Wallace*	*Gates*	*Proctor*	*White*
								Ref: B Hill	A big crowd turns up to sing City towards Division One, but the game is an anti-climax. There's precious little entertainment as Norwich leave their shooting boots at home. The nearest to a goal is early on when Drinkell and Deehan both have attempts blocked with Andy Dibble beaten.											
38	A	BRADFORD C		1	W	2-0	1-0	Drinkell, Biggins	Woods	Culverhouse	Van Wijk	Bruce	Phelan	Watson	Barham	Drinkell	Biggins	Deehan	Williams	
		12/4	*7,190*	*15*	80				*Litchfield*	*Oliver*	*Evans*	*McCall*	*Jackson*	*Clegg*	*Hendrie*	*Goodman*	*Campbell*	*Abbott*	*Graham**	*Thorpe*
								Ref: T Fitzharris	A win will clinch promotion at the Odsal Stadium, but there are less than 1,000 City fans present - maybe a reflection on Wednesday's goalless flop? Drinkell nets an early breakthrough at the far post after a long throw by Bruce. Biggins clinches the points with a fierce shot on the run.											
39	H	STOKE		1	D	1-1	0-0	Gordon 75	Woods	Culverhouse	Van Wijk	Bruce	Phelan	Watson	Gordon	Drinkell	Biggins*	Deehan	Williams	Brooke
		19/4	17,757	*13*	81			*Bertschin 65*	*Fox*	*Mills**	*Hemming*	*Bonnyman*	*Bould*	*Berry*	*Adams*	*Saunders*	*Bertschin*	*Painter*	*Heath*	*Shaw*
								Ref: M Scott	City swarm all over Stoke but struggle in front of goal. Ex-Norwich favourite Keith Bertschin heads in against the run of play. Stoke player-boss Mick Mills comes off, and City save a point via Gordon. Results elsewhere confirm that the title is definitely bound for Carrow Road.											
40	A	GRIMSBY		1	L	0-1	0-0		Woods	Culverhouse	Van Wijk	Bruce	Phelan	Watson	Gordon*	Drinkell	Biggins	Deehan	Williams	Brooke
		26/4	*8,090*	*15*	81			*Hobson 54*	*Batch*	*Bonnyman*	*Crombie*	*Peake*	*Lyons*	*Moore K*	*Henshaw*	*Matthews**	*Hobson*	*Robinson*	*Cummings*	*Lund*
								Ref: N Midgley	Around 3,000 City fans make the trip to Blundell Park and there are nine arrests after fighting breaks out. Ken Brown appeals at half-time for calm. After the interval Gordon Hobson fastens on to long-serving Bob Cumming's excellent through pass and blasts a great drive past Woods.											
41	A	HULL		1	L	0-1	0-0		Woods	Haylock	Van Wijk	Bruce	Phelan	Watson	Brooke	Drinkell	Biggins*	Deehan	Williams	Spearing
		29/4	*6,146*	*7*	81			*Williams 80*	*Norman*	*Jobson*	*Swann*	*Doyle*	*Skipper*	*McEwan*	*Williams*	*Bunn*	*Flounders**	*Heard*	*Pearson*	*Saville*
								Ref: D Allison	Everyone wants to beat the champions, and Brian Horton's side try to emulate Grimsby. City look in control for much of the match, if a little subdued. Brooke's dipping shot is acrobatically cleared off the line by Pat Heard. Near the end Neil Williams 25-yard volley goes in off a post.											
42	H	LEEDS		1	W	4-0	1-0	Ormsby 33(og), Drinkell 59, Bruce 66,	Woods	Culverhouse	Van Wijk	Bruce	Phelan	Watson	Brooke	Drinkell	Deehan	Mendham	Williams	
		3/5	17,942	*14*	84			[Williams 79]	*Day*	*Aspin*	*Hamson*	*Robinson*	*Ormsby*	*Rennie*	*Ritchie*	*Sellars*	*Baird*	*Swan*	*Stiles*	
		Home	Away					Ref: K Millar	After two losses, the season ends on a high. The trophy is handed over amid a carnival atmosphere. Brendan Ormsby nets a comical own goal with a fierce header. Drinkell's fine header and Bruce's well-taken shot raise noise levels. The trophy is to be paraded in Norwich the next day.											
Average		14,528	8,059																	

CANON DIVISION 2 (CUP-TIES) Manager: Ken Brown SEASON 1985-86

Milk Cup	Att		F-A	H-T	Scorers, Times, and Referees	1	2	3	4	5	6	7	8	9	10	11	12 sub used
2:1 A PRESTON	8	D	1-1	1-1	Bruce 45	Woods	Haylock	Spearing	Bruce	Phelan	Van Wijk	Barham	Drinkell	Rosario	Mendham	Williams	
30/9	*4,330 4:19*				*Brazil 20p*	*Platt*	*Twentyman*	*Jones*	*Atkins*	*Gibson*	*Welsh*	*Keen*	*Greenwood*	*Thomas*	*Gray*	*Brazil*	
					Ref: G Tyson	Thrashed 0-6 by Northampton recently and with major injury worries, Tommy Booth is having a tough managerial baptism at Deepdale. His side raise their game tonight, however, and it takes a 30-yard free-kick by Bruce to cancel out Gary Brazil's goal. City have to fight all the way.											
2:2 H PRESTON	9	W	2-1	0-1	Brooke 64, Rosario 87	Woods	Culverhouse	Van Wijk	Bruce	Phelan	Watson	Barham	Drinkell	Rosario	Mendham	Brooke	
9/10	11,537 *4:20*				*Brazil 5*	*Platt*	*Twentyman*	*Jones*	*Atkins*	*Gibson*	*Welsh*	*Keen*	*Foster*	*Thomas*	*Gray**	*Brazil*	*Greenwood*
					Ref: G Napthine (Norwich win 3-2 on aggregate)	Culverhouse hesitates and Gary Brazil nips in to volley home Nigel Keen's cross. It's miserable viewing for the home fans until Brooke curls a rebound superbly into the roof of John Platt's net after his first effort is blocked. Rosario glances in very late winner from a Van Wijk centre.											
3 A LUTON	5	W	2-0	2-0	Mendham 28, Bruce 34	Woods	Culverhouse	Van Wijk	Bruce	Phelan	Watson	Barham	Drinkell	Rosario	Mendham	Williams	
29/10	*8,202 1:13*					*Sealey*	*Breacker*	*Johnson**	*Parker*	*Foster*	*Donaghy*	*Hill*	*Stein B*	*Harford*	*Nwajiobi*	*Daniel*	*Grimes*
					Ref: B Hill	David Pleat's men hit seven goals past Peter Shilton in their last home match, but City rise to the occasion and inflict Luton's first defeat on the new artificial surface. Mendham nips in for a close-range goal, then Bruce doubles the lead with a fierce free-kick. The Hatters look off-colour.											
4 A OXFORD	5	L	1-3	1-1	Drinkell 15	Woods	Culverhouse	Van Wijk	Bruce	Phelan	Watson	Barham	Drinkell	Rosario	Mendham	Williams*	Brooke
20/11	*7,851 1:19*				*Aldridge 20, Thomas 51, Phillips 63*	*Hardwick*	*Langan**	*Slatter*	*Trewick*	*Hebberd*	*Shotton*	*Brock*	*Aldridge*	*Thomas*	*Phillips*	*Rh-Brown*	*Jones*
					Ref: A Robinson	Norwich dominate early on and Drinkell puts them ahead. Maurice Evans' team hit back through a John Aldridge header and press forward in search of more. Bruce slips up to allow Andy Thomas to chip home and then Les Phillips sweeps a third. Brown blasts his players afterwards.											

FA Cup																	
3 A LIVERPOOL	1	L	0-5	0-2	*[Whelan 78, Wark 81]*	Woods	Culverhouse	Van Wijk	Bruce	Phelan	Watson	Barham	Drinkell	Biggins	Mendham	Williams*	Deehan
4/1	*29,082 1:3*				*Macdon'd 23, Walsh 37, McMahon 73,*	*Grobbelaar*	*Nicol*	*Macdonald*	*Lawrenson*	*Whelan*	*Hansen*	*Walsh**	*Johnston*	*Rush*	*Molby*	*McMahon*	*Wark*
					Ref: D Hutchinson	In atrocious blizzard conditions, the Canaries look ill at ease on a slippery surface. Macdonald shoots the Reds ahead and Walsh, playing in place of player-manager Kenny Dalglish, heads a second. A late three-goal burst in a spell of just eight minutes finishes Norwich's cup hopes.											

		P	W	D	L	F	A	W	D	L	F	A	Pts
			Home					Away					
1	NORWICH	42	16	4	1	51	15	9	5	7	33	22	84
2	Charlton	42	14	5	2	44	15	8	6	7	34	30	77
3	Wimbledon	42	13	6	2	38	16	8	7	6	20	21	76
4	Portsmouth	42	13	4	4	43	17	9	3	9	26	24	73
5	Crys Palace	42	12	3	6	29	22	7	6	8	28	30	66
6	Hull	42	11	7	3	39	19	6	6	9	26	36	64
7	Sheffield Utd	42	10	7	4	36	24	7	4	10	28	39	62
8	Oldham	42	13	4	4	40	28	4	5	12	22	33	60
9	Millwall	42	12	3	6	39	24	5	5	11	25	41	59
10	Stoke	42	8	11	2	29	16	6	4	11	19	34	57
11	Brighton	42	10	5	6	42	30	6	3	12	22	34	56
12	Barnsley	42	9	6	6	29	26	5	8	8	18	24	56
13	Bradford C	42	14	1	6	36	24	2	5	14	15	39	54
14	Leeds	42	9	7	5	30	22	6	1	14	26	50	53
15	Grimsby	42	11	4	6	35	24	3	6	12	23	38	52
16	Huddersfield	42	10	6	5	30	23	4	4	13	21	44	52
17	Shrewsbury	42	11	5	5	29	20	3	4	14	23	44	51
18	Sunderland	42	10	5	6	33	29	3	6	12	14	32	50
19	Blackburn	42	10	4	7	30	20	2	9	10	23	42	49
20	Carlisle	42	10	2	9	30	28	3	5	13	17	43	46
21	Middlesbro	42	8	6	7	26	23	4	3	14	18	30	45
22	Fulham	42	8	3	10	29	32	2	3	16	16	37	36
		924	242	108	112	767	497	112	108	242	497	767	1278

Odds & ends

Double wins: (7) Carlisle, Leeds, Oldham, Fulham, Crystal Palace, Shrewsbury and Sheffield Utd.
Double losses: (1) Wimbledon.

Won from behind: (4) C Palace (h), Shrewsbury (h), Charlton (h), Preston (h) (LC).
Lost from in front: (5) Blackburn (a), Wimbledon (h&a), Oxford (a) (LC).

High spots: Bouncing back from relegation in style, to win the title.
Setting a new club record of ten successive league victories.
A run of 18 unbeaten league games between October and February.
Reaching the semi-finals of the Screen Sports Super Cup.
The first-half display against Millwall on 21 December.
The excellent form of new signings Drinkell, Williams and Phelan.

Low spots: Two defeats by Wimbledon after taking the lead.
Major squabbles at Boardroom level in November.

Player of the Year: Kevin Drinkell.
Ever-presents: (4) Watson (Leagee only), Bruce, Phelan, Woods.
Hat-tricks: (0).
Hat-tricks against: (0).
Leading scorer: (23) Kevin Drinkell.

	Appearances						Goals			
	Lge	*Sub*	LC	*Sub*	FAC	*Sub*	**Lge**	LC	FAC	**Tot**
Barham, Mark	**35**		4		1		**9**			**9**
Biggins, Wayne	**28**				1		**7**			**7**
Brooke, Garry	**8**	*5*	1	*1*			**2**	1		**3**
Bruce, Steve	**42**		4		1		**8**	2		**10**
Clayton, Paul	**1**									
Culverhouse, Ian	**30**		3		1					
Deehan, John	**22**	*4*				*1*	**4**			**4**
Donowa, Louie		*2*								
Drinkell, Kevin	**41**		4		1		**22**	1		**23**
Gordon, Dale	**3**	*3*					**1**			**1**
Haylock, Paul	**12**		1				**1**			**1**
Mendham, Peter	**35**		4		1		**8**	1		**9**
Phelan, Mike	**42**		4		1		**3**			**3**
Rosario, Robert	**8**		4				**2**	1		**3**
Spearing, Tony	**7**	*1*	1							
Van Wijk, Dennis	**27**	*2*	4		1		**1**			**1**
Watson, Dave	**42**		3		1		**3**			**3**
Williams, David	**37**	*2*	3		1		**8**			**8**
Woods, Chris	**42**		4		1					
(own-goals)							**5**			**5**
19 players used	**462**	***19***	**44**	***1***	**11**	***1***	**84**	**6**		**90**

No	Date		Att	Pos	Pt	F-A	H-T	Scorers, Times, and Referees	1	2	3	4	5	6	7	8	9	10	11	12 sub used
1	A	CHELSEA			D	0-0	0-0		Benstead	Culverhouse	Spearing	Bruce	Phelan	**Elliott**	Williams	Drinkell	Biggins	**Crook**	**Putney***	Gordon
	23/8		*19,887*		1				*Godden*	*Wood*	*Pates*	*Bumstead*	*McLaughlin*	*Wicks*	*Durie*	*Spackman*	*Dixon*	*Speedie*	*Murphy*	
								Ref: A Gunn	It's all change, with two big names departed and three debutants. Bruce has a fine game in his new role as skipper. Watson has left for Everton after much wrangling, Woods has joined Rangers. Benstead makes point-saving saves from Kerry Dixon. Fosters Lager are new shirt sponsors.											
2	H	SOUTHAMPTON		11	W	4-3	0-2	Drink' 47, Gor' 49, Wil' 69, Bruce 82	Benstead	Culverhouse	Spearing	Bruce	Phelan	Elliott	Williams	Drinkell	Biggins	Crook	Gordon	
	30/8		15,205	*15*	4			*Wallace 31, Blake 41, Dennis 80*	*Shilton*	*Forrest*	*Dennis*	*Case*	*Blake*	*Bond*	*Lawrence**	*Cockerill*	*Clarke*	*Holmes*	*Wallace*	*LeTissier*
								Ref: K Barratt	The new Main Stand opens for business. Danny Wallace bursts clear to score and Mark Blake nets a header. Drinkell and Gordon net emphatic shots to level. Williams' drive is wiped out by Mark Dennis' 30-yarder. Matt Le Tissier makes his senior debut. Bruce drills a dramatic winner.											
3	A	MANCHESTER C		7	D	2-2	1-2	Barham 10, Elliott 78	Benstead	Culverhouse	Spearing	Bruce	Phelan	Elliott	Williams	Drinkell	Biggins	Barham*	Gordon	Brooke
	3/9		*19,122*	*15*	5			*Christie 6p, 39*	*Suckling*	*May*	*Wilson*	*Baker*	*McCarthy*	*Redmond*	*Hopkins*	*McNab*	*Christie*	*Davies*	*Simpson*	
								Ref: L Robinson	Culverhouse pushes Trevor Christie, who nets the penalty. Barham volleys Norwich level, but Christie - on a short-lived stay at Maine Road - scores again after Bruce's goalline clearance falls for him. New central defender Shaun Elliott levels with a fine header, his first Norwich goal.											
4	A	CHARLTON		6	W	2-1	1-1	Drinkell 6, Williams 84	Benstead	Culverhouse	Spearing	Bruce	Phelan	Elliott	Williams	Drinkell	Biggins	Barham	Gordon	
	6/9		***5,312***	*18*	8			*Aizlewood 1*	*Johns*	*Humphreys*	*Reid*	*Shipley*	*Thompson*	*Shirtliff*	*Lee*	*Gritt*	*Pearson*	*Aizlewood*	*Stuart*	
								Ref: B Hill	Benstead takes his time in possession in the first minute and, astonishingly a free-kick is given for time-wasting! The ball is played to Mark Aizlewood, who buries a left-foot drive. Drinkell beats Nicky Johns with a firm header. Williams nets a downward header from Phelan's pass.											
5	H	WATFORD		11	L	1-3	1-0	Williams 18	Benstead	Culverhouse	Spearing	Bruce	Phelan	Elliott	Williams	Drinkell	Biggins	Barham*	Gordon	**Hodgson**
	13/9		15,487	*13*	8			*Richards'n 55, Sterling 60, Bliss't 88*	*Coton*	*Franklin**	*Rostron*	*Richardson*	*Terry*	*McClelland*	*Bardsley*	*Blissett*	*Callaghan*	*Jackett*	*Sterling*	*Talbot*
								Ref: D Reeves	Williams sweeps Norwich ahead. Kevin Richardson fires a deserved equaliser and Worrell Sterling converts from close range after a Nigel Callaghan free-kick. Luther Blissett hooks a third for Graham Taylor's men. City's bid for Aberdeen keeper Bryan Gunn has been put on ice.											
6	H	LEICESTER		2	W	2-1	1-1	Barham 33, Biggins 78	Benstead	Culverhouse	Spearing	Bruce	Phelan	Elliott*	Williams	Drinkell	Biggins	Barham	Gordon	Hodgson
	17/9		14,814	*14*	11			*Smith A 22*	*Andrews*	*Ramsey*	*Venus*	*Osman*	*Walsh*	*McAllister*	*Kelly**	*Moran*	*Smith A*	*Wilson*	*Morgan*	*Sealy*
								Ref: K Hackett	Alan Smith puts new manager Bryan Hamilton's side in front with a header. Barham lashes in after a Williams' corner-kick to even things up. With time fast running out, Barham's deep cross into the danger zone is headed on by Drinkell and Biggins swoops to break his scoring duck.											
7	A	ASTON VILLA		2	W	**4-1**	2-0	Phelan 29, Biggins 44, Gordon 54, [Bruce 62]	Benstead	Culverhouse	Spearing	Bruce	Phelan	**Butterw'rth**	Williams	Drinkell	Biggins	Barham*	Gordon	Crook
	20/9		*12,304*	*22*	14			*Stainrod 88*	*Poole*	*Keown*	*Dorigo*	*Evans*	*Elliott*	*Hunt*	*Birch*	*Stainrod*	*Thompson*	*Hodge*	*Daley*	
								Ref: K Hackett	Managerless and bottom of the table, Villa are brushed aside by eager City. Steve Hodge's poor back-pass is snapped up by Phelan. Biggins shoots in from ten yards, then Gordon cuts in and makes it three. Bruce strokes home another from a corner. Barham departs with knee trouble.											
8	H	NEWCASTLE		2	W	2-0	1-0	Drinkell 4, 68	Benstead	Culverhouse	Spearing	Bruce	Phelan	Butterworth	Williams	Drinkell	Biggins	Barham	Gordon	
	27/9		15,735	*20*	17				*Thomas M*	*Anderson**	*Bailey*	*McCreery*	*Clarke*	*Roeder*	*Stephenson*	*Thomas A*	*Allon*	*Beardsley*	*McDonald*	*Gascoigne*
								Ref: C Downey	Drinkell rises high to head home a Williams corner. Martin Thomas blocks a Gordon shot, but Drinkell bags his second goal from the rebound. Coach Mel Machin is rumoured to be a target for Manchester City. Aberdeen boss Alex Ferguson is delaying the deal involving keeper Gunn.											
9	H	QP RANGERS		2	W	1-0	0-0	Gordon 78	Benstead	Culverhouse	Spearing	Bruce	Phelan	Butterworth	Williams	Drinkell	Biggins	Barham	Gordon	
	4/10		15,984	*15*	20				*Seaman*	*Fereday*	*Daws*	*Allen*	*Fenwick*	*Chivers*	*Neill*	*James*	*Bannister**	*Byrne*	*Channing*	*Walker*
								Ref: V Callow	Jim Smith's side pose Norwich a few problems, particularly via winger Clive Walker, who comes on as sub. The game is heading for goalless deadlock when Gordon jinks into space and sends a cracking shot past young David Seaman. Williams celebrates the 400th game of his career.											
10	A	LUTON		1	D	0-0	0-0		Benstead	Culverhouse	Spearing	Bruce	Phelan	Butterworth	Williams*	Drinkell	Biggins	Barham	Gordon	Crook
	11/10		*10,022*	*11*	21				*Sealey*	*Johnson*	*Grimes*	*Nicholas*	*Foster*	*Donaghy*	*Hill*	*Stein M*	*Newell*	*North M**	*Preece*	*McDonough*
								Ref: J Ashworth	Norwich's unbeaten away run continues in a game of few chances and they soar to the top of the table. John Moore's side maintain their own unbeaten home record and go closest as Marc North sends a lob against the bar. Williams picks up an injury that will keep him out for weeks.											

11	H	WEST HAM	2	D	1-1	0-0	Drinkell 58	Benstead	Culverhouse	Spearing	Bruce	Phelan	Elliott	Crook	Drinkell	Biggins	Barham	Gordon*	Hodgson
	18/10	22,884	*5*	22			*Goddard 76*	*Parkes*	*Stewart*	*Parris*	*Gale*	*Hilton*	*Keen*	*Ward**	*Goddard*	*Dickens*	*Cottee*	*Orr*	*Bonds*
							Ref: A Seville	An excellent contest in front of the biggest gate for more than a year. Biggins' cross is touched in by Drinkell. John Lyall's side respond when Tony Gale's deep cross is headed back by Tony Cottee for Paul Goddard to convert. In the last minute Benstead saves superbly from Goddard.											
12	A	WIMBLEDON	2	L	0-2	0-2		Benstead	Culverhouse	Spearing	Bruce	Phelan	Elliott	Crook	Drinkell	Biggins*	Barham	Gordon	Putney
	25/10	*6,172*	*14*	22			*Fashanu 13, Gayle 38*	*Beasant*	*Kay*	*Winterburn*	*Galliers*	*Gayle*	*Thorn*	*Cork*	*Fairweather*	*Fashanu*	*Sanchez*	*Hodges**	*Downes*
							Ref: P Vanes	Dave Bassett's eager Dons seem to relish playing Norwich and record their third successive win over the Canaries, ending the unbeaten run. Their unpopular long ball game and 'get-amongst-them' attitude rattles City in a the first half and Benstead looks particularly uncomfortable.											
13	A	LIVERPOOL	4	L	**2-6**	0-2	Phelan 72, Hodgson 84 *[Rush 49, 71]*	Benstead	Culverhouse	Spearing	Bruce	Phelan	Elliott	Crook*	Drinkell	Hodgson	Mendham	Gordon	Putney
	1/11	*36,915*	*3*	22			*Nicol 16, Walsh 31, 58, 76,*	*Grobbelaar*	*Gillespie*	*Beglin*	*Lawrenson*	*Whelan*	*Hansen*	*Walsh*	*Nicol**	*Rush*	*Molby*	*McMahon*	*Dalglish*
							Ref: J Bray	Unmarked Steve Nicol launches a rout. Paul Walsh's stunning drive is followed by a second set up by Alan Hansen's chip, and then a simple tap-in. Ian Rush weighs in with two. Norwich net twice near the end to save a little face, including one from ex-Red Hodgson on his full debut.											
14	H	TOTTENHAM	4	W	2-1	0-0	Crook 59, Elliott 76	**Gunn**	Culverhouse	Spearing	Bruce	Phelan	Elliott	Crook	Drinkell	Hodgson	Mendham	Gordon	
	8/11	22,139	*11*	25			*Claesen 72*	*Clemence*	*Hughton**	*Thomas M*	*Roberts*	*Miller*	*Gough*	*Allen C*	*Claesen*	*Waddle*	*Mabbutt*	*Allen P*	*Hoddle*
							Ref: K Baker	Gunn's debut sees an excellent team performance, to banish memories of Anfield. Crook's first Norwich goal comes against his old team and is an immaculate finish after a sweeping move. Clive Allen sets up Nico Claeasen, but Shaun Elliott has the last laugh, heading home a free-kick.											
15	H	MANCHESTER U	6	D	0-0	0-0		Gunn	Culverh'se*	Spearing	Bruce	Phelan	Elliott	Putney	Drinkell	Hodgson	Mendham	Gordon	Biggins
	15/11	22,684	*21*	26				*Turner*	*Sivebaeck**	*Duxbury*	*Moses*	*McGrath*	*Hogg*	*Olsen*	*Blackmore*	*Stapleton*	*Davenport*	*Barnes*	*Moran*
							Ref: J McAulay	United are revitalised now that Alex Ferguson has replaced Ron Atkinson. Norwich have a let-off when a clearance hits their bar. Hodgson goes off in agony after his back seizes up. His exit is prolonged because at first he can't be moved. Biggins hits the bar nine minutes from time.											
16	A	COVENTRY	7	L	1-2	1-1	Biggins 19	Gunn	Culverhouse	**Seagraves**	Bruce	Phelan*	Elliott	Crook	Drinkell	Biggins	Putney	Gordon	Barham
	22/11	*11,029*	*8*	26			*Phillips 7, 56*	*Ogrizovic*	*Borrows*	*Downs*	*McGrath*	*Sedgley*	*Peake*	*Bennett*	*Phillips*	*Regis*	*Emerson*	*Pickering*	
							Ref: D Hutchinson	Liverpool allow England youth cap Mark Seagraves to join City on loan. David Phillips thumps George Curtis' outfit into an early lead, but Biggins swoops to level. Phillips fires the Sky Blues ahead and has a third disallowed. Cyrille Regis and Dean Emerson miss decent chances.											
17	H	OXFORD	6	W	2-1	2-1	Drinkell 13, Gordon 22	Gunn	Culverhouse	Seagraves	Bruce	Crook	Elliott	**Fox**	Drinkell	Biggins*	Putney	Gordon	**Brown**
	29/11	**13,610**	*14*	29			*Aldridge 35*	*Hardwick*	*Langan*	*McDonald*	*Phillips*	*Briggs*	*Dreyer*	*Leworthy*	*Aldridge*	*Whitehurst*	*Reck**	*Brock*	*Mustoe*
							Ref: D Phillips	On a foggy day, Ruel Fox debuts in place of the injured Phelan. Drinkell nets a firm header, then Steve Hardwick drops a Crook free-kick and Gordon pounces. Putney has to put up with more barracking. Latest back injury victim is Biggins, who is replaced by the manager's son Kenny.											
18	A	EVERTON	9	L	0-4	0-2	*[Heath 81]*	Gunn	Culverhouse	Seagraves	Bruce	Crock	Butterworth	Goss	Drinkell	Rosario	Putney	Gordon	
	6/12	*26,746*	*3*	29			*Power 18, Steven 29p, Pointon 76,*	*Southall*	*Stevens*	*Pointon*	*Ratcliffe*	*Watson*	*Power*	*Steven*	*Heath*	*Sharp**	*Harper*	*Sheedy*	*Wilkinson*
							Ref: J Lovatt	Injury-plagued City now have nine out. Bruce handles a Kevin Sheedy shot for the crucial second goal by Howard Kendall's outfit. Adrian Heath's fourth is a superb volley from Sheedy's chipped pass. Ian Butterworth signs from Nottingham Forest for £160,000 after a spell on loan.											
19	H	ARSENAL	7	D	1-1	0-0	Drinkell 79	Gunn	Culverhouse	Spearing	Bruce	Phelan	Butterworth	Crook	Drinkell	Biggins	Rosario	Gordon	
	13/12	21,409	*1*	30			*Hayes 55p*	*Lukic*	*Anderson*	*Sansom*	*Williams*	*O'Leary*	*Adams*	*Rocastle**	*Davis*	*Quinn*	*Groves*	*Hayes*	*Caesar*
							Ref: T Mills	Butterworth tangles with Niall Quinn and a penalty results, tucked in by Martin Hayes. Gunners' coach Theo Foley is 'sent off' by Mr Mills for his antics in the dug-out. With Norwich hopes beginning to dwindle, Drinkell sweeps the ball past John Lukic after a cross is only half-cleared.											
20	A	WATFORD	8	D	1-1	1-1	Terry 23(og)	Gunn	Culverhouse	Spearing	Bruce	Phelan	Butterworth	Crook	Drinkell	Biggins	Rosario	Gordon	
	19/12	*12,900*	*12*	31			*Barnes 2*	*Coton*	*Bardsley*	*Rostron*	*Richardson*	*Terry*	*McClelland*	*Callaghan*	*Barnes*	*Falco**	*Jackett*	*Porter*	*Sinnott*
							Ref: J Lloyd	The Friday night entertainment is delayed for 15 minutes after a power failure in the ground. The gloom continues for City when John Barnes' half-hit shot deceives Gunn with less than two minutes gone. City get back on terms when Phelan's low cross flies into the net off Steve Terry.											
21	H	NOTT'M FOREST	6	W	2-1	0-0	Crook 75, Rosario 79	Gunn	Culverhouse	Spearing	Bruce	Phelan	Butterworth	Crook	Drinkell	Biggins	Rosario	Gordon	
	26/12	22,131	*3*	34			*Pearce 64*	*Segers*	*Fleming*	*Pearce*	*Walker*	*Fairclough*	*Bowyer*	*Carr*	*Metgod*	*Clough*	*Campbell*	*Webb*	
							Ref: J Ashworth	Forest boss Brian Clough ignores the game for two minutes to berate rowdy fans behind his dugout. Stuart Pearce nets after Johnny Metgod sets him up. City hit back as Crook's 25-yarder deflects in off David Campbell. Chris Fairclough hesitates and Rosario grabs the winning goal.											

No	Date		Att	Pos	Pt	F-A	H-T	Scorers, Times, and Referees	1	2	3	4	5	6	7	8	9	10	11	12 sub used
22	A	MANCHESTER U		4	W	1-0	0-0	Drinkell 80	Gunn	Culverhouse	Spearing	Bruce	Phelan	Butterworth	Crook	Drinkell	Biggins	Rosario	Gordon	
	27/12		*44,610*	*15*	37				*Walsh*	*Sivebaeck*	*Gibson C*	*Whiteside*	*Garton*	*Duxbury*	*Robson**	*Strachan*	*Stapleton*	*Davenport*	*Olsen*	*O'Brien*
								Ref: T Simpson	In driving, freezing rain, the big crowd is warmed by an entertaining game. Old Trafford is stunned when Culverhouse's near-post cross is met by the diving figure of Drinkell. It's Norwich's first league win at this stadium in 16 visits and it comes 24 hours after United win at Liverpool.											
23	A	SHEFFIELD WED		6	D	1-1	0-0	Drinkell 90	Gunn	Culverhouse	Spearing	Bruce	Phelan	Butterworth	Crook	Drinkell	Biggins	Rosario	Gordon	
	1/1		*20,956*	*10*	38			*Shelton 81*	*Hodge*	*Sterland**	*Worthington*	*Knight*	*Madden*	*Jonsson*	*Snodin*	*Chamberlain*	*Chapman*	*Shutt*	*Shelton*	*Morris*
								Ref: J Worrall	Gary Shelton buries a header to put Howard Wilkinson's men in the driving seat. Moments later Martin Hodge makes a sensational save from a powerful close-range header by Biggins. In the dying seconds, Drinkell wins a deserved point for City by sweeping in his tenth goal this term.											
24	H	CHARLTON		6	D	1-1	0-1	Biggins 74	Gunn	Culverhouse	Spearing	Bruce	Phelan	Butterworth	Crook	Drinkell	Biggins	Rosario*	Gordon	Putney
	3/1		16,827	*19*	39			*Stuart 22*	*Bolder*	*Humphreys*	*Reid*	*Shipley*	*Thompson*	*Shirtliff*	*Stuart*	*Peake*	*Melrose*	*Aizlewood*	*Walsh*	
								Ref: D Axcell	Mark Stuart's drive puts Lennie Lawrence's men ahead. After Bob Bolder drops a corner, a Biggins effort is ruled to have crossed the line. All hell is let loose and amid the jostling, the referee is knocked to the ground. He is carried off semi-conscious, but later agrees it was an accident.											
25	H	CHELSEA		6	D	2-2	1-1	Rosario 30, Drinkell 62	Gunn	Culverhouse	Spearing	Bruce	Phelan	Elliott	Crook	Drinkell	Biggins	Rosario	Gordon	
	24/1		16,562	*17*	40			*Bumstead 2, Wicks 46*	*Godden*	*Wood*	*Dublin*	*Pates*	*Wicks*	*Bumstead*	*Nevin*	*Spackman*	*Durie*	*Speedie**	*Hazard*	*Clarke*
								Ref: J Moules	Gordon Durie robs Elliott and Bruce's attempted clearance falls for John Bumstead to score after just 79 seconds. Biggins' pass is converted by Rosario, but Steve Wicks is left unmarked to head in. John Hollins' men are foiled as Drinkell scores after a Crook free-kick causes a scramble.											
26	A	SOUTHAMPTON		6	W	2-1	0-0	Phelan 55, Drinkell 79	Gunn	Brown	Spearing	Bruce	Phelan	Butterworth	Crook	Drinkell	Rosario	Putney	Gordon*	Barham
	7/2		*12,754*	*17*	43			*Cockerill 69*	*Flowers*	*Forrest*	*Dennis*	*Case*	*Wright*	*Bond*	*Holmes**	*Cockerill*	*Clarke*	*Armstrong*	*Hobson*	*Townsend*
								Ref: K Cooper	In a game of six bookings, Mark Dennis is carded for a tackle on Gordon that appears to have broken his leg, but the news later is good. Phelan thumps home a shot from 15 yards. Glenn Cockerill's first attempt hits Brown, but he nets the rebound. Putney's cross is converted by Drinkell.											
27	H	MANCHESTER C		7	D	1-1	1-1	Crook 44	Gunn	Brown	Spearing	Bruce	Phelan	Butterworth	Crook	Drinkell	Rosario	Putney	Barham*	Fox
	14/2		16,094	*18*	44			*Brightwell 42*	*Suckling*	*Gidman*	*Wilson*	*Clements*	*McCarthy*	*Redmond*	*Brightwell*	*McNab*	*Varadi*	*Lake**	*Barnes*	*White*
								Ref: R Lewis	The Duchess of Kent officially opens the new Main Stand. Gunn races out of goal, but his kick strikes Ian Brightwell for a real gift goal. Two minutes later Crook is fouled, takes the kick himself and curls it past Perry Suckling. Mick McCarthy and Rosario are booked after a flare-up.											
28	A	LEICESTER		6	W	2-0	1-0	Crook 1, Putney 61	Gunn	Brown	Spearing	Bruce	Phelan	Butterworth	Crook	Drinkell	Rosario	Putney	Gordon	
	21/2		*8,742*	*19*	47				*Andrews*	*Morgan*	*Venus**	*O'Neill*	*Walsh*	*McAllister*	*Mauchlen*	*D'Avray*	*Smith A*	*Ramsey*	*Wilson*	*Horner*
								Ref: J Ireland	A top quality display by Norwich. Bruce taps aside an early free-kick for Crook to blast a handsome goal past Ian Andrews. Putney cocks a snook at his Carrow Road barrackers by cutting in and slotting in a tremendous second goal after the break. Now it's ten games without defeat.											
29	H	ASTON VILLA		5	D	1-1	0-1	Phelan 72	Gunn	Brown	Spearing*	Bruce	Phelan	Butterworth	Crook	Drinkell	Rosario	Putney	Gordon	Biggins
	28/2		15,070	*21*	48			*Elliott 34*	*Spink*	*Norton*	*Williams*	*Keown*	*Elliott*	*Glover*	*Cooper*	*Aspinall*	*Thompson*	*Hunt*	*Daley*	
								Ref: D Hedges	Struggling Villa go ahead when a Gary Williams free-kick finds Paul Elliott unmarked and he heads home. A wild tackle by Warren Aspinall on Crook has Ken Brown leaping from the dug-out, but the boss is booked for his dissent. City level through Phelan after Rosario sets him up.											
30	H	WIMBLEDON		7	D	0-0	0-0		Gunn	Brown	Spearing	Bruce	Phelan	Butterworth	Crook	Drinkell	Rosario	Putney	Gordon*	Biggins
	7/3		14,293	*9*	49				*Beasant*	*Gage*	*Winterburn*	*Jones*	*Gayle*	*Thorn*	*Wise*	*Sayer*	*Fashanu*	*Downes*	*Hodges*	
								Ref: K Hackett	The unbeaten run never looks in real danger, but Wimbledon have had the measure of City's forwards for four games now. Windy conditions, added to the Dons' usual uncomplicated game-plan, means this is not one for the purists. Beasant is in good form and Drinkell fires just wide.											
31	A	WEST HAM		5	W	2-0	1-0	Bruce 2, Drinkell 90	Gunn	Brown	Spearing	Bruce	Phelan	Butterworth	Crook	Drinkell	Rosario	Putney	Gordon	
	14/3		*21,531*	*14*	52				*Parkes*	*Stewart*	*Parris*	*Gale*	*Bonds*	*Dickens*	*Brady*	*Ince*	*Pike**	*Cottee*	*Robson*	*Keen*
								Ref: M Bailey	Liam Brady arrives from Italy to make his West Ham debut, but City steal the limelight. Bruce pokes home after a Crook free-kick. After withstanding huge pressure, Drinkell nets a late shot on the turn. It's a fine result after midweek misery in the Full Members' Cup semi-final.											

32	H	LUTON	5	D	0-0	0-0		Gunn	Brown	Spearing	Bruce*	Phelan	Butterworth	Crook	Drinkell	Rosario	Putney	Gordon	Biggins
	21/3	16,440	*4*	53				*Sealey*	*Breacker*	*Johnson*	*Nicholas*	*North S*	*Donaghy*	*Hill*	*Stein B*	*Newell*	*Harford*	*Grimes!*	
							Ref: M James	These two sides, normally known for open football, produce a goalless draw for a second successive meeting. Luton's Ashley Grimes and Rob Johnson have a bust-up and the former is red-carded for spitting at his colleague. Mike Newell goes close and Rosario hits Les Sealey's bar.											
33	A	QP RANGERS	7	D	1-1	1-1	Drinkell 20	Gunn	Brown	Spearing	Bruce	Phelan	Butterworth	Crook	Drinkell	Rosario	Putney	Gordon*	Biggins
	28/3	*9,834*	*13*	54			*Rosenior 40*	*Seaman*	*Neill*	*James*	*Lee*	*McDonald*	*Fenwick*	*Rosenior*	*Fillery*	*Bannister*	*Byrne*	*Fereday*	
							Ref: L Shapter	The 100th clash of these clubs ends with spoils shared. Drinkell dispossesses Terry Fenwick and opens the scoring by getting on the end of the move himself. Wayne Fereday does well to get a cross over and it is volleyed in by Leroy Rosenior. Veteran Williams gets a call-up by Wales.											
34	A	TOTTENHAM	7	L	0-3	0-0		Gunn	Brown	Spearing	Bruce	Phelan	Butterworth	Crook	Drinkell	Rosario	Putney*	Gordon	Biggins
	4/4	*22,400*	*4*	54			*Allen C 75, 81, 87*	*Clemence*	*Hughton*	*Thomas M*	*Hodge*	*Mabbutt*	*Gough*	*Allen C*	*Allen P*	*Waddle*	*Ardiles*	*Claesen*	*Galvin*
							Ref: V Callow	Clive Allen is having a wonderful season under David Pleat and he takes his goals tally to 43 with a late hat-trick. The first is a toe-poke past Gunn, the second a far-post conversion and the last a crashing drive. Playmaker Glenn Hoddle is missing, but City still fall to a first loss in 16.											
35	A	NEWCASTLE	7	L	1-4	1-1	Drinkell 17 *[Jackson D 90]*	Gunn	Brown	Spearing	Bruce	Phelan	Butterworth	Crook	Drinkell	Rosario	Biggins	Gordon	
	8/4	*24,534*	*18*	54			*Goddard 40, Gasc' 62, McDon'ld 71p,*	*Thomas M*	*McDonald*	*Wharton*	*McCreery**	*Jackson P*	*Roeder*	*Stephenson*	*Gascoigne*	*Goddard*	*Beardsley*	*Anderson*	*Jackson D*
							Ref: D Allison	Drinkell covers 70 yards to net a superb solo goal. Paul Goddard's header equalises for Willie McFaul's lowly side and a deflected shot by Paul Gascoigne puts them in front. Bruce handles to concede a penalty and Darren Jackson adds a late fourth after a good run by Peter Beardsley.											
36	H	LIVERPOOL	6	W	2-1	0-1	Putney 70, Drinkell 88	Gunn	Brown	Spearing	Bruce*	Phelan	Butterworth	Crook	Drinkell	Rosario	Putney	Gordon	Biggins
	11/4	22,879	*2*	57			*Rush 37*	*Grobbelaar*	*Gillespie*	*Venison*	*Lawrenson*	*Whelan*	*Hansen*	*Walsh*	*Johnston*	*Rush*	*Molby*	*McMahon*	
							Ref: C Downey	The Reds look dangerous early on and Ian Rush's first-time shot skids in off a post. They've never lost when Rush has scored, but City show scant respect after the break and get their reward. Putney sweeps in a clever Drinkell cross and Drinkell suprises Grobbelaar with a fierce drive.											
37	H	SHEFFIELD WED	6	W	1-0	1-0	Putney 2	Gunn	Brown	Spearing	Elliott	Phelan	Butterworth	Crook !	Drinkell	Rosario	Putney	Gordon	
	18/4	17,924	*17*	60				*Hodge*	*Sterland**	*Snodin !*	*May*	*Madden*	*Worthington*	*Marwood*	*Megson*	*Chapman*	*Hirst*	*Shelton*	*Morris*
							Ref: A Buksh	David Hirst hits the Norwich bar in the first minute, but moments later Crook, looking well offside, crosses for Putney to net at the near post. After 72 minutes a flare-up between Ian Snodin and Crook sees fists flying and both men are sent off. It's Wednesday's fourth defeat in a row.											
38	A	NOTT'M FOREST	6	D	1-1	0-0	Rosario 62	Gunn	Brown	Spearing	Bruce	Phelan	Butterworth	Crook	Drinkell	Rosario	Putney	Gordon	
	20/4	*14,446*	*7*	61			*Clough 78*	*Sutton*	*Fleming*	*Pearce*	*Walker*	*Foster*	*Bowyer*	*Carr**	*Metgod*	*Clough*	*Wilkinson*	*Mills*	*Fairclough*
							Ref: N Butler	Rosario crashes in a low cross from Phelan and City look all set for a three-point haul. The home side are let off the hook when Stuart Pearce's cross is moved on by Johnny Metgod for Nigel Clough to turn smartly and blast in. Veteran Ian Bowyer, 35, plays his last game at senior level.											
39	H	COVENTRY	6	D	1-1	1-0	Drinkell 26	Gunn	Brown	Spearing	Bruce	Phelan	Butterworth	Crook*	Drinkell	Rosario	Putney	Gordon	Biggins
	25/4	14,610	*10*	62			*Butterworth 81 (og)*	*Ogrizvic*	*Borrows**	*Downs*	*McGrath*	*Kilcline*	*Peake*	*Bennett*	*Phillips*	*Regis*	*Houchen*	*Gynn*	*Rodger*
							Ref: T Ward	Ex-Canary Greg Downs gets a mixed reaction on his return to Carrow Road. Drinkell's 19th goal of the season seems to have wrapped up three points, but the Sky Blues keep fighting and are rewarded late on. Cyrille Regis' cross is turned past his keeper by the unfortunate Butterworth.											
40	A	OXFORD	6	W	1-0	1-0	Gordon 2	Gunn	Brown	Spearing	Bruce	Phelan	Butterworth	Williams	Drinkell	Rosario	Putney	Gordon	
	2/5	*8,394*	*18*	65				*Hucker*	*Langan*	*Dreyer*	*Phillips*	*Briggs*	*Caton*	*Houghton**	*Saunders*	*Mustoe*	*Hebberd*	*Brock*	*Slatter*
							Ref: K Baker	Gordon cuts in and drills home a fine left-foot shot in the opening exchanges. It's frustration all the way for a grumbling home crowd. Maurice Evans' side have a late penalty appeal turned down. Williams returns to the Norwich side after several months out due to an Achilles operation.											
41	H	EVERTON	6	L	0-1	0-1		Gunn	Brown	Spearing	Bruce	Phelan	Butterworth	Williams	Drinkell	Rosario	Biggins*	Gordon	Fox
	4/5	**23,489**	*1*	65			*Van den Hauwe 1*	*Southall*	*Stevens*	*V d Hauwe*	*Ratcliffe*	*Watson*	*Reid*	*Steven*	*Heath*	*Sharp*	*Snodin*	*Power*	
							Ref: J Bray	Former Canary favourite Dave Watson makes a triumphant return. Pat Van den Hauwe nets from close range with only 45 seconds gone. The three points, combined with a Liverpool defeat at Coventry, confirm what we've known for some time now - Everton are the new champions.											
42	A	ARSENAL	5	W	2-1	1-0	Crook 8, Putney 72	Gunn	Brown	Spearing	Bruce	Phelan	Butterworth	Crook	Drinkell	Rosario	Putney	Gordon	
	9/5	*24,001*	*4*	68			*Merson 61*	*Wilmot*	*Anderson**	*Thomas*	*Williams*	*O'Leary*	*Adams*	*Hayes*	*Davis*	*Merson*	*NIcholas*	*Rix*	*Groves*
	Home	Away					Ref: R Milford	Gunn sends a huge punt downfield and Crook finds space to receive a knockdown and score. City miss several chances to notch a second goal before Paul Merson nets a sharp half-volley. A corner reaches Putney who heads home the winner. City attain their highest-ever league finish.											
Average	17,564	17,743																	

Littlewoods Cup	Att			F-A	H-T	Scorers, Times, and Referees	1	2	3	4	5	6	7	8	9	10	11	12 sub used
2:1 A PETERBOROUGH		2	D	0-0	0-0		Benstead	Culverhouse	Spearing	Bruce	Phelan	Rosario*	Williams	Drinkell	Biggins	Barham	Gordon	Crook
24/9	*6,956*	*4:22*					*Beasley*	*Paris*	*Doyle**	*Gunn*	*Price*	*Gage*	*Gregory*	*Fuccillo*	*Lawrence*	*Gallagher*	*Nightingale*	*Nuttell*
						Ref: G Napthine	This game turns into a perfect illustration of how the two-legged system often takes away the cut-and-thrust of cup football. Rosario goes off with a knee injury. In the last third of the game City look dangerous, but Andy Beasley keeps them at bay and Noel Cantwell's side survive.											
2:2 H PETERBOROUGH		2	W	1-0	0-0	Biggins 48	Benstead	Culverhouse	Spearing	Bruce	Phelan	Crook	Williams	Drinkell	Biggins	Barham	Gordon	
8/10	10,027	*4:20*					*Shoemake*	*Nightingale*	*Collins*	*Gunn*	*Price*	*Gage*	*Gregory*	*Fuccillo*	*Doyle*	*Gallagher*	*Paris*	
						Ref: M Scott (Norwich win 1-0 on aggregate)	Biggins produces an acrobatic header from Gordon's cross to end the resistance of plucky Fourth Division Posh. Alan Paris tangles with Bruce in the area, but City calls for a penalty are ignored. 86 league places separate these two sides, but Peterborough go out with heads held high.											
3 H MILLWALL		2	W	4-1	2-1	Hodgson 2, 77, 90, Drinkell 11p	Benstead	Culverhouse	Spearing	Bruce	Phelan	Elliott	Crook	Drinkell	Hodgson	Barham*	Gordon	Mendham
29/10	10,277	*2:13*				*Byrne 14*	*Sansome*	*Stevens*	*Coleman N*	*Briley*	*Walker*	*McLeary*	*Byrne*	*Morgan*	*Sheringham*	*Marks**	*Salman*	*Leslie*
						Ref: J Key	On his full debut, Hodgson nets with his first touch - a free header. Drinkell is pulled down by Nicky Coleman for a penalty. David Byrne pulls one back with a solo effort. Hodgson settles the tie, drilling in his second. He completes a hat-trick with a firm header from Culverhouse's pass.											
4 H EVERTON		6	L	1-4	1-2	Barham 30 *[Heath 84]*	Gunn	Culverhouse	Spearing*	Bruce	Phelan	Elliott	Putney	Drinkell	Biggins	Mendham	Gordon	Barham
19/11	17,988	*7*				*Sheedy 21, Sharp 35, Steven 78p,*	*Southall*	*Harper*	*Power*	*Ratcliffe*	*Mountfield*	*Langley*	*Steven*	*Heath*	*Sharp*	*Adams*	*Sheedy*	
						Ref: C Downey	City are disrupted by Spearing's departure. Barham's equaliser is a splendid effort, but they are caught on the break and Putney fouls Adrian Heath for the decisive penalty. Coach Machin is booked for dissent. Champions-elect Everton are revving up after a mixed start to the season.											

FA Cup																		
3 H HUDDERSFIELD		6	D	1-1	0-0	Drinkell 87	Gunn	Culverhouse	Spearing	Bruce	Phelan	Butterworth	Crook	Drinkell	Hodgson	Biggins	Gordon	
10/1	11,524	*2:19*				*Shearer 73*	*Cox*	*Brown*	*Burke*	*Banks*	*Webster*	*Mitchell*	*Winter*	*Cork*	*Shearer*	*Wilson*	*Cowling*	
						Ref: A Seville	A pre-match blizzard leaves the pitch covered in snow. Steve Smith's Terriers withstand City pressure and break out from defence for Duncan Shearer to rifle home Ian Banks' pass. With full-time approaching, Drinkell saves City, latching on to a chance after Gordon's shot is blocked.											
3R A HUDDERSFIELD		6	W	4-2	2-1	Phelan 30, Rosario 45, Gordon 48, [Drinkell 48]	Gunn	Culverhouse	Spearing	Bruce	Phelan	Butterworth	Crook	Drinkell	Rosario	Biggins !	Gordon	
21/1	*8,970*	*2:19*				*Brown 13p, Cork 78*	*Cox*	*Brown*	*Burke*	*Banks*	*Webster*	*Mitchell*	*Winter**	*Cork*	*Shearer*	*Wilson*	*Cowling^*	*Raynor/Cooper*
						Ref: A Seville	Bruce's foul on David Cork gives the home side an ideal start. Phelan volleys an equaliser and Rosario races down the left flank to crash in a marvellous goal. Gordon sweeps home another excellent effort after the restart. Biggins is sent off after retaliating to a Paul Raynor challenge.											
4 A WIGAN		6	L	0-1	0-0		Gunn	Culverhouse	Spearing	Bruce	Phelan	Butterworth	Crook	Drinkell	Rosario	Biggins	Gordon	
31/1	*8,095*	*3:7*				*Jewell 78*	*Tunks*	*Hamilton*	*Knowles*	*Cook*	*Cribley*	*Holden*	*Lowe*	*Thompson*	*Campbell*	*Jewell*	*Hilditch*	
						Ref: M Reed	On a frosty pitch, the deadlock is broken when Paul Jewell's powerful shot is deflected in by Butterworth. City go close to an equaliser in a late scramble. The giant-killing sparks a pitch invasion at the end. Ray Mathias's Wigan are through to Round 5 for the first time in their history.											

		P	W	D	L	F	A	W	D	L	F	A	Pts
			Home					Away					
1	Everton	42	16	4	1	49	11	10	4	7	27	20	86
2	Liverpool	42	15	3	3	43	16	8	5	8	29	26	77
3	Tottenham	42	14	3	4	40	14	7	5	9	28	29	71
4	Arsenal	42	12	5	4	31	12	8	5	8	27	23	70
5	NORWICH	42	9	10	2	27	20	8	7	6	26	31	68
6	Wimbledon	42	11	5	5	32	22	8	4	9	25	28	66
7	Luton	42	14	5	2	29	13	4	7	10	18	32	66
8	Nott'm For	42	12	8	1	36	14	6	3	12	28	37	65
9	Watford	42	12	5	4	38	20	6	4	11	29	34	63
10	Coventry	42	14	4	3	35	17	3	8	10	15	28	63
11	Manchester U	42	13	3	5	38	18	1	11	9	14	27	56
12	Southampton	42	11	5	5	44	24	3	5	13	25	44	52
13	Sheffield Wed	42	9	7	5	39	24	4	6	11	19	35	52
14	Chelsea	42	8	6	7	30	30	5	7	9	23	34	52
15	West Ham	42	10	4	7	33	28	4	6	11	19	39	52
16	QP Rangers	42	9	7	5	31	27	4	4	13	17	37	50
17	Newcastle	42	10	4	7	33	29	2	7	12	14	36	47
18	Oxford	42	8	8	5	30	25	3	5	13	14	44	46
19	Charlton	42	7	7	7	26	22	4	4	13	19	33	44
20	Leicester	42	9	7	5	39	24	2	2	17	15	52	42
21	Manchester C	42	8	6	7	28	24	0	9	12	8	33	39
22	Aston Villa	42	7	7	7	25	25	1	5	15	20	54	36
		924	238	123	101	756	459	101	123	238	459	756	1263

Odds & ends

Double wins: (3) Leicester, Oxford, Southampton.
Double losses: (1) Everton.

Won from behind: (6) Southampton (h), Charlton (a), Leicester (h), Nott'm For (h), Liverpool (h), Huddersfield (a) (FAC).
Lost from in front: (2) Watford (h), Newcastle (a).

High spots: The club's highest-ever finishing position.
The thrilling victory over Liverpool in April.
December's first-ever league win a t Old Trafford.
Kevin Drinkell's marvellous solo goal at Newcastle in April.

Low spots: The European ban on English clubs again affecting City.
Two late Charlton goals prevent Wembley trip in the Full Members Cup.
Losing Woods, Watson, Deehan, Haylock, Van Wijk before season starts.
The FA Cup giant-killing by Wigan Athletic.
Coach Mel Machin being lured away by Manchester City.
The ref knocked semi-conscious by Charlton players at Carrow Road.
Damage caused to the new Main Stand during Everton's visit.

Player of the Year: Kevin Drinkell.
Ever-presents: (1) Kevin Drinkell.
Hat-tricks: (1) David Hodgson (Millwall, h, LC).
Hat tricks against: (2) Clive Allen (Spurs, a), Paul Walsh (Liverpool, a).
Leading scorer: (19) Kevin Drinkell.

	Appearances						Goals			
	Lge	*Sub*	LC	*Sub*	FAC	*Sub*	**Lge**	LC	FAC	**Tot**
Benstead, Graham	**13**		3							
Barham, Mark	**11**	*2*	3	*1*			**2**	1		**3**
Biggins, Wayne	**23**	*8*	3		3		**4**	1		**5**
Brooke, Garry		*1*								
Brown, Kenny	**17**	*1*								
Bruce, Steve	**41**		4		3		**3**			**3**
Butterworth, Ian	**28**				3					
Crook, Ian	**31**	*2*	2	*1*	3		**5**			**5**
Culverhouse, Ian	**25**		4		3					
Drinkell, Kevin	**42**		4		3		**16**	1	2	**19**
Elliott, Shaun	**15**		2				**2**			**2**
Fox, Ruel	**1**	*2*								
Gordon, Dale	**40**	*1*	4		3		**5**		1	**6**
Goss, Jeremy	**1**									
Gunn, Bryan	**29**		1		3					
Hodgson, David	**3**	*3*	1		1		**1**	3		**4**
Mendham, Peter	**3**		1	*1*						
Phelan, Mike	**40**		4		3		**4**		1	**5**
Putney, Trevor	**20**	*3*	1				**4**			**4**
Rosario, Robert	**25**		1		2		**3**		1	**4**
Seagraves, Mark	**3**									
Spearing, Tony	**39**		4		3					
Williams, David	**12**		2				**3**			**3**
(own-goals)							**1**			**1**
23 players used	**462**	*23*	**44**	*3*	**33**		**53**	**6**	**5**	**64**

No	Date		Att	Pos	Pt	F-A	H-T	Scorers, Times, and Referees	1	2	3	4	5	6	7	8	9	10	11	subs used
1	A	EVERTON		18	L	0-1	0-1		Gunn	Brown*	Spearing	Bruce	Phelan	Butterworth	Gordon	Drinkell	Biggins	Williams	Putney	Crook
	15/8		*31,728*	*8*	0			*Power 35*	*Mimms*	*V d Hauwe*	*Pointon*	*Ratcliffe*	*Watson*	*Harper*	*Steven*	*Clarke*	*Sharp*	*Adams*	*Power*	
								Ref: G Tyson	No new faces for the big kick-off and City are second best in the first half. Paul Power heads Graeme Sharp's cross past Gunn. City improve after a half-time reshuffle, but the nearest to a goal is when Drinkell stretches and just misses a teasing cross. Ex-Canary Watson hits the post.											
2	H	SOUTHAMPTON		19	L	0-1	0-0		Gunn	Culverhouse	Spearing	Bruce	Phelan	Butterworth	Fox	Drinkell	Biggins	Crook	**Bowen***	Rosario
	19/8		14,429	*6*	0			*Moore 61*	*Flowers*	*Forrest*	*Cook*	*Case*	*Moore*	*Bond*	*Townsend*	*Cockerill*	*Clarke*	*Hobson*	*Baker G*	
								Ref: K Hackett	Andy Townsend's curling corner is headed in at the far post by Kevin Moore. Townsend also hits the bar with a free-kick. Biggins gives the crowd something to shout about, hitting the underside of the bar. Gloomy Brown admits City have a lot of work to do to get their season going.											
3	H	COVENTRY		12	W	3-1	1-0	Bruce 20, Drinkell 54, 84	Gunn	Culverhouse	Spearing	Bruce	Phelan	Butterworth	Fox	Drinkell	Biggins	Crook	Bowen	
	22/8		13,726	*5*	3			*Kilcline 58p*	*Ogrizovic*	*Borrows^*	*Downs*	*McGrath*	*Kilcline*	*Peake*	*Bennett*	*Gynn*	*Regis**	*Speedie*	*Pickering*	*Houchen/Phillips*
								Ref: A Buksh	After 264 minutes without a Norwich goal at Carrow Road, Bruce breaks the hoodoo. Drinkell heads a second to put City in the comfort zone, but Bruce handles to let John Sillett's men back into the game. Brian Kilcline nets from the spot. Nerves are finally settled by Drinkell's header.											
4	A	WEST HAM		16	L	0-2	0-0		Gunn	Culverhouse	Spearing	Bruce	Phelan	Butterworth	Fox	Drinkell	Biggins	Crook	Bowen*	Gordon
	29/8		*16,394*	*14*	3			*Cottee 51, 65*	*McAlister*	*Stewart*	*McQueen*	*Strodder*	*Martin*	*Brady*	*Ward*	*McAvennie*	*Ince*	*Cottee*	*Robson*	
								Ref: M Reed	Quicksilver Tony Cottee torments Norwich. He turns in a cross by Mark Ward and shortly afterwards tops this by leaping to volley a superb second from Ray Stewart's pass. Bruce and Drinkell bring stunning saves from Tom McAlister as City bid in vain to get back into the match.											
5	H	NEWCASTLE		15	D	1-1	0-0	Biggins 73	Gunn	Culverhouse	Spearing	Bruce	Phelan	Butterw'th*	Fox	Drinkell	Biggins	Crook	Bowen	**Ratcliffe**
	1/9		16,636	*16*	4			*Jackson D 76*	*Thomas M*	*McDonald*	*Wharton*	*McCreery*	*Jackson P*	*Roeder*	*Jackson D*	*Gascoigne*	*Mirandinha*	*Anderson*	*Hodges*	
								Ref: B Hill	Ex-Manchester U kid Simon Ratcliffe debuts for City, but is overshadowed by the hoopla surrounding the first game of Brazilian Mirandinha for the visitors. Sixty pressmen and 2,000 away fans come to see him. Biggins nets a fine goal, but unmarked Darren Jackson heads a leveller.											
6	A	WATFORD		11	W	1-0	0-0	Bruce 48	Gunn	Culverhouse	Spearing	Bruce	Phelan	Butterworth	Fox	Drinkell	Biggins	Crook	Bowen	
	5/9		*11,724*	*19*	7				*Coton*	*Gibbs*	*Jackett**	*Hill^*	*Morris*	*McClelland*	*Bardsley*	*Blissett*	*Senior*	*Porter*	*Agana*	*Rostron/Roberts*
								Ref: L Shapter	Steve Harrison has replaced Graham Taylor as Hornets boss and things aren't going well. Big-money signing Trevor Senior has yet to score. Bruce shows him how it's done with a header from a Crook corner. The margin of victory could have been wider, but City lack ruthlessness.											
7	H	DERBY		15	L	1-2	0-0	Rosario 78	Gunn	Culverhouse	Spearing	Bruce	Phelan	Butterworth	Fox	Drinkell	Biggins	Crook	Bowen*	Rosario
	12/9		14,402	*12*	7			*Davison 50, Gregory 67p*	*Shilton*	*Sage*	*Forsyth*	*Williams*	*Wright*	*MacLaren*	*Micklewhite*	*Gee**	*Davison*	*Gregory*	*Callaghan*	*Garner*
								Ref: D Hedges	Birthday-boy Nigel Callaghan crosses for Bobby Davison to open the scoring with his head. Phelan pulls down Callaghan for John Gregory's spot-kick. Rosario brings Norwich back into the game, forcing home from six yards. Peter Shilton foils equalising attempts by Fox and Bruce.											
8	A	CHELSEA		17	L	0-1	0-1		Gunn	Culverhouse	Spearing^	Bruce	Phelan	Butterworth	Fox*	Drinkell	Biggins	Crook	Bowen	Rosario/Ratcliffe
	19/9		*15,242*	*3*	7			*Dixon 4*	*Niedzwiecki*	*Clarke^*	*Dorigo*	*Pates*	*McLaughlin*	*Wood*	*Nevin*	*Hazard**	*Dixon*	*Wilson K*	*Wilson C*	*West/Coady*
								Ref: J Martin	Master-goalscorer Kerry Dixon looks offside as he receives the ball and dances round Gunn to score. Norwich argue furiously and Bruce is booked. Butterworth misses a glorious opportunity midway through the first period. Both goalkeepers are kept on their toes in an even contest.											
9	H	NOTT'M FOREST		19	L	0-2	0-2		Gunn	Culverhouse	Elliott	Bruce	Phelan	Ratcliffe	Fox	Drinkell	Rosario	Crook^	Putney*	Gordon/Williams
	26/9		13,755	*4*	7			*Webb 28, 31*	*Sutton*	*Chettle*	*Pearce*	*Walker*	*Foster*	*Wilson*	*Carr*	*Webb*	*Clough*	*Wilkinson*	*Rice**	*Glover*
								Ref: P Don	England prospect Neil Webb sidefoots home Franz Carr's low cross. With Norwich reeling, he adds a second, crashing the ball in after Putney is dispossessed in his own penalty box. Carr has a tremendous game on the wing. City allow Steve Sutton in the Forest goal a quiet afternoon.											
10	A	OXFORD		20	L	**0-3**	0-1		Gunn	Brown	Elliott	Bruce	Phelan	Ratcliffe	Gordon	Drinkell	Rosario	Williams	Putney	
	3/10		*6,847*	*10*	7			*Slatter 14, Foyle 68, Hill 68*	*Hardwick*	*Bardsley*	*Dreyer*	*Shelton*	*Slatter*	*Caton*	*Houghton*	*Foyle*	*Saunders*	*Phillips*	*Hill*	
								Ref: A Gunn	Brown tries to stem the bad run by playing Williams at sweeper, but it turns into a miserable day at the poorly-attended Manor Ground. Neil Slatter forces home a Ray Houghton corner. Richard Hill sidefoots in Houghton's pass and Martin Foyle is on hand as Gunn parries a Hill shot.											

11	H	TOTTENHAM	14	W	2-1	1-1	Drinkell 23, Biggins 63	Gunn	Culverhouse	Elliott	Bruce	Phelan	Ratcliffe	Fox	Drinkell	Biggins	Williams*	Bowen	Crook
10/10		18,669	*6*	10			*Claesen 34*	*Clemence*	*Stevens*	*Thomas*	*Samways*	*Fairclough*	*Mabbutt*	*Close*	*Allen P*	*Ardiles**	*Hodge*	*Claesen*	*Howells*
							Ref: K Barrett	Norwich's best home display so far this term. Bowen's run sets up Drinkell, whose vicious shot goes in off the bar. A Paul Allen effort is well saved by Gunn, but Belgian Nico Claesen fastens onto the loose ball to score. Biggins brushes off a challenge and cuts in to net a fine winner.											
12	A	MANCHESTER U	19	L	1-2	1-0	Biggins 29	Gunn	Culverhouse	Elliott	Bruce	Phelan	Ratcliffe	Fox	Drinkell	Biggins	Williams*	Bowen	Crook
17/10		***39,345***	*14*	10			*Davenport 46, Robson 80*	*Walsh*	*Garton*	*Gibson*	*Duxbury*	*McGrath*	*Davenport*	*Robson*	*Blackmore*	*McClair*	*Whiteside*	*Olsen*	
							Ref: G Alpin	Biggins stuns Old Trafford, swiftly turning and firing in. A mix-up between Culverhouse and Gunn hands Peter Davenport a simple equaliser. Davenport then takes a tumble, but Brian McClair's spot-kick is saved. Bryan Robson collides with a post as his brave header wins the points.											
13	A	SHEFFIELD WED	19	L	0-1	0-1		Gunn	Culverhouse	Elliott	Bruce^	Phelan	Ratcliffe*	Fox	Drinkell	Biggins	Williams	Bowen	Butterworth/Crook
24/10		*15,861*	*20*	10			*Pearson 12*	*Hodge*	*Sterland*	*Worthington*	*Madden*	*Pearson*	*Proctor*	*Chamb'lain^*	*Megson*	*Chapman*	*West**	*Galvin*	*Bradshaw/Fee*
							Ref: M Peck	Howard Wilkinson's side have won just one league game thus far, but take an early lead through Nigel Pearson. Biggins hits the crossbar and Bowen passes up a glorious chance for a leveller. Eight minutes from the whistle, Bruce is carried off after tangling with Mark Chamberlain.											
14	H	QP RANGERS	20	D	1-1	0-0	Biggins 64	Gunn	Brown	Spearing	Bruce	Phelan	Butterworth	Fox	Drinkell	Biggins	Putney	Crook	
31/10		14,522	*2*	11			*Allen 81*	*Seaman*	*Neill*	*Dawes*	*Parker*	*O'Neill*	*Fenwick*	*Allen*	*Coney*	*Fereday*	*Byrne**	*Channing*	*Pizanti*
							Ref: D Axcell	After the midweek cup defeat by Stoke, pressure from unhappy fans is building on Ken Brown. He enquires about Justin Fashanu, but the ex-Canary is not fully fit. Putney capitalises on Rangers hesitancy and Biggins pounces to score. Martin Allen heads in a Wayne Fereday corner.											
15	A	CHARLTON	20	L	0-2	0-2		Gunn	Brown	Spearing*	Bruce	Phelan	Butterworth	Fox	Drinkell	Biggins	Ratcliffe^	Crook	Williams/Rosario
7/11		*5,044*	*21*	11			*Bennett 15, Jones 22*	*Bolder*	*Humphrey*	*Gritt*	*Mortimer*	*Shirtliff*	*Thompson*	*Bennett*	*Campbell*	*Jones*	*Walsh*	*McKenzie*	
							Ref: J Ashworth	An awful start as errors by Bruce and Crook allow Michael Bennett and Andy Jones to net. In a pitiful display, Drinkell even sees a penalty saved. City fans stage a 'white hankie' protest, mocking another surrender by their side. It leads to a dramatic press conference two days later.											
16	H	ARSENAL	21	L	2-4	1-0	Drinkell 31, 81 *[Groves 61]*	Gunn	Brown	Elliott	Bruce	Phelan	Butterworth	Crook*	Drinkell	Rosario	Goss	Gordon	Biggins
14/11		20,558	*1*	11			*Rocastle 49, 54, Thomas 52,*	*Lukic*	*Thomas*	*Sansom*	*Williams*	*O'Leary*	*Adams**	*Rocastle*	*Davis*	*Smith*	*Groves*	*Richardson*	*Caesar*
							Ref: J Key	Brown has departed and Stringer is caretaker. Hostile protests continue, with many fans sympathising with Brown and turning on chairman Chase. The game takes a back seat. Drinkell poaches an opener, but the leaders produce a devastating burst of four in 12 minutes to sink City.											
17	A	LIVERPOOL	21	D	0-0	0-0		Gunn	Brown	Elliott	Bruce	Phelan	Butterworth	Crook	Drinkell	Rosario	Putney	Gordon	
21/11		*37,446*	*2*	12				*Grobbelaar*	*Gillespie*	*Lawrenson*	*Nicol*	*Whelan*	*Hansen*	*Beardsley**	*Aldridge*	*Houghton*	*Barnes*	*McMahon*	*Johnston*
							Ref: J Deakin	Stringer boosts his chances of a permanent appointment, inspiring a heroic Anfield display. Gunn makes a series of fine saves. Crook scores, but handball is called. Ex-player Mick Channon publicly puts his name forward for the manager's position, offering to work initially for free!											
18	H	PORTSMOUTH	21	L	0-1	0-1		Gunn	Brown*	Elliott	Bruce	Phelan	Butterworth	Crook	Drinkell	Rosario	Putney	Gordon	Bowen
28/11		13,099	*20*	12			*Horne 36*	*Knight*	*Swain*	*Hardyman*	*Dillon*	*Ball*	*Whitehead*	*Horne*	*Kennedy*	*Baird*	*Quinn*	*Hilaire*	
							Ref: T Holbrook	Ian Baird cuts in and shoots, Gunn beating the ball straight to Barry Horne, who drills in. In a gloomy atmosphere, chanting alternates between 'what a load of rubbish' and 'Chase out'. The only ones smiling are Alan Ball's struggling outfit. A new power struggle emerges at board level.											
19	A	LUTON	20	W	2-1	0-1	Gordon 61, Crook 88	Gunn	Culverhouse	Elliott	Bruce	Phelan	Butterworth	Crook	Drinkell	Rosario	Putney	Gordon*	Fox
5/12		*7,002*	*14*	15			*Stein B 20*	*Sealey*	*Breacker*	*Grimes*	*McDonough*	*Foster*	*Donaghy*	*Wilson D*	*Stein B*	*Nwajiobi**	*Weir*	*Allinson*	*Hill*
							Ref: D Scott	Ray Harford's men take it easy after Brian Stein's opener and are punished. Ian Crook lobs a neat winning goal near the end. With their ban on away fans, this is Luton's lowest-ever Division One crowd. The ban means only a handful of Norwich fans witness the first win in nine games.											
20	A	WIMBLEDON	20	L	0-1	0-1		Gunn	Culverhouse	Elliott^	**O'Neill***	Phelan	Butterworth	Crook	Drinkell	**Fleck**	Putney	Gordon	Goss/O'Neill
18/12		***4,026***	*8*	15			*Fashanu 14*	*Beasant*	*Goodyear*	*Scales*	*Jones*	*Young*	*Thorn*	*Fairweather*	*Cork*	*Fashanu**	*Sanchez*	*Wise*	*Turner*
							Ref: A Seville	Skipper Bruce goes to Man U (£900k) and Fleck signs from Rangers for a club record £580k. Ex-Canary John Fashanu heads the Dons ahead. New man O'Neill's debut is ended by a knee injury, inflicted by Fashanu's challenge. It subsequently ends his career and leads to legal action.											
21	A	DERBY	21	W	2-1	1-0	Fleck 33, Gordon 52	Gunn	Culverhouse	Bowen	Elliott	Phelan	Butterworth	Fox	Drinkell	Fleck	Goss	Gordon	
26/12		*15,452*	*15*	18			*Wright 49*	*Shilton*	*MacLaren*	*Forsyth*	*Williams*	*Wright*	*Blades*	*Callaghan*	*Gee*	*Garner*	*Gregory*	*Penney*	
							Ref: V Callow	Late call-offs further deplete an injury-hit City squad. Fleck bags his first goal, converting a Fox centre. Mark Wright levels, heading home a corner. Three minutes later Gordon fires past Peter Shilton from close in. Three points are a welcome Christmas present for the caretaker boss.											

No	Date		Att	Pos	Pt	F-A	H-T	Scorers, Times, and Referees	1	2	3	4	5	6	7	8	9	10	11	subs used
22	H	CHELSEA		18	W	3-0	0-0	Fox 51, Goss 71, Drinkell 76p	Gunn	Culverhouse	Elliott*	Bowen	Phelan	Butterworth	Fox	Drinkell	Rosario	Goss	Gordon	Putney
	28/12		19,668	8	21				*Freestone*	*Hall*	*Dorigo**	*Clarke*	*McLaughlin*	*Wood*	*Nevin*	*Wegerle*	*Durie*	*Wilson K*	*Wilson C*	*Coady*
								Ref: K Morton	John Hollins' inconsistent side crumple as City go on a second-half rampage. After this third victory, Stringer is confirmed as new boss, with Williams as player-coach. These two have won the fans over, but not so chairman Chase, subject of a 'no confidence' motion by shareholders.											
23	H	WEST HAM		15	W	**4-1**	0-1	Gordon 47, Drinkell 67, Bowen 79,	Gunn	Culverhouse	Bowen	Putney	Phelan	Butterworth	Fox	Drinkell	Rosario	Goss	Gordon	
	1/1		20,059	14	24			*Cottee 27* [Rosario 86]	*McAlister*	*Bonds*	*Parris*	*Hilton*	*Stewart*	*Keen^*	*Ward*	*Dickens*	*Ince**	*Cottee*	*Robson*	*Dolan/Gale*
								Ref: B Hall	Another entertaining second-half rally wins the day. Tony Cottee nets for John Lyall's men, but Tom McAlister makes a mess of Gordon's shot to open the floodgates. Drinkell bags a typical opportunist effort and Bowen heads in the third. Rosario fires home through a ruck of defenders.											
24	H	EVERTON		19	L	**0-3**	0-1		Gunn	Culverhouse	Bowen	Putney	Phelan	Butterworth	Fox*	Drinkell	Fleck	Goss	Gordon	Elliott
	16/1		15,750	3	24			*Sharp 21, 87, Heath 90*	*Southall*	*Stevens*	*Pointon*	*V d Hauwe*	*Watson*	*Reid**	*Steven*	*Heath*	*Sharp*	*Snodin*	*Wilson*	*Harper*
								Ref: S Lodge	Graeme Sharp finds himself with space galore to give Colin Harvey's side the lead. The victory is clinched in the closing stages when Gunn fumbles an Alan Harper long-range shot and Sharp pounces again. The scorer turns provider in the final minute when he sets up Adrian Heath.											
25	A	SOUTHAMPTON		16	D	0-0	0-0		Benstead	Culverhouse	Bowen	Putney	Phelan	Butterworth	Fox	Drinkell	Fleck	Goss	Gordon	
	23/1		*12,002*	11	25				*Burridge*	*Forrest*	*Statham*	*Case*	*Moore*	*Bond*	*Townsend*	*Le Tissier*	*Clarke*	*Baker G*	*Wallace D*	
								Ref: R Lewis	Norwich are boosted by a midweek 3-2 Simod Cup win at Millwall. Heavy rain leads to two pitch inspections before this game can go ahead. Gunn is missing due to a knee injury, but his deputy Benstead has a tremendous match. Bruised and battered, Fleck also gives a heroic display.											
26	H	WATFORD		17	D	0-0	0-0		Benstead	Culverhouse	Bowen	Putney	Phelan	Butterworth	Fox	Drinkell	Fleck	Goss	Gordon*	Elliott
	6/2		13,316	21	26				*Coton*	*Gibbs*	*Rostron*	*Jackett*	*Morris*	*McClelland*	*Sterling*	*Allen*	*Senior*	*Porter*	*Hodges**	*Blissett*
								Ref: M Bailey	City fans show their displeasure when the goals fail to come against a Watford outfit heading for relegation. Drinkell goes closest with a late header. Malcolm Allen wins Man of the Match, but it was a tough task finding a candidate! Many fans leave early; those left jeer the teams off.											
27	A	NEWCASTLE		17	W	3-1	1-1	Fleck 2, 58, Drinkell 85	Gunn	Culverhouse	Bowen	Putney*	Phelan	Butterworth	Fox	Drinkell	Fleck	Elliott	Gordon	Goss
	13/2		*21,068*	13	29			*Gascoigne 34*	*Kelly*	*Anderson*	*Wharton*	*Jackson D*	*Jackson P*	*Roeder*	*McDonald*	*Gascoigne*	*Goddard*	*Mirandinha*	*O'Neill*	
								Ref: A Flood	Fleck converts a Fox cross in an early raid. Paul Gascoigne whips home a breathtaking free-kick to equalise. Fleck's close-range header beats Gary Kelly to restore the lead. Drinkell finishes the Geordies off late on with a smartly taken effort. The only black spot is an injury to Putney.											
28	A	COVENTRY		15	D	0-0	0-0		Gunn	Culverhouse	Bowen	Goss	Phelan	Butterworth	Fox*	Drinkell	Fleck	Elliott !	Gordon	Crook
	20/2		*15,577*	17	30				*Ogrizovic*	*Borrows*	*Downs*	*Sedgley*	*Kilcline*	*Peake^*	*Bennett*	*Phillips*	*Emerson**	*Speedie*	*Smith D*	*Houchen/Smith K*
								Ref: E Parker	On a sandy pitch, this goalless bore springs to life when a flare-up between David Speedie and Elliott sees the latter sent packing for use of an elbow. Ten-man Norwich go closest to a winner when a Fleck shot hits the underside of the bar and is hooked off the line by Brian Borrows.											
29	H	MANCHESTER U		14	W	1-0	0-0	Fleck 76	Gunn	Culverhouse	Bowen	**Linighan**	Phelan	Putney	Fox	Drinkell	Fleck	Goss	Gordon*	Crook
	5/3		19,129	2	33				*Turner*	*Blackmore**	*Duxbury*	*Bruce*	*O'Brien*	*Moran*	*Robson*	*Strachan*	*McClair*	*Davenport*	*Gibson*	*Olsen*
								Ref: M Reed	Andy Linighan signs from Oldham (£300k), a much-needed replacement for Bruce and O'Neill. A midweek 0-2 Simod Cup defeat at Swindon is forgotten as this cut-and-thrust battle (five bookings) gets underway. Crook's centre is set up by Drinkell for Fleck to bury a low half-volley.											
30	A	TOTTENHAM		14	W	3-1	1-0	Goss 37, Fleck 67, Drinkell 75	Gunn	Culverhouse	Bowen	Linighan	Phelan	Butterworth	Fox	Drinkell	Fleck	Goss	Putney	
	12/3		*19,322*	8	36			*Claesen 85*	*Mimms*	*Statham*	*Thomas*	*Fenwick*	*Fairclough*	*Mabbutt*	*Allen C*	*Allen P*	*Ardiles*	*Samways**	*Walsh*	*Claesen*
								Ref: G Tyson	Fielding three ex-Spurs men, City end their London hoodoo in great style. Goss is injured in the process of netting a fine header. Fleck lets fly to punish a ragged home side. Drinkell, said to be a Spurs transfer target, swoops on a loose ball after Mimms denied Fleck. A pivotal victory.											
31	H	OXFORD		9	W	4-2	1-1	Linighan 10, Fleck 65, 80, Drinkell 72	Gunn	Culverhouse	Bowen	Linighan	Phelan	Butterworth	Fox	Drinkell	Fleck	Goss	Putney	
	16/3		12,260	21	39			*Bardsley 45, Hebberd 82*	*Judge*	*Bardsley*	*Dreyer*	*Shelton*	*Briggs*	*Caton*	*Hebberd*	*Foyle*	*Saunders*	*Phillips !*	*Hill**	*Brown R*
								Ref: K Miller	Relegation now looks highly unlikely and City play with freedom. Linighan heads in an early corner and minutes later Les Phillips is sent off for dissent. David Bardsley rockets one in, but Fleck finishes a nice move to restore the lead. Drinkell and Fleck headers clinch all three points.											

No	Date	Opponent	Att	Pos	Res	Pts	FT	HT	Scorers, Times, and Referees	1	2	3	4	5	6	7	8	9	10	11	subs used
32		A QPR		10	L		**0-3**	0-1		Gunn	Culverhouse	Bowen^	Linighan	Phelan*	Butterworth	Fox	Drinkell	Fleck	Goss	Putney	Crook/Biggins
	19/3		*9,033*	*6*		39			*Channing 25, Coney 47, Fereday 81*	*Seaman*	*Neill*	*Dawes*	*Parker*	*McDonald*	*Maddix*	*Allen**	*Kerslake*	*Coney^*	*Fereday*	*Channing*	*Byrne/Dennis*
									Ref: D Allison	Young Justin Channing scores his career-first goal after Gunn blocked his first attempt. City's cause isn't helped when Phelan limps off injured in the first period. Jim Smith's side increase their lead through a Dean Coney 20-yard drive. Wayne Fereday nods home a cross by Ian Dawes.											
33		H SHEFFIELD W		13	L		**0-3**	0-1		Gunn	Culverhouse	Bowen	Linighan	Crook*	Butterworth	Fox	Drinkell	Fleck	Goss	Putney	Spearing
	26/3		13,280	*9*		39			*Sterland 43, Jons'n 75, Chapman 80*	*Pressman*	*Sterland*	*Worthington*	*Madden*	*Cranson*	*Proctor*	*Chamberlain*	*Megson*	*Chapman*	*Hirst**	*Jonsson*	*Bradshaw*
									Ref: D Hutchison	Gunn hauls down Mark Chamberlain for Mel Sterland to crack in a penalty. Sterland fouls Fox after the break, but Fleck's penalty is weak and young Kevin Pressman saves. Siggi Jonsson nets a wonderful 30-yarder and even home fans applaud. Lee Chapman's third follows a scramble.											
34		H CHARLTON		13	W		2-0	0-0	Fox 50, Drinkell 58	Gunn	Culverhouse	Spearing	Linighan	Williams	Butterworth	Fox	Drinkell	Fleck	Goss	Putney	
	2/4		15,015	*20*		42				*Bolder*	*Humphrey*	*Reid*	*McKenzie*	*Shirtliff*	*Miller*	*Stuart^*	*Leaburn**	*Gritt*	*Campbell*	*Crooks*	*Jones/Williams*
									Ref: B Stevens	Veteran player-coach Williams, 33, and full-back Spearing return to the side after lengthy lay-offs. Williams is architect of the victory. He sets up Fox's opening goal with a precise through ball and then he floats over a free-kick for the unsettled Drinkell to head the decisive second goal.											
35		A ARSENAL		15	L		0-2	0-1		Gunn	Culverhouse	Spearing	Linighan	Williams*	Butterworth	Fox	Drinkell	Fleck	Goss	Putney	Biggins
	4/4		*19,341*	*6*		42			*Smith 38, Groves 59*	*Lukic*	*Winterburn*	*Sansom*	*Williams*	*Caesar*	*Adams*	*Rocastle*	*Davis*	*Smith*	*Groves*	*Hayes*	
									Ref: B Stevens	A gloomy Easter Monday for Norwich who can't muster a single worthwhile attempt on goal. The travelling fans are disgruntled to see some players struggling and others strolling. The Gunners, who soon face a Littlewoods Cup final, clinch the points with a fine Perry Groves strike.											
36		H LIVERPOOL		15	D		0-0	0-0		Gunn	Culverhouse	Spearing	Linighan	Phelan	Butterworth	Fox	Drinkell	Fleck	Goss	Putney	
	20/4		**22,509**	*1*		43				*Grobbelaar*	*Gillespie*	*Ablett*	*Nicol*	*Spackman*	*Hansen*	*Beardsley*	*Aldridge*	*Houghton*	*Johnston*	*McMahon*	
									Ref: R Hart	A capacity crowd squeezes into Carrow Road, but a much-anticipated contest proves a big disappointment. Kenny Dalglish's all-star side is a long way ahead of the pack and could have clinched the title tonight by taking three points, but Peter Beardsley is uncharacteristically wasteful.											
37		H PORTSMOUTH		13	D		2-2	1-0	Linighan 31, Biggins 90p	Gunn	Culverhouse	Spearing	Linighan	Phelan	Butterworth	Fox^	Rosario	Fleck*	Goss	Putney	Biggins/Gordon
	23/4		12,762	*20*		44			*Quinn 59, Mariner 68*	*Gosney*	*Swain*	*Sandford*	*Dillon*	*Blake*	*Ball*	*Horne*	*Whitehead*	*Mariner*	*Quinn*	*Hilaire*	
									Ref: P Don	Pompey are scrapping desperately near the bottom. Linighan heads in a Goss free-kick, but Mick Quinn levels from close range. Paul Mariner powers home a Noel Blake centre. There is fury over a last-minute penalty, given for a handball that few saw. Biggins ignores the fuss to net.											
38		H LUTON		13	D		2-2	0-0	Drinkell 51, Putney 63	Gunn	Culverhouse	Spearing	Linighan	Phelan	Butterworth	Fox^	Drinkell*	Fleck	Goss	Putney	Biggins/Gordon
	30/4		12,700	*12*		45			*Stein M 87, Wilson D 89p*	*Dibble*	*Breacker*	*Johnson R*	*Hill*	*Foster*	*Donaghy**	*Wilson D*	*Stein M*	*Allinson^*	*Grimes*	*Black*	*Johnson M/Oldfield*
									Ref: A Ward	Six days after winning the Milk Cup, the Hatters are hit by a double blast via Drinkell's diving header and Putney's interception of a back-pass. David Oldfield comes on as a sub and they storm back. He sets up Mark Stein and a minute from time is pulled down by Gunn for a penalty.											
39		A NOTT'M FOREST		14	L		0-2	0-2		Gunn	Culverhouse	Spearing	Linighan	Phelan	Butterworth	Fox	Biggins	Fleck^	Goss*	Putney	Gordon/Ratcliffe
	4/5		*11,610*	*4*		45			*Webb 9, Glover 41*	*Sutton*	*Fleming*	*Williams*	*Chettle*	*Foster*	*Wilson^*	*Carr*	*Webb*	*Clough**	*Glover*	*Rice*	*Wilkinson/Parker*
									Ref: A Robinson	Discontent is evident in the ranks, with six Norwich players now on the transfer list: Biggins, Drinkell, Spearing, Brown, Elliott and Benstead. Teenager Lee Glover lays on Neil Webb's opener for Forest and notches the second himself. Steve Sutton makes two fine saves from Biggins.											
40		H WIMBLEDON		14	L		0-1	0-0		Gunn	Culverhouse	Spearing	Linighan	Phelan	Butterworth	Fox	Drinkell	Biggins	Goss*	Putney	Gordon
	7/5		**11,782**	*7*		45			*Gibson 82*	*Beasant*	*Goodyear*	*Phelan*	*Jones*	*Young*	*Gayle*	*Gibson**	*Gannon^*	*Fashanu*	*Sanchez*	*Cunningham*	*Hazel/Sayer*
		Home	Away						Ref: J Martin	After four draws in a row, the Dons pinch all the points when Spearing's weak back-pass lets in Terry Gibson. It's a frustrating climax to the season for City's lowest gate, who spend most of their energy chanting anti-Robert Chase slogans. Gunn collects his Player of the Year award.											
Average		16,397	15,703																		

Littlewoods Cup

Littlewoods Cup	Att		F-A	H-T	Scorers, Times, and Referees	1	2	3	4	5	6	7	8	9	10	11	subs used
2:1 A BURNLEY	17	D	1-1	1-1	Biggins 15	Gunn	Culverhouse	Elliott	Bruce	Phelan	Butterworth	Gordon	Drinkell	Biggins	Crook	Bowen	
22/9	*7,912 4:3*				*Oghani 7*	*Pearce*	*Leebrook*	*Deakin*	*Malley*	*James*	*Gardner*	*Farrell*	*Grewcock*	*Oghani*	*Comstive*	*Taylor*	
					Ref: G Courtney												

A tremendous shot by George Oghani gives Brian Miller's men the lead. Biggins, back at his former club, is barracked by home fans, but has the last laugh, equalising by heading home Crook's cross. Chris Pearce makes several fine saves. The Clarets get a standing ovation at the end.

Littlewoods Cup	Att		F-A	H-T	Scorers, Times, and Referees	1	2	3	4	5	6	7	8	9	10	11	subs used
2:2 H BURNLEY	20	W	1-0	0-0	Bowen 48	Gunn	Culverhouse	Elliott	Bruce	Phelan	Ratcliffe	Fox	Drinkell	Biggins	Williams	Bowen	
7/10	6,168 *4:10*					*Pearce*	*Leebrook*	*McGrory*	*James*	*Davis*	*Gardner*	*Farrell*	*Grewcock*	*Oghani !*	*Comstive*	*Taylor*	
					Ref: I Hemley (Norwich win 2-1 on aggregate)												

City look purposeful - not always the case against lower division opposition in recent years. Bowen has his best game yet, netting a first-time shot after Williams' corner is cleared to him. George Oghani is sent off for a series of fouls on Bruce. Andy Farrell strikes the bar near the end.

Littlewoods Cup	Att		F-A	H-T	Scorers, Times, and Referees	1	2	3	4	5	6	7	8	9	10	11	subs used
3 A STOKE	18	L	1-2	0-2	Bruce 76	Gunn	Culverhouse	Elliott	Bruce	Phelan	Ratcliffe	Fox	Drinkell	Biggins	Williams*	Bowen^	Crook/Butterworth
27/10	*8,603 2:10*				*Daly 14, Talbot 17*	*Fox*	*Dixon*	*Carr*	*Talbot*	*Hemming*	*Berry*	*Ford*	*Parkin*	*Shaw*	*Daly*	*Heath*	
					Ref: J Moules												

Mick Mills' side storm into an early lead at the Victoria Ground. Gerry Daly's 25-yarder skids in off the post and then Brian Talbot races in to convert Graham Shaw's cross. Bruce gives sorry City a chance with a late header but it's not to be. Unhappy Brown plans major team changes.

FA Cup

FA Cup	Att		F-A	H-T	Scorers, Times, and Referees	1	2	3	4	5	6	7	8	9	10	11	subs used
3 A SWINDON	16	D	0-0	0-0		Gunn	Culverhouse	Bowen	Putney	Phelan	Butterworth	Fox	Drinkell	Rosario	Goss	Gordon	
9/1	*12,807 2:11*					*Hammond*	*Hockaday*	*King*	*Kamara*	*Parkin*	*Calderwood*	*Bamber**	*Gittens*	*Quinn*	*Foley*	*White^*	*Wade/O'Regan*
					Ref: K Walmsley												

Fox shaves the woodwork after just five minutes. However, this is not a taste of things to come, and the tie degenerates into a dull affair played out in heavy conditions. Jimmy Quinn nets just before the break for Lou Macari's side, but it is ruled out because of handball by Steve Foley.

FA Cup	Att		F-A	H-T	Scorers, Times, and Referees	1	2	3	4	5	6	7	8	9	10	11	subs used
3R H SWINDON	16	L	0-2	0-0		Gunn	Culverhouse	Bowen	Putney	Phelan	Butterworth	Fox	Drinkell	Rosario*	Goss	Gordon	Fleck
13/1	12,501 *2:11*				*Bamber 67, 87*	*Hammond*	*Hockaday*	*King*	*Kamara*	*Parkin*	*Calderwood*	*Bamber*	*Gittens*	*Quinn*	*Barnes*	*O'Regan*	
					Ref: J Moules												

Norwich's luck is out tonight as Bowen hits the bar after five minutes and three further efforts are cleared off the line by defenders. Big Dave Bamber swoops twice in the second half to take his side through to face Newcastle. Tonight is one of 14 cup-ties Swindon will tackle this term.

		Home					Away					
	P	W	D	L	F	A	W	D	L	F	A	Pts
1 Liverpool	40	15	5	0	49	9	11	7	2	38	15	90
2 Manchester U	40	14	5	1	41	17	9	7	4	30	21	81
3 Nott'm For	40	11	7	2	40	17	9	6	5	27	22	73
4 Everton	40	14	4	2	34	11	5	9	6	19	16	70
5 QP Rangers	40	12	4	4	30	14	7	6	7	18	24	67
6 Arsenal	40	11	4	5	35	16	7	8	5	23	23	66
7 Wimbledon	40	8	9	3	32	20	6	6	8	26	27	57
8 Newcastle	40	9	6	5	32	23	5	8	7	23	30	56
9 Luton	40	11	6	3	40	21	3	5	12	17	37	53
10 Coventry	40	6	8	6	23	25	7	6	7	23	28	53
11 Sheffield Wed	40	10	2	8	27	30	5	6	9	25	36	53
12 Southampton	40	6	8	6	27	26	6	6	8	22	27	50
13 Tottenham	40	9	5	6	26	23	3	6	11	12	25	47
14 NORWICH	40	7	5	8	26	26	5	4	11	14	26	45
15 Derby	40	6	7	7	18	17	4	6	10	17	28	43
16 West Ham	40	6	9	5	23	21	3	6	11	17	31	42
17 Charlton	40	7	7	6	23	21	2	8	10	15	31	42
18 Chelsea *	40	7	11	2	24	17	2	4	14	26	51	42
19 Portsmouth	40	4	8	8	21	27	3	6	11	15	39	35
20 Watford	40	4	5	11	15	24	3	6	11	12	27	32
21 Oxford	40	5	7	8	24	34	1	6	13	20	46	31
	840	182	132	106	610	439	106	132	182	439	610	1128

* relegated after play-offs

Odds & ends
Double wins: (1) Tottenham.
Double losses: (5) Arsenal, Everton, Nott'm For, Sheff Wed, Wimbledon.
Won from behind: (2) Luton (a) and West Ham (h).
Lost from in front: (2) Manchester U (a) and Arsenal (h).
High points: Steering clear of relegation under new boss Stringer.
Successful big-money buys in Robert Fleck and Andy Linighan.
Doing the 'double' over Tottenham.
Holding the near-unbeatable Liverpool side at Anfield.
Hosting the high-profile debut of Newcastle's Brazilian star, Mirandinha.
Low points: The unpopular sacking of manager Ken Brown.
The climate of conflict, featuring anti-Robert Chase demonstrations.
John O'Neill's career-ending injury after 34 minutes of his debut.
Losing skipper Steve Bruce to Manchester U.
The run of poor results in the autumn.
Losing to lower division sides in FA, League and Simod Cups.
Player of the Year: Bryan Gunn.
Ever-presents: (0).
Hat-tricks: (0).
Hat-tricks against: (0).
Leading scorer: (12) Kevin Drinkell.

	Appearances						Goals			
	Lge	*Sub*	LC	*Sub*	FAC	*Sub*	Lge	LC	FAC	Tot
Benstead, Graham	**2**									
Biggins, Wayne	**15**	*5*	3				**5**	1		**6**
Bowen, Mark	**23**	*1*	3		2		**1**	1		**2**
Brown, Kenny	**7**									
Bruce, Steve	**19**		3				**2**	1		**3**
Butterworth, Ian	**34**	*1*	1	*1*	2					
Crook, Ian	**16**	*7*	1	*1*			**1**			**1**
Culverhouse, Ian	**33**		3		2					
Drinkell, Kevin	**38**		3		2		**12**			**12**
Elliott, Shaun	**14**	*2*	3							
Fleck, Robert	**18**					*1*	**7**			**7**
Fox, Ruel	**33**	*1*	2		2		**2**			**2**
Gordon, Dale	**16**	*5*	1		2		**3**			**3**
Goss, Jeremy	**20**	*2*			2		**2**			**2**
Gunn, Bryan	**38**		3		2					
Linighan, Andy	**12**						**2**			**2**
O'Neill, John	**1**									
Phelan, Mike	**37**		3		2					
Putney, Trevor	**25**	*1*			2		**1**			**1**
Ratcliffe, Simon	**6**	*3*	2							
Rosario, Robert	**9**	*5*			2		**2**			**2**
Spearing, Tony	**17**	*1*								
Williams, David	**7**	*2*	2							
23 players used	**440**	***36***	**33**	***2***	**22**	***1***	**40**	**3**		**43**

No	Date			Att	Pos	Pt	F-A	H-T	Scorers, Times, and Referees	1	2	3	4	5	6	7	8	9	10	11	subs used
1		H	NOTT'M FOREST			W	2-1	2-0	Fleck 13, Bowen 15	Gunn	Culverhouse	Bowen	Butterworth	Linighan	Crook	Gordon	Fleck*	Rosario	Phelan	Putney	**Allen**
	27/8			13,488		3			*Chettle 66*	*Sutton*	*Chettle*	*Pearce*	*Walker*	*Foster*	*Wilson*	*Crosby*	*Webb*	*Clough*	*Hodge*	*Rice**	*Carr*
									Ref: R Lewis	Six summer departures (including young Dion Dublin to Cambridge) and three arrivals, including today's debutant Malcolm Allen. A flying start as Fleck touches in Gordon's cross-shot and Bowen, surprise choice at No 3, rifles a shot home. Steve Chettle dives to head a consolation.											
2		A	MIDDLESBROUGH		4	W	3-2	2-1	Rosario 2, Fleck 35, 53	Gunn	Culverhouse	Bowen	Butterworth	Linighan	Crook	Gordon^	Fleck*	Rosario	Phelan	Putney	Allen/**Townsend**
	3/9			*18,259*	*19*	6			*Mowbray 10, Burke 58*	*Pears*	*Parkinson*	*Cooper*	*Mowbray*	*Hamilton*	*Pallister*	*Slaven*	*Brennan*	*Senior**	*Ripley*	*Burke*	*Kernaghan*
									Ref: D Allison	Rosario's speculative shot flies past Stephen Pears, but Tony Mowbray cracks a fine 25-yard equaliser. Fleck regains the lead, stabbing home off the woodwork. The points are in the bag as Mark Brennan blocks Fleck, only for his clearance to rebound into the net off the striker's shins.											
3		H	QP RANGERS		2	W	1-0	0-0	Phelan 83	Gunn	Culverhouse	Bowen	Butterworth	Linighan	Crook*	Gordon	Fleck	Rosario	Phelan	Putney	Townsend
	10/9			**11,174**	*17*	9				*Seaman*	*Fereday*	*Dennis*	*Parker*	*McDonald*	*Maddix*	*Allen M*	*Barker^*	*Coney*	*Stein*	*Brock**	*Falco/Ardiles*
									Ref: G Courtney	Defence-minded Rangers look like they've grabbed a point until Phelan strikes late in the day. The midfielder surges through and combines with Fleck before blasting a fine effort past David Seaman. Andy Townsend (£300k from Southampton) replaces Crook and looks impressive.											
4		A	NEWCASTLE		1	W	2-0	1-0	Gordon 38, Fleck 67	Gunn	Culverhouse	Bowen	Butterworth	Linighan	Crook	Gordon	Fleck	Rosario*	Phelan	Putney	Allen
	17/9			*22,801*	*20*	12				*Beasant*	*Anderson*	*Tinnion*	*McCreery*	*Scott*	*Thorn*	*Hendrie*	*Bogie*	*O'Neill**	*Jackson D*	*Robertson*	*Stephenson*
									Ref: K Breen	Norwich's best-ever start to a season - four straight wins - sees them surge to the top of the league. Gordon's lofted cross-shot deceives Dave Beasant for the first, crossing the line before being hooked clear by new signing Andy Thorn. Fleck lobs the keeper to makes sure of the points.											
5		H	MILLWALL		1	D	2-2	0-0	Crook 47, Rosario 73	Gunn	Culverhouse	Bowen	Butterworth	Linighan	Crook	Gordon	Fleck	Rosario	Phelan	Putney*	Townsend
	24/9			16,616	*3*	13			*Cascarino 48, O'Callaghan 74*	*Horne*	*Stevens*	*Dawes*	*Hurlock*	*Wood*	*McLeary*	*Lawrence*	*Briley*	*Sheringham*	*Cascarino*	*O'Callaghan*	
									Ref: J Key	City twice go ahead, but are pegged back within a minute each time by John Docherty's newly promoted outfit. Crook curls in a free-kick, only for Tony Cascarino to finish coolly seconds later. Rosario's firm header is followed by Jim Carter crossing for Kevin O'Callaghan to volley in.											
6		H	CHARLTON		2	L	1-3	1-1	Linighan 16	Gunn	Culverhouse	Bowen^	Butterworth	Linighan	Crook	Gordon	Fleck*	Rosario	Phelan	Putney	Allen/Townsend
	1/10			11,470	*13*	13			*Williams 23, 66, Mortimer 60*	*Bolder*	*Humphrey*	*Reid*	*MacKenzie*	*Shirtliff*	*Peake*	*Bennett*	*Williams*	*Gritt*	*Leaburn*	*Mortimer*	
									Ref: P Vanes	Linighan powers in a far-post header, but after this Norwich are outfought and outgunned by Lennie Lawrence's men. Paul Williams stoops to head an equaliser. Paul Mortimer, previously anonymous, scores with a marvellous solo effort. Carl Leaburn hits a post and Williams pounces.											
7		A	DERBY		1	W	1-0	0-0	Wright 53 (og)	Gunn	Culverhouse	Bowen	Butterworth	Linighan	Crook^	Gordon	Fleck*	Rosario	Phelan	Putney !	Allen/Townsend
	8/10			*14,117*	*12*	16				*Shilton*	*Sage*	*Forsyth*	*Williams*	*Wright !*	*Blades*	*McMinn*	*Penney*	*Goddard*	*Hebberd*	*Pickering*	
									Ref: A Seville	Putney fires a firm low cross into the danger area and it bobbles into his own net off hapless Mark Wright. Putney kicks out at Ted McMinn and Wright steams in with fists flying. Putney and Wright both walk. Norwich, Millwall and Coventy are the unlikely top three this evening.											
8		H	TOTTENHAM		1	W	**3-1**	2-0	Rosario 34, Fleck 43, Linighan 69	Gunn	Culverhouse	Bowen	Butterworth	Linighan	Crook	Gordon	Fleck	Rosario	Phelan	Townsend	
	22/10			20,330	*19*	19			*Fairclough 57*	*Mimms*	*Stevens*	*Thomas*	*Fenwick*	*Fairclough*	*Mabbutt*	*Stewart*	*Gascoigne*	*Waddle*	*Howells**	*Allen*	*Samways*
									Ref: K Hackett	Rosario heads home a Gordon corner-kick. Fleck scores with a shot on the turn from Rosario's pull-back. Paul Gascoigne's clever chip allows Chris Fairclough to pull one back with a crisp shot. Linighan powers in a cracking header to clinch the win and City open up a three-point lead.											
9		A	MANCHESTER U		1	W	2-1	0-0	Phelan 84, Townsend 85	Gunn	Culverhouse	Bowen	Butterworth	Linighan	Crook*	Gordon	Fleck	Rosario	Phelan	Townsend	Fox
	26/10			***36,998***	*11*	22			*Hughes 58*	*Leighton*	*Blackmore*	*Sharpe*	*Bruce*	*Garton*	*Duxbury*	*Robson*	*Strachan*	*McClair*	*Hughes*	*Davenport**	*Olsen*
									Ref: D Phillips	Mark Hughes fires United ahead, but Brian McClair has a penalty saved. A thrilling finale as Fleck equalises with a brilliant volley and then Townsend stuns Old Trafford with the winner. Next day, chairman Chase beats Bobby Charlton for a place on the FL management committee.											
10		H	SOUTHAMPTON		1	D	1-1	0-0	Fleck 47	Gunn	Culverhouse	Bowen	Butterworth	Linighan	Crook	Gordon	Fleck	Rosario	Phelan	Townsend*	Fox
	29/10			14,808	*6*	23			*Wallace D 68*	*Burridge*	*Wallace Ray*	*Statham*	*Baker*	*Moore*	*Osman*	*Wallace Rod*	*Cockerill*	*Le Tissier**	*Benali*	*Wallace D*	*Maddison*
									Ref: A Buksh	A cracking 20-yard volley comes from in-form Fleck. Saints hit back as Danny Wallace weaves through and stabs in. Townsend is carried off unconscious after a clearance hits him in the face. The Wallace trio represent the first three brothers to play in the league together for 68 years.											

11	A	WIMBLEDON	1	W	2-0	1-0	Linighan 36, Allen 72	Gunn	Culverhouse	Bowen	Butterworth	Linighan	Townsend	Gordon	Fleck*	Rosario	Phelan	Putney	Allen
5/11		*5,853*	*17*	26				*Segers*	*Joseph*	*Phelan*	*Jones*	*Young*	*Scales*	*Wise**	*Gibson*	*Fashanu*	*Sanchez*	*Fairw'ther^*	*Cork/Curle*
							Ref: J Rushton	The bludgeoning tactics of Bobby Gould's side are eclipsed by confident Norwich. Two superbly executed goals mean the gap between the Canaries and the rest is now an astonishing seven points. Phelan and Townsend look a cut above the physical endeavours of Vin Jones and Co.											
12	H	SHEFFIELD WED	1	D	1-1	1-0	Putney 29	Gunn	Culverhouse	Bowen	Butterworth	Linighan	Townsend	Gordon	Fleck*	Allen	Phelan	Putney	Taylor
12/11		14,353	*13*	27			*Sterland 88*	*Turner*	*Sterland*	*Worthington*	*Cranson*	*Pearson*	*Jonsson*	*Megson*	*Proctor*	*West*	*Reeves*	*Hodgson**	*Hirst*
							Ref: J Moules	Taylor, 35 in two days' time, asked to train with Norwich to keep fit, but gets a call-up after impressing in the reserves. Putney nets against the run of play after his ex-Ipswich mate Ian Cranson misplaces a header. Mel Sterland's fine run ends with a deflected shot bamboozling Gunn.											
13	A	EVERTON	1	D	1-1	0-0	Allen 61	Gunn	Culverhouse	Bowen	Butterworth	Linighan	Townsend	Gordon	Fleck*	Allen	Phelan	Putney	Taylor
19/11		*28,118*	*10*	28			*Steven 74p*	*Southall*	*Snodin*	*V d Hauwe*	*Ratcliffe*	*Watson*	*Reid*	*Steven*	*McCall*	*Sharp*	*Cottee*	*Wilson*	
							Ref: J Penrose	In his second full game, Welshman Allen buries an impressive far-post header from Gordon's cross. Norwich are furious when Putney's tackle on Ian Snodin prompts the ref to point to the spot. Steven scores and Everton launch a late, unsuccessful bid to end the unbeaten away record.											
14	H	LUTON	1	D	2-2	1-1	Johnson R 3 (og), Gordon 62	Gunn	Culverhouse	Bowen	Butterworth	Linighan	Townsend	Gordon	Fleck	Allen*	Phelan	Putney	Rosario
26/11		13,541	*15*	29			*Wegerle 38, 57*	*Sealey*	*Johnson R*	*Harvey*	*Preece*	*Foster*	*Johnson M*	*Wilson*	*Wegerle*	*Harford*	*Oldfield*	*Black*	
							Ref: P Danson	More misery for Rob Johnson - attacked by a teammate on a previous visit - as he deflects into his own net. Ray Harford's team look lively in attack and skilful, South African-born Roy Wegerle nets two fine goals, both with the aid of David Preece. Gordon's equaliser is a huge relief.											
15	A	ASTON VILLA	1	L	1-3	1-1	Putney 39	Gunn	Culverhouse	Bowen	Butterworth	Linighan	Townsend	Gordon^	Fleck*	Allen	Phelan	Putney	Rosario/Crook
3/12		*19,653*	*14*	29			*Gage 21,74, Platt 59*	*Spink*	*Price*	*Gray S*	*Gage*	*Evans*	*Keown*	*Gray A*	*Platt*	*McInally*	*Cowans*	*Daley*	
							Ref: J Martin	Kevin Gage has only hit three goals in 58 league matches for Villa thus far, but today he nets two volleys within an hour. David Platt has a penalty saved by Gunn, but makes amends five minute later with a header. Putney equalises Gage's first goal, firing through a ruck of players.											
16	H	ARSENAL	1	D	0-0	0-0		Gunn	Culverhouse	Bowen	Butterworth	Linighan	Townsend	Gordon	Fleck*	Rosario	Phelan	Putney	Allen
10/12		23,069	*2*	30				*Lukic*	*Dixon*	*Winterburn*	*Thomas*	*Bould*	*Adams*	*Rocastle*	*Thomas*	*Smith*	*Merson**	*Marwood*	*Hayes*
							Ref: K Morton	A much-anticipated clash between the top two clubs turns into a real anti-climax. The nearest to a goal comes when Gunn brings down Brian Marwood. The winger nets his penalty, but a re-take is ordered and he shoots over the bar. Tony Lormer joins City on loan from Newcastle.											
17	A	LIVERPOOL	1	W	1-0	0-0	Townsend 60	Gunn	Culverhouse	Bowen	Crook	Linighan	Townsend	Gordon	Fleck	Rosario	Phelan	Putney	
17/12		*34,325*	*6*	33				*Hooper*	*Ablett*	*Venison**	*Nicol*	*Whelan*	*Burrows*	*Beardsley*	*Houghton*	*Rush*	*Barnes*	*McMahon*	*Spackman*
							Ref: F Roberts	Watched by Ireland boss Jack Charlton, Townsend produces a ruthless close-range finish after an error by Reds skipper Ronnie Whelan. After this, it's backs-to-the-wall stuff to foil Kenny Dalglish's side. It's a stunning result for those who think Norwich won't last long in first place.											
18	H	WEST HAM	1	W	2-1	0-0	Gordon 53, Townsend 61	Gunn	Culverhouse	Bowen	Crook	Linighan	Townsend*	Gordon	Fleck	Rosario	Phelan	Putney	Butterworth
27/12		17,491	*20*	36			*Stewart 71p*	*McKnight*	*Potts*	*Parris*	*Gale*	*Martin**	*Devonshire*	*Brady*	*Kelly*	*Rosenior*	*Dickens^*	*Ince*	*Stewart/Keen*
							Ref: M Bailey	The club's first appearance on live TV in this top-versus-bottom clash. Erratic keeper Allen McKnight dashes out of goal but Gordon sidesteps him to score. Man-of-the-match Townsend steers in the second. David Kelly is impeded and Ray Stewart pulls one back from the penalty spot.											
19	H	MIDDLESBROUGH	2	D	0-0	0-0		Gunn	Culverhouse	Bowen	Crook	Linighan	Townsend	Gordon	Fleck*	Rosario	Phelan	Putney^	Taylor/Butterworth
31/12		16,021	*15*	37				*Pears*	*Parkinson*	*Cooper*	*Mowbray*	*Hamilton*	*Pallister*	*Slaven*	*Brennan*	*Glover*	*Davenport*	*Ripley*	
							Ref: D Elleray	A hugely disappointing display against Bruce Rioch's side, who haven't won in six games. Two efforts by Gordon are saved by Stephen Pears. Boro improve after the interval and Crook and Bowen both have to make goalline clearances. Arsenal beat Villa and go top on goal difference.											
20	A	QP RANGERS	2	D	1-1	0-0	Taylor 59	Gunn	Culverhouse	Bowen	Butterworth	Linighan^	Crook	Gordon	Taylor	Rosario*	Phelan	Townsend	Fleck/Putney
2/1		*12,410*	*14*	38			*Falco 88*	*Seaman*	*McDonald*	*Pizanti*	*Parker*	*Law*	*Maddix*	*Falco*	*Francis*	*Barker*	*Stein**	*Allen M*	*Kerslake*
							Ref: D Axcell	Veteran Taylor is now on a monthly contract, and his first full league game after eight years away from Norwich nearly has a fairytale ending. He toe-pokes past David Seaman, but Trevor Francis' men win a point at the death when Mark Falco is left free to head in Paul Parker's cross.											
21	H	COVENTRY	2	L	1-2	0-0	Gordon 56	Gunn	Culverhouse	Bowen	Butterworth	Linighan	Townsend	Gordon	Fleck	Rosario	Phelan	Putney	
14/1		14,399	*3*	38			*Speedie 65, 88*	*Ogrizovic*	*Borrows*	*Phillips*	*Sedgley*	*Kilcline*	*Peake*	*Emerson*	*Speedie*	*Regis*	*McGrath**	*Smith D*	*Clark*
							Ref: P Alcock	Gordon earns the lead, but John Sillett's Sky Blues are having a fine season and respond in style. David Speedie, the scourge of opposing fans, poaches two goals, his winner a superb chip over Gunn close to the end. Norwich apply plenty of pressure but Brian Kilcline is in great form.											

No	Date		Att	Pos	Pt	F-A	H-T	Scorers, Times, and Referees	1	2	3	4	5	6	7	8	9	10	11	subs used
22	A	MILLWALL		2	W	3-2	2-2	Butterworth 2, Bowen 7, Fleck 90	Gunn	Culverhouse	Bowen	Butterworth	Linighan	Townsend	Gordon	Fleck	Rosario	Phelan	Putney	
	22/1		*13,687*	*6*	41			*Cascarino 11, Carter 42*	*Horne*	*Salman*	*Dawes*	*Hurlock*	*Wood*	*McLeary*	*Carter*	*Morgan*	*Sheringham*	*Cascarino*	*O'Callaghan*	
								Ref: V Callow	Sunday action at Cold Blow Lane sees Norwich get off to a red-hot start. Butterworth nets his first goal in 201 league games and Bowen makes it two. Tony Cascarino and Jimmy Carter get Lions fans roaring again. In the last minute Fleck nets a cracking winner from a very tight angle.											
23	A	CHARLTON		2	W	2-1	0-0	Allen 51, Townsend 65	Gunn	Culverhouse	Bowen	Butterworth	Linighan	Townsend	Gordon	Fleck	Allen	Phelan	Putney	
	4/2		*7,518*	*17*	44			*Crooks 48*	*Bolder*	*Humphrey*	*Gritt^*	*Shirtliff*	*Pates*	*Peake*	*Lee*	*Williams*	*MacKenzie*	*Mortimer*	*Crooks**	*Leaburn/Minto*
								Ref: K Barrett	Robert Lee hits the Norwich bar, but Garth Crooks pounces to net the rebound. Norwich are soon back on terms when Allen volleys a Phelan cross past Bob Bolder. Townsend wins it by sending a sweet volley whistling in after a defender heads his free-kick straight back into his path.											
24	H	DERBY		2	W	1-0	0-0	Fleck 52	Gunn	Culverhouse	Bowen*	Butterworth	Linighan	Townsend	Gordon	Fleck	Allen	Phelan	Putney	Crook
	11/2		17,227	*8*	47				*Shilton*	*Blades*	*Forsyth*	*Williams*	*Wright*	*Hindmarch*	*McMinn*	*Saunders**	*Goddard*	*Hebberd^*	*Micklewhite*	*Penney/Cross*
								Ref: D Phillips	Arthur Cox's side have not lost an away league game for five months. City look the better side for long periods and deservedly go ahead via Fleck's backheel after good work by Allen. Stringer unloads Ratcliffe to Brentford and goes to spy on teenager Alan Shearer of Southampton.											
25	A	TOTTENHAM		2	L	1-2	0-1	Putney 53	Gunn	Culverhouse	Bowen	Butterw'th*	Linighan	Townsend	Gordon	Rosario	Allen	Phelan	Putney	Crook
	21/2		*19,120*	*11*	47			*Gascoigne 14, Waddle 66*	*Thorstvedt*	*Butters*	*Thomas*	*Nayim*	*Hughton*	*Mabbutt*	*Walsh*	*Gascoigne*	*Waddle*	*Robson**	*Allen*	*Howells*
								Ref: T Holbrook	City start the day eight points clear of third-placed Manchester U and three behind leaders Arsenal. Moroccan-born Nayim, on loan from Barcelona, makes his English debut and Spurs look to be on the up. Consolation for this narrow defeat is that Arsenal also suffer a rare loss.											
26	H	MANCHESTER U		2	W	2-1	2-0	Butterworth 18, Allen 39	Gunn	Culverhouse	Bowen	Butterworth	Linighan	Townsend	Gordon	Rosario	Allen	Phelan	Putney	
	25/2		23,155	*5*	50			*McGrath 81*	*Leighton*	*Blackmore^*	*Sharpe*	*Bruce*	*McGrath*	*Donaghy*	*Robson*	*Strachan*	*McClair*	*Hughes*	*Milne**	*Martin/Beardsmore*
								Ref: P Don	A rather subdued United are hit by two first-half goals which light up Carrow Road. Butterworth flicks the ball over Jim Leighton for the first and Allen taps in after Putney's shot was parried. United's 10-match unbeaten run ends, despite a late rally when Paul McGrath rifles a shot in.											
27	H	WIMBLEDON		2	W	1-0	0-0	Putney 52	Gunn	Culverhouse	Bowen	Butterworth	Linighan	Townsend	Gordon	Rosario	Allen	Phelan	Putney	
	11/3		15,159	*9*	53				*Segers*	*Joseph*	*Phelan*	*Jones*	*Young*	*Scales*	*Wise**	*Gibson*	*Fashanu*	*Sanchez*	*Fairw'ther^*	*Cork/Curle*
								Ref: D Hedges	Norwich maintain pressure on the leaders, but - inevitably - the points are not easily taken from Wimbledon's grasp. Just back from a break in Tenerife, the Dons crack as Roger Joseph dithers and Putney sets up Fleck. Angry boss Bobby Gould boycotts the post-game press conference.											
28	H	NEWCASTLE		2	L	0-2	0-1		Gunn	Culverhouse	Bowen	Butterworth	Linighan	Townsend	Gordon	Rosario*	Allen	Phelan	Putney	Fleck
	25/3		22,440	*19*	53			*Mirandinha 27, O'Brien 52*	*Kelly*	*Ranson*	*Sansom*	*McCreery*	*Scott*	*Thorn*	*Hendrie*	*Pingel^*	*Mirandinha**	*O'Brien*	*Brock*	*Brazil/O'Neill*
								Ref: I Hemley	Jim Smith's relegation-threatened side take advantage of a sluggish Norwich display. Two well-worked goals put a big dent in the Canaries' hopes of a league and cup double. Neat approach play by Liam O'Brien and Dane Frank Pingel leads to O'Brien thrashing home a 30-yarder.											
29	A	WEST HAM		2	W	2-0	0-0	Linighan 61, Allen 86	Gunn	Culverhouse	Bowen	Butterworth	Linighan	Townsend	Gordon	Fleck*	Allen	Phelan^	Putney	**Coney**/Crook
	27/3		*27,265*	*20*	56				*Parkes*	*Parris*	*Dicks*	*Gale*	*Hilton*	*Brady**	*Ward*	*McAvennie*	*Slater*	*Dickens*	*Ince*	*Rosenior*
								Ref: J Deakin	Dean Coney, £300k from QPR, comes on for his debut in place of Fleck, who has not scored for more than six weeks. Coney blends well with his new teammates and peps up the attack. Linighan heads the breakthrough goal and Allen wriggles into the box to make sure of the victory.											
30	H	LIVERPOOL		3	L	0-1	0-1		Gunn	Culverhouse	Bowen	Butterworth	Linighan	Townsend	Gordon	Coney	Allen*	Phelan	Putney	Fleck
	1/4		**26,338**	*2*	56			*Whelan 20*	*Grobbelaar*	*Ablett*	*Staunton*	*Nicol*	*Whelan*	*Gillespie*	*Beardsley*	*Aldridge*	*Houghton*	*Barnes*	*McMahon*	
								Ref: J Ashworth	John Barnes fails to control a Steve Staunton centre properly, but Ronnie Whelan is on hand to blast the ball home. After the interval, Barnes misses a sitter. Defeat in this 'six-pointer' - City's fifth big game in a 15-day period - is a major setback. Liverpool leapfrog into second place.											
31	A	NOTTINGHAM F		3	L	0-2	0-2		Gunn	Culverhouse	Bowen	Butterworth	Linighan	Townsend	Gordon	Coney	Allen*	Phelan	Putney	Fleck
	5/4		*19,872*	*5*	56			*Clough 27, Pearce 37*	*Sutton*	*Chettle*	*Pearce*	*Walker*	*Wilson*	*Hodge*	*Gaynor*	*Webb*	*Clough*	*Chapman**	*Parker*	*Foster*
								Ref: D Vickers	Disappointingly slack defending costs Norwich two first-half goals, put away clinically Nigel Clough and Stuart Pearce. Bowen thumps a 25-yarder against a Forest post. It's far from over yet, but most observers now feel the title race is a two-way fight between Arsenal and Liverpool.											

32	A	COVENTRY	3	L	1-2	1-1	Fleck 14	Gunn !	Culverhouse	Bowen	Butterworth	Linighan	Townsend	Gordon	Coney	Fleck	Phelan*	Putney	Crook
8/4		*12,740*	*6*	56			*Phillips 24, Speedie 67*	*Ogrizovic*	*Borrows*	*Dobson*	*Emerson*	*Kilcline*	*Peake*	*Phillips*	*Speedie*	*Regis*	*Sedgley*	*Smith D*	
							Ref: D Elleray	Fleck nets an early chance, but the Sky Blues recover well, inspired by David Speedie - once again a major thorn in Norwich's side. In the last minute Speedie is felled and Gunn is sent off for arguing about the penalty decision. Brian Kilcline blasts the kick wide with Bowen in goal.											
33	A	SOUTHAMPTON	3	D	0-0	0-0		Gunn	Culverhouse	Putney*	Butterworth	Linighan	Townsend	Gordon	Coney	Allen	Crook	Fox^	Phelan/**Cook**
19/4		*14,403*	*16*	57				*Burridge*	*Wallace Ray*	*Adams*	*Case*	*Ruddock*	*Osman*	*Wallace Rod*	*Cockerill*	*Rideout*	*Horne*	*Le Tissier*	
							Ref: B Hamer	A tame draw that seems in keeping with a sombre national mood after the Hillsborough disaster. Dumped out of the FA Cup four days earlier, the championship now slips further from Norwich's grasp. Gordon has a goal disallowed and brings a great save from acrobatic John Burridge.											
34	H	ASTON VILLA	3	D	2-2	0-0	Coney 48, Townsend 49	**Sheffield**	Culverhouse	Bowen	Butterworth	Linighan	Townsend	Gordon*	Coney	Allen	Crook	Phelan	Fox
22/4		14,550	*13*	58			*Olney 62, McInally 69*	*Spink*	*Price*	*Gray S*	*Evans*	*Sims*	*Keown*	*Callaghan*	*Platt*	*McInally*	*Cowans**	*Olney*	*Ormondroyd*
							Ref: T Ward	Sheffield, the last apprentice signed before YTS was introduced, plays his first and last game in place of the suspended Gunn. Nigel Spink races out to clear but the ball hits Coney and loops in. Gordon's great run sets up Townsend, but Norwich allow the comfortable lead to vanish.											
35	A	ARSENAL	3	L	**0-5**	0-2	*[Rocastle 54, 82]*	Gunn	Culverhouse	Bowen	Butterworth	Linighan	Townsend	Gordon	Fleck	Coney	Phelan	Putney	
1/5		*28,449*	*1*	58			*Winterburn 15, Smith 37, 80,*	*Lukic*	*Dixon*	*Winterburn*	*Thomas*	*Bould*	*Adams*	*Rocastle*	*Thomas*	*Smith*	*Merson**	*Marwood*	*Hayes*
							Ref: G Courtney	The league leaders outclass Norwich. This mauling is the worst defeat in over eight years and leaves Stringer visibly upset in media interviews later on. George Graham's rampant side are never in any trouble. David Rocastle caps things with a magical run down the right before scoring.											
36	H	EVERTON	3	W	1-0	0-0	Gordon 88	Gunn	Culverhouse	Crook	Butterworth	Linighan*	Townsend	Gordon	Fleck	Rosario	Phelan	Cook	Putney
6/5		13,239	*12*	61				*Southall*	*McDonald*	*Pointon*	*Ratcliffe*	*Watson*	*Bracewell*	*Steven*	*McCall*	*Clarke*	*Cottee*	*Sheedy*	
							Ref: A Buksh	Norwich create the best opportunities and Townsend sees three cracking drives all superbly saved by Neville Southall. Gordon was presented with the Player of the Year award before the start and becomes hero of the day when he sweeps home a stylish goal two minutes from the end.											
37	A	LUTON	4	L	0-1	0-0		Gunn	Culverhouse	Crook	Butterworth	Putney	Townsend	Gordon*	Fleck	Rosario	Phelan^	Cook	Allen/Coney
13/5		*10,862*	*16*	61			*Wilson 62p*	*Chamberlain*	*Breacker*	*Dreyer*	*Preece*	*Foster*	*Beaumont*	*Wilson*	*Wegerle*	*Harford*	*Hill*	*Black*	
							Ref: M Bailey	This game means far more to Luton, who need to win to avoid the drop. An early penalty is blasted wide by Danny Wilson. Mick Harford hits a post with a header for the anxious Hatters. Rosario pushes Harford and Wilson bravely steps up to score with his second penalty of the game.											
38	A	SHEFFIELD WED	4	D	2-2	0-0	Rosario 68, Fleck 84	Gunn	Culverhouse	Bowen	Butterworth	Linighan	Townsend	Gordon	Fleck	Rosario	Crook	Cook	
17/5		*16,238*	*15*	62			*Linighan 73 (og), Reeves 82*	*Turner*	*Harper*	*Wood*	*Palmer*	*Pearson*	*Madden*	*Bennett*	*Fee*	*Whitton*	*Hirst*	*Galvin**	*Reeves*
	Home	Away					Ref: R Wiseman	Delayed by the Hillsborough tragedy, this fixture proves surprisingly entertaining for an end-of-season affair. Rosario ends his goal drought with a curling shot. Linighan stabs an attempted clearance past Gunn and David Reeves shoots a second. Fleck's looping header saves a point.											
Average	16,785	19,089																	

Littlewoods Cup		Att			F-A	H-T	Scorers, Times, and Referees	1	2	3	4	5	6	7	8	9	10	11	subs used
2:1	H PRESTON		1	W	2-0	1-0	Rosario 15, Crook 57	Gunn	Culverhouse	Bowen	Butterworth	Linighan	Crook*	Gordon	Fleck^	Rosario	Phelan	Putney	Townsend/Allen
	28/9	7,484	*3:19*					*Brown*	*Rathbone*	*McAteer*	*Atkins*	*Jones*	*Allardyce*	*Miller**	*Swann*	*Ellis*	*Brazil*	*Patterson*	*Mooney*
							Ref: D Vickers	Rosario's header sets the Canaries on their way. Tony Ellis looks impressive for John McGrath's side. Preston have several opportunities and from one, Ellis's header brings an acrobatic save out of Gunn. Stringer warns that the tie is not over yet, despite the comfortable-looking lead.											
2:2	A PRESTON		1	W	3-0	1-0	Fleck 9, Gordon 47, Rosario 71	Gunn	Culverhouse	Bowen	Butterworth	Linighan	Crook	Gordon	Fleck	Rosario	Phelan	Putney	
	11/10	*7,002*	*3:13*					*Brown*	*Rathbone*	*Williams N*	*Atkins*	*Wrightson*	*Hughes**	*Mooney*	*Swann*	*Ellis*	*Joyce*	*Patterson*	*Jones*
							Ref: V Callow (Norwich win 5-0 on aggregate)	Fleck converts a knockdown by Linighan early on to knock the stuffing out of Preston. This kills off any chance of a cup shock and, befitting the league leaders, Norwich knock the ball around stylishly on the artificial surface. Manager McGrath is critical of his side's slack defending.											
3	A LEICESTER		1	L	0-2	0-1		Gunn	Culverhouse	Bowen*	Butterworth	Linighan	Crook^	Gordon	Fleck	Rosario	Phelan	Putney	Allen/Fox
	2/11	*14,586*	*2:14*				*Newell 16, Reid 81*	*Cooper*	*Paris*	*Spearing*	*Mauchlen*	*Walsh*	*Morgan*	*Reid*	*Cross*	*Newell*	*McAllister*	*Russell*	
							Ref: D Wiseman	David Pleat's side go ahead when Mike Newell nets a thunderous header from Nicky Cross's centre. Leicester are outplayed for long spells, but the Canaries can produce no end result. Putney strikes the bar with a fine shot from 25 yards. Paul Reid's goal ensures the Foxes' passage.											

FA Cup																			
3	A PORT VALE		2	W	3-1	0-1	Townsend 64, 73, Fleck 66	Gunn	Culverhouse	Bowen	Butterworth	Linighan	Townsend	Gordon	Taylor*	Rosario	Phelan	Putney	Fleck
	8/1	*15,697*	*3:2*				*Webb 33*	*Grew*	*Webb*	*Hughes*	*Walker*	*Hazell*	*Sproson*	*Mills*	*Earle*	*Futcher*	*Beckford*	*Riley*	
							Ref: G Tyson	Alan Webb's fine strike has Canaries fans fearing that another giant-killing is on the way. Enter Townsend, whose equaliser is a gem of a shot. Fleck comes on as sub for veteran Taylor and soon ends an 11-game barren spell. Townsend surges clear and produces a deft chip for the third.											
4	H SUTTON UNITED		2	W	8-0	3-0	Putney 13, Allen 15, 46, 72, 84, [Fleck 36, 50, 55]	Gunn	Culverhouse	Bowen	Butterworth	Linighan	Townsend*	Gordon	Fleck	Allen	Phelan	Putney	Crook
	28/1	23,073	*NL*					*Roffey*	*Jones*	*Rains*	*Golley*	*Pratt*	*Rogers*	*Stephens*	*Dawson*	*Dennis*	*McKinnon*	*Hanlon*	
							Ref: V Callow	Conference side Sutton beat Coventry in Round 3, but City show no mercy in this club-record cup win. It's the biggest fourth round victory by anyone in 30 years. Allen and Fleck run riot after Putney's volley starts the rout. On a wet pitch, Sutton are caught square time and time again.											
5	H SHEFFIELD U		2	W	3-2	1-1	Thomps'n 11(og), Allen 71p, Gordon 81	Gunn	Culverhouse	Bowen	Butterworth	Linighan	Townsend	Gordon	Fleck*	Allen	Phelan	Putney	Rosario
	18/2	24,139	*3:4*				*Deane 37, Agana 72*	*Benstead*	*Smtih*	*Pike*	*Booker*	*Stancliffe*	*Thompson*	*Duffield*	*Todd*	*Agana*	*Deane*	*Bryson*	
							Ref: R Groves	Steve Thompson slides in to intercept a cross, but pokes the ball past ex-Canary Graham Benstead. Brian Deane levels for Dave Bassett's men. Phelan is upended to give Allen his chance from the spot. Another equaliser is followed by Gordon's super-cool finish to win a real cup thriller.											
QF	A WEST HAM		2	D	0-0	0-0		Gunn	Culverhouse	Bowen	Butterworth	Linighan	Townsend	Gordon	Allen*	Rosario	Phelan	Putney	Fox
	18/3	*29,119*	*20*					*Parkes*	*Potts*	*Dicks*	*Gale*	*Strodder*	*Devonshire**	*Kelly*	*Dickens*	*Slater*	*Brady*	*Ince*	*Keen*
							Ref: L Shapter	Norwich frustrate John Lyall's men and the Upton Park crowd with a dominant display. Townsend and Phelan run things stylishly in midfield. Gordon is highly unlucky not to break the deadlock, forcing a tremendous save from Phil Parkes. He also hits the bar. Fox gets a rare run-out.											
QF R	H WEST HAM		2	W	3-1	2-0	Allen 25, 27, Gordon 85	Gunn	Culverhouse	Bowen	Butterworth	Linighan	Townsend*	Gordon	Allen	Rosario	Phelan	Putney	Crook
	22/3	25,785	*20*				*Ince 74*	*Parkes*	*Potts*	*Dicks*	*Gale*	*Strodder*	*Devonshire**	*Kelly^*	*Dickens*	*Slater*	*Brady*	*Ince*	*Keen/Hilton*
							Ref: L Shapter	A fine cup-tie in a lively atmsophere sees Rosario set up two for Allen in a two-minute spell. Allen knows he is under pressure from new recruit Coney and fit-again Fleck, but he blots his copybook by letting in Paul Ince with a poor back-pass. Gordon's goal eases any worries.											
SF	N EVERTON		3	L	0-1	0-1		Gunn	Culverhouse	Bowen	Butterworth	Linighan	Townsend	Gordon	Allen*	Rosario	Crook	Putney	Fox
	15/4	*46,533*	*11*				*Nevin 26*	*Southall*	*McDonald*	*V d Hauwe*	*Ratcliffe*	*Watson*	*Bracewell*	*Nevin*	*Steven*	*Sharp*	*Cottee*	*Sheedy*	
	(At Villa Park)						Ref: G Courtney	Fleck is missing after the sudden death of his father and Phelan fails a fitness test. Pat van den Hauwe's cross is sliced by Crook against the bar, Kevin Sheedy hits a post with the rebound and Nevin pokes it in. The misery of defeat is soon overshadowed by the news from Hillsborough.											

		Home						Away					
		P	W	D	L	F	A	W	D	L	F	A	Pts
1	Arsenal	38	10	6	3	35	19	12	4	3	38	17	76
2	Liverpool	38	11	5	3	33	11	11	5	3	32	17	76
3	Nott'm For	38	8	7	4	31	16	9	6	4	33	27	64
4	NORWICH	38	8	7	4	23	20	9	4	6	25	25	62
5	Derby	38	9	3	7	23	18	8	4	7	17	20	58
6	Tottenham	38	8	6	5	31	24	7	6	6	29	22	57
7	Coventry	38	9	4	6	28	23	5	9	5	19	19	55
8	Everton	38	10	7	2	33	18	4	5	10	17	27	54
9	QP Rangers	38	9	5	5	23	16	5	6	8	20	21	53
10	Millwall	38	10	3	6	27	21	4	8	7	20	31	53
11	Manchester U	38	10	5	4	27	13	3	7	9	18	22	51
12	Wimbledon	38	10	3	6	30	19	4	6	9	20	27	51
13	Southampton	38	6	7	6	25	26	4	8	7	27	40	45
14	Charlton	38	6	7	6	25	24	4	5	10	19	34	42
15	Sheffield Wed	38	6	6	7	21	25	4	6	9	13	26	42
16	Luton	38	8	6	5	32	21	2	5	12	10	31	41
17	Aston Villa	38	7	6	6	25	22	2	7	10	20	34	40
18	Middlesbro	38	6	7	6	28	30	3	5	11	16	31	39
19	West Ham	38	3	6	10	19	30	7	2	10	18	32	38
20	Newcastle	38	3	6	10	19	28	4	4	11	13	35	31
		760	157	112	111	538	424	111	112	157	424	538	1028

Odds & ends

Double wins: (4) Derby, Manchester U, West Ham, Wimbledon.
Double losses: (1) Coventry.

Won from behind: (3) Charlton (a), Manchester U (a), Port Vale (a) (FAC).
Lost from in front: (3) Charlton (h), Coventry (h) and Coventry (a).

High points: The best ever League position – despite the late slump.
Topping the Football League for more than three months.
Maintaining the chance of a League and Cup double until mid-April.
A club record FA Cup win of 8-0 over Sutton.
Six successive away wins at the start of the season.

Low points: Losing an FA Cup semi-final, on the day of Hillsborough.
The disappointing end to a season: 1 win from the last 10 games.
The five-goal humiliation at Arsenal on 1 May.

Player of the Year: Dale Gordon.
Ever-presents: (2) Ian Culverhouse and Dale Gordon.
Hat-tricks: (2) Malcolm Allen (4), Robert Fleck (both v Sutton, FAC).
Hat-tricks against: (0).
Leading scorer: (15) Robert Fleck.

	Appearances						Goals			
	Lge	*Sub*	LC	*Sub*	FAC	*Sub*	**Lge**	LC	FAC	**Tot**
Allen, Malcolm	**15**	*8*		*2*	5		**5**		7	**12**
Bowen, Mark	**35**		3		6		**2**			**2**
Butterworth, Ian	**35**	*2*	3		6		**2**			**2**
Coney, Dean	**6**	*2*					**1**			**1**
Cook, Paul	**3**	*1*								
Crook, Ian	**19**	*7*	3		1	*3*	**1**	1		**2**
Culverhouse, Ian	**38**		3		6					
Fleck, Robert	**29**	*4*	3		2	*1*	**10**	1	4	**15**
Fox, Ruel	**1**	*3*		*1*		*2*				
Gordon, Dale	**38**		3		6		**5**	1	2	**8**
Gunn, Bryan	**37**		3		6					
Linighan, Andy	**37**		3		6		**4**			**4**
Phelan, Mike	**36**	*1*	3		5		**2**			**2**
Putney, Trevor	**31**	*2*	3		6		**4**		1	**5**
Rosario, Robert	**25**	*2*	3		4	*1*	**4**	2		**6**
Sheffield, Jon	**1**									
Taylor, Alan	**1**	*3*			1		**1**			**1**
Townsend, Andy	**31**	*5*		*1*	6		**5**		2	**7**
(own-goals)							**2**		1	**3**
18 players used	**418**	***40***	**33**	***4***	**66**	***7***	**48**	**5**	**17**	**70**

No	Date		Att	Pos	Pt	F-A	H-T	Scorers, Times, and Referees	1	2	3	4	5	6	7	8	9	10	11	subs used
1	A	SHEFFIELD WED			W	**2-0**	1-0	Phillips 3, Fleck 71	Gunn	Culverhouse	Bowen	Butterworth	Linighan	Townsend	Gordon	Fleck	Coney	Crook	**Phillips**	
	19/8		*19,142*		3				*Turner*	*Harper*	*Worthington*	*Palmer*	*Pearson*	*Madden*	*Bennett*	*Barrick*	*Whitton**	*Atkinson*	*Shakespeare*	*Hirst*
								Ref: A Buksh	Skipper Phelan has joined Manchester U (£750k). His place goes to new signing Phillips (£550k) from Coventry. It's a dream start for Phillips as he tucks away Culverhouse's cross. Ron Atkinson's men are sunk without trace after Coney touches on Gordon's centre for Fleck to convert.											
2	H	NOTT'M FOREST			D	1-1	1-0	Gordon 27	Gunn	Culverhouse	Bowen	Butterw'th*	Linighan	Townsend	Gordon	Fleck	Coney	Crook	Phillips	Cook
	23/8		18,267		4			*Chapman 67*	*Sutton*	*Laws*	*Pearce*	*Walker*	*Foster*	*Hodge*	*Carr*	*Parker*	*Clough*	*Chapman*	*Crosby*	
								Ref: D Vickers	Gordon fires Norwich ahead, but the defence has to reorganise when Butterworth goes off with concussion. Lee Chapman levels for Brian Clough's side, exploiting defensive hesitation. Culverhouse's tackle on Gary Crosby looks worthy of a penalty, but Mr Vickers is unmoved.											
3	H	QP RANGERS		7	D	0-0	0-0		Gunn	Culverhouse	Bowen	**Sherwood**	Linighan	Townsend	Gordon	Fleck	Coney	Crook	Phillips	
	26/8		14,021	*8*	5				*Seaman*	*Channing*	*Sansom*	*Parker*	*McDonald*	*Spackman*	*Barker*	*Reid*	*Clarke**	*Wright^*	*Sinton*	*Kerslake/Falco*
								Ref: K Barratt	Both sides remain unbeaten, but there's little to entertain the fans. Sherwood, signed from Watford (£175k) debuts. Linighan snuffs out any threat from Rangers, while David Seaman is in commanding form at the other end. Trevor Francis is having a rocky start as QPR manager.											
4	A	MANCHESTER U		2	W	**2-0**	1-0	Gordon 44, Fleck 78p	Gunn	Culverh'se*	Bowen	Butterworth	Linighan	Townsend	Gordon	Fleck	Rosario	Cook	Phillips	Sherwood
	30/8		***39,610***	*14*	8				*Leighton*	*Duxbury*	*Blackmore**	*Bruce*	*Phelan*	*Pallister*	*Robson^*	*Webb*	*McClair*	*Hughes*	*Sharpe*	*Robins/Martin*
								Ref: K Cooper	Superb work by Townsend and Fleck fashions the opening goal, which is nicely taken by Gordon. Alex Ferguson's men suffer a blow as Bryan Robson exits with a rib injury. Costly signing Gary Pallister (£2.3m) makes his debut, but hauls down Rosario for Fleck to clinch the victory.											
5	H	SOUTHAMPTON		3	D	4-4	1-2	Rosario 27, 84, Sherw'd 48, Fleck 77	Gunn	Sherwood*	Bowen	Butterworth	Linighan	Townsend	Gordon	Fleck	Rosario	Crook	Phillips	Cook
	9/9		14,259	*9*	9			*Rideout 7, 50, Wallace Rod 39, 47*	*Flowers*	*Wallace Ray*	*Adams*	*Case*	*Ruddock*	*Moore**	*Wallace Rod*	*Cockerill*	*Rideout*	*Horne*	*Wallace D*	*Osman*
								Ref: T Ward	A breathless thriller that banishes memories of the last two dull home games. Paul Rideout's headed goal is cancelled out by a stunning 30-yard dipper from Rosario, which subsequenlty wins ITV Goal of the Season. A game of ebb and flow ends level as Fleck volleys in Crook's cross.											
6	A	LIVERPOOL		7	D	0-0	0-0		Gunn	Sherwood	Bowen	Butterworth	Linighan	Townsend	Gordon	Fleck	Rosario	Crook	Phillips	
	16/9		*36,885*	*2*	10				*Grobbelaar*	*Hysen*	*Burrows*	*Nicol*	*Whelan*	*Hansen*	*Beardsley*	*Gillespie*	*Rush*	*Barnes*	*McMahon*	
								Ref: R Milford	A disciplined performance by Norwich wins a point at Anfield, just four days after the Reds hit nine against Palace. Gunn is star of the show with excellent saves from Nicol and Beardsley. It's his third successive clean sheet against Liverpool. Skipper Butterworth is outstanding too.											
7	H	TOTTENHAM		7	D	2-2	0-2	Phillips 48, Bowen 57	Gunn	Sherwood	Bowen	Butterworth	Linighan	Townsend	Gordon	Fleck	Rosario	Crook	Phillips	
	23/9		20,095	*19*	11			*Gascoigne 20, Lineker 34*	*Thorstvedt*	*Butters*	*V d Hauwe*	*Fenwick*	*Thomas*	*Mabbutt*	*Samways**	*Gascoigne*	*Stewart*	*Lineker^*	*Sedgley*	*Robson/Walsh*
								Ref: V Callow	Gary Lineker scores his first Spurs goal since signing from Barcelona to put Terry Venables men two ahead. City surge back after the break with Phillips powering through and netting an unstoppable shot. Bowen, against his former club, adds the finishing touch to a move he started.											
8	A	MILLWALL		4	W	1-0	0-0	Bowen 60	Gunn	Sherwood	Bowen	Butterworth	Linighan	Townsend	Gordon	Fleck	Rosario	Crook	Phillips	
	30/9		*13,295*	*5*	14				*Horne*	*Stevens*	*Dawes*	*Hurlock*	*Thompson*	*Wood*	*Carter^*	*Waddock*	*Sheringham*	*Cascarino*	*Anthrobus**	*Torpey/Sparham*
								Ref: L Shapter	The Lions were top at the beginning of September, but this is their third defeat since then. A cool finish by Bowen sees Norwich leapfrog them in the table. City have gone six hours-plus without conceding an away goal. A £1m plan for a 24-acre training HQ at Little Melton is revealed.											
9	H	CHELSEA		3	W	**2-0**	1-0	Bowen 14, Fleck 50p	Gunn	Sherwood	Bowen	Butterworth	Linighan	Townsend	Gordon	Fleck	Rosario	Crook	Phillips	
	14/9		19,042	*5*	17				*Beasant*	*Clarke*	*Dorigo*	*Bumstead*	*Lee*	*Monkou*	*Dickens**	*NIcholas*	*Dixon*	*Wilson K*	*Hazard^*	*Wilson C/McAllister*
								Ref: T Simpson	Full-back Bowen's purple patch continues as he lashes a powerful left-footer into the roof of Dave Beasant's net. Steve Clarke trips Gordon for Fleck to convert the penalty. Bobby Campbell's newly promoted side go close when Gunn pushes a Kevin Wilson header against the crossbar.											
10	A	LUTON		6	L	1-4	0-1	Allen 83p *[Williams 76]*	Gunn	Sherwood	Bowen	Butterworth	Linighan	Fox*	Gordon	Fleck^	Rosario	Crook	Phillips	Goss/Allen
	21/10		*9,038*	*12*	17			*Black 4, Dreyer 54, Wilson 65,*	*Chamberlain*	*Breacker*	*Dreyer*	*Wilson*	*Rodger**	*Beaumont*	*Williams*	*Wegerle*	*Elstrup*	*Preece*	*Black^*	*Harvey/Dowie*
								Ref: B Stevens	Kingsley Black's deflected shot ends the run of away clean sheets. After the injured ref is replaced, John Dreyer converts achipped pass from Steve Williams. Danny Wilson rockets in a fine shot and Williams wallops an even better fourth. Dreyer pushes Goss for Allen's consolation.											

11	H	EVERTON		3	D	1-1	1-0	Linighan 45	Gunn	Culverhouse	Bowen	Butterworth	Linighan	Townsend*	Gordon	Fleck	Rosario	Crook^	Phillips	Allen/Sherwood
28/10			18,637	*1*	18			*Cottee 67*	*Southall*	*Ebbrell*	*McDonald*	*Keown*	*Watson*	*Whiteside*	*Nevin*	*McCall*	*Newell*	*Cottee*	*Sheedy*	
								Ref: D Hedges	Leaders Everton are stunned as Linighan produces a towering header from Phillips' free-kick just before the interval. After the break Phillips is guilty of a bad miss and Fleck hits a post. Colin Harvey's men then level, when Tony Cottee's mis-hit shot fools Gunn and trickles into the net.											
12	A	ARSENAL		6	L	3-4	2-0	Allen 19, Phillips 30, Sherwood 76	Gunn	Culverhouse	Bowen	Butterworth	Linighan	Sherwood	Gordon	Allen	Rosario	Goss	Phillips	
4/11			*35,338*	*3*	18			*Quinn 55, Dixon 62p, 90, O'Leary 78*	*Lukic*	*Dixon*	*Winterburn*	*Thomas*	*O'Leary*	*Adams*	*Rocastle*	*Richardson*	*Smith*	*Quinn*	*Merson**	*Groves*
								Ref: G Tyson	An amazing tale of two disputed penalties. The first, for handball by Linighan, brings the Gunners back to 2-2. The next, for a pull on Lee Dixon in the last minute, leads to their winner. Gunn saves the kick, but the rebound is scrambled in by Dixon, sparking an ugly 20-man brawl.											
13	H	ASTON VILLA		6	W	**2-0**	0-0	Mountfield 46 (og), Linighan 68	Gunn	Culverhouse	Bowen	Butterworth	Linighan	Sherwood	Gordon	Allen	Coney	Townsend	Phillips	
11/11			18,186	*5*	21				*Spink*	*Price*	*Comyn*	*McGrath**	*Mountfield*	*Nielsen*	*Callaghan*	*Platt*	*Olney*	*Cowans*	*Ormond'yd^*	*Blake/Williams*
								Ref: H King	Dererk Moutfield's unlucky intervention is a blow for Graham Taylor's outfit and Norwich maintain their top-six place. Also unlucky is Coney, being barracked for a lack of goals. The FA is looking into the Highbury brawl and a fine of £50k is on the way for City and £20k for Arsenal.											
14	H	CHARLTON		6	D	0-0	0-0		Gunn	Culverhouse	Bowen	Butterworth	Linighan	Townsend*	Gordon	Allen	Coney^	Sherwood	Phillips	Crook/Rosario
18/11			16,084	*17*	22				*Bolder*	*Humphrey*	*Reid*	*Peake*	*Caton*	*Minto*	*Lee R*	*Williams*	*Leaburn*	*Mortimer*	*Walsh*	
								Ref: K Barratt	Norwich are in control for long periods against Lennie Lawrence's unadventurous side. Bob Bolder makes an outstanding save from Coney. Gunn is hardly troubled. Danish U-21 forward Henrik Mortensen, who cost £360k from Aarhus last month, is waiting patiently for a call-up.											
15	A	COVENTRY		8	L	0-1	0-0		Gunn	Culverhouse	Bowen	Butterworth	Linighan	Townsend	Gordon	Allen	Rosario	Sherwood	Phillips	
25/11			*11,999*	*6*	22			*Regis 84*	*Ogrizovic*	*Borrows*	*Downs*	*MacDonald*	*Billing*	*Peake*	*Gynn*	*Speedie*	*Regis*	*Drinkell*	*Smith*	
								Ref: A Dilkes	Former Canaries Kevin Drinkell and Greg Downs line up against City. The former misses three good chances to score, before the in-form Cyrille Regis converts a Drinkell flick-on. Big Steve Ogrizonic keeps Norwich at bay with great saves from Linighan, Gordon and Rosario.											
16	H	SHEFFIELD W		5	W	2-1	2-1	Townsend 22p, King 42 (og)	Gunn	Sherwood*	Bowen	Butterworth	Linighan	Townsend	Gordon	**Mortensen**	Rosario^	Crook	Phillips	Culverhouse/Coney
2/12			15,341	*17*	25			*Hirst 14*	*Pressman*	*King*	*Worthington*	*Palmer*	*Pearson*	*Shirtliff*	*Bennett*	*Sheridan*	*Hirst*	*Atkinson*	*Shakesp're**	*Whitton*
								Ref: R Lewis	Mortensen's midweek scoring debut in the ZDS Cup 5-0 win over Brighton convinces Stringer he's now ready for the top flight. David Hirst is teed up by Dalian Atkinson, but Mortensen is brought down by Nigel Worthington for a penalty equaliser. Phil King's blunder proves decisive.											
17	A	NOTTINGHAM F		4	W	1-0	1-0	Bowen 45	Gunn	Culverhouse	Bowen	Butterworth	Linighan	Townsend	Gordon	Mortensen	Rosario	Crook	Phillips	
9/12			*18,939*	*11*	28				*Sutton*	*Laws*	*Pearce*	*Walker*	*Chettle*	*Hodge*	*Crosby*	*Parker*	*Clough*	*Chapman*	*Rice*	
								Ref: D Allison	Lee Chapman and Steve Hodge both strike the frame of Gunn's goal, but Norwich stay cool and surge ahead with a cracking left-foot drive by Bowen on the stroke of half-time. Forest are held at bay after the interval and the Canaries' drought at the City Ground is over after 15 years.											
18	H	DERBY		4	W	1-0	1-0	Rosario 16	Gunn	Culverhouse	Bowen	Butterworth	Linighan	Townsend	Gordon	Mortensen	Rosario	Crook	Phillips	
16/12			16,184	*9*	31				*Shilton*	*Sage*	*Forsyth*	*Williams*	*Wright*	*Hindmarch^*	*Pickering*	*Saunders*	*Goddard*	*Hebberd**	*Micklewhite*	*Cross/Blades*
								Ref: M Bailey	One of the tightest defences in the league is unlocked early on when Mortensen sets up a close-range goal for Rosario. Norwich produce some flowing football and the passing is excellent. Arthur Cox's side hadn't been beaten in seven matches before this, including six successive wins.											
19	A	MANCHESTER C		4	L	0-1	0-0		Gunn	Culverhouse	Bowen	Butterworth	Linighan	Townsend	Gordon	Mortensen*	Rosario	Crook	Phillips	Sherwood
26/12			*29,534*	*19*	31			*Allen 86*	*Dibble*	*Harper*	*Hinchcliffe*	*Reid*	*Hendrey*	*Redmond*	*White*	*Bishop*	*Morley^*	*Megson**	*Lake*	*Brightwell/Allen*
								Ref: M Reed	Ex-Canaries' coach Mel Machin was sacked as Blues manager last month and Howard Kendall is now in charge. Norwich ended their Forest hoodoo recently, but sub Clive Allen's late goal means it's 25 years since a win on this ground. The home side enjoy a first win in eight games.											
20	A	CRYSTAL PALACE		6	L	0-1	0-0		Gunn	Culverhouse	Bowen	Butterworth	Linighan	Townsend	Gordon	Mortensen*	Rosario	Crook^	Phillips	Fleck/Sherwood
30/12			*14,250*	*12*	31			*Wright 58*	*Martyn*	*Pemberton*	*Dennis*	*Gray*	*Hopkins*	*Thorn*	*McGoldrick*	*Barber*	*Wright*	*Bright*	*Pardew*	
								Ref: R Lewis	More holiday gloom for lack-lustre Norwich on their travels. Ian Wright and Andy Gray work tirelessly and Wright is rewarded with his 11th goal of the season when his header from John Pemberton's cross is deflected over Gunn. Nigel Martyn makes an excellent save from Bowen.											
21	H	WIMBLEDON		6	L	0-1	0-0		Gunn	Culverhouse	Bowen	Butterworth	Linighan	Townsend	Gordon	Fleck	Rosario	Crook	Phillips	
1/1			16,680	*12*	31			*Gibson 90*	*Segers*	*Kruszynski*	*Phelan*	*Scales*	*Young*	*Curle*	*Fairweather*	*Fashanu*	*Gibson*	*Ryan*	*Wise**	*Cork*
								Ref: D Phillips	Norwich enjoy far more possession but find Hans Segers in fine form. Three saves in particular are top drawer. With City pushing forward in seach of a winner, Keith Curle joins a Dons attack and Terry Gibson snatches a soul-destroying late goal. It's City's fifth successive 1-0 result.											

No	Date		Att	Pos	Pt	F-A	H-T	Scorers, Times, and Referees	1	2	3	4	5	6	7	8	9	10	11	subs used
22	A	QP RANGERS		9	L	1-2	0-0	Gordon 70	Gunn	Culverhouse	Bowen*	Butterworth	Linighan	Townsend	Gordon	Fleck	Rosario	Crook	Phillips	Sherwood
	13/1		*11,439*	*13*	31			*Falco 49, Clarke 83*	*Seaman*	*Bardsley*	*Sansom*	*Parker*	*McDonald*	*Maddix*	*Barker*	*Wilkins*	*Falco**	*Wegerle*	*Sinton*	*Clarke*
								Ref: G Courtney	Rangers are climbing the table after a troubled autumn, and open the scoring when Kenny Sansom's cross is blasted in on the volley by Mark Falco. Gordon raises Norwich hopes with a well-worked equaliser. Sub Colin Clarke wins it with his first touch after a poor pass by Linighan.											
23	H	MANCHESTER U		8	W	**2-0**	0-0	Fleck 70, 85	Gunn	Culverhouse	Bowen	Butterworth	Linighan	Townsend	Gordon	Fleck	Rosario	Crook	Phillips	
	21/1		17,370	*17*	34				*Leighton*	*Anderson*	*Martin*	*Bruce*	*Phelan**	*Pallister*	*Robins*	*Ince^*	*McClair*	*Hughes*	*Wallace*	*Blackm're/Beards're*
								Ref: T Holbrook	Stringer keeps faith with the same line-up, despite four successive defeats. A thrilling finale in front of the live TV cameras sees Fleck pounce twice to sink United. Scotland manager Andy Roxburgh is in the crowd and shortly afterwards selects Fleck for a World Cup warm-up game.											
24	A	TOTTENHAM		9	L	**0-4**	0-2		Gunn	Culverhouse	Bowen	Sherwood	Linighan	Townsend	Gordon	Fleck	Rosario^	Crook	Phillips*	Goss/Coney
	4/2		*19,599*	*5*	34			*Lineker 24, 47p, 63, Howells 44*	*Thorstvedt*	*Hughton*	*V d Hauwe*	*Polston*	*Howells*	*Mabbutt*	*Walsh*	*Gascoigne*	*Nayim*	*Lineker**	*Sedgley*	*Moran*
								Ref: R Groves	Lethal Gary Lineker is simply too sharp for City today. His lightning reactions and speed off the mark play a key part in all three of his goals. He was pulled down by Gunn for the penalty. But it's not all one-way traffic - Townsend and Coney both strike Erik Thorstvedt's woodwork.											
25	H	LIVERPOOL		10	D	0-0	0-0		Gunn	Culverhouse	Bowen	Sherwood	Linighan	Townsend	Gordon	Fleck	Coney*	Crook	Phillips	Allen
	10/2		**20,210**	*1*	35				*Grobbelaar*	*Hysen !*	*Venison*	*Nicol*	*Whelan*	*Hansen*	*Beardsley*	*Burrows*	*Rush*	*Barnes*	*McMahon*	
								Ref: D Phillips	Another battling display against The Reds, but again no goals. It's the fifth goalless draw between these sides in their last seven meetings - and the other two ended 1-0. Glenn Hysen departs the field after two yellow cards - both for fouls on Fleck. A Coventry bid for Crook is rejected.											
26	A	SOUTHAMPTON		12	L	1-4	1-0	Allen 18	Gunn	Culverhouse	Bowen	**Pennock**	Linighan*	Townsend	Gordon^	Fleck	Allen	Crook	Phillips	Mortensen/Goss
	27/2		*13,668*	*6*	35			*Le Tissier 55, 62, 87, Moore 82*	*Flowers*	*Dodd*	*Benali*	*Davis*	*Osman*	*Moore*	*Wallace Rod*	*Cockerill*	*Shearer*	*Horne*	*Le Tissier*	
								Ref: R Hamer	City are hampered by injuries to Linighan and Gordon, the latter suffering a dislocated shoulder. Recalled Allen's first goal since November is soon obliterated by superb Matt Le Tissier finishing. His second is an awesome solo effort and the third a chip. Kevin Moore nets a fine volley.											
27	A	CHARLTON		11	W	1-0	1-0	Fleck 25	Gunn	Culverhouse	Bowen	**Tanner**	Rosario	Townsend	Mortensen	Fleck	Allen	Crook	Phillips	
	3/3		*7,918*	*20*	38				*Bolder*	*Humphrey*	*Minto*	*Peake*	*McLaughlin*	*Caton*	*Lee R**	*Williams*	*Jones*	*Mortimer*	*McKenzie^*	*Watson/Reid*
								Ref: P Foakes	Nick Tanner arrives on loan from Liverpool to alleviate a defensive crisis, with Rosario standing in as centre-back alongside him. Townsend's cross reaches Fleck, who swivels to shoot City ahead. Fleck misses four other chances, though, two being saved and two sailing over the top.											
28	A	CHELSEA		9	D	0-0	0-0		Gunn	Culverhouse	Bowen	Tanner	Linighan	Townsend	Mortensen*	Fleck	Allen	Crook	Phillips	Rosario
	10/3		*18,796*	*5*	39				*Beasant*	*Hall*	*Dorigo*	*Bumstead*	*Johnston*	*Monkou*	*McAllister*	*NIcholas*	*Dixon*	*Wilson K*	*Durie*	
								Ref: N Midgley	At a windy Stamford Bridge, Chelsea have the better opportunities in the first half and Norwich after the interval. All go begging. The best of all falls to City, but Allen and Fleck both go for the same ball and collide. The recent shortage of goals is worrying - just four in eight matches.											
29	H	COVENTRY		9	D	0-0	0-0		Gunn	Culverhouse	Bowen	Tanner	Linighan	Townsend	Allen	Fleck	Rosario*	Crook	Phillips	Mortensen
	14/3		13,673	*4*	40				*Ogrizovic*	*Borrows*	*Dobson*	*Gynn*	*Billing*	*Peake*	*Gallacher*	*Speedie*	*Regis*	*Drinkell*	*Smith*	
								Ref: J Moules	Rosario comes back in place of Allen but Norwich continue to fire blanks. In a collision with Rosario, Steve Ogrizovic fractures his nose, but bravely carries on and makes some heroic saves. The Canaries do most of the attacking but John Sillett's men go close through Kevin Drinkell.											
30	H	MILLWALL		10	D	1-1	0-0	Townsend 79	Gunn	Culverhouse	Bowen	Tanner	Linighan	Townsend	Allen	Fleck !	Mortensen	Crook	Phillips	
	17/3		14,699	*19*	41			*Sheringham 59*	*Branagan*	*Cunningham*	*Dawes*	*Wood !*	*Thompson*	*McLeary*	*Reid*	*Briley*	*Sheringham*	*Goddard*	*Stephens'n**	*Morgan*
								Ref: J Kirkby	Teddy Sheringham nets a near-post header. Unlucky City see a Mortensen goal disallowed, Bowen hits the bar and three efforts are cleared off the line. Fleck and Steve Wood are dismissed for a punch-up. Townsend's header saves the day. Kenny Cunningham makes his senior debut.											
31	A	EVERTON		11	L	1-3	1-0	Phillips 44	Gunn	Culverhouse	Bowen	Tanner	Linighan	Townsend	Sherwood	Fleck	Rosario	Crook	Phillips	
	24/3		*21,707*	*4*	41			*Cottee 47, 60, Sharp 85*	*Southall*	*Snodin*	*Pointon*	*Ratcliffe**	*Keown*	*Whiteside*	*Atteveld*	*McCall*	*Sharp*	*Cottee*	*Sheedy^*	*Nevin/Beagrie*
								Ref: R Hart	Good work by Rosario sets up Phillips, who tucks a shot past Neville Southall. Transfer-listed Tony Cottee bags a couple of headers. Tanner goes close and the score is a little harsh on City. Coney goes on the transfer list, saying 'the fans have it in for me'. Sympathetic Stringer agrees.											

32	H	LUTON		8	W	**2-0**	1-0	Townsend 27p, Bowen 48	Gunn	Culverhouse	Bowen	Tanner	Linighan	Townsend	Sherwood	Mortensen*	Rosario^	Crook	Phillips	Fox/Coney
	31/3		14,451	*18*	44				*Chamberlain*	*Breacker*	*McDonough*	*Kennedy*	*James*	*Dreyer*	*Wilson*	*Nogan**	*Dowie*	*Preece*	*Black*	*Rees*
								Ref: D Hedges	Mortensen tumbles theatrically over the diving Alec Chamberlain and Townsend tucks in the penalty after furious protests. After Wilson's slip, Rosario seizes the ball and squares for Bowen to curl a neat shot into the corner of the net. Relegation worries increase for Jim Ryan's Hatters.											
33	H	CRYSTAL PALACE		8	W	**2-0**	2-0	Sherwood 14, O'Reilly 37 (og)	Gunn	Culverhouse	Bowen	Sherwood	Linighan	Townsend	Fox	Mortensen	Rosario	Crook	Phillips	
	4/4		**12,640**	*15*	47				*Martyn*	*Pemberton*	*Shaw*	*Gray*	*O'Reilly*	*Hedman**	*Thomas*	*Barber*	*Bright*	*Thompson*	*Pardew*	*Salako*
								Ref: P Wright	Sherwood stabs home from close range after a fumble by £1m man Nigel Martyn. Both keepers are kept busy throughout. Gary Thompson hits the crossbar for Steve Coppell's side. Fleck makes his full international debut for Scotland against Argentina and Gunn plays for the 'B' team.											
34	A	WIMBLEDON		8	D	1-1	1-0	Bowen 42	Gunn	Culverhouse	Bowen	Sherwood	Linighan	Fox*	Townsend	Mortensen	Rosario	Crook	Phillips	Goss
	14/4		*4,638*	*12*	48			*Fashanu 55*	*Segers*	*Scales*	*Phelan*	*Ryan*	*Young*	*Curle*	*Anthrobus**	*Kruszynski*	*Fashanu*	*Gibson*	*Wise*	*Cork*
								Ref: K Burge	A scrappy affair in front of a tiny crowd. Was this really a top-division fixture? Crook's through pass sends Bowen clear to open the scoring. Fashanu equalises after the break, heading home a chip forward by Terry Gibson. Han Segers' huge up-and-under kicks keep Gunn on his toes.											
35	H	MANCHESTER C		9	L	0-1	0-1		Gunn	Culverhouse	Bowen	Sherwood	Linighan	Townsend	Goss	Mortensen*	Rosario	Crook	Phillips	Fleck
	16/4		18,914	*14*	48			*Heath 14*	*Dibble*	*Harper*	*Brightwell*	*Reid*	*Hendrey*	*Redmond*	*Heath*	*Ward*	*Allen^*	*Megson*	*Quinn**	*Clarke/Hinchcliffe*
								Ref: D Elleray	Howard Kendall has brought old colleague Adrian Heath to Maine Road and the little man hits a winner in his third full game. Ian Brightwell and Niall Quinn, another new boy, go close to extending the lead. Crook nearly equalises with a 30-yard rocket which Andy Dibble tips over.											
36	A	DERBY		8	W	**2-0**	1-0	Rosario 7, Fox 73	Gunn	Culverhouse	Bowen	Sherwood	Linighan	Townsend	Fox	Fleck*	Rosario^	Crook	Phillips	Mortensen/**Smith**
	21/4		*13,758*	*16*	51				*Shilton*	*Sage*	*Forsyth*	*Williams*	*Wright^*	*Hindmarch*	*Patterson**	*Saunders*	*Harford*	*Williams P*	*Briscoe*	*Francis/Davidson*
								Ref: P Don	Arthur Cox's side have slumped down the table and lack confidence. Rosario heads Norwich into the lead. He seals the win by setting up Fox, who coolly shoots past Peter Shilton at his near post. Gunn makes an excellent last-minute save to keep out a misdirected header by Linighan.											
37	A	ASTON VILLA		8	D	3-3	1-0	Fox 30, Mountf'ld 79 (og), Rosario 83	**Walton**	Culverhouse	Bowen	Sherwood	Linighan	Townsend	Fox	Fleck*	Rosario	Crook	Phillips	**Power**
	28/4		*28,998*	*2*	52			*McGrath 63, Cascarino 65, Platt 68*	*Spink*	*Price*	*Gray*	*McGrath*	*Mountfield*	*Nielsen*	*Daley*	*Platt*	*Olney*	*Cowans*	*Cascarino*	
								Ref: R Milford	Gunn's wife goes into labour, so Walton is rushed up the M6 for his debut. Graham Taylor is being lined up for the England job, but today still harbours outside hopes of the title. After Fox's volley, Villa hit three in five minutes. Rosario races clear to level and thus ends the title dream.											
38	H	ARSENAL		10	D	2-2	2-1	Bowen 13, Fox 45	Gunn	Culverhouse	Bowen	Sherwood	Linighan	Goss	Fox	Fleck	Rosario	Crook	Phillips	
	5/5		19,256	*4*	53			*Smith 44, 77*	*Lukic*	*Dixon*	*Winterburn*	*Hayes*	*Bould**	*Adams*	*Rocastle*	*Davis^*	*Smith*	*Campbell*	*Groves*	*O'Leary/Thomas*
		Home	Away					Ref: J Martin	In blazing sunshine, Bowen celebrates his Player of the Year award by rocketing home a pull-back. Alan Smith's tap-in levels matters, but Fox immediately restores the lead, netting a rebound off John Lukic. Smith curls a superb shot beyond Gunn to preserve a point for the Gunners.											
Average		16,737	19,397																	

Littlewoods Cup			Att			F-A	H-T	Scorers, Times, and Referees	1	2	3	4	5	6	7	8	9	10	11	subs used
2:1	H	ROTHERHAM		7	D	1-1	1-1	Fleck 32	Gunn	Sherwood	Bowen	Butterworth	Linighan	Townsend	Gordon	Fleck	Rosario	Crook	Phillips	
		20/9	9,531	*3:4*				*Williamson 41*	*O'Hanlon*	*Russell*	*Robinson*	*Grealish*	*Johnson*	*Barnsley*	*Buckley*	*Dempsey*	*Williamson*	*Haycock*	*Hazel*	
								Ref: R Wiseman	Billy McEwan's Millers fall behind to Fleck's close-range header, but level through an angled shot by prolific Glaswegian Bobby Williamson. The unbeaten Third Division outfit embarrass City by holding their own in the second half and fully deserve to leave Norfolk on level terms.											
2:2	A	ROTHERHAM		4	W	2-0	2-0	Gordon 7, Fleck 29	Gunn	Sherwood	Bowen	Butterworth	Linighan	Townsend	Gordon	Fleck	Rosario	Crook	Phillips	
		3/10	*13,295*	*3:7*					*O'Hanlon*	*Russell*	*Robinson*	*Grealish*	*Johnson*	*Barnsley*	*Hazel*	*Scott^*	*Williamson*	*Mendonca**	*Buckley*	*Thompson/Goodwin*
								Ref: R Wiseman (Norwich win 3-1 on aggregate)	Norwich put on a vastly improved display compared to the first leg, and are in control throughout. Gordon's early strike extingushes some of the Millers' fire and City end up cruising through. The third round draw pits Stringer against his former Norwich coaching colleague Machin.											
3	A	MANCHESTER C		6	L	1-3	0-1	Fleck 90	Gunn	Sherwood*	Bowen	Butterworth	Linighan	Townsend	Gordon	Fleck	Rosario	Crook	Phillips	Allen
		25/10	*20,126*	*16*				*White 31, Bishop 51, Allen 85*	*Dibble*	*Fleming*	*Hinchcliffe*	*Bishop*	*Gayle*	*Redmond*	*White*	*Morley*	*Allen*	*McNab*	*Lake*	
								Ref: T Holbrook	Still reeling from the hammering by Luton, their first loss in 15 games all told, Norwich never look likely winners after falling behind to David White's effort. Million-pound man Clive Allen, recently arrived from Bordeaux, has had a quiet return to English football, but pounces late on.											

FA Cup																				
3	A	EXETER		6	D	1-1	0-0	Fleck 86	Gunn	Culverhouse	Bowen	Butterworth	Linighan	Townsend	Gordon	Fleck	Rosario	Crook	Phillips	
		6/1	*9,061*	*4:1*				*Rowbotham 85*	*Miller*	*Hiley*	*Benjamin*	*McNichol*	*Taylor*	*Whitehead*	*Rowbotham*	*Bailey*	*Neville*	*McDermott*	*Frankland*	
								Ref: P Foakes	Terry Cooper is putting together a Grecians side that will win the Fourth Division title - the first real success in their 86-year history. They relish this chance of a giant-killing and St James Park goes wild when Darren Rownbotham puts them ahead. But the lead lasts mere seconds.											
3R	H	EXETER		6	W	2-0	1-0	Rosario 7, Gordon 76	Gunn	Culverhouse	Bowen	Butterworth	Linighan	Townsend	Gordon	Fleck	Rosario	Crook	Phillips	
		10/1	18,202	*4:1*					*Miller*	*Hiley*	*Benjamin*	*McNichol*	*Taylor*	*Whitehead*	*Rowbotham*	*Bailey*	*Neville**	*McDerm'tt^*	*Frankland*	*Cooper/Batty*
								Ref: P Foakes	The replay lacks the drama and raw excitement of Saturday's full-blooded affair. As against Rotherham, the early goal proves crucial. Exeter put themselves about and it becomes a bruising battle. One flare-up threatens to reprise the infamous Highbury brawl. Gordon's goal settles it.											
4	H	LIVERPOOL		8	D	0-0	0-0		Gunn	Culverhouse	Bowen	Butterworth	Linighan	Townsend	Gordon	Fleck	Rosario	Crook	Phillips	
		28/1	23,152	*1*					*Grobbelaar*	*Hysen*	*Venison*	*Nicol*	*Whelan*	*Hansen*	*Beardsley*	*Staunton*	*Rush*	*Barnes*	*McMahon*	
								Ref: K Hackett	Not too many Sunday thrills for the live TV audience. The nearest to a goal is when Rosario rises to beat Bruce Grobbelaar and Glenn Hysen in the air, but his header skims the bar. The draw is a huge improvement on the midweek 4-1 defeat by Swindon in the ZDS Cup quarter-finals.											
4R	A	LIVERPOOL		8	L	1-3	1-1	Fleck 20	Gunn	Culverhouse	Bowen	Butterworth	Linighan	Townsend	Gordon	Fleck	Rosario	Crook	Phillips	
		31/1	*29,339*	*1*				*Nicol 18, Barnes 56, Beardsley 64p*	*Grobbelaar*	*Hysen*	*Venison*	*Nicol*	*Whelan*	*Hansen*	*Beardsley*	*Staunton**	*Rush*	*Barnes*	*McMahon*	*Burrows*
								Ref: K Hackett	Nicol arrives in the danger area late to force home the opening goal at the far post. Norwich match the home side for much of the game, but find Peter Beardsley in superb form. John Barnes nets a diving header to regain the lead. Linghan fells Beardsley for the decisive penalty-kick.											

		Home						Away					
	P	W	D	L	F	A	W	D	L	F	A	Pts
1 Liverpool	38	13	5	1	38	15	10	5	4	40	22	79
2 Aston Villa	38	13	3	3	36	20	8	4	7	21	18	70
3 Tottenham	38	12	1	6	35	24	7	5	7	24	23	63
4 Arsenal	38	14	3	2	38	11	4	5	10	16	27	62
5 Chelsea	38	8	7	4	31	24	8	5	6	27	26	60
6 Everton	38	14	3	2	40	16	3	5	11	17	30	59
7 Southampton	38	10	5	4	40	27	5	5	9	31	36	55
8 Wimbledon	38	5	8	6	22	23	8	8	3	25	17	55
9 Nott'm For	38	9	4	6	31	21	6	5	8	24	26	54
10 NORWICH	38	7	10	2	24	14	6	4	9	20	28	53
11 QP Rangers	38	9	4	6	27	22	4	7	8	18	22	50
12 Coventry	38	11	2	6	24	25	3	5	11	15	34	49
13 Manchester U	38	8	6	5	26	14	5	3	11	20	33	48
14 Manchester C	38	9	4	6	26	21	3	8	8	17	31	48
15 Crys Palace	38	8	7	4	27	23	5	2	12	15	43	48
16 Derby	38	9	1	9	29	21	4	6	9	14	19	46
17 Luton	38	8	8	3	24	18	2	5	12	19	39	43
18 Sheffield Wed	38	8	6	5	21	17	3	4	12	14	34	43
19 Charlton	38	4	6	9	18	25	3	3	13	13	32	30
20 Millwall	38	4	6	9	23	25	1	5	13	16	40	26
	760	183	99	98	580	406	98	99	183	406	580	1041

Odds & ends

Double wins: (4) Chelsea, Derby, Manchester U, Sheffield Wed.
Double losses: (1) Manchester C.

Won from behind: (1) Sheffield Wed (h).
Lost from in front: (3) Arsenal (a), Everton (a), Southampton (a).

High spots: The 4-4 thriller with Southampton, including ITV's 'Goal of the Season' by Robert Rosario.
Top-six status throughout November and December.
No goals conceded in the first five away games.
Mark Bowen's goalscoring raids down the left flank.

Low spots: Losing key players Phelan, Townsend and Linighan.
Disappointing post-Xmas form – 5 wins from 20 league games.
The ugly 20-man brawl at Highbury, leading to a heavy fine.
Three ex-Canaries favourites – Bond, Brown and Machin – sacked by other clubs during the season.
The harsh barracking by some fans of Dean Coney.
Two hotly disputed penalties helping Arsenal beat City 4-3

Player of the Year: Mark Bowen.
Ever-presents: (2) Mark Bowen and David Phillips.
Hat-tricks: (0).
Hat-tricks against: (2) Lineker (Tottenham, a), Tissier (Southampton, a).
Leading scorer: (12) Robert Fleck.

	Appearances						Goals			
	Lge	*Sub*	LC	*Sub*	FAC	*Sub*	Lge	LC	FAC	Tot
Allen, Malcolm	**9**	*3*		*1*			**3**			**3**
Bowen, Mark	**38**		3		4		**7**			**7**
Butterworth, Ian	**22**		3		4					
Coney, Dean	**6**	*3*								
Cook, Paul		*2*								
Crook, Ian	**34**	*1*	3		4					
Culverhouse, Ian	**31**	*1*			4					
Fleck, Robert	**25**	*2*	3		4		**7**	3	2	**12**
Fox, Ruel	**6**	*1*					**3**			**3**
Gordon, Dale	**26**		3		4		**3**	1	1	**5**
Goss, Jeremy	**3**	*4*								
Gunn, Bryan	**37**		3		4					
Linighan, Andy	**37**		3		4		**2**			**2**
Mortensen, Henrik	**12**	*3*								
Pennock, Adrian	**1**									
Phillips, David	**38**		3		4		**4**			**4**
Power, Lee		*1*								
Rosario, Robert	**29**	*2*	3		4		**5**		1	**6**
Sherwood, Tim	**22**	*5*	3				**3**			**3**
Smith, David		*1*								
Tanner, Nick	**6**									
Townsend, Andy	**35**		3		4		**3**			**3**
Walton, Mark	**1**									
(own-goals)							**4**			**4**
23 players used	**418**	***29***	**33**	***1***	**44**		**44**	**4**	**3**	**52**

No	Date		Opponent	Att	Pos	Pt	F-A	H-T	Scorers, Times, and Referees	1	2	3	4	5	6	7	8	9	10	11	subs used
1		H	SUNDERLAND			W	3-2	2-0	Gordon 10, Sherwood 44, Fox 72	Gunn	**Blades**	Bowen	Butterworth	**Polston**	Sherwood	Gordon	Fox	Crook	Rosario	Phillips	
	25/8			17,247		3			*Davenport 54, Gabbiadini 63*	*Norman*	*Kay*	*Agboola*	*Bennett*	*MacPhail*	*Owers*	*Bracewell*	*Armstrong*	*Davenport*	*Gabbiadini^*	*Atkinson**	*Cullen/Hauser*
									Ref: P Don	With Townsend and Linighan sold, City splash £1 million on Polston (Spurs) and Blades (Derby). Gordon buries Fox's flicked header and Sherwood touches in Fox's cross. Peter Davenport grabs a debut goal and Marco Gabbiadini's rocket levels it. Fox cracks in a deserved winner.											
2		A	SOUTHAMPTON			L	0-1	0-0		Gunn	Blades	Bowen	Butterworth	Polston	Sherwood	Gordon	Fox*	Crook^	Rosario	Phillips	Fleck/Goss
	28/8			*17,206*		3			*Polston 63 (og)*	*Flowers*	*Cherednik*	*Adams*	*Case*	*Moore*	*Osman*	*Le Tissier*	*Horne*	*Rideout*	*Cockerill*	*Wallace Rod*	
									Ref: A Buksh	New boy Polston attempts to cut out a Rod Wallace cross but can only thump a header past bewildered Gunn. Crook exits with an ankle injury. Sherwood's fierce drive is well saved by Tim Flowers. Spurs boss Terry Venables is amazed when a tribunal fixes the Polston fee at £300,000.											
3		A	LEEDS		15	L	0-3	0-2		Gunn	Blades	Bowen^	Butterworth	Polston	Sherwood	Gordon	Fox*	Goss	Rosario	Phillips	Fleck/**Minett**
	1/9			*25,684*	*2*	3			*Chapman 12, 36, Varadi 72*	*Lukic*	*Sterland*	*Snodin**	*Batty*	*Fairclough*	*Whyte*	*Stachan*	*Varadi*	*Chapman*	*McAllister^*	*Speed*	*Whitlow/Haddock*
									Ref: D Allison	City are outplayed by Howard Wilkinson's newly promoted side. Lee Chapman converts a Gary Speed cross and slots home a second before half-time. Imre Varadi seals the victory when he nets a simple chance after Bowen's poor back-pass. Bowen is carried off injured near the end.											
4		H	CRYSTAL PALACE		17	L	0-3	0-2		Gunn	Blades	Bowen	Butterworth	Polston	Sherwood^	Gordon	Fleck	Goss	Rosario*	Phillips	Fox/Minett
	8/9			15,306	*2*	3			*Barber 7, Wright 13, Salako 55*	*Martyn*	*Humphrey*	*Shaw*	*Gray*	*Young*	*Thorn*	*Salako*	*Thorne*	*Thompson*	*Wright*	*Barber*	
									Ref: K Cooper	Norwich's worst home defeat in over two years. Gunn's error is exploited by Phil Barber for the first. Geoff Thomas' shot rebounds off Bowen to give Ian Wright his chance. Man-of-the-match John Salako shows superb control to net a third and ensure the win for Steve Coppell's outfit.											
5		A	MANCHESTER C		17	L	1-2	0-2	Fleck 77	Gunn	Culverhouse	Bowen	Butterworth	Blades	Sherwood	Gordon	Fleck	Crook	Fox	Phillips	
	15/9			*26,247*	*6*	3			*Quinn 22, Brennan 26*	*Coton*	*Brightwell*	*Pointon*	*Redmond*	*Hendry*	*Reid**	*White*	*Harper*	*Quinn*	*Heath*	*Ward M^*	*Allen/Brennan*
									Ref: A Wilkie	Adrian Heath's volley is blocked, but falls nicely for Niall Quinn. Howard Kendall's men are undaunted by early injuries and Quinn sets up sub Mark Brennan for the second. Norwich rally late in the game, inspired by Fleck's superb half-volley. Transfer speculation is surrounding Fleck.											
6		H	DERBY		16	W	2-1	0-0	Phillips 58, Fox 66	Gunn	Culverhouse	Bowen	Butterworth	Blades	Sherwood	Gordon	Fleck	Crook	Fox	Phillips	
	22/9			13,258	*19*	6			*Patterson 62*	*Shilton*	*Patterson**	*Forsyth*	*Williams G*	*Wright*	*Watson*	*Mick'white^*	*Saunders*	*Harford*	*Hebberd*	*Davidson*	*Sage/Francis*
									Ref: P Danson	A dull affair bursts into life midway through the second half. City go ahead through a fierce low shot from Phillips. Defender Mark Patterson rifles in the first goal of his career to level. Fox cracks a fine winner from distance past Peter Shilton. Blades is delighted to beat his old pals.											
7		H	LUTON		17	L	1-3	1-0	Gordon 4	Gunn	Culverhouse	Bowen	Butterworth	Blades^	Crook	Gordon*	Fleck	Sherwood	Fox	Phillips	Power/Goss
	29/9			12,794	*6*	6			*Elstrup 48, 53, 62*	*Chamberlain*	*Breacker*	*Harvey*	*Williams*	*Beaumont*	*Dreyer*	*Elstrup*	*Preece*	*Dowie*	*Hughes*	*Black*	
									Ref: R Pawley	Gordon's early boost is cancelled out by a dramatic hat-trick in a 14-minute spell by Dane Lars Elstrup. One is a superb finish after he outstrips the defence and the others headers from free-kicks by Steve Williams, playing his first game of the season. Stringer hits out at slack defending.											
8		A	ARSENAL		17	L	0-2	0-2		Gunn	Culverhouse	Bowen	Butterworth	Blades	Crook	Gordon	Fleck*	Sherwood	Fox	Phillips	Power
	6/10			*36,048*	*2*	6			*Davis 26, 29*	*Seaman*	*Dixon*	*Winterburn*	*Jonsson*	*Bould*	*Adams*	*Rocastle*	*Davis*	*Smith*	*Merson^*	*Limpar**	*Groves/Hillier*
									Ref: G Courtenay	Paul Davis' first-half double gives George Graham's men the points. They are chasing Liverpool, who today equalled a 96-year-old record by winning a 12th successive game. Norwich's lack of goal-power is worrying. Canaries fans voice concerns over the club's 'lack of ambition'.											
9		H	LIVERPOOL		17	D	1-1	1-1	Fox 8	Gunn	Culverhouse	Bowen	Butterworth	Blades	Crook	Gordon	Power	Sherwood	Fox	Phillips	
	20/10			**21,275**	*1*	7			*Gillespie 2*	*Grobbelaar*	*Hysen*	*Burrows*	*Nicol*	*Venison**	*Gillespie*	*Beardsley*	*Houghton*	*Rush*	*Barnes*	*McMahon*	*Staunton*
									Ref: J Moules	City end The Reds run of victories with their best display of the season so far. Power gets a full debut in place of Fleck. Gary Gillespie is left free to head Kenny Dalglish's men ahead early on. City hit back when Fox unleashes a cracking shot in off the bar, after a one-two with Power.											
10		A	QP RANGERS		16	W	3-1	2-0	Power 15, 69, Phillips 39	Gunn	Culverhouse	Bowen	Butterworth	Blades	Crook	Gordon	Power	Sherwood	Fox*	Phillips	Goss
	27/10			*11,103*	*11*	10			*Wegerle 57p*	*Stejskal*	*Bardsley*	*Sansom*	*Parker*	*McDonald^*	*Maddix*	*Wilkins*	*Barker*	*Ferdinand**	*Wegerle*	*Sinton*	*Falco/Channing*
									Ref: P Jones	Power shows remarkable composure and deadly finishing skills for one so young when he puts City ahead. Phillips increases the lead before skilful Roy Wegerle is fouled by Culverhouse and converts the penalty himself. Power clinches the win, cracking a fine shot past Jan Stejskal.											

11	H	SHEFFIELD UTD	12	W	3-0	1-0	Sherw'd 30, Jones 50(og), Phillips 74	Gunn	Culverhouse	Bowen	Butterworth	Blades	Crook	Gordon	Power	Sherwood	Fox	Phillips	
3/11		14,806	20	13				Tracey	Pemberton	Lake^	Jones	Morris*	Beesley	Bradshaw	Gannon	Agana	Deane	Rostron	Bryson/Booker
							Ref: P Foakes	Dave Bassett's Blades are blunted by an impressive display. Sherwood, a target for barracking recently, heads home a Phillips cross to chalk up the first. Visiting skipper Vinnie Jones blunders as he puts a Crooks cross past Simon Tracey. Phillips slides in a loose ball to complete the job.											
12	A	CHELSEA	12	D	1-1	1-1	Gordon 13	Gunn	Culverhouse	Bowen	Butterworth	Blades	Crook	Gordon	Power	Sherwood	Fox	Phillips*	Fleck
10/11		16,925	11	14			Wise 26p	Hitchcock	Hall	Dorigo	Townsend	Cundy	Lee	Wise	Bumstead*	Dixon	Durie	Wilson	Le Saux
							Ref: V Callow	Gordon stuns Stamford Bridge with a jinking run that ends with a left-foot drive into the net. Butterworth handles, allowing Dennis Wise to put Chelsea back on terms. Kerry Dixon misses a great chance. When Kevin Hitchcock strays out of goal, Crook tries a 45-yarder, but is off-target.											
13	H	ASTON VILLA	9	W	2-0	1-0	Crook 4, Fox 71	Gunn	Culverhouse	Bowen	Butterworth	Blades	Crook	Gordon	Power*	Sherwood	Fox	Phillips	Fleck
17/11		17,243	13	17				Spink	Price	Gray	McGrath	Mountield !	Nielsen	Daley	Platt	Olney	Cowans	Cascarino	
							Ref: D Elleray	Recent improvement is maintained. In the opening exchanges, Crook sends a 25-yarder past Nigel Spink and in off a post. Derek Mountifeld is red-carded for a 'professional foul' on Gordon. Fox and Gordon beat five players between them in a gem of a move that brings the second goal.											
14	A	TOTTENHAM	11	L	1-2	1-1	Crook 32	Gunn	Culverhouse	Bowen	Butterworth	Blades	Crook	Gordon	Power*	Sherwood	Fox	Phillips	Fleck
24/11		33,942	3	17			Lineker 29, 52	Thorstvedt	Thomas	V d Hauwe	Sedgley	Howells	Mabbutt	Stewart	Gascoigne	Nayim	Lineker	Allen	
							Ref: R Milford	The unbeaten league run ends in a good quality contest. City complain about handball in the build-up to both Spurs goals. Gary Lineker later admits he handled just before netting his winner, although it was still a fine piece of finishing. Crook's goal is a free-kick that goes in off a post.											
15	H	WIMBLEDON	13	L	0-4	0-4		Gunn	Culverhouse	Bowen	Butterworth	Blades	Crook^	Gordon	Power*	Sherwood	Fox	Phillips	Fleck/Goss
1/12		12,324	8	17			Fashanu 1, 28, Barton 19, Scales 21	Segers	Joseph	Phelan	Barton	Blackwell	Curle	McGee	Kruszynski*	Fashanu	Scales	Gibson	Sanchez
							Ref: J Ashworth	A horrendous opening half-hour. Ex-Canary John Fashanu streaks clear and scores on 26 seconds to launch a battering. City's passing game is brushed aside. Disenchanted fans stage a sit-down protest in the Barclay End. Caretaker Ray Harford is confirmed as Dons manager after this.											
16	H	SOUTHAMPTON	10	W	3-1	1-1	Phillips 36, Rud'ck 54(og), Bowen 56	Gunn	Culverhouse	Bowen	Butterworth	Polston	Crook	Gordon	Rosario	Sherwood	Fox*	Phillips	Power
8/12		11,705	17	20			Le Tissier 6	Flowers	Cockerill	Adams	Case*	Ruddock	Osman	Le Tissier	Horne	Shearer	Rideout	Benali	Banger
							Ref: R Milford	Stringer recalls Polston and Rosario. A bad start on the frosty pitch as Matt Le Tissier shoots under Gunn, but Phillips levels with a long-range shot. Neil Ruddock's back-pass flies past Tim Flowers. Glenn Cockerill is more careful, but his back-pass too weak, and Bowen nips in to net.											
17	A	SUNDERLAND	10	W	2-1	0-1	Sherwood 59, Gordon 75	Gunn	Culverhouse	Bowen	Butterworth	Polston	Crook	Gordon	Power	Sherwood	Rosario	Phillips	
15/12		18,693	17	23			Armstrong 14	Norman	Kay	Hardyman	Ord	Ball	Owers	Bracewell	Armstrong	Davenport	Gabbiadini	Pascoe	
							Ref: N Midgley	Marco Gabbiadini's cross is headed home by Gordon Armstrong. Sherwood equalises by deftly floating in a clever shot. Tony Norman is in great form, but can't prevent Gordon drilling in a Rosario knock-down. City play some quality stuff. Fleck is out of action after knee surgery.											
18	H	EVERTON	9	W	1-0	1-0	Polston 38	Gunn	Culverhouse	Bowen	Butterworth	Polston	Crook	Gordon	Power*	Sherwood	Rosario	Phillips	Goss
22/12		14,294	16	26				Southall	McDonald	Keown^	Ratcliffe	Watson	Ebbrell	Nevin	Atteveld	Newell	Cottee*	Hinchliffe	Sharp/Youds
							Ref: R Wiseman	An early bang in the face leaves Polston covered in blood. When a Gordon shot hits a post, the blood-stained defender snaps up the rebound. Gunn ensures a City win by making crucial late saves from sub Graeme Sharp, Mike Newell and Pat Nevin. Butterworth has asked for a move.											
19	A	MANCHESTER U	9	L	0-3	0-0		Gunn	Culverhouse	Bowen	Butterworth	Polston	Crook	Gordon	Power*	Sherwood	Fox	Phillips	Sutch
26/12		39,801	6	26			Hughes 53, McClair 69, 90	Sealey	Irwin	Blackmore	Bruce	Webb	Pallister	Robson*	Ince	McClair	Hughes	Sharpe^	Phelan/Donaghy
							Ref: A Seville	Alex Ferguson overcomes his Norwich hoodoo at last. In fierce wind and rain, Mark Hughes is set up by Gary Pallister's chip. Boxing Day's biggest crowd of the day applauds fine finishing by Brian McClair. Lowestoft-born utility player Daryl Sutch, 19, comes on for a senior debut.											
20	A	COVENTRY	9	L	0-2	0-0		Gunn	Culverhouse	Bowen	Butterworth	Polston	Crook	Gordon	Rosario	Sherwood	Fox*	Phillips	Sutch
29/12		12,039	16	26			Borrows 56p, Speedie 58	Ogrizovic	Borrows	Edwards	Emerson	Butcher	Peake	Gallacher	Gynn	Regis	Speedie*	Smith	Drinkell
							Ref: M Peck	Coventry's new player-manager Terry Butcher inspires his second win in a row. The Lowestoft-born stopper enjoys putting one over Norwich. In driving rain, Polston hauls down David Speedie for a penalty. Ex-Canary Drinkell replaces Speedie when the Scot limps off after scoring.											
21	H	NOTT'M FOREST	11	L	2-6	1-2	Sh' 10, Fl' 71 [Keane 68,78, C'sby 87]	Gunn	Culverhouse	Bowen	Butterworth	Polston	Crook	Gordon	Fleck	Sherwood	Rosario	Phillips	
2/1		17,043	10	26			Wilson 26, Clough 28, Polston 53(og),	Crossley	Laws	Pearce	Walker	Chettle	Wilson*	Carr	Keane	Parker	Clough	Crosby	Woan
							Ref: J Martin	This game is switched to avoid heavy policing costs, but City are made to pay in other ways by Brian Clough's slick young outfit. Sherwood curls in a free-kick, but Terry Wilson nets a low drive and Forest never look back. Polston's sliced own goal seems to sum up this nightmare.											

No	Date	Att	Pos	Pt	F-A	H-T	Scorers, Times, and Referees	1	2	3	4	5	6	7	8	9	10	11	subs used
22	H LEEDS		11	W	2-0	1-0	Sherwood 17, Gordon 53	Gunn	Culverhouse	Bowen	Butterworth	Polston	Crook	Gordon	Fleck	Sherwood	Goss	Phillips	
	12/1	17,786	*4*	29				*Lukic*	*Sterland*	*Snodin*	*Batty*	*Fairclough*	*Whyte*	*Stachan*	*Shutt^*	*Chapman*	*McAllister*	*Whitlow**	*Speed/Pearson*
							Ref: T Ward	Unpredictable City put the Forest thrashing behind them and give high-flying Leeds a tough afternoon. Sherwood fires home a low drive after a run from his own half. The vital second goal is a splendid 12-yard volley past John Lukic by Gordon, finishing off a move he started himself.											
23	A CRYSTAL PALACE		10	W	3-1	1-0	Goss 18, Fleck 57, 72	Gunn	Culverhouse	Bowen	Butterworth	Polston	Crook	Gordon	Fleck	Sherwood	Goss	Phillips	
	19/1	*17,201*	*3*	32			*Bright 53*	*Martyn*	*Humphrey*	*Shaw*	*Gray*	*Young*	*Thorn*	*Salako*	*Thomas*	*Bright*	*Wright*	*McGoldr'k**	*Barber*
							Ref: A Gunn	Eight wins from their last 10 games, but in-form Palace find Norwich in confident mood. Goss produces an excellent finish from a tight angle. After Mark Bright's header, Fleck chases a lost cause and forces in a remarkable goal. Then he finishes off an excellent move from close range.											
24	H MANCHESTER C		10	L	1-2	0-2	Polston 80	Gunn	Culverhouse	Bowen	Butterworth	Polston	Crook	Gordon	Fleck	Sherwood*	Smith	Phillips	Mortensen
	2/2	15,194	*8*	32			*Quinn 2, White 43*	*Coton*	*Brightwell*	*Pointon*	*Harper*	*Hendry*	*Redmond*	*White*	*Allen**	*Quinn*	*Megson*	*Ward M*	*Heath*
							Ref: D Phillips	David White's cross is headed in by Niall Quinn and White's volley makes it two. Polston rams the ball in from close range, but it's too little, too late. Norwich haven't beaten the Maine Road club in 10 years now. Crook gets a surprise call-up for an England 'B' fixture against Wales.											
25	A DERBY		10	D	0-0	0-0		Gunn	Culverhouse	Bowen	Blades	Polston	Crook*	Gordon	Fleck	Sherwood	Goss	Phillips	Fox
	23/2	*14,102*	*20*	33				*Shilton*	*Sage*	*Cross*	*Williams G*	*Wright*	*Forsyth*	*Micklewhite*	*Saunders*	*Harford*	*Wilson*	*McMinn**	*Hebberd*
							Ref: T Fitzharris	Gunn puts in a marvellous display to keep Arthur Cox's side at bay. He needs lengthy treatment after one buffeting from big Mick Harford. His saves include a penalty stop from Dean Saunders on 72 minutes, after Crook had brought the Welshman down. Ian Wilson debuts for Derby.											
26	A WIMBLEDON		10	D	0-0	0-0		Gunn	Culverhouse	Bowen	Blades	Polston	Smith	Gordon	Fleck	Sherwood	Goss	Phillips	
	2/3	**4,041**	*6*	34				*Segers*	*Joseph*	*Elkins*	*Barton*	*Sanchez*	*Curle*	*McGee**	*Kruszynski*	*Fashanu*	*Scales*	*Gibson^*	*Cork/Clarke*
							Ref: R Dilkes	Rarely can a top-flight game between two top-ten sides have been such a non-event. No atmosphere, no goals, no thrills. Norwich are unable to emulate the recent victory over the Dons achieved by ex-manager John Bond, now with Shrewsbury. Debutant Andy Clarke looks a good find.											
27	A LUTON		10	W	1-0	1-0	Sherwood 21	Gunn	Culverhouse	Bowen	Blades	Polston	Crook	Gordon	Fleck	Sherwood	Goss	Phillips	
	16/3	*8,604*	*14*	37				*Chamberlain*	*Johnson**	*McDon'gh^*	*Beaumont*	*Rodger*	*Dreyer*	*Elstrup*	*Preece*	*Dowie*	*Pembridge*	*Black*	*Farrell/Harvey*
							Ref: M Bodenham	It's one-way traffic towards the Norwich goal for most of the game, but Jim Ryan's side can't hit the target. A break down the left by Phillips sets up Sherwood to fire past Alec Chamberlain. Gunn has an excellent match to keep the Hatters out and keeps a third successive clean sheet.											
28	H ARSENAL		10	D	0-0	0-0		Gunn	Culverhouse	Bowen	Blades	Polston	Crook	Gordon	Fleck	Sherwood	Fox	Phillips	
	23/3	20,131	*2*	38				*Seaman*	*Dixon*	*Winterburn*	*Rocastle^*	*Bould*	*Adams*	*O'Leary*	*Davis*	*Smith*	*Campbell*	*Limpar**	*Groves/Linighan*
							Ref: J Ashworth	City employ a 3-4-3 system and Fox is a constant threat to the high-flying Gunners. Man-of-the-match Sherwood hits a post. David O'Leary has a close-range effort well saved. Arsenal's title hopes are dented as Liverpool win 7-1 at Derby and go top. Rosario leaves to join Coventry.											
29	H MANCHESTER U		11	L	0-3	0-2		Gunn	Culverhouse	Bowen	Blades	Polston	Crook	Gordon	Fleck	Sherwood	Fox	Phillips	
	30/3	18,282	*5*	38			*Bruce 18, 75p, Ince 30*	*Sealey*	*Irwin**	*Blackmore*	*Bruce*	*Phelan*	*Pallsiter*	*Robson*	*Ince*	*Webb*	*Hughes*	*Sharpe^*	*McClair/Robins*
							Ref: K Barrett	From United's first corner, Steve Bruce thumps home a header. Paul Ince doubles the lead with a well-placed 20-yarder. Polston's challenge on Mark Hughes is harshly deemed worthy of a penalty, which Bruce puts away. The ex-Canary defender will end up joint-leading scorer with 13.											
30	A EVERTON		13	L	0-1	0-0		Gunn	Culverhouse	Bowen	Blades	Polston	Crook	Goss	Fleck	Sherwood*	Fox	Phillips	Mortensen
	1/4	*20,485*	*9*	38			*Newell 62*	*Southall*	*McDonald*	*Hinchcliffe*	*Youds*	*Keown*	*Milligan*	*Warzycha**	*McCall*	*Newell*	*Cottee*	*Sheedy^*	*Nevin/Ebbrell*
							Ref: G Ashby	April Fool's Day brings few smiles at a wet and windy Goodison. Gunn has a fine match and is only beaten when he parries Robert Warzycha's cross-shot straight into the path of Mike Newell. It's exactly 18 months since Mortensen joined City but this is only his 17th league appearance.											
31	H COVENTRY		13	D	2-2	1-1	Sherwood 40, Fleck 49	Gunn	Culverhouse	Bowen	Butterworth	Polston	Goss	Gordon	Fleck	Sherwood	Power*	Phillips	Fox
	6/4	**11,550**	*11*	39			*Gallacher 29, Gynn 60*	*Ogrizovic*	*Borrows*	*Sansom*	*Emerson*	*Pearce*	*Peake*	*McGrath**	*Gynn*	*Regis^*	*Gallacher*	*Smith*	*Rosario/Drinkell*
							Ref: A Buksh	Kevin Gallacher beats Gunn, but Norwich hit back against the run of play, scoring either side of the break. Both visiting subs are ex-Canaries and get the inevitable hostile welcome. Rosario responds by setting up Micky Gynn. It's Rosario's debut after his £650,000 move 15 days ago.											

No	Date	H/A	Opponent	Att	Pos	Pts	F-A	H-T	Scorers, Times, and Referees	1	2	3	4	5	6	7	8	9	10	11	Subs used
32		H	TOTTENHAM		10	W	2-1	1-1	Power 12, Crook 81	Gunn	Culverhouse	Bowen	Butterworth	Polston	Crook	Gordon*	Fleck	Sherwood	Power	Phillips	Fox
	10/4			19,014	*8*	42			*Hendry 43*	*Walker*	*Howells*	*V d Hauwe**	*Sedgley*	*Thomas*	*Tuttle*	*Nayim*	*Gascoigne^*	*Walsh*	*Hendry*	*Moncur*	*Hendon/Garland*
									Ref: S Lodge	With an FA Cup semi-final looming, Terry Venables fields a very weakened Spurs side. Ian Walker, son of City reserve coach Mike, makes his debut. Power's near-post finish is followed by John Hendry's debut goal from a Nayim cross. Crook wins the points with a 25-yard dipper.											
33		H	CHELSEA		13	L	1-3	0-2	Polston 79	Gunn	Culverhouse	Bowen	Butterworth	Polston	Crook	Gordon	Fleck	Sherwood	Power	Phillips*	Fox
	17/4			12,301	*9*	42			*Wise 18, Durie 38, 65*	*Beasant*	*Hall*	*Sinclair*	*Townsend*	*Cundy*	*Monkou*	*Le Saux*	*Dickens*	*Dixon*	*Durie*	*Wise*	
									Ref: J Kirkby	A miserable home display: maybe City were dazzled by Chelsea's bizarre red-and-white strip? Dennis Wise's header is followed by Gordon Durie blasting a 20-yarder and then finishing clinically Polston scrambles a consolation. It's Bobby Campbell's side's first win in seven games.											
34		A	LIVERPOOL		15	L	0-3	0-2		Gunn	Culverhouse	Bowen	Butterworth	Polston	Goss	Sutch	Fleck	Sherwood	Fox	Phillips	
	20/4			*37,065*	*2*	42			*Barnes 30, Houghton 35, Rush 85*	*Grobbelaar*	*Ablett*	*Burrows*	*Nicol*	*Molby*	*Staunton*	*Beardsley*	*Houghton*	*Rush*	*Barnes*	*Gillespie*	
									Ref: V Callow	A surprise full debut for Sutch as Gordon and Crook are dropped. John Barnes heads in Steve Staunton's free-kick and Ray Houghton strikes a killer second. Ian Rush heads his 200th league goal. Gunn prevents more goals. England youth cap Goss, born in Cyprus, wins a Wales call-up.											
35		A	NOTT'M FOREST		16	L	**0-5**	0-2	*[Crosby 75, Woan 88]*	Walton	Culverhouse	**Ullathorne**	Butterworth	Polston	Goss	Sutch	Fleck*	Sherwood^	Fox	Phillips	Gordon/Crook
	24/4			*17,641*	*8*	42			*Glover 17, Clough 35, Pearce 58,*	*Crossley*	*Charles**	*Pearce*	*Walker*	*Chettle*	*Keane*	*Crosby*	*Parker*	*Clough^*	*Glover*	*Woan*	*Laws/Gemmill*
									Ref: P Alcock	Lee Glover heads his first goal in nearly three years - on his 21st birthday. Stuart Pearce blasts in a free-kick and City crumble after the break. After conceding 18 goals in seven games, Stringer admits he is perplexed by the recent dip in form. He says goalkeeper Walton is not to blame.											
36		H	QP RANGERS		13	W	1-0	0-0	Gordon 50	Walton	Culverhouse	Bowen	Butterworth	Polston	Goss	Gordon	Fleck*	Sherwood	Fox	Phillips	**Sutton**
	4/5			13,469	*12*	45				*Stejskal*	*Bardsley*	*Brevett*	*Parker*	*Peacock*	*McDonald**	*Wilkins*	*Barker*	*Allen*	*Wegerle*	*Sinton*	*Iorfa*
									Ref: K Hackett	Before kick-off Culverhouse is presented with the Player of the Year award. A nice pass by Phillips is slid into the bottom corner by Gordon to win the three points. Chris Sutton, 18, son of former Norwich utility player Mike (64 games in the 1960s), comes on for Fleck for his debut.											
37		A	ASTON VILLA		13	L	1-2	1-1	Gordon 41	Walton	Culverhouse	Bowen	Butterworth	Polston	Goss	Gordon	Fleck	Sherwood	Crook*	Phillips	Sutton
	8/5			*16,697*	*17*	45			*Bowen 9 (og), Yorke 65*	*Spink*	*Price*	*Gage*	*McGrath*	*Mountfield*	*Nielsen*	*Penrice*	*Platt*	*Cascarino*	*Cowans*	*Blake**	*Yorke*
									Ref: W Flood	Bowen helps a David Platt cross into the Norwich net. Gordon equalises, rifling in a Crook centre. Tony Cascarino's clever pass is glanced in by Dwight Yorke. Nigel Spink makes a superb late save to prevent a rare goal from Culverhouse. Canaries fought hard and feel hard done by.											
38		A	SHEFFIELD UTD		15	L	1-2	1-2	Polston 8	Walton	Culverhouse	Bowen	**Woodth'pe**	Polston	Goss^	Gordon	Fleck	Ullathorne*	Crook	Phillips	Mortensen/Smith
	11/5			*21,019*	*13*	45			*Agana 11, 18*	*Tracey*	*Wilder**	*Barnes*	*Lake*	*Beesley*	*Pemberton*	*Ward^*	*Whitehouse*	*Agana*	*Deane*	*Hoyland*	*Sayer/Booker*
	Home		Away						Ref: L Shapter	Colin Woodthorpe, who cost £225k from Chester 10 months ago, gets a long-awaited debut. Polston rattles in a volley after a Phillips corner. Tony Agana has had a goalless season so far, but drills two shots past Walton in seven minutes. Referee Shapter takes his 500th major match.											
Average	15,468		20,765																		

Rumbelows Cup			Att		F-A	H-T	Scorers, Times, and Referees	1	2	3	4	5	6	7	8	9	10	11	subs used
2:1	H	WATFORD	16	W	2-0	1-0	Crook 4, Sherwood 90	Gunn	Culverhouse	Bowen	Butterworth	Blades	Crook	Gordon	Fleck !	Sherwood	Fox	Phillips	
		26/9	7,720 2:24					James	Dublin	Drysdale	Roeder	McLoughlin	Holdsworth	Williams	Wilkinson	Inglethorpe*	Falconer	Porter	Bazeley
							Ref: A Bennett	Bottom of Division Two, The Hornets have failed to win so far this season and don't give City much difficulty this evening. Manager Colin Lee has lost the services of stalwarts Tony Coton and Kenny Jackett and things look bleak. Fleck was sent off after lashing out at Dublin (85).											
2:2	A	WATFORD	17	W	3-0	1-0	Goss 9, 64, Fleck 53	Gunn	Culverhouse	Goss	Butterworth	Blades	Crook	Gordon*	Fleck	Sherwood	Fox	Phillips	Sutch
		9/10	6,148 2:24					James	Ashby*	Williams	Porter^	Roeder	Holdsworth	Thomas	Wilkinson	Falconer	Devonshire	Bazeley	Drysdale/Ing'thorpe
							Ref: A Gunn (Norwich win 5-0 on aggregate)	Goss is star of the show at Vicarage Road. He sidefoots home a Fox cross and later shows great control to net his second after being supplied by Fox again. Fleck guides in a Fox pass for City's second. Under-pressure Colin Lee admits the match was just shooting practice for Norwich.											
3	A	MIDDLESBROUGH	16	L	0-2	0-2		Gunn	Culverhouse	Bowen	Butterworth	Blades	Crook	Gordon	Power	Sherwood	Fox	Phillips	
		30/10	17,024 2:7				Kerr 21, Hendrie 35	Pears	Cooper	Phillips	Mowbray	Kernaghan	Putney	Slaven	Mustoe	Baird	Kerr	Hendrie	
							Ref: R Nixon	Paul Kerr's volley gives Colin Todd's side the lead. John Hendrie nets a fine solo effort. Ex-Canary Trevor Putney returns for his first full game since breaking his leg eight months ago. Norwich's big-money bid for Forest midfield man Terry Wilson is put on ice as he is currently injured.											

FA Cup																			
3	H	BRISTOL CITY	11	W	2-1	1-1	Rosario 4, Fleck 70	Gunn	Culverhouse	Bowen	Butterw'th*	Polston	Crook	Gordon	Fleck	Sherwood	Rosario	Phillips	Goss
		5/1	12,630 2:9				Allison 41	Leaning	Llewellyn*	Bailey	May	Shelton	Aizlewood	Rennie	Newman	Allison	Taylor^	Smith	Bent/Donowa
							Ref: R Lewis	City take the lead through a freak goal as Phillips' 25-yard shot is deflected in off Rosario's thigh. Wayne Allison levels with a header from David Smith's cross. Jimmy Lumsden's outfit are beaten when man-of-the-match Gordon combines with Fleck for an excellent winning goal.											
4	H	SWINDON	10	W	3-1	0-0	Gordon 63, Mortensen 86, Fleck 89	Gunn	Culverhouse	Bowen	Butterworth	Polston	Crook	Gordon	Fleck	Sherwood	Smith*	Phillips	Mortensen
		26/1	14,408 2:10				White 50	Digby	Kerslake	Bodin	Hazard	Lorenzo !	Gittens !	Jones	Shearer*	White^	MacLaren	Foley	Summerbee/Viveash
							Ref: I Hemley	Argentine Nestor Lorenzo is sent off for a 'professional foul' before evergreen Steve White puts Ossie Ardiles' team ahead from a tight angle. Swindon go down to nine men after Jon Gittens elbows Fleck. City take charge and hit three, including Mortensen's first-timer from close in.											
5	H	MANCHESTER U	10	W	2-1	1-1	Fleck 26, Gordon 68	Gunn	Culverhouse	Bowen	Butterworth	Polston	Crook	Gordon	Fleck	Sherwood	Smith*	Phillips	Fox
		18/2	23,058 5				McClair 37	Sealey	Irwin	Martin*	Bruce	Blackmore	Pallister	Robson	Ince	McClair	Hughes	Sharpe	Wallace
							Ref: J Moules	In a frantic cup-tie, Sherwood nods down Gordon's corner for Fleck to swivel and shoot home. Lee Sharpe does well to set up Brian McClair's equaliser. A low cross by Culverhouse is touched by lively sub Fox to Gordon, who fires a winner under Les Sealey, sparking jubilant scenes.											
6	H	NOTTINGHAM F	10	L	0-1	0-0		Gunn	Culverhouse	Bowen	Blades	Polston	Crook*	Gordon	Fleck	Sherwood	Goss	Phillips	Fox
		9/3	24,018 12				Keane 61	Crossley	Charles	Pearce	Walker	Chettle	Keane	Crosby	Wilson	Clough	Jemson	Parker	
							Ref: A Gunn	Norwich enjoy much possession but can't find a way through. Gary Charles blocks a Phillips shot on the line. Roy Keane nets a fierce drive - Forest's first effort on target - which puts them into the semi-finals. The game is a huge anti-climax after the excitement of the previous round.											

		Home						Away					
		P	W	D	L	F	A	W	D	L	F	A	Pts
1	Arsenal*	38	15	4	0	51	10	9	9	1	23	8	83
2	Liverpool	38	14	3	2	42	13	9	4	6	35	27	76
3	Crys Palace	38	11	6	2	26	17	9	3	7	24	24	69
4	Leeds	38	12	2	5	46	23	7	5	7	19	24	64
5	Manchester C	38	12	3	4	35	25	5	8	6	29	28	62
6	Manch' U**	38	11	4	4	34	17	5	8	6	24	28	59
7	Wimbledon	38	8	6	5	28	22	6	8	5	25	24	56
8	Nott'm For	38	11	4	4	42	21	3	8	8	23	29	54
9	Everton	38	9	5	5	26	15	4	7	8	24	31	51
10	Tottenham	38	8	9	2	35	22	3	7	9	16	28	49
11	Chelsea	38	10	6	3	33	25	3	4	12	25	44	49
12	QP Rangers	38	8	5	6	27	22	4	5	10	17	31	46
13	Sheffield Utd	38	9	3	7	23	23	4	4	11	13	32	46
14	Southampton	38	9	6	4	33	22	3	3	13	25	47	45
15	NORWICH	38	9	3	7	27	32	4	3	12	14	32	45
16	Coventry	38	10	6	3	30	16	1	5	13	12	33	44
17	Aston Villa	38	7	9	3	29	25	2	5	12	17	33	41
18	Luton	38	7	5	7	22	18	3	2	14	20	43	37
19	Sunderland	38	6	6	7	15	16	2	4	13	23	44	34
20	Derby	38	3	8	8	25	36	2	1	16	12	39	24
		760	189	103	88	629	420	88	103	189	420	629	1034

* 2pts deducted
** 1pt deducted

Odds & ends

Double wins: (2) QP Rangers, Sunderland.
Double losses: (3) Manchester C, Manchester U, Nott'm Forest.

Won from behind: (3) South'pton (h), Sunderland (a), Swindon (h)(FAC).
Lost from in front: (3) Luton (h), Nott'm Forest (h), Sheffield Utd (a).

High spots: The FA Cup win over Man U, to reach the last eight.
The emergence of youngsters Power, Sutch, Sutton and Ullathorne.
Putting an end to Liverpool's 100 per cent record in October.

Low spots: Two almighty hammerings by Nottingham Forest.
A first-half nightmare at home to Wimbledon.
The lack of a serious challenge for a UEFA Cup place.
The pre-season sale of established stars Townsend and Linighan.
Defeat by Crystal Palace in the Zenith Data Systems Cup area final.

Player of the Year: Ian Culverhouse.
Ever-presents: (1) David Phillips.
Hat-tricks: (0)
Hat-tricks against: (1) Lars Elstrup (v Luton, h).
Leading scorer: (9) Robert Fleck.

	Appearances						Goals			
	Lge	*Sub*	LC	*Sub*	FAC	*Sub*	**Lge**	LC	FAC	**Tot**
Blades, Paul	**21**		3		1					
Bowen, Mark	**37**		2		4		**1**			**1**
Butterworth, Ian	**31**		3		3					
Crook, Ian	**31**	*1*	3		4		**3**	1		**4**
Culverhouse, Ian	**34**		3		4					
Fleck, Robert	**23**	*6*	2		4		**5**	1	3	**9**
Fox, Ruel	**23**	*5*	3			*2*	**4**			**4**
Gordon, Dale	**35**	*1*	3		4		**7**		2	**9**
Goss, Jeremy	**14**	*5*	1		1	*1*	**1**	2		**3**
Gunn, Bryan	**34**		3		4					
Minett, Jason		*2*								
Mortensen, Henrik		*3*				*1*			1	**1**
Phillips, David	**38**		3		4		**4**			**4**
Polston, John	**27**				4		**4**			**4**
Power, Lee	**13**	*3*	1				**3**			**3**
Rosario, Robert	**9**				1				1	**1**
Sherwood, Tim	**37**		3		4		**7**	1		**8**
Smith, David	**2**	*1*			2					
Sutch, Daryl	**2**	*2*		*1*						
Sutton, Chris		*2*								
Ullathorne, Robert	**2**									
Walton, Mark	**4**									
Woodthorpe, Colin	**1**									
(own-goals)							**2**			**2**
23 players used	**418**	***31***	**33**	***1***	**44**	***4***	**41**	**5**	**7**	**53**

No	Date		Att	Pos	Pt	F-A	H-T	Scorers, Times, and Referees	1	2	3	4	5	6	7	8	9	10	11	subs used
1	H	SHEFFIELD UTD			D	2-2	0-1	Fleck 75, 89	Gunn	Culverhouse	Bowen	Butterworth	Blades	Crook	Gordon	Fleck	**Newman**	**Beckford***	Phillips	Fox
	17/8		16,380		1			*Deane 4, Hill 73*	*Tracey*	*Pemberton*	*Cowan*	*Jones*	*Beesley*	*Hill*	*Hoyland*	*Whiteh'se**	*Agana*	*Deane*	*Bryson*	*Booker*
								Ref: P Don	City splash a club record £925k on Port Vale's Darren Beckford but fail to get Robbie Earle. Rob Newman (Bristol C) signs for £600k. Brian Deane blasts an early shock and Colin Hill's low drive makes it two. Fleck cracks home two excellent late goals to transform the atmosphere.											
2	A	QP RANGERS			W	2-0	1-0	Gordon 29, Newman 75	Gunn	Culverhouse	Bowen	Butterworth	Blades	Crook	Gordon	Fleck	Newman	Beckford*	Phillips	Fox
	21/8		*10,726*		4				*Stejskal*	*Bardsley*	*Brevett*	*Holloway*	*Peacock*	*Maddix*	*Bailey**	*Barker*	*Ferdinand*	*Wegerle*	*Sinton*	*Thompson*
								Ref: D Axcell	On a hot and humid evening, 'Disco Dale' Gordon dances in to net a sweet, side-foot volley from a Phillips cross. Newman makes the points safe from close-range after another Phillips cross. It's an unhappy first home match in charge for Rangers' new boss, the popular Gerry Francis.											
3	A	OLDHAM		5	D	2-2	1-2	Crook 21, Newman 49	Gunn	Culverhouse	Bowen	Butterworth	Blades	Crook	Gordon	Fleck	Newman	Beckford	Phillips	
	24/8		*13,548*	*7*	5			*Marshall 3, Barrett 24*	*Hallworth*	*Halle*	*Snodin*	*Henry*	*Barrett*	*Jobson^*	*Adams**	*Marshall*	*Sharp*	*Milligan*	*Holden*	*Currie/Fleming*
								Ref: K Lupton	Ex-Canary Joe Royle has done a fine job to get the Latics back in the top flight after 68 years. Ian Marshall nets a cracking drive from the edge of the box, but Crook levels from a free-kick. Earle Barrett's volley is cancelled out when Newman touches in a Phillips cross after the break.											
4	H	MANCHESTER C		7	D	0-0	0-0		Gunn	Culverhouse	Bowen	Butterworth	Blades	Crook	Gordon	Fleck	Newman	Beckford*	Phillips	Fox
	28/8		15,376	*2*	6				*Coton*	*Hill*	*Pointon*	*Reid*	*Curle*	*Redmond*	*White*	*Brightwell*	*Heath*	*Megson*	*Brennan*	
								Ref: A Buksh	A solid display by Butterworth and Blades keeps Peter Reid's men at bay. They've won their first three games and lead the table, but Norwich are not overawed. One point almost becomes three in the last minute when a thunderbolt from Newman is tipped on to the crossbar by Coton.											
5	H	TOTTENHAM		15	L	0-1	0-1		Gunn	Culverh'se*	Bowen	Butterworth	Blades	Crook	Gordon	Fleck	Newman	Beckford	Phillips	Fox
	31/8		19,460	*5*	6			*Lineker 38*	*Walker*	*Fenwick*	*V d Hauwe*	*Nayim*	*Howells*	*Mabbutt*	*Stewart*	*Durie*	*Samways*	*Lineker*	*Bergsson*	
								Ref: I Hemley	Gary Lineker heads home unchallenged from a Paul Stewart cross. City drive forward in search of an equaliser but lack finesse in the final third and Ian Walker is rarely troubled. Newman is looking good value, but record-buy Beckford has failed to impress in five goalless games.											
6	A	EVERTON		13	D	1-1	0-0	Phillips 85	Gunn	Culverhouse	Bowen	Butterworth	Blades	Crook	Gordon	Fleck	Newman	Beckford*	Phillips	Fox
	3/9		*19,197*	*17*	7			*Ward 49*	*Southall*	*Harper*	*Hinchcliffe*	*Ratcliffe*	*Watson*	*Ebbrell*	*Warzycha*	*Beardsley*	*Newell*	*Sheedy*	*Ward*	
								Ref: S Bell	New signing Mark Ward continues his good start at Goodison by skipping round Gunn to put Howard Kendall's men ahead. City leave it late but draw level when Phillips nets Gordon's cross with a stunning left-foot volley. After five hours without a goal, this was well worth the wait.											
7	A	MANCHESTER U		16	L	0-3	0-3		Gunn	Culverhouse	Bowen	Butterworth	Blades	Crook	Gordon	Fleck	Newman	Beckford*	Phillips^	Fox/Goss
	7/9		***44,986***	*1*	7			*Irwin 20, McClair 23, Giggs 28*	*Schmeichel*	*Parker*	*Irwin*	*Bruce*	*Webb^*	*Pallister*	*Robson*	*Kanch'skis**	*McClair*	*Hughes*	*Giggs*	*Blackmore/Phelan*
								Ref: V Callow	The league leaders hit three in eight minutes in the opening half-hour. Dennis Irwin shoots through a crowd and Brian McClair converts Mark Hughes' pass three minutes later. Ryan Giggs nets from an angle after a poor back-pass by Blades. Phillips is carried off with an ankle injury.											
8	H	WEST HAM		14	W	2-1	2-1	Fox 13, Gordon 39	Gunn	Culverhouse	Bowen	Butterworth	Blades	Crook	Gordon	Fleck	Newman	Fox	Ullathorne*	Goss
	14/9		15,348	*18*	10			*Small 15*	*Miklosko*	*Brown*	*Thomas*	*Breacker*	*Foster*	*Parris^*	*Bishop*	*Slater*	*Small*	*Potts*	*Morley**	*Rosenior/Rush*
								Ref: T West	Out-of-luck Beckford is axed after an unhappy start at Carrow Road. He must have winced to see his replacement, Fox, hammer home a pass from Bowen. Mick Small taps the equaliser after Trevor Morley hits the bar. Man-of-the-match Bowen sets up Gordon for the decisive goal.											
9	H	SHEFFIELD WED		8	W	1-0	1-0	Fleck 24p	Gunn	Phillips	Bowen	Butterworth	Blades	Crook	Gordon	Fleck	Newman	Fox	Ullathorne*	Goss
	18/9		12,503	*7*	13				*Woods*	*Nilsson*	*King*	*Palmer*	*Pearson*	*Warhurst*	*Wilson*	*Hyde^*	*Watson**	*Williams*	*Worthington*	*Jemson/Harkes*
								Ref: T Ward	Norwich have gone 65 games in an 18-month period without being awarded a penalty. Perhaps this explains why the ex-Canary Chris Woods looks so bemused when Mr Ward penalises his challenge on Fox. The kick is confidently stroked home by Fleck to sink Trevor Francis' outfit.											
10	A	NOTTS CO		10	D	2-2	0-1	Ullathorne 62, Bowen 90p	Gunn	Phillips	Bowen	Butterworth	Blades	Crook	Gordon*	Fleck !	Newman	Fox	Ullathorne^	Beckford/**Ball**
	21/9		*9,488*	*11*	14			*Rideout 21, Bowen 72 (og)*	*Cherry*	*Short Ch*	*Paris*	*Short Cr*	*Yates*	*Draper^*	*Thomas*	*Dryden*	*Rideout*	*Bartlett*	*Johnson T**	*Palmer/Turner*
								Ref: R Dilkes	Fleck, angry when a free-kick is awarded against him, jumps up and handles the ball when the kick is taken. He is sent off when the linesman reminds the ref this was his second yellow-card offence. Beckford returns as sub and is bundled over to give Norwich a last-minute equaliser.											

No	Venue	Opponent / Date	Att	Pos	Res / Pts	FT	HT	Scorers, Times, Referees												Subs used
11	H	LEEDS		10	D	2-2	0-0	Gordon 58, 74	Gunn	Phillips	Bowen	Butterworth	Blades	Crook	Gordon	Fleck	Newman	Fox	Ullathorne	
		28/9	15,828	*2*	15			*Dorigo 62, Speed 72*	*Lukic*	*Sterland*	*Dorigo*	*Batty*	*McClelland*	*Whyte*	*Varadi**	*Hodge^*	*Chapman*	*McAllister*	*Speed*	*Shutt/Whitlow*
								Ref: P Jones	Fox slides a pass through to Gordon who beats John Lukic. Full-back Tony Dorigo steps up to thunder a free-kick into the top left corner of Gunn's goal. Gordon hooks City back into the lead, but Gary Speed springs the offside trap to equalise again for Howard Wilkinson's outfit.											
12	A	WIMBLEDON		15	L	1-3	0-1	Beckford 69	Gunn	Phillips	Bowen	Butterworth	Blades	Crook*	Gordon	Beckford	Newman	Fox	Ullathorne	Goss
		5/10	***3,531***	*7*	15			*Fitzgerald 3, Fashanu 73, Clarke 75*	*Segers*	*Joseph*	*Phelan*	*Barton*	*Scales*	*Fitzgerald*	*Bennett**	*Earle*	*Fashanu*	*Newhouse^*	*Elkins*	*Clarke/Blackwell*
								Ref: R Groves	Sweeper Scott Fitzgerald nods his career-first goal. Beckford (at last) follows suit to level. Two quickfire late goals sink City. The tiny crowd is, amazingly, 400 higher than at the Dons' previous home game. Their manager, Ray Harford, bids farewell after this game to join Blackburn.											
13	A	SOUTHAMPTON		15	D	0-0	0-0		Gunn	Phillips	Bowen	Butterworth	Blades	Goss	Gordon*	Fleck	Newman	Fox	Ullathorne	Beckford
		19/10	*12,516*	*20*	16				*Flowers*	*Dodd*	*Adams*	*Hurlock*	*Wood*	*Ruddock*	*Lee**	*Cockerill*	*Shearer*	*Gray*	*Le Tissier*	*Dowie*
								Ref: L Shapter	A dull affair is played out at The Dell. It's Norwich's seventh draw in 13 league games. There is little flowing football on view and Fox misses City's best opening. Glenn Cockerill fluffs an easy chance, heading over the bar on 31 minutes. Steve Wood, from Millwall, debuts for Saints.											
14	H	LUTON		11	W	1-0	1-0	Newman 41	Gunn	Phillips	Bowen	Butterworth	Blades	Goss	Gordon	Fleck	Newman	Ullathorne*	Fox	Beckford
		26/10	**10,541**	*21*	19				*Chamberlain*	*Telfer*	*Dreyer*	*Hughes*	*Rodger**	*Peake*	*Rees^*	*James*	*Nogan*	*Pembridge*	*Oakes*	*Linton/Harvey*
								Ref: K Hackett	The Canaries dominate but find Alec Chamberlain in great form. Newman slots home a Fleck cross to end Norwich anxiety. David Pleat has so far only inspired two wins in 15 games in this second spell at Luton. He gives a debut to winger Scott Oakes, who hits the bar from 30 yards.											
15	H	NOTTINGHAM F		11	D	0-0	0-0		Gunn	Phillips	Bowen	Butterworth	Blades	Goss	Gordon	Fleck	Newman	Fox	Phillips	
		2/11	13,014	*17*	20				*Crossley*	*Charles*	*Pearce*	*Walker*	*Chettle*	*Gemmill*	*Crosby*	*Parker*	*Glover*	*Sheringham*	*Black*	
								Ref: D Gallacher	Forest netted 11 goals in the matches between these sides last season, so a clean sheet this time represents pride salvaged for City. Phillips is denied by the woodwork with Mark Crossley beaten. Phillips and Bowen are called into the Wales senior squad, but there's no place for Goss.											
16	A	CHELSEA		8	W	3-0	2-0	Fleck 11, 63, Bowen 26	Gunn	Phillips	Bowen	Butterworth	Blades	Goss	Ullathorne	Fleck	Newman	Sherwood	Beckford	
		16/11	*15,755*	*10*	23				*Beasant*	*Clarke*	*Myers**	*Jones*	*Elliott*	*Monkou*	*Le Saux*	*Matthew^*	*Dixon*	*Wilson*	*Wise*	*Stuart/Pearce*
								Ref: P Foakes	Gordon is sold to Glasgow Rangers for £1.2 million. It was a bid too good to turn down, but many fans are fed up with Norwich selling their best men. Fleck's 20-yarder squeezes past Dave Beasant, who then parries a Goss drive straight to Bowen. Fleck's second is a fine half-volley.											
17	H	COVENTRY		8	W	3-2	0-1	Bowen 46, Fleck 85, Sutton 90	Gunn	Phillips	Bowen	Butterworth	Blades	Goss	Ullathorne	Fleck	Newman	Sherwood*	Beckford^	Sutton/Crook
		23/11	12,056	*14*	26			*Gallagher 29, 47*	*Ogrizovic*	*Booty*	*Hurst*	*Robson**	*Pearce*	*Greenman*	*McGrath*	*Gynn*	*Furlong*	*Gallacher*	*Emerson*	*Ndlovu*
								Ref: R Lewis	Terry Butcher's side are on a losing run and he rings the changes. Coach Mick Mills is replaced by Don Howe and youngsters play in defence. Kevin Gallacher's goals look decisive until two substitutions enliven Norwich. Sutton's dramatic winner comes in his first game of the season.											
18	A	LIVERPOOL		8	L	1-2	1-2	Beckford 35	Gunn	Phillips	Bowen	Butterw'th*	Blades	Goss	Ullathorne	Fleck	Newman	Sherwood	Beckford	Sutton
		30/11	*34,881*	*9*	26			*Molby 3, Houghton 30*	*Grobbelaar*	*Ablett*	*Burrows*	*Nicol*	*Wright*	*Tanner*	*Saunders*	*Houghton*	*McManam'n*	*Molby*	*McMahon**	*Marsh*
								Ref: B Hill	Jan Molby nets an early thunderbolt to register his first goal of the season and put The Kop in good voice. Ray Houghton swoops to double the lead after Gunn parried another Molby effort. City pull a goal back straight away when Ullathorne's cross is powerfully headed in by Beckford.											
19	H	CRYSTAL PALACE		9	D	3-3	1-1	Thorn 20(og), Beckf'd 48, Newm'n 90	Gunn	Phillips	Bowen	Sutton	Crook	Goss	Ullathorne*	Fleck	Newman	Sherwood	Beckford	Fox
		7/12	12,667	*8*	27			*Newm'n 30(og), McGold' 49, Osb'n 50*	*Martyn*	*Southgate*	*Coleman*	*Gray*	*Young !*	*Thorn*	*Mortimer*	*Osborn*	*Bright*	*Gabbiadini**	*McGoldrick*	*Rodger*
								Ref: G Pooley	A Phillips drive deflects in off Andy Thorn. Newman's knee gives Palace an equaliser. Beckford, Eddie McGoldrick and Simon Osborn net in a hectic two-minute spell. City are saved by a 90th-minute goal for the third successive home match. Eric Young is sent off for arguing about it.											
20	H	QP RANGERS		11	L	0-1	0-0		Gunn	Phillips	Bowen	Sutton	Blades	Goss	Ullathorne	Fleck	Newman	Sherwood*	Beckford	Fox
		21/12	11,436	*13*	27			*Bailey 90*	*Stejskal*	*Bardsley*	*Wilson*	*Wilkins*	*Peacock*	*McDonald*	*Holloway*	*Barker*	*Bailey*	*Wegerle*	*Sinton*	
								Ref: A Smith	Rangers gain revenge for the Loftus Road result with a well-taken last-minute winning goal. Ray Wilkins puts Dennis Bailey in the clear and he calmly chips the advancing Gunn. Norwich rue second-half misses by Beckford, whose effort went wide, and Goss, foiled by Jan Stejskal.											
21	A	MANCHESTER C		13	L	1-2	1-2	Newman 5	Gunn	Phillips	Bowen	Sutton	Blades	Goss	Ullathorne*	Fleck	Newman	Sherwood	Beckford^	Fox/Polston
		26/12	*28,164*	*4*	27			*Quinn 27, White 45*	*Coton*	*Brightwell*	*Pointon*	*Reid*	*Curle*	*Redmond*	*White*	*Heath*	*Quinn*	*McMahon**	*Hughes*	*Megson*
								Ref: K Redfern	Steve McMahon is injured on his Manchester City debut after signing from Liverpool. Newman is left unmarked to head in a Phillips corner. Niall Quinn levels, heading in a White cross. On the stroke of half-time, Adrian Heath miscues a great chance, but it falls for White to convert.											

No	Date		Att	Pos	Pt	F-A	H-T	Scorers, Times, and Referees	1	2	3	4	5	6	7	8	9	10	11	subs used
22	A	TOTTENHAM		14	L	0-3	0-1		Gunn	Phillips	Bowen	Sutton	Blades	Goss	Woodth'pe*	Fleck	Newman	Sherwood	Fox	Beckford
	28/12		*27,969*	*8*	27			*Allen 31, Lineker 65, Nayim 87*	*Thorstvedt*	*Fenwick*	*V d Hauwe*	*Sedgley*	*Nayim*	*Mabbutt*	*Stewart*	*Walsh**	*Samways*	*Lineker*	*Allen*	*Houghton*
								Ref: K Burge	Paul Allen fires a cracking goal after combining neatly with Vinnie Samways. Gary Lineker, who always seems to score against Norwich, gets clear of the defence and floats a shot over Gunn. The icing on the cake for Peter Shreeves' side is when Nayim scores directly from a free-kick.											
23	H	ASTON VILLA		12	W	2-1	0-0	Fleck 56p, Ullathorne 78	Gunn	Phillips	Bowen	Sutton*	Blades	Goss	Fox	Fleck	Newman	Beckford	Ullathorne	Polston
	1/1		15,318	*6*	30			*Regis 74*	*Sealey*	*Kubicki*	*Price*	*Teale*	*McGrath*	*Richardson*	*Daley*	*Blake**	*Regis*	*Parker*	*Yorke*	*Olney*
								Ref: J Martin	Chris Price pulls Ullathorne to concede a penalty. Les Sealey saves Fleck's kick, but as Dariusz Kubicki had encroached he gets another chance and scores. Veteran Cyrille Regis outstrips the defence to hammer an equaliser. Ullathorne coolly slots home the winner from a Phillips cross.											
24	H	OLDHAM		14	L	1-2	1-1	Beckford 38	Gunn	Phillips	Bowen	Sutton	Blades	Crook	Fox	Fleck	Newman	Beckford*	Ullathorne	Sutch
	11/1		10,986	*15*	30			*Holden 45, Bernard 65*	*Hallworth*	*Fleming*	*Bernard*	*Henry*	*Barrett*	*Jobson*	*Adams*	*Marshall*	*Sharp*	*Palmer*	*Holden*	
								Ref: J Rushton	Jon Hallworth fumbles a Fleck cross and Beckford pounces to put Norwich ahead. Andy Holden equalises with a close-range header after City are undone by a long throw. Holden's second-half cross is flicked on by Graeme Sharp for unmarked youngster Paul Bernard to hammer home.											
25	A	SHEFFIELD UTD		14	L	0-1	0-0		Gunn*	Woodthorpe	Bowen	Sutton	Polston	Goss	Sutch	Fleck	Newman	Crook	Ullathorne	Beckford
	18/1		*17,549*	*19*	30			*Bryson 74*	*Tracey*	*Gage*	*Hill*	*Gannon*	*Gayle*	*Beesley*	*Bradshaw*	*Lake*	*Bryson*	*Deane*	*Whiteh'se**	*Hodges*
								Ref: R Hamer	Gunn injures his back early on and is replaced in goal for the second-half by Beckford. The stand-in makes saves from Ian Bryson and Brian Deane. He is well protected by the defence, but is finally beaten when Kevin Gage's long-range shot hits the bar and Bryson nets the rebound.											
26	H	SOUTHAMPTON		12	W	2-1	0-0	Ullathorne 49, Fleck 74	Walton	Phillips	Bowen	Sutton	Polston	Goss	Beckford	Fleck	Newman	Crook*	Ullathorne	Fox
	1/2		10,660	*21*	33			*Cockerill 71*	*Flowers*	*Kenna*	*Adams*	*Horne**	*Hall*	*Ruddock*	*Le Tissier*	*Hurlock*	*Shearer*	*Dowie*	*Benali^*	*Cockerill/Gray*
								Ref: P Banes	Beckford neatly evades Tim Flowers and pulls the ball back for Ullathorne to head City ahead. Glenn Cockerill fires in a spectacular equaliser for Ian Branfoot's side, his 25-yarder going in off the bar. Flowers parries Bowen's shot into the path of Fleck, who nets a close-range winner.											
27	A	LUTON		16	L	0-2	0-0		Walton	Culverhouse	Bowen	Butterworth	Polston	Goss	Fox	Fleck	Beckford*	Crook	Phillips	Sutch
	8/2		*8,554*	*21*	33			*Preece 67, Harford 88*	*Sutton*	*James*	*Harvey*	*Kamara**	*Dreyer*	*Peake*	*Oakes*	*Hughes*	*Harford*	*Pembridge*	*Preece*	*Stein*
								Ref: P Jones	Relegation-threatened Luton come out after the break looking much sharper after an appalling first-half display by both sides. David Preece beats ex-Luton keeper Walton after a slip by Bowen. Mark Pembridge's cross is tapped in by Mick Harford to clinch the points for the Hatters.											
28	A	ARSENAL		14	D	1-1	0-0	Fox 58	Walton	Culverhouse	Woodthorpe	Butterworth	Polston	Goss	Fox	Fleck	Newman	Sutton	Phillips	
	11/2		*22,352*	*6*	34			*Merson 63*	*Seaman*	*Dixon*	*Winterburn^*	*Hillier*	*Bould*	*Adams*	*Pates*	*Wright*	*Smith*	*Merson*	*Limpar**	*Campbell/Parlour*
								Ref: J Key	A reshuffle by Stringer works well at Highbury. Fox hits the crossbar in the tenth minute, but is on target later with a cool finish. Paul Merson equalises, lobbing in Lee Dixon's through ball. Sherwood departs for Blackburn, having earlier this season had a dispute with the management.											
29	H	LIVERPOOL		10	W	**3-0**	0-0	Woodthorpe 66, Fleck 70, 90	Walton	Culverhouse	Woodthorpe	Butterworth	Polston	Goss	Fox	Fleck	Newman	Sutton	Phillips	
	22/2		**20,411**	*5*	37				*Grobbelaar*	*Hysen*	*Harkness*	*Marsh*	*Wright*	*Kozma**	*Saunders^*	*Houghton*	*Rush*	*Redknapp*	*McManam'n*	*Rosenthal/Walters*
								Ref: M Bailey	Graeme Souness' men are crushed in the last half hour. Woodthorpe's first Norwich goal sees him steers the ball in at the second attempt. Mark Wright's poor back-pass is pounced on by Fleck for the second. With the last kick of the game, Fleck slots in after dispossessing Glenn Hysen.											
30	A	CRYSTAL PALACE		10	W	4-3	4-2	Sutton 14, Newman 32, Polston 43,	Walton	Culverhouse	Woodthorpe	Butterworth	Polston	Goss	Fox	Fleck	Newman	Sutton	Phillips	
	29/2		*14,201*	*11*	40			*Osborn 17, Bright 22, 65* [Goss 45]	*Martyn*	*Humphrey*	*Shaw*	*Osborn*	*Young*	*Thorn*	*Mortimer*	*Thomas**	*Bright*	*Whyte^*	*McGoldrick*	*Southgate/Coleman*
								Ref: B Nixon	Chris Sutton shoots under Nigel Martyn to get a thriller underway. City then fall behind, only to bounce back with three goals in 13 minutes. Newman and Polston are set up by Phillips crosses and Goss knocks into an empty net. Mark Bright pulls one back to ensure a tense finale.											
31	A	COVENTRY		10	D	0-0	0-0		Walton	Culverhouse	Woodthorpe	Butterworth	Polston	Goss	Fox*	Sutch	Newman	Sutton^	Phillips	Fleck/Ball
	4/3		*8,549*	*17*	41				*Ogrizovic*	*Burrows*	*Sansom*	*Robson*	*Pearce*	*Atherton*	*Flynn*	*Emerson^*	*Rosario**	*Gallacher*	*Furlong*	*Drinkell/McGrath*
								Ref: C Trussell	Don Howe is now in charge at Coventry and although they've not conceded in 400 minutes' play, this goalless draw is their fourth in a row and a club record. It's drab fare for the tiny crowd. Goss blasts the best chance over the bar. Ex-Canary Drinkell gets his first action in six months.											

32	H	CHELSEA		13	L	0-1	0-0		Walton	Culverhouse	Woodthorpe	Butterworth	Polston	Goss	Fox	Fleck	Newman	Sutch*	Phillips	Sutton
	11/3		13,413	*7*	41			*Dixon 84*	*Beasant*	*Clarke*	*Sinclair*	*Jones*	*Cundy*	*Monkou*	*Le Saux*	*Townsend*	*Dixon*	*Cascarino*	*Stuart*	
								Ref: D Axcell	Stringer drops Sutton and plays Sutch in attack. Kerry Dixon misses an easy chance early on, but has the last laugh near the end. He swivels and fires home Steve Clarke's cross in terrific style. Afterwards he says his worst-ever miss had been followed by one of his best five goals.											
33	A	NOTT'M FOREST		14	L	0-2	0-2		Walton	Culverhouse	Woodthorpe	Butterworth	Polston	Goss	Fox	Fleck	Newman	Sutton	Phillips*	Bowen
	14/3		*20,721*	*13*	41			*Keane 37, Gemmill 42*	*Crossley*	*Charles*	*Pearce*	*Walker*	*Tiler*	*Keane*	*Crosby*	*Gemmill*	*Clough*	*Sheringham*	*Black*	
								Ref: R Dilkes	Forest play accurate and fast-flowing football and Norwich have to settle for their fourth successive game without a goal. At the end of a fine move Roy Keane slides a shot under Walton. Gary Crosby's shot is blocked after a Stuart Pearce cross, but Scott Gemmill is on hand to score.											
34	H	EVERTON		13	W	4-3	1-2	Beckford 2, 83, 86, Newman 46	Walton	Culverhouse	Bowen^	Butterworth	Polston*	Goss	Fox	Beckford	Newman	Sutton	Crook	Woodthorpe/Sutch
	21/3		11,900	*8*	44			*Johnston 10, 50, Beardsley 29*	*Southall*	*Jackson*	*Ablett**	*Ebbrell*	*Atteveld*	*Keown*	*Warzycha*	*Beardsley*	*Johnston*	*Harper*	*Ward*	*Barlow*
								Ref: G Willard	Beckford coolly slots home the first, but City are behind by the half-hour mark. Newman's powerful header is followed by a second Mo Johnson strike. Roared on by a small crowd, City leave it late again. Expensive Beckford silences his critics by shooting home two late goals.											
35	A	ASTON VILLA		14	L	0-1	0-0		Walton	Culverhouse	Bowen	Butterworth	Woodthorpe	Goss	Fox	Sutch	Newman	Sutton	Crook	
	28/3		*16,985*	*10*	44			*Staunton 79*	*Spink*	*Barrett*	*Staunton*	*Teale*	*McGrath*	*Richardson*	*Carruthers**	*Parker*	*Regis*	*Atkinson*	*Yorke^*	*Daley/Olney*
								Ref: A Buksh	Nigel Spink makes some fine saves to keep Ron Atkinson's side on level terms. Villa have scored just one goal in 11 league games, but strike gold in the late stages here with a real fluke. Steve Staunton floats a cross over and Walton is deceived by the flight, the ball ending in the net.											
36	H	MANCHESTER U		15	L	1-3	0-1	Power 62	Walton	Culverhouse	Bowen	Butterworth	Polston	Goss	Fox	Phillips*	Newman	Sutton	Crook^	Power/Polston
	31/3		17,489	*1*	44			*Ince 40, 59, McClair 66*	*Schmeichel*	*Donaghy*	*Irwin*	*Bruce*	*Giggs*	*Pallister*	*Robson**	*Ince*	*McClair*	*Hughes*	*Sharpe*	*Blackmore*
								Ref: M James	Paul Ince is on target for the first time in six months, as he cracks two fierce drives past Walton either side of the interval. Power races on to a through pass to blast home a fine response. Brian McClair's volley four minutes later is enough to put the points well out of Norwich's reach.											
37	H	ARSENAL		17	L	1-3	0-1	Butterworth 59	Walton	Culverhouse	Bowen	Butterworth	Polston	Goss	Fox	Power*	Newman	Beckford	Ullathorne	Sutton
	8/4		12,971	*4*	44			*Wright 33p, 82, Campbell 55*	*Seaman*	*O'Leary^*	*Lydersen*	*Hillier*	*Bould*	*Adams*	*Rocastle*	*Wright*	*Campbell*	*Merson*	*Limpar**	*Smith/Morrow*
								Ref: P Wright	Ian Wright tangles with Ullathorne and converts the penalty himself. Kevin Campbell increases the lead, drilling his shot inside the near post. Butterworth converts the rebound from a Beckford effort, only his third goal in 182 City league appearances. Wright neatly clinches the points.											
38	A	WEST HAM		17	L	**0-4**	0-2		Walton	Bowen	Ullathorne	Butterworth	Polston	Goss	Fox	Power*	Newman	Beckford	Smith	Sutton^/Sutch
	11/4		*16,896*	*22*	44			*Rush 14, 36, Dicks 72p, Bishop 79*	*Miklosko*	*Breacker*	*Dicks*	*Potts*	*Martin*	*Thomas*	*Bishop*	*Rush*	*Small**	*Allen C*	*Slater*	*Keen*
								Ref: P Foakes	A humiliating defeat by bottom-of-the-table West Ham. It's their first win in 10. Youngster Matthew Rush converts two headers and City never recover. Walton brings down Mitchell Thomas for the penalty. Ian Bishop gets on the end of a neat move to net a fourth for Billy Bonds' side.											
39	H	NOTTS CO		18	L	0-1	0-0		Walton	Bowen	Woodthorpe	Butterworth	Polston	Goss	Fox	Fleck	Newman	Beckford	Sutch	
	18/4		12,100	*21*	44			*Matthews 87*	*Cherry*	*Palmer*	*Dryden*	*Short Cr*	*Johnson M*	*Draper*	*Williams**	*Harding*	*Thomas*	*Bartlett^*	*Wilson*	*Short Ch/Matthews*
								Ref: P Don	Serious relegation fears surround the club after this fifth successive league defeat. Fleck's volley is brilliantly saved as lowly County hang on grimly. Walton's earlier heroics in goal amount to nothing as student Rob Matthews, yet to start a match, sees a late shot deflect in off Polston.											
40	A	SHEFFIELD WED		18	L	0-2	0-2		Walton	Bowen	Woodthrope	Blades	Polston	Goss	Fox	Fleck	Newman	Beckford*	**Johnson**	Power
	20/4		*27,362*	*3*	44			*Nilsson 10, Sheridan 45*	*Woods*	*Nilsson*	*King*	*Palmer*	*Pearson*	*Warhurst*	*Wilson*	*Sheridan**	*Johnson^*	*Williams*	*Worthington*	*Harkes/Francis*
								Ref: J Worrall	The FA Cup semi-final hangover continues as City return to the scene of their defeat. This time they have 250 followers, instead of 17,000. Roland Nilsson curls in a low shot for the first goal and John Sheridan sweeps in the second in first-half injury-time. Andy Johnson, 17, debuts.											
41	H	WIMBLEDON		18	D	1-1	1-0	Fleck 20	Walton	Culverhouse	Bowen	Blades	Polston	Goss	Fox	Fleck	Newman	Beckford*	Phillips	Woodthorpe
	25/4		11,061	*17*	45			*Elkins 52*	*Segers*	*Joseph*	*Elkins*	*Barton*	*Scales**	*McAllister*	*Miller*	*Earle*	*Fashanu*	*Fitzgerald*	*Clarke*	*Castledine*
								Ref: I Hemley	Joe Kinnear has re-invigorated the Dons and they are clear of the drop, but for City one more point will ensure survival. Fleck ends the team's goal drought after Newman's header comes back off Hans Segers. Gary Elkins nets his first Dons goal after a free-kick is touched aside to him.											
42	A	LEEDS		18	L	0-1	0-1		Walton	Culverhouse	Ullathorne*	Blades	Polston	Goss	Fox	Fleck	Newman	Johnson	Phillips	Woodthorpe
	2/5		*32,673*	*1*	45			*Rod Wallace 25*	*Lukic*	*Newsome*	*Dorigo*	*Batty*	*Fairclough*	*Whyte*	*Cantona**	*Wallace Rod*	*Chapman^*	*McAllister*	*Speed*	*Strachan/Hodge*
		Home	Away					Ref: R Milford	Stringer shocks the club by resigning on 1 May, saying it's time for a new man to take over. Coach Mike Walker emerges as favourite to take over. Leeds have already clinched the title and their fans create a party atmosphere. Rod Wallace wins the game with a marvellous solo effort.											
Average		13,858	19,362																	

Rumbelows Cup			Att			F-A	H-T	Scorers, Times, and Referees	1	2	3	4	5	6	7	8	9	10	11	subs used
2:1	A	CHARLTON		10	W	2-0	1-0	Gordon 40, Newman 57	Gunn	Phillips*	Bowen	Butterworth	Blades	Crook	Gordon	Fleck^	Newman	Fox	Ullathorne	Woodth'pe/Beckf'd
		25/9	*2,886*	*2:14*					*Bolder*	*Pitcher*	*Barness*	*Peake*	*Webster*	*Gatting*	*Lee*	*Bacon*	*Leaburn*	*Nelson*	*Dyer**	*Grant*
								Ref: M Pierce	At sparsely populated Upton Park, the class gap is clear. Not a good night for Charlton's new management duo of Alan Curbishley and Steve Gritt. Fleck dummies a Fox pass for Gordon to score and victory is assured as Newman stabs in at the second attempt following a slick move.											
2:2	H	CHARLTON		15	W	3-0	2-0	Fleck 9, 35, Beckford 69	Gunn	Goss	Bowen*	Butterworth	Blades	Fleck^	Gordon	Beckford	Newman	Fox	Ullathorne	Woodthorpe/Ball
		9/10	5,507	*2:7*					*Bolder*	*Pitcher*	*Barness*	*Peake*	*Webster*	*Gatting*	*Bacon**	*Grant*	*Salako*	*Minto*	*Dyer*	*Gorman*
								Ref: R Wiseman (Norwich win 5-0 on aggregate)	Fleck returns hungry from a one-match suspension and notches two first-half strikes. He knocks the first into an empty net and sweeps in the second after combining well with Newman. Record signing Beckford heads his first Norwich goal from a Fox corner-kick to seal an easy win.											
3	H	BRENTFORD		11	W	4-1	0-0	Fox 50, Fleck 51, Beckford 74, 84	Gunn	Phillips	Bowen	Butterworth	Blades*	Goss^	Gordon	Fleck	Newman	Beckford	Fox	Polston/Ball
		30/10	7,394	*3:2*				*Manuel 90*	*Bayes*	*Bates*	*Manuel*	*Millen*	*Evans*	*Ratcliffe**	*Godfrey^*	*Gayle*	*Holdsworth*	*Blissett*	*Smillie*	*Rostron/Buckle*
								Ref: A Gunn	The Bees' stubborn resistance begins to crumble after a Fox shot is helped into the net by Keith Millen's stumble. Seconds later Fleck rounds Ashley Bayes for the second. Beckford finds his shooting boots to see off Phil Holders' men with a double. Billy Manuel grabs a consolation.											
4	H	WEST HAM		8	W	2-1	0-0	Fleck 64, 90p	Gunn	Phillips	Bowen	Sutton	Blades*	Goss	Ullathorne	Fleck	Newman	Beckford^	Sherwood	Crook/Fox
		4/12	16,325	*17*				*Small 73*	*Miklosko*	*Breacker*	*Thomas*	*Gale*	*Potts*	*Parris*	*Bishop*	*McAvennie*	*Small*	*Allen*	*Slater*	
								Ref: K Morton	A spectacular volley from 20 yards by Fleck opens the scoring, but Mick Small nips in for the equaliser after a slip-up by Blades. After nearly four minutes of injury-time, Mitchell Thomas pushes Bowen and Fleck squeezes his penalty-kick past the despairing dive of Ludek Miklosko.											
5	A	TOTTENHAM		12	L	1-2	1-0	Fleck 32	Gunn	Phillips	Bowen	Sutton	Blades	Goss	Fox	Fleck	Newman	Crook*	Ullathorne	Beckford
		8/1	*29,471*	*8*				*Walsh 77, Lineker 85*	*Thorstvedt*	*Fenwick**	*V d Hauwe*	*Sedgley*	*Nayim*	*Mabbutt*	*Stewart*	*Walsh*	*Samways^*	*Lineker*	*Allen*	*Bergsson/Houghton*
								Ref: M Bodenham	A Fleck shot is deflected in by Gary Mabbutt to give City an interval lead. It's the Scotsman's 23rd goal in 31 cup-ties. Spurs storm back in the later stages and Paul Walsh flicks in a Pat Van den Hauwe long throw. Minutes later Gary Lineker pounces after a corner to net the winner.											

FA Cup																				
3	H	BARNSLEY		12	W	1-0	0-0	Fleck 88	Gunn	Phillips	Bowen	Sutton	Blades*	Goss	Fox	Fleck	Newman	Beckford^	Ullathorne	Polston/Crook
		4/1	12,189	*2:18*					*Butler*	*Fleming*	*Bishop*	*Bullimore*	*Smith**	*Williams*	*Robinson*	*Redfearn*	*O'Connell*	*Rammell*	*Archdeacon*	*Currie^/Saville*
								Ref: A Buksh	Lee Butler heroically keeps Norwich at bay until the dying minutes. Mark Robinson brings down Goss and Flecks nets from the spot to break Barnsley hearts. Moments later Owen Archdeacon fires a 25-yarder against he bar. Tykes boss and ex-Canary Mel Machin just can't believe it.											
4	H	MILLWALL		12	W	2-1	1-0	Bowen 3, Fleck 63	Walton	Phillips	Bowen	Sutton	Polston	Goss	Ullathorne	Fleck	Newman	Beckford	Crook	
		5/2	16,500	*2:13*				*Kerr 85*	*Davison*	*Cooper*	*Dawes*	*Stevens*	*Thompson*	*Rae*	*Colquhoun*	*Verveer*	*Kerr*	*McGinlay*	*Falco**	*Goodman*
								Ref: T Holbrook	Etienne Verveer's poor clearance is converted by the alert Bowen. Sutton is penalised for handball, but Paul Kerr's first-half penalty is saved by Walton, who also blocks Alex Rae's follow-up. After Rae strikes a post, Fleck produces a neat finish. Kerr's volleyed goal is too late to matter.											
5	H	NOTTS CO		14	W	3-0	2-0	Sutton 19, 56, Phillips 41	Walton	Culverhouse	Woodthorpe	Butterworth	Polston	Goss	Fox	Fleck	Newman	Sutton	Phillips	
		15/2	14,511	*19*					*Cherry*	*Palmer*	*Paris*	*Short Cr*	*Short Ch*	*Draper*	*Thomas*	*Turner*	*Harding**	*Bartlett*	*Agana^*	*Johnson T/Dryden*
								Ref: D Gallacher	Teenager Sutton tucks home the first after a Newman shot is only parried by Steve Cherry. The all-important second goal comes when Phillips latches on to a through-ball from Culverhouse just before the interval. Neil Warnock's men are on the ropes when Sutton nets a diving header.											
QF	A	SOUTHAMPTON		11	D	0-0	0-0		Walton	Culverhouse	Woodthorpe	Butterworth	Polston	Goss	Fox	Fleck	Newman	Sutton	Phillips	
		7/3	*20,088*	*21*					*Flowers*	*Dodd*	*Benali*	*Horne*	*Moore*	*Ruddock*	*Le Tissier*	*Cockerill*	*Shearer*	*Dowie*	*Hurlock*	
								Ref: G Ashby	Walton makes a good save from Iain Dowie after ten minutes, but Norwich go on to have the better of the first half. Tim Flowers makes an excellent save from Fleck. Best chance of all is missed by Glenn Cockerill. Portsmouth are the only team definitely through after today's ties.											
QF R	H	SOUTHAMPTON		14	W	2-1	0-1	Newman 54, Sutton 116	Walton	Culverhouse	Woodthorpe	Butterworth	Polston	Goss	Fox	Fleck	Newman	Sutton*	Bowen	Sutch
		18/3	21,017	*19*		*aet*		*Ruddock 45*	*Flowers*	*Dodd**	*Benali*	*Horne !*	*Moore*	*Ruddock*	*Le Tissier !*	*Cockerill*	*Shearer*	*Dowie*	*Hurlock*	*Kenna*
								Ref: G Ashby	In a red-hot atmosphere, Neil Ruddock heads home at the near post. After the break, Le Tissier kicks out at Fleck and is red-carded. Newman lashes a fine goal to force extra-time. Barry Horne kicks Woodthorpe and is also sent off. Sutton heads home a loose ball for a late winner.											
SF	N	SUNDERLAND		15	L	0-1	0-1		Walton	Culverhouse	Woodthorpe	Butterworth	Polston	Goss	Fox	Fleck	Newman	Sutton*	Bowen	Sutch
		5/4	*40,102*	*2:18*				*Byrne 33*	*Norman*	*Kay*	*Rogan*	*Ball**	*Hardyman*	*Bracewell*	*Davenport*	*Rush*	*Armstrong*	*Byrne*	*Atkinson*	*Bennett*
		(At Hillsborough)						Ref: N Midgley	Loud appeals for offside are ignored as Brian Atkinson's cross floats beyond Walton and is headed home by John Byrne. Fleck passed a late fitness test, but has a quiet game and City never get going. A third FA Cup semi-final defeat means heartbreak for the 17,000 travelling fans.											

			Home					Away					
		P	W	D	L	F	A	W	D	L	F	A	Pts
1	Leeds	42	13	8	0	38	13	9	8	4	36	24	82
2	Manchester U	42	12	7	2	34	13	9	8	4	29	20	78
3	Sheffield Wed	42	13	5	3	39	24	8	7	6	23	25	75
4	Arsenal	42	12	7	2	51	22	7	8	6	30	24	72
5	Manchester C	42	13	4	4	32	14	7	6	8	29	34	70
6	Liverpool	42	13	5	3	34	17	3	11	7	13	23	64
7	Aston Villa	42	13	3	5	31	16	4	6	11	17	28	60
8	Nott'm For	42	10	7	4	36	27	6	4	11	24	31	59
9	Sheffield Utd	42	9	6	6	29	23	7	3	11	36	40	57
10	Crys Palace	42	7	8	6	24	25	7	7	7	29	36	57
11	QP Rangers	42	6	10	5	25	21	6	8	7	23	26	54
12	Everton	42	8	8	5	28	19	5	6	10	24	32	53
13	Wimbledon	42	10	5	6	32	20	3	9	9	21	33	53
14	Chelsea	42	7	8	6	31	30	6	6	9	19	30	53
15	Tottenham	42	7	3	11	33	35	8	4	9	25	28	52
16	Southampton	42	7	5	9	17	28	7	5	9	22	27	52
17	Oldham	42	11	5	5	46	36	3	4	14	17	31	51
18	NORWICH	42	8	6	7	29	28	3	6	12	18	35	45
19	Coventry	42	6	7	8	18	15	5	4	12	17	29	44
20	Luton	42	10	7	4	25	17	0	5	16	13	54	42
21	Notts Co	42	7	5	9	24	29	3	5	13	16	33	40
22	West Ham	42	6	6	9	22	24	3	5	13	15	35	38
		924	208	135	119	678	496	119	135	208	496	678	1251

Odds & ends

Double victories: (0).
Double losses:(2) Tottenham, Manchester U.

Won from behind: (4) Coventry (h), Crystal Palace (a), Everton (h), Southampton (h)(FAC).
Lost from in front: (3) Manchester C (a), Oldham (h), Tottenham (a)(LC).

High points: Lengthy runs in both major cup competitions.
Avoiding relegation, to ensure a place in the new Premier League.
The emphatic home win over Liverpool in February.
Two thrilling 4-3 victories (over Crystal Palace and Everton).

Low points: The disappointing FA Cup semi-final defeat thanks to a disputed goal and a below-par display.
The shock resignation of popular manager Dave Stringer.
A 10% drop in average crowds at Carrow Road.
The miserable end to the season: 9 losses in the last 12 games.
Demolition of the old Barclay Stand – a 'home from home' for many.
The embarrassing 0-4 defeat by bottom-of-the-table West Ham.

Player of the Year: Robert Fleck.
Ever-presents: (0).
Hat-tricks: (1) Darren Beckford (v Everton, h).
Hat-tricks against: (0).
Leading scorer: (19) Robert Fleck.

	Appearances						Goals			
	Lge	*Sub*	LC	*Sub*	FAC	*Sub*	Lge	LC	FAC	Tot
Ball, Steve		*2*		*2*						
Beckford, Darren	**25**	*5*	3	*2*	2	*1*	**7**	3		**10**
Blades, Paul	**26**		5		1					
Bowen, Mark	**35**	*1*	5		4		**3**		1	**4**
Butterworth, Ian	**31**		3		4		**1**			**1**
Crook, Ian	**20**	*1*	2	*1*	1	*2*	**1**			**1**
Culverhouse, Ian	**21**				4					
Fleck, Robert	**35**	*1*	5		6		**11**	6	2	**19**
Fox, Ruel	**27**	*10*	4	*1*	5		**2**	1		**3**
Gordon, Dale	**15**		3				**4**	1		**5**
Goss, Jeremy	**29**	*4*	4		6		**1**			**1**
Gunn, Bryan	**25**		5		1					
Johnson, Andy	**2**									
Newman, Rob	**41**		5		6		**7**	1	1	**9**
Phillips, David	**34**		4		4		**1**		1	**2**
Polston, John	**16**	*3*		*1*	5	*1*	**1**			**1**
Power, Lee	**2**	*2*					**1**			**1**
Sherwood, Tim	**7**		1							
Smith, David	**1**									
Sutch, Daryl	**5**	*4*				*1*				
Sutton, Chris	**16**	*5*	2		6		**2**		3	**5**
Ullathorne, Robert	**20**		4		2		**3**			**3**
Walton, Mark	**17**				5					
Woodthorpe, Colin	**12**	*3*		*2*	4		**1**			**1**
(own-goals)							**1**			**1**
24 players used	**462**	***41***	**55**	***9***	**66**	***5***	**47**	**12**	**8**	**67**

No	Date		Att	Pos	Pt	F-A	H-T	Scorers, Times, and Referees	1	2	3	4	5	6	7	8	9	10	11	subs used
1	A	ARSENAL		1	W	4-2	0-2	Robins 69, 84, Phillips 72, Fox 82	Gunn	Culverhouse	Bowen	Butterworth	Polston	**Megson**^	Fox	Newman	Sutton*	Goss	Phillips	**Robins**/Crook
	15/8		*24,030*	*22*	3			*Bould 28, Campbell 39*	*Seaman*	*Dixon*	*Winterburn*	*Hillier*	*Bould*	*Adams*	*Jensen*	*Smith*	*Campbell*	*Merson**	*Limpar*	*Wright*
								Ref: A Gunn	An amazing afternoon as Norwich become the new Premier League's first leaders and leading scorers. New boss Walker brings on debutant Mark Robins and he sparks a sensational last 21 minutes to obliterate the two-goal deficit. His second goal is an exquisite chip from 30 yards.											
2	H	CHELSEA		1	W	2-1	0-1	Phillips 57, Robins 59	Gunn	Culverhouse	Bowen	Butterworth	Polston*	Megson	Fox	Newman	Robins	Goss	Phillips	Sutton
	19/8		15,164	*16*	6			*Stuart 15*	*Beasant*	*Clarke*	*Hall*	*Jones*	*Elliott*	*Donaghy*	*Stuart*	*Allon*^	*Harford*	*Townsend*	*Matthew**	*Newton/Spencer*
								Ref: G Ashby	Fleck has joined Chelsea for £2.1 million with a contract clause preventing him playing tonight. Graham Stuart's header gives the Blues the lead. Polston clashes with Mick Harford and exits with a broken nose. Phillips nets a fierce volley and Robins wins it with a deftly lofted shot.											
3	H	EVERTON		2	D	1-1	0-0	Fox 67	Gunn	Culverhouse	Bowen	Butterworth	Sutton	Megson^	Fox	Newman*	Robins	Goss	Phillips	Crook/Power
	22/8		14,150	*6*	7			*Beardsley 55*	*Southall*	*Harper*	*Hinchcliffe*	*Ebbrell*^	*Watson*	*Ablett*	*Warzycha**	*Beardsley*	*Rideout*	*Horne*	*Ward*	*Beagrie/Johnston*
								Ref: J Key	Peter Beardsley answers the home fans, who were singing unkind songs, by firing in a loose ball. Norwich equalise when Fox gets above much taller opponents to head past Neville Southall. A gritty display by City nearly wins three points when a late Robins shot curls narrowly wide.											
4	A	MANCHESTER C		6	L	1-3	0-1	Megson 55	Gunn	Culverhouse	Bowen	Butterworth	Sutton	Megson	Fox*	Goss	Robins^	Crook	Phillips	Newman/Power
	26/8		*23,182*	*14*	7			*White 45, 79, McMahon 90*	*Coton*	*Brightwell*	*Phelan*	*Simpson*	*Curle*	*Vonk*	*White*	*Sheron*	*Quinn*	*Holden*	*McMahon*	
								Ref: D Elleray	David White's low shot beats Gunn just before the break. Unmarked Megson heads his first Norwich goal against the club he came from, after a Phillips corner. White blasts home from six yards, then Steve McMahon finishes City off in the last minute by lashing into the roof of the net.											
5	A	CRYSTAL PALACE		3	W	2-1	1-1	Power 15, Phillips 74	Gunn	Culverhouse	Bowen	Butterworth	Sutton	Megson	Crook	Newman	Power	Goss*	Phillips	Sutch
	29/8		*12,033*	*18*	10			*McGoldrick 19*	*Martyn*	*Humphrey*^	*Sinnott*	*Southgate*	*Young*	*Thorn*	*Coleman**	*Thomas*	*Bright*	*Gordon*	*McGoldrick*	*Salako/Osborn*
								Ref: D Allison	Power swoops to score from what looks like a miscued Phillips shot. A long throw is not cleared properly and Eddie McGoldrick brings Steve Coppell's men level. The home side exert plenty of pressure, but Norwich snatch the points when Phillips buries a spectacular overhead kick.											
6	H	NOTT'M FOREST		1	W	3-1	1-1	Crook 2, Power 76, Phillips 90	Gunn	Culverhouse	Bowen	Butterworth	Sutton	Megson	Crook	Newman	Power	Goss	Phillips	
	31/8		14,104	*20*	13			*Clough 31*	*Crossley*	*Laws*	*Pearce*	*Wilson*	*Chettle*	*Keane*	*Orlygsson*	*Gemmill*	*Clough*	*Bannister*	*Black*	
								Ref: B Hill	Fireworks, celebrity guests and dancing girls - all part of the live TV razzmatazz. Crook gets on with the real business, firing a free-kick into the top corner. Nigel Clough levels from an angle, but Power and Phillips crack home fierce drives in the final 15 minutes to put Norwich top.											
7	H	SOUTHAMPTON		1	W	1-0	0-0	Robins 87	Gunn	Culverhouse	Bowen	Butterw'th*	Sutton	Megson	Crook	Newman	Power	Goss	Phillips	Robins
	5/9		**12,452**	*18*	16				*Flowers*	*Dodd*	*Benali*	*Hurlock*	*Monkou*	*Moore*	*Le Tissier*	*Maddison*	*Dowie*	*Speedie*	*Groves*	
								Ref: K Hackett	Walker picks up the Manager of the Month award for August - his first active month as boss. A bad-tempered and lack-lustre contest ensues with Ian Branfoot's unattractive side. Robins is quiet until pouncing to grab the winner near the end, after Phillips knocked back a Goss centre.											
8	A	CHELSEA		1	W	3-2	0-2	Robins 46, 73, Phillips 76	Gunn	Culverhouse	Bowen	Polston	Sutton	Megson	Crook*	Newman	Robins	Goss	Phillips	Sutch
	12/9		*16,880*	*13*	19			*Harford 3, Townsend 28*	*Beasant*	*Barness*	*Hall*	*Townsend**	*Lee*	*Donaghy*	*Newton*	*Fleck*	*Harford*	*Spackman*	*Wise*	*Stuart*
								Ref: K Barrett	The team arrives late due to traffic and are caught cold as ex-City hero Fleck sets up Mick Harford. It gets worse as ex-Canary Townsend hits another. Dave Beasant has a dreadful second half, at fault with two Robins efforts and then allowing a Phillips shot to creep in under his body.											
9	H	SHEFFIELD WED		1	W	1-0	1-0	Newman 44	Gunn	Culverhouse	Bowen	Butterworth	Sutton	Megson	Crook	Newman	Robins	Goss	Phillips	
	19/9		13,367	*16*	22				*Woods*	*Harkes*	*Worthington*	*Palmer*	*Shirtliff*	*Anderson*	*Wilson*	*Waddle*	*Bright*	*B't-Williams*	*Francis**	*Pearson*
								Ref: R Nixon	A fine cross by Robins is met by a powerful header from Newman to beat Chris Woods. Norwich rarely look in any trouble after this and play some attractive football. This fifth successive win is a new club record for the top division and maintains Walker's wonderful start as manager.											
10	A	COVENTRY		1	D	1-1	1-1	Crook 13	Gunn	Culverhouse	Bowen	Polston	Sutton	Sutch	Crook	Newman	Robins	Goss	Phillips	
	26/9		*16,436*	*3*	23			*Ndlovu 37*	*Ogrizovic*	*Borrows*	*Sansom**	*Atherton*	*Pearce*	*Ndlovu*	*McGrath*	*Hurst*	*Rosario*	*Gallacher*	*Williams J*	*Babb*
								Ref: A Buksh	Bobby Gould's men look uncomfortable against City's slick passing. Crook finishes well to grab the lead. Peter Ndlovu nets a superb equaliser as he beats three men, dummies Gunn and chips in. Even Norwich fans applaud. Sutton is lucky to stay on after pulling back Kevin Gallacher.											

11	A	BLACKBURN	2	L	1-7	1-4	Newman 39 [Cowans 63, Ripley 70]	Gunn	Culverhouse	Bowen	Butterworth	Sutton	Sutch	Crook	Newman	Robins	Goss	Phillips*	Power
3/10		16,312	1	23			Weg' 8, 32, Sher' 27, Shea'r 43, 76,	Mimms	Brown	Wright	Sherwood	Hendry	Moran*	Ripley^	Atkins	Shearer	Wegerle	Cowans	Marker/Wilcox
							Ref: R Dilkes	Alan Shearer goes on the rampage as Rovers leapfrog City to go top. Shearer sets up the elusive Roy Wegerle twice and Sherwood, unpopular when at Norwich, heads another. A fine Shearer chip after a long run makes it four. This demolition job continues unabated after the interval.											
12	H	QP RANGERS	1	W	2-1	0-0	Bowen 53p, Sutton 64	Gunn	Culverhouse	Bowen	Butterworth	Polston	Sutch	Crook	Phillips	Robins*	Goss	Sutton	Power
17/10		16,009	4	26			Allen 77	Stejskal	Bardsley	Wilson	Wilkins	Peacock	McDonald	Impey	Holloway	Bailey	Penrice^	Sinton*	Maddix/Allen
							Ref: D Gallagher	Gunn decides to play despite the death of his daughter after illness - he receives a huge ovation. With a fortnight to recover from the Ewood mauling, City go ahead after Sutton is hauled down. Sutton heads a second but a bad back-pass by Phillips lets in Bradley Allen. Back on top!											
13	A	LIVERPOOL	2	L	1-4	1-2	Butterworth 2 [Walters 89p]	Gunn	Culverhouse	Bowen	Butterworth	Polston	Newman	Crook	Phillips	Robins^	Goss*	Sutton	Sutch/Fox
25/10		36,318	13	26			Thomas 14, Hutchison 20, Burrows 52,	Grobbelaar	Marsh*	Burrows	Nicol	Piechnik	Hutchison	McManam'n	Walters	Rosenthal	Redknapp	Thomas	Wright
							Ref: R Lewis	More comfort for those convinced City's leadership is a flash in the pan. Butterworth scrambles a goal after 65 seconds, but Graeme Souness' men storm back. Bruce Grobbelaar delays a Norwich penalty and Bowen hits it into the Kop! Culverhouse's foul concedes one at the other end.											
14	H	MIDDLESBROUGH	2	D	1-1	0-0	Sutch 86	Gunn	Sutton^	Bowen	Butterworth	Polston*	Sutch	Crook	Newman	Robins	Goss	Phillips	Beckford/Fox
31/10		14,499	11	27			Wilkinson 64	Pears	Fleming	Phillips	Kernaghan	Whyte	Gittens	Wright*	Falconer	Wilkinson	Proctor	Hendrie	Morris
							Ref: S Lodge	Lennie Lawrence's side take the lead when Paul Wilkinson rises unmarked to convert a Jimmy Phillips' cross. Norwich pile on the pressure in search of an equaliser. It finally comes via Sutch - his first goal for the club - a firm shot after Bowen's cross is headed down by sub Beckford.											
15	A	OLDHAM	1	W	3-2	2-2	Robins 14, 28, 90	Gunn	Culverhouse	Bowen	Butterworth	Polston	Sutch	Crook	Beckford*	Robins	Fox	Phillips	Sutton
9/11		11,081	18	30			Sharp 26, Marshall 43	Hallworth	Halle	Pointon	Henry	Jobson	Redmond	Olney*	Marshall	Sharp	Milligan	Bernard	Adams
							Ref: R Hart	Robins is back on song with his first senior hat-trick - watched by his father, a local policeman on crowd control duty. Graeme Sharp's volley and Ian Marshall's lob peg City back, but Robins regains the league leadership with an exquisite 22-yard chipped shot in the very last minute.											
16	H	SHEFFIELD UTD	1	W	2-1	0-0	Beesley 60 (og), Robins 80	Gunn	Culverhouse	Bowen	Butterworth	Polston	Sutch	Crook	Beckford	Robins	Fox	Phillips	
21/11		14,874	16	33			Cork 72	Kelly	Gage	Gannon	Cowan	Pemberton	Beesley	Ward^	Rogers	Littlejohn*	Deane	Hodges	Cork/Kamara
							Ref: M Peck	A fast and furious contest in heavy rain and the teams are applauded off after a goalless first half. Beckford breaks the deadlock when his low shot crosses the line after deflecting off Paul Beesley. Unmarked Alan Cork levels but Robins pops up to volley in a first-time cross from Fox.											
17	A	ASTON VILLA	1	W	3-2	2-1	Phillips 17, Beckford 30, Sutch 48	Gunn	Culverhouse	Bowen	Butterworth	Polston	Sutch	Crook	Beckford*	Robins	Fox	Phillips	Sutton
28/11		28,837	4	36			Houghton 45, Parker 46	Spink	Barrett	Staunton	Ehiogu*	McGrath	Richardson	Houghton	Parker	Saunders	Atkinson	Small	Regis
							Ref: A Buksh	A fine run by Sutch sets up Phillips and Beckford stabs home a second. In first-half injury-time Ray Houghton's shot squeezes under Gunn. Garry Parker equalises 22 seconds after the re-start. Villa's celebrations are halted within two minutes when Sutch drives in the decisive goal.											
18	H	WIMBLEDON	1	W	2-1	0-0	Robins 77, Phillips 88	Gunn	Culverhouse	Bowen	Butterworth	Polston	Sutch^	Crook	Beckford*	Robins	Fox	Phillips	Megson/Sutton
5/12		14,161	20	39			Sanchez 53	Segers	Talboys	Joseph	Jones*	Scales	McAllister	Blackwell	Earle	Holdsw'th^	Sanchez	Miller	Fashanu/Gibson
							Ref: R Groves	City struggle against Joe Kinnear's spoilers and things look grim when Lawrie Sanchez rises to head in a Brian McAllister corner. Unpopular ex-Canary sub John Fashanu nearly makes it two before Robins levels from six yards. Fox's cross finds Phillips at the far post for a late winner.											
19	A	MANCHESTER U	1	L	0-1	0-0		Gunn	Culverhouse	Bowen	Butterworth	Polston	Sutch	Crook^	Beckford*	Robins	Fox	Phillips	Megson/Sutton
12/12		34,500	3	39			Hughes 59	Schmeichel	Parker	Irwin	Bruce	Sharpe	Pallister	Cantona	Ince	McClair	Hughes	Giggs	
							Ref: R Milford	Eric Cantona makes his full United debut after signing from Leeds. The home side take the lead when Sutch accidentally knocks a Lee Sharpe cross into the path of Mark Hughes. Schmeichel saves a Robins effort with his feet. Walker celebrates another Manager of the Month award.											
20	H	IPSWICH	1	L	0-2	0-0		Gunn	Culverhouse	Bowen	Butterw'th^	Polston	Sutch	Megson	Beckford*	Robins	Fox	Phillips	Newman/Sutton
21/12		20,032	6	39			Kiwomya 52, Thompson 88	Baker	Johnson	Thompson	Stockwell	Wark	Linighan	Williams	Goddard*	Whitton	Dozzell	Kiwomya	Whelan
							Ref: D Elleray	Under Mick McGiven, Ipswich don't display much flair these days, but they hit two in the second half to inflict a hugely disappointing defeat. Ex-Canary Clive Baker keeps City at bay. Chris Kiwomya nods home from a corner and Neil Thompson blasts the clincher from a tight angle.											
21	H	TOTTENHAM	1	D	0-0	0-0		Gunn	Culverhouse	Bowen	Newman	Polston	Megson	Crook	Sutton	Robins	Fox	Phillips	
26/12		19,413	13	40				Thorstvedt	Austin	Edinburgh	Samways	Mabbutt	Ruddock	Howells	Barmby*	Anderson	Sheringham	Allen	Moran
							Ref: J Martin	City enjoy plenty of possession but everything breaks down before reaching the danger area. Norwich get a let-off when Neil Ruddock crashes home a free-kick, only for a re-take to be ordered as the ref wasn't ready. Erik Thorstvedt somehow blocks a Sutton effort from close range.											

No	Date	Opponent	Att	Pos	Pt	F-A	H-T	Scorers, Times, and Referees	1	2	3	4	5	6	7	8	9	10	11	subs used
22	A	LEEDS		1	D	0-0	0-0		Gunn	Culverhouse	Bowen	Newman*	Polston	Megson	Crook	Sutton	Robins	Fox	Phillips	Sutch
	28/12		30,282	16	41				Lukic	Sterland	Dorigo	Batty	Fairclough	Wetherall*	Strachan	Varadi	Chapman	McAllister	Speed	Newsome
								Ref: P Don	Fox is brought down but Bowen repeats his glaring miss from the spot at Liverpool. Again it came after delaying tactics by the opposition. He later vows never to take another. Newman breaks his ankle and will be out until May. City go close when a Robins effort is cleared off the line.											
23	A	SHEFFIELD WED		3	L	0-1	0-1		Gunn	Culverhouse	Bowen	Butterworth	Polston	Megson	Crook	Power	Robins*	Fox	Phillips	Sutch
	10/1		23,360	11	41			Worthington 41	Woods	Nilsson	Worthington	Harkes	Shirtliff	Anderson*	Wilson	Waddle	Bright	Hirst^	Sheridan	Warh'st/B't-Williams
								Ref: D Allison	A miserable Sunday in South Yorkshire. Knocked off the top of the table, five games without a goal and leading scorer Robins hobbling away on crutches. Trevor Francis' men win the points after Nigel Worthington's powerful shot rebounds to him and he scores at the second attempt.											
24	H	COVENTRY		1	D	1-1	1-0	Sutton 13	Gunn	Culverhouse	Bowen	Butterworth	Polston^	Goss	Crook*	Beckford	Sutton	Fox	Phillips	Sutch/Woodthorpe
	16/1		13,613	11	42			Quinn 57	Ogrizovic	Borrows	Babb	Atherton	Busst	Williams J	Greenman*	Gynn	Rosario	Quinn	Gallacher	Rowland
								Ref: A Gunn	A neat passing move ends with Sutton shooting in. Gunn brings down John Williams, escapes even a booking, and then saves Brian Borrows' penalty, Mick Quinn hitting the bar with the rebound. Minutes later Quinn atones by hammering the equaliser. Polston is carried off injured.											
25	H	CRYSTAL PALACE		3	W	4-2	2-2	Power 9, 89, Sutton 26, Goss 50	Gunn	Culverhouse	Bowen	Butterworth	Polston	Megson	Goss	Power	Sutton	Fox	Phillips	
	27/1		13,543	18	45			Armstrong 2, Thomas 45	Martyn	Humphrey*	Sinnott	Coleman	Sinnott	Thorn	Osborn	Thomas	Armstrong	Rodger	McGoldrick	Ndah
								Ref: V Callow	Palace score at either end of the first half, but City reply with four goals of outstanding quality. Power and Sutton net excellent headers within the first half hour. Geoff Thomas' equaliser is a soft one, but Goss hammers a beauty and a lively evening is rounded off by Power's solo gem.											
26	A	EVERTON		1	W	1-0	1-0	Sutton 15	Gunn	Culverhouse	Bowen	Butterworth	Polston	Megson	Goss	Power*	Sutton	Fox	Phillips	Robins
	30/1		20,301	12	48				Southall	Jackson	Harper	Snodin^	Watson	Ablett	Radosav'ic*	Beardsley	Cottee	Horne	Kenny	Barlow/Rideout
								Ref: R Lewis	Sutton swoops to score a well-taken goal after a blunder by ex-Canary skipper Dave Watson. Howard Kendall's side go close to an equaliser in injury-time, but Gunn makes a brilliant save, tipping Tony Cottee's overhead kick against a post. Everton's run of three wins in a row is ended.											
27	A	SOUTHAMPTON		3	L	0-3	0-2		Gunn	Culverhouse	Bowen	Butterworth	Polston	Megson	Goss	Power	Robins*	Fox	Phillips	Sutch
	10/2		12,969	14	48			Hall 8, Adams 24, Banger 78	Flowers	Kenna	Adams	Widdrington	Monkou	Hall	Le Tissier*	Dodd	Dowie	Maddison	Benali	Banger
								Ref: J Worrall	A poor display by Norwich, particularly in the first half. Ipswich-born Richard Hall heads the Saints in front and Micky Adams doubles the lead, finishing coolly with defenders screaming for offside. Robins and Power strike the woodwork before Nicky Banger finishes things off.											
28	H	MANCHESTER C		3	W	2-1	2-0	Robins 29, Power 30	Gunn	Culverhouse	Bowen	Butterworth	Polston	Megson	Goss*	Power^	Robins	Fox	Phillips	Sutch/Johnson
	20/2		16,386	10	51			Sheron 46	Coton	Ransom	Phelan*	Ingebritsen^	Curle	Vonk	White	Sheron	Quinn	Holden	Flitcroft	Hill/Quigley
								Ref: B Hill	Robins bundles the ball in from close range and seconds later Power nets a cracking drive after a slick move. Peter Reid's side are stunned but re-group at the interval and pull one back through Mike Sheron just 40 seconds from the re-start. White fluffs a chance to level from close in.											
29	H	BLACKBURN		3	D	0-0	0-0		Gunn	Culverhouse	Bowen	Sutton	Polston	Smith	Sutch	Power	Robins	Fox	Phillips	
	28/2		15,821	5	52				Mimms	May	Dobson	Sherwood	Hendry	Moran	Ripley	Andersson	Wegerle	Newell	Wilcox	
								Ref: P Don	City have five regulars injured for this Sunday afternoon televised game. An orange ball is called for after snow begins falling before the start. Rovers fail to take the game's best two chances and Fox has a penalty appeal turned down. Home fans taunt ex-Canary Sherwood mercilessly.											
30	H	ARSENAL		3	D	1-1	1-0	Fox 35	Gunn	Culverhouse	Bowen	Sutton	Polston	Smith	Sutch	Power	Robins	Fox	Phillips	
	3/3		14,802	11	53			Wright 82	Seaman	Dixon	Winterburn	Davis	Linighan	Keown	Jensen	Wright	Parlour	Carter	Limpar*	Campbell
								Ref: J Martin	Fox heads home a Sutch cross to put Norwich ahead. Ian Wright has an eventful evening: he is booked for patting the referee's face and later sees a penalty well saved by Gunn. He has the last laugh, however, being left in space to net the equaliser from a cross by sub Kevin Campbell.											
31	A	QP RANGERS		3	L	1-3	1-2	Robins 38	Gunn	Culverhouse	Bowen	Sutton	Woodthorpe	Sutch	Crook	Power*	Robins	Fox	Phillips	Minett
	6/3		13,892	4	53			Ferdinand 18, 34, Wilson 78	Roberts	Bardsley	Brevett	Doyle	Maddix	McDonald	Wilson	Impey	Ferdinand	White*	Meaker	Allen
								Ref: R Gifford	With Polston out, Walker tries the sweeper system, but Les Ferdinand is left unmarked to nod an opening goal. He runs at the defence in direct fashion to crash home his second. Robins pulls one back with a shot that creeps over the line, but Clive Wilson's late strike settles the outcome.											

No	Date	Opponent / Att	Pos	Res / Pts	FT	HT	Scorers, Times, and Referees	1	2	3	4	5	6	7	8	9	10	11	12 sub used
32	A	SHEFFIELD UTD	3	W	1-0	0-0	Fox 55	Gunn	Culverhouse	Bowen	Sutton	Polston	Sutch*	Crook	Woodthorpe	Robins	Fox	Phillips	Smith
	10/3	*15,583*	*19*	56				*Kelly*	*Gage*	*Ward*	*Hoyland*	*Gayle*	*Pemberton*	*Carr^*	*Hartfield**	*Bryson*	*Deane*	*Hodges*	*Littlejohn/Bradshaw*
							Ref: R Lewis	A very poor first half is forgotten when sub Smith starts a fine move that ends with Fox rifling a shot past Alan Kelly. Fox ignores unmarked Robins and tries for a second goal, but his effort flies off target. Title hopes are boosted by the news that Manchester U went down to Oldham.											
33	H	OLDHAM	3	W	1-0	1-0	Henry 13 (og)	Gunn	Culverhouse	Bowen	Sutton	Polston	Megson	Crook	Woodthorpe	Robins*	Fox	Phillips	Power
	13/3	19,597	*22*	59				*Gerrard*	*Halle*	*Pointon*	*Henry*	*Jobson^*	*Fleming*	*Adams**	*Bernard*	*Olney*	*Milligan*	*Brennan*	*Palmer/Redmond*
							Ref: R Milford	A volley from Phillips hits Tony Henry on the head and loops over Paul Gerrard into the net. It's hard luck on Joe Royle's side, who play some good football. Robins nets before the break but is ruled offside. With Villa and Manchester U both drawing, City make ground in the title race.											
34	A	NOTT'M FOREST	1	W	**3-0**	1-0	Robins 45, Power 72, Crook 78	Gunn	Culverhouse	Bowen	Sutton	Polston	Smith	Crook	Woodthorpe	Robins*	Fox	Phillips	Power
	17/3	20,799	*21*	62				*Crossley*	*Laws*	*Charles*	*Tiler*	*Chettle*	*Crosby**	*Orlygsson*	*Stone*	*Clough*	*Bannister^*	*Woan*	*Black/Glover*
							Ref: S Lodge	Forest are heading for relegation and Brian Clough is contemplating retirement. Norwich show no mercy and Robins outpaces two defenders before driving in off the post. Power volleys Phillips' corner into the net. Crook shoots in off Carl Tiler after getting on the end of a Fox cross.											
35	A	WIMBLEDON	3	L	0-3	0-2		Gunn	Culverhouse	Bowen	Sutton	Polston	Smith	Crook	Woodth'pe*	Robins	Fox	Phillips	Power
	20/3	***10,875***	*12*	62			*Holdsworth 16, 82, Ardley 29*	*Segers*	*Elkins*	*Joseph*	*Jones*	*Scales*	*McAllister*	*Ardley*	*Earle*	*Fashanu*	*Holdsworth*	*Dobbs*	
							Ref: K Cooper	John Fashanu's cross is netted by Dean Holdsworth and John Scales flicks on for Neil Ardley to score at the second attempt. City never look likely to come back from this and Vinnie Jones sets up the third. The referee withdraws a late Norwich penalty award after lengthy discussions.											
36	H	ASTON VILLA	1	W	1-0	0-0	Polston 81	Gunn	Culverhouse	Bowen	Sutton	Polston	Megson	Crook	Goss	Robins*	Fox	Phillips	Power
	24/3	19,528	*2*	65				*Bosnich*	*Barrett*	*Staunton*	*Teale*	*McGrath*	*Richardson*	*Houghton*	*Parker**	*Saunders*	*Yorke*	*Regis*	*Daley*
							Ref: R Hart	Defeat against title rivals Villa would be disastrous. A fine game keeps the fans spellbound. Dean Saunders has a goal disallowed. Both sides go close before Polston nets from close range after Megson's diving header is saved. Cue pandemonium. City are now a point clear at the top.											
37	H	MANCHESTER U	3	L	1-3	0-3	Robins 61	Gunn	Culverhouse	Bowen	Sutton	Polston	Megson*	Crook	Goss	Robins	Fox	Phillips	**Ekoku**
	5/4	20,582	*2*	65			*Giggs 13, Kanch'skis 17, Cantona 20*	*Schmeichel*	*Parker*	*Irwin*	*Bruce*	*Sharpe*	*Pallister*	*Cantona*	*Ince*	*McClair*	*Kanch'skis**	*Giggs*	*Robson*
							Ref: T Ward	An epic title battle gets off to an horrendous start. United are three up within 20 minutes. Ryan Giggs races though to round Gunn and Andrei Kanchelskis does the same after a slick move. Eric Cantona sweeps in a third. Robins heads home a Fox cross, but it's too late to really matter.											
38	A	TOTTENHAM	3	L	1-5	0-2	Ekoku 85 *[Nayim 82]*	Gunn	Culverhouse	Bowen	Sutton	Polston	Megson	Crook	Goss	Robins	Fox	Phillips*	Ekoku
	9/4	*31,425*	*5*	65			*Rud' 26, Shering' 30,76, Barmby 54,*	*Thorstvedt*	*Austin*	*Edinburgh*	*Barmby**	*Mabbutt*	*Ruddock*	*Sedgley*	*Nayim*	*Anderson^*	*Sheringham*	*Allen*	*Turner/Nethercott*
							Ref: K Barratt	Sheer misery in the pouring rain. Neil Rudddock cracks in a free-kick and Teddy Sheringham arrows a shot past Gunn. Nick Barmby's diving header ends any lingering hopes. Sub Efan Ekoku pulls one back. He was signed from Bournemouth to replace Beckford (now with Oldham).											
39	H	LEEDS	3	W	4-2	3-1	Sutton 10, 13, 78, Phillips 15p	Gunn	Culverhouse	Bowen	Butterworth	Polston	Goss	Crook	Sutton	Robins	Fox	Phillips	
	14/4	18,613	*16*	68			*Chapman 3, Rod Wallace 47*	*Lukic*	*Kerslake*	*Kerr*	*Tinkler*	*Fairclough**	*Whyte*	*Strachan*	*Wallace Rod*	*Chapman*	*Forrester^*	*Speed*	*Newsome/Hodge*
							Ref: K Burge	Norwich respond superbly to two horrific defeats and a soft early goal by Lee Chapman. Two by Sutton and a Phillips penalty - after Dylan Kerr barged into Fox - gives a 3-1 lead after only 15 minutes. Rod Wallace nets a fine goal, but Sutton shows great composure for his hat-trick.											
40	A	IPSWICH	3	L	1-3	1-1	Sutton 41	Gunn	Culverhouse	Bowen	Butterworth	Polston	Goss	Crook	Sutton	Robins	Fox	Phillips	
	19/4	*21,081*	*16*	68			*Dozzell 21, 56, Stockwell 54*	*Baker*	*Youds*	*Johnson*	*Williams*	*Wark*	*Linighan*	*Whitton*	*Stockwell*	*Milton*	*Dozzell*	*Kiwomya*	
							Ref: R Milford	Faint title hopes disappear in this live TV game as Town end a long winless run. Geraint Williams' cross is missed by Gunn and Jason Dozzell pounces. Sutton heads in Crook's free-kick. Persistent Mick Stockwell stabs home and Dozzell nets a fine third. Two City headers hit the post.											
41	H	LIVERPOOL	3	W	1-0	0-0	Phillips 62p	Gunn	Culverhouse	Bowen	Newman	Polston	Goss	Crook	Sutton	Robins*	Fox	Phillips	Ekoku/Megson
	1/5	**20,610**	*7*	71				*James !*	*Jones*	*Burrows*	*Nicol*	*Wright*	*Redknapp^*	*Stewart**	*Hutchison*	*Rush*	*Barnes*	*Walters*	*Rosenthal/Hooper*
							Ref: D Elleray	Gunn is awarded the Player of the Year trophy. City are still chasing a UEFA Cup place. The big breakthrough comes thanks to David James' petulance. Having been booked earlier, James collects a corner but kicks the challenging Polston. He is sent off and Phillips nets the spot-kick.											
42	A	MIDDLESBROUGH	3	D	3-3	1-1	Ekoku 21, 65 Johnson 68	Gunn	Culverhouse	Bowen	Newman	Polston	Johnson	Crook	Sutton	Ekoku	Fox	Phillips	
	8/5	*15,155*	*21*	72			*Falconer 33, Wilkinson 64, Hendrie 73*	*Collett*	*Fleming^*	*Phillips*	*Kernaghan*	*Whyte*	*Peake*	*Hendrie*	*Falconer*	*Wilkinson*	*Hignett**	*Mustoe*	*Marshall/Moore*
Average	Home 16,154	Away 20,730					Ref: G Ashby	Norwich need a point to ensure finishing third. Then, if Arsenal win the FA Cup, City will be in the UEFA Cup. This topsy-turvy thriller sees City take the lead, fall 1-2 behind, then recover to go 3-2 up via Johnson's fine volley. There is unbearable late tension before the point is won.											

Coca-Cola Cup	Att			F-A	H-T	Scorers, Times, and Referees	1	2	3	4	5	6	7	8	9	10	11	subs used
2:1 A CARLISLE		1	D	2-2	0-1	Robins 46, Goss 57	Gunn	Culverhouse	Bowen	Polston	Sutton	Sutch	Crook	Newman	Robins	Goss	Phillips	
22/9	*10,328*	*3:15*				*Barnsley 25p, Edmondson 62*	*O'Hanlon*	*Williams*	*Thorpe*	*Holmes*	*Walling*	*Barnsley*	*Gabbiadini*	*Davey*	*Oghani**	*Watson*	*Edmondson*	*Sendall*
						Ref: I Hendrick	The Cumbrians pile on the pressure, but Norwich believe Andy Barnsley's first-half penalty was the result of a dive. Robins scores a fine goal just 12 seconds into the second half, and a Goss shot squeezes under Kelham O'Hanlon. Defender Darren Edmondson's heads past Gunn.											
2:2 H CARLISLE		2	W	2-0	0-0	Sutton 67, 77	Walton	Culverhouse	Bowen	Butterworth	Polston	Sutch	Crook	Newman	Robins	Goss	Sutton	
7/10	8,489	*3:19*					*O'Hanlon*	*Williams*	*Thorpe*	*Holmes**	*Barnsley*	*Edmondson*	*Sendall*	*Davey*	*Oghani*	*Watson*	*Potts*	*McCreery*
						Ref: D Axcell (Norwich win 4-2 on aggregate)	Norwich are rarely troubled, but miss a host of chances and the decisive goals come late in the day. Two identical headers by Sutton from Culverhouse crosses do the trick. Sutton hits the bar with another header. Gunn is away on compassionate leave, due to his daughter's illness.											
3 A BLACKBURN		2	L	0-2	0-1		Gunn	Culverh'se^	Bowen	Butterworth	Polston	Sutch	Crook	Newman	Sutton	Goss*	Phillips	Robins/Fox
28/10	*14,216*	*1*				*Shearer 33, May 61*	*Mimms*	*May*	*Wright*	*Sherwood*	*Hendry*	*Dobson*	*Ripley**	*Atkins*	*Shearer*	*Newell*	*Wilcox*	*Makel*
						Ref: M Peck	City return to the scene of their 1-7 hammering 25 days ago. A disputed free-kick is curled in from 22 yards by Alan Shearer. He takes it quickly, catching all and sundry by surprise, but it stands. Goss hits the post. David May seals victory by heading home a second-half corner.											

FA Cup																		
3 H COVENTRY		1	W	1-0	0-0	Beckford 46	Gunn	Culverhouse	Bowen	Butterworth	Polston	Megson*	Crook	Beckford	Sutton	Fox	Phillips	Goss
13/1	15,301	*10*					*Ogrizovic*	*Borrows*	*Babb*	*Atherton*	*Pearce*	*Ndlovu*	*McGrath**	*Williams J*	*Rosario*	*Quinn^*	*Gallacher*	*Busst/Gynn*
						Ref: K Hackett	After 496 minutes play without a Norwich goal, Beckford stabs the ball in from close range. It had been the longest barren spell in 66 years. The relief inspires the Canaries to create more chances. Coventry manager Bobby Gould is banished from the dugout for berating a linesman.											
4 H TOTTENHAM		1	L	0-2	0-0		Gunn	Culverhouse	Bowen	Butterworth	Polston	Megson	Goss*	Beckford	Sutton	Fox	Phillips	Power
24/1	15,003	*14*				*Sheringham 47, 49*	*Thorstvedt*	*Austin*	*Edinburgh*	*Samways*	*Mabbutt*	*Ruddock*	*Barmby*	*Durie**	*Anderton*	*Sheringham*	*Allen*	*Howells*
						Ref: R Dilkes	Time off from league business, but Norwich look out of touch and put in a hugely disappointing display. Teddy Sheringham nets two excellent goals in two minutes. First he combines with Gordon Durie to beat Gunn, then sends in a deft glancing header. Erik Thorstvedt has a quiet day.											

		Home						Away					
		P	W	D	L	F	A	W	D	L	F	A	Pts
1	Manchester U	42	14	5	2	39	14	10	7	4	28	17	84
2	Aston Villa	42	13	5	3	36	16	8	6	7	21	24	74
3	NORWICH	42	13	6	2	31	19	8	3	10	30	46	72
4	Blackburn	42	13	4	4	38	18	7	7	7	30	28	71
5	QP Rangers	42	11	5	5	41	32	6	7	8	22	23	63
6	Liverpool	42	13	4	4	41	18	3	7	11	21	37	59
7	Sheffield Wed	42	9	8	4	34	26	6	6	9	21	25	59
8	Tottenham	42	11	5	5	40	25	5	6	10	20	41	59
9	Manchester C	42	7	8	6	30	25	8	4	9	26	26	57
10	Arsenal	42	8	6	7	25	20	7	5	9	15	18	56
11	Chelsea	42	9	7	5	29	22	5	7	9	22	32	56
12	Wimbledon	42	9	4	8	32	23	5	8	8	24	32	54
13	Everton	42	7	6	8	26	27	8	2	11	27	28	53
14	Sheffield Utd	42	10	6	5	33	19	4	4	13	21	34	52
15	Coventry	42	7	4	10	29	28	6	9	6	23	29	52
16	Ipswich	42	8	9	4	29	22	4	7	10	21	33	52
17	Leeds	42	12	8	1	40	17	0	7	14	17	45	51
18	Southampton	42	10	6	5	30	21	3	5	13	24	40	50
19	Oldham	42	10	6	5	43	30	3	4	14	20	44	49
20	Crys Palace	42	6	9	6	27	25	5	7	9	21	36	49
21	Middlesbro	42	8	5	8	33	27	3	6	12	21	48	44
22	Nott'm Forest	42	6	4	11	17	25	4	6	11	24	37	40
		924	214	130	118	723	499	118	130	214	499	723	1256

Odds & ends

Double victories: (6) Palace, Chelsea, Oldham, Villa, Nott' F, Sheffield U.
Double losses:(2) Manchester U, Ipswich.

Won from behind: (6) Arsenal (a), Chelsea (h&a), Wimbledon (h), Palace (h), Leeds (h).
Lost from in front: (1) Liverpool (a).

High points: The club's highest-ever league finish, and into UEFA Cup.
Being serious title contenders from August until early April.
Two Manager-of-the-Month awards for Mike Walker.
A series of top-quality goals: e.g. all four in the win over Palace.
The 'easy-on-the-eye' passing game under new boss Mike Walker.

Low points: Heavy defeats by Man U and Spurs in five days.
Bryan Gunn's ordeal in losing his daughter to leukaemia.
The 1-7 hammering at Blackburn.
The spell of five games without a goal at the turn of the year.

Player of the Year: Bryan Gunn.
Ever-presents: (3) Bowen, Gunn (League only), Phillips (League only).
Hat-tricks: (2) Mark Robins (Oldham, h), Chris Sutton (Leeds, h).
Hat-tricks against: (0).
Leading scorer: (16) Mark Robins.

	Appearances						Goals			
	Lge	*Sub*	LC	*Sub*	FAC	*Sub*	Lge	LC	FAC	Tot
Beckford, Darren	7	*1*			2		1		1	2
Bowen, Mark	42		3		2		1			1
Butterworth, Ian	26		2		2		1			1
Crook, Ian	32	*2*	3		1		3			3
Culverhouse, Ian	41		3		2					
Ekoku, Efan	1	*3*					3			3
Fox, Ruel	32	*2*		*1*	2		4			4
Goss, Jeremy	25		3		1	*1*	1	1		2
Gunn, Bryan	42		2		2					
Johnson, Andy	1	*1*					1			1
Megson, Gary	20	*3*			2		1			1
Minett, Jason		*1*								
Newman, Rob	16	*2*	3				2			2
Phillips, David	42		2		2		9			9
Polston, John	34		3		2		1			1
Power, Lee	11	*7*				*1*	6			6
Robins, Mark	34	*3*	2	*1*			15	1		16
Smith, David	5	*1*								
Sutch, Daryl	14	*8*	3				2			2
Sutton, Chris	32	*5*	3		2		8	2		10
Walton, Mark			1							
Woodthorpe, Colin	5	*2*								
(own-goals)							2			2
22 players used	**462**	***41***	**33**	***2***	**22**	***2***	**61**	**4**	**1**	**66**

No	Date		Att	Pos	Pt	F-A	H-T	Scorers, Times, and Referees	SQUAD	NUMBERS	IN	USE								subs used
1	H	MANCHESTER U			L	0-2	0-1		Gunn	Culverhouse	Bowen	Butterworth	Polston	Goss	Crook	Newman	Robins*	Fox	Sutton	Ekoku
	15/8		19,705		0			*Giggs 25, Robson 57*	*Schmeichel*	*Parker*	*Irwin*	*Bruce*	*Kanchelskis*	*Pallister*	*Robson*	*Keane*	*Ince*	*Hughes*	*Giggs*	
								Ref: K Hackett	The reigning champions generally look sharper than Norwich. After Gunn pushes the ball on to the bar, Ryan Giggs nets the rebound. United are on their way to a seventh successive top-flight win over City. Mark Hughes' cute backheel sets up Bryan Robson, who drove in the second.											
2	A	BLACKBURN		11	W	3-2	1-1	Sutton 44, 65, Newman 63	Gunn	Culverhouse	Bowen	Butterworth	Polston	Goss	Crook	Newman	Robins	Fox	Sutton	
	18/8		*14,260*	*9*	3			*Atkins 7, Wilcox 54*	*Mimms*	*May*	*Le Saux*	*Sherwood*	*Moran**	*Marker*	*Ripley*	*Atkins*	*Newell*	*Gallacher^*	*Wilcox*	*Berg/Shearer*
								Ref: R Hart	City overcome an early strike from Mark Atkins to chalk up a fine win over Kenny Dalglish's big spenders. Sutton nods back a Crook free-kick for Newman to make it 2-2. Two minutes later, Sutton turns neatly past Kevin Moran on the flank, cuts in and slips a shot past Bobby Mimms.											
3	A	LEEDS		6	W	4-0	2-0	Fox 2, 69, Sutton 41, Goss 61	Gunn	Culverhouse	Bowen	Butterworth	Polston	Goss	Crook	Newman	Robins	Fox	Sutton*	Ekoku
	21/8		*32,008*	*12*	6				*Lukic*	*Kelly*	*Dorigo*	*Batty*	*Fairclough*	*O'Leary**	*Strachan*	*Whelan*	*Deane*	*McAllister*	*Speed*	*Newsome*
								Ref: M Reed	Fox provides an early boost after Tony Dorigo's poor clearance. Sutton's right-foot drive makes it two before the break. Fox's cross is met just inside the area by Goss, whose spectacular volley screams into the net. City are on a high and a John Lukic blunder allows Fox to make it four.											
4	H	IPSWICH		4	W	1-0	1-0	Goss 30	Gunn	Culverhouse	Bowen	Butterworth	Polston	Goss	Crook	Newman	Robins	Fox	Sutton	
	25/8		18,976	*5*	9				*Baker*	*Stockwell*	*Thompson*	*Whelan^*	*Wark*	*Linighan*	*Williams*	*Guentchev**	*Whitton*	*Palmer*	*Kiwomya*	*Milton/Yallop*
								Ref: A Gunn	Mick McGiven's side has gone around 300 minutes without conceding until Robins slips the ball to Goss, who conjures up an emphatic finish. Geraint Williams nets after the break but the offside flag is aloft. Robins hits the bar and ex-Canary keeper Clive Baker prevents a bigger win.											
5	H	SWINDON		4	D	0-0	0-0		Gunn	Culverhouse	Bowen	Butterw'th^	Polston	Goss	Crook	Newman	Robins*	Fox	Sutton	Ekoku/Megson
	28/8		17,614	*22*	10				*Digby*	*Summerbee*	*Nijholt*	*Moncur*	*Whitbread*	*Taylor*	*Hazard*	*Mutch**	*Horlock*	*Ling*	*MacLaren*	*Fjortoft*
								Ref: D Elleray	Frustration for Canaries fans as Swindon - four defeats out of four thus far - survive to take their first top-flight point. John Gorman's outfit occasionally look dangerous on swift breaks. The closest to a goal is when Newman's cross finds Polston, but his shot strikes the woodwork.											
6	A	SHEFFIELD WED		5	D	3-3	0-0	Bowen 62, Ekoku 72, Sutton 75	Gunn	Culverhouse	Bowen	**Prior**	Polston	Goss	Crook	Newman	Robins*	Fox	Sutton	Ekoku
	1/9		*25,175*	*21*	11			*B't-Williams 53, Bright 58, Sinton 61*	*Woods*	*Nilsson*	*Worthington*	*B't-Williams*	*Pearson*	*Walker*	*Sheridan*	*Waddle*	*Bright*	*Hyde*	*Sinton*	
								Ref: A Wilkie	An astonishing second-half spell sees Trevor Francis' men hit three in eight minutes, only for City to reply instantly with three in 13. Bowen begins the comeback with a stunning shot from 30 yards. Ekoku nets a near-post cross by Fox. Bowen feeds Sutton, whose finish is super-cool.											
7	H	WIMBLEDON		8	L	0-1	0-0		Gunn	Culverhouse	Bowen	Prior*	Polston	Goss	Crook	Newman	Ekoku	Fox	Sutton	Robins
	11/9		**14,851**	*7*	11			*Sanchez 57*	*Segers*	*Joseph*	*Fitzgerald*	*Scales*	*Kimble*	*Barton*	*Earle*	*Sanchez*	*Jones*	*Fashanu*	*Holdsworth*	
								Ref: G Ashby	Goals are proving hard to come by in home games and Joe Kinnear's hard-working Dons hold City at bay without too much trouble. Spencer Prior, a summer recruit from Southend, makes a home debut, but slips to allow Warren Barton to get in a cross, converted by Lawrie Sanchez.											
8	A	QP RANGERS		10	D	2-2	2-1	McDonald 25 (og), Eadie 39	Gunn	Culverhouse	Bowen	Newman	Polston	Goss	Crook	**Eadie**	Ekoku	Fox	Sutton	
	18/9		*13,359*	*15*	12			*Sinclair 33, Ferdinand 83*	*Stejskal*	*Bardsley*	*Wilson*	*Wilkins*	*Peacock*	*McDonald*	*Impey*	*Barker*	*Ferdinand*	*Penrice*	*Sinclair*	
								Ref: R Milford	Alan McDonald loops a header high over his own keeper, but Trevor Sinclair gets Rangers back on terms. City debutant Darren Eadie, a lively 18-year-old winger, coolly slots home a Sutton flick-on. City look set for a win until Les Ferdinand strikes late, hooking in Ray Wilkins' cross.											
9	A	EVERTON		5	W	**5-1**	1-1	Ekoku 41, 57, 63, 69, Sutton 77	Gunn	Culverhouse	Bowen	Butterworth	Polston	Goss	Crook	Newman	Ekoku	Fox	Sutton	
	25/9		*20,631*	*8*	15			*Rideout 13*	*Southall*	*Holmes^*	*Hinchcliffe*	*Ebbrell*	*Jackson*	*Ablett*	*Ward**	*Horne*	*Cottee*	*Rideout*	*Beagrie*	*Radosav'ic/Angell*
								Ref: P Durkin	Paul Rideout puts them ahead, but Everton collapse to lethal finishing by four-goal Ekoku, known as 'The Chief'. He nets a header, a tap-in, a stunning solo effort and a well-placed shot after sprinting clear. Sutton finishes matters off and Norwich have now hit 17 in five away games.											
10	H	COVENTRY		4	W	1-0	1-0	Fox 45	Gunn	Culverhouse	Bowen	Megson	Polston	Goss	Crook	Newman	Ekoku	Fox	Sutton	
	2/10		16,239	*11*	18				*Ogrizovic*	*Morgan*	*Williams PR*	*Sheridan**	*Babb*	*Atherton*	*Williams J*	*Boland*	*Quinn^*	*Wegerle*	*Jenkinson*	*Flynn/Kruszynski*
								Ref: D Gallacher	City look weary after their midweek efforts in Holland. Bobby Gould, who three weeks later will quit the Sky Blues, is grateful to his keeper for a number of fine saves, especially from in-form Ekoku. Fox speeds past Paul Williams and nets the only goal in first-half stoppage time.											

No	Date	Opponent	Att	Pos	Res	FT	HT	Scorers, Times, and Referees	1	2	3	4	5	6	7	8	9	10	11	subs used
11	A	CHELSEA		2	W	2-1	1-0	Fox 22, Sutton 69	Gunn	Culverhouse	Bowen	Butterworth	Prior	Goss	Crook	Newman	Robins	Fox	Sutton	
	16/10		*16,923*	*15*	21			*Peacock 83*	*Kharine*	*Clarke*	*Sinclair*	*Kjeldbjerg*	*Dow*	*Hall*	*Hoddle*	*Peacock*	*Shipperley*	*Cascarino**	*Newton*	*Fleck*
								Ref: V Callow	Bowen combines with Crook to set up Fox, who nets a low shot. Dmitri Kharine comes out and blocks a Robins shot, but the ball falls loose and Sutton increases the lead. Gavin Peacock's stooping header from close range livens things up near the end. The unbeaten away run goes on.											
12	H	WEST HAM		2	D	0-0	0-0		Gunn	Culverhouse	Bowen	Butterworth	Newman	Goss	Crook	Megson	Sutch*	Fox	Sutton	Eadie
	23/10		20,175	*17*	22				*Miklosko*	*Breacker*	*Burrows*	*Potts*	*Gale**	*Bishop*	*Butler*	*Morley*	*Chapman*	*Marsh*	*Holmes*	*Rowland*
								Ref: J Worrall	A full house welcomes City back after the heroics at Bayern Munich. Megson returns and works hard to drive the team forward. A series of fine saves by Ludek Miklosko keeps City out. The Hammers nearly pinch victory when Lee Chapman's effort brings a great save from Gunn.											
13	A	ARSENAL		2	D	0-0	0-0		Gunn	Culverhouse	Bowen	Butterworth	Prior	Megson	Crook	Newman	Eadie	Fox	Sutton	
	30/10		*30,516*	*3*	23				*Seaman*	*Dixon*	*Winterburn^*	*Davis*	*Bould*	*Adams*	*Jensen*	*Wright*	*Smith**	*Merson*	*Limpar*	*Campbell/Keown*
								Ref: R Dilkes	Norwich keep their unbeaten away run intact but George Graham's side apply heavy pressure and can't believe they didn't win this one. Two efforts are cleared desperately off the City line and Ian Wright strikes the bar with a header. It's the Gunners' fourth successive goalless draw.											
14	A	SHEFFIELD UTD		2	W	2-1	1-1	Goss 26, Eadie 57	Gunn	Culverhouse	Ullathorne	Butterworth	Polston	Goss	Crook	Newman	Eadie	Fox	Sutton	
	6/11		*18,254*	*19*	26			*Whitehouse 43p*	*Tracey*	*Bradshaw*	*Nilsen*	*Falconer^*	*Tuttle*	*Hoyland*	*Carr*	*Rogers*	*Flo*	*Littlejohn**	*Whitehouse*	*Cork/Hodges*
								Ref: K Burge	Goss produces an excellent header to beat Simon Tracey from a Fox cross. Polston's handball gives Dane Whitehouse the opportunity to level the scores from the spot. Polston's second-half cross is knocked down by Sutton and Eadie spins to fire home a fine winning goal for Norwich.											
15	H	MANCHESTER C		3	D	1-1	0-0	Fox 57	Gunn	Culverhouse	Bowen	Butterworth	Polston	Goss	Crook	Newman	Sutton	Fox*	Megson	Sutch
	20/11		16,626	*16*	27			*Quinn 59*	*Coton*	*Edghill*	*Phelan*	*McMahon*	*Curle*	*Kernaghan*	*White*	*Sheron**	*Quinn*	*Simpson*	*Lomas*	*Griffiths*
								Ref: K Hackett	Sutton and Fox combine to set up Fox, who nets a snapshot past Tony Coton. Norwich are pegged back almost immediately by Brian Horton's outfit thanks to a deft back-header by Niall Quinn. Ticketing arrangements for the Inter Milan trip are causing major unrest among City fans.											
16	A	OLDHAM		7	L	1-2	0-0	Sutton 55	Gunn	Culverhouse	Bowen	Butterworth	Polston	Goss	Crook	Newman*	Power	Fox	Sutton	Ullathorne
	27/11		*10,198*	*21*	27			*Sharp 46, Makin 61*	*Beresford*	*Fleming*	*Makin !*	*Halle*	*Jobson*	*Redmond*	*Adams*	*Ritchie**	*Sharp*	*Bernard*	*Holden*	*Palmer*
								Ref: P Don	Graeme Sharp sidefoots home a Craig Fleming pass. Sutton is left unmarked at a Crook free-kick to level. Andy Ritchie lays the ball back for Chris Makin to slide home from 20 yards. For the second week running, Makin departs after a second yellow card. The fine away run is ended.											
17	A	MANCHESTER U		7	D	2-2	1-2	Sutton 31, Fox 47p	Gunn	Culverhouse	Bowen	Butterw'th^	Woodthorpe	Goss	Megson	Newman	Power	Fox*	Sutton	Eadie/Sutch
	4/12		***44,694***	*1*	28			*Giggs 30, McClair 41*	*Schmeichel*	*Parker*	*Irwin*	*Bruce*	*Kanchelskis*	*Pallister*	*Cantona*	*McClair*	*Ince*	*Hughes**	*Giggs*	*Sharpe*
								Ref: M Bodenham	Eric Cantona's cross is half-volleyed in by Ryan Giggs, but Sutton levels instantly, his 20-yarder whistling past Peter Schmeichel. Cantona's chip into the area is bundled home by Brian McClair. Fox puts brave City on terms again, netting a penalty after Gary Pallister impedes Sutton.											
18	H	LEEDS		6	W	2-1	1-0	Sutton 45, Ekoku 80	Gunn	Culverhouse	Bowen	Megson	Prior^	Woodthorpe	Smith	Newman	Ekoku*	Fox	Sutton	Power/Ullathorne
	13/12		16,586	*2*	31			*Wallace Rd 67*	*Beeney*	*Kelly*	*Dorigo*	*Sharp**	*Fairclough*	*Wetherall*	*Strachan*	*Wallace Rd*	*Deane*	*McAllister*	*Hodge*	*Whelan*
								Ref: R Milford	Before today, only three of City's 27 league goals have come at home. Sutton improves the situation by netting Bowen's pull-back off a post. Rod Wallace squeezes past two defenders to net a half-hit effort. Ekoku decides a lively end-to-end contest, netting a rebound off the keeper.											
19	A	IPSWICH		6	L	1-2	1-1	Bowen 40	Gunn	Culverhouse	Bowen	Butterworth	Newman	Woodthorpe	Megson	Smith	Ekoku*	Fox	Sutton	Power !
	18/12		*19,751*	*10*	31			*Wark 7p, Megson 90 (og)*	*Forrest*	*Stockwell*	*Thompson*	*Williams*	*Wark**	*Linighan*	*Youds*	*Slater*	*Palmer*	*Whelan*	*Kiwomya*	*Guentchev*
								Ref: M Reed	Butterworth brings down Chris Kiwomya and old-stager John Wark scores from the spot. Bowen nets a fierce drive to level. A nightmare of a finale sees sub Power pick up his second yellow card. Then Megson miscues a header into his own net from a late Neil Thompson corner-kick.											
20	A	TOTTENHAM		6	W	3-1	2-0	Sutton 27, 90, Ekoku 36	Gunn	Culverhouse	Bowen	Butterworth	Woodthorpe	Newman	Crook	Megson	Ekoku	Fox*	Sutton	Ullathorne
	27/12		*33,130*	*14*	34			*Barmby 74*	*Thorstvedt*	*Kerslake*	*Edinburgh*	*Samways*	*Calderwood*	*Sedgley*	*Caskey*	*Barmby*	*Anderton*	*Dozzell*	*Hazard*	
								Ref: A Gunn	A great attacking display as City have 15 shots on target. Sutton fires in a low Fox cross and Ekoku cuts in to surprise Erik Thorstvedt with a firm shot. Nick Barmby pulls one back with a cracking drive, but a long run by Ekoku ends with his shot parried to the feet of grateful Sutton.											
21	H	ASTON VILLA		7	L	1-2	1-0	Sutton 26	Gunn	Culverhouse	Bowen	Butterw'th^	Woodthorpe	Newman	Crook	Smith*	Ekoku	Fox	Sutton	Ullathorne/Johnson
	29/12		20,650	*8*	34			*Houghton 55, Saunders 58*	*Bosnich*	*Barrett*	*Staunton*	*Teale*	*McGrath*	*Richardson*	*Houghton*	*Townsend*	*Saunders*	*Whitting'm**	*Cox*	*Yorke*
								Ref: D Elleray	A slip by Shaun Teale lets in Sutton for his 13th of the season. Ray Houghton collects a poor back-pass by Culverhouse to equalise. Dean Saunders cracks a fine winner from 25 yards. Rumours circulate that manager Walker is at odds with the chairman over his contract and wages.											

No	Date		Att	Pos	Pt	F-A	H-T	Scorers, Times, and Referees	SQUAD	NUMBERS	IN USE									subs used
22	A	SOUTHAMPTON		6	W	1-0	1-0	Sutton 45	Gunn	Culverhouse	Bowen	Butterworth	Woodthorpe	Megson	Crook	Newman	Ekoku	Fox	Sutton	
	1/1		*16,556*	*21*	37				*Beasant*	*Dodd^*	*Adams*	*Benali !*	*Wood*	*Moore*	*Le Tissier*	*Wid'ring'on**	*Dowie*	*Maddison*	*Allen*	*Bennett/Kenna*
								Ref: G Poll	The topsy-turvy results continue as a home loss is followed by an away win. Sutton beats Dave Beasant with a quality strike from 20 yards. Francis Benali is sent off after tangling with Fox near a corner flag and using his elbow. Gossip continues over Walker's managerial future.											
23	H	NEWCASTLE		7	L	1-2	1-1	Bowen 4	Gunn	Culverhouse	Bowen	Butterworth	Woodthorpe	Newman	Crook	Megson	Ekoku	Fox	Sutton	
	4/1		19,564	*4*	37			*Beardsley 20, Cole 80*	*Hooper*	*Robinson*	*Beresford*	*Elliott*	*Scott*	*Howey*	*Lee*	*Beardsley*	*Cole*	*Clark*	*Sellars*	
								Ref: T Holbrook	Everton admit their interest in Walker and City fans await developments. Bowen turns in a low Fox cross. Peter Beardsley is in supreme form and nets a neat chip. He also tries to a catch Gunn out with outrageous efforts from distance. Andy Cole rounds Gunn for a deserved winner.											
24	H	CHELSEA		7	D	1-1	0-1	Ekoku 59	Gunn	Culverhouse	Bowen	Butterworth	Woodthorpe	Megson*	Crook	Newman	Ekoku	Fox	Sutton	Johnson
	15/1		19,472	*17*	38			*Stein 42*	*Kharine*	*Clarke*	*Sinclair*	*Myers*	*Johnsen*	*Spackman*	*Newton**	*Peacock*	*Shipperley*	*Burley*	*Stein*	*Dow*
								Ref: K Cooper	Coach John Deehan is put in charge after Walker resigns to join Everton. Mark Stein breaks the deadlock just before half-time, poking the ball in from close range after Eddie Newton's shot is blocked. Crook's free-kick is headed on by Sutton and Ekoku pounces to score at the far post.											
25	A	WEST HAM		8	D	3-3	1-1	Sutton 5, 57, Fox 79	Gunn	Culverhouse	Bowen	Butterworth	Woodthorpe	Megson*	Crook	Newman	Sutton	Fox	Goss	Ekoku
	24/1		*20,738*	*11*	39			*Sutton 35(og), Jones 46, Morley 84*	*Miklosko*	*Breacker*	*Rowland*	*Potts*	*Gale^*	*Bishop*	*Allen M*	*Jones*	*Chapman**	*Marsh*	*Holmes*	*Morley/Brown*
								Ref: J Worrall	A Sutton shot is fumbled over the line by Ludek Miklosko. Martin Allen's shot is deflected past Gunn by Sutton, and Steve Jones shoots the home side ahead. Sutton heads an equaliser and Fox volleys home from a Crook corner. Sub Trevor Morley wins a point with his first touch.											
26	H	LIVERPOOL		8	D	2-2	1-0	Sutton 12, 63	Gunn !	Culverhouse	Bowen	Megson*	Polston	Woodthorpe	Crook	Newman	Sutton	Ekoku	Goss	Eadie^/**Howie**
	5/2		19,746	*5*	40			*Culverhouse 53 (og), Barnes 76*	*Grobbelaar*	*Jones*	*Dicks*	*Harkness*	*Wright*	*Whelan*	*Clough*	*Walters*	*Rush*	*Barnes*	*McMan'm 'n*	
								Ref: D Gallagher	Sutton stabs in from close range to give City a great start, but Culverhouse deflects in an Ian Rush cross-shot at the other end. A superb curling shot regains the lead. Julian Dicks' lob sets up John Barnes' equaliser. Gunn handles outside the box to foil Steve McManaman and is sent off.											
27	H	ARSENAL		9	D	1-1	0-1	Ekoku 57	Gunn	Culverhouse	Bowen	Woodth'pe*	Polston	Goss	Crook	Newman	Ekoku	Megson^	Sutton	Eadie/Power
	13/2		17,667	*3*	41			*Campbell 33*	*Seaman*	*Dixon*	*Winterburn*	*Davis*	*Bould*	*Adams*	*Jensen*	*Campbell*	*Smith*	*Merson*	*Parlour*	
								Ref: R Dilkes	Ekoku swoops to save a point and the youthful new-look management team (Deehan, 36, and coach Megson, 34) chalk up another draw. Fox refuses a contract offer and joins Newcastle for £2.25 million. Many fans are upset at this - the eighth million-pound departure from Norwich.											
28	A	SWINDON		9	D	3-3	2-2	Sutton 14, Newman 41, Goss 83	Howie	Culverhouse	Bowen	Woodth'pe*	Polston	Goss	Crook	Newman	Ekoku	Sutton	**Adams**	Eadie
	19/2		*15,341*	*22*	42			*Taylor 16, Fjortoft 42, 49*	*Sheffield^*	*Summerbee*	*Bodin*	*Nijholt*	*Whitbread*	*Taylor*	*Moncur*	*Horlock*	*Fjortoft*	*Scott**	*Kilcline*	*McAven'/Hammond*
								Ref: R Gifford	In a real blood-and-thunder clash, Sutton turns past Brian Kilcline to fire the first. Newman steals in at the far post to net a volley. Jan Fjortoft puts the Robins ahead before Crooks' 35-yard lob hits the bar and falls for the alert Goss. Ex-City keeper Jon Sheffield goes off with an injury.											
29	H	BLACKBURN		9	D	2-2	1-1	Sutton 40p, 57	Gunn	Culverhouse	Bowen	Crook	Polston !	Ullathorne	Adams*	Newman	Ekoku^	Sutton	Goss	Butterworth/Eadie
	22/2		15,124	*2*	43			*Gallacher 32, 58*	*Flowers*	*Berg*	*Le Saux*	*Batty*	*Moran*	*May*	*Ripley*	*Atkins*	*Shearer*	*Gallacher*	*Wilcox*	
								Ref: K Barrett	An even first half ends with Polston red-carded after hauling down goalbound Alan Shearer. Ten-man City score through Sutton's well-taken goal, but within seconds Kevin Gallacher brings Kenny Dalglish's men level. Neil Adams, £250k from Oldham, goes close on his home debut.											
30	H	SHEFFIELD W		9	D	1-1	0-0	Sutton 90	Gunn	Culverhouse	Bowen*	Ullathorne	Polston !	Goss	Crook	Newman	Ekoku	Sutton	Adams	Buttterworth
	26/2		18,311	*8*	44			*Watson 75*	*Pressman*	*Nilsson*	*Coleman*	*Palmer*	*Pearce*	*Walker*	*B't-Will'ms^*	*Hyde*	*Hirst*	*Bright**	*Sinton*	*Watson/Poric*
								Ref: V Callow	Sub Gordon Watson cracks in a ten-yard drive through a forest of legs. It looks to be a winner until last-minute drama at the other end. Keeper Gunn goes up for a corner and panic ensues before Sutton fires a shot in. It's seven draws from seven league games since Deehan took charge.											
31	A	WIMBLEDON		9	L	1-3	1-1	Ekoku 6	Gunn	Culverhouse	Bowen	Butterworth	Newman	Goss	Crook	Ullathorne	Ekoku	Sutton	Adams	
	5/3		***7,206***	*11*	44			*Earle 37, 65, Holdsworth 75*	*Segers*	*Barton*	*Fitzgerald*	*Scales*	*McAllister*	*Fear*	*Earle*	*Blissett*	*Jones*	*Fashanu*	*Holdsworth*	
								Ref: A Gunn	Butterworth takes over the captaincy from the missing Polston again and Deehan tastes defeat in the league for the first time as a boss. A weak Warren Barton back-pass is seized on by Ekoku to put Norwich ahead, but Robbie Earle and Dean Holdsworth's ruthless finishing is decisive.											

32	H	QP RANGERS	9	L	3-4	1-0	Ekoku 9, 55, Bowen 88 *[White 84]*	Gunn	Culverhouse	Bowen	Crook	Woodthorpe	Goss*	Adams	Newman^	Ekoku	Sutton	Smith	Ullathorne/**Akinbiyi**
12/3		16,499	*10*	44			*Barker 49, Peacock 64, Penrice 70,*	*Stejskal*	*Ready*	*Wilson*	*Wilkins*	*Peacock*	*Yates*	*Meaker**	*Barker*	*White*	*Penrice*	*Sinclair*	*Holloway*
							Ref: D Allison	City lead for 40 minutes after Ekoku's firm header - then things go pear-shaped. Four second-half strikes by Gerry Francis' side shock home fans. Ekoku hits back with a lob and Bowen with a fine 25-yarder, but it's not enough. Rumours that Spurs have bid £4m for Sutton are denied.											
33	H	EVERTON	8	W	3-0	1-0	Culverh'se 40, Sutton 49, Bowen 70	Gunn	Culverhouse	Bowen	Butterworth	Polston	Goss	Crook	Megson*	Sutton	Eadie	Adams	Smith
21/3		16,432	*15*	47				*Southall*	*Jackson*	*Hinchcliffe*	*Ebbrell*	*Watson*	*Snodin*	*Radosav'ic**	*Stuart*	*Cottee*	*Rideout*	*Beagrie*	*Angell*
							Ref: K Burge	Walker returns with his new club in the same week a tribunal considers the 'illegal approach' allegations. He gets the full Judas treatment from City fans. Culverhouse shoots only his second goal in 360 games. Sutton rattles in the second and Bowen is coolness personified with his goal.											
34	A	COVENTRY	9	L	1-2	0-1	Eadie 46	Gunn	Culverhouse	Bowen	Butterworth	Polston*	Goss	Crook	Megson	Sutton	Eadie	Adams	Woodthorpe
26/3		*13,515*	*12*	47			*Flynn 28, Quinn 70*	*Ogrizovic*	*Morgan*	*Borrows*	*Darby*	*Babb*	*Atherton*	*Williams J**	*Rennie*	*Quinn*	*Ndlovu*	*Flynn*	*Boland*
							Ref: D Frampton	Deehan returns to his native Midlands for the first time as a manager. Sky Blues boss Phil Neal tries Sean Flynn as an emergency striker and his plan comes up trumps. Flynn is on the spot after Gunn spills a Peter Ndlovu shot. Eadie levels, but Ndlovu sets up Mick Quinn's winner.											
35	A	NEWCASTLE	10	L	**0-3**	0-1		Gunn	Culverhouse	Bowen	Woodthorpe	Prior	Goss	Crook	Megson	Eadie	Ullathorne	Aams*	Akinbiyi
29/3		*32,228*	*3*	47			*Cole 37, Lee 50, Beardsley 70*	*Srnicek*	*Robinson*	*Beresford*	*Bracewell^*	*Peacock*	*Neilson*	*Lee*	*Beardsley*	*Cole*	*Fox**	*Sellars*	*Mathie/Holland*
							Ref: T Holbrook	Ex-Canary Fox has a major hand in the Toon's victory. He sets up Andy Cole for the first. Cole lays the ball to Robert Lee who nets a fine effort. An error by Prior sets a move in motion, ending with Peter Beardsley beating Gunn. London teenager Ade Akinbiyi gets another outing.											
36	H	TOTTENHAM	11	L	1-2	0-0	Sutton 70	Gunn	Culverhouse	Bowen	Woodthorpe	Prior	Goss*	Crook	Megson	Sutton	Eadie	Adams	Robins
2/4		**21,181**	*16*	47			*Sheringham 55, Woodthorpe 76 (og)*	*Walker*	*Kerslake*	*Campbell*	*Samways*	*Scott*	*Sedgley*	*Mabbutt*	*Barmby*	*Anderton*	*Dozzell*	*Rosenthal**	*Sheringham*
							Ref: A Wilkie	Teddy Sheringham returns after a five-month lay-off. He flicks the ball up and shoots a clever goal past Gunn. Robins, also returning after a lengthy injury absence, sets up Sutton's equaliser with his first touch. Woodthorpe deflects a Darren Anderton pass past a wrong-footed Gunn.											
37	A	ASTON VILLA	11	D	0-0	0-0		Gunn	Culverhouse	Bowen	Woodthorpe	Prior	Goss	Crook	Megson*	Sutton	Eadie^	Ullathorne	Johnson/Adams
4/4		*25,416*	*9*	48				*Bosnich*	*Barrett*	*Staunton*	*Teale*	*Ehiogu*	*Richardson*	*Daley*	*Townsend*	*Saunders*	*Atkinson*	*Fenton**	*Yorke*
							Ref: M Bodenham	Norwich go close to stealing victory with Sutton hitting a post and Mark Bosnich making several fine saves to keep them out. Deehan is back where his career began and is delighted to win a point. Ron Atkinson's Villa are finding goals hard to come by and are slipping down the table.											
38	H	SOUTHAMPTON	11	L	4-5	1-1	Robins 37, Goss 48, Sutton 55, 63	Gunn	Culverhouse	Bowen	Ullathorne	Prior	Goss	Crook	Megson*	Sutton	Eadie^	Adams	Robins/Woodthorpe
9/4		17,150	*20*	48			*Ulla' 44(og), Le T' 57,63p,72, Monk 90*	*Beasant*	*Kenna*	*Bound*	*Benali*	*Charlton*	*Monkou*	*Le Tissier*	*Magilton*	*Dowie*	*Maddison*	*Allen*	
							Ref: K Cooper	Robins nets a stunner, flicking the ball up and swivelling to shoot past Dave Beasant. Ullathorne's ugly slice flies past Gunn for the equaliser. Goss's glancing header sparks a second-half goal-feast. An amazing game ends with big defender Ken Monkou winning it in the dying seconds.											
39	A	MANCHESTER C	11	D	1-1	1-0	Ullathorne 14	Gunn	Culverhouse	Bowen	Ullathorne	Polston	Prior	Crook	Smith^	Sutton	Robins*	Goss	Ekoku/Adams
16/4		*28,020*	*15*	49			*Rosler 46*	*Dibble*	*Hill*	*Brightwell D*	*McMahon*	*Curle*	*Vonk*	*Shutt**	*Karl*	*Rosler*	*Walsh*	*Lomas*	*Griffiths*
							Ref: D Elleray	Robins' neat pass sets up Ullathorne, who cracks a fine 20-yard shot past Andy Dibble. German striker Uwe Rosler steals in front of Polston to poach a clever equaliser just after the break. Andy Hill nearly wins it in the dying moments, but his header brings an excellent save from Gunn.											
40	H	SHEFFIELD UTD	11	L	0-1	0-1		Gunn	Culverhouse	Bowen	Prior	Polston	Goss	Crook	Ullathorne	Sutton	Robins	Adams*	Ekoku
23/4		18,474	*20*	49			*Blake 31*	*Tracey*	*Bradshaw*	*Nilsen*	*Gannon*	*Beasley*	*Gayle*	*Ward**	*Rogers*	*Flo*	*Blake*	*Whitehouse*	*Hodges*
							Ref: R Hart	Blades' new signing Nathan Blake stabs in a Dane Whitehouse cross from close range to inflict Norwich's eighth home defeat of the season. Battling against the drop, Dave Bassett's side always look the more likely winners. It's just two wins from 19 games since Deehan took charge.											
41	A	LIVERPOOL	11	W	1-0	1-0	Goss 35	Gunn	Culverhouse	Bowen	Woodthorpe	Polston	Prior	Crook	Ullathorne	Sutton	Ekoku	Goss	
30/4		*44,339*	*8*	52				*James*	*Jones*	*Dicks*	*Redknapp*	*Wright*	*Ruddock*	*Clough**	*Whelan*	*Rush*	*Barnes*	*Fowler*	*Hutchison*
							Ref: B Hill	The famous Kop is to be replaced by seated accommodation, so Liverpool use this match as a 'farewell' party. Goss silences the revellers as he smacks in a magnificent 20-yarder. It's his third truly spectacular goal of the season and helps a mixed campaign end on a more optimistic note.											
42	H	OLDHAM	12	D	1-1	0-1	Ullathorne 72	Gunn	Culverhouse	Bowie	Woodthorpe	Polston	Prior^	Ulalthorne	Megson*	Sutton	Ekoku	Goss	Robins/Adams
7/5		20,394	*21*	53			*McCarthy 13*	*Gerrard*	*Makin*	*Pointon*	*Henry*	*Jobson*	*Fleming*	*Beckford**	*Ritchie*	*McCarthy*	*Brennan*	*Holden*	*Barlow*
Average	Home 18,164	Away 22,869					Ref: D Frampton	To have any chance of staying up, Joe Royle's desperate Latics must win this and hopes rivals lose elsewhere. Their large following celebrate when Mark Brennan's mishit shot falls perfectly for Sean McCarthy to convert. Adams feeds Ullathorne, who nets a stunning volley to level it.											

Coca-Cola Cup

Rd	Ven	Opponent / Date	Att	Pos	Res	F-A	H-T	Scorers, Times, and Referees	SQUAD NUMBERS IN USE										
2:1	A	BRADFORD C		10	L	1-2	0-1	Fox 80	Gunn	Culverhouse	Bowen	Crook	Polston	Newman	Ekoku*	Johnson	Robins	Fox	Sutch	Sutton
		22/9	*8,988*	*2:12*				*McCarthy 23, 46*	*Tomlinson*	*Ford*	*Lawford*	*Duxbury*	*Oliver*	*Richards*	*Jewell**	*Robson*	*McCarthy*	*Stapleton^*	*Showler*	*McHugh/Steele*
								Ref: K Lipton	Sean McCarthy nods his 14th goal of the season, leaving Polston floundering behind him. Frank Stapleton's side go further ahead just after the break when McCarthy swivels and shoots past Gunn. Fox pulls a goal back after a fine 40-yard run, but Norwich deserve to be beaten tonight.											
2:2	H	BRADFORD C		4	W	3-0	0-0	Ekoku 65, Fox 67, Sutton 67	Gunn	Culverhouse	Bowen	Crook	Polston	Newman	Ekoku*	Megson	Sutton	Fox	Goss	Robins
		6/10	12,787	*2:13*					*Bowling*	*Ford*	*Lawford*	*Duxbury*	*Oliver*	*Richards*	*Jewell**	*Robson*	*McCarthy*	*Williams*	*Showler*	*Partridge*
								Ref: I Hemley (Norwich win 4-2 on aggregate)	Player-manager Stapleton sits this one out. After more than an hour of stubborn resistance, Ekoku calmly shoots Norwich level on aggregate after a Fox nod-back. Moments later Fox drives home another after Gavin Oliver heads straight to him. Sutton rises to head in an Ekoku cross.											
3	A	ARSENAL		2	D	1-1	1-0	Crook 33	Gunn	Culverhouse	Bowen	Butterworth	Prior	Newman	Crook	Eadie	Sutton	Fox	Goss	
		26/10	*24,539*	*3*				*Wright 78*	*Seaman*	*Dixon*	*Winterburn*	*Parlour*	*Linighan*	*Adams*	*Jensen*	*Wright*	*Smith*	*Merson**	*McGoldrick^*	*Campbell/Davis*
								Ref: A Gunn	City employ a sweeper system and give the Gunners a fright. John Jensen's miscued clearance hands Crook the opening goal. Tony Adams is lucky to only see yellow after bringing down Sutton, who was round Seaman and about to score. Ian Wright levels, shooting high into the net.											
3R	H	ARSENAL		2	L	0-3	0-2		Gunn	Culverhouse	Bowen	Butterworth	Polston	Newman	Crook	Eadie*	Sutton	Fox	Goss	Sutch
		10/11	16,319	*6*				*Wright 14, 65, Merson 34*	*Seaman*	*Dixon*	*Keown*	*Selley*	*Linighan*	*Bould*	*Jensen*	*Wright*	*Smith*	*Merson*	*Limpar*	
								Ref: P Foakes	The irrepressible Ian Wright latches on to a huge David Seaman drop-kick to slot home. Alan Smith turns past Butterworth, finds Paul Merson wide, and the cross is converted by Wright. An unhappy night for the fans, who can't understand why City's away form deserts them at home.											

FA Cup

Rd	Ven	Opponent / Date	Att	Pos	Res	F-A	H-T	Scorers, Times, and Referees												
3	A	WYCOMBE W		7	W	2-0	1-0	Sutton 37, 87	Gunn	Culverhouse	Bowen	Butterworth	Woodthorpe	Megson^	Crook	Ekoku*	Sutton	Fox	Newman	Ullathorne/Smith
		8/1	*7,802*	*3:4*					*Hyde*	*Cousins*	*Stapleton*	*Crossley*	*Evans*	*Ryan*	*Carroll*	*Hodges**	*Thompson*	*Hemmings^*	*Guppy*	*Langford/Horton*
								Ref: P Vanes	John Deehan is asked to take charge when Mike Walker walks out 24 hours before this tie to join Everton. League newcomers Wycombe, led by ex-Canary Martin O'Neill, fall behind to Sutton's diving header from an Ekoku cross. Near the end Sutton sidefoots home his second goal.											
4	H	MANCHESTER U		8	L	0-2	0-1		Gunn	Culverhouse	Bowen	Megson	Polston	Woodthorpe	Crook*	Goss	Newman	Fox	Sutton	Ekoku
		30/1	21,060	*1*				*Keane 19, Cantona 73*	*Schmeichel*	*Parker*	*Irwin*	*Bruce*	*Kanchelskis*	*Pallister*	*Cantona*	*Ince*	*Keane*	*Hughes**	*Giggs*	*McClair*
								Ref: P Durkin	Disappointment and bitterness after this defeat. Eric Cantona commits a dreadful tackle on Goss and tramples on Polston, but instead of being sent off, the Frenchman goes on to score a clinching goal. Earlier Goss, returning to the side, and Polston have shots beaten out by Schmeichel.											

UEFA Cup

Rd	Ven	Opponent / Date	Att	Pos	Res	F-A	H-T	Scorers, Times, and Referees												
1:1	H	VITESSE ARNHEM		8	W	3-0	0-0	Ekoku 51, Goss 68, Polston 71	Gunn	Culverhouse	Bowen	Newman	Polston	Megson^	Ekoku	Crook	Sutton*	Fox	Goss	Robins/Eadie
		15/9	16,818						*V der Gouw*	*Straal*	*V der Looi*	*Bos*	*Vermeulen*	*Laamers*	*Cocu*	*Loeffen*	*Latuheru*	*Gillhuas*	*Helder*	
		(Holland)						Ref: R Sedlacek (Aus)	Norwich's European debut starts worryingly with the Dutch looking faster and slicker in the first period. Walker's half-time pep talk does the trick and from a Crook free-kick, Ekoku nets a sizzling volley. Goss cracks the second after Megson's backheel. Poston stabs in a Fox centre.											
1:2	A	VITESSE ARNHEM		5	D	0-0	0-0		Gunn	Culverhouse	Bowen	Newman	Polston	Butterworth	Ekoku*	Crook	Sutton	Fox	Goss	Megson
		29/9	*9,133*						*V der Gouw*	*Sturing*	*V der Looi*	*Bos*	*Vermeulen*	*Laamers*	*Cocu*	*Straal**	*Latuheru*	*Gillhuas*	*Helder*	*Pothuizen*
								Ref: T Kefalos (Greece) (Norwich win 3-0 on aggregate)	A heroic defensive display sees Norwich safely through. Around 1,500 City fans travel to Holland, but find the humble Arnhem stadium is no great shakes. Four yellow cards are collected along the way as City battle hard. Ekoku has three chances to ease the pressure but misses the lot.											
2:1	A	BAYERN MUNICH		2	W	2-1	2-1	Goss 13, Bowen 30	Gunn	Culverhouse	Bowen	Newman	Prior	Butterworth	Robins*	Crook	Sutton	Fox	Goss	Sutch
		20/10	*28,500*					*Nerlinger 41*	*Aumann*	*Jorginho*	*Ziege**	*Kreuzer*	*Helmer*	*Nerlinger*	*Wouters*	*Witeczek*	*Valencia*	*Matthaus*	*Scholl^*	*Sternkopf/Labbadia*
		(Germany)						Ref: L Sundell (Sweden)	Unbeaten at home for over a year, Bayern are stunned as Newman's cross is headed by Lother Matthaus straight to Goss, who volleys a superb goal from 20 yards. Bowen's far-post header makes it two before Christian Nerlinger heads in Jorginho's cross. An unforgettable night for City.											

2:2	H	BAYERN MUNICH	2	D	1-1	0-1	Goss 50	Gunn	Culverhouse	Bowen	Newman	Polston	Butterworth	Eadie^	Crook	Sutton	Fox*	Goss	Sutch/Akinbiyi
	3/11	20,829					*Valencia 4*	*Aumann*	*Jorginho*	*Ziege*	*Kreuzer*	*Helmer*	*Nerlinger*	*Wouters*	*Schupp*	*Valencia*	*Matthaus*	*Witeczek*	
							Ref: F Vandenwijngaert (Belg) (Norwich win 3-2 on aggregate)	Ebullient after the first leg, City fans are temporary silenced as Adolfo Valencia makes no mistake after two ricochets off defenders. That man Goss comes to the rescue again, shooting home after Sutton's deft flick. Lother Matthaus is booked for argy-bargy with Gunn as City hold firm.											
3:1	H	INTER MILAN	3	L	0-1	0-0		Gunn	Culverhouse	Bowen	Newman	Polston	Butterworth	Sutch*	Crook	Sutton	Fox	Goss	Power
	24/11	20,805					*Bergkamp 80p*	*Zenga*	*Bergomi*	*Orlando*	*Manniconi*	*Battistini*	*Paganin M*	*Paganin A*	*Dell'Anno*	*Fontolan*	*Bergkamp*	*Sosa**	*Ferri*
	(Italy)						Ref: S Muhmenthaler (Switz)	City look positive in the first-half but fail to break through. Goss slams a fierce shot against the underside of the bar near the end. Newman's tackle on Ruben Sosa in the dying minutes brings a penalty winner from Dennis Bergkamp. Bookings put three City men out of the second leg.											
3:2	A	INTER MILAN	7	L	0-1	0-0		Gunn	Ullathorne	Bowen	Newman	Prior^	Megson	Ekoku*	Woodthorpe	Sutton	Fox	Goss	Sutch/Power
	8/12	*30,000*					*Bergkamp 88*	*Zenga*	*Bergomi*	*Orlando*	*Shalimov*	*Battistini*	*Paganin M*	*Paganin A*	*Dell'Anno*	*Fontolan*	*Bergkamp*	*Sosa*	
							Ref: V Krondl (RCS) (Norwich lose 0-2 on aggregate)	Severely depleted by suspensions, City need something special in the San Siro. They have plenty of the ball, but conjure few chances. Three fine saves by Gunn keeps them alive. The heroic effort is snuffed out as Bergkamp explodes down the left and calmly curls a shot into the net.											

			Home						Away					
		P	W	D	L	F	A	W	D	L	F	A	Pts
1	Manchester U	42	14	6	1	39	13	13	5	3	41	25	92
2	Blackburn	42	14	5	2	31	11	11	4	6	32	25	84
3	Newcastle	42	14	4	3	51	14	9	4	8	31	27	77
4	Arsenal	42	10	8	3	25	15	8	9	4	28	13	71
5	Leeds	42	13	6	2	37	18	5	10	6	28	21	70
6	Wimbledon	42	12	5	4	35	21	6	6	9	21	32	65
7	Sheffield Wed	42	10	7	4	48	24	6	9	6	28	30	64
8	Liverpool	42	12	4	5	33	23	5	5	11	26	32	60
9	QP Rangers	42	8	7	6	32	29	8	5	8	30	32	60
10	Aston Villa	42	8	5	8	23	18	7	7	7	23	32	57
11	Coventry	42	9	7	5	23	17	5	7	9	20	28	56
12	NORWICH	42	4	9	8	26	29	8	8	5	39	32	53
13	West Ham	42	6	7	8	26	31	7	6	8	21	27	52
14	Chelsea	42	11	5	5	31	20	2	7	12	18	33	51
15	Tottenham	42	4	8	9	29	33	7	4	10	25	26	45
16	Manchester C	42	6	10	5	24	22	3	8	10	14	27	45
17	Everton	42	8	4	9	26	30	4	4	13	16	33	44
18	Southampton	42	9	2	10	30	31	3	5	13	19	35	43
19	Ipswich	42	5	8	8	21	32	4	8	9	14	26	43
20	Sheffield Utd	42	6	10	5	24	23	2	8	11	18	37	42
21	Oldham	42	5	8	8	24	33	4	5	12	18	35	40
22	Swindon	42	4	7	10	25	45	1	8	12	22	55	30
		924	192	142	128	663	532	128	142	192	532	663	1244

Odds & ends

Double victories: (2) Everton, Leeds.
Double losses:(2) Newcastle, Wimbledon.

Won from behind: (2) Blackburn (a), Everton (a).
Lost from in front: (5) Aston Villa (h), Wimbledon (a), QP Rangers (h), Southampton (h), Newcastle (h).

High points: The tremendous victory at Bayern Munich.
Superb away form throughout the first half of the season.
Goss' wonder-goal and the 4-0 humbling of Leeds at Elland Road.
Victory at Anfield thanks to another spectacular Goss goal.
The Ekoku-inspired 5-1 thrashing of Everton at Goodison.
A fine display at Old Trafford, against the runaway leaders.
The 12% rise in average Carrow Road league crowds.
Low points: Losing Mike Walker to Everton in mid-season.

Erratic home form – only 4 wins from 21 league games.
The slow slide down the table after the turn of the year.
The sale of another key player (Ruel Fox) – albeit for a huge profit.
Mark Robins' and Daryl Sutch's long injury absences.

Player of the Year: Chris Sutton.
Ever-presents: (1) Ian Culverhouse (not including UEFA Cup).
Hat-tricks: (1) Efan Ekoku (4 v Everton, a).
Hat-tricks against: (1) Matt Le Tissier (v Southampton, a).
Leading scorer: (28) Chris Sutton.

	Appearances								Goals				
	Lge	Sub	LC	Sub	FAC	Sub	Eur	Sub	Lge	LC	FAC	Eur	Tot
Adams, Neil	11	3											
Akinbiyi, Ade		2											
Bowen, Mark	41		4		2		6		5			1	6
Butterworth, Ian	23	2	2		1		4						
Crook, Ian	38		4		2		5				1		1
Culverhouse, Ian	42		4		2		5		1				1
Eadie, Darren	9	6	3				1	1	3				3
Ekoku, Efan	20	7	2		1	1	3		12	1		1	14
Fox, Ruel	25		4		2		6		7	2			9
Goss, Jeremy	34		3		1		6		6			3	9
Gunn, Bryan	41		4		2		6						
Howie, Scott	1	1											
Johnson, Andy		2	1										
Megson, Gary	21	1	1		2		2	1					
Newman, Rob	32		4		2		6		2				2
Polston, John	24		3		1		4					1	1
Power, Lee	2	3						2					
Prior, Spencer	13		1				2						
Robins, Mark	9	4	1	1			1	1	1				1
Smith, David	5	2				1							
Sutch, Daryl	1	2		1			1	3					
Sutton, Chris	41		3	1	2		6		25	2	1		28
Ullathorne, Robert	11	5				1	1		2				2
Woodthorpe, Colin	18	2			2		1						
(own-goals)									1				1
24 players used	**462**	*42*	**44**	*3*	**22**	*3*	**66**	*8*	**65**	**5**	**2**	**6**	**78**

No	Date		Att	Pos	Pt	F-A	H-T	Scorers, Times, and Referees	SQUAD	NUMBERS	IN	USE								subs used
1	A	CHELSEA			L	0-2	0-1		Gunn	**Bradshaw**	Bowen	**Newsome**	Polston	Newman*	Crook	Ullathorne	Robins	Ekoku^	Goss	Adams/Sutch
	20/8		*23,098*		0			*Sinclair 43, Furlong 75*	*Kharine*	*Clarke*	*Sinclair**	*Kjeldbjerg*	*Johnsen*	*Spackman*	*Rocastle*	*Shipperley^*	*Furlong*	*Peacock*	*Wise*	*Newton/Hoddle*
								Ref: T Holbrook	Deehan gives debuts to Carl Bradshaw (£450k from Sheffield U) and Jon Newsome (club record £1m from Leeds). Frank Sinclair hits a fine volley past Gunn before the break. Paul Furlong nets a low shot, with City protesting that Gavin Peacock impeded Bradshaw in the build-up.											
2	H	CRYSTAL PALACE		17	D	0-0	0-0		Gunn	Bradshaw	Bowen	Newsome	Polston	Goss	Crook	Ullathorne	Robins*	Ekoku	Adams	Eadie
	25/8		19,015	*20*	1				*Martyn*	*Patterson*	*Gordon*	*Southgate*	*Shaw*	*Coleman*	*Rodger**	*Bowry*	*Armstrong*	*Dyer^*	*Salako*	*Newman/Cox*
								Ref: B Hill	Happily settled in a new state-of-the-art training HQ at Trowse on the edge of the city, the team are unable to put a smile on fans' faces at the first home game. Alan Smith's side conceded six goals at home four days ago, but City do everything but score and are unfortunate not to win.											
3	H	WEST HAM		11	W	1-0	0-0	Robins 64	Gunn	Bradshaw	Bowen	Newsome	Polston	Goss	Crook	Ullathorne	Robins*	Ekoku^	Adams	Newman/Akinbiyi
	27/8		19,110	*19*	4				*Miklosko*	*Breacker*	*Burrows*	*Potts*	*Martin*	*Allen*	*Bishop*	*Moncur*	*Jones*	*Marsh**	*Rowland^*	*Whitbread/Chapman*
								Ref: P Jones	Sub Ade Akinbiyi comes on and produces a fine cross, knocked past Ludek Miklosko by Robins, pouncing like lightning on the chance. It's enough to ensure Norwich's first home win in five months. More good news when striker Mike Sheron signs from Manchester City for £800k.											
4	A	SHEFFIELD WED		11	D	0-0	0-0		Gunn	Bradshaw	Bowen	Newsome	Polston	Goss	Crook	Ullathorne	Robins*	Akinbiyi^	Adams	Newman/**Sheron**
	31/8		*25,072*	*12*	5				*Pressman*	*Atherton*	*Nolan*	*Taylor^*	*Pearce*	*Walker*	*Sheridan*	*Petrescu*	*Hirst*	*Bright**	*Sinton*	*Watson/B't-Williams*
								Ref: K Cooper	Deehan surprisingly gives Akinbiyi a full debut in place of Ekoku, said to be a target for Wimbledon. Sheron makes his debut from the bench. Andy Pearce saves the home side by knocking a Polston header off the goalline. Wednesday hit the net twice, but both efforts are disallowed.											
5	H	ARSENAL		11	D	0-0	0-0		Gunn	Bradshaw	Bowen	Newsome	Polston	Goss	Crook	Ullathorne	Newman	Ekoku*	Adams^	Robins/Sutch
	10/9		17,768	*12*	6				*Seaman*	*Dixon*	*Winterburn*	*Schwarz*	*Keown*	*Adams*	*Selley*	*Wright*	*Campbell**	*Parlour*	*McGoldrick*	*Smith*
								Ref: R Hart	New boy Sheron will have to wait for his home debut after picking up an injury. Ullathorne gets the best opportunities to breach the Gunners' defences as he twice breaks into the box, but fails to beat David Seaman each time. The defence chalks up its fourth clean sheet in succession.											
6	A	IPSWICH		9	W	2-1	1-1	Newman 12, Bradshaw 53	Gunn	Bradshaw	Bowen	Newsome	Polston	Goss	Crook	**Milligan^**	Newman	Sheron*	Adams	Ekoku/Eadie
	19/9		*21,031*	*16*	9			*Wark 45p*	*Forrest*	*Johnson*	*Yallop*	*Sedgley*	*Wark*	*Linighan*	*Williams*	*Slater*	*Milton*	*Marshall*	*Kiwomya**	*Guentchev*
								Ref: R Dilkes	Expensive signings Milligan and Ipswich's Steve Sedgley both debut. Newman slides in to net the opening goal. Ian Marshall is fouled for John Wark to level from the spot. Crook is fouled by Simon Milton and Bradshaw hits the winner after his penalty is parried by Craig Forrest.											
7	A	MANCHESTER C		11	L	0-2	0-0		Gunn	Bradshaw	Bowen	Newsome	Polston	Goss	Crook	Ullathorne^	Newman	Sheron	Adams*	Robins/Milligan
	24/9		*21,031*	*7*	9			*Quinn 53, Rosler 62*	*Coton*	*Edghill*	*Phelan*	*Flitcroft*	*Curle**	*Brightwell*	*Summerbee*	*Walsh*	*Rosler^*	*Quinn*	*Beagrie*	*Hill/Lomas*
								Ref: G Poll	Terry Phelan crosses for big Niall Quinn to put Norwich behind. Nine minutes later Quinn heads down a Peter Beagrie cross and Uwe Rosler is on hand to convert. Shortly after this, Gunn saves a Beagrie penalty. The Canaries haven't won a league fixture at Maine Road for 30 years.											
8	H	BLACKBURN		9	W	2-1	1-1	Bowen 30, Newsome 55	Gunn	Bradshaw	Bowen	Newsome	Polston	Crook	Eadie	Milligan	Newman	Ekoku^	Adams*	Goss/Robins
	1/10		18,146	*3*	12			*Sutton 4*	*Flowers*	*Berg*	*Le Saux*	*Sherwood**	*Hendry*	*Warhurst*	*Ripley*	*Atkins*	*Shearer*	*Sutton*	*Wilcox*	*Slater*
								Ref: P Jones	Sold for £5m in July, Chris Sutton returns to Carrow Road to prod home an Alan Shearer pass in the opening minutes. Bowen swaps passes with Ekoku and drives in an equaliser. Defender Newsome nets an extraordinary winner, cutting in skilfully and crashing home a dipping shot.											
9	H	LEEDS		8	W	2-1	0-0	Robins 61, Adams 90	Gunn	Bradshaw	Bowen	Newsome	Newman^	Crook	Eadie	Milligan*	Robins	Sheron	Adams	Goss/Prior
	8/10		17,390	*9*	15			*Wallace 89*	*Lukic*	*Kelly*	*Dorigo*	*Palmer*	*Wetherall*	*McAllister*	*White*	*Wallace*	*Deane*	*Whelan^*	*Worthingt'n**	*Faircl'gh/Pemberton*
								Ref: P Don	Gunn is at it again, diving to save a 48th-minute penalty by Gary McAllister. Robins puts City ahead with a sweetly-taken sidefooted goal. Rod Wallace equalises late on from a Gary Speed cross, but in the dying moments Adams gleefully heads in Robins' cross to send home fans wild.											
10	A	ASTON VILLA		6	D	1-1	0-0	Milligan 49	Gunn	Bradshaw^	Bowen	Newman	Prior	Crook	Eadie	Milligan	Robins	Sheron*	Adams	Akinbiyi/**Wright**
	15/10		*22,468*	*16*	16			*Saunders 62*	*Bosnich*	*Barrett*	*King*	*Ehiogu*	*McGrath*	*Richardson*	*Yorke*	*Parker*	*Saunders*	*Atkinson^*	*Staunton**	*Houghton/Whit'g'm*
								Ref: A Wilkie	Eadie and Sheron both hit the woodwork during a frantic scramble before Milligan heads his first City goal. Dean Saunders levels with a fierce header from Gary Parker's cross. Dwight Yorke hits a post as Villa press hard for a winner. Bradshaw is carried off as the injury crisis deepens.											

No	Venue	Opponent / Date	Att	Pos	Res / Pts	FT	HT	Scorers, Times, and Referees	1	2	3	4	5	6	7	8	9	10	11	Subs used
11	H	QP RANGERS		6	W	4-2	0-1	Robins 46, Bowen 54, Sheron 57,	Gunn	Wright	Bowen*	Newsome	Polston	Crook	Eadie	Milligan	Robins	Sheron	Adams^	Newman/Goss
		22/10	19,431	20	19			*Barker 24, Gallen 61* [White 62 (og)]	*Dykstra*	*Bardsley*	*Wilson*	*Barker*	*Yates*	*McDonald*	*Meaker**	*Holloway*	*White*	*Gallen*	*Sinclair*	*Allen*
								Ref: M Reed	Simon Barker is left unmarked to give Rangers the lead, but City are inspired by a brilliant wing display from Eadie. Robins poaches the first before Bowen flashes home a fine shot. Sheron pounces to make it three and Devon White slides Robins' cross into his own net to settle things.											
12	A	WIMBLEDON		8	L	0-1	0-0		Gunn	Sutch	Bowen	Milligan	Polston	Ullathorne*	Milligan	Newman	Akinbiyi^	Sheron	Goss	Crook/Adams
		30/10	*8,242*	17	19			*Ekoku 63*	*Segers*	*Barton*	*Thorn*	*Reeves*	*Joseph*	*Talboys*	*Jones*	*Elkins*	*Gayle**	*Blissett*	*Ekoku*	*Clarke*
								Ref: D Gallagher	A rainy Sunday afternoon gets more depressing for Norwich when Efan 'The Chief' Ekoku bursts through to score from a tight angle - his first goal since joining the Dons from City just a fortnight ago. It ends the home side's run of four losses, but is City's sixth in a row in this fixture.											
13	A	SOUTHAMPTON		7	D	1-1	0-0	Robins 48	Gunn	Newman	Bowen^	Goss	Polston	Prior	Crook	Milligan	Robins	Akinbiyi*	Adams	Sutch/**O'Neill**
		2/11	*12,876*	13	20			*Le Tissier 89p*	*Grobbelaar*	*Kenna*	*Benali**	*Magilton*	*Hall*	*Monkou*	*Le Tissier*	*Ekelund*	*Dowie*	*Maddison*	*Heaney*	*McDonald*
								Ref: P Durkin	Newman's badly gashed leg means a debut for 18-year-old winger Keith O'Neill. Robins jinks inside two challenges and shoots low past Bruce Grobbelaar. Near the end Prior is penalised for handball and Matt Le Tissier levels from the spot. Furious City players insist Prior was pushed.											
14	H	EVERTON		7	D	0-0	0-0		Gunn	Sutch	Bowen	Milligan	Polston	Goss	Crook	Newman	Robins*	Milligan	Adams	**Cureton**
		5/11	18,377	22	21				*Southall*	*Jackson*	*Burrows*	*Ablett*	*Watson*	*Unsworth**	*Horne*	*Stuart*	*Ferguson*	*Rideout*	*Parkinson*	*Limpar*
								Ref: P Danson	Norwich have the better of the first half but Mike Walker's Everton look stronger after the break. Prolific reserve scorer Jamie Cureton, 19, debuts and goes close minutes after coming on, but is foiled by Neville Southall. Everton sack ex-City hero Walker two days after this match.											
15	A	COVENTRY		9	L	0-1	0-0		Gunn	Polston	Bowen*	Crook	Polston	Prior	Eadie	Newman	Robins	Milligan	Adams^	Goss/Sutch
		19/11	*11,891*	13	21			*Jones 62*	*Ogrizovic*	*Darby*	*Morgan*	*Busst*	*Borrows*	*Pressley*	*Jones*	*Cook*	*Dublin*	*Ndlovu*	*Flynn*	
								Ref: G Willard	The home team are without the injured Roy Wegerle and big Mick Quinn, who has joined Plymouth. Goss and Sutch make way for Eadie and Newsome but to no avail.A mediocre contest comes to life after an hour when American winger Cobi Jones converts his first Coventry goal.											
16	H	LEICESTER		9	W	2-1	0-1	Newsome 56, Sutch 89	Gunn	Sutch	Bowen	Newsome	Polston	Crook	Eadie	Milligan*	Newman	Sheron^	Adams	Goss/Cureton
		26/11	20,657	21	24			*Draper 22*	*Poole*	*Blake*	*Whitlow*	*Mohan*	*Willis*	*Draper*	*Oldfield*	*Thompson*	*Walsh*	*Lowe**	*Ormondroyd*	*Gee*
								Ref: R Gifford	David Lowe drives in a low cross for Mark Draper to open the scoring for Mark McGhee's side. Newsome puts City back on terms, rising to head in Adams' free-kick. In the nick of time Adams' deep cross leads to a scramble, the ball spilling free for Sutch to knock in a bobbling ball.											
17	A	MANCHESTER U		9	L	0-1	0-1		Gunn	Bradshaw	Bowen	Newsome	Polston	Ullathorne	Sutch	Newman*	Robins	Crook	Goss	Cureton
		3/12	*43,789*	2	24			*Cantona 36*	*Walsh*	*Neville*	*Irwin*	*May*	*Kanch'skis^*	*Pallister*	*Cantona*	*Ince*	*McClair*	*Hughes*	*Davies**	*Gillespie/Butt*
								Ref: T Holbrook	Robins has the ball in the net against his former team, but a hairline offside decision rules it out. When Bowen slips, Brian McClair races in and pulls the ball back for Eric Cantona to side-foot home. YTS trainee Danny Mills, a 17-year-old local lad, signs professional forms for City.											
18	H	CHELSEA		9	W	**3-0**	2-0	Ward 23, 45, Cureton 58	Gunn	Bradshaw	Ullathorne	Newsome	Polston	Crook*	Sutch	Milligan	Robins^	**Ward**	Sutch	Newman/Cureton
		10/12	18,246	8	27				*Kharine*	*Barness**	*Minto*	*Sinclair*	*Johnsen*	*Spackman*	*Newton*	*Spencer*	*Furlong*	*Peacock*	*Wise*	*Burley*
								Ref: J Worrall	Ashley Ward signs from Crewe for just over one-third of the £900k received for Ekoku, the man he replaces. Ward is an instant hero, slipping in Eadie's cross and tapping in after Dmitri Kharine blocks Robins' effort. Cureton nods in a swirling cross, 20 seconds after coming on as sub.											
19	A	CRYSTAL PALACE		7	W	1-0	0-0	Ward 47	Gunn	Bradshaw*	Ullathorne	Newsome	Polston	Crook^	Sutch	Milligan	Robins	Ward	Sutch	Bowen/Newman
		17/12	*12,473*	16	30				*Martyn*	*Humphrey*	*Gordon*	*Southgate*	*Shaw^*	*Coleman*	*Bowry**	*Preece*	*Armstrong*	*Newman*	*Salako*	*Dyer/Pitcher*
								Ref: R Hart	A superb 50-yard run by Eadie and neat cross by Robins sees Ward blast home from close range. The goal proves to be the highlight of a drab game. Ward has now hit 13 goals in his last eight outings. Ian Culverhouse, a model of consistency in 369 Norwich games, signs for Swindon.											
20	H	TOTTENHAM		7	L	0-2	0-1		Gunn	Bowen*	Ullathorne	Newsome	Polston	Crook^	Sutch	Eadie	Robins	Ward	Goss	Newman/Adams
		26/12	21,814	8	30			*Barmby 11, Sheringham 90*	*Walker*	*Austin*	*Campbell*	*Popescu*	*Calderwood*	*Mabbutt*	*Anderton*	*Barmby*	*Klinsmann*	*Sheringham*	*Howells**	*Nethercott*
								Ref: R Dilkes	The best crowd for nearly four years sees the first home loss of the season. Darren Anderton beats the offside trap to run through and square for Nicky Barmby to net. Newsome snuffs out Jurgen Klinsmann, but Teddy Sheringham goes on a long run and his shot is deflected over Gunn.											
21	A	NOTT'M FOREST		7	L	0-1	0-0		Gunn*	Sutch	Ullathorne	Newsome	Polston	Crook	Cureton^	Newman	Sheron	Ward	Goss	**Marshall**/Adams
		27/12	*21,010*	4	30			*Bohinen 50*	*Crossley*	*Lyttle*	*Pearce*	*Cooper*	*Chettle*	*Stone*	*Haaland*	*Roy*	*Bohinen*	*Collymore*	*Woan**	*Black*
								Ref: S Lodge	Gunn collapses in agony after blocking an early Ian Woan shot. Stuart Pearce is near the incident and immediately calls for a stretcher as the keeper has clearly broken his leg. His replacement, teenage debutant Andy Marshall, flaps at a Lars Bohinen corner-kick and it goes straight in.											

No	Date		Att	Pos	Pt	F-A	H-T	Scorers, Times, and Referees	SQUAD	NUMBERS	IN	USE								subs used
22	H	NEWCASTLE		7	W	2-1	2-1	Adams 1, Ward 10	Marshall	Sutch	Ullathorne	Newsome	Polston	Goss	Crook*	Milligan	Sheron^	Ward	Adams	Newman/Cureton
	31/12		21,172	*4*	33			*Fox 39p*	*Srnicek*	*Venison*	*Beresford*	*Howey*	*Peacock*	*Watson**	*Lee*	*Bracewell*	*Cole*	*Fox*	*Kitson*	*Clark*
								Ref: B Hill	Worries about young Marshall are banished as he has a superb home debut, winning praise from Magpies boss Kevin Keegan. Another hero is Newsome, who shrugs off a broken nose. Adams' looping header and Ward's shot give a dream start. Ullathorne trips Kitson for the spot-kick.											
23	A	LIVERPOOL		8	L	0-4	0-2		Marshall	Sutch	Ullathorne	Newman^	Polston	Prior	Crook	Milligan	Sheron	Ward	Goss*	Adams/Eadie
	2/1		*34,709*	*3*	33			*Scales 14, Fowler 37, 46, Rush 81*	*James*	*Jones*	*Bjornbye*	*Scales*	*Babb*	*Ruddock*	*McManam'n*	*Redknapp*	*Rush*	*Barnes*	*Fowler*	
								Ref: K Cooper	Marshall is brought back down to earth by Roy Evans' men. John Scales converts an early header and the Red tide advances. A slick move ends with Robbie Fowler making it two. The hammering is complete when Ian Rush produces a majestic near-post header from a Fowler cross.											
24	H	WIMBLEDON		9	L	1-2	1-1	Goss 22	Marshall	Sutch	Bowen	Newsome	Polston	Goss	Crook*	Ullathorne	Sheron	Ward	Adams^	Akinbiyi/Prior
	14/1		18,261	*7*	33			*Reeves 44, Ekoku 49*	*Segers*	*Cunningham*	*Perry*	*Reeves*	*Kimble*	*Barton*	*Jones*	*Earle*	*Goodman**	*Ekoku*	*Holdsw'th^*	*Elkins/Clarke*
								Ref: M Bodenham	Another sale enrages City fans - Robins joins Leicester for £1m. Goss, last season's goal hero, grabs his first in more than eight months. Joe Kinnear's men hit back as City reject Alan Reeves equalises, then Efan Ekoku heads his fifth goal since his recent move from Carrow Road.											
25	H	COVENTRY		9	D	2-2	1-1	Adams 32p, Ward 55	**Tracey**	Sutch*	Bowen	Newsome	Polston	Prior	Milligan	Newman	Sheron	Ward	Adams	Eadie
	25/1		14,024	*19*	34			*Dublin 22, Jenkinson 76*	*Ogrizovic*	*Borrows*	*Pickering*	*Cook*	*Rennier*	*Williams*	*Darby**	*Marsh*	*Dublin*	*Ndlovu*	*Jenkinson*	*Wegerle*
								Ref: P Don	Simon Tracey arrives on loan from Sheffield U to allow young Marshall a break from the firing line, but has a largely unhappy debut. Paul Cook handles for a penalty and Ward swoops on David Rennie's misplaced header. Winger Leigh Jenkinson levels with his first Coventry goal.											
26	A	EVERTON		10	L	1-2	0-1	Milligan 80	Marshall	Sutch^	Bowen	Newsome	Polston	Ullathorne	Crook	Milligan	Sheron*	Ward	Eadie	Goss/Adams
	4/2		*23,295*	*18*	34			*Stuart 42, Rideout 66*	*Southall*	*Barrett*	*Ebbrell*	*Ablett*	*Watson*	*Unsworth*	*Horne*	*Stuart*	*Hinchliffe*	*Rideout*	*Parkinson**	*Samways*
								Ref: A Wilkie	Andy Hinchcliffe's through ball slices City apart and finds Graham Stuart in acres of space to net the opening goal. Paul Rideout heads home unchallenged at the far post to clinch the vcitory for Joe Royle's side. Milligan side-foots home to briefly raise Norwich's hopes near the end.											
27	H	SOUTHAMPTON		10	D	2-2	1-2	Newsome 38, Ward 90	Marshall	Bradshaw	Bowen	Newsome	Prior^	Ullathorne	Crook*	Eadie	Sheron	Ward	Goss	Sutch/Adams
	11/2		18,361	*15*	35			*Hall 33, Magilton 36*	*Grobbelaar*	*Kenna*	*Dodd*	*Widdrington*	*Hall*	*Monkou*	*Le Tissier**	*Magilton*	*Shipperley*	*Maddison*	*Heaney*	*Hughes*
								Ref: R Hart	Ipswich-born Richard Hall puts Saints ahead from a Matt Le Tissier corner and Jim Magilton stuns Carrow Road with a low drive. Newsome brings City back into it, netting from close in after Prior heads on a corner. Ward's fierce drive in the final minute completes a fine comeback.											
28	H	MANCHESTER U		12	L	0-2	0-2		Marshall	Bradshaw	Bowen	Newsome	Polston	Johnson	Adams	Milligan	Sheron	Ward	Eadie	
	22/2		21,824	*2*	35			*Ince 2, Kanchelskis 16*	*Schmeichel*	*Keane*	*Sharpe*	*Bruce*	*Kanchelskis*	*Pallister*	*Cole*	*Ince*	*McClair*	*Hughes*	*Giggs*	
								Ref: T Holbrook	Deehan makes five team changes but has to suffer more misery. Lightning early strikes by United kill the game. Newsome heads the ball clear but Paul Ince picks it up and races forward to shoot home. A sweeping counter-attack sees Andrei Kanchelskis power home a cracking drive.											
29	A	BLACKBURN		14	D	0-0	0-0		Marshall	Bradshaw	Bowen	Newsome	Polston	Johnson	Adams^	Milligan*	Sheron	Ward	Eadie	Cureton/Sutch
	25/2		*25,579*	*1*	36				*Flowers*	*Berg*	*Le Saux*	*Sherwood*	*Hendry*	*Pearce*	*Ripley*	*Atkins**	*Shearer*	*Newell*	*Wilcox*	*Warhurst*
								Ref: M Reed	Chris Sutton is suspended, but league leaders Rovers still start odds-on favourites. A resolute defensive display sees City become the first side to keep a clean sheet at Ewood this season. Free-scoring Rovers are almost beaten near the end when lively sub Cureton goes desperately close.											
30	H	MANCHESTER C		14	D	1-1	0-0	Cureton 82	Marshall	Bradshaw	Bowen	Newman	Polston	Johnson	Adams	Milligan*	Cureton^	Ward	Eadie	Sheron/Prior
	4/3		16,266	*15*	37			*Simpson 86*	*Coton*	*Summ'bee**	*Phelan*	*Kernaghan*	*Curle*	*Vonk^*	*Gaudino*	*Walsh*	*Brightwell*	*Quinn*	*Simpson*	*Hill/Griffiths*
								Ref: D Gallagher	A Norwich side desperate for a first win in 1995 versus a five-man defence: it's the perfect formula for a poor game. The stalemate finally ends as Ward sets up Cureton's confident finish. Just minutes later Fitzroy Simpson levels with a smart half-volley from Niall Quinn's knockdown.											
31	H	SHEFFIELD WED		15	D	0-0	0-0		Marshall	Bradshaw^	Bowen	Newsome	Polston	Ullathorne	Crook*	Sutch	Cureton	Ward	Eadie	Newman/Johnson
	8/3		**13,530**	*8*	38				*Woods*	*Atherton*	*Nolan*	*B't-Williams*	*Pearce*	*Walker*	*Williams*	*Waddle**	*Hyde*	*Bright*	*Briscoe*	*Watson*
								Ref: P Danson	The slide continues amidst more hostility directed towards the chairman. This is not currently a pleasant place to play football, says Deehan, with a degree of understatement. His comments are later criticised by fans. Ex-Canary Chris Woods makes one superb save from Bradshaw.											

No	H/A	Opponent / Date / Att	Pos	Res / Pts	F-A	H-T	Scorers, Times, Referees	1	2	3	4	5	6	7	8	9	10	11	subs used
32	A	WEST HAM	14	D	2-2	1-0	Eadie 22, Ullathorne 53	Marshall	Sutch	Ullathorne	Newsome	Polston	Prior	Johnson !	Newman	Cureton*	Ward	Eadie^	Adams/Akinbiyi
	11/3	21,464	18	39			*Cottee 82, 88*	*Miklosko*	*Breacker*	*Dicks*	*Potts*	*Reiper*	*Bishop**	*Morley*	*Moncur*	*Cottee*	*Hutchison*	*Williamson*	*Hughes*
							Refs: A Wilkie/M Sims	Ref Wilkie is injured in the first period and his replacement blunders by sending off Johnson after a bad tackle by Prior. City build a two-goal lead, but the Hammers blast back after the mistaken identity incident. Their equaliser loops over Marshall's head off the knee of Tony Cottee.											
33	A	QP RANGERS	15	L	0-2	0-0		Marshall	Sutch	Ullathorne	Newman	Polston	Prior	Johnson*	Milligan	Cureton^	Ward	Eadie	Adams/Akinbiyi
	15/3	10,519	11	39			*Ferdinand 66, Gallen 86*	*Roberts*	*Bardsley*	*Wilson*	*Barker*	*Maddix*	*McDonald*	*Impey*	*Holloway*	*Ferdinand*	*Gallen*	*Sinclair*	
							Ref: G Ashby	A Les Ferdinand tap-in puts City behind. The points are secure for Ray Wilkins' side when Kevin Gallen blasts in an Andrew Impey cross, knocked back to him by Ferdinand. Norwich are now well and truly in the relegation mire, having taken just nine points from a possible 42.											
34	H	IPSWICH	14	W	**3-0**	0-0	Cureton 53, Ward 58, Eadie 78	Marshall	Crook	Bowen	Newsome	Polston	Ullathorne	Adams^	Milligan	Cureton*	Ward	Eadie	Newman/Sutch
	20/3	17,510	21	42				*Forrest*	*Thompson*	*Yallop*	*Whelan*	*Wark !*	*Williams*	*Thomsen*	*Slater**	*Mathie*	*Marshall*	*Milton*	*Chapman*
							Ref: P Durkin	Struggling Town drop million-pound misfit skipper Steve Sedgley. Veteran player-coach John Wark hauls down Eadie in midfield and gets a harsh red card. City's depressing run ends as they jubilantly hit two in five minutes. Cureton skips round Craig Forrest to set the ball rolling.											
35	A	ARSENAL	14	L	**1-5**	1-3	Cureton 32 *[Newman 90 (og)]*	Marshall	Bradshaw	Bowen	Newsome	Newman	Ullathorne*	Adams	Johnson	Cureton	Ward	Eadie	Sutch
	1/4	36,942	10	42			*Hartson 4, 13, Dixon 6, Merson 75,*	*Bartram*	*Dixon*	*Winterburn*	*Hillier*	*Bould*	*Adams*	*Morrow**	*Wright*	*Hartson^*	*Merson*	*Helder*	*Keown/Kiwomya*
							Ref: P Jones	John Hartson sidefoots home Glenn Helder's pass and Lee Dixon's curling cross freakishly ends up in the net. Hartson gets clear unchallenged for his second. Cureton hammers home to restore a little pride. Merson's volley is followed by an embarrassing headed own-goal by Newman.											
36	A	LEICESTER	14	L	0-1	0-0		Marshall	Bradshaw	Ullathorne*	Newsome	Polston	Megson^	Sutch	Newman	Cureton	Ward	Eadie	Bowen/Prior
	5/4	15,992	21	42			*Parker 48*	*Poole*	*Grayson*	*Whitlow*	*Hill*	*Willis*	*Carey*	*Lawrence*	*Lowe*	*Robins*	*Roberts*	*Parker*	
							Ref:T Holbrook	Jamie Lawrence's cross is driven decisively past Marshall by Garry Parker. Ward nets but offside is given. Speculation is inevitably mounting about the future of under-pressure manager Deehan. This was only the fifth victory in their last 39 league games for Mark McGhee's outfit.											
37	A	NEWCASTLE	14	L	0-3	0-2		Marshall	Bradshaw	Bowen	Newsome	Polston^	Prior	Crook*	Ullathorne	Ward	Milligan	Eadie	Sutch/Cureton
	8/4	35,518	3	42			*Beardsley 8p, 42, Kitson 74*	*Srnicek*	*Hottiger*	*Elliott*	*Venison*	*Peacock*	*Howie*	*Lee*	*Beardsley*	*Kitson*	*Fox*	*Bracewell*	
							Ref: M Reed	Newsome tugs Paul Kitson for Peter Beardsley to net from the spot. Beardsley spots Marshall off his line and nets a beauty from 35 yards. He goes close with two other crafty efforts. Kitson races through for the third. Deehan resigns the next day after 15 months in charge of the team.											
38	H	NOTT'M FOREST	16	L	0-1	0-0		Marshall	Bradshaw	Bowen	Newsome	Polston	Crook	Adams	Milligan	Cureton^	Ward	Eadie*	Prior/Akinbiyi
	12/4	19,005	3	42			*Stone 85*	*Crossley*	*Lyttle*	*Pearce*	*Cooper*	*Chettle*	*Stone*	*Phillips*	*Roy**	*Bohinen*	*Collymore*	*Woan*	*Lee*
							Ref: K Morton	Just two wins from the last five games will probably save City from relegation, but new caretaker boss Gary Megson knows it will be tough. Crook hits the bar with a free-kick but City are hit by a late sucker punch. Stan Collymore catches them on the break and sets up Steve Stone.											
39	A	TOTTENHAM	20	L	0-1	0-1		Marshall	Bradshaw	Bowen	Newsome	Polston	Prior	Crook	Milligan	Sheron^	Ward	Newman*	Sutch/Akinbiyi
	17/4	32,304	7	42			*Sheringham 35*	*Walker*	*Austin*	*Edinburgh*	*Popescu*	*Calderwood*	*Mabbutt*	*Anderton*	*Barmby**	*Klinsmann*	*Sheringham*	*Rosenthal*	*Caskey*
							Ref: R Gifford	Teddy Sheringham looks well offside when he receives Darren Anderton's cross to score the only goal. City battle hard to level and in the final minute Newsome's 30-yarder smashes against the bar. This year four will go down and tonight City drop into the bottom four for the first time.											
40	H	LIVERPOOL	20	L	1-2	1-1	Ullathorne 17	Marshall	Bradshaw^	Bowen	Newsome	Polston	Ullathorne	Sutch	Milligan	Akinbiyi	Ward	Crook*	Adams/Cureton
	29/4	**21,843**	4	42			*Harkness 7, Rush 84*	*James*	*Thomas*	*Harkness*	*Scales*	*Babb*	*Wright*	*McManam'n*	*Redknapp*	*Rush*	*Barnes**	*Fowler^*	*Clough/Walters*
							Ref: B Hill	Temporary speakers belt out rock music in an attempt to jolly up the atmosphere. Most believe it's a bid to drown out the anti-Chase protests. Ullathorne's thumping drive cancels out Steve Harkness's first senior goal. Ian Rush walks in the winner after a rebound off brave Marshall.											
41	A	LEEDS	20	L	1-2	1-0	Ward 35	Marshall	Newman	Bowen	Newsome	Polston	Goss	Sutch	Ullathorne	Akinbiyi^	Ward	Crook*	Bradshaw/Sheron
	6/5	31,981	6	42			*McAllister 79p, Palmer 90*	*Lukic*	*Kelly*	*Dorigo*	*Palmer*	*Wetherall*	*Pemberton*	*Yeboah**	*Wallace^*	*Deane*	*McAllister*	*Speed*	*Whelan/Sharp*
							Ref: A Wilkie	A win will set up a 'winner-takes-all' final day versus Villa. Anything less means relegation. John Lukic's howler hands City a goal. A shock win is prevented when Newsome is very harshly penalised in a scramble. City are down and the game ends in a turmoil of dissent and misery.											
42	H	ASTON VILLA	20	D	1-1	0-1	Goss 56	Marshall	Bradshaw	Bowen	Newsome	Polston	Goss	Crook	Ullathorne	Akinbiyi*	Ward	Sutch	Sheron
	14/5	19,374	18	43			*Staunton 7*	*Spink*	*Charles*	*Wright*	*Teale*	*McGrath*	*Ehiogu*	*Yorke*	*Townsend*	*Saunders^*	*Fenton**	*Staunton*	*King/Johnson*
	Home	Away					Ref: K Cooper	A flying header by Steve Staunton and City look to be on their way to a new club record of eight league losses in a row. Goss brings back memories of better times with a fine second-half volley. An above-average crowd has turned up, largely, it seems, to protest against Chase.											
Average	18,625	22,393																	

Coca-Cola Cup			Att		F-A	H-T	Scorers, Times, and Referees	SQUAD	NUMBERS	IN	USE								subs used
2:1	H	SWANSEA	11	W	3-0	1-0	Sheron 36, Bradshaw 48p, Adams 63	Gunn	Bradshaw	Johnson^	Newsome	Polston*	Goss	Eadie	Ullathorne	Robins	Sheron	Adams	Newman/Crook
		21/9	8,053 *2:15*					*Freestone*	*Jenkins*	*Clode*	*Ford*	*Harris*	*Pascoe^*	*Bowen*	*Penney*	*Torpey*	*Cornforth*	*Perrett**	*Ampadu/Hodge*
							Ref: T West	Sheron combines with Polston to curl home his first City goal. John Ford chops down Adams for Bradshaw to net from the spot. Adams buries a low drive to sink Frank Burrows' side and chalk up his first strike. There are cup shocks galore elsewhere, but City never look in any danger.											
2:2	A	SWANSEA	9	L	0-1	0-0		Gunn	Bradshaw	Bowen	Newsome	Prior	Goss	Eadie	Milligan^	Newman	Ekoku*	Adams	Robins/Crook
		4/10	*3,568 2:17*				*Pascoe 54*	*Freestone*	*Jenkins*	*Clode*	*Ford*	*Harris*	*Pascoe*	*Ampadu !*	*Penney*	*Torpey*	*Cornforth**	*Hodge*	*Bowen*
							Ref: G Ashby (Norwich win 3-1 on aggregate)	Colin Pascoe cracks a 20-yarder past the diving Gunn. A handful of City fans endure a miserable night in South Wales, although an aggregate win is never in doubt. Kwame Ampadu is sent off for two bookable offences. Assistant boss Megson calls it the worst display so far this term.											
3	A	TRANMERE	6	D	1-1	1-0	Polston 45	Gunn	Polston	Bowen	Crook	Prior	Newman	Adams*	Milligan	Robins	Sheron	Eadie^	Sutch/Goss
		26/10	*10,232 1:4*				*Aldridge 69*	*Nixon*	*Stevens*	*Mungall*	*McGreal*	*Garnett*	*O'Brien**	*Morrissey*	*Aldridge*	*Malkin*	*Brannan*	*Nevin*	*Irons*
							Ref: S Lodge	Following an Eadie corner-kick, Polston is on hand at the far post to give Norwich the lead. After this it's hair-raising stuff as Tranmere press forward relentlessly. John Aldridge converts a Pat Nevin cross and John King's side twice hit the bar, but City somehow hold on for a replay.											
3R	H	TRANMERE	7	W	4-2	0-1	Prior 56, McGreal 61(og), Polston 65, [Newman 85]	Gunn	Sutch	Bowen	Newman	Polston	Prior	Crook*	Milligan	Robins	Eadie	Adams	Goss
		9/11	13,311 *1:3*				*Irons 12, Nevin 51*	*Nixon*	*Stevens*	*Mungall*	*McGreal*	*Garnett*	*Irons*	*Morrissey*	*Aldridge*	*Malkin*	*Brannan*	*Nevin*	
							Ref: B Hill	A spectacular long-range effort from Kenny Irons stuns the home fans, but three goals in a nine-minute spell in the second half settles it. Goss comes on as sub and within seconds has set up the first goal. Eadie's 30-yard shot cannons home off John McGreal's head to give City the lead.											
4	H	NOTTS CO	9	W	1-0	1-0	Eadie 1	Gunn	Sutch	Bowen	Newsome	Polston	Crook	Eadie^	Milligan	Newman	Sheron*	Adams	Cureton/Goss
		30/11	14,030 *1:24*					*Cherry*	*Mills*	*Legg*	*Turner*	*Yates*	*Johnson*	*Devlin*	*Butler*	*Lund*	*McSwegan*	*Agana*	
							Ref: K Morton	Eadie is brought down in the game's first real attack. He gets up to curl the free-kick past Steve Cherry with just 42 seconds gone. Later in the game Eadie goes off feeling unwell. Norwich reach the last eight after bad-tempered late exchanges, in which three County men are cautioned.											
QF	A	BOLTON	8	L	0-1	0-0		Marshall	Sutch	Bowen	Newsome	Polston	Goss	Eadie*	Crook	Newman	Sheron	Adams^	Akinbiyi/Ullathorne
		11/1	*17,029 1:4*				*Lee 66*	*Branagan*	*Green*	*Phillips*	*McAteer*	*Coleman*	*Stubbs*	*Lee*	*Sneekes*	*Paatalainen*	*McGinlay*	*Thompson*	
							Ref: D Elleray	Eadie is stretchered off after a firm tackle by Scott Green. David Lee nets a superb goal, accelerating past three defenders before unleashing a ferocious shot from 15 yards past Gunn. It's another great night of giant-killing for Bruce Rioch's outfit, who ultimately make it to Wembley.											

FA Cup																			
3	A	GRIMSBY	8	W	1-0	0-0	Crook 54	Marshall	Sutch	Ullathorne !	Newsome	Polston	Crook	Eadie	Milligan	Newman	Sheron^	Adams*	Goss/Cureton
		7/1	*11,198 1:13*					*Crichton*	*McDermott*	*Croft*	*Handyside*	*Rodger !*	*Groves*	*Childs**	*Shakespeare*	*Woods*	*Mendonca*	*Gilbert^*	*Jobling/Lester*
							Ref: G Poll	A bad-tempered affair at chilly Blundell Park sees Graham Rodger dismissed early on for lunging at Eadie with upraised arm. After the break Paul Crichton misjudges a 30-yard shot from Crook and it sails past him into the net. Near the end Ullathorne departs after a bout of wrestling.											
4	A	COVENTRY	9	D	0-0	0-0		Tracey*	Ullathorne	Bowen	Newsome	Polston	Sutch	Eadie	Milligan	Newman^	Sheron"	Adams	Marsh'l/Akin'/Curet'n
		28/1	*15,122 19*					*Ogrizovic*	*Pickering*	*Morgan**	*Rennie*	*Borrows*	*Pressley*	*Marsh*	*Cook*	*Dublin*	*Ndlovu*	*Jenkinson*	*Wegerle*
							Ref: G Willard	The first half is a dull affair, but the under-pressure home side step up a gear after Marshall replaces injured keeper Tracey. The teenager plays superbly, saving well from ex-Canary Dion Dublin and Peter Ndlovu. Sub Roy Wegerle comes on and looks a threat, but Norwich hold firm.											
4R	H	COVENTRY	10	W	3-1 *aet*	1-1	Sheron 8, 108, Eadie 103	Marshall	Ullathorne	Bowen	Newsome	Polston	Sutch	Eadie	Milligan	Crook^	Sheron	Adams*	Akinbiyi/Goss
		8/2	14,673 *20*				*Ndlovu 32*	*Ogrizovic*	*Pickering*	*Morgan*	*Rennie*	*Borrows*	*Pressley*	*Marsh*	*Flynn*	*Dublin^*	*Ndlovu*	*Wegerle**	*Jones/Darby*
							Ref: G Willard	A fairly even contest goes into extra-time. Marshall is again in top form against the Sky Blues. Dion Dublin and Roy Wegerle limp off and Norwich look more likely winners as the minutes tick by. Sheron and Eadie finish off a team whose boss, Phil Neal, is sacked a few days later.											
5	A	EVERTON	10	L	0-5	0-2	*[Ferguson 62, Stuart 88]*	Tracey	Bradshaw	Bowen	Newsome !	Newman	Johnson	Sutch	Ullathorne*	Eadie	Sheron	Goss	Prior
		18/2	*31,616 18*				*Limpar 6, Parkinson 23, Rideout 55,*	*Southall*	*Jackson*	*Hinchcliffe*	*Ebbrell*	*Watson*	*Ablett*	*Stuart*	*Parkinson*	*Ferguson*	*Rideout**	*Limpar*	*Barlow*
							Ref: M Bodenham	Anders Limpar's powerful shot is followed by strikes from Joe Parkinson and Paul Rideout which loan keeper Simon Tracey looks at fault with. Newsome is sent off for an ugly lunge at Limpar. City's travelling army give Deehan and Tracey the sort of stick normally reserved for Chase.											

		Home						Away					
		P	W	D	L	F	A	W	D	L	F	A	Pts
1	Blackburn	42	17	2	2	54	21	10	6	5	26	18	89
2	Manchester U	42	16	4	1	42	4	10	6	5	35	24	88
3	Nott'm Forest	42	12	6	3	36	18	10	5	6	36	25	77
4	Liverpool	42	13	5	3	38	13	8	6	7	27	24	74
5	Leeds	42	13	5	3	35	15	7	8	6	24	23	73
6	Newcastle	42	14	6	1	46	20	6	6	9	21	27	72
7	Tottenham	42	10	5	6	32	25	6	9	6	34	33	62
8	QP Rangers	42	11	3	7	36	26	6	6	9	25	33	60
9	Wimbledon	42	9	5	7	26	26	6	6	9	22	39	56
10	Southampton	42	8	9	4	33	27	4	9	8	28	36	54
11	Chelsea	42	7	7	7	25	22	6	8	7	25	33	54
12	Arsenal	42	6	9	6	27	21	7	3	11	25	28	51
13	Sheffield Wed	42	7	7	7	26	26	6	5	10	23	31	51
14	West Ham	42	9	6	6	28	19	4	5	12	16	29	50
15	Everton	42	8	9	4	31	23	3	8	10	13	28	50
16	Coventry	42	7	7	7	23	25	5	7	9	21	37	50
17	Manchester C	42	8	7	6	37	28	4	6	11	16	36	49
18	Aston Villa	42	6	9	6	27	24	5	6	10	24	32	48
19	Crys Palace	42	6	6	9	16	23	5	6	10	18	26	45
20	NORWICH	42	8	8	5	27	21	2	5	14	10	33	43
21	Leicester	42	5	6	10	28	37	1	5	15	17	43	29
22	Ipswich	42	5	3	13	24	34	2	3	16	12	59	27
		924	205	134	123	697	498	123	134	205	498	697	1252

Odds & ends

Double victories: (1) Ipswich.
Double losses:(5) Liverpool, Manch U, Nott'm F, Tottenham, Wimbledon.

Won from behind: (4) Blackburn (h), Leicester (h), QP Rangers (h), Tranmere (h) (CCC).
Lost from in front: (2) Leeds (a), Wimbledon (h).

High points: The first local derby 'double' for 43 years.
The fighting spirit shown in the last five matches under Megson.
The move to a vastly improved training HQ at Colney.
Newsome's extraordinary winner at home to Blackburn.

Low points: Relegation after nine seasons, with just one win from the final 20 games.
More big-money departures (Sutton, Robins and Ekoku).
Bryan Gunn's broken leg at Nott'm Forest – the season's turning point?
The iffy penalty award at Leeds, which virtually confirmed relegation.
The failure to invest in new blood, despite the threat of relegation.
The departure, perhaps inevitable, of popular John Deehan.
Humiliating five-goal thrashings at Arsenal and Everton.
Ian Butterworth having to quit, following a water-skiing injury.

Player of the Year: Jon Newsome.
Ever-presents: (0).
Hat-tricks: (0).
Hat-tricks against: (0).
Leading scorer: (8) Ashley Ward.

	Appearances						Goals			
	Lge	*Sub*	LC	*Sub*	FAC	*Sub*	Lge	LC	FAC	Tot
Adams, Neil	**23**	*10*	6		3		**3**	1		**4**
Akinbiyi, Ade	**6**	*7*		*1*		*2*				
Bowen, Mark	**34**	*2*	5		3		**2**			**2**
Bradshaw, Carl	**25**	*1*	2		1		**1**	1		**2**
Crook, Ian	**33**	*1*	4	*2*	2				1	**1**
Cureton, Jamie	**9**	*8*		*1*		*2*	**4**			**4**
Eadie, Darren	**22**	*4*	6		4		**2**	1	1	**4**
Ekoku, Efan	**5**	*1*	1							
Goss, Jeremy	**19**	*6*	3	*3*	1	*2*	**2**			**2**
Gunn, Bryan	**21**		5							
Johnson, Andy	**6**	*1*	1		1					
Marshall, Andy	**20**	*1*	1		2	*1*				
Megson, Gary	**1**									
Milligan, Mike	**25**	*1*	4		3		**2**			**2**
Newman, Rob	**23**	*9*	5	*1*	3		**1**	1		**2**
Newsome, Jon	**35**		4		4		**3**			**3**
O'Neill, Keith		*1*								
Polston, John	**38**		5		3			2		**2**
Prior, Spencer	**12**	*5*	3			*1*		1		**1**
Robins, Mark	**14**	*3*	3	*1*			**4**			**4**
Sheron, Mike	**17**	*4*	4		4		**1**	1	2	**4**
Sutch, Daryl	**20**	*10*	3	*1*	4		**1**			**1**
Tracey, Simon	**1**				2					
Ullathorne, Robert	**27**		1	*1*	4		**2**			**2**
Ward, Ashley	**25**						**8**			**8**
Wright, Johnny	**1**	*1*								
(own-goals)							**1**	1		**2**
26 players used	**462**	***76***	**66**	***11***	**44**	***8***	**37**	**9**	**4**	**50**

No	Date	Att	Pos	Pt	F-A	H-T	Scorers, Times, and Referees	1	2	3	4	5	6	7	8	9	10	11	subs used
1	A LUTON			W	3-1	1-0	Newsome 14, 55, Adams 69	Gunn	**Mills**	Bowen	Milligan*	Newsome	Prior	Adams	Akinbiyi	Ward	Eadie	Johnson^	Sutch"/Ullathorne/Polston
	13/8	*7,848*		3			*Guentchev 53p*	*Davis*	*Thomas*	*Johnson*	*Waddock*	*Hughes*	*Peake*	*Alexander*	*Oldfield*	*Thorpe*	*Guentchev**	*Harvey*	*Taylor*
							Ref: M Pierce	Two nervous new managers face each other on the opening day. Newsome thumps in two right in front of celebrating Norwich fans. Local lad Danny Mills, on his debut, pulls down Graham Alexander for Bontcho Guentchev's debut penalty. Adams secures the victory from 25 yards.											
2	H SUNDERLAND		5	D	0-0	0-0		Gunn	Mills	Bowen	Milligan	Newsome	Prior	Adams	Akinbiyi	Sheron^	Johnson*	Eadie	Newman/**Rush**
	19/8	16,739	*21*	4				*Chamberlain*	*Kubicki*	*Gray Mtn*	*Bracewell*	*Ball*	*Ord*	*Gray Mcl*	*Atkinson*	*Smith**	*Gray P*	*Angell^*	*Rusell/Howey*
							Ref: I Hemley	Akinbiyi heads a decent chance over the bar, but City are generally second best and the visitors strike the woodwork twice. Gunn hobbles for most of the game with a thigh injury. New face Mathew Rush debuts as a sub, but a knee injury means this will be his only action this season.											
3	A BIRMINGHAM		13	L	**1-3**	0-1	Sheron 85	Gunn	Mills	Bowen	Milligan*	Newsome	Prior	Adams	Sheron	Akibiyi	Johnson^	Eadie	Sutch/Cureton
	26/8	*19,267*	*4*	4			*Hunt 22, 48, 70p*	*Bennett*	*Poole*	*Frain*	*Ward**	*Edwards*	*Whyte*	*Hunt*	*Claridge*	*Bowen*	*Donowa^*	*Hiley*	*Forsyth/Castle*
							Ref: R Poulain	Ward is sorely missed in attack and Milligan goes off with a hip injury. Norwich are undone by a clinical Jonathan Hunt hat-trick. Sheron hits the bar and later gets a consolation near the end, heading in an Adams cross. O'Neill signs former favourite Robert Fleck on loan from Chelsea.											
4	H OLDHAM		8	W	2-1	0-0	Bowen 56, Johnson 80	Gunn	Sutch	Bowen	Newsome	Polston	Ullathorne	Adams	Fleck*	Akinbiyi	Johnson	Eadie	Sheron
	30/8	14,816	*10*	7			*Halle 46*	*Gerrard*	*Redmond*	*Makin*	*Henry^*	*Jobson*	*Fleming*	*Halle*	*Rickers**	*McCarthy*	*Pointon*	*Brennan*	*Banger/McNiven*
							Ref: A D'Urso	Norwich are on top in the first half but have no success until past the hour mark. Returning hero Fleck sets up Bowen, who nets from a tight angle to equalise a Gunner Halle goal. Ten minutes from the end Johnson nods in a close-range winner. It's the first home victory since March.											
5	H PORT VALE		5	W	2-1	2-1	Johnson 19, Fleck 24	Gunn	Sutch	Bowen	Ullathorne	Newsome	Polston^	Adams	Fleck	Ward	Johnson*	Eadie	Sheron/Prior
	2/9	13,908	*20*	10			*Mills 40*	*Musselwhite*	*Hill*	*Tankard*	*Bogie**	*Griffiths*	*Glover D*	*McCarthy^*	*Porter*	*Mills*	*Glover L*	*Guppy*	*Walker/Naylor*
							Ref: D Orr	A fine header from Johnson sets City on their way. Within minutes Fleck nets a brave diving header that sends the fans into raptures. Lee Mills hits the bar, but a minute later heads in a Steve Guppy corner. This was our best yet, says O'Neill, who is chasing Hull striker Dean Windass.											
6	A SHEFFIELD UTD		8	L	1-2	1-1	Ward 18	Gunn !	Mills	Bowen	Crook*	Newsome	Prior	Adams	Fleck"	Ward	Johnson^	Eadie	Milligan/Akinbiyi/Newman
	9/9	*11,205*	*24*	10			*Blake 45, Veart 72*	*Kelly*	*Beard*	*Nilsen*	*Rodgers**	*Tuttle^*	*Blount*	*Ward*	*Flo*	*Blake*	*Hodges*	*Whitehouse*	*Holland/Veart*
							Ref: A Butler	Ward slides into an empty net. Nathan Blake looks offside as he levels and a row ensues as the teams leave the field at the break. Gunn is red-carded for dissent at this point. Carl Veart's header beats Gunn's stand-in Newman. Fleck is ordered from the touchline by the card-happy ref.											
7	A WOLVERHAMPTON		3	W	2-0	0-0	Johnson 59, Ward 69	Gunn	Mills	Bowen	Crook*	Newsome	Prior	Adams	Fleck	Ward	Johnson	Eadie	Milligan
	13/9	***27,064***	*16*	13				*Stowell*	*Thompson*	*Pearce**	*Rankine*	*De Wolf*	*Richards*	*Daley*	*Goodman^*	*Bull !*	*Ferguson"*	*Froggatt*	*Emblen/Kelly/Cowans*
							Ref: T West	Johnson's low drive is a big setback for Graham Taylor's Wolves. Ten minutes later Ward doubles the lead with a crisp 20-yard shot, set up by in-form Fleck. Wolves' frustration grows and five minutes from time Steve Bull is sent off for head-butting Ward in an off-the-ball incident.											
8	H MILLWALL		5	D	0-0	0-0		Gunn	Mills	Bowen	Crook*	Newsome	Prior	Adams	Fleck	Ward^	Johnson	Eadie	Milligan/Akinbiyi
	16/9	15,962	*2*	14				*Keller*	*Newman*	*Thatcher*	*Bowry*	*Witter*	*Stevens*	*McRobert^*	*Doyle**	*Malkin*	*Dixon*	*Van Blerk*	*Fuchs/Forbes*
							Ref: J Kirkby	Mick McCarthy's high-flying Lions go home with a point from a drab game. Some light relief comes via Martin O'Neill's witty programme notes, in which he talks about the pressure he is under to sign loanee Fleck on a permanent basis. Ward is forced off with a hamstring problem.											
9	A GRIMSBY		5	D	2-2	1-2	Fleck 19, Akinbiyi 90	Marshall	Sutch*	Bowen	Crook	Newsome	Prior	Adams^	Fleck"	Akinbiyi	Johnson	Eadie !	Ullathorne/Sheron/Newman
	23/9	*5,901*	*12*	15			*Childs 31, Southall 32*	*Crichton*	*McDermott*	*Croft*	*Handyside*	*Smith*	*Groves*	*Childs**	*Dobbin*	*Woods*	*Livingstone*	*Southall*	*Watson*
							Ref: T Heilbron	Fleck nets a half-volley, but Brian Laws' men roar back with two in 60 seconds. Gary Childs beats Marshall with a dipper from 30 yards and Nicky Southall cuts in and cracks a beauty. Eadie is sent off for clattering into Childs. Akinbiyi pounces in stoppage time to fire an equaliser.											
10	H LEICESTER		9	L	0-1	0-0		Mashall	Ullathorne	Bowen	Crook	Newsome	Prior	Adams^	Fleck*	Akinbiyi	Johnson	Eadie	Sheron/O'Neill
	30/9	18,435	*1*	15			*Heskey 87*	*Poole*	*Grayson*	*Whitlow*	*Rollin*	*Walsh*	*Parker*	*Joachim*	*Taylor*	*Robins**	*Lowe*	*Hill*	*Heskey*
							Ref: N Barry	Fleck signs permanently for £650k, but cannot oblige with a goal against a team unbeaten away from home. Seventeen-year-old Emile Heskey comes on for his second appearance as a sub and prods in his first senior goal in the dying minutes. The Foxes go three points clear at the top.											
11	A STOKE		11	D	1-1	1-0	Akinbiyi 32	Gunn	Ullathorne	Bowen	Crook	Newsome	Prior	Adams*	Akinbiyi	Fleck"	Johnson	O'Neill^	Milligan/Polston/Sheron
	7/10	*12,016*	*21*	16			*Wallace 67*	*Prudhoe*	*Clarkson*	*Sandford*	*Sigurdsson*	*Overson*	*Potter*	*Sturridge*	*Wallace*	*Peschisolido*	*Carruthers*	*Gleghorn*	
							Ref: G Cain	Lou Macari's side have picked up lately after a bad spell, but City go ahead as Akinbiyi taps in after Mark Prudhoe parries a Johnson effort. A slick move culminates in Ray Wallace slotting past Gunn. Stoke look lightweight in attack, but within a month will be joined by City's Sheron.											

No Date	Venue	Opponent	Att	Pos	Res/Pts	F-A	H-T	Scorers, Times, and Referees												subs used
12	H	BARNSLEY		6	W	3-1	0-1	Newsome 53, Johnson 61, Fleck 72	Gunn	Ullathorne	Bowen	Crook	Newsome	Prior	**Simpson***	Fleck	Ward	Johnson	O'Neill	Milligan
14/10			14,002	*7*	19			*Eaden 20*	*Watson*	*Eaden*	*Moses*	*Molby*	*Davis**	*Bishop*	*Sheridan*	*Redfearn*	*Liddell^*	*Jackson*	*Archdeacon*	*Rammell/Bullock*
								Ref: E Lomas	Nicky Eaden scores from 20 yards after a neat one-two. City are jeered off at the interval, but tactical changes bring about a transformation. Newsome levels with a tap-in, then Johnson curls a spectacular goal past diving David Watson. Fleck sidefoots a third to make the points safe.											
13	A	CHARLTON		8	D	1-1	0-0	Bowen 71	Gunn	Ullathorne	Bowen	Crook	Newsome	Prior	Milligan	Fleck	Ward	Johnson	O'Neill	
21/10			*13,369*	*10*	20			*Bowyer 67*	*Salmon*	*Humphrey^*	*Stuart*	*Walsh**	*Chapple*	*Rufus*	*Robinson !*	*Newton*	*Williams*	*Leaburn*	*Bowyer*	*Robson/Nelson*
								Ref: P Rejer	Keith O'Neill's cross finds the net, going in off the shins of Bowen. Alan Curbishley's outfit draw level four minutes later when teenager Lee Bowyer snakes in a 30-yard daisy-cutter. Hard-working John Robinson departs after picking up a second yellow card three minutes from time.											
14	H	TRANMERE		7	D	1-1	1-0	Johnson 11	Gunn	Ullathorne	Bowen^	Crook*	Newsome	Prior	Eadie	Fleck"	Ward	Johnson	O'Neill	Milligan/Polston/Akinbiyi
29/10			15,513	*6*	21			*Moore 46*	*Coyne*	*Stevens*	*Thomas*	*McGreal*	*Teale*	*Jones*	*Brannan*	*Aldridge*	*Bennett*	*Moore*	*Nevin*	
								Ref: G Singh	Johnson chips past Danny Coyne, but City are pegged back as Ian Moore heads in Tony Thomas' cross. Rush has a long-term injury and a new signing looks essential. The chairman won't agree a deal with Hull for Windass and the fans protest over his 'broken promises' to release funds.											
15	A	HUDDERSFIELD		10	L	2-3	0-1	Ward 65, 77	Gunn	Ullathorne	Polston	Crook	Newsome	Prior	Mills	Akinbiyi*	Ward	Johnson	Eadie	Fleck
4/11			*13,747*	*11*	21			*Jepson 16, Jenkins 50, Dalton 82*	*Francis*	*Dyson**	*Cowan*	*Bullock*	*Scully*	*Gray*	*Dalton*	*Makel*	*Booth*	*Jepson*	*Jenkins*	*Reid*
								Ref: E Lomas	After falling two behind, City launch a rousing second-half fightback. Ward nets a near-post flick and then equalises with a glancing header. Brian Horton's men are undaunted and snatch a late winner. Paul Dalton forces home from close-range after the ball squirms away from Gunn.											
16	H	CRYSTAL PALACE		6	W	1-0	1-0	Johnson 44	Gunn	Bradshaw	Ullathorne	Crook*	Newsome	Prior	Bowen	Fleck	Ward	Johnson^	Eadie	Adams/Akinbiyi
11/11			14,156	*20*	24				*Martyn*	*Edworthy*	*Vincent*	*Roberts*	*Coleman*	*Shaw*	*Hopkin*	*Pitcher*	*Freedman*	*Taylor*	*Dyer**	*McKenzie*
								Ref: T West	Johnson nets a downward header from Eadie's corner, but moments later is carried off with an ankle injury. It's his sixth goal in 16 games since O'Neill became manager. His previous tally was one in 13. Akinbiyi nets but is called offside. Johnson and Crook both require hospital X-rays.											
17	H	IPSWICH		6	W	2-1	1-0	Newsome 9, Fleck 72	Gunn	Ullathorne	Bowen	Bradshaw^	Newsome	Prior	Adams	Ward	Fleck	Milligan*	O'Neill	Akinbiyi/Sutch
19/11			**17,862**	*15*	27			*Wark 82p*	*Forrest*	*Stockwell*	*Vaughan*	*Mowbray*	*Wark*	*Williams*	*Thomsen*	*Milton**	*Uhlenbeek^*	*Mathie*	*Mason*	*Gregory/Tanner*
								Ref: K Lynch	Newsome beats Tony Mowbray to head in O'Neill's free-kick. Fleck fastens on to Ward's header to extend the lead. Ullathorne impedes Alex Mathie for John Wark to pull one back from the spot. In a frantic finale, Mr Lynch awards a second Town penalty, but then changes his mind.											
18	A	WEST BROM		4	W	**4-1**	1-1	Fleck 45, Scott 48, Adams 58, Ward 66	Gunn	Sutch	Ullathorne	Polston	Newsome	Prior	Bowen^	Fleck*	Ward	**Scott**	Adams	Akinbiyi/**Carey**
21/11			*13,680*	*12*	30			*Hunt 4*	*Fettis*	*Burgess*	*King**	*Coldicott*	*Marden*	*Raven*	*Donovan*	*Gilbert*	*Taylor"*	*Hunt*	*Hamilton*	*Edwards^/Ashcroft/Smith*
								Ref: J Kirkby	Andy Hunt rounds Gunn to put Alan Buckley's men ahead early. A blitz of four in 21 minutes turns the tables. New signing from Stoke, Keith Scott, nets a well-taken debut goal to put City ahead. After Adams' volley, the result is never in doubt. Hunt's late penalty-kick is well saved.											
19	A	WATFORD		2	W	2-0	1-0	Ward 31, Scott 46	Gunn	Sutch"	Ullathorne	Polston	Newsome	Prior	Bowen	Fleck*	Ward	Scott	Adams^	Eadie/Crook/Bradshaw
26/11			*7,798*	*21*	33				*Miller*	*Bazeley*	*Caskey*	*Millen*	*Holdsworth*	*Ramage*	*Hessenthaler*	*Palmer*	*Mooney*	*Moralee*	*Phillips*	
								Ref: S Bennett	Fleck nods down a Bowen cross for Ward to sweep past Kevin Miller. Ward's nine goals this term have all come away from home. Scott pounces just after the break to put the result beyond doubt. He buries a volley from a tight angle and City surge into second place in the table.											
20	H	STOKE		4	L	0-1	0-0		Gunn	Ullathorne	Bowen	Sutch*	Newsome	Prior	Adams	Ward	Fleck	Scott	Eadie	Akinbiyi
2/12			15,707	*7*	33			*Gleghorn 53*	*Prudhoe*	*Clarkson*	*Sandford*	*Sigurdsson*	*Cranson*	*Potter^*	*Dreyer*	*Wallace*	*Peschis'lido**	*Sturridge*	*Gleghorn*	*Sheron/Beeston*
								Ref: P Taylor	A fifth successive win would put City on top of the table, but they find keeper Mark Prudhoe in great form. He and Ian Cranson have superb games in defence. Ex-Ipswich man Nigel Gleghorn's winner is set up by Paul Peschisolido. Stoke look far better than they did two months ago.											
21	H	GRIMSBY		3	D	2-2	1-1	Ward 34, Eadie 62	Gunn	Polston	Ullathorne	Adams	Newsome	Prior	Bowen	Fleck*	Ward	Carey	Eadie	Scott
9/12			13,283	*6*	34			*Livingstone 6, Groves 77*	*Crichton*	*McDermott*	*Croft*	*Handyside*	*Lever*	*Groves*	*Childs*	*Dobbin*	*Forrester**	*Livingstone*	*Bonetti*	*Laws*
								Ref: R Furnandiz	Steve Livingstone heads in a deep cross. Ward levels with a header from Adams' cross. Akinbiyi takes a 25-yard pot-shot and puts City ahead. Brilliant wing-play by Ivano Bonetti sets up Paul Groves' late leveller. Martin O'Neill is being linked with the vacant Leicester manager's job.											
22	A	LEICESTER		7	L	2-3	2-1	Eadie 2, Fleck 31	Gunn	Polston	Ullathorne	Milligan	Newsome	Prior	Bowen	Fleck^	Ward	Carey	Eadie*	Adams/Scott
17/12			*14,251*	*3*	34			*Whitlow 36, Roberts 66, Heskey 80*	*Poole*	*Hill*	*Whitlow*	*Carey*	*Walsh*	*Parker*	*Corica*	*Taylor*	*Robins**	*Roberts*	*Rollin^*	*Joachim/Heskey*
								Ref: T Heilbron	O'Neill quits shortly before kick-off at a brief hotel meeting with the chairman. Chase refuses to accept his resignation. Eadie and Fleck give City a great start, but things go pear-shaped when Iwan Roberts scrambles an equaliser. A bad back-pass by Newsome sets up Emile Heskey.											
23	A	PORTSMOUTH		9	L	0-1	0-0		Gunn	Polston	Bowen	Carey	Newsome	Prior	Adams	Fleck^	Ward	Johnson*	Ullathorne	Sutch/Scott
23/12			*9,960*	*17*	34			*Durnin 55*	*Knight*	*Gittens*	*Stimson*	*McLoughlin*	*Whitbread*	*Butters*	*Walsh*	*Allen*	*Durnin*	*Hall*	*Carter**	*Igoe*
								Ref: G Pooley	Gary Megson returns to the club as manager after a spell as coach at Bradford City. Three clear-cut chances for Norwich to take the lead are wasted before Terry Fenwick's men hit the target. Jimmy Carter sets up John Durnin, who has plenty of time to fire home from a tight angle.											

No		Date	Att	Pos	Pt	F-A	H-T	Scorers, Times, and Referees	1	2	3	4	5	6	7	8	9	10	11	subs used
24	H	SOUTHEND		11	L	0-1	0-0		Gunn	Bowen	Ullathorne	Milligan"	Newsome	Prior	Adams	Fleck^	Ward	Johnson	O'Neill*	Newman/Scott/Goss
		26/12	17,029	6	34			Jones 55	Royce	Dublin	Powell	Lapper*	McNally	Gridelet	Marsh	Byrne	Regis	Jones	Hails	Hone
								Ref: D Orr	A hostile atmosphere as the home fans vent their anger on Chase. Ronnie Whelan's side exploit the situation and stretch their unbeaten run to eight games. Gary Jones nets a cute backheel to win it. Three arrests are made and two police injured in ugly scenes at a big post-match demo.											
25	H	READING		10	D	3-3	1-1	Johnson 20, Ward 48, Fleck 51	Gunn	Bowen	Ullathorne	**Molby***	Newsome	Prior	Adams	Fleck	Ward	Johnson^	O'Neill	Newman/Goss
		30/12	13,556	19	35			Lambert 41, Nogan 72, Kerr 83	Hammond	Brown	Lambert"	Wdowczyk	Williams	McPherson*	Gilkes^	Parkinson	Morley	Nogan	Holsgrove	Quinn/Jones/Kerr
								Ref: W Burns	Johnson heads City ahead but James Lambert brings Jimmy Quinn and Mick Gooding's side level before the break. Ward steers City's second and they are firmly in the driving seat when Fleck nets a glancing header. But the bright football fails to yield a win as sub Dylan Kerr levels.											
26	A	DERBY		11	L	1-2	0-1	Fleck 62	Gunn	Sutch	Bowen	Carey"	Polston	Prior^	Adams	Goss	Ward	Ullathorne	O'Neill*	Milligan/Newman/Fleck
		1/1	16,714	10	35			Willems 36, Gabbiadini 89	Hoult	Rowett	Nicholson	Powell	Yates	Stimac	V der Laan^	Flynn	Willems	Gabbiadini"	Carsley*	Trollope/Simpson/Wrack
								Ref: J Rushton	Prior is carried off with an ankle problem and Carey goes off with a bloodied face. Megson is ordered from the dug-out after a heated debate during this spell with only nine men. Fleck equalises by diving full length to head home a rebound, but Marco Gabbiadini heads a late winner.											
27	A	SUNDERLAND		6	W	1-0	1-0	Ward 12	Gunn	Bradshaw	Bowen	Molby	Polston	Prior	Adams	Fleck^	Ward	Eadie	O'Neill*	Ullathorne/Scott
		14/1	14,983	8	38				Chamberlain	Kubicki*	Scott	Bracewell	Agnew	Melville	Gray Mcl	Ord	Russell	Gray P	Kelly^	Howey/Smith
								Ref: G Cain	Andy Melville blunders by being caught in possession to allow Ward to nip in and net a powerful shot. City hold on grimly and Megson can celebrate his first win in 12 as manager. Peter Reid's side hit six in their last home match, but indifferent form has seen them slip off the top.											
28	H	LUTON		9	L	0-1	0-1		Gunn	Bradshaw*	Bowen^	Molby	Polston	Prior	Adams	Fleck	Ward	Eadie"	O'Neill	Newman/Scott/Goss
		20/1	12,474	23	38			Guentchev 33p	Feuer	Thomas	James	Waddock	Davis	Johnson	Alexander	Oakes*	Taylor	Guentchev	Harvey	Oldfield
								Ref: C Wilkes	The lowly-placed Hatters are being revived by new boss Lennie Lawrence. They defend in numbers and frustrate City. Bontcho Guentchev breaks clear from halfway and comes crashing down after dribbling round Gunn. Norwich claim he dived, but the Bulgarian nets from the spot.											
29	H	BIRMINGHAM		10	D	1-1	0-0	Ward 73	Gunn	Bradshaw	Bowen*	Crook	Polston	Prior	Adams	Fleck	Ward	Johnson"	Akinbiyi^	Newman/Scott/Goss
		4/2	12,612	11	39			Otto 75	Griemink	Hiley	Frain	Forsyth	Johnson	Daish	Cooper	Claridge	Francis	Tait*	Bowen^	Otto/Barnes
								Ref: A Butler	Big Kevin Francis puts Bowen out of the game with a clumsy tackle and City are up against it. A Fleck effort is deflected into the path of Ward and he grabs the lead. Two minutes later Francis hits the crossbar and the ball falls perfectly for Ricky Otto to save a point for Barry Fry's men.											
30	A	OLDHAM		12	L	0-2	0-1		Gunn	Bradshaw	Newman	Crook*	Polston	Prior	Adams	Fleck"	Ward	Johnson !	Akinbiyi^	Mills/Cureton/Goss
		10/2	5,604	16	39			Makin 12, Barlow 63	Gerrard	Serrant	Makin	Hughes	Graham	Redmond	Halle	Orlygsson	Beckford*	Barlow	Brennan	McCarthy
								Ref: T West	Chris Makin drives in a cross-shot and the Norwich heads drop. The travelling fans gloomily witness a spineless display. The contest is all but over when Stuart Barlow prods in following some woeful defending. Johnson is sent off after 71 minutes for collecting his second yellow card.											
31	H	WOLVERHAMPTON		12	L	2-3	2-2	Crook 24, Eadie 25	Gunn	Bradshaw	Bowen	Crook^	Polston	Prior	Adams	Fleck*	Ward	Johnson	Eadie	Cureton/Carey
		17/2	14,691	17	39			Bull 12, 37, Goodman 74	Stowell	Thompson	Young	Atkins	De Wolf	Emblen	Corica	Goodman	Bull	Ferguson	Emblen*	Birch
								Ref: A D'Urso	There's more urgency and determination today after the Oldham debacle. Two City goals in a minute cap an entertaining first half. Either side of this double blast, Steve Bull displays his renowned clinical finishing. It's ten home games without a win when Don Goodman curls a winner.											
32	A	MILLWALL		14	L	1-2	0-0	Milligan 83	Gunn	Newman	Bowen	Crook^	Polston	Prior	Adams	O'Neill	Ward*	Milligan	Eadie	Akinbiyi/Goss
		24/2	8,218	9	39			Bowry 56, Fuchs 69	Keller	Lavin	Thatcher	Bowry	Witter	Stevens*	Neill	Kulkov^	Fuchs	Yuran"	Van Blerk	Rogan/Newman/Dolby
								Ref: K Leach	The fall from grace continues. City look to be hurtling towards relegation. Fleck and Bradshaw are dropped, but Millwall surge ahead when Bobby Bowry prods in from close range and Uwe Fuchs nets a glancing header. Sergei Yuran hits the bar. Milligan steers in a pass from Ward.											
33	H	SHEFFIELD UTD		13	D	0-0	0-0		Gunn	Newman	Bradshaw	Crook	Polston	Prior	Adams^	Johnson	Akinbiyi*	Milligan	Eadie	Fleck/O'Neill
		28/2	**10,945**	21	40				Kelly	Ward	Nilsen	Cowans	Vonk	Tuttle*	White	Patterson	Angell	Walker^	Whitehouse	Starbuck/Short
								Ref: N Barry	An awful night for the Carrow Road faithful. Chants of 'what a load of rubbish' ring round the ground. Alan Kelly keeps City at bay in the first-half, but a victory rarely looks likely. The fans turn on the players in addition to their usual barracking of Chase. A demo is staged at the end.											
34	A	SOUTHEND		13	D	1-1	0-1	Bradshaw 64	Gunn	Newman	Bradshaw	Crook	Polston	Prior	Adams	Goss	Ward	Carey*	Eadie	Newsome
		2/3	6,208	9	41			Byrne 42	Royce	Dublin	Brown	Bodley	McNally	Gridelet	Marsh	Byrne	Boere	Rammell*	Hails	Thomson
								Ref: W Burns	A three-man central defence looks strong, but Southend take the lead when Paul Byrne lets rip a real thunderbolt from around 35 yards. A welcome equaliser arrives after the interval when Ward's shot is blocked by ex-Canary Kenny Brown and falls for Bradshaw, who curls home.											

35	H	PORTSMOUTH		14	D	1-1	1-1	Milligan 13	Gunn	Bradshaw	Newman	Crook	Newsome	Prior	Adams	Goss*	Ward	Milligan	Eadie	Fleck
	9/3		13,004	*11*	42			*Hall 38*	*Knight*	*Pethick*	*Awford*	*McLoughlin*	*Thomson*	*Butters*	*Wood**	*Allen*	*Burton^*	*Hall*	*Carter*	*Durnin/Griffiths*
								Ref: P Taylor	Hopes of a rare home win are raised when Milligan nets a fine shot after a corner is cleared to him. Defensive chaos ensues as Dean Burton finds Paul Hall, who drives home an equaliser. The fans, miserable of late, get behind the side much more today, but City can't find a winner.											
36	A	READING		13	W	3-0	1-0	Prior 17, Eadie 55, O'Neill 90	Gunn	Bradshaw	Newman	Crook*	Polston	Prior	Adams	Fleck	Goss	Milligan	Eadie^	Mills/O'Neill
	16/3		*8,501*	*22*	45				*Shepherd*	*Booty*	*Bernal**	*Caskey*	*Williams*	*Hopkin*	*Meaker*	*Parkinson^*	*Gooding*	*Lovell*	*Gilkes*	*Holsgrove/Quinn*
								Ref: J Brandwood	Another massive blow as Newsome and Ward are sold for a combined £2.6 million. Megson is as livid as the fans. The reshuffled side rallies and Prior powers in a corner with his head. Goss sets up Eadie, who finishes nicely. O'Neill puts icing on the cake as he gallops clear to score.											
37	A	PORT VALE		13	L	0-1	0-1		Gunn	Bradshaw	Newman"	Crook^	Polston	Prior	Adams	Fleck	Goss*	Milligan	O'Neill	Mills/Johnson/Cureton
	20/3		*6,085*	*17*	45			*Foyle 16*	*Musselwhite*	*Hill*	*Stokes*	*Bogie*	*Griffiths*	*Aspin*	*McCarthy**	*Walker*	*Foyle*	*Naylor*	*Guppy*	*Talbot*
								Ref: C Wilkes	Martin Foyle sprints through to lob John Rudge's side into an early lead. City huff and puff in response, but don't muster enough penetration. Paul Musselwhite makes a fine save from Fleck just after half-time. Vale's unbeaten run extends to eight and they look set to avoid relegation.											
38	H	DERBY		11	W	1-0	0-0	Goss 66	Gunn	Bradshaw	Newman	Crook*	Polston	Prior	Adams	Fleck"	Goss	Milligan	Cureton^	Mills/Akinbiyi/O'Neill
	23/3		15,341	*2*	48				*Hoult*	*Wassall*	*Powell**	*Hodges^*	*Yates*	*Stimac*	*Ward*	*Flynn*	*Willems*	*Gabbiadini"*	*Carsley*	*Rowett/Simpson/Sturridge*
								Ref: I Hemley	Goss turns the clock back with a 25-yard thunderbolt that is reminiscent of his celebrated goals of several years ago. Ex-Canary Ward is kept off the scoresheet on his Rams debut, but picks up a nasty cut. The win means City don't equal their worst run without a home win - 13 games.											
39	H	CHARLTON		14	L	0-1	0-0		Gunn	Bradshaw	Newman	Crook	Polston	Prior	Adams	Fleck	Goss^	Milligan	Cureton*	Bowen/Eadie
	30/3		13,434	*4*	48			*Allen 53*	*Ammann*	*Jackson*	*Sturgess**	*Mortimer*	*Rufus*	*Whyte*	*Robinson !*	*Newton*	*Allen*	*Leaburn*	*Bowyer*	*Robson*
								Ref: R Poulain	The Derby win proves a false dawn and City remain in relegation danger after this loss. Charlton look rather ordinary, but still have too much for City. After a drab first half, two new signings combine for the winner: Matt Jackson's shot is parried and Bradley Allen steers the ball in.											
40	A	BARNSLEY		14	D	2-2	1-1	Fleck 3, Newman 88	Gunn	Bradshaw	Ullathorne	Newman	Polston	Prior	Adams	Fleck^	Goss"	Milligan	Eadie*	Mills/Cureton/O'Neill
	2/4		*6,375*	*10*	49			*Redfearn 8, Payton 62*	*Watson*	*Eaden*	*Bullock*	*Sheridan*	*Moses*	*De Zeeuw*	*Regis**	*Redfearn*	*O'Connell*	*Payton*	*V d Velden*	*Hurst*
								Ref: K Lynch	David Watson blocks a thundering Newman drive, but Fleck is on hand to net. Neil Redfearn quickly levels, shooting in unchallenged. Mr Lynch overrules a linesman to allow Andy Payton to go on and score. Stand-in striker Newman has a good game and nods home a point-saver.											
41	A	TRANMERE		16	D	1-1	1-0	Eadie 28	Gunn	Bradshaw	Ullathorne	Crook	Newsome	Newman	Adams^	Fleck	Scott*	Milligan	Eadie	O'Neill/Goss
	6/4		*6,613*	*17*	50			*Aldridge 60*	*Coyne*	*Stevens*	*Irons**	*McGreal*	*Teale*	*Cook*	*Brannan*	*Aldridge*	*Rogers*	*Moore*	*Nevin*	*Branch*
								Ref: T Heilbron	After another week of turmoil, Megson recalls Scott to the attack, but this plan is foiled when he is injured in the early stages. A well-worked Eadie goal boosts City's chances, but pressure by the home side pays off after the break with a classy finish by player-manager John Aldridge.											
42	H	HUDDERSFIELD		14	W	2-0	0-0	Fleck 62, Akinbiyi 81	Gunn	Bradshaw	Ullathorne	Crook"	Polston	Newman	Adams	Fleck	Akinbiyi^	Milligan	Eadie*	Mills/Cureton/Sutch
	8/4		13,021	*6*	53				*Francis*	*Jenkins*	*Cowan*	*Ward*	*Scully*	*Gray*	*Edwards*	*Makel*	*Booth*	*Jepson*	*Thornley**	*Collins*
								Ref: A Butler	In a game of very few goalscoring chances, Fleck breaks the stalemate by drilling in a Carl Bradshaw cross. Akinbiyi makes the three points safe when he nets a glorious header near the end which gives Steve Francis no chance. Norwich seem to be edging their way towards safety.											
43	A	IPSWICH		15	L	1-2	0-1	Cureton 62	Gunn	Ullathorne	Bradshaw	Crook	Newman	Polston	Adams	Akinbiyi*	Fleck	Milligan"	Eadie^	Prior/Johnson/Cureton
	14/4		*20,355*	*6*	53			*Marshall 23, Ullathorne 86 (og)*	*Wright*	*Uhlenbeek*	*Taricco*	*Stockwell^*	*Wark**	*Williams*	*Mason*	*Sedgley*	*Scowcroft*	*Marshall*	*Milton*	*Vaughan/Appleby*
								Ref: J Rushton	A long punt by Richard Wright finds Ian Marshall, who opens the scoring. Sub Cureton fires in Eadie's pass to level. Ipswich's play-off hopes are boosted in the dying minutes when Gunn completely misses his kick and Ullathorne's back-pass trickles into the net. An awful way to lose.											
44	H	WEST BROM		16	D	2-2	0-1	Cureton 78, Eadie 84	Gunn	Prior	Ullathorne	Crook	Polston^	Newman	Adams	Fleck	Scott"	Milligan*	Eadie	Johnson/Bradshaw/Cureton
	20/4		14,667	*13*	54			*Taylor 30, Sneekes 61*	*Spink*	*Burgess*	*Nicholson*	*Sneekes**	*Mardon*	*Gilbert*	*Butler*	*Holmes*	*Taylor*	*Hunt^*	*Hamilton*	*Donovan/Angell*
								Ref: U Rennie	Two down with 12 minutes left and all three subs on, things look desperate for City. Then comes a lucky break as Nigel Spink makes a mess of a back-pass and Cureton nips in to net. This is followed by a poor Bob Taylor pass which allows Eadie to swoop and crack home an equaliser.											
45	H	WATFORD		17	L	1-2	0-1	Crook 55	Gunn	Prior	Ullathorne	Crook"	Polston	Newman	Adams	Fleck	Cureton*	Milligan	Carey^	Bradshaw/O'Neill/Carey
	27/4		14,188	*23*	54			*Connolly 2p, Porter 67*	*Miller*	*Bazeley*	*Barnes**	*Hessenthaler*	*Page*	*Connolly*	*Porter*	*Palmer*	*Mooney*	*Ramage*	*White*	*Ludden*
								Ref: S Mathieson	Another game overshadowed by dissent from the terraces. Ullathorne sends David Connolly flying for an early penalty. Crook curls in a free-kick but Gary Porter's long-range shot wins it. Results elsewhere ensure City won't be relegated, but the miserable atmosphere is not dispelled.											
46	A	CRYSTAL PALACE		16	W	1-0	1-0	Hopkin 5 (og)	Marshall	Wright*	Ullathorne	Mills	Polston	Prior	Adams	Fleck	Cureton	Milligan	Goss	Sutch
	5/5		*19,354*	*3*	57				*Martyn*	*Boxall*	*Vincent*	*Tuttle*	*Davies*	*Rodger**	*Quinn*	*Dyer*	*Ndah*	*Veart*	*Hopkin*	*Brown*
		Home	Away					Ref: G Singh	City are safe from the drop and Palace already in the play-offs, so today's result is academic. A large and very colourful away following is in fine voice because chairman Chase resigned in midweek and a new era is dawning. David Hopkin's misdirected header wins a scrappy game.											
Average		14,581	12,079																	

Coca-Cola Cup

Rd		Opponent	Att		F-A	H-T	Scorers, Times, and Referees	1	2	3	4	5	6	7	8	9	10	11	subs used
2:1	H	TORQUAY	5	W	6-1	3-0	Akinbiyi 15, 46, Crook 19, Sheron 44, 61,	Marshall	Sutch	Bowen	Crook*	Newsome	Prior	Simpson !	Sheron	Akinbiyi	Johnson^	Eadie"	Carey/Mills/O'Neill
	20/9		7,542 3:19				*Hathaway 57* [Gore 81(og)]	*Bayes*	*Barrow*	*Stamps*	*O'Riordan*	*Gore*	*Curran*	*Kelly*	*Buckle*	*Ndah**	*Hathaway*	*Hall*	*Hancox*
							Ref: R Furnandiz	Akinbiyi's first senior goal is a fine piece of finishing and quickly followed by Crook's 20-yard volley. Ian Hathaway grabs a consolation for Eddie May's men. Ian Gore heads over colleague Ashley Bayes to make it six. Debutant Karl Simpson, 18, is sent off after two yellow cards.											
2:2	A	TORQUAY	9	W	3-2	0-0	Ullathorne 61, Eadie 85, Mills 87	Gunn	Mills	Ullathorne	Carey	Newman	Polston	Adams	Sheron^	Akinbiyi*	Milligan	O'Neill	Eadie/Fleck
	4/10		*1,790 3:21*				*Barrow 57, 68*	*Bayes*	*Winter*	*Kelly*	*Stamps*	*Gore*	*Barrow*	*Hawthorne*	*Buckle*	*Ndah**	*Hathaway*	*Hall^*	*Byng"/Mateu/Laight*
							Ref: J Rushton (Norwich win 9-3 on aggregate)	Keith O'Neill and Shaun Carey get full debuts. Defender Lee Barrow gets forward to score two rare goals, but Ullathorne hits back with a bizarre effort as his deep cross sails over Ashley Bayes. Eadie and Mills - his first senior goal - blast home from 25 yards in the closing stages.											
3	H	BRADFORD C	10	D	0-0	0-0		Gunn	Ullathorne	Bowen	Crook	Newsome	Prior	Milligan*	Eadie	Ward	Johnson	O'Neill	Fleck
	25/10		11,649 2:8					*Ward*	*Liburd*	*Jacobs*	*Mitchell !*	*Mohan*	*Ford*	*Wright**	*Youds*	*Orm'droyd^*	*Hamilton*	*Showler*	*Murray/Shutt*
							Ref: D Orr	Ward misses a great chance after just 50 seconds. Lennie Lawrence's men battle hard after Graham Mitchell is harshly sent off on 66 minutes. Ex-policeman Paul Showler is lucky to avoid punishment after bundling Gunn into the advertising hoardings in his hurry to get a corner taken.											
3R	A	BRADFORD C	10	W	5-3	2-1	Ward 10, 34, 87, Fleck 91, Johnson 109	Gunn	Ullathorne	Bradshaw	Crook	Newman*	Prior^	Milligan	Fleck	Ward	Johnson	Eadie	Akinbiyi/Mills
	7/11		*8,665 2:8*		*aet*		*Showler 23, Ormondroyd 48, Tolson 56*	*Ward*	*Huxford^*	*Jacobs*	*Mitchell*	*Mohan*	*Ford*	*Wright**	*Hamilton*	*Ormondroyd*	*Tolson"*	*Showler*	*Murray/Liburd/Robson*
							Ref: N Barry	A real thriller almost goes Bradford's way, but after Fleck's 85th-minute penalty miss, Ward heads past his namesake to force extra-time and complete a hat-trick. Just 14 seconds after the restart, Fleck drives home from six yards. Johnson shoots home City's fifth after being put clear.											
4	H	BOLTON	2	D	0-0	0-0		Gunn	Ullathorne	Bowen	Crook*	Newsome	Polston	Prior	Fleck	Ward	Adams	Eadie	Scott
	29/11		13,820 P:20					*Branagan*	*Green*	*Phillips*	*Curcic*	*Bergsson*	*Taggart*	*Fairclough*	*Todd*	*Patterson*	*McGinlay*	*Thompson*	
							Ref: G Singh	Roy McFarland's men have lost their last four Premiership games, but they defend desperately to bring an end to City's five-match winning run. Bolton occasionally look dangerous in the closing stages, but Eadie goes nearest to a winning goal as his shot clips the outside of a post.											
4R	A	BOLTON	7	D	0-0	0-0		Gunn	Ullathorne	Bowen	Milligan	Newsome	Polston	Prior	Fleck*	Ward	Carey	Sutch	Adams
	20/12		*8,736 P:20*		*aet*			*Branagan*	*Green*	*Phillips**	*Curcic*	*Bergsson*	*Taggart*	*Fairclough*	*Todd*	*De Fretias*	*McGinlay*	*Patterson*	*Whittaker*
							Ref: D Allison (Norwich win 3-2 on penalties)	210 blank minutes means penalties. Adams nets but McGinlay hits wide. Milligan's goes over and De Freitas' is saved. Ward's is saved, Green scores. Sutch hits wide but Whittaker scores. Bowen nets but Curcic's is saved. Newsome scores and Gunn wins it by saving from Patterson.											
5	H	BIRMINGHAM	11	D	1-1	0-0	Fleck 69	Gunn	Bradshaw	Bowen	Molby	Newsome*	Polston	Adams	Fleck	Ward^	Eadie	O'Neill"	Prior/Scott/Ullathorne
	10/1		13,028 *5*				*Francis 65*	*Sansome*	*Poole*	*Frain*	*Forsyth*	*Edwards*	*Daish*	*Hunt**	*Claridge*	*Francis*	*Richards'n^*	*Donowa*	*Bowen/Cooper*
							Ref: R Poulain	Barry Fry's side find Gunn in brilliant form. He stops an early Jonathan Hunt penalty and makes a string of other crucial saves. Kevin Francis nets after a misdirected pass by Ward. Norwich level soon afterwards, Fleck's sliced volley deceiving Paul Sansome and bouncing into the net.											
5R	A	BIRMINGHAM	8	L	1-2	0-0	Molby 78	Gunn	Bradshaw	Bowen	Molby	Prior	Polston	Adams	Fleck	Ward	Eadie*	O'Neill	Johnson
	24/1		*21,097 9*				*Bowen 53, Daish 88*	*Griemink*	*Poole !*	*Frain*	*Forsyth*	*Edwards*	*Daish*	*Donowa*	*Claridge*	*Francis"*	*Castle**	*Doherty^*	*Tait/Bull/Bowen*
							Ref: R Gifford	Norwich dominate early on, but fall behind when Jason Bowen volleys home. Gary Poole is sent off after two yellow cards, the second for handball. Molby levels with a marvellous 25-yard free-kick in the last game of his loan spell. Liam Daish's powerful late header wins the tie.											

FA Cup

Rd		Opponent	Att		F-A	H-T	Scorers, Times, and Referees	1	2	3	4	5	6	7	8	9	10	11	subs used
3	H	BRENTFORD	11	L	1-2	0-1	Newsome 65	Gunn	Bradshaw*	Bowen^	Ullathorne	Newsome	Polston	Adams	Fleck"	Ward	Goss	O'Neill	Prior/Sutch/Eadie
	6/1		10,082 *2:21*				*Newsome 20 (og), Bent 60*	*Dearden*	*Harvey**	*Grainger*	*Hutchings*	*Bates*	*Ashby*	*McGhee*	*Smith*	*Forster*	*Bent^*	*Taylor*	*Martin/Anderson*
							Ref: J Kirkby	Newsome backheels the ball into his own net under pressure from Bees forwards. Things get even worse when 17-year-old Marcus Bent tucks home a cross. The jeers are temporarily halted as Newsome heads in an O'Neill cross. It's an embarrassing defeat by David Webb's merry men.											

		Home						Away					
		P	W	D	L	F	A	W	D	L	F	A	Pts
1	Sunderland	46	13	8	2	32	10	9	9	5	27	23	83
2	Derby	46	14	8	1	48	22	7	8	8	23	29	79
3	Crys Palace	46	9	9	5	34	22	11	6	6	33	26	75
4	Stoke	46	13	6	4	32	15	7	7	9	28	34	73
5	Leicester*	46	9	7	7	32	29	10	7	6	34	31	71
6	Charlton	46	8	11	4	28	23	9	9	5	29	22	71
7	Ipswich	46	13	5	5	45	30	6	7	10	34	39	69
8	Huddersfield	46	14	4	5	42	23	3	8	12	19	35	63
9	Sheffield Utd	46	9	7	7	29	25	7	7	9	28	29	62
10	Barnsley	46	9	10	4	34	28	5	8	10	26	38	60
11	West Brom	46	11	5	7	34	29	5	7	11	26	39	60
12	Port Vale	46	10	5	8	30	29	5	10	8	29	37	60
13	Tranmere	46	9	9	5	42	29	5	8	10	22	31	59
14	Southend	46	11	8	4	30	22	4	6	13	22	39	59
15	Birmingham	46	11	7	5	37	23	4	6	13	24	41	58
16	NORWICH	46	7	9	7	26	24	7	6	10	33	31	57
17	Grimsby	46	8	10	5	27	25	6	4	13	28	44	56
18	Oldham	46	10	7	6	33	20	4	7	12	21	30	56
19	Reading	46	8	7	8	28	30	5	10	8	26	33	56
20	Wolves	46	8	9	6	34	28	5	7	11	22	34	55
21	Portsmouth	46	8	6	9	34	32	5	7	11	27	37	52
22	Millwall	46	7	6	10	23	28	6	7	10	20	35	52
23	Watford	46	7	8	8	40	33	3	10	10	22	37	48
24	Luton	46	7	6	10	30	34	4	6	13	10	30	45
		1104	233	177	142	804	613	142	177	233	613	804	1479

* promoted after play-offs

Odds & ends

Double wins: (0).
Double losses: (1) Leicester.

Won from behind: (5) Oldham (h), Barnsley (h), West Brom (a), Torquay (a) (LC), Bradford C (a) (LC).
Lost from in front: (3) Sheffield U (a), Leicester (a), Wolves (h).

High points: The arrival of Martin O'Neill as manager in June 1995.
The departure of unpopular chairman Robert Chase in May 1996.
The eight-goal Coca-Cola Cup thriller at Bradford City.
Three penalty saves by Bryan Gunn in the Bolton cup shoot-out.
Four successive wins in November to go second in the table.

Low points: Losing manager Martin O'Neill after just four months.
Sliding from second place into the relegation zone mid-season.
Bryan Gunn's horrendous blunder at Ipswich in April.
The violence and ugly atmosphere at the Southend home match.
The sorry saga of the failure to sign Dean Windass from Hull.
The board decision to sell two more key men (Ward and Newsome).

Player of the Year: Spencer Prior.
Ever-presents: (0).
Hat-tricks: (1) Ashley Ward (v Bradford C a, LC).
Hat-tricks against: (1) Jonathan Hunt (v Birmingham, a).
Leading scorer: (13) Ashley Ward.

	Appearances						Goals			
	Lge	*Sub*	LC	*Sub*	FAC	*Sub*	Lge	LC	FAC	Tot
Adams, Neil	**40**	*2*	4	*1*	1		**2**			**2**
Akinbiyi, Ade	**13**	*9*	2	*1*			**3**	2		**5**
Bowen, Mark	**30**	*1*	6		1		**2**			**2**
Bradshaw, Carl	**18**	*3*	3		1		**1**			**1**
Carey, Shaun	**6**	*3*	2	*1*						
Crook, Ian	**27**	*1*	4				**2**	1		**3**
Cureton, Jamie	**4**	*8*					**2**			**2**
Eadie, Darren	**29**	*2*	6	*1*		*1*	**6**	1		**7**
Fleck, Robert	**37**	*4*	5	*2*	1		**10**	2		**12**
Goss, Jeremy	**9**	*7*			1		**1**			**1**
Gunn, Bryan	**43**		7		1					
Johnson, Andy	**23**	*3*	3	*1*			**7**	1		**8**
Marshall, Andy	**3**		1							
Milligan, Mike	**21**	*7*	4				**2**			**2**
Mills, Danny	**8**	*6*	1	*2*				1		**1**
Molby, Jan	**3**		2					1		**1**
Newman, Rob	**15**	*8*	2				**1**			**1**
Newsome, Jon	**26**	*1*	5		1		**4**		1	**5**
O'Neill, Keith	**12**	*7*	4	*1*	1		**1**			**1**
Polston, John	**27**	*3*	5		1					
Prior, Spencer	**42**	*2*	6	*1*			**1**			**1**
Rush, Matthew		*1*								
Scott, Keith	**5**	*7*		*2*			**2**			**2**
Sheron, Mike	**2**	*5*	2				**1**	2		**3**
Simpson, Karl	**1**		1							
Sutch, Daryl	**7**	*6*	2			*1*				
Ullathorne, Robert	**26**	*3*	5	*1*	1			1		**1**
Ward, Ashley	**28**		6		1		**10**	3		**13**
Wright, Johnny	**1**									
(own-goals)							**1**	1		**2**
29 players used	**506**	***99***	**88**	***14***	**11**	***2***	**59**	**16**	**1**	**76**

No	Date	Opponent	Att	Pos	Pt	F-A	H-T	Scorers, Times, and Referees	1	2	3	4	5	6	7	8	9	10	11	subs used
1	H	SWINDON			W	2-0	2-0	Johnson 26, Fleck 37	Gunn	Mills	Newman	Eadie	Polston	Crook	Adams	Fleck*	Milligan^	Johnson	O'Neill	Akinbiyi/Sutch
	17/8		15,165		3				*Talia*	*Darras*	*Drysdale*	*Leitch*	*Allen*	*Taylor"*	*Robinson*	*Walters*	*Finney**	*Allison*	*Horlock^*	*Thorne/Watson/Seagraves*
								Ref: N Barry	Norwich are 28-1 to win the title even though 'messiah' Mike Walker is back in the hot seat. He re-introduces a passing game and puts Crook at sweeper. Johnson knocks home a rebound and Fleck makes it two with a superb volley after deftly flicking the ball over the head of a defender.											
2	A	BOLTON		13	L	1-3	0-1	Eadie 56	Gunn	Mills	Newman	Eadie	Polston	Crook	Adams	Fleck*	Milligan	Johnson	O'Neill	Akinbiyi
	24/8		*13,507*	*1*	3			*Blake 30, 76, Johansen 46*	*Branagan*	*Green*	*Phillips*	*Frandsen*	*Taggart*	*Fairclough*	*Johansen*	*Sellars**	*Blake*	*McGinlay*	*Thompson*	*Lee*
								Ref: T Heilbron	Newman stops Nathan Blake in his tracks, but when Gunn slips, he gets a second chance. Another soft goal is conceded after the break. Eadie takes Milligan's pass to round the keeper. A body-check on O'Neill goes unpunished and Bolton break to the other end and finish the game off.											
3	A	OXFORD		7	W	1-0	1-0	Adams 12	Gunn	Mills	Newman	Bradshaw !	Polston	Crook	Adams	Fleck*	Milligan	Johnson	Eadie	Akinbiyi
	27/8		*7,436*	*11*	6				*Whitehead*	*Robinson*	*Ford M*	*Smith*	*Elliott*	*Gilchrist*	*Ford B*	*Massey^*	*Moody*	*Jemson**	*Beauchamp*	*Rush ! /Gray*
								Ref: A Wiley	Mills' perfect cross is nodded in by Adams to crown a confident opening spell by City. Eadie heads in a Johnson cross but a linesman rules the ball went out before being crossed. The game has an ugly end after Bradshaw retaliates to a vicious David Rush tackle and both are sent off.											
4	H	WOLVERHAMPTON		4	W	1-0	1-0	Adams 21p	Gunn	Mills	Newman	Bradshaw	Polston	Crook	Adams	Fleck*	Milligan	Johnson^	Sutch"	Akinbiyi/Carey/**Forbes**
	31/8		14,456	*7*	9				*Stowell*	*Smith*	*Froggatt*	*Atkins*	*Venus*	*Richards*	*Thompson*	*Corica*	*Bull*	*Roberts*	*Osborn*	
								Ref: R Harris	The ref baffles most observers by giving a penalty and Adams gratefully tucks in City's first league spot-kick for around 18 months. Johnson goes off concussed when a free-kick hits him full in the face. Young winger Adrian Forbes debuts. Mark McGhee's outfit are disappointing.											
5	A	BRADFORD C		2	W	2-0	2-0	Sutch 9, Eadie 31	Gunn	Mills	Newman	Eadie	Polston	Crook	Adams	Fleck*	Milligan	Sutch	O'Neill^	Akinbiyi/Carey
	7/9		*10,054*	*14*	12				*Gould !*	*Jacobs*	*Cowans*	*Mohan*	*Sas*	*Hamilton^*	*Duxbury**	*Regtop"*	*Stallard*	*Kiwomya*	*Liburd*	*Wright/Shutt/Ormondroyd*
								Ref: A Leake	Sutch slots a neat goal after combining with Fleck. Eadie cracks a second into the corner of Jonathan Gould's net from outside the box. Mike Walker's liking for a passing game is paying dividends and City look classy and dominant. Gould is sent off for bringing Eadie down late on.											
6	H	QP RANGERS		3	D	1-1	1-0	Adams 16	Gunn	Mills !	Newman	Carey	Polston	Crook	Adams	Sutch	Akinbiyi	Milligan	Eadie	
	11/9		14,000	*10*	13			*Impey 81*	*Sommer*	*Jackson*	*Brevett*	*Barker*	*McDonald*	*Yates*	*Challis**	*Quashie*	*Dichio*	*Impey*	*Sinclair*	*Murray*
								Ref: M Bailey	Rangers recently parted company with manager Ray Wilkins. A free-kick routine ends with Adams firing low into the net. Mills is red-carded for his second bookable offence. The free-kick for his second offence is played into the box and volleyed in by Andy Impey for a late leveller.											
7	H	SOUTHEND		4	D	0-0	0-0		Gunn	Mills	Newman	Carey	Polston	Crook	Adams	Sutch	Akinbiyi	Milligan	Eadie	
	14/9		12,461	*23*	14				*Royce*	*Hails*	*Dublin*	*McInally*	*Harris*	*Gridelet*	*Marsh*	*Byrne**	*Boere*	*Williams*	*Tilson*	*Lapper*
								Ref: B Burns	The failure to punish Ronnie Whelan's workmanlike side irritates the home fans, who direct most of their abuse at poor Akinbiyi. Loud jeers greet the final whistle, which is a little harsh. The Shrimpers came to spoil City's passing game and shut up shop - and they succeed perfectly.											
8	A	PORTSMOUTH		3	W	1-0	1-0	Crook 36	Gunn	Mills	Newman	Eadie	Polston	Crook*	Adams	Sutch	Akinbiyi	Milligan	O'Neill	Carey
	21/9		*7,511*	*16*	17				*Flahaven*	*Pethick*	*Russell*	*McLoughlin*	*Igoe*	*Awford*	*Carter*	*Simpson^*	*Bradbury*	*Hall**	*Turner*	*Durnin/Perrett*
								Ref: D Orr	After withstanding early pressure, City look purposeful and Eadie's long-range drive crashes against the bar. Akinbiyi somehow fails to net the rebound. Akibiyi does well, however, to supply Adams, who finds Crook and a 25-yarder flies past Aaron Flahavan. Crook picks up an injury.											
9	H	TRANMERE		3	D	1-1	0-1	Fleck 46	Gunn	Newman	Wright	Eadie	Polston	Carey*	Adams	Fleck	Sutch	Milligan	O'Neill	Johnson
	28/9		14,511	*7*	18			*Aldridge 19*	*Coyne*	*Stevens*	*Brannan*	*Thorn*	*Teale*	*O'Brien*	*Irons*	*Aldridge^*	*Cook*	*Branch**	*Bonetti*	*Morrissey/Jones*
								Ref: B Knight	Chances galore are created but Danny Coyne is in great form, saving from Eadie, Milligan and Adams. Ex-Canary Paul Cook miskicks a chance, but it falls to John Aldridge who makes no mistake. Straight after the break City level when Johnson nods to Fleck, who volleys home.											
10	A	GRIMSBY		1	W	**4-1**	3-1	Eadie 2, 8, McDermott 29(og), O'Neill 81	Gunn	Mills	Newman^	Eadie"	Polston	Sutch	Adams	Fleck*	Milligan	Johnson	O'Neill	Akinbiyi/Wright/Rush
	1/10		*5,266*	*21*	21			*Fickling 6*	*Pearcey*	*McDermott*	*Jobling**	*Fickling*	*Shakespeare*	*Widdringt'n^*	*Childs !*	*Forrester"*	*Llvingstone*	*Mendonca*	*Black*	*Gallimore/Woods/Trollope*
								Ref: S Mathieson	Eadie rounds Jason Pearcey for an early goal. Unmarked Ashley Fickling turns in a corner. Pearcey makes a mess of a back-pass and Eadie pounces. John McDermott turns Fleck's cross into his own net. Gary Childs lunges at Milligan to get sent off. O'Neill volleys in a neat fourth.											
11	H	IPSWICH		1	W	3-1	2-0	Johnson 19, 34, Polston 67	Gunn	Mills	Newman	Eadie	Polston	Sutch	Adams	Fleck^	Milligan	Johnson*	O'Neill	Crook/Akinbiyi
	11/10		**20,256**	*9*	24			*Sonner 46*	*Wright*	*Taricco*	*Vaughan*	*Mowbray*	*Sedgley*	*Williams*	*Stockwell*	*Sonner*	*Mathie*	*Scowcroft*	*Milton**	*Naylor*
								Ref: C Wilkes	Johnson becomes the hero of Norfolk. He fires in a beauty and then grabs another to set up this fine win. Danny Sonner pulls one back with a fierce drive, but City keep their cool. Crook comes on to loud jeers from Ipswich fans, following his remarkable U-turn after signing for them.											

12	H	OLDHAM		2	W	2-0	0-0	Eadie 71, Adams 74	Gunn	Mills	Newman	Eadie	Polston	Sutch	Adams	Fleck*	Milligan	Crook	O'Neill	Scott Kt
	16/10		12,271	*24*	27				*Kelly*	*Fleming*	*Halle*	*Rickers*	*Garnett*	*Redmond*	*Orlygsson*	*Hughes*	*Orm'droyd^*	*Serrant*	*Beresford**	*McNiven/Allott*
								Ref: G Singh	The first goal is a long time coming but worth the wait. Eadie combines neatly with Fleck before firing in. Oldham go forward in search of an equaliser and leave gaps at the back. Eadie catches a defender in possession and sets up Adams who converts at the near post to ensure the win.											
13	A	MANCHESTER C		2	L	1-2	0-1	Scott Kt 88	Gunn	Mills^	Newman	Eadie	Polston	Sutch	Adams	Fleck*	Milligan	Crook	O'Neill	Johnson/Scott Kt
	19/10		***28,269***	*13*	27			*Clough 31, Dickov 54*	*Dibble*	*Brightwell*	*McGoldrick*	*Lomas*	*Symonds*	*Wassall*	*Summerbee*	*Clough*	*Dickov*	*Kinkladze**	*Rosler*	*Whitley*
								Ref: K Leach	Andy Dibble makes a brilliant save from O'Neill. At the other end Nigel Clough's shot is deflected past Gunn by Sutch. Polston's weak back-header is seized upon by Paul Dickov and he lobs home the second. Dibble saves the home side again before sub Scott pulls a late goal back.											
14	A	BIRMINGHAM		2	W	3-2	1-1	Johnson 19, Adams 48p, Scott Kt 54	Gunn	Mills	Newman	Sutch	Polston	Crook*	Adams	Johnson	Milligan	Scott Kt	Eadie	O'Neill
	26/10		*18,869*	*15*	30			*Devlin 40, 86*	*Bennett*	*Poole*	*Ablett**	*Bruce*	*Breen*	*Holland*	*Devlin*	*Castle"*	*Furlong*	*Horne^*	*Bowen*	*Newell/Tait/Legg*
								Ref: M Pierce	Johnson heads in Adams' perfect cross, but Paul Devlin volleys in from a tight angle to equalise. Adams converts a penalty after Johnson is tripped, then Scott powers home a Johnson free-kick. The home side press very hard but their only reward is Devlin's late consolation goal.											
15	H	SHEFFIELD UTD		2	D	1-1	0-1	Adams 71	Gunn	Newman	Mills	Eadie	Polston	Sutch	Adams	Johnson*	Milligan	Scott Kt^	O'Neill	Crook/Fleck
	30/10		14,534	*7*	31			*Katchuro 24*	*Kelly*	*Short*	*Nilsen*	*Hutchinson*	*Vonk*	*Holdsworth*	*Ward*	*Patterson*	*Taylor**	*Katchuro^*	*Whitehouse*	*White/Walker*
								Ref: A Leake	Petr Katchuro rises to head the opener. Five are booked as the visitors attempts to muscle their way to victory, but they are foiled as a foul on O'Neill leads to a free-kick, curled directly in by Adams. This produces a bizarre celebration, apparently a dance routine from the film Grease.											
16	H	CHARLTON		2	L	1-2	0-0	Milligan 70	Gunn	Mills	Newman	Sutch	Polston	Crook	Adams	Fleck*	Milligan	Forbes^	Eadie	Akinbiyi/Scott Kt
	2/11		14,145	*21*	31			*Allen 64, Kinsella 82*	*Salmon*	*Brown*	*Barness*	*O'Connell*	*Balmer*	*Rufus*	*Newton*	*Leaburn*	*Robinson*	*Allen*	*Kinsella*	
								Ref: P Rejer	Flying winger Adrian Forbes starts a game for the first time. Charlton slowly take command of the game and Bradley Allen nods them into the lead. Milligan soon equalises with a low drive, but Mark Kinsella powers home a cracking shot. Sub Scott rattles the crossbar with a header.											
17	A	BARNSLEY		3	L	1-3	0-0	Newman 73	Gunn	Newman	Mills	Crook^	Polston	Sutch	Adams	Fleck	Milligan	Johnson*	Eadie	Bradshaw/Forbes
	12/11		*9,697*	*4*	31			*Moses 55, Wilkinson 61, Hendrie 71*	*Watson*	*Eaden*	*Appleby*	*Sheridan*	*Moses*	*De Zeeuw*	*Hendrie**	*Redfearn*	*Wilkinson*	*Liddell*	*Jones*	*Bosancic*
								Ref: G Frankland	The Tykes miss golden opportunities early on, but break the deadlock when a cross is half-cleared and Adrian Moses thumps in a fierce volley. Slipshod defending and half-hearted offside claims accompany two more goals. Newman taps home a consolation, but City are already beaten.											
18	H	READING		3	D	1-1	0-0	Scott Kt 79	Gunn	Newman	Bradshaw*	Eadie	Polston	Sutch	Adams	Fleck	Milligan	Johnson	O'Neill	Scott Kt
	16/11		14,412	*20*	32			*Morley 56*	*Wright*	*Bernal*	*Bodin*	*McPherson*	*Hunter*	*Parkinson*	*Gilkes*	*Caskey*	*Morley**	*Nogan^*	*Gooding !*	*Williams/Meaker*
								Ref: A Butler	Reading look to be there for the taking, but are allowed to go ahead when Trevor Morley heads in a free-kick. Joint-manager Mick Gooding is red-carded for preventing Eadie's run on goal. Sub Keith Scott scrambles home an equaliser with his first touch. This was two points dropped.											
19	H	BIRMINGHAM		6	L	0-1	0-0		Gunn	Newman	Bradshaw*	Eadie	Polston	Sutch	Adams"	Fleck	Milligan	Johnson^	O'Neill	Mills/Crook/Scott Kt
	30/11		12,764	*7*	32			*O'Connor 62*	*Sutton*	*Jackson*	*Johnson*	*Ablett*	*Breen*	*Holland*	*Holland*	*Furlong^*	*O'Connor**	*Horne*	*Bowen*	*Tait/Otto"/Cooke*
								Ref: S Bennett	TV chef Delia Smith joins the board, but City can't find the ingredients to overcome Birmingham. A bright start amounts to nothing and the visitors take the lead when debutant Martin O'Connor blasts in a loose ball. A handball gives Fleck a late penalty, but his weak effort is saved.											
20	A	HUDDERSFIELD		7	L	0-2	0-1		Gunn	Mills	Newman	Eadie	Polston	Sutch	Adams	Fleck	Milligan	Johnson	O'Neill*	Scott Kt
	7/12		*10,749*	*13*	32			*Payton 34, 56*	*Francis*	*Jenkins*	*Cowan*	*Bullock*	*Sinnott*	*Gray*	*Makel*	*Dalton**	*Dyson*	*Payton*	*Crosby*	*Edwards*
								Ref: B Burns	Polston's bad tackle gives the Terriers a free-kick which is headed in by Andy Payton. O'Neill loses possession and Payton breaks clear to go round Gunn and clinch the victory. The 1,128 miserable fans who have travelled north to support Norwich give the team the slow handclap.											
21	H	CRYSTAL PALACE		8	D	1-1	0-1	Adams 71	Gunn	Mills	Newman	Eadie	Polston	Crook	Adams	Fleck*	Scott Kt	Johnson	Sutch	O'Neill
	14/12		16,395	*4*	33			*Shipperley 3*	*Day*	*Edworthy*	*Muscat !*	*Roberts*	*Tuttle*	*Gordon*	*Quinn^*	*Houghton !*	*Shipperley*	*Dyer**	*Veart*	*Freedman/Davies*
								Ref: K Lynch	Early Palace pressure pays off as Neil Shipperley fires past Gunn. Two City 'goals' are ruled out for offside before an Adams free-kick flies in after at least two deflections. Kevin Muscat is sent off for a body-check on Eadie and Ray Houghton follows for his part in the ensuing melee.											
22	A	WEST BROM		7	L	1-5	0-2	O'Neill 89	Gunn	Newman	Wright^	Sutch	Mills !	Scott*	Adams	Fleck	Crook	Johnson	Eadie	O'Neill/Carey
	18/12		*12,620*	*17*	33			*Hamilton 24, 51, Hunt 44, 64, Pesch' 64*	*Crichton*	*Holmes*	*Agnew*	*Sneekes**	*Burgess*	*Darby*	*Groves*	*Smith*	*Peschisolido*	*Hunt*	*Hamilton*	*Butler*
								Ref: A D'Urso	City crumble badly in an appalling display. Walker admits the Baggies could have had ten and he says he won't stand for this sort of standard of performance. Ian Hamilton can even afford to miss a penalty. Gunn is lucky not to be sent off for a blatant foul, but Mills is not so fortunate.											
23	A	PORT VALE		10	L	**1-6**	0-2	Fleck 90 *[Mills 69]*	Gunn	Mills	Newman	Sutch	Wright	Crook	Adams	Carey*	O'Neill	Johnson	Eadie	Fleck
	21/12		*6,278*	*9*	33			*Porter 7, Talbot 43, 62, Foyle 47, 90,*	*Musselwhite*	*Aspin*	*Tankard*	*Talbot^*	*Griffiths*	*Glover*	*McCarthy*	*Porter*	*Mills*	*Naylor**	*Guppy*	*Foyle/Jansson*
								Ref: S Mathieson	Three days on and things get even worse. Martin Foyle slips home the sixth and final humiliation after a Lee Mills dummy. The *EDP* calls this an insult to the supporters. The makeshift defence looks a shambles and immediately afterwards Walker goes out and signs Matthew Jackson.											

No	Date		Att	Pos	Pt	F-A	H-T	Scorers, Times, and Referees	1	2	3	4	5	6	7	8	9	10	11	Subs used
24	A	QP RANGERS		13	L	2-3	1-2	Crook 39, Eadie 74	Gunn	Newman	**Jackson**	Sutch	Polston	Crook	Adams	Milligan	Eadie	Johnson	O'Neill	
	26/12		*15,699*	*6*	33			*Peacock 22, Dichio 40, McDermott 85*	*Roberts*	*McDermott*	*Brevett*	*Barker*	*McDonald^*	*Ready*	*Spencer*	*Peacock*	*Dichio*	*Brazier**	*Sinclair*	*Impey/Maddix*
								Ref: M Pierce	Gavin Peacock volleys Rangers ahead, but City look in better shape thanks to Jackson and Polston's presence. Crooks' 25-yarder squeezes past Tony Roberts, but Daniel Dichio converts a through ball. Eadie lashes an equaliser, but Andy McDermott grabs a rather fortunate late winner.											
25	H	BRADFORD C		10	W	2-0	1-0	Adams 35p, O'Neill 60	Gunn	Newman	Jackson	Eadie"	Polston	Sutch	Adams	Fleck^	Milligan	Johnson*	O'Neill	Mills/Scott Kt/Forbes
	28/12		13,473	*23*	36				*Schwartzer*	*Jacobs*	*Hamilton*	*Kiwomya*	*Mohan*	*O'Brien**	*Waddle*	*Duxbury*	*Sundgot^*	*Steiner*	*Dreyer*	*Shutt/Pinto*
								Ref: D Orr	It's virtually a completely changed Bradford line-up since the sides met less than four months ago. Chris Waddle, 36, looks classy but City go ahead as Johnson is floored and Adams tucks in the penalty. After a touchline fracas involving the two managers, O'Neill turns in Fleck's pass.											
26	H	PORTSMOUTH		6	W	1-0	0-0	Jackson 77	Gunn	Newman	Jackson	Eadie	Polston*	Sutch	Adams	Fleck	Milligan	Johnson	O'Neill	Akinbiyi
	1/1		**11,946**	*17*	39				*Knight*	*Whitbread*	*Pethick*	*McLoughlin*	*Perrett^*	*Awford*	*Hall*	*Simpson*	*Durnin*	*Svensson**	*Cook"*	*Carter/Thomson/Dobson*
								Ref: A Wiley	City go close in the first half but appear to be running out of steam by the time an Eadie corner finds Johnson. His effort is cleared off the line but Jackson pounces to stab the winner. Sub Akinbiyi balloons a good chance over and City have to cling on fiercely to take the three points.											
27	H	GRIMSBY		6	W	2-1	2-1	Polston 27, Sutch 45	Gunn	Newman	Jackson	Eadie	Polston*	Sutch	Mills	Crook	**Rocastle**	Carey	O'Neill	**Ottosson**
	18/1		16,687	*24*	42			*Lester 20*	*Pearcey*	*McDermott*	*Gallimore*	*Fickling*	*Lever*	*Jobling**	*Appleton*	*Lester*	*Woods^*	*Mendonca*	*Southall*	*Black/Oster*
								Ref: M Fletcher	David Rocastle and Swede Olf Ottossun join on loan. The Mariners sail into the lead when Jack Lester is given the space to advance and beat Gunn. Polston sidefoots in a corner. Poor defensive work allows Sutch to nip in and put City ahead. Ottossun comes on to a hearty welcome.											
28	A	STOKE		5	W	2-1	2-1	O'Neill 4, Eadie 11	Gunn	Newman	Jackson	Eadie	Scott Kv	Sutch	Adams	Crook^	Rocastle	Carey	O'Neill*	Scott Kt/Ottossun
	21/1		*10,179*	*7*	45			*Stein 14*	*Prudhoe*	*Pickering^*	*Griffin*	*Sigurdsson*	*Whittle*	*Forsyth**	*McMahon*	*Wallace*	*Stein*	*Sheron*	*Kavanagh*	*Macari/Mackenzie*
								Ref: M Bailey	Twice in the early stages Lou Macari's side are caught square at the back and O'Neill and Eadie race clear to score. In his farewell match, Mark Stein pulls a goal back with a tap-in. Ex-Canary Mike Sheron has been named Sky TV's Nationwide Player of the Year runner-up for 1996.											
29	A	TRANMERE		5	L	1-3	1-2	Eadie 2	Gunn	Newman	Jackson	Eadie	Scott Kv	Sutch	Adams	Fleck*	Rocastle	Carey^	Milligan	Forbes/Ottossun
	28/1		*5,891*	*7*	45			*Cook 9, 65, Moore 45*	*Nixon*	*Stevens*	*Thomas*	*McGreal*	*Thorn*	*Irons*	*Brannan"*	*Moore*	*Cook*	*Branch^*	*Nevin**	*Rogers/Bonetti/Jones*
								Ref: N Barry	Eadie puts City ahead only for Paul Cook to equalise, but many fans fail to see the goals due to very thick fog. The ref says later he could see both goals from the centre circle, so played on. Ian Moore heads Rovers ahead and ex-Canary Cook kills off any lingering chances of a point.											
30	H	BARNSLEY		5	D	1-1	0-1	Eadie 89	Gunn	Newman	Jackson	Crook	Scott Kv	Sutch	Adams	Fleck	Rocastle*	Milligan	Eadie	Johnson
	1/2		17,001	*3*	46			*Eaden 18*	*Watson*	*Eaden*	*Appleby*	*Sheridan*	*Moses*	*Shirtliff*	*Hendrie*	*Redfearn*	*Wilkinson*	*Liddell**	*Thompson*	*Marcelle*
								Ref: T Lunt	Nicky Eaden thumps a 20-yarder goalwards and it hits Jackson and Crook on the way in. Fleck's deft flick from Eadie's cross goes in, but ref Lunt pulls play back for a City free-kick. An unjust defeat looks likely until Milligan's quickly-taken free-kick is thrashed in late on by Eadie.											
31	A	SHEFFIELD UTD		5	W	3-2	0-0	J'hns'n 56, Ottos'n 74, Holdsw'th 83(og)	Gunn	Mills	Sutch	Crook	Scott Kv	Rocastle	Adams	Fleck	Ottosson*	Johnson	Milligan	Bradshaw
	9/2		*15,301*	*4*	49			*Katchuro 46, Walker 79*	*Kelly**	*Short*	*Nilsen*	*Hutchinson"*	*Hodgson^*	*Holdsworth*	*White*	*Spackman*	*Fjortoft*	*Katchuro*	*Ward*	*Walker/Taylor/Beard*
								Ref: K Leach	Petr Katchuro pokes United into the lead but Alan Kelly drops a cross and Johnson pounces. In the scramble, Kelly is injured and goes off. Fleck's cross is thumped in by Ottossun but Andy Walker equalises. David Holdsworth heads the winner into his own net from Adams' cross.											
32	H	WEST BROM		6	L	2-4	0-1	Sutch 65, Adams 78p	Gunn	Mills	Sutch	Crook	Scott Kv	Rocastle^	Adams	Milligan	Ottosson*	Johnson	Eadie	Bradshaw/Forbes
	15/2		14,845	*15*	49			*Peschisolido 9, 56, 68, Sneekes 49*	*Crichton*	*Holmes*	*Agnew*	*Sneekes*	*Burgess^*	*Raven*	*Donovan*	*Smith**	*Peschisolido*	*Hunt"*	*Hamilton*	*Butler/Murphy/Potter*
								Ref: R Furnandiz	Kevin Scott's weak back-pass is netted by Paul Peschisolido. Richard Sneekes pounces after Andy Hunt's low shot is parried by Gunn. After Peschisolido twice beats Gunn in one-on-ones, Sutch's curling shot and Adams' penalty - after Eadie was brought down - are merely academic.											
33	A	CHARLTON		5	D	4-4	2-2	Adams 29, 64p, Eadie 45, 84 *[Leaburn 88]*	Gunn	Newman*	Sutch	Eadie	Mills	Rocastle	Adams	Crook	Ottosson	Johnson	Milligan	Bradshaw
	22/2		*12,405*	*18*	50			*Kinsella 31, Robson 36, Lee 87,*	*Petterson*	*Brown*	*Barness*	*Jones*	*Balmer*	*Chapple !*	*Robson**	*Lee"*	*Robinson*	*Jones^*	*Kinsella*	*Newton/Leaburn/Poole*
								Ref: J Brandwood	Phil Chapple trips Eadie and is sent off, Adams curling the free-kick in. Mark Kinsella and Mark Robson both emulate Adams with free-kicks. Newman goes off after Gunn falls on him. Fine finishing by Eadie and an Adams penalty are cancelled out by dramatic late close-range goals.											
34	A	SOUTHEND		5	D	1-1	0-0	Fleck 87	Gunn	Newman	Jackson	Eadie	Scott Kv	Sutch	Adams	Rocastle^	Ottosson*	Johnson	Milligan !	Fleck/Bradshaw
	25/2		***5,169***	*22*	51			*Thomson 51*	*Royce*	*Harris*	*Dublin*	*McInally*	*Roget*	*Gridelet*	*Poric**	*Marsh*	*Boere^*	*Thomson*	*Hails*	*Byrne/Rammell*
								Ref: B Knight	Kevin Scott signs permanently and, with Jackson and Newman back, City look stronger at the back. Andy Thomson's poorly-hit shot somehow eludes the groping Gunn, who is struggling for form lately. Milligan is sent off for two yellow card offences. Fleck poaches a late equaliser.											

No	Ven	Opponent / Date	Att	Pos	Res / Pts	F-A	H-T	Scorers, Times, and Referees	1	2	3	4	5	6	7	8	9	10	11	Subs used
35	H	HUDDERSFIELD		5	W	2-0	1-0	Eadie 32, 53	Marshall	Newman	Jackson	Eadie	Scott Kv !	Sutch	Adams	Fleck	Rocastle	Johnson	Milligan	
		1/3	13,001	*17*	54				*Francis*	*Edwards**	*Cowan !*	*Browning*	*Burnett"*	*Gray*	*Makel*	*Crosby^*	*Stewart*	*Payton !*	*Reid*	*Dalton/Baldry/Ryan*
								Ref: A D'Urso	Off-form Gunn is dropped for the first time in 1[illegible] years at Norwich. Card-happy referee D'Urso angers both sets of fans. Tom Cowans departs for two yellows and is followed by Scott and Andy Payton after flare-ups. Eadie scores two glorious goals to prise the limelight from the ref.											
36	A	READING		5	L	1-2	1-1	Adams 27p	Marshall	Newman	Jackson	Eadie	Scott Kv	Sutch	Adams	Fleck	Rocastle	Johnson*	Milligan	Crook
		4/3	*8,174*	*16*	54			*Morley 20, Adams 86 (og)*	*Mautone*	*Bernal*	*Bodin**	*Gooding*	*Hunter*	*McPherson*	*Gilkes*	*Meaker*	*Morley*	*Quinn^*	*Caskey*	*Parkinson/Williams*
								Ref: M Halsey	Trevor Morley's overhead kick loops over stranded Marshall. Eadie is felled for Adams to equalise from the spot. Eadie hits the post and later the side-netting and Jackson misses a sitter. Marshall is beaten by a low cross and Adams hammers it into his own net in an attempt to clear.											
37	H	PORT VALE		5	D	1-1	1-1	Jackson 11	Marshall	Newman^	Jackson	Eadie	Scott Kv	Sutch	Adams	Fleck	Rocastle*	Crook	Milligan	Carey/Bradshaw
		8/3	16, 101	*8*	55			*McCarthy 26*	*Musselwhite*	*Hill*	*Tankard*	*Bogie*	*Aspin*	*Glover*	*McCarthy*	*Porter*	*Talbot*	*Naylor**	*Koordes*	*Mills*
								Ref: P Taylor	A Rocastle corner is headed in at the near post by Jackson and more goals should have followed. City pay the penalty when Jon McCarthy runs on to a through pass and clips his shot past the advancing Marshall. City fade after this and are not resembling serious promotion contenders.											
38	A	CRYSTAL PALACE		6	L	0-2	0-2		Gunn	Newman	Jackson	Crook*	Bradshaw	Sutch	Adams	Fleck	Carey^	Scott Kt"	Forbes	Rush/**Bellamy/Broughton**
		15/3	*17,378*	*5*	55			*Gordon 30p, McKenzie 35*	*Nash*	*Edworthy*	*Gordon*	*Roberts*	*Veart*	*Linighan*	*Muscat*	*Hopkin*	*McKenzie*	*Dyer*	*Freedman**	*Houghton*
								Ref: S Baines	Dean Gordon puts away a penalty, the award of which surprises even Dave Bassett's men. Leon MacKenzie heads a second despite a posse of defenders around him. Young prospects Drewe Broughton and Craig Bellamy come on for their debuts, but Palace are never in much danger.											
39	H	BOLTON		8	L	0-1	0-1		Gunn	Newman	Jackson	Crook^	Bradshaw	Sutch	Adams	Fleck	Milligan	Eadie	O'Neill*	Forbes/Broughton
		22/3	17,585	*1*	55			*Sellars 24*	*Branagan*	*McAnespie*	*Phillips*	*Frandsen*	*Taggart*	*Fairclough*	*Pollock*	*Sellars*	*Blake*	*McGinlay*	*Thompson*	
								Ref: B Burns	Fleck misses a great opportunity before Nathan Blake squares for Scott Sellars to give Colin Todd's men the lead. In the second half Norwich pound the Bolton defence but simply cannot score. It's another disappointing result, but the manner of the performance was more encouraging.											
40	A	SWINDON		7	W	3-0	1-0	Eadie 12, 75, O'Neill 48	Gunn	Newman	Jackson"	Crook	Bradshaw^	Sutch	Adams	Fleck	Milligan	Eadie	O'Neill*	Mills/Polston/Broughton
		29/3	*10,249*	*13*	58				*Digby*	*Robinson^*	*King*	*Bullock*	*Seagraves*	*Coughlan**	*Culverhouse*	*Cowe"*	*Thorne*	*Finney*	*Smith*	*Darras/Watson/Goooden*
								Ref: R Poulain	City's luck changes at last, against a poor-looking Swindon outfit. A marvellous 30-yard thunderbolt from Eadie breaks the deadlock. After the break Eadie and Fleck combine to set up O'Neill, who cuts in and curls home a beauty. Eadie skips past Fraser Digby to slot home a third goal.											
41	H	OXFORD		7	D	1-1	1-1	Eadie 9	Gunn	Newman	Jackson	Crook	Bradshaw*	Sutch	Adams	Fleck	Broughton^	Milligan	Eadie	Polston/Forbes
		31/3	14,644	*14*	59			*Massey 31*	*Whitehead*	*Robinson*	*Ford M*	*Smith*	*Purse*	*Gilchrist*	*Murphy^*	*Gray*	*Moody**	*Jemson*	*Massey*	*Aldridge/Beauchamp*
								Ref: J Kirkby	Realistically only a win will do if City are to reach the play-offs. Early pressure yields an Eadie goal, but City fail to get the vital second. Stuart Massey is left unmarked and equalises. Norwich dominate for spells, but miss clearcut chances. Luckily, other play-off contenders also slip up.											
42	A	WOLVERHAMPTON		9	L	2-3	2-2	Broughton 43, Adams 45p	Gunn	Newman	Jackson	Crook*	Bradshaw	Sutch	Adams	Fleck^	Broughton	Milligan	Eadie	Mills/Carey
		5/4	*26,938*	*3*	59			*Thomas 19, Curle 35p, Roberts 78*	*Stowell*	*Smith*	*Froggatt*	*Atkins*	*Curle*	*Thomas*	*Gilkes*	*Ferguson*	*Roberts*	*Goodman*	*Osborn**	*Robinson*
								Ref: K Lynch	Geoff Thomas converts after Gunn blocks a Don Goodman shot. Bradshaw impedes Goodman for Keith Curle's penalty. Broughton side-foots his first senior goal, then Newman is pulled over and Adams levels from the spot. Iwan Roberts wins it for Wolves, sliding in a left-wing cross.											
43	H	STOKE		7	W	2-0	1-0	O'Neill 1, Eadie 53	Marshall	Newman	Jackson	Crook	Bradshaw	Sutch	Adams	Fleck^	Milligan*	Eadie	O'Neill"	Mills/Polston/Broughton
		12/4	13,805	*13*	62				*Muggleton*	*McNally*	*Griffin**	*Sigurdsson*	*Whittle^*	*Forsyth*	*Kavanagh"*	*Wallace*	*Macari*	*McMahon*	*Mackenzie*	*Pickering/Beeston/Devlin*
								Ref: M Bailey	Graham Kavanagh's poor back-pass is fired home by O'Neill after just 12 seconds - one of the quickest City goals on record. City dominate and could have had a hatful. O'Neill's through-ball finds Eadie for the second goal. Marshall has just the one save to make - from Richard Forsyth.											
44	A	IPSWICH		9	L	0-2	0-2		Marshall	Newman	Jackson	Crook	Bradshaw*	Sutch	Adams	Fleck	Eadie	Mills	O'Neill^	Polston/Simpson
		18/4	*22,397*	*5*	62			*Taricco 32, Mason 42*	*Wright*	*Stockwell*	*Taricco*	*Sedgley*	*Swailes*	*Williams*	*Uhlenbeek*	*Vaughan*	*Gregory*	*Gudmunds'n*	*Mason**	*Dyer*
								Ref: U Rennie	Ipswich are close to clinching a play-off place, but City are rank outsiders for this prize and are really just playing for local pride. Mauricio Taricco fires in a beauty from Steve Sedgley's pass. An overhead kick from Geraint Williams falls for Paul Mason, who slams home a second.											
45	H	MANCHESTER C		10	D	0-0	0-0		Marshall	Simpson	Sutch	**Moore**	Newman	Polston	Adams	Mills	Broughton	Crook	Forbes*	Bellamy
		25/4	14,080	*14*	63				*Margetson*	*Brightwell*	*Horlock*	*McGoldrick*	*Symonds*	*Brannan*	*Summerbee*	*Atkinson*	*Heaney**	*Whitley*	*Crooks*	*Dickov*
								Ref: J Brandwood	A play-off place is now definitely out of reach, but City battle well - particularly after the interval - and win back some pride against Frank Clark's unpredictable side. After the final whistle, the squad and management do a lap of honour and thank the fans for their support in 1996-7.											
46	A	OLDHAM		13	L	0-3	0-2		Marshall	Newman	Jackson	Crook*	Moore	Polston^	Adams	Fleck"	Sutch	Mills	Eadie	Bellamy/Broughton/Simpson
		4/5	*5,562*	*23*	63			*Moore 27 (og), Rush 29, Barlow 74*	*Kelly*	*McNiven*	*Serrant*	*Duxbury*	*Garnett*	*Fleming*	*Rush**	*Rickers*	*McCarthy"*	*Barlow^*	*Reid*	*McNiven/Allott/Ritchie*
		Home	Away					Ref: F Stretton	Moore, on loan from Everton, blasts an attempted clearance into his own net. Graeme Sharp's relegated side get a second when Newman presents the ball to ex-Canary Matthew Rush and he slots home gratefully. Rush pulls the ball back for Stuart Barlow to complete the scoring.											
Average		14,719	12,334																	

Coca-Cola Cup			Att			F-A	H-T	Scorers, Times, and Referees	1	2	3	4	5	6	7	8	9	10	11	subs used
1:1	A	OXFORD			D	1-1	1-1	Johnson 29	Gunn	Mills	Newman	Eadie	Polston	Crook	Adams	Fleck*	Milligan	Johnson^	O'Neill	Akinbiyi/Bradshaw
	20/8		*6,062*					*Jemson 31*	*Whitehead*	*Robinson*	*Ford M*	*Smith*	*Elliott*	*Gilchrist*	*Ford R*	*Massey*	*Aldridge**	*Jemson^*	*Beauchamp*	*Moody/Rush*
								Ref: J Brandwood	City have to tackle a first-round tie for the first time since winning this competition in 1962. They look a class above the home side with their slick passing. Johnson seizes Fleck's through ball and clips a shot in. Nigel Jemson heads an instant response. Eadie hits a post after a solo run.											
1:2	H	OXFORD		4	L	2-3	1-0	Adams 11p, 116	Gunn	Mills	Newman	Eadie !	Polston	Crook^	Adams	Fleck !	Milligan	Sutch	O'Neill*	Akinbiyi/Carey
	4/9		7,301	*17*		*aet*		*Elliott 52, Ford M 95, Aldridge 103*	*Whitehead*	*Robinson*	*Ford M*	*Smith"*	*Elliott^*	*Gilchrist*	*Ford R*	*Gray*	*Moody*	*Massey**	*Beauchamp*	*Aldridge/Purse/Angel*
								Ref: T West (Norwich lose 3-4 on aggregate)	After City go ahead, Fleck tangles with Martin Gray and later Eadie joins him for an early bath. Angered and disrupted by various refeering decisions, nine-man City are taken into extra-time and the numerical disadvantage tells. Adams curls in a free-kick, but it's too little, too late.											

FA Cup																				
3	H	SHEFFIELD UTD		6	W	1-0	1-0	Polston 32	Gunn	Jackson	Newman	Eadie	Polston	Crook	Adams	Johnson*	Milligan^	Sutch	O'Neill	Carey/Scott Kt
	4/1		12,356	*3*					*Kelly*	*Beard*	*Sandford*	*Spackman*	*Hodgson^*	*Holdsworth*	*White*	*Patterson*	*Walker*	*Katchuro*	*Scott**	*Hartfield/Nilsen*
								Ref: R Pearson	O'Neill flicks on a Newman long throw and Polston hooks the ball in after his first attempt is blocked. Minutes later the Blades are unlucky not to level in an amazing scramble in which the ball strikes the woodwork four times and is cleared off the line before ending up in Gunn's hands.											
4	A	LEICESTER		5	L	1-2	1-1	Adams 39p	Gunn	Mills	Newman	Jackson !	Carey^	Sutch	Adams	Fleck*	Milligan	Eadie	Forbes	Ottossun/Scott Kt
	25/1		*16,703*	*12*				*Marshall 32, Parker 67p*	*Keller*	*Lawrence**	*Kamark^*	*Parker*	*Elliott*	*Prior*	*Lennon !*	*Izzet*	*Claridge*	*Marshall*	*Heskey*	*Robins/Watts*
								Ref: A Wilkie	Ian Marshall fires Martin O'Neill's men ahead from a corner. Neil Lennon and Jackson clash and are sent off. Forbes is fouled on the edge of the box and City are handed a rather fortunate penalty. Gary Parker and Newman take a tumble and this time the Foxes get the rub of the green.											

		P	W	D	L	Home F	Home A	W	D	L	Away F	Away A	Pts
1	Bolton	46	18	4	1	60	20	10	10	3	40	33	98
2	Barnsley	46	14	4	5	43	19	8	10	5	33	36	80
3	Wolves	46	10	5	8	31	24	12	5	6	37	27	76
4	Ipswich	46	13	7	3	44	23	7	7	9	24	27	74
5	Sheffield Utd	46	13	5	5	46	23	7	8	8	29	29	73
6	Crys Palace*	46	10	7	6	39	22	9	7	7	39	26	71
7	Portsmouth	46	12	4	7	32	24	8	4	11	27	29	68
8	Port Vale	46	9	9	5	36	28	8	7	8	22	27	67
9	QP Rangers	46	10	5	8	33	25	8	7	8	31	35	66
10	Birmingham	46	11	7	5	30	18	6	8	9	22	30	66
11	Tranmere	46	10	9	4	42	27	7	5	11	21	29	65
12	Stoke	46	15	3	5	34	22	3	7	13	17	35	64
13	NORWICH	46	9	10	4	28	18	8	2	13	35	50	63
14	Manchester C	46	12	4	7	34	25	5	6	12	25	35	61
15	Charlton	46	11	8	4	36	28	5	3	15	16	38	59
16	West Brom	46	7	7	9	37	33	7	8	8	31	39	57
17	Oxford	46	14	3	6	44	26	2	6	15	20	42	57
18	Reading	46	13	7	3	37	24	2	5	16	21	43	57
19	Swindon	46	11	6	6	36	27	4	3	16	16	44	54
20	Huddersfield	46	10	7	6	28	20	3	8	12	20	41	54
21	Bradford C	46	10	5	8	29	32	2	7	14	18	40	48
22	Grimsby	46	7	7	9	31	34	4	6	13	29	47	46
23	Oldham	46	6	8	9	30	30	4	5	14	21	36	43
24	Southend	46	7	9	7	32	32	1	6	16	10	54	39
		1104	262	150	140	872	604	140	150	262	604	872	1506

* promoted after play-offs

Odds & ends

Double wins: (5) Bradford C, Grimsby, Portsmouth, Stoke, Swindon.
Double losses: (2) Bolton, West Brom.

Won from behind: (2) Grimsby (h), Sheffield Utd (a).
Lost from in front: (2) Tranmere (h), Oxford (h) (LC).

High points: Some tremendous goals from Darren Eadie.
The return of Mike Walker and an attractive passing game.
The local derby win over Ipswich in October to remain top of the table.
The arrival of Delia Smith and new supporter liaison initiatives.

Low Points: The new red away kit – highly unpopular with many fans.
Thrashings at West Brom and Port Vale within days of each other.
Losing a two-goal lead at Charlton in the dying moments.
The fading away of the play-off challenge.
Losing to Oxford in a cup-tie marred by refereeing controversies.
The shortage of goals from Robert Fleck.
Financial cut-backs by the new board.
The dropping of popular, but out-of-form keeper Bryan Gunn.

Player of the Year: Darren Eadie.
Ever-presents: (0).
Hat-tricks: (0).
Hat-tricks against: (1) Paul Peschisolido (v West Brom, H).
Leading scorer: (17) Darren Eadie.

	Appearances Lge	*Sub*	LC	*Sub*	FAC	*Sub*	Goals Lge	LC	FAC	Tot
Adams, Neil	**45**		2		2		**13**	2	1	**16**
Akinbiyi, Ade	**3**	*9*		*2*						
Bellamy, Craig		*3*								
Bradshaw, Carl	**11**	*6*		*1*						
Broughton, Drewe	**3**	*5*					**1**			**1**
Carey, Shaun	**8**	*6*		*1*	1	*1*				
Crook, Ian	**33**	*4*	2		1		**2**			**2**
Eadie, Darren	**42**		2		2		**17**			**17**
Fleck, Robert	**33**	*3*	2		1		**4**			**4**
Forbes, Adrian	**3**	*7*			1					
Gunn, Bryan	**39**		2		2					
Jackson, Matt	**19**				2		**2**			**2**
Johnson, Andy	**24**	*3*	1		1		**5**	1		**6**
Marshall, Andy	**7**									
Milligan, Mike	**37**		2		2		**1**			**1**
Mills, Danny	**27**	*5*	2		1					
Moore, Neil	**2**									
Newman, Rob	**44**		2		2		**1**			**1**
O'Neill, Keith	**23**	*3*	2		1		**6**			**6**
Ottossun, Ulf	**4**	*3*				*1*	**1**			**1**
Polston, John	**27**	*4*	2		1	*1*	**2**		1	**3**
Rocastle, David	**11**									
Rush, Matthew		*2*								
Scott, Keith	**5**	*8*				*2*	**3**			**3**
Scott, Kevin	**9**									
Simpson, Karl	**1**	*2*								
Sutch, Daryl	**43**	*1*	1		2		**3**			**3**
Wright, Johnny	**3**	*1*								
(own-goals)							**2**			**2**
28 players used	**506**	***75***	**22**	***4***	**22**	***5***	**63**	**3**	**2**	**68**

No	Date		Att	Pos	Pt	F-A	H-T	Scorers, Times, and Referees	1	2	3	4	5	6	7	8	9	10	11	subs used
1	H	WOLVERHAMPTON			L	0-2	0-1		Marshall A	**Fleming**	Newman*	Sutch	**Segura**	Polston	Adams	Mills	**Roberts^**	Eadie	O'Neill	Bellamy/Fleck
	9/8		17,230		0			*Keane 34, 64*	*Stowell*	*Smith*	*Kubicki*	*Atkins*	*Sedgley*	*Curle*	*Keane*	*Ferguson*	*Bull*	*Goodman*	*Froggatt*	
								Ref: M Bailey	Johnson and Crook have gone and three new faces take a bow, including Roberts, playing against his old team. But 17-year-old wonder-kid Robbie Keane takes centre stage on his debut. He volleys home after a Keith Curle free-kick and later on cuts in and buries a fierce low drive.											
2	A	NOTT'M FOREST	21		L	1-4	1-1	O'Neill 7 *[Campbell 59]*	Marshall A	Newman	Scott^	Bradshaw*	Segura	Polston	Adams	Sutch	Roberts	Eadie	O'Neill	Bellamy/Mills
	15/8		*16,524*	*1*	0			*Van Hooijdonk 22, Thomas 57, 61,*	*Pascolo*	*Lyttle*	*Rogers*	*Hjelde*	*Chettle*	*Thomas^*	*Stone**	*Gemmill*	*V Hooijdonk*	*Campbell*	*Bonalair*	*Johnson/Saunders*
								Ref: J Kirkby	City crumble in the second half after snatching an early goal from O'Neill. Kevin Campbell's fierce shot flies past Marshall for the pick of the four goals. Steve Stone is left covered in blood after a clash of heads. The way we caved in was a disgrace, storms manager Walker afterwards.											
3	H	CREWE	24		L	0-2	0-1		Marshall A	Mills*	Newman	**Grant^**	Sutch	Polston	Adams	Fleck	Roberts	Milligan	Eadie	Segura/Forbes
	23/8		11,821	*14*	0			*Rivers 29, Smith S 60*	*Kearton*	*Rivers**	*Smith S*	*Westwood*	*Lightfoot*	*Charnock*	*Whalley*	*Lunt^*	*Adebola*	*Johnson*	*Moralee"*	*Garvey/Wright/Anthrobus*
								Ref: T Lunt	Mark Rivers is allowed acres of space to open the scoring. Shaun Smith's free-kick somehow squeezes past the grasp of Marshall and narrowly crosses the line. Inspired goalkeeping by Jason Kearton keeps City at bay. Peter Grant, signed from Celtic, is injured on his Canaries debut.											
4	A	SUNDERLAND	19		W	1-0	0-0	Sutch 76	Marshall A	Segura	Newman	Grant	Sutch	Polston	Adams	Fleck*	Roberts	Milligan^	Eadie	O'Neill/Jackson
	30/8		*29,204*	*17*	3				*Perez*	*Makin*	*Scott*	*Clark*	*Ball**	*Melville*	*Agnew^*	*Ord*	*Quinn*	*Phillips*	*Gray*	*Byrne/Alston*
								Ref: R Furnandiz	Peter Reid's newly relegated Sunderland are frustrated by a series of great saves from Marshall. Delight for City as Sutch exchanges passes with Eadie and shoots past Frenchman Lionel Perez. The Stadium of Light is stunned and the Canaries move off the bottom of Division One.											
5	A	PORTSMOUTH	16		D	1-1	0-0	Adams 90p	Marshall A	Segura"	Newman	Grant	Sutch	Polston	Adams	Fleck*	Roberts	Milligan	Eadie	O'Neill^/Scott/Jackson
	2/9		*10,577*	*6*	4			*Turner 65*	*Flahaven*	*Pethick*	*Russell*	*McLaughlin*	*Whitbread*	*Perrett*	*Allen !*	*Turner**	*Aloisi^*	*Svensson*	*Igoe*	*Thorp/Durnin*
								Ref: B Knight	Martin Allen is sent off for two bookable offences. Terry Fenwick's side go ahead via Andy Turner. The quest for an equaliser pays off four minutes into stoppage time. With two men looking offside, Eadie is up-ended by Aaron Flahaven. The disputed penalty is put away by Adams.											
6	H	PORT VALE	16		W	1-0	0-0	Fleck 59	Marshall A	Jackson	Newman	Grant	Sutch	Polston	Adams	Fleck*	Roberts^	Milligan	Forbes	Bellamy/**Coote**
	13/9		11,269	*15*	7				*Musselwhite*	*Hill*	*Tankard*	*Talbot*	*Aspin*	*Snijders*	*Jansson**	*Porter*	*Mills*	*Naylor*	*Foyle*	*Ainsworth*
								Ref: S Baines	Hard-working Vale make life difficult for City, but man-of-the-match Fleck finds a way through when he picks up a quickly-taken Forbes free-kick and streaks clear to beat Paul Musselwhite with a fine finish. Vale's best chance sees Stuart Talbot's effort saved by the feet of Marshall.											
7	H	CHARLTON	16		L	0-4	0-3		Marshall A	Jackson	Newman	Grant	Sutch	Polston*	Adams	Fleck	Coote	Milligan^	Forbes	Fleming/Bellamy
	17/9		10,157	*9*	7			*Mendonca 7, 22, 28, Chapple 84*	*Petterson*	*Brown*	*Barness*	*Jones K*	*Chapple"*	*Balmer*	*Mortimer*	*Kinsella**	*Robinson*	*Mendonca^*	*Jones S*	*Nicholls/Lisbie/Bowen*
								Ref: A D'Urso	City do plenty of attacking but get a lesson in finishing from Alan Curbishley's men. Clive Mendonca grabs a hat-trick in 21 first-half minutes. Near the end, ex-City apprentice Phil Chapple rubs salt into the wounds with the fourth. It's the Canaries worst home defeat in over six years.											
8	A	MANCHESTER C	15		W	2-1	1-1	Adams 38, Coote 64	Marshall A	Fleming	Sutch	Grant	Scott	Jackson	Adams	Fleck*	Coote^	Bellamy"	Forbes	Newman/Polston/Mills
	20/9		*27,258*	*20*	10			*Bradbury 27*	*Margetson*	*Brightwell*	*Van Blerk*	*Wiekens*	*Symons*	*Edghill*	*Summ'bee**	*Horlock*	*Bradbury*	*Kinkladze^*	*Brannan*	*Dickov/Scully*
								Ref: A Butler	Walker makes three changes and City bounce back superbly to break their 33-year-old Maine Road jinx. Lee Bradbury rifles in a low shot, but Adams levels with a fine finish from 18 yards. Bellamy lays the ball square and local teenager Coote taps in his first senior goal to win the day.											
9	H	IPSWICH	14		W	2-1	1-0	Eadie 8, Cundy 59 (og)	Marshall A	Fleming	Sutch	Grant	Scott	Jackson	Adams	Fleck	Eadie	Milligan*	Forbes^	Bellamy/Coote
	26/9		18,911	*22*	13			*Stein 73*	*Wright*	*Stockwell*	*Venus^*	*Williams*	*Mowbray*	*Cundy*	*Dyer*	*Holland*	*Stein*	*Scowcroft**	*Petta*	*Mathie/Kerslake*
								Ref: J Brandwood	Fleming's defence-splitting pass is netted by Eadie. Things gets worse for George Burley's struggling side as Tony Mowbray heads a free-kick against Jason Cundy and the ball flies in. On-loan Mark Stein heads past Marshall. James Scowcroft exits with a serious-looking neck injury.											
10	A	TRANMERE	14		L	0-2	0-1		Marshall A	Mills	Sutch	Grant	Newman !	Jackson	Adams	Fleck*	Eadie	Milligan !	Forbes^	Coote/**Kenton**
	4/10		*6,674*	*18*	13			*Kelly 12, Jones L 68*	*Coyne*	*Stevens*	*Thompson*	*McGreal*	*Challinor"*	*Irons*	*Morrissey*	*Branch^*	*Kelly*	*Jones G*	*Jones L**	*Aldridge/Mahon/Morgan*
								Ref: E Wolstenholme	David Kelly strikes an early blow with a well-hit shot. Shortly afterwards Kelly is pulled back by Newman and the City man is sent off. It's down to nine men when Milligan sees red for an horrendous high tackle on Dave Challinor. Lee Jones nets an easy header to clinch the points.											
11	H	STOCKPORT	17		D	1-1	0-1	Eadie 73	Marshall A	Fleming"	Sutch	Grant	Scott	Jackson	Adams	Fleck	Eadie*	Bellamy	Forbes^	Mills/Coote/Simpson
	18/10		12,689	*10*	14			*Angell 34*	*Nixon*	*Connelly*	*Woodthorpe*	*Bennett^*	*McIntosh*	*Dinning*	*Gannon*	*Angell*	*Armstrong**	*Cooper*	*Searle*	*Mutch/Nash*
								Ref: P Taylor	Brett Angell puts Gary Megson's men ahead after a ricochet off Scott. The equaliser's a long time coming, but it's a cracking effort from Eadie. He takes the ball forward and cracks in a tremendous shot from 25 yards. Fleck nearly wins all three points, but his header strikes the crossbar.											

12	H	READING		17	D		0-0	0-0		Marshall A	Simpson^	Sutch	Grant	Scott	Jackson	Adams	Fleck*	Milligan	Bellamy	Forbes	Newman/Coote
		21/10	17,781	19		15				Mautone	Bernal	Swailes	Williams*	McPherson	Primus	Parkinson	Lambert	Caskey	Houghton	Meaker	Roach
									Ref: F Stretton	A special cut-price ticket scheme boosts the attendance. City look solid in defence with Jackson and Scott in good form, but the attack lacks guile. Bellamy looks promising in his third full game and Forbes' hard running troubles Terry Bullivant's outfit. Grant misses the best chance.											
13	A	SWINDON		17	L		0-1	0-0		Marshall A	Simpson	Sutch*	Grant	Scott	Jackson	Adams	Fleck"	Milligan	Bellamy	Forbes^	Newman/Mills/Coote
		25/10	9,256	2		15			Hay 84	Digby	Borrows	Culverhouse	Bullock	Taylor	Casper	Watson	Walters*	Hay	Allison	Gooden	Smith
									Ref: M Halsey	Chris Hay drifts between Jackson and Grant and sends an exquisite 40-yard chip over Marshall and into the net. It's his tenth goal in 12 starts since arriving from Celtic. Steve McMahon's side maintain their fine start to the season. Bellamy should have levelled but lacked composure.											
14	H	BURY		16	D		2-2	2-1	Bellamy 2, Adams 23	Marshall A	**Marshall L**	Sutch	Grant	Scott	Jackson	Adams	Coote^	Milligan	Bellamy	Forbes*	Simpson/Broughton
		1/11	14,419	15		16			Battersby 40, Johnrose 90	Kiely	Hughes*	Peake"	Daws	Lucketti	Butler	Gray	Johnson	Woodward	Johnrose	Battersby^	Jepson/Armstrong/Swan
									Ref: J Kirkby	Bellamy produces a confident early finish and the lead is increased when Coote lays the ball back to Adams, who nets from 12 yards. Things start to go pear-shaped when Marshall drops a ball, giving Tony Battersby an easy goal. In stoppage time, Lenny Johnrose nets a sharp volley.											
15	A	WEST BROM		17	L		0-1	0-0		Marshall A	Marshall L"	Sutch	Grant	Scott	Jackson*	Adams	Coote^	Roberts	Bellamy	Forbes	Newman/Roberts/Simpson
		4/11	13,949	4		16			Hughes 85	Miller	Holmes	Smith	Sneekes	Dobson	Mardon	Flynn*	Hamilton	Butler	Hunt	Kilbane^	Coldicott/Hughes
									Ref: D Laws	Adams is unlucky to hit a post with a pot-shot from 35 yards. In his second game, defender Lee Marshall departs with an ankle injury. Great saves foil Richard Sneekes and Lee Hughes. Andy Hunt sets up Hughes, who goes round the keeper to score. It's another sickening late blow.											
16	A	BIRMINGHAM		16	W		2-1	2-1	Forbes 23, 36	Marshall A	Segura*	Sutch	Mills	Scott	Newman	Adams	Fleck	Roberts	Milligan	Forbes	Simpson
		8/11	16,464	14		19			Devlin 27p	Bennett	Bass	Grainger	Bruce	Ablett	Marsden	Devlin	McCarthy	Furlong	Hughes*	Johnson^	Francis/Robinson
									Ref: R Pearson	After good work by Roberts and Fleck, Forbes drills in his first senior goal. Segura lunges at Paul Devlin, who picks himself up to level from the spot. Fleck's cross is thrashed in by Forbes minutes later. Chris Marsden's 40-yard volley hits a post and bounces clear off Marshall's back.											
17	H	MIDDLESBROUGH		16	L		1-3	1-1	Roberts 32	Marshall A	Segura	Sutch	Grant*	Scott	Newman	Adams	Fleck"	Roberts	Milligan	Forbes	Mills^/**Fugelstad**/Bellamy
		15/11	16,011	4		19			Beck 39, Merson 52, Ormerod 55	Schwarzer	Baker*	Vickers	Festa	Pearson	Emerson	Hignett	Summerbell	Beck	Merson	Ormerod	Harrison
									Ref: S Mathieson	Roberts finds himself in space to head home his first league goal for Norwich. Mikkel Beck levels with a shot that goes in off both posts. Paul Merson's classy finish puts Boro ahead. Tony Ormerod, 18, slips the third goal just inside a post to clinch the points for Bryan Robson's side.											
18	H	OXFORD		15	W		2-1	1-0	Fleck 31, Bellamy 61	Marshall A	Segura	Fugelstad	Bellamy	Scott	Jackson	Adams	Fleck	Roberts	Milligan	Forbes	
		22/11	11,241	22		22			Powell 80	V Heusden	Remy	Ford	Robinson	Purse	Gilchrist	Ford	Massey^	Banger*	Jemson	Angel	Murphy/Powell
									Ref: B Coddington	Forbes puts Fleck in the clear and his cool finish delights the home fans. Paul Powell scrambles a shot past the diving figure of Adams on the Norwich goalline for the first goal of his career. To great relief all round, Fleck sends Bellamy sprinting through to fire City back into the lead.											
19	A	BRADFORD C		15	L		1-2	0-1	Bellamy 75	Marshall A	Segura	Sutch	Bellamy	Scott	Jackson	Adams*	Fleck	Roberts	Milligan	Fugelstad	Forbes
		29/11	16,637	10		22			Steiner 13, 48	Walsh	Dreyer	O'Kane	Kulcsar	Youds	Moore	Lawrence	Pepper	Steiner	McGinlay	Murray	
									Ref: P Richards	Chris Kamara's men go ahead when Rob Steiner nips round Jackson and shoots under the diving Marshall. Steiner lashes a second when he makes the most of hesitation by Marshall. The nippy Bellamy gets clear and neatly sidefoots the ball over the advancing figure of Gary Walsh.											
20	A	QP RANGERS		15	D		1-1	0-0	Forbes 51	Marshall A	Segura	Sutch^	Bellamy	Scott	Jackson	Adams	Fleck	Roberts	Milligan*	Fugelstad	Newman/Forbes
		3/12	10,141	11		23			Peacock 71	Roberts	Maddix	Brazier !	Barker*	Ready	Morrow	Quashie	Peacock	Murray	Sheron	Sinclair	Brevett
									Ref: P Rejer	Matt Brazier is sent off after receiving a second yellow card. City make numerical advantage count as Forbes nets a smart strike. Bellamy and Nigel Quashie both strike the woodwork. Gavin Peacock is left unmarked to head in the equaliser. Milligan and Sutch both join the injury list.											
21	H	SHEFFIELD UTD		15	W		2-1	0-0	Vonk 61 (og), Fugelstad 84	Marshall A	Segura	Mills	Bellamy	Scott	Jackson	Adams	Fleck	Roberts	Forbes	Fugelstad	
		6/12	11,745	4		26			Deane 51	Tracey	Borbokis	Woodhouse	Ford	Vonk !	Holdsworth	Saunders	Marker	Fjortoft*	Deane	Stuart	Taylor
									Ref: S Bennett	Brian Deane shrugs off the attentions of Jackson to squeeze a low shot past Marshall. Bellamy's shot deflects past the despairing keeper off the chest of Michel Vonk. A foul on Forbes gets Vonk his second yellow card. Forbes' cross is superbly volleyed in by Fugelstad to win the points.											
22	A	HUDDERSFIELD		12	W		3-1	2-0	Forbes 3, Bellamy 40, Grant 90	Marshall A	Segura	Mills	Bellamy	Scott	Jackson	Adams	Fleck*	Roberts	Forbes^	Fugelstad	Grant/Carey
		13/12	11,436	24		29			Stewart 58	Bartram	Phillips	Edmondson*	Dyson	Morrison	Gray	Dalton	Horne	Stewart	Allison	Johnson^	Edwards/Richardson
									Ref: T Leake	A great run and delicate chip by Forbes gives City a dream start at the McAlpine Stadium. Bellamy wrong-foots Vince Bartram to fire in the second. Marcus Stewart knocks in a rebound off Marshall. Grant has the last word by prodding in from close range. Nine players are booked.											
23	H	STOKE		13	D		0-0	0-0		Marshall A	Segura	Mills	Grant	Scott	Jackson	Forbes	Carey*	Roberts	Bellamy	Fugelstad	O'Neill
		20/12	12,265	15		30				Muggleton	Pickering	Griffin	Sigurdsson	Tweed	Keen	Forsyth	Mackenzie	Thorne	Stewart	Kavanagh	
									Ref: R Harris	After successive wins, Canaries fans have high hopes this afternoon but it's a drab, frustrating game against Chic Bates' side. Many wish they'd gone Christmas shopping instead. Segura goes closest, but his effort is booted off the line by Andy Griffin. Adams is sorely missed in midfield.											

No	Date		Att	Pos	Pt	F-A	H-T	Scorers, Times, and Referees	1	2	3	4	5	6	7	8	9	10	11	subs used
24	A	CHARLTON		13	L	1-2	0-0	Bellamy 81p	Marshall A	Segura	Mills	Grant	Scott	Jackson	Forbes	Fugelstad	Roberts*	Bellamy	Milligan !	O'Neill
	26/12		*14,472*	*3*	30			*Kinsella 59, Robinson 62*	*Salmon*	*Brown*	*Bowen*	*Jones K*	*Rufus*	*Chapple*	*Newton*	*Kinsella*	*Robinson*	*Mendonca*	*Leaburn*	
								Ref: P Danson	Mark Kinsella nets a dipping volley to end nearly an hour of stalemate. Milligan's lunge at Kinsella produces his second yellow card. John Robinson pounces on a rebound off Scott to grab the vital second goal. City's only attempt on target is the penalty consolation from Bellamy.											
25	H	PORTSMOUTH		12	W	2-0	1-0	Jackson 14, Bellamy 56	Marshall A	Segura	Mills	Grant	Scott	Jackson	Forbes	Fugelstad*	Milligan	Bellamy	O'Neill	Fleck
	30/12		16,441	*24*	33				*Knight*	*Pethick*	*Thomson*	*McLaughlin*	*Waterman"*	*Awford*	*Hall*	*Foster*	*Aloisi^*	*Svensson*	*Turner**	*Igoe/Durnin/Enes*
								Ref: K Lynch	Winger O'Neill is welcomed back from injury. Forbes' corner is headed home by Jackson. Grant's free-kick finds Bellamy and his shot from 22 yards sails past Alan Knight. Pompey dish out some rugged treatment, particularly to Forbes, who eventually has to be helped from the pitch.											
26	A	WOLVERHAMPTON		12	L	**0-5**	0-4	*[Freedman 43, 45, 77]*	Gunn	Fugelstad	Mills	Grant	Scott*	Jackson	Sutch	Carey^	Roberts	Bellamy	O'Neill	Fleming/**Llewellyn**
	10/1		*23,703*	*6*	33			*Keane 22, Goodman 24,*	*Stowell*	*Muscat*	*Froggatt*	*Atkins*	*Richards*	*Curle*	*Goodman^*	*Keane"*	*Freedman*	*Osborn**	*Ferguson*	*Paatelainen/Robinson/Daley*
								Ref: D Pugh	Marshall is injured and Gunn returns for his first game in eight months. Robbie Keane nets a gentle header and Don Goodman makes it two. Dougie Freedman nets a fine solo goal and heads a fourth just before the interval. He completes a hat-trick by tucking the ball in at the far post.											
27	H	NOTT'M FOREST		12	W	1-0	0-0	Roberts 46	Gunn	Sutch	Fugelstad	Grant	Fleming	Jackson	Forbes	Coote	Roberts	Eadie	O'Neill	
	17/1		17,059	*1*	36				*Beasant*	*Lyttle*	*Rogers*	*Cooper*	*Chettle*	*Johnson*	*Bonalair**	*Gemmill*	*V Hooijdonk*	*Campbell*	*Woan^*	*Thomas/Moore*
								Ref: M Pearce	Leaders Forest come to Town and find veteran Gunn in heroic form between the sticks. Undaunted by his Molineux nightmare, he makes a string of fine saves. Roberts has the crowd on its feet just after the break when he stabs in a Forbes cross. City hang on for a welcome victory.											
28	H	SUNDERLAND		12	W	2-1	1-0	Eadie 32, Craddock 62 (og)	Gunn	Sutch	Fugelstad	Grant	Fleming	Jackson	Forbes^	Coote	Roberts	Milligan*	Eadie	Segura/Mills
	28/1		15,940	*5*	39			*Clark 84*	*Perez*	*Makin*	*Holloway*	*Clark*	*Craddock*	*Williams*	*Summerbee*	*Rae*	*Quinn**	*Phillips*	*Gray*	*Dichio*
								Ref: J Brandwood	City are buoyed up by the Forest win and go on to inflict Sunderland's first defeat in 17 games. Eadie nets a glorious 40-yard lob after an error by keeper Lionel Perez. Jody Craddock helps a Fugelstad cross into his own net. Coote hits a post with a header. Lee Clark nets a consolation.											
29	A	CREWE		12	L	0-1	0-0		Gunn	Sutch	Fugelstad	Grant	Fleming	Jackson	Forbes	Coote	Roberts	Bellamy	Eadie	
	31/1		*5,559*	*14*	39			*Fugelstad 62(og)*	*Kearton*	*Bignot*	*Unsworth^*	*Foran*	*Walton*	*Lunt*	*Whalley*	*Garvey*	*Anthrobus**	*Johnson*	*Little*	*Lightfoot/Street*
								Ref: M Dean	This was not as bad as the awful displays at Wolves and Grimsby (FA Cup), but City still look an unhappy lot on their travels. They contain Dario Gradi's skilful outfit until a Dele Adebola shot cannons in off the shins of poor Fugelstad after appearing to be going wide of the target.											
30	H	MANCHESTER C		12	D	0-0	0-0		Marshall A	Sutch	Fugelstad*	Grant	Segura	Jackson	Kenton	Coote	Roberts	Bellamy !	Eadie^	Mills/Forbes
	7/2		15,274	*21*	40				*Wright*	*Brightwell*	*Tskhadadze*	*Brown^*	*Symons*	*Edghill*	*Crooks*	*Russell*	*Bradbury*	*Kinkladze**	*Rosler*	*Van Blerk/Whitley*
								Ref: B Knight	City look off-colour and this is a frustrating afternoon against Frank Clark's side. Main talking point is the sending-off of young Bellamy. He is booked early on for a bad tackle and is later seen to spit at the retreating figure of Georgi Kinkladze. The ref has no choice but to brandish red.											
31	A	PORT VALE		13	D	2-2	0-1	Grant 64, Jackson 68	Marshall A	Sutch	Fleming	Grant	Segura	Jackson	Kenton^	Coote	Roberts*	Bellamy	Fugelstad	Fleck/Llewellyn
	14/2		*6,664*	*21*	41			*Mills 34, 85*	*Musselwhite*	*Hill*	*Tankard*	*Bogie^*	*Aspin**	*Snijders*	*Ainsworth*	*Porter*	*Mills*	*Naylor"*	*Jansson*	*Glover/Corden/Foyle*
								Ref: A Wiley	Lee Mills nets a fierce header, but City draw level when Grant steals in and produces a calm finish. Minutes later Jackson's glancing header from a Fugelstad free-kick gives City the lead. Five minutes from time Mills takes a lengthy run-up and blasts a 30-yard free-kick into the net.											
32	H	TRANMERE		13	L	0-2	0-0		Marshall A	Sutch	Segura	Grant^	Fleming	Jackson	Mills*	Fleck"	Coote	Bellamy	Eadie	Kenton/Carey/Llewellyn
	18/2		12,105	*17*	41			*O'Brien 66, Kelly 75*	*Simonsen*	*Morgan^*	*Thompson*	*McGreal*	*Challinor*	*Irons*	*Morrissey*	*Hill*	*Kelly*	*O'Brien*	*Parkinson**	*Jones G/Mellon*
								Ref: D Crick	A depressing defeat against ordinary opposition. Liam O'Brien gets the freedom of the six-yard box to net the first goal. Bellamy slices a cross straight to David Kelly, who hits Rovers' second. Eadie tries to inject some class into proceedings but receives some very physical attention.											
33	A	IPSWICH		14	L	**0-5**	0-3		Marshall A	Sutch	Segura^	Grant	Fleming	Jackson	Forbes"	Fleck*	Coote	Carey	Eadie	Mills/Kenton/Llewellyn
	21/2		*21,858*	*10*	41			*Mathie 2, 27, 42, Petta 56, 81*	*Wright*	*Stockwell^*	*Clapham*	*Dyer*	*Mowbray*	*Cundy*	*Uhlenbeek*	*Holland*	*Johnson*	*Mathie**	*Petta*	*Scowcroft/Sonner*
								Ref: C Wilkes	With barely 11 fit men, this awful hammering was always on the cards against an in-form side. Alex Mathie scores after 64 seconds and bags a first-half hat-trick before departing to protect an injury. Fleck misses a sitter. City supporters have rarely been so depressed by a single result.											
34	A	STOCKPORT		14	D	2-2	0-1	Grant 56, Coote 89	Marshall A	Sutch	Segura	Grant	Fleming	Jackson	Forbes*	Kenton	Llewellyn	Carey	Eadie	Coote
	24/2		*7,471*	*6*	42			*Dinning 19, Grant 46*	*Nixon*	*Connelly*	*Woodthorpe*	*Dinning*	*McIntosh*	*Flynn*	*Phillips*	*Cook*	*Angell*	*Grant^*	*Cooper**	*Gannon/Nash*
								Ref: A Robinson	Fleck cries off with a ricked neck - City's 37th injury of the season. Tony Dinning nets a fine volley from 30 yards and Stephen Grant tucks in a second. Peter Grant knocks in Eadie's pass and in the last minute Coote nods home an unexpected equaliser to complete a spirited fightback.											

No	H/A	Opponent	Pos	Res	F-A	H-T	Scorers, Times, and Referees	1	2	3	4	5	6	7	8	9	10	11	subs used
35	H	QP RANGERS	14	D	0-0	0-0		Marshall A	Sutch	Segura	Grant	Fleming	Jackson	Forbes*	Kenton	Llewellyn	Carey	Eadie^	Fleck/Coote
	28/2	12,730	16	43				Harper	Bardsley	Rowland*	Kulcsar	Ready	Morrow	Murray^	Peacock	Dowie	Sheron	Kennedy	Yates/Heinola
							Ref: G Singh	The injury crisis is a major factor in recent results but the fans are an unforgiving lot and it's hard to disagree with them after this dull affair. A match of five yellow cards is enlivened only by the occasional glimpses of cavalier wing-play by Forbes and Rangers' on-loan Mark Kennedy.											
36	H	BIRMINGHAM	14	D	3-3	0-2	Bellamy 47, 68, Llewellyn 58	Marshall A	Sutch	Segura^	Grant	Fleming	Jackson	Forbes	Fleck*	Llewellyn	Carey	Bellamy	Coote/Kenton
	4/3	**9,819**	8	44			Ndlovu 13, 88, Adebola 44	Bennett	Johnson	Charlton	Bruce	Ablett	Marsden	Robinson	McCarthy*	Adebola	Hughes	Ndlovu	Forster
							Ref: A Bates	The lowest home league crowd for 26 years sees Peter Ndlovu head Blues ahead and Dele Adebola add a second as Marshall slips up. Norwich battle back and Bellamy's neat finish is followed by Llewellyn's first senior goal. Bellamy fires a third, but Ndlovu pops up to square it again.											
37	A	BURY	15	L	0-1	0-0		Marshall A	Sutch	Kenton	Grant^	Fleming	Jackson	Forbes"	Fleck*	Llewellyn	Carey	Bellamy	Mills/Coote/Marshall L
	7/3	5,154	17	44			Jemson 60p	Kiely	Rigby	Small	Daws	Luckett	Butler	Jemson*	Patterson	Armstrong	Johnrose^	Matthews"	Battersby/Woodward/Ellis
							Ref: R Pearson	The little Gigg Lane club are holding their own in their first season at this level in nearly 30 years. The pivotal moment comes when Fleck is harshly judged to have handled a cross from Nick Daws. Nigel Jemson tucks the penalty in. A good chance is floated over the bar by Bellamy.											
38	H	WEST BROM	15	D	1-1	1-0	Bellamy 5	Marshall A	Sutch	Kenton	Grant	Fleming	Jackson	Forbes^	Fleck*	Bellamy	Carey	Fugelstad"	Roberts/Marshall L/Llew'yn
	14/3	**19,069**	10	45			Hughes 50	Miller	Holmes*	Van Blerk	Sneekes	Burgess	Beesley	Flynn	Nicol	Hughes	Quinn^	Kilbane	Hamilton/Taylor
							Ref: P Danson	Bellamy gets home fans roaring with a fabulous goal. He nods forward and outstrips the defence in an amazing run before hammering his shot in. Jackson skies a clearance and Lee Hughes manages to head the ball in from out of the grasp of Marshall. Relegation remains a possibility.											
39	A	MIDDLESBROUGH	16	L	0-3	0-1		Marshall A	Sutch	Kenton*	Grant	Fleming	Jackson	Adams	Bellamy	Roberts	Carey	Fugelstad	Forbes
	22/3	30,040	2	45			Maddison 22, Armstrong 71, Beck 90	Beresford	Fleming	Harrison	Festa	Pearson	Emerson*	Ricard	Armstrong	Branca^	Maddison	Thomas	Hignett/Beck
							Ref: F Stretton	The club is still beset by money trouble and Danny Mills is sold to Charlton. Neil Maddison nets a smartly taken effort and Alun Armstrong doubles the lead at a crucial time. Mikkel Beck adds a late third after a real comedy - four separate attempts to clear the ball fail to do the trick.											
40	A	OXFORD	18	L	0-2	0-0		Marshall A	Sutch	Fugelstad	Grant	Fleming	Jackson	Adams	Bellamy	Roberts	Carey^	Forbes*	Polston/**Fenn**
	28/3	7,869	10	45			Francis 64, Beauchamp 80p	Whitehead	Robinson	Marsh	Gray	Davis	Gilchrist	Murphy*	Smith	Francis	Powell^	Beauchamp	Banger/Cook
							Ref: K Leach	It's nip and tuck for more than an hour, but then a Kevin Francis effort sneaks into the net after Jackson leaves the ball alone, thinking that Marshall will collect it. Forbes clips the heels of Nicky Banger and Joey Beauchamp knocks in the penalty. The slide downwards continues.											
41	H	BRADFORD C	20	L	2-3	0-1	Llewellyn 64, Bellamy 89	Marshall A	Sutch	Fugelstad	Grant*	Fleming	Jackson	Adams	Bellamy	Roberts	Fenn	Llewellyn	Eadie
	4/4	13,260	9	45			Jacobs 41, Lawrence 46, Blake 47p	Walsh	McAnespie	Jacobs^	Ramage	Sinnott	Moore	Lawrence	O'Brien	Davies*	Edinho	Blake	Bolland/Bower
							Ref: P Taylor	Things are going badly wrong for Walker and there are some cries for his head. Wayne Jacobs' cross sails straight in and Jamie Lawrence nets a fierce header. Craig Ramage tumbles for a penalty. A mini-revival sees Llewellyn net a superb effort and a mix-up hands Bellamy a second.											
42	A	SHEFFIELD UTD	19	D	2-2	0-2	Bellamy 72, Llewellyn 78	Marshall A	Sutch	Fugelstad	Eadie	Fleming	Jackson	Adams	Bellamy	Roberts	Fenn	Llewellyn	
	11/4	16,915	5	46			Stuart 28, Borbokis 33	Kelly	Borbokis	Nilsen	Quinn	Sandford	Holdsworth	Saunders	Hamilton*	Taylor^	Ford	Stuart	Dellas/Devlin
							Ref: K Lynch	Graham Stuart thumps the Blades ahead and Greek international Vassilis Borbokis curls a fine second. Norwich come back into the game as Bellamy finishes nicely after he is set up by Neale Fenn, on loan from Spurs. A marvellous individual goal by Llewellyn wins a valuable point.											
43	H	HUDDERSFIELD	17	W	**5-0**	2-0	Fleming 12, Adams 30p, Roberts 57, 67, [Fugelstad 90]	Marshall A	Sutch	Fugelstad	Eadie*	Fleming^	Jackson	Adams	Bellamy	Roberts	Fenn	Llewellyn	Segura/Scott
	13/4	16,550	16	49				Harper	Phillips	Edwards	Jenkins	Collins	Gray	Richardson	Horne	Stewart*	Allison	Johnson	Lawson
							Ref: S Bennett	After 14 games without a win, City get off to a great start with Fleming's headed goal and Adams' penalty after Eadie is hauled over. Roberts heads the third from Llewellyn's cross and then grabs his second from an Eadie pull-back. Fugelstad gets on the end of a sweeping late move.											
44	A	STOKE	17	L	0-2	0-1		Marshall A	Sutch	Fugelstad*	Segura^	Scott	Jackson	Adams	Bellamy	Roberts"	Fenn	Llewellyn	Polston/Coote/Grant
	18/4	13,098	21	49			Sigurdsson 19, Lightbourne 50	Southall	Pickering	Tiatto	Sigurdsson	Tweed	Keen	Heath	Wallace	Lightbourne*	Crowe	Kavanagh	Thorne
							Ref: G Cain	Both sides are relegation candidates, but Chris Kamara's team are in the worst trouble. Larus Sigurdsson heads in Graham Kavanagh's cross as the Stokies press hard. Robert Heath's fine cross is converted by Kyle Lightbourne. Veteran Neville Southall saves brilliantly to foil Adams.											
45	H	SWINDON	15	W	**5-0**	2-0	Llewellyn 16, Jackson 34, Roberts 51, [Bellamy 68, Fenn 76]	Marshall A	Sutch	Fugelstad	Milligan"	Scott	Jackson	Adams	Bellamy^	Roberts	Fenn	Llewellyn*	Polston/Coote/Carey
	25/4	18,443	17	52				Digby	Kerslake	Davis	Taylor	Bullock	Borrows	Walters	Watson	Onoura	Ndah*	Robinson^	Cowe/McAreavey
							Ref: T Heilbron	A win will ensure safety. Llewellyn ghosts in to head the first and Jackson rises to make it two. Roberts guides in a free-kick and celebrations intensify. Bellamy calmly slots a fourth and Fenn cracks home a smart fifth. Successive 5-0 wins at home is an unexpected treat for City fans.											
46	A	READING	15	W	1-0	0-0	Bellamy 57	Marshall A	Sutch	Fugelstad	Carey	Scott	Jackson	Adams	Bellamy	Roberts*	Fenn^	Llewellyn	Polston/**Russell**
	3/5	14,817	24	55				Howie	Bernal	Gray	Parkinson	Primus	Kelly^	Meaker*	Caskey	Fleck	O'Neill	Lovell	Lambert/Brayson
	Home	Away					Ref: T Jones	The drop is avoided but the new board expects more than this and Walker departs on 30 April. Reading have lost 14 of their last 16 and are already doomed. Fleck is up against his old mates, but they have the last laugh of a troubled season, courtesy of a swirling shot from Bellamy.											
Average	14,444	14, 156																	

Coca-Cola Cup	Att			F-A	H-T	Scorers, Times, and Referees	1	2	3	4	5	6	7	8	9	10	11	subs used
1:1 H BARNET			W	2-1	2-1	Roberts 13, Adams 37	Marshall A	Fleming*	Segura	Sutch	Scott	Polston	Adams	Fleck	Roberts	Bradshaw	Bellamy	Newman
12/8	5,429					*Polston 35 (og)*	*Harrison*	*Stockley"*	*Harle*	*Heald*	*Howarth*	*Ford*	*Manuel**	*Goodhind*	*Charlery*	*Devine^*	*Mills*	*Wilson/Samuels/McDonald*
						Ref: C Finch	Roberts' first Norwich goal is a thundering header from an Adams free-kick. Marshall fails to reach a corner and the ball ends up hitting the net off Polston. Adams then fires City ahead from 16 yards. New signing Fleming suffers a nasty facial injury and is taken off for dental treatment.											
1:2 A BARNET		24	L	1-3	0-0	Roberts 46	Marshall A	Newman	Segura	Grant	Polston	Sutch	Adams	Fleck*	Roberts	Milligan	Eadie	O'Neill
26/8	*2,846*	*3:7*				*Heald 68, Devine 69, 80*	*Harrison*	*Stockley^*	*Harle*	*Heald*	*Howarth*	*Ford"*	*Manuel**	*Simpson*	*Charlery*	*Devine*	*Wilson*	*Onwere/Goodhind/Mustafa*
						Ref: M Fletcher (Norwich lose 3-4 on aggregate)	Grant looks good in midfield and, after Roberts' goal, City look all set for an easy win. But John Still's men grab three in 12 minutes late in the game to leave City red-faced and humiliated. Greg Heald's header launches the comeback and the winning goal is a tame shot by Sean Devine.											

FA Cup																		
3 A GRIMSBY		12	L	0-3	0-1		Marshall A	Mills	Segura	Grant	Scott	Fleming	Bellamy	Fleck*	Fugelstad	Milligan	O'Neill	Llewellyn
3/1	*8,161*	*2:4*				*McDermott 25, Woods 48, Donovan 76*	*Davison*	*McDermott*	*Gallimore*	*Handyside*	*Rodger*	*Jobling*	*Donovan**	*Black*	*Nogan"*	*Clare^*	*Groves*	*Butterfield/Lever/Woods*
						Ref: M Bailey	Norwich play second fiddle at chilly Blundell Park. John McDermott gets clear and arrows home the first goal. Neil Woods sends a looping header over Marshall. Kevin Donovan hits the third goal after Marshall parries a shot. It's hapless Norwich's second giant-killing of the season.											

	Home						Away					
	P	W	D	L	F	A	W	D	L	F	A	Pts
1 Nott'm For	46	18	2	3	52	20	10	8	5	30	22	94
2 Middlesbro	46	17	4	2	51	12	10	6	7	26	29	91
3 Sunderland	46	14	7	2	49	22	12	5	6	37	28	90
4 Charlton*	46	17	5	1	48	17	9	5	9	32	32	88
5 Ipswich	46	14	5	4	47	20	9	9	5	30	23	83
6 Sheffield Utd	46	16	5	2	44	20	3	12	8	25	34	74
7 Birmingham	46	10	8	5	27	15	9	9	5	33	20	74
8 Stockport	46	14	6	3	46	21	5	2	16	25	48	65
9 Wolves	46	13	6	4	42	25	5	5	13	15	28	65
10 West Brom	46	9	8	6	27	26	7	5	11	23	30	61
11 Crewe	46	10	2	11	30	34	8	3	12	28	31	59
12 Oxford	46	12	6	5	36	20	4	4	15	24	44	58
13 Bradford C	46	10	9	4	26	23	4	6	13	20	36	57
14 Tranmere	46	9	8	6	34	26	5	6	12	20	31	56
15 NORWICH	46	9	8	6	32	27	5	5	13	20	42	55
16 Huddersfield	46	9	5	9	28	28	5	6	12	22	44	53
17 Bury	46	7	10	6	22	22	4	9	10	20	36	52
18 Swindon	46	9	6	8	28	25	5	4	14	14	48	52
19 Port Vale	46	7	6	10	25	24	6	4	13	31	42	49
20 Portsmouth	46	8	6	9	28	30	5	4	14	23	33	49
21 QP Rangers	46	8	9	6	28	21	2	10	11	23	42	49
22 Manchester C	46	6	6	11	28	26	6	6	11	28	31	48
23 Stoke	46	8	5	10	30	40	3	8	12	14	34	46
24 Reading	46	8	4	11	27	31	3	5	15	12	47	42
	1104	262	146	144	835	575	144	146	262	575	835	1510

* promoted after play-offs

Odds & ends

Double wins: (2) Huddersfield, Sunderland.
Double losses: (6) Bradford C, Charlton, Crewe, Middlesbrough, Tranmere, Wolves.

Won from behind: (2) Manchester C (a), Sheffield Utd (h).
Lost from in front: (3) Barnet (a) (LC), Nott'm For (a), Middlesbrough (h).

High points: Two 5-0 wins in April, which staved off relegation.
Successive wins in January against high-flying opposition.
The immense promise shown by youngsters like Craig Bellamy.

Low points: The bad start to the season.
Two humiliating giant-killings in the cups – particularly at Barnet.
The 0-5 hammerings at Ipswich and Wolves.
The crippling series of injuries to key players.
Mike Walker's departure after less than two years back at the club.
The first sub-10,000 crowd for a home league game in 26 years.

Player of the Year: Matt Jackson.
Ever-presents: (0).
Hat-tricks: (0).
Hat-tricks against: (3) Mendonca (v Charlton, h), Freedman (v Nott'm Forest, a), Mathie (v Ipswich, a).
Leading scorer: (13) Craig Bellamy.

	Appearances						Goals			
	Lge	*Sub*	LC	*Sub*	FAC	*Sub*	Lge	LC	FA	Tot
Adams, Neil	**30**		2				**4**	1		**5**
Bellamy, Craig	**30**	*6*	1		1		**13**			**13**
Bradshaw, Carl	**1**		1							
Broughton, Drewe		*1*								
Carey, Shaun	**11**	*3*								
Coote, Adrian	**11**	*12*					**2**			**2**
Eadie, Darren	**18**	*1*	1				**3**			**3**
Fenn, Neale	**6**	*1*					**1**			**1**
Fleck, Robert	**23**	*4*	2		1		**2**			**2**
Fleming, Craig	**20**	*2*	1		1		**1**			**1**
Forbes, Adrian	**28**	*5*					**4**			**4**
Fugelstad, Erik	**23**	*1*			1		**2**			**2**
Grant, Peter	**33**	*2*	1		1		**3**			**3**
Gunn, Bryan	**4**									
Jackson, Matt	**39**	*2*					**3**			**3**
Kenton, Darren	**7**	*4*								
Llewellyn, Chris	**10**	*5*				*1*	**4**			**4**
Marshall, Andy	**42**		2		1					
Marshall, Lee	**2**	*2*								
Milligan, Mike	**20**		1		1					
Mills, Danny	**11**	*9*			1					
Newman, Rob	**10**	*5*	1	*1*						
O'Neill, Keith	**5**	*4*		*1*	1		**1**			**1**
Polston, John	**7**	*5*	2							
Roberts, Iwan	**29**	*2*	2				**5**	2		**7**
Russell, Darel		*1*								
Scott, Kevin	**22**	*2*	1		1					
Segura, Victor	**22**	*3*	2		1					
Simpson, Karl	**2**	*4*								
Sutch, Daryl	**40**		2			*1*	**1**			**1**
(own-goals)							**3**			**3**
30 players used	**506**	***86***	**22**	***2***	**11**	***2***	**52**	**3**		**55**

No	Date		Att	Pos	Pt	F-A	H-T	Scorers, Times, and Referees	1	2	3	4	5	6	7	8	9	10	11	subs used
1	H	CREWE			W	2-1	2-1	Bellamy 31, Kenton 35	Marshall A	Sutch	Kenton	Grant	Fleming	Jackson	Adams	Bellamy	Carey	Eadie	O'Neill	
	8/8		15,016		3			*Rivers 36*	*Kearton*	*Bignot*	*Smith S*	*Lightfoot**	*Walton*	*Wright*	*Lunt*	*Johnson^*	*Rivers*	*Little*	*Street"*	*Unsworth/Charnock/Smith P*
								Ref: S Bennett	New manager Bruce Rioch is delighted as a glorious 40-yard pass from Sutch sees Bellamy time his run to perfection and clip a shot home. Kenton robs Kenny Lunt and cuts in to crash in a great shot. Mark Rivers gets past Jackson and rolls his shot past Marshall and in off a post.											
2	A	STOCKPORT		2	W	2-0	1-0	Bellamy 31, Woodthorpe 74 (og)	Marshall A	Sutch	Kenton	Grant	Fleming	Jackson	Marshall L	Bellamy	Carey*	Eadie	O'Neill"	Milligan^/Llewellyn/Roberts
	15/8		*6,538*	*12*	6				*Nash*	*Phillips**	*Woodthorpe*	*Dinning*	*Flynn*	*Gannon*	*Alsaker^*	*Byrne*	*Angell*	*Cooper*	*Moore*	*Cook/Branch*
								Ref: T Heilbron	Early injury blows hit City with Carey tearing his Achilles tendon and his replacement Milligan damaging a knee. Bellamy takes O'Neill's pass and fires under Carlo Nash. The points are made safe as ex-Canary Colin Woodthrope inadvertently slides Eadie's cross-shot into his own net.											
3	H	QP RANGERS		1	W	4-2	3-2	Bellamy 2, 6p, 57p, Jackson 8	Marshall A	Sutch	Kenton	Grant	Fleming	Jackson	Marshall L	Bellamy	Llewellyn^	Eadie*	O'Neill	Roberts/**Brannan**
	22/8		16,317	*20*	9			*Peacock 4p, Sheron 37*	*Harper*	*Heinola^*	*Rowland*	*Yates**	*Ready*	*Maddix*	*Murray*	*Peacock*	*Sheron*	*Gallen*	*Scully*	*Slade/Rose*
								Ref: P Rejer	An early goal-rush delights the fans. Tony Scully tumbles over Marshall for a penalty equaliser. Antti Heinloa impedes Grant and Norwich go ahead again. Jackson hammers another after a melee. Mike Sheron quietens his barrackers with a fine goal, before another Bellamy spot-kick.											
4	A	WEST BROM		5	L	0-2	0-0		Marshall A	Sutch	Kenton	Grant	Fleming	Jackson	Marshall L	Bellamy	Brannan	Eadie*	O'Neill	Roberts
	29/8		*17,401*	*3*	9			*De Freitas 59, 72*	*Miller*	*Mardon*	*Van Blerk*	*Flynn*	*Murphy"*	*Carbon*	*Quinn**	*Sneekes*	*Evans^*	*Hughes*	*Kilbane*	*Bortolazzi/De Freitas/Burgess*
								Ref: F Stretton	A drab first half ends goalless, but City look livelier after the re-start. However, Denis Smith's side knock the Canaries off the top of the table with two in 13 minutes. Fabian De Freitas nets after the ball is bundled out of Marshall's grasp and then scoops in Jimmy Quinn's knockdown.											
5	A	BARNSLEY		6	W	3-1	0-1	Marshall L 58, Roberts 86, Bellamy 90	Marshall A^	Sutch	Kenton*	Grant	Fleming	Jackson	Marshall L	Bellamy	Roberts	Eadie	Brannan	Llewellyn/**Watt**
	8/9		*15,695*	*7*	12			*Ward 6*	*Watson*	*Eaden*	*Morgan !*	*Richardson**	*Moses*	*Appleby*	*Bullock*	*V der Laan*	*Bullock*	*Ward^*	*Fjortoft*	*Liddell/Sheridan*
								Ref: D Laws	Wearing a garish blue change strip, City fall behind early to ex-Canary Ashley Ward's tap-in. Chris Morgan is sent off for two fouls on lively Bellamy, but City lose keeper Marshall to a back injury. Scot Michael Watt debuts. Lee Marshall nods an equaliser and his lob sets up Roberts.											
6	H	BURY		7	D	0-0	0-0		Marshall A	Sutch	Llewellyn	Grant	Fleming	Jackson*	Marshall L	Bellamy	Roberts	Eadie	Brannan^	Segura/Forbes
	13/9		16,919	*4*	13				*Kiely*	*Woodward*	*Barrick*	*Daws*	*Lucketti*	*Redmond*	*Swailes*	*Matthews**	*D'Jaffo*	*Johnrose*	*Preece*	*Ellis*
								Ref: B Knight	Neil Warnock's team of journeymen have conceded just two goals in their previous seven league games, so a goalless draw was always on the cards. In his first league appearance of the season, Forbes comes under attack from a lunging Andy Woodward, but Bellamy's penalty is saved.											
7	A	SHEFFIELD UTD		11	L	1-2	0-1	Brannan 63	Marshall A	Sutch^	Fugelstad	Grant	Fleming	Segura"	Marshall L	Bellamy	Roberts*	Eadie	Brannan	Llewellyn/Forbes/**Mackay**
	19/9		*16,155*	*6*	13			*Marcelo 27, 72*	*Goram*	*Borbokis*	*Quinn*	*Ford*	*Dellas**	*Sandford*	*Saunders*	*Marker*	*Marcelo^*	*Hamilton*	*Stuart*	*Nilsen/Devlin*
								Ref: G Laws	Marcelo's early penalty is well saved by Marshall. The Brazilian makes up for his miss when his half-hit shot scuttles past the keeper. Brannan, on loan from Manchester C, dives to head Norwich level, but Marcelo has the last laugh, lashing in a corner to win it for Steve Bruce's Blades.											
8	H	BIRMINGHAM		6	W	2-0	0-0	Bellamy 79, Roberts 88	Marshall A	Sutch	Kenton	Grant	Fleming	Mackay	Marshall L	Bellamy	Roberts	Eadie	Brannan*	Forbes
	26/9		16,584	*7*	16				*Bennett*	*Rowett*	*Charlton*	*Marsden*	*Johnson*	*McCarthy*	*O'Connor^*	*Adebola*	*Grainger**	*Ndlovu*	*Ablett*	*Forster/Robinson*
								Ref: M Halsey	Malky Mackay makes his full debut after his £350k capture from Celtic. An entertaining contest is decided by late goals. Eadie's cross is nodded in by Bellamy. Roberts settles the nerves by sidefooting in a free-kick from Eadie. It's a third successive loss for Trevor Francis' side.											
9	H	SUNDERLAND		6	D	2-2	2-1	Eadie 19, Mackay 23	Marshall A	Sutch	Kenton^	Grant	Fleming	Mackay	Marshall L	Bellamy	Roberts	Eadie*	Brannan	Forbes/Fugelstad
	29/9		17,504	*1*	17			*Quinn 2, Marshall A 47 (og)*	*Sorensen*	*Makin*	*Gray*	*Ball*	*Melville*	*Butler*	*Summerbee*	*Rae*	*Dichio*	*Quinn*	*Johnston*	
								Ref: S Baines	Niall Quinn puts the table-toppers ahead after collecting Alex Rae's looping pass. Thomas Sorensen pushes Roberts' effort against a post and Eadie swoops. Mackay pokes in an Eadie cross. Chris Makin's hopeful lofted ball forward is punched into his own net by a red-faced Marshall.											
10	A	PORT VALE		10	L	0-1	0-0		Marshall A	Sutch	Kenton^	Grant	Fleming	Mackay !	Marshall L	Bellamy	Roberts	Eadie	Brannan*	Coote/Fugelstad
	3/10		*5,580*	*20*	17			*Ainsworth 61*	*Musselwhite*	*Walsh*	*Tankard*	*Barker*	*Bennett*	*Beesley*	*Ainsworth*	*Talbot^*	*Beadle*	*Naylor**	*Koordes*	*Bogie/Snijders*
								Ref: P Robinson	A rather flat and lifeless affair at Vale Park. Gareth Ainsworth is stopped in his tracks, but Tony Naylor gathers the ball and returns it back to him and he powers a shot past Marshall. Near the end Mackay kicks out at Ainsworth and gets his marching orders, having been carded earlier.											
11	A	CRYSTAL PALACE		13	L	**1-5**	1-2	Roberts 36 *[Lombardo 79]*	Marshall A	Sutch	Kenton	Grant*	Fleming	Fugelstad	Marshall L	Bellamy^	Roberts	Eadie	Brannan	Adams/Llewellyn
	17/10		*18,100*	*14*	17			*Rizzo 38, Jansen 42, 50, Svensson 48,*	*Digby*	*Jihal*	*Smith*	*Zhiyi*	*Moore*	*Foster"*	*Lombardo*	*Rizzo*	*Svensson^*	*Jansen**	*Mullins*	*Curcic/Butron/Thomson*
								Ref: A Bates	Bellamy chases what looks like a lost cause and his low cross is netted by Roberts. Aussie Nicky Rizzo cancels it out with a 35-yard drive that comes right out of the blue. After this, City crumble and suffer a series of defensive disasters. Skipper Attilio Lombardo cracks a superb fifth.											

12	A	IPSWICH	9	W	1-0	0-0	Bellamy 53	Marshall A	Fugelstad	Kenton	Forbes*	Fleming	Segura^	Marshall L	Bellamy	Roberts	Eadie	Brannan	Sutch/Adams
20/10		22,079	4	20				Wright	Stockwell	Taricco	Clapham	Mowbrey	Venus	Vernazza*	Holland	Johnson	Scowcroft	Petta	Hunt
							Ref: J Kirkby	A deadlocked derby explodes into life when Fugelstad's cross is headed in by Bellamy. It's the first conceded by Ipswich in 410 minutes. Jamie Scowcroft and Roberts both strike the woodwork. This hard-earned win is tainted by serious outbreaks of trouble in and outside the stadium.											
13	H	HUDDERSFIELD	6	W	4-1	3-0	Bellamy 2, 30, Roberts 41, 46	Marshall A	Kenton	Fugelstad	Sutch*	Fleming	Jackson	Marshall L	Bellamy^	Roberts	Eadie	Brannan	Adams/O'Neill
24/10		15,403	3	23			Beresford 59	Vaesen	Jenkins	Edwards	Dyson	Morrison	Gray"	Beresford	Horne	Stewart	Allison^	Phillips*	Browning/Thornley/Barnes
							Ref: P Taylor	Bellamy sprints clear in typical style to net an early goal. He drills home a smart second, but spurns a hat-trick chance by unselfishly setting up Roberts. Bellamy comes off to a huge ovation. Terriers' boss Peter Jackson rues his decision to play three centre-backs against a nippy attack.											
14	A	WATFORD	10	D	1-1	1-1	Eadie 34	Marshall A	Mackay	Fugelstad	Grant	Fleming	Jackson	Marshall L	Bellamy	Roberts	Eadie	Sutch	
3/11		10,011	4	24			Jackson 8 (og)	Chamberlain	Gibbs	Kennedy	Page	Palmer	Robinson	Hazan^	Hyde	N'l-Williams	Johnson	Wright*	Mooney/Gudmundsson
							Ref: T Leake	Jackson slides a Gifton Noel-Williams cross into his own net, in an attempt to intercept it. Marshall, in his 100th game, makes a fine save to prevent another own goal, from Fleming. Mackay is unlucky when his effort hits the bar. Eadie powers forward and cracks in a fine equaliser.											
15	H	BRADFORD C	9	D	2-2	0-1	O'Brien 77 (og), Adams 90p	Marshall A	Sutch	Fugelstad	Grant*	Fleming	Jackson	Marshall L	Bellamy	Roberts	Eadie	Adams	O'Neill
7/11		14,722	7	25			Rankin 19, Mills 88	Walsh	Lawrence	Jacobs	McCall	Moore	O'Brien	Rankin	Blake	Mills	Whalley	Beagrie	
							Ref: A Butler	Isaiah Rankin's shot goes under Marshall. After an hour of toil, Norwich level when O'Brien slices a low cross into his own net. Lee Mills restores the Bantams' lead with a snapshot. After a bout of wrestling between Darren Moore and Roberts, Adams coolly slots in a late penalty.											
16	A	PORTSMOUTH	8	W	2-1	0-1	Roberts 52, Eadie 73	Marshall A	Sutch^	Mackay	Adams	Fleming	Jackson	Marshall L	Bellamy*	Roberts	Eadie	O'Neill	Grant/Llewellyn
10/11		9,335	20	28			Aloisi 29	Knight	Thogersen	Simpson	McLoughlin	Waterman*	Awford	Perrett	Peron	Aloisi	Claridge	Igoe	Phillips
							Ref: E Wolstenholme	Australian John Aloisi swoops at the near post for Pompey. Roberts thrashes in a fine left-foot shot. In all, Roberts hits the woodwork three times and Bellamy once as City chase more goals. Roberts has a magnificent game. City snatch a deserved winner thanks to an Eadie tap-in.											
17	H	WOLVERHAMPTON	8	D	0-0	0-0		Marshall A	Llewellyn	Mackay	Grant	Fleming	Jackson !	Marshall L	Bellamy*	Roberts	Eadie	Adams	O'Neill
14/11		17,275	7	29				Stowell	Atkins	Naylor	Richards	Emblen	Curle	Corica	Robinson	Connolly	Whit'gham*	Osborn	Keane
							Ref: P Richards	Jackson is sent off after tangling with Lee Naylor. The officials believe he stamped on the full-back, but Jackson claims he was hurdling over him as he got up. A potential ban is later lifted after the video is studied. Mackay and Fleming put in fine displays in a game of few chances.											
18	A	TRANMERE	6	W	3-1	2-0	O'Neill 10, Bellamy 39, Roberts 83	Marshall A	Kenton	Mackay	Grant	Fleming	Jackson	Marshall L	Bellamy	Roberts	O'Neill	Adams	
21/11		6,319	19	32			Irons 50	Achterberg	Allen	Thompson	Mahon	Challinor	Irons	Morrissey^	Santos	Kelly	Mellon*	Taylor	Parkinson/Gibson
							Ref: T Jones	O'Neill calmly lofts the ball into the net over Dave Challinor and John Achterberg after a Bellamy raid causes havoc. Bellamy taps a second after another Challinor misjudgement. Kenny Irons lashes in a poor punch by Marshall. Mackay's knock-down sets up Roberts for a late third.											
19	H	OXFORD	7	L	1-3	1-2	Bellamy 3	Marshall A	Kenton	Mackay	Grant^	Fleming	Jackson	Marshall L*	Bellamy	Roberts	O'Neill	Adams	Forbes/Russell
29/11		17,851	18	32			Wilsterman 34, Windass 45, Thoms'n 48	Whitehead	Robinson	Marsh	Gray	Wilsterman	Gilchrist	Murphy	Smith	Thompson*	Windass	Powell	Banger
							Ref: M Pierce	A great start as Bellamy slots in Jackson's pass. Brian Wilsterman nods in a corner after it is missed by Marshall. The keeper saves an Andy Thomson effort, but Dean Windass is on hand to net the rebound. Les Robinson heads the ball on for Thomson to put Norwich further behind.											
20	H	GRIMSBY	4	W	3-1	1-0	Adams 11, Roberts 80, Bellamy 84	Watt	Kenton	Mackay	Grant	Fleming	Jackson	Marshall L	Bellamy	Roberts	O'Neill	Adams	
2/12		12,024	12	35			Smith D 83	Davison	McDermott	Gallimore	Handyside	Black*	Widdrington	Clare"	Smith D	Ashcroft^	Lester	Groves	Coldicott/Nogan/Donovan
							Ref: B Burns	Bellamy sets up Adams, who cracks home an 18-yard drive. Roberts prods in an O'Neill cross with ten minutes left, to spark a three-goal burst. David Smith pulls one back for Alan Buckley's men with a rising drive. Lee Marshall lobs into the path of Bellamy who cracks home another.											
21	A	SWINDON	4	D	1-1	1-1	Roberts 17	Watt	Kenton	Mackay	Grant	**Wilson**	Jackson	Marshall L	Bellamy	Roberts	Russell	Llewellyn	
5/12		9,262	19	36			Walters 41	Talia	Robinson	Hall^	Leitch	Willis	Borrows	Walters*	Watson	Onoura	Fenn"	Davis	Bullock/Taylor/Hay
							Ref: B Coddington	A very young-looking Norwich side takes the lead when Roberts rises high to head home a Llewellyn free-kick. After a clever run, winger Mark Walters fires the equaliser. Bellamy misses three reasonable opportunities. Club chairman Barry Lockwood is succeeded by Bob Cooper.											
22	A	WOLVERHAMPTON	6	D	2-2	1-0	Adams 31p, Roberts 60	Watt	Kenton	Mackay	Grant	Wilson^	Jackson	Adams	Bellamy*	Roberts	Russell	Llewellyn"	Eadie/Marshall L/Segura
12/12		21,014	12	37			Keane 84, 89	Stowell	Muscat	Naylor	Richards	Sedgley"	Curle	Corica	Robinson	Whit'gham^	Keane	Osborn*	Emblen/Connolly/Gilkes
							Ref: J Kirkby	Dean Richards climbs over Roberts and City go ahead from the spot. Roberts' downward header makes it two. Kevin Muscat's dreadful lunge at Bellamy goes unpunished and inflicts a gash needing ten stitches. Furious City crumble - Robbie Keane lashes a shot in, then nods a second.											
23	H	BRISTOL C	5	W	2-1	2-1	Roberts 18, 36	Watt	Kenton	Mackay	Grant	Wilson	Jackson	Adams*	Eadie	Roberts	Russell^	Llewellyn	Sutch/Marshall L
19/12		17,022	23	40			Akinbiyi 20	Phillips	Brennan	Bell	Hutchings	Shail	Carey	Edwards*	Thorpe	Akinbiyi	Murray	Goodridge^	Andersen/Torpey
							Ref: J Brandwood	Adams' superb volleyed pass to Llewellyn is crossed for Roberts to head in. Ex-Canary Ade Akinbiyi strokes an equaliser as the Bristolians respond instantly. An Adams corner is headed down powerfully by Jackson and as it bounces up Roberts calmly guides it home with his head.											

No	Date		Att	Pos	Pt	F-A	H-T	Scorers, Times, and Referees	1	2	3	4	5	6	7	8	9	10	11	subs used
24	A	QP RANGERS		8	L	0-2	0-2		Watt	Kenton^	Mackay	Grant	Wilson	Jackson	Adams	Marshall L*	Roberts	Coote"	Llewellyn	Fleming/Forbes/Russell
	26/12		*15,251*	*18*	40			*Murray 11, Peacock 18*	*Miklosko*	*Heinola*	*Barrowcl'gh*	*Morrow*	*Ready*	*Maddix*	*Rose*	*Peacock*	*Sheron**	*Gallen*	*Murray*	*Steiner*
								Ref: A Wiley	It's the same old story for City as promising pre-Christmas form evaporates over the holiday period. Paul Murray's volley from a Kevin Gallen cross bounces into the net. Gavin Peacock nets an inch-perfect drive. Rioch brings on subs and changes his formation early, but to little effect.											
25	H	WATFORD		7	D	1-1	0-0	Roberts 54	Watt	Sutch	Fugelstad	Grant	Mackay	Jackson	Adams	Marshall L	Roberts	Eadie	Llewellyn	
	29/12		19,259	*5*	41			*Palmer 81*	*Chamberlain*	*Bazeley*	*Kennedy*	*Page*	*Palmer*	*Iroha"*	*Smart^*	*Hyde*	*N'l-Williams*	*Johnson*	*Gudm'ds'n**	*Mooney/Rosenthal/Robinson*
								Ref: C Wilkes	Two of the leading sides go head to head, but this is certainly no classic. City take the lead when Eadie whips in a good cross and Roberts chests it over the line. Watt claws a Peter Kennedy free-kick off Tommy Mooney's head, but it falls nicely for Steve Palmer to drill into goal.											
26	A	CREWE		10	L	2-3	2-0	Llewellyn 10, Marshall L 33	Watt	Sutch	Fugelstad	Grant	Mackay	Jackson	Adams	Marshall L	Roberts	Eadie	Llewellyn*	Coote
	9/1		*4,782*	*24*	41			*Street 82, 90, Rivers 87*	*Kearton*	*Bignot*	*Smith S*	*Foran*	*Walton*	*Wright*	*Charnock^*	*Johnson*	*Jack*	*Little"*	*Rivers**	*Lunt/Unsworth/Street*
								Ref: P Walton	Llewellyn's tap-in and Lee Marshall's smart finish subdue lowly Crewe. City are cruising until an astonishing collapse in the closing minutes. Kevin Street leaps to volley in and Mark Rivers nets Seth Johnson's centre. Three minutes into added time Street scores after a hectic scramble.											
27	H	WEST BROM		9	D	1-1	0-0	Marshall L 78	Marshall A	Sutch	Fugelstad	Wilson	Fleming	Jackson	Adams	Marshall L	Roberts	Eadie	Llewellyn	
	16/1		15,411	*8*	42			*Bortolazzi 50*	*Whitehead*	*Holmes*	*Porter*	*Bortolazzi**	*Murphy*	*Carbon*	*Quinn*	*Sneekes*	*De Freitas*	*Hughes*	*Flynn^*	*Angel/Maresca*
								Ref: B Burns	Llewellyn cheekily heads the ball out of Phil Whitehead's hands and scores, but the whistle sounds and he is booked. Mario Bortolazzi lashes a free-kick goalwards from 35 yards and it flies in after a deflection. Denis Smith's men are pegged back when Lee Marshall prods the equaliser.											
28	A	BOLTON		11	L	0-2	0-1		Marshall A	Wilson	Kenton	Sutch	Fleming	Jackson	Adams	Marshall L*	Llewellyn^	O'Neill		Grant/Bellamy
	30/1		*17,269*	*3*	42			*Holdsworth 38, Cox 65*	*Jaaskalainen*	*Cox*	*Whitlow*	*Frandsen"*	*Warhurst^*	*Fish*	*Johansen*	*Jensen*	*Holdsw'th**	*Taylor*	*Sellars*	*Gunlaugsson/Elliott/Gardner*
								Ref: F Stretton	Looking offside, Dean Holdsworth sweeps a Claus Jensen cross past Marshall. Llewellyn is guilty of a glaring miss. Neil Cox takes advantage of a deflection into his path to knock home the clincher. Bellamy returns after his Muscat-inflicted absence. Kevin Scott departs for Darlington.											
29	H	STOCKPORT		12	L	0-2	0-2		Marshall A	Wilson	Kenton"	Grant^	Fleming	Jackson	Adams*	Bellamy	Roberts	Sutch	O'Neill	Marshall L/Llewellyn/Mackay
	6/2		14,675	*17*	42			*Angell 9, Wilson 36 (og)*	*Nash*	*Gannon*	*Byrne D*	*Smith*	*Flynn*	*McIntosh*	*Matthews**	*Hughes*	*Angell*	*Ellis*	*Woodthorpe*	*Travis*
								Ref: D Crick	Gary Megson has an enjoyable return to Carrow Road as City's depressing slide goes on. Brett Angell taps in a Tony Ellis cross. Rob Matthews robs Kenton and his cross is turned into his own goal by Wilson. Martin McIntosh impedes Roberts, but O'Neill slides the penalty-kick wide.											
30	H	BARNSLEY		12	D	0-0	0-0		Marshall A	Sutch	Fugelstad	Grant	Fleming	Jackson	Marshall L	Bellamy	Roberts	Llewellyn	Forbes	
	16/2		13,232	*13*	43				*Bullock*	*Eaden*	*De Zeeuw*	*Richardson*	*Tinkler*	*Appleby*	*Sheridan*	*Jones*	*Turner*	*Dyer*	*Hignett*	
								Ref: P Rejer	Another frustrating 90 minutes for Canaries fans. Forbes has a lively game on the wing, but Roberts, Llewellyn and Lee Marshall all waste good chances. The club gets a £1 million windfall after Tim Sherwood is sold on by Blackburn, but the board says it won't be available for transfers.											
31	A	BURY		10	W	2-0	1-0	Bellamy 29, Fleming 72	Marshall A	Sutch	Fugelstad^	Grant*	Fleming	Jackson	Marshall L	Bellamy	Roberts	Llewellyn	Forbes"	Mackay/Wilson/Russell
	20/2		***4,285***	*22*	46				*Kiely*	*Woodward*	*Serrant*	*Daws"*	*Lucketti*	*Bullock !*	*Swailes*	*Patterson*	*Jemson^*	*Hall*	*D'Jaffo**	*Preece/Littlejohn/West*
								Ref: M Warren	The Shakers' uncompromising midfielder Darren Bullock gets his marching orders after hurdling over the fallen Grant and catching him in the face with his studs. Forbes' low drive is blocked by Dean Kiely, but the rebound flies in off Bellamy. Fleming joyfully nods in a corner-kick.											
32	H	SHEFFIELD UTD		10	D	1-1	1-0	Llewellyn 20	Marshall A	Sutch	Fugelstad	Grant	Fleming	Jackson	Marshall L	Bellamy	Roberts	Llewellyn*	Forbes	O'Neill
	27/2		14,224	*11*	47			*Devlin 55*	*Kelly*	*Derry*	*Quinn**	*Woodhouse*	*Holdsworth*	*Sandford*	*Morris*	*Jacobsen*	*Marcelo*	*Devlin*	*Ford*	*Henry*
								Ref: P Jones	Blades boss Steve Bruce and assistant John Deehan are welcomed back to their old stamping ground. Grant's looping pass to the far post is netted by Llewellyn. Paul Devlin cracks a shot past Marshall with the aid of a big deflection. Lee Sandford hooks a Roberts effort off the line.											
33	A	BIRMINGHAM		11	D	0-0	0-0		Marshall A	Sutch	Fugelstad*	Grant	Fleming	Jackson	Marshall L	Bellamy	Roberts	O'Neill	Forbes^	Llewellyn/Wilson
	2/3		*20,749*	*5*	48				*Poole*	*Bass*	*Charlton*	*Rowett*	*Johnson*	*McCarthy**	*O'Connor*	*Furlong^*	*Hughes*	*Ndlovu*	*Hyde !*	*Adebola/Robinson*
								Ref: A D'Urso	On a miserable wet night at St Andrews, Norwich's outside hopes of a play-off place are kept alive. Andy Marshall keeps his third clean sheet in four matches. Mr D'Urso brandishes his cards freely and Graham Hyde is unlucky to get marching orders for two relatively minor offences.											
34	A	SUNDERLAND		12	L	0-1	0-1		Marshall A	Sutch	Fugelstad	Grant^	Fleming	Jackson	Marshall L	Bellamy*	Roberts	Wilson	O'Neill	Llewellyn/Russell
	6/3		***39,004***	*1*	48			*Phillips 7*	*Sorensen*	*Makin*	*Gray*	*Ball**	*Melville*	*Butler*	*Summerbee*	*Williams*	*Phillips*	*Quinn*	*Johnston*	*McCann*
								Ref: D Pugh	Peter Reid's runaway leaders never look in trouble from the moment Kevin Phillips arrows a fierce shot onto the corner of Norwich's net in the early stages. It was set up by a clever backheel by Darren Williams. Marshall has a good game and restricts the champions-elect to one goal.											

No	Venue / Date	Opponent	Att	Pos	Res / Pts	F-A	H-T	Scorers, Times, and Referees	1	2	3	4	5	6	7	8	9	10	11	Subs used
35	H	PORT VALE		12	L	3-4	1-2	Fleming 30, Roberts 68, Bellamy 83	Marshall A	Sutch	Fugelstad*	Grant	Fleming !	Jackson	Marshall L	Bellamy	Roberts	Wilson	O'Neill	Llewellyn
	9/3		12,960	20	48			Tank' 14, Russell 35, Walsh 50, Bogie 87	Musselwhite	Walsh	Tankard*	Bogie	Aspin	Gardiner	Barker	Talbot	Bent^	Beesley	Russell	Barnett/Lee
								Ref: B Knight	City have a dreadful first half, but the tide turns and they roar back from 1-3 down, only to toss it all away at the death. Fleming is sent off for deliberate handball. Play-off hopes disappear when Allen Tankard finds Ian Bogie in space and he picks his spot to steal an unlikely winner.											
36	A	BRADFORD C		12	L	1-4	0-4	Roberts 48 [Lawrence 45]	Marshall A	Sutch	Wilson	Grant*	Fleming	Mackay	Marshall L	Bellamy	Roberts	Milligan	O'Neill^	Llewellyn/Forbes
	13/3		13,331	3	48			Moore 13, Beagrie 25p, Mills 34,	Walsh	Todd*	Jacobs	McCall	Moore	Dreyer !	Lawrence	Blake^	Mills	Whalley	Beagrie	O'Brien/Windass
								Ref: A Wiley	Rioch recalls Milligan and tries Lee Marshall at sweeper. It all goes horribly wrong. Darren Moore nets a free header. Lee Mills' header and then Jamie Lawrence's solo run see City four-down by the break. Roberts pulls one back with a header and John Dreyer is sent off for a foul.											
37	H	PORTSMOUTH		13	D	0-0	0-0		Marshall A	Sutch	Wilson	Russell	Fleming	Jackson	Forbes	Bellamy	Roberts*	Marshall L	Llewellyn	Coote
	20/3		16,662	16	49				Knight	Robinson	Simpson	McLoughlin	Whitbread	Waterman	Claridge	Peron	Miglioranzi	Durnin	Igoe	
								Ref: K Hill	Winger O'Neill signs for Middlesbrough for £1 million. Pompey boss Alan Ball complains about the state of the pitch after this very lacklustre affair. Rioch turns to youth and City end the game with seven players of 20 or under. New boy Darel Russell nearly scores after a fine solo run.											
38	A	HUDDERSFIELD		12	D	1-1	1-0	Russell 3	Marshall A !	Sutch	Wilson	Russell	Fleming	Jackson	Forbes^	Bellamy	Roberts	Marshall L	Llewellyn*	Carey/**Hughes**
	24/3		9,717	8	50			Hughes 83 (og)	Vaesen	Edmondson*	Edwards	Johnson	Armstrong	Gray	Beresford^	Hamilton	Stewart	Allison	Thornley	Facey/Baldry
								Ref: R Pearson	Russell charges down a Nico Vaesen clearance and coolly tucks it in. Five minutes later keeper Marshall is red-carded after a mistimed lunge at Marcus Stewart. Sutch goes in goal and has a magnificent match. He keeps everything out until Ben Thornley's corner ricochets past him.											
39	H	CRYSTAL PALACE		14	L	0-1	0-1		Marshall A	Sutch	Wilson	Russell	Mackay	Jackson	Marshall L*	Bellamy	Roberts	Hughes^	Llewellyn"	Forbes/**Mulryne/Dalglish**
	3/4		16,754	10	50			Austin 13	Miller	Jihai^	Frampton	Austin	Woozley	Foster	Thomson	Zhiyi	Martin	Morrison*	Mullins	Carlisle/Hibburt
								Ref: A Hall	Craig Foster's hopeful forward ball is nodded home by Dean Austin. Three players make their home debuts for City and there are encouraging signs for the home fans, despite the lack of goals. Mulryne (ex-Manchester U) and Dalglish (ex-Newcastle) both have Premiership experience.											
40	A	GRIMSBY		12	W	1-0	1-0	Mulryne 35	Marshall A	Sutch	Fugelstad	Russell	Mackay	Jackson	**Anselin**	Bellamy	Dalglish*	Mulryne	Carey	Roberts
	5/4		6,302	13	53				Love	McDermott	Gallimore	Livingstone	Lever^	Coldicott	Donovan	Nogan	Ashcroft"	Lester*	Groves	Black/Burnett/Clare
								Ref: T Heilbron	Carey hits the post early at Blundell Park with a low volley. After a Steve Livingstone foul, new boy Mulryne steps up and sweeps in a superb free-kick past young keeper Andrew Love. Bellamy clips the bar with a fine shot. City fans celebrate as the run of eight without a win ends.											
41	H	IPSWICH		11	D	0-0	0-0		**Green**	Sutch	Fugelstad	Mackay	Fleming	Jackson*	Anselin	Bellamy	Carey	Mulryne	Dalglish^	Marshall L/Roberts
	11/4		**19,511**	2	54				Wright	Wilnis	Tanner*	Clapham	Mowbray	Venus	Stockwell	Holland	Johnson	Scowcroft	Magilton	Cundy
								Ref: P Taylor	Teenage keeper Robert Green is plunged into the fray for his senior debut. He has a fine game against promotion-chasers Ipswich, who posed Norwich problems. David Johnson misses a sitter and Mick Stockwell is halted by a whistle when the advantage rule should have been applied.											
42	H	TRANMERE		13	D	2-2	1-1	Bellamy 15, Mulryne 62	Green	Sutch	Fugelstad	Mackay	Marshall L	Hughes*	Anselin^	Bellamy	Roberts	Mulryne	Russell	Carey/Dalglish
	17/4		14,735	15	55			Kelly 9, Hill 75	Achterberg	Allen	Hill	McGreal	Challinor	Irons	Taylor*	Santos	Mahon	Kelly	Koumas^	Jones/O'Brien
								Ref: R Furnandiz	The game is preceded by a lap of honour by the re-united 1959 FA Cup semi-final team, to mark the 40th anniversary. Sloppy defending lets in David Kelly, but Hughes neatly sets up Bellamy. Mulryne's assured second-half strike is cancelled out as Clint Hill nets Georges Santos' flick.											
43	H	BOLTON		12	D	2-2	2-0	Roberts 3, 5	Marshall A	Sutch	Fugelstad	Marshall L	Mackay	Jackson*	Anselin	Carey	Roberts	Dalglish^	Llewellyn"	Fleming/Bellamy/Russell
	20/4		**11,137**	5	56			Cox 48, Frandsen 74	Banks	Cox	Phillips	Frandsen	Warhurst	Fish	Johansen	Jensen	Gudjohnsen	Taylor	Gardner	
								Ref: A D'Urso	The new-look side gets off to a superb start against Colin Todd's promotion-chasers. Roberts rises high to head in Dalglish's cross, then he nets a fierce 12-yard drive from Dalglish's cut-back. Neil Cox's hopeful effort squeezes in and later Per Frandsen muscles in to force an equaliser.											
44	A	OXFORD		9	W	4-2	1-1	Anselin 34, Roberts 65, Fleming 70,	Marshall A	Sutch"	Fugelstad	Carey	Mackay	Fleming	Anselin*	Bellamy	Roberts^	Mulryne	Llewellyn	Marshall L/Coote/Wilson
	24/4		7,345	23	59			Wilsterman 29, Francis 77 [Bellamy 88]	Lundin	Robinson	Powell	Gray	Watson	Gilchrist^	Banger	Tait	Weath'st'ne*	Murphy"	Beauchamp	Thomson/Wilsterman/Francis
								Ref: G Cain	Brian Wilsterman heads home and Malcolm Shotton's side hit the woodwork twice in the first half. Anselin nets a deft lob from 30 yards and races over for 'high fives' with the manager. Roberts nets after Lee Marshall hits the bar and Bellamy's flicked header clinches a welcome win.											
45	H	SWINDON		9	W	2-1	0-0	Roberts 62, Hughes 90	Marshall A	Sutch"	Fugelstad*	Carey^	Mackay	Fleming	Anselin	Coote	Roberts	Mulryne	Llewellyn	Jackson/Marshall L/Hughes
	1/5		17,306	17	62			Onoura 47p	Talia	Linton	Hall	Watson	Robinson	Borrows	Howe^	Ndah	Onoura	Hay*	Taylor	Bradley/McAreavey
								Ref: G Frankland	Bobby Howe falls over the keeper for Iffy Onoura to net a penalty. Roberts goes round Frank Talia to drill an equaliser. Loanee Hughes cracks in a superb acrobatic vollley to win the points in the last minute. It's the first home victory for nearly five months and is rapturously received.											
46	A	BRISTOL C		9	L	0-1	0-1		Marshall A	Sutch	Fugelstad	Marshall L	Jackson	Mackay	Anselin*	Bellamy	Roberts	Mulryne	Llewellyn	Carey
	9/5		11,362	24	62			Pinamonte 40	Phillips	Brennan	Bell*	Jordan	Sebok	Carey	Goodridge^	Doherty	Akinbiyi	Pinamonte	Brown	Andersen/Meechan
		Home	Away					Ref: M Halsey	Roberts misses an open goal after a defensive mix-up. Lorenzo Pinamonte nets on his debut after Ade Akinbiyi's downward header finds him from a corner. The home side have had an awful season under Benny Lennartsson, but this rare victory sees them celebrating in defiant style.											
	Average	15,761	12,801																	

Worthington Cup			Att			F-A	H-T	Scorers, Times, and Referees	1	2	3	4	5	6	7	8	9	10	11	subs used
1:1	A	SWANSEA			D	1-1	0-0	Bellamy 76	Marshall A	Marshall L	Kenton	Grant	Fleming^	Jackson	Adams	Bellamy	Carey	Eadie*	O'Neill	Roberts/Scott
	11/8		*3,803*					*Cusack 88*	*Freestone*	*Price*	*Howard*	*Cusack*	*Smith*	*Bound*	*O'Gorman^*	*Thomas*	*Alsop*	*Watkin*	*Coates**	*Roberts/Casey*
								Ref: N Fletcher	Roger Freestone hauls down Eadie, but Adams' spot-kick is saved - his first miss in 13 attempts for City. Bellamy breaks the deadlock when his shot is deflected in off Jason Smith. Nick Cusack equalises late on when he volleys home from ten yards after a cross from Stuart Roberts.											
1:2	H	SWANSEA		2	W	1-0	0-0	Roberts 91	Marshall A	Marshall L	Kenton	Grant	Fleming	Jackson	Sutch	Bellamy	Llewellyn	Eadie	O'Neill*	Roberts
	18/8		13,146	*3:8*		*aet*			*Freestone*	*Price*	*Howard*	*Cusack*	*Smith*	*Bound*	*Casey^*	*Thomas**	*Alsop*	*Watkin"*	*Coates*	*Bird/Jenkins/Roberts*
								Ref: A Butler (Norwich win 2-1 on aggregate)	John Hollins' men cling on gamely as they come under siege. City's finishing isn't up to scratch and shots galore go off target. A Lee Marshall header hits the crossbar. The tie goes into extra-time and within seconds sub Roberts finds the net, flicking in a header from Llewellyn's cross.											
2:1	H	WIGAN		7	W	1-0	1-0	Bradshaw 22 (og)	Marshall A	Marshall L	Kenton	Grant	Fleming	Segura	Sutch	Bellamy	Llewellyn*	Eadie	Roberts^	Forbes/Coote
	16/9		11,426	*2:19*					*Carroll*	*Green*	*Bradshaw*	*Griffiths*	*McGibbon*	*Rogers*	*Lee*	*Greenall*	*Lowe*	*Martinez*	*Barlow**	*Warne*
								Ref: D Crick	As with Swansea, City struggle to break down a dogged lower division defence. City enjoy plenty of possession, but find Ray Mathias' side in mean mood. The only goal of a dull affair comes when Bellamy's low shot is sliced into the roof of his own net by ex-Canary Carl Bradshaw.											
2:2	A	WIGAN		11	W	3-2	2-0	Bellamy 10, Roberts 37, 66	Marshall A	Marshall L*	Kenton	Grant	Fleming	Mackay	Sutch	Bellamy	Brannan	Eadie	Roberts	Forbes
	22/9		*3,402*	*2:17*				*Griffiths 78, Barlow 89*	*Carroll*	*Green*	*Jenkinson**	*Griffiths*	*Balmer*	*Rogers*	*Lee*	*Greenall*	*Lowe*	*O'Neill*	*Barlow*	*Smeets*
								Ref: K Lynch (Norwich win 4-2 on aggregate)	Bellamy's re-taken free-kick is deflected past Roy Carroll. Scott Green's blunder sets up Roberts, who later makes it three with a near-post header. City inevitably take their foot off the pedal with a 4-0 aggregate lead and Wigan hit back with late goals, which leaves Rioch furious.											
3	H	BOLTON		6	L	1-1	0-0	O'Neill 104	Marshall A	Marshall L	Kenton	Fugelstad	Fleming	Jackson*	Sutch	Bellamy	Adams^	Eadie	Roberts	Mackay/O'Neill
	27/10		14,189	*7*				*Elliott 96*	*Branagan*	*Aljofree*	*Phillips*	*Todd*	*Bergsson*	*Fish*	*Johansen*	*Jensen*	*Blake^*	*Elliott*	*Gunlaugs'n**	*Holdsworth/Taylor B*
								Ref: T Heilbron (Norwich lose 1-3 on penalties)	O'Neill cancels out a stunning opening goal in extra-time by Robbie Elliott. The tie goes to penalties. Bellamy skies his over, but Marshall saves Bolton's first effort. The visitors net their next three, but after Roberts scores for Norwich, Fleming's is saved and Fugelstad's goes over.											

FA Cup																				
3	A	SHEFFIELD WED		7	L	1-4	1-3	Roberts 45 *[Stefanovic 73]*	Watt	Marshall L*	Sutch	Grant	Fugelstad	Mackay^	Jackson	Adams	Llewellyn	Eadie	Roberts	Forbes/Fleming
	3/1		*18,737*	*P:15*				*Humphreys 18, 33, Rudi 40,*	*Srnicek*	*Atherton*	*Hinchcliffe*	*Stefanovic*	*Emerson^*	*Walker*	*Jonk**	*Carbone*	*Humphreys*	*Rudi*	*Alexanders'n*	*Sonner/Briscoe*
								Ref: P Rejer	A large City following heads for Hillsborough, but the tie is lost in the first half. Benito Carbone sets up Richie Humphreys for the first two and Petter Rudi squeezes the ball past brave Watt. Roberts nets a near-post header from a corner, but Dejan Stefanovic scrambles in the fourth.											

		Home					Away					
	P	W	D	L	F	A	W	D	L	F	A	Pts
1 Sunderland	46	19	3	1	50	10	12	9	2	41	18	105
2 Bradford C	46	15	4	4	48	20	11	5	7	34	27	87
3 Ipswich	46	16	1	6	37	15	10	7	6	32	17	86
4 Birmingham	46	12	7	4	32	15	11	5	7	34	22	81
5 Watford *	46	12	8	3	30	19	9	6	8	35	37	77
6 Bolton	46	13	6	4	44	25	7	10	6	34	34	76
7 Wolves	46	11	10	2	37	19	8	6	9	27	24	73
8 Sheffield Utd	46	12	6	5	42	29	6	7	10	29	37	67
9 NORWICH	46	7	12	4	34	28	8	5	10	28	33	62
10 Huddersfield	46	11	9	3	38	23	4	7	12	24	48	61
11 Grimsby	46	11	6	6	25	18	6	4	13	15	34	61
12 West Brom	46	12	4	7	43	33	4	7	12	26	43	59
13 Barnsley	46	7	9	7	35	30	7	8	8	24	26	59
14 Crys Palace	46	11	10	2	43	26	3	6	14	15	45	58
15 Tranmere	46	8	7	8	37	30	4	13	6	26	31	56
16 Stockport	46	7	9	7	24	21	5	8	10	25	39	53
17 Swindon	46	7	8	8	40	44	6	3	14	19	37	50
18 Crewe	46	7	6	10	27	35	5	6	12	27	43	48
19 Portsmouth	46	10	5	8	34	26	1	9	13	23	47	47
20 QP Rangers	46	9	7	7	34	22	3	4	16	18	39	47
21 Port Vale	46	10	3	10	22	28	3	5	15	23	47	47
22 Bury	46	9	7	7	24	27	1	10	12	11	33	47
23 Oxford	46	7	8	8	31	30	3	6	14	17	41	44
24 Bristol C	46	7	8	8	35	36	2	7	14	22	44	42
	1104	250	163	139	846	609	139	163	250	609	846	1493

* promoted
after play-offs

Odds & ends

Double wins: (1) Grimsby.
Double losses: (2) Crystal Palace, Port Vale.

Won from behind: (4) Barnsley (a), Oxford (a), Portsm'th (a), Swind'n (h).
Lost from in front: (3) Crewe (a), Oxford (h), C Palace (a)..

High points: The goalscoring form of Iwan Roberts.
The away win at Ipswich in October.
Stand-in Daryl Sutch's goalkeeping heroics at Huddersfield.
Paul Hughes' winning goal against Swindon in May.
The rise in home league crowds of nearly 10%.

Low points: Sliding down the table after reaching fourth in December.
The run of 11 home games (19 weeks) without a win.
Miserable home defeats by Port Vale and Gary Megson's Stockport.
Collapsing at Crewe after being 2-0 up with eight minutes left.
The 'tackle' at Wolves put Craig Bellamy out for seven weeks.

Player of the Year: Iwan Roberts.
Ever-presents: (0).
Hat-tricks: (1) Craig Bellamy (v QPR, h).
Hat-tricks against: (0).
Leading scorer: (23) Iwan Roberts.

	Appearances						Goals			
	Lge	*Sub*	LC	*Sub*	FAC	*Sub*	Lge	LC	FAC	Tot
Adams, Neil	**15**	*3*	2		1		**3**			**3**
Anselin, Cedric	**7**						**1**			**1**
Bellamy, Craig	**38**	*2*	5				**17**	2		**19**
Brannan, Ged	**10**	*1*	1				**1**			**1**
Carey, Shaun	**7**	*2*	1							
Coote, Adrian	**2**	*4*		*1*						
Dalglish, Paul	**3**	*2*								
Eadie, Darren	**21**	*1*	5		1		**3**			**3**
Fleming, Craig	**35**	*2*	5			*1*	**3**			**3**
Forbes, Adrian	**7**	*8*		*2*		*1*				
Fugelstad, Erik	**22**	*2*	1		1					
Grant, Peter	**31**	*2*	4		1					
Green, Robert	**2**									
Hughes, Paul	**2**	*2*					**1**			**1**
Jackson, Matt	**36**	*1*	3		1		**1**			**1**
Kenton, Darren	**22**		5				**1**			**1**
Llewellyn, Chris	**21**	*10*	2	*1*	1		**2**			**2**
Mackay, Malky	**24**	*4*	1	*1*	1		**1**			**1**
Marshall, Andy	**37**		5							
Marshall, Lee	**38**	*6*	5		1		**3**			**3**
Milligan, Mike	**1**	*1*		*1*						
Mulryne, Phil	**6**	*1*					**2**			**2**
O'Neill, Keith	**14**	*4*	2	*1*			**1**	1		**2**
Roberts, Iwan	**40**	*5*	3	*2*	1		**19**	3	1	**23**
Russell, Darel	**8**	*5*					**1**			**1**
Scott, Kevin				*1*						
Segura, Victor	**2**	*2*	1							
Sutch, Daryl	**34**	*2*	4		1					
Watt, Michael	**7**	*1*			1					
Wilson, Che	**14**	*3*								
(own-goals)							**2**	1		**3**
30 players used	**506**	***76***	**55**	***10***	**11**	***2***	**62**	**7**	**1**	**70**

No	Date		Att	Pos	Pt	F-A	H-T	Scorers, Times, and Referees	SQUAD NUMBERS IN USE											subs used
1	A	WEST BROM		11	D	1-1	0-0	Dalglish 49	Marshall A	Sutch	Fugelstad	Fleming	Jackson	Mulryne	**De Blasiis**	Llewellyn*	Roberts	Dalglish	Anselin	Marshall L
	7/8		*16,196*	*12*	1			*Raven 73*	*Miller*	*Gabbidon**	*Potter*	*Flynn*	*Burgess*	*Carbon*	*Maresca^*	*Sneekes*	*Evans"*	*Hughes*	*Kilbane*	*Raven/Quinn/De Freitas*
								Ref: D Pugh	Dalglish misses a chance created by Anselin. Marshall produces a superb save to defy Enzo Maresca. Alan Miller drops a Sutch cross and Dalglish nets his first Norwich goal. Sub Paul Raven levels with his first touch. West Brom boss Brian Little admits City deserved the points.											
2	H	BIRMINGHAM		17	L	0-1	0-1		Marshall A	Sutch	Fugelstad^	Fleming	Jackson*	De Blasiis	Anselin	Dalglish	Roberts	Mulryne	Llewellyn"	Mackay/**Diop**/Marshall L
	14/8		15,261	*5*	1			*McCarthy 11*	*Poole*	*Rowett*	*Grainger*	*Hughes*	*Holdsworth*	*Johnson M*	*McCarthy*	*O'Connor*	*Furlong**	*Johnson A*	*Lazaridis^*	*Adebola/Hyde*
								Ref: A Butler	Jon McCarthy latches on to Stan Lazaridis' pass on halfway and races through to fire into the corner of the net. Jackson sustains a knee injury when he lands badly after leaping for a header. Kevin Poole blocks Mulryne's free-kick and makes a double save to foil Anselin and Roberts.											
3	A	CHARLTON		22	L	0-1	0-0		Marshall A	Sutch	Fugelstad	Fleming	Anselin"	De Blasiis	Mulryne*	Mackay	Roberts	Dalglish	Llewellyn^	Marshall L/Coote/Diop
	21/8		*19,623*	*4*	1			*Rufus 73*	*Kiely*	*Brown*	*Powell*	*Stuart*	*Rufus*	*Youds*	*Newton*	*Kinsella*	*Hunt^*	*Mendonca**	*Robinson*	*Pringle/Jones*
								Ref: D Gallagher	Marshall foils John Robinson with a diving save, but his opposite number Dean Kiely enjoys a quiet day. A pinpoint cross by Graham Stuart is fired into the roof of the net by Richard Rufus - his third goal in nearly 200 Charlton matches. Powell foils Roberts when a late chance arises.											
4	H	BLACKBURN		24	L	0-2	0-1		Marshall A	Sutch	Fugelstad	Fleming	Mackay	De Blasiis"	Anselin	Dalglish	Roberts	Mulryne*	Llewellyn^	Marshall L/Coote/Carey
	28/8		15,407	*16*	1			*Ostenstad 6, 51*	*Filan*	*Kenna*	*Grayson*	*Short*	*Dailly*	*Carsley*	*Dunn**	*Jansen^*	*Ward*	*Ostenstad"*	*Wilcox*	*Gillespie/Gallacher/Johnson*
								Ref: K Leach	Mulryne becomes the fourth long-term injury victim of the season when his right leg is broken after a tackle which gains Christian Dailly a yellow card. A flick by Ashley Ward gives Egil Ostenstad his first goal since signing. Ostenstad later diverts Keith Gillespie's shot into goal.											
5	A	WALSALL		24	D	2-2	1-1	Marshall L 35, Coote 90	Marshall A	Sutch*	Fugelstad^	Fleming	Mackay	Carey	Anselin	Coote	Roberts"	Marshall L	Wilson	Diop/Llewllyn/Dalglish
	30/8		*6,187*	*11*	2			*Barras 3, Wrack 50*	*Walker*	*Marsh*	*Pointon*	*Viveash*	*Barras*	*Bukran*	*Wrack*	*Robins^*	*Rammell*	*Keates*	*Brissett**	*Daley/Eyjolfsson*
								Ref: A Leake	Dean Keates' free-kick is diverted past Marshall to give the Saddlers a good start. Lee Marshall nets at the far post for City and celebrates with the away fans. Darren Wrack shoots in after the break, but City level in the dying seconds via Coote. It's not enough to lift them off the bottom.											
6	H	CREWE		21	W	2-1	1-1	Roberts 19, Eadie 83	Marshall A	Sutch	Fugelstad	Fleming	Mackay	Carey	Anselin"	Dalglish*	Roberts	Marshall L^	Wilson	Eadie/Coote/Diop
	11/9		13,172	*19*	5			*Cramb 31*	*Kearton*	*Wright D**	*Smith S*	*Wright S*	*Macauley*	*Charnock*	*Little"*	*Lunt*	*Cramb*	*Sorvel*	*Rivers*	*Unsworth^/Lightfoot/Jack*
								Ref: N Barry	Fugelstad's floated cross is glanced home by the head of Roberts. Seconds after a bad Dalglish miss, Colin Cramb nips in to flick the equaliser. After a penalty appeal is turned down, Eadie marks his return after eight months out by lashing in a late winner, set up by Roberts and Coote.											
7	A	HUDDERSFIELD		22	L	0-1	0-0		Marshall A	Sutch	Fugelstad^	Fleming	Mackay	Carey	Marshall L	Coote*	Roberts	Eadie	Russell	Dalglish/Llewellyn
	18/9		*12,823*	*4*	5			*Wijnhard 51*	*Vaesen*	*Armstrong*	*Dyson^*	*Irons*	*Lucketti*	*Monkou*	*Donis*	*Beech*	*Stewart**	*Sellars*	*Wijnhart*	*Gorre/Hodouto*
								Ref: A Wilkie	At the end of a poor first half, Terriers' new signing Clyde Wijnhard is set up by Kenny Irons but produces an amazing miss in front of an open goal. He compensates by chipping Marshall after Chris Beech's through ball. Good efforts by Mackay and Dalglish are saved by Nico Vaesen.											
8	A	STOCKPORT		20	D	2-2	1-1	Roberts 40, Dalglish 50	Marshall A	Sutch	Kenton	Fleming	Jackson	Carey	Marshall L	Dalglish	Roberts	Russell	Llewellyn	
	25/9		*7,603*	*8*	6			*D'Jaffo 27, Dinning 87*	*Nash*	*Connelly*	*Nicholson*	*Dinning*	*Flynn*	*McIntosh*	*Bergersen**	*Moore*	*D'Jaffo*	*Gannon*	*Wilbraham^*	*Cooper/Ellis*
								Ref: M Warren	Laurent D'Jaffo heads home a pinpoint cross at the end of a flowing move. Roberts levels by firing home Russell's fine through ball. Dalglish's sweet volley looks to have won the game until the dying minutes when Tony Dinning smashes a 25-yarder which leaves Marshall flat-footed.											
9	H	MANCHESTER C		16	W	1-0	1-0	Roberts 37	Marshall A	Sutch	Kenton	Fleming	Jackson	Carey	Marshall L	Dalglish*	Roberts	Eadie	Russell	Llewellyn
	28/9		15,130	*4*	9				*Weaver*	*Crooks*	*Granville*	*Morrison*	*Jobson"*	*Horlock*	*Kennedy*	*Whitley*	*Dickov**	*Goater*	*Bishop*	*Taylor^/Allsopp/Cooke*
								Ref: M Fletcher	An entertaining contest under the Carrow Road lights. After a Jeff Whitley effort is disallowed for offside, Norwich go ahead when Roberts nips in to beat Carlo Nash amid offside appeals. Ian Bishop is sent tumbling by Carey but nothing given. Russell is off target after a long run.											
10	H	FULHAM		19	L	1-2	1-0	Forbes 29	Marshall A	Marshall L^	Kenton	Fleming	Jackson	Carey	Forbes*	Dalglish	Roberts	Eadie	Russell	Llewellyn/Sutch
	2/9		16,332	*3*	9			*Riedle 73, Hayles 89*	*Taylor*	*Finnan*	*Brevett**	*Melville*	*Coleman*	*Symons*	*Trollope*	*Clark*	*Horsfield"*	*Riedle^*	*Hayward*	*Collymore/Davis/Hayles*
								Ref: G Cain	Forbes, in his first game of the season, lashes a shot in after Eadie's corner is not cleared. Paul Bracewell's side turn on the style after the break to stay unbeaten. Debutant Karl-Heinz Riedle stabs home to level and in the last minute Barry Hayles breaks City hearts by slotting the winner.											
11	A	PORT VALE		17	W	1-0	0-0	Fleming 82	Marshall A	Marshall L	Kenton	Fleming	Jackson	Carey	Forbes	De Blasiis	Roberts	Eadie	Russell	
	16/9		*5,790*	*21*	12				*Musselwhite*	*Walsh*	*Butler*	*Brammer*	*Carragher**	*Gardner*	*Widdrington*	*Foyle*	*Naylor"*	*Minton^*	*Eyre*	*Tankard/Bent/Aldridge*
								Ref: D Elleray	Vale boss Brian Horton is furious as a penalty appeal is turned down during a scrappy first half and then Marcus Bent has a header kicked off the line by Kenton. Norwich pinch the points when a dipping cross by Eadie is headed beyond the flat-footed Paul Musselwhite by Fleming.											

No	Venue	Opponent / Date	Att	Pos	Res	F-A	H-T	Scorers, Times, Referees	1	2	3	4	5	6	7	8	9	10	11	subs used
12	A	SHEFFIELD UTD		18	D	0-0	0-0		Marshall A	Sutch	Kenton	Fleming	Jackson	Carey	Forbes^	De Blasiis	Roberts	Eadie*	Russell	Dalglish/Llewellyn
		19/10	*11,907*	*15*	13				*Tracey*	*Kozluk*	*Quinn*	*Derry**	*Craddock*	*Sandford*	*Ford*	*Devlin*	*Marcelo*	*Smith*	*Woodhouse*	*Katchuro*
								Ref: M Jones	A battling display keeps the Blades at bay. Marshall is in good form and acrobatically turns aside a Marcelo header. From the corner, on-loan Jody Craddock cracks a 20-yarder against a Norwich post. A Roberts header goes close and Forbes fails to hit the net after going clear on goal.											
13	H	BOLTON		13	W	2-1	0-0	Russell 50, 82	Marshall A	Sutch	Kenton	Fleming	Jackson	Carey	Forbes*	De Blasiis	Roberts	Eadie	Russell	Dalglish
		24/10	**12,468**	*12*	16			*Gardner 74*	*Jaaskalainen*	*Cox*	*Phillips**	*Todd*	*Bergsson*	*Fish"*	*Johansen^*	*Jensen*	*Gudjohnsen*	*Holdsworth*	*Gardner*	*Whitlow/Hansen/Warhurst*
								Ref: B Knight	Third-choice keeper Jussi Jaaskelainen keeps City at bay until Russell rounds Neil Cox and plants a shot low into the net. Eidur Gudjohnsen slips a pass to Ricardo Gardner for the equaliser. Carey's chip finds Eadie and after Andy Todd blocks Roberts' shot, Russell tucks in a winner.											
14	H	STOCKPORT		11	W	2-0	1-0	Flynn 42 (og), Roberts 89	Marshall A	Sutch	Kenton	Fleming	Jackson	Carey	Forbes	De Blasiis	Roberts	Eadie	Russell	
		26/10	16,880	*8*	19				*Nash*	*Connelly*	*Nicholson**	*Dinning*	*Flynn*	*McIntosh*	*Cooper*	*Moore*	*D'Jaffo*	*Byrne*	*Woodth'pe^*	*Gannon/Wilbraham*
								Ref: G Frankland	A much more scrappy affair than Sunday's fine win over Bolton. Forbes' cross is headed past his own keeper by ex-Canary Mike Flynn. Forbes and Kenton both hit the woodwork in the second half. A cross from Eadie is miscued by Forbes, but Roberts pounces to net from close range.											
15	A	FULHAM		19	D	1-1	0-1	Roberts 53	Marshall A	Sutch	Kenton	Fleming^	Jackson	Carey*	Forbes	De Blasiis	Roberts	Eadie	Russell	Milligan"/Mackay/Anselin
		30/10	*13,552*	*6*	20			*Symons 9*	*Taylor*	*Uhlenbeek*	*Brevett*	*Morgan*	*Coleman*	*Symons*	*Trollope**	*Clark*	*Riedle*	*Davis*	*Hayward*	*Collins*
								Ref: C Wilkes	Hit by injuries and suspension, the Cottagers take an early lead through Kit Symons' header. Marshall is booked for bringing down Sean Davis in the first half, but then saves the resultant penalty from Lee Clark. Good work by Eadie and De Blasiis sets up a simple header for Roberts.											
16	H	NOTT'M FOREST		17	W	1-0	1-0	Sutch 27	Marshall A	Sutch	Kenton	Fleming	Mackay	Milligan	Forbes*	De Blasiis	Roberts	Eadie	Marshall L	Dalglish
		6/11	15,818	*16*	23				*Crossley*	*Louis-Jean*	*Brennan*	*Johnson*	*Chettle*	*Hjelde*	*Petrachi**	*Prutton*	*Freedman*	*B't-Williams*	*Woan*	*Gray*
								Ref: R Furnandiz	A cross by Gianluca Petrachi is goalbound until teammate Chris Bart-Williams gets in the way. Moments later man-of-the-match Eadie whips in a cross, neatly converted by Sutch. Dougie Freedman strikes the bar with a header and misses a sitter when Marshall's clearance hits Kenton.											
17	A	SWINDON		11	D	0-0	0-0		Marshall A	Sutch	Kenton	Fleming	Mackay	Milligan	Forbes*	De Blasiis	Roberts	Eadie^	Russell	Marshall L/Llewellyn
		12/11	*7,405*	*23*	24				*Talia*	*Robinson*	*Hall**	*Leitch^*	*Reeves*	*Davis*	*Howe*	*Carrick*	*Onoura"*	*Hay*	*Williams A*	*Willis/Williams J/Quinn*
								Ref: R Styles	The unbeaten run extends to seven and City climb to halfway. The best chance falls to Roberts who heads wide from six yards out. Russell, in for Lee Marshall, also heads wide. In a game of limited goalmouth action, player-manager Jimmy Quinn has a shot deflected against the bar.											
18	H	IPSWICH		12	D	0-0	0-0		Marshall A	Sutch	Kenton	Fleming	De Blasiis	Jackson	Marshall L^	Russell	Llewellyn*	Forbes	Milligan	Dalglish/Anselin
		21/11	**19,948**	*5*	25				*Wright*	*Wilnis*	*Clapham*	*Thetis*	*Mowbray*	*Brown*	*Holland*	*Stockwell**	*Johnson*	*Scowcroft*	*Magilton*	*Naylor*
								Ref: T Heilbron	Ipswich have most of the possession but City go close when Forbes shoots wide after going clear on goal. Manu Thetis puts Jamie Scowcroft through but his lob clears the City bar. A De Blasiis free-kick is headed against the bar by Jackson. Overall, a fair result with defences on top.											
19	A	CRYSTAL PALACE		12	L	0-1	0-0		Marshall A	Sutch	Kenton	Fleming	Jackson	Milligan^	Carey	De Blasiis	Roberts	Dalglish*	Russell	Forbes/Llewellyn
		23/11	*12,110*	*16*	25			*Svensson 90*	*Digby*	*Austin*	*Phelan*	*Zhiyi*	*Foster*	*Linighan^*	*Mullins*	*Rodger*	*Svensson*	*Martin**	*McKenzie"*	*Carlisle/Woozley/De Ornelas*
								Ref: K Hill	Russell fires a chance over in the early stages. Leon McKenzie looks dangerous and goes close with opportunities either side of the break. City fail to impress in attack, but look like stealing a point until the dying seconds. Then Tony Phelan crosses to Mattias Svensson, who blasts in.											
20	A	GRIMSBY		14	L	1-2	1-1	Kenton 11	Marshall A	Sutch	Kenton^	Fleming	Jackson	Milligan	Forbes*	De Blasiis	Roberts	Eadie	Russell	Dalglish/Mackay
		28/11	*5,333*	*15*	25			*Ashcroft 25p, 60*	*Coyne*	*Butterfield*	*Gallimore*	*Hamilton*	*Lever*	*Coldicott*	*Donovan*	*Buckley**	*Ashcroft*	*Lester*	*Smith*	*Black*
								Ref: G Laws	Kenton fires City ahead, but the hero turns villain when he brings down winger Kevin Donovan. Lee Aschroft blasts in the penalty. Jack Lester races on to Ian Hamilton's through ball and after Marshall parries his shot, Aschroft nets the rebound. Eadie and Dalglish miss chances to level.											
21	H	WEST BROM		13	W	2-1	1-1	Roberts 45, Russell 87	Marshall A	Sutch	Kenton	Fleming	Jackson	Dalglish*	Anselin	De Blasiis	Roberts	Eadie	Russell	Forbes
		4/12	15,183	*15*	28			*Kilbane 28*	*Miller*	*Raven*	*Townsend*	*Sigurdsson**	*Burgess !*	*Carbon*	*Maresca^*	*Sneekes*	*Evans"*	*Hughes*	*Kilbane*	*De Freitas/V Blerk/McDerm't*
								Ref: L Cable	Richard Sneekes sets up Irish winger Kevin Kilbane, who lashes Albion ahead. Roberts dives to head an equaliser from Sutch's cross. Darryl Burgess is sent-off after two yellow cards. Late celebrations for home fans when Eadie pulls the ball back for Russell to sidefoot the winner.											
22	A	TRANMERE		12	W	2-1	0-1	Roberts 63, 89	Marshall A	Sutch	Kenton	Fleming	Jackson	Forbes*	Anselin	De Blasiis	Roberts	Llewellyn	Russell	Diop
		17/12	*5,863*	*14*	31			*Allison 14*	*Achterberg*	*Hazell*	*Roberts*	*Henry"*	*Morgan*	*Challinor*	*Mahon**	*Parkinson*	*Jones G*	*Allison*	*Kelly^*	*Allen/Taylor/Koumas*
								Ref: R Pearson	Rovers are on a high after beating Middlesbrough and West Ham in the cups. Wayne Allison nets from 15 yards after a trademark long-throw by Dave Challinor. Fuglestad's cross is headed in by Roberts. Rovers pressure is resisted and Roberts pounces on a miskick for a surprise win.											
23	H	QP RANGERS		8	W	2-1	1-1	Breacker 25 (og), Llewellyn 87	Marshall A	Sutch	Kenton	Fleming	Jackson	Diop	Anselin	De Blasiis	Roberts	Llewellyn !	Russell	
		26/12	17,823	*10*	34			*Wardley 40*	*Miklosko*	*Breacker*	*Baraclough*	*Langley !*	*Darlington*	*Plummer*	*Ward*	*Murray**	*Steiner*	*Wardley*	*Kiwomya*	*Gallen*
								Ref: D Laws	Jackson's shot flies in off Tim Breacker, but Rangers level when Stuart Wardley heads in a cross. Late on, Roberts jumps with keeper Ludek Miklosko and the ball falls for jubilant Llewellyn to stab in. Llewellyn and Richard Langley are both sent off for second bookable offences.											

No	Date		Att	Pos	Pt	F-A	H-T	Scorers, Times, and Referees	SQUAD	NUMBERS	IN	USE								Subs used
24	A	WOLVERHAMPTON		12	L	0-1	0-0		Marshall A	Sutch	Kenton	Fleming	Jackson	Diop	Anselin*	De Blasiis^	Roberts	Llewellyn	Russell	Marshall L/Carey
	28/12		*25,072*	*10*	34			*Branch 57*	*Oakes*	*Naylor*	*Muscat*	*Robinson*	*Curle*	*Pollett*	*Bazeley*	*Emblen*	*Akinbiyi*	*Branch**	*Sinton*	*Flo*
								Ref: F Stretton	City work hard at Molineux but have a frustrating day. Lady Luck smiles on Wolves as Llewellyn's attempted clearance hits Michael Branch and ends up in the net. The run of wins is over and this seems a depressing way to end the 20th century. The two teams swap places in the table.											
25	H	PORTSMOUTH		10	W	2-1	2-0	Fleming 9, Roberts 25p	Marshall A	Sutch	Kenton	Fleming	Jackson	De Blasiis"	Anselin*	Russell^	Roberts	Llewellyn	Fugelstad	Forbes/Marshall L/Wilson
	3/1		16,637	*22*	37			*Bradbury 60*	*Knight*	*Crowe*	*Robinson*	*Moore*	*Whitbread*	*Awford*	*Phillips**	*Miglioranzi*	*Bradbury*	*Claridge*	*Igoe*	*Whittingham*
								Ref: P Rejer	Against managerless Pompey, without a win in 12, Fleming gets things off to a great start, heading in a Llewellyn cross. Stefani Miglioranzi trips Kenton and Roberts blasts in the penalty. Miglioranzi hits the bar before Lee Bradbury latches on to a poor clearance to pull a goal back.											
26	H	BARNSLEY		9	D	2-2	1-0	Roberts 3, 50	Marshall A	Sutch	Kenton	Fleming	Jackson	De Blasiis	Anselin^	Russell	Roberts	Llewellyn	Fugelstad*	Coote/Marshall L
	8/1		14,039	*4*	38			*Dyer 58, Hignett 88*	*Miller*	*Curtis*	*Barker*	*Morgan*	*Chettle*	*Eaden*	*Appleby"*	*Hignett*	*Sheron**	*Tinkler*	*Barnard^*	*Shipperley/Dyer/McClare*
								Ref: D Crick	Roberts, locked in a contract dispute, nets from close range after Fugelstad's flick-on. He heads a second from Russell's cross. Dave Bassett's side enjoy long periods of possession and deservedly get back in the game when Bruce Dyer stabs in. Craig Hignett dives to head an equaliser.											
27	A	BIRMINGHAM		12	L	0-2	0-2		Marshall A !	Sutch	Kenton	Mackay	Jackson	De Blasiis*	Anselin^	Carey	Roberts	Coote	Marshall L	Green/Dalglish
	15/1		*21,007*	*11*	38			*Grainger 16, 30*	*Bennett*	*Rowett*	*Charlton*	*Hughes*	*Holdsworth*	*Purse*	*Hyde*	*O'Connor**	*Marcelo*	*Robinson^*	*Grainger*	*Adebola/Lazaridis*
								Ref: B Burns	An attempted clearance by Marshall falls for Martin Grainger, who lobs the home side ahead. City's task gets harder as Grainger glances in a header from a corner. Marshall handles outside his area and is red-carded. Coote nearly pulls a goal back, but is deprived by the woodwork.											
28	H	CHARLTON		12	L	**0-3**	0-1		Marshall A	Sutch	Kenton	Mackay	Jackson	Forbes	Fugelstad*	Carey^	Roberts	Llewellyn	Russell	Dalglish/Marshall L
	22/1		15,642	*1*	38			*Hunt 42, 73, 77*	*Kiely*	*Shields*	*Powell*	*Stuart*	*Rufus*	*Todd*	*Newton*	*Brown*	*Hunt*	*Pringle*	*Robinson*	
								Ref: M Jones	Norfolk-born City reject Andy Hunt comes back to haunt Norwich. He sidefoots a Graham Stuart corner in off the bar. His second squeezes past Marshall after he was put clear by John Robinson. He completes his hat-trick by nodding in a Robinson cross. The score flatters Charlton.											
29	H	WALSALL		13	D	1-1	1-1	Llewellyn 11	Green	Sutch	Fugelstad	Mackay	Jackson	Forbes^	Dalglish*	Carey	Roberts	Llewellyn	Marshall L	Coote/Wilson
	5/2		16,837	*21*	39			*Ricketts 36*	*Walker*	*Marsh**	*Padula*	*Roper"*	*Barras*	*Bukran*	*Wrack*	*Robins^*	*Ricketts*	*Keates*	*Harper*	*Viveash/Larusson/Gadsby*
								Ref: S Baines	Roberts hits the bar early on but is soon on target when he drives in a Llewellyn cross. A fine effort by Dalglish hits the inside of a post. Stand-in Green is beaten as Michael Ricketts nets a neat pass by ex-Canary Mark Robins. Ricketts misses an easy chance, firing over from close in.											
30	A	MANCHESTER C		14	L	1-3	1-1	Roberts 15	Green	Sutch	Fugelstad	Mackay	Jackson	Milligan*	Dalglish	Carey^	Roberts	Llewellyn	Russell"	Marshall L/De Blasiis/Forbes
	12/2		***32,681***	*2*	39			*Goater 2, Kennedy 83, 85*	*Weaver*	*Edghill**	*Granville*	*Wiekens*	*Jobson*	*Horlock*	*Kennedy*	*Whitley*	*Dickov^*	*Goater*	*Bishop*	*Pollock/Allsopp*
								Ref: T Bates	The division's top scorer, Shaun Goater, puts Joe Royle's men ahead from a fine Mark Kennedy cross. Roberts powers home a fine header to equalise. Two late goals kill off the Canaries. Kennedy fires in after picking up a loose ball and then strikes his second past an exposed Green.											
31	H	GRIMSBY		14	W	**3-0**	1-0	McDermott 11 (og), Russell 64, [Llewellyn 74]	Marshall A	Sutch*	Fugelstad	Mackay	Jackson	De Blasiis^	Dalglish	Carey	Roberts	Llewellyn	Sutch	Wilson/Russell
	19/2		13,533	*15*	42				*Coyne*	*McDermott*	*Smith**	*Livingstone*	*Lever*	*Coldicott*	*Donovan*	*Pouton*	*Ashcroft^*	*Allen*	*Groves*	*Butterfield/Clare*
								Ref: A Kaye	John McDermott gets in the way of Dalglish's cross and heads into his own net. Mackay strikes the crossbar with a header. Carey goes close with a powerful shot, but Russell beats Danny Coyne from a Dalglish cross. Llewellyn's looping header finishes off the miserable Mariners.											
32	H	HUDDERSFIELD		13	D	1-1	0-0	Roberts 75	Marshall A	Sutch	Fugelstad	Mackay	Jackson^	Russell	Dalglish	Carey"	Roberts	Llewellyn*	Sutch	Forbes/Fleming/De Blasiis
	26/2		16,464	*6*	43			*Vincent 65*	*Vaesen*	*Jenkins*	*Vincent*	*Armstrong*	*Lucketti*	*Monkou*	*Irons**	*Holland*	*Gorre*	*Smith^*	*Wijnhart*	*Sellars/Thornley*
								Ref: A Butler	Marshall does well to stop Clyde Wijnhard and Dean Gorre opening the scoring for Steve Bruce's men. A bloodied Jackson is carried off after a clash of heads. Marshall blocks Martin Smith, but the ball falls for Jamie Vincent to net. Roberts nets a diving header from a Forbes cross.											
33	A	BLACKBURN		12	D	1-1	1-0	Sutch 25	Marshall A	Sutch*	Fugelstad	Fleming	Mackay	De Blasiis	Dalglish	Kenton	Roberts	Llewellyn	Russell	Forbes
	29/2		*15,671*	*9*	44			*Frandsen 90*	*Kelly*	*Davidson*	*Grayson*	*Broomes*	*Dailly*	*Flitcroft^*	*McAteer*	*Gillespie*	*Ward*	*Ostenstad**	*Duff*	*Jansen/Frandsen*
								Ref: M Warren	Fugelstad's left-flank run leads to Roberts and Russell setting up Sutch, who drives a fierce shot in. Marshall and his defenders then face a lengthy battle as Rovers pile on the pressure. A brave and heroic victory looks likely until sub Per Frandsen's injury-time header brings it level.											
34	A	CREWE		12	L	0-1	0-1		Marshall A	Sutch*	Fugelstad	Fleming	Mackay	De Blasiis	Dalglish	Kenton	Roberts	Llewellyn	Russell	Forbes
	4/3		***5,450***	*19*	44			*Sorvel 5*	*Kearton*	*Wright S*	*Bignot*	*Wright D*	*Macauley*	*Tait^*	*Rivers*	*Lunt*	*Cramb*	*Sorvel*	*Newby**	*Street/Hulse"/Walton*
								Ref: G Frankland	A late play-off bid now looks highly unlikely as City slip up again. Neil Sorvel's early strike is the only time man-of-the-match Marshall is beaten, however, as the Canaries struggle to contain inventive Alex. City's best opportunity falls to Mackay, who heads wide from six yards.											

35	A	NOTT'M FOREST	13	D	1-1	1-1	Roberts 28	Marshall A	Kenton*	Fugelstad	Fleming	Jackson	De Blasiis	Dalglish^	Russell	Roberts	Llewellyn	Sutch	Milligan/Marshall L
	8/3	15,640	17	45			Lester 1	Beasant	Louis-Jean	Rogers	Scimeca	Vaughan	B't-Williams"	Prutton^	Quashie !	Freedman	Lester*	Johnson	Harewood/Brennan/Gray
							Ref: J Brandwood	Dougie Freedman puts Jack Lester clear and he nets after 15 seconds - one of the quickest goals City have ever conceded. Roberts deservedly levels after a Russell cross is half-cleared. Dave Beasant foils sub Milligan with a fine save. Nigel Quashie is sent off for two bookable fouls.											
36	H	CRYSTAL PALACE	15	L	0-1	0-0		Marshall A	Sutch	Fugelstad	Fleming	Jackson	De Blasiis*	Dalglish^	Milligan	Roberts	Llewellyn	Russell	Forbes/Marshall L
	11/3	15,064	17	45			Morrison 79	Digby	Austin	Cole	Zhiyi	Carlisle	Linighan	Mullins	Thomson	Morrison	Forssell	McKenzie	
							Ref: G Barber	A one-sided first half sees Norwich saved from embarrassment by more Marshall heroics. Steve Thompson finds Morrison who calmly fires a winner. Dalglish is visibly angry when Rioch hauls him off to be substituted. Ominously, Rioch says this defeat has left him feeling 'empty'.											
37	A	IPSWICH	13	W	2-0	2-0	Roberts 19, 45	Marshall A	Sutch	Fugelstad	Fleming	Milligan	Jackson	Marshall L	Russell	Roberts^	Dalglish*	Llewellyn	Anselin/Coote
	19/3	21,760	3	48				Wright	Wilnis	Clapham	Thetis*	Mowbray	Venus	Holland	Stewart^	Johnson	Scowcroft	Magilton	Stockwell/Naylor
							Ref: R Styles	Rioch quits, apparently unhappy over lack of transfer funds, and Bryan Hamilton takes over as caretaker. His first match is against his former team and he has a dream start. Roberts' shot deflects past Richard Wright. Roberts latches on to Dalglish's pass before converting a slick goal.											
38	H	SWINDON	13	L	0-2	0-0		Marshall A	Sutch	Fugelstad	Fleming	Jackson	Marshall L	Dalglish	Milligan*	Coote	Llewellyn^	Russell	Anselin/Forbes
	22/3	13,662	24	48			Hay 56p, 65	Talia	Robinson	Hall*	Leitch	Reeves	Willis	Collins	Cowe^	Gray"	Hay	Williams A	Davis/Williams J/Grazioli
							Ref: P Danson	Boosted by the local derby win, fans hope for a new dawn, but this is a scrappy affair. Fleming brings down Steve Cowe and Chris Hay sends Marshall the wrong way from the spot. Hay latches on to Wayne Gray's pass and fires in from 20 yards. Suspended Roberts is badly missed.											
39	A	QP RANGERS	13	D	2-2	1-0	Marshall L 14, 58	Marshall A	Sutch	Fugelstad	Fleming	Jackson	Marshall L	Dalglish*	**Hamilton**	Roberts	**Brady**	**De Waard**^	Carey/Llewellyn
	25/3	11,918	11	49			Kiwomya 47, 85	Harper	Perry	Baraclough	Ready	Rose"	Jeanne*	Langley	Murray	Beck^	Wardley	Kiwomya	Peacock/Gallen/Taylor
							Ref: K Lynch	Three new faces and Lee Marshall's looping header gets City off to a great start. Ex-Ipswich man Chris Kiwomya levels just after half-time. In an absorbing game, Marshall's second sets up real hopes of a fine away win, but Kiwomya pounces again near the end for Gerry Francis' outfit.											
40	H	TRANMERE	12	D	1-1	1-1	Marshall L 15	Marshall A	Sutch	Fugelstad	Fleming	Jackson"	Marshall L	Llewellyn*	Hamilton	Roberts	Brady*	De Waard	Kenton/Coote/Mackay
	1/4	13,734	14	50			Sutch 38 (og)	Achterberg*	Hazell	Roberts	Morgan	Allen	Challinor	Taylor	Parkinson	Jones G	Allison	Kelly	Nixon
							Ref: P Jones	New Dutch winger De Waard sends over a cross for Lee Marshall to head his third in two games. The goal comes just moments after Wayne Allison hit the bar. Keeper John Achterberg limps off after a collision. Unlucky Sutch hits Andy Parkinson's probing cross into his own goal.											
41	A	PORTSMOUTH	13	L	1-2	1-0	Marshall L 44	Marshall A	Sutch	Kenton !	Fleming	Jackson	Marshall L	Mulryne"	Hamilton	Roberts	Brady^	De Waard*	Llewellyn/Mackay/Russell
	8/4	14,003	15	50			Harper 51, Moore 71	Hoult	Waterman	Edinburgh"	Moore	Whitbread	Thorgerson	Derry	Claridge^	Harper*	Hughes	Bradbury	Awford/Allen/Myers
							Ref: P Richards	Lee Marshall does the trick again, rising high to head in a Sutch cross. City survive two penalty appeals and Marshall brings off fine saves in the first half. Kevin Harper levels with a header and Darren Moore's looping shot puts Pompey ahead. Kenton departs after two yellow cards.											
42	H	WOLVERHAMPTON	12	W	1-0	0-0	Roberts 50	Marshall A	Sutch	**Derveld***	Fleming	Jackson	Marshall L	Forbes	Hamilton^	Roberts	Brady	Llewellyn"	Kenton/Mulryne/**Giallanza**
	15/4	15,910	7	53				Oakes	Emblen	Muscat	Sedgley	Curle	Pollett	Bazeley	Nielsen	Flo	Branch	Taylor*	Osborn
							Ref: A D'Urso	Marshall saves City in the first minute, brilliantly tipping over Michael Branch's 22-yard shot. Roberts, against his former team, produces an excellent near-post header from Forbes' corner. City survive late pressure and the win puts a real dent in the play-off hopes of Colin Lee's men.											
43	H	PORT VALE	12	D	0-0	0-0		Marshall A	Sutch	Derveld	Fleming	Jackson	Marshall L	Anselin"	Hamilton^	Roberts	Brady	Giallanza*	Bellamy/Mulryne/Forbes
	22/4	15,526	23	54				Pilkington	Brisco	Tankard	Widdrington	Burns	Burton	Eyre	Healy	Viljanen*	Cummins	Rougier	Naylor
							Ref: M Halsey	City welcome back long-term injury victim Bellamy and give a full debut to Swiss-born forward Gaetano Giallanza, who has been loaned from Nantes. Relegation-threatened Vale scrap determinedly for their point but are nearly foiled when returning hero Bellamy shoots against the bar.											
44	A	BARNSLEY	12	L	1-2	0-2	Bellamy 67	Marshall A	Sutch	Derveld	Fleming	Mackay	Marshall L	Forbes*	Hamilton"	Roberts	Brady^	Dalglish	Bellamy/Mulryne/Russell
	24/4	15,253	3	54			Chettle 41, Shipperley 45	Miller	Curtis	Barker	Morgan	Chettle	V der Laan	Eaden	Hignett	Shipperley	Dyer*	Appleby^	Barnard/Tinkler
							Ref: R Pearson	A foul on Bruce Dyer gives the Tykes a free-kick which is fired past Marshall by defender Steve Chettle. Minutes later the game is over as a contest when Neil Shipperley rises to head in at the far post. Sub Bellamy pulls one back, but the home side hang on to clinch a play-off place.											
45	H	SHEFFIELD UTD	12	W	2-1	2-0	Fleming 4, Bellamy 11	Marshall A	Sutch	Derveld*	Fleming	Jackson	Marshall L	Mulryne	Hamilton^	Roberts	Bellamy	De Waard^	Kenton/Llewellyn/Russell
	29/4	16,921	16	57			Devlin 75p	Tracey	Kozluk	Quinn	Woodhouse	Gijsbrechts"	Sandford	Devlin	Ribeiro^	Bent	Wilson*	Ford	Hamilton/Brown/D'Jaffo
							Ref: K Leach	A superb start for City as Fleming is left unmarked and heads Mulryne's cross in after a short corner. Simon Tracey dashes out of his goal recklessly and Bellamy nips in to score from a tight angle. United make a late fight of it, and Paul Devlin pulls one back from the penalty spot.											
46	A	BOLTON	12	L	0-1	0-0		Marshall A	Sutch	Derveld	Fleming	Jackson	Marshall L	Mulryne	Anselin^	Roberts	Bellamy	Giallanza*	**McVeigh**/Russell"/Llewellyn
	7/5	17,987	6	57			Holdsworth 72	Jaaskalainen	Bergsson	Whitlow	Warhurst	Fish	Ritchie	Johansen^	Jensen	Gudjohnsen"	Hansen*	Johnston	Holdsworth/Elliott/Passi
	Home	Away					Ref: J Kirkby	Sam Allardyce's men need the points for their play-off bid, but Norwich look more likely winners in an uninhibited display. Injuries intervene and even sub Russell is forced off. Hamilton has now fielded six debutants in nine games. Dean Holdsworth's strike brings Bolton late relief.											
Average	15,539	13,923																	

Worthington Cup			Att			F-A	H-T	Scorers, Times, and Referees	SQUAD	NUMBERS	IN	USE								subs used
1:1	H	CHELTENHAM		11	W	2-0	2-0	Roberts 14, 37	Marshall A	Sutch	Fugelstad	De Blasiis	Fleming	Jackson	Anselin"	Dalglish^	Roberts	Mulryne	Llewellyn*	Marshall L/Coote/Diop
	10/8		12,276	*3:22*					*Book*	*Griffin*	*Victory*	*Banks*	*Freeman*	*Howarth*	*Howells*	*McAuley**	*Grayson^*	*Daveney"*	*Yates*	*Watkins/Brough/Bloomer*
								Ref: F Stretton	After an Anselin goal is ruled out, Roberts heads home a pinpoint cross by Mulryne. Good work by Dalglish sets up Roberts to hammer home another. City take it easy after the break. Jamie Victory fires a good chance over the bar and Mulryne is just wide with a powerful 25-yarder.											
1:2	A	CHELTENHAM		22	L	1-2	0-0	Marshall L 100	Marshall A	Sutch	Wilson	Marshall L	Fleming	Mackay	Anselin*	Dalglish^	Roberts	Mulryne	Llewellyn	De Blasiis/Diop
	24/8		*4,203*	*3:9*		*aet*		*Grayson 47p, Victory 69*	*Book*	*Griffin*	*Victory*	*Banks*	*Freeman*	*Howarth*	*Howells*	*McAuley**	*Grayson*	*Daveney^*	*Yates"*	*Watkins/Bloomer/Jackson*
								Ref: P Dowd (Norwich win 3-2 on aggregate)	Steve Cotterill's side make the most of a controversial penalty award against Fleming. Jamie Victory brings the aggregate scores level with a powerful header from a corner. Ten minutes into extra-time City silence the Whaddon Road crowd as Lee Marshall touches in a Roberts pass.											
2:1	H	FULHAM		21	L	0-4	0-1		Marshall A	Sutch	Wilson*	Diop	Fleming	Mackay	Russell	Eadie	Roberts	Carey	Coote	Fugelstad
	14/9		11,760	*6*				*Peschisolido 24, Coote 64 (og), Clark 74, [Collins 82]*	*Taylor*	*Finnan*	*Brevett*	*Melville*	*Coleman*	*Symons*	*Trollope*	*Clark"*	*Horsfield**	*Peschi'lido^*	*Hayward*	*Hayles/Collymore/Collins*
								Ref: J Robinson	Dakaar-born full-back Pape Diop, on loan from Racing Club de Paris, gets a full debut. Paul Peschisolido opens the scoring after a Coote error and Coote unluckily heads into his own net at a corner. Lee Clark streaks clear for a third and sub Wayne Collins heads in with his first touch.											
2:2	A	FULHAM		22	L	0-2	0-1		Marshall A	Sutch	Wilson"	Jackson	Fleming	Mackay	Marshall L	Eadie*	Roberts^	Carey	Russell	Llewellyn/Kenton/Dalglish
	21/9		*5,246*	*5*				*Hayles 20, Davis 84*	*Taylor*	*Finnan*	*Brevett*	*Melville*	*Coleman*	*Morgan*	*Hayward**	*Clark*	*Horsfield^*	*Trollope*	*Hayles*	*Davis/Uhlenbeek*
								Ref: P Taylor (Norwich lose 0-6 on aggregate)	Four goals down at the start, this looks like 'mission impossible'. Steve Hayward's corner is headed goalwards by Simon Morgan and Barry Hayles gets the last touch. Russell hits the post and Chris Coleman the crossbar. Sean Davis slides in Gus Uhlenbeek's cross to finish City off.											

FA Cup																				
3	H	COVENTRY		13	L	1-3	0-0	Llewellyn 66	Marshall A	Sutch	Fugelstad	De Blasiis	Fleming	Jackson	Anselin^	Dalglish*	Roberts	Llewellyn	Russell	Forbes/Kenton
	11/12		15,702	*P:11*				*Whelan 58, Russell 76 (og), Eustace 84*	*Hedman*	*Telfer*	*Froggatt*	*Williams^*	*Breen*	*Chippo*	*Whelan**	*Palmer*	*Keane*	*McAllister*	*Hadji*	*Roussel/Eustace*
								Ref: P Alcock	On a wet pitch, Marshall blots his copybook with two blunders. Noel Whelan's header slips through his hands before Llewellyn scores with a deflected drive. Marshall slips up again when a deflection off Russell sneaks under him. Sub John Eustace finishes off Norwich's cup dreams.											

		Home						Away					
		P	W	D	L	F	A	W	D	L	F	A	Pts
1	Charlton	46	15	3	5	37	18	12	7	4	42	27	91
2	Manchester C	46	17	2	4	48	17	9	9	5	30	23	89
3	Ipswich *	46	16	3	4	39	17	9	9	5	32	25	87
4	Barnsley	46	15	4	4	48	24	9	6	8	40	43	82
5	Birmingham	46	15	5	3	37	16	7	6	10	28	28	77
6	Bolton	46	14	5	4	43	26	7	8	8	26	24	76
7	Wolves	46	15	5	3	45	20	6	6	11	19	28	74
8	Huddersfield	46	14	5	4	43	21	7	6	10	19	28	74
9	Fulham	46	13	7	3	33	13	4	9	10	16	28	67
10	QP Rangers	46	9	12	2	30	20	7	6	10	32	33	66
11	Blackburn	46	10	9	4	33	20	5	8	10	22	31	62
12	NORWICH	46	11	6	6	26	22	3	9	11	19	28	57
13	Tranmere	46	10	8	5	35	27	5	4	14	22	41	57
14	Nott'm For	46	9	10	4	29	18	5	4	14	24	37	56
15	Crys Palace	46	7	11	5	33	26	6	4	13	24	41	54
16	Sheffield Utd	46	10	8	5	38	24	3	7	13	21	47	54
17	Stockport	46	8	8	7	33	31	5	7	11	22	36	54
18	Portsmouth	46	9	6	8	36	27	4	6	13	19	39	51
19	Crewe	46	9	5	9	27	31	5	4	14	19	36	51
20	Grimsby	46	10	8	5	27	25	3	4	16	14	42	51
21	West Brom	46	6	11	6	25	26	4	8	11	18	34	49
22	Walsall	46	7	6	10	26	34	4	7	12	26	43	46
23	Port Vale	46	6	6	11	27	30	1	9	13	21	39	36
24	Swindon	46	5	6	12	23	37	3	6	14	15	40	36
		1104	260	159	133	821	570	133	159	260	570	821	1497

* promoted after play-offs

Odds & ends

Double wins: (0).

Double losses: (3) Birmingham, Charlton, Crystal Palace.

Won from behind: (2) West Brom (h), Tranmere (a).

Lost from in front: (3) Fulham (h), Grimsby (a), Portsmouth (a).

High points: The shock win at Ipswich, after Bruce Rioch's departure.

Darren Eadie's come-back goal against Crewe.

A series of superb displays by goalkeeper Andy Marshall.

Low points: Long-term injuries early on to Bellamy, Mulryne and Eadie.

The late goal at Blackburn which prevented a heroic victory.

Bruce Rioch quitting over the lack of funds for new players.

Having to suffer Ipswich's promotion celebrations.

Player of the Year: Iwan Roberts

Ever-presents: (0).

Hat-tricks: (0).

Opposing hat-tricks: (1) Andy Hunt (v Charlton, h).

Leading scorer: (19) Iwan Roberts.

	Appearances						Goals			
	Lge	*Sub*	LC	*Sub*	FAC	*Sub*	Lge	LC	FAC	Tot
Anselin, Cedric	**15**	*4*	2		1					
Bellamy, Craig	**2**	*2*					**2**			**2**
De Blasiis, Jean-Yves	**26**	*2*	1	*1*	1					
Brady, Garry	**6**									
Carey, Shaun	**18**	*3*	2							
Coote, Adrian	**4**	*7*	1	*1*			**1**			**1**
Dalglish, Paul	**22**	*9*	2	*1*	1		**2**			**2**
Derveld, Fernando	**5**									
Diop, Pape	**2**	*5*	1	*2*						
Eadie, Darren	**12**	*1*	2				**1**			**1**
Fleming, Craig	**38**	*1*	4		1		**3**			**3**
Forbes, Adrian	**15**	*10*				*1*	**1**			**1**
Fugelstad, Erik	**26**		1	*1*	1					
Giallanza, Gaetano	**2**	*1*								
Green, Robert	**2**	*1*								
Hamilton, Des	**7**									
Jackson, Matt	**38**		2		1					
Kenton, Darren	**23**	*3*		*1*		*1*	**1**			**1**
Llewellyn, Chris	**24**	*12*	2	*1*	1		**3**		1	**4**
Mackay, Malky	**16**	*5*	3							
Marshall, Andy	**44**		4		1					
Marshall, Lee	**21**	*12*	2	*1*			**5**	1		**6**
McVeigh, Paul		*1*								
Milligan, Mike	**9**	*2*								
Mulryne, Phil	**7**	*2*	2							
Roberts, Iwan	**44**	*17*	4	*2*	1		**17**	2		**19**
Russell, Darel	**28**	*5*	2		1		**4**			**4**
Sutch, Daryl	**44**	*1*	4		1		**2**			**2**
De Waard, Raymond	**4**									
Wilson, Che	**2**	*3*	3							
(own-goals)							**3**			**3**
30 players used	**506**	***109***	**44**	***11***	**11**	***2***	**45**	**3**	**1**	**49**

No	Date		Att	Pos	Pt	F-A	H-T	Scorers, Times, and Referees	SQUAD	NUMBERS	IN	USE								subs used
1	A	BARNSLEY			L	0-1	0-0		Marshall	Sutch	Derveld	Marshall L	Fleming	Bellamy	Roberts	Mulryne	Russell″	Kenton*	Llewellyn^	De Waard/Forbes/Giallanza
	12/8		*15,640*		0			*Jones 64*	*Miller*	*Moses*	*Regan !*	*Morgan*	*Chettle*	*Kay**	*Appleby*	*Jones^*	*Shipperley*	*Sheron″*	*Barnard*	*O'Callaghan/Dyer/McClare*
								Ref: P Richards	Making his debut for the Tykes, England youth cap Carl Regan is sent off after only 16 minutes for a bad tackle on Sutch. Another debutant, Lee Jones, gives Dave Bassett's outfit the lead. Norwich create some promising moves but fail to take a number of reasonable scoring chances.											
2	H	NOTT'M FOREST	17	D		0-0	0-0		Marshall	Sutch	Derveld*	Marshall L	Fleming	Kenton	Roberts	Mulryne	Russell	Giallanza	Llewellyn	De Waard
	19/8		18,059	*9*	1				*Beasant*	*Louis-Jean*	*Brennan*	*B't-Williams*	*Hjelde**	*Doig*	*Prutton*	*Scimeca*	*Jones*	*Lester^*	*Rogers*	*Vaughan/Gray*
								Ref: S Tomlin	Craig Bellamy departs for Coventry for a record-equalling £5 million. It's a fee Norwich can hardly refuse, but it leaves them clearly short of firepower. Veteran Dave Beasant, now 41 and with 600-plus league games to his name, makes some great saves to keep the Canaries at bay.											
3	A	BLACKBURN	21	L		2-3	0-1	Roberts 55, Giallanza 90	Marshall	Sutch	Derveld	Marshall L	Fleming	Jackson″	Roberts	Mulryne*	Russell	Kenton^	Llewellyn	Giallanza/Forbes/**McGovern**
	26/8		*19,542*	*3*	1			*Dunn 25p, Blake 52, Jansen 82*	*Kelly*	*Curtis*	*Bjornbye*	*Short*	*Dailly*	*Dunn*	*McAteer*	*Flitcroft**	*Blake*	*Jansen*	*Duff^*	*Carsley/Diawara*
								Ref: C Foy	Marshall's foul on Nathan Blake hands David Dunn a penalty. Blake's header doubles the lead. Mulryne's injury is a serious blow. City battle hard but Giallanza's goal after a neat dummy is a mere consolation. Emotions are running high at Ewood after benefactor Jack Walker's death.											
4	H	FULHAM	23	L		0-1	0-0		Marshall	Sutch	Derveld	Marshall L	Fleming	Kenton	Roberts	**Whitley**	Russell	Giallanza″	Llewellyn*	Forbes^/De Waard/McVeigh
	28/8		16,678	*1*	1			*Boa Morte 88*	*Taylor*	*Finnan*	*Brevett*	*Melville*	*Coleman*	*Davis*	*Goldbaek**	*Clark″*	*Saha*	*Collins*	*Hayles^*	*Lewis/Boa Morte/Fernandes*
								Ref: M Fletcher	Jeff Whitley, on loan from Manchester City, makes his bow. There's no joy for shot-shy City who look the better side for much of the game. In a match of nine bookings, Jean Tigana's men maintain their 100 per cent record with a crushing injury-time winner from Lusi Boa Morte.											
5	A	CREWE	24	D		0-0	0-0		Marshall	Sutch	Derveld	Marshall L	Fleming	Jackson*	Roberts	Whitley	Russell	Giallanza″	Brady^	Forbes/McGov'n/**Nederga'rd**
	9/9		*5,955*	*16*	2				*Kearton*	*Wright*	*Smith S*	*Sodje*	*Macauley*	*Street*	*Hulse^*	*Lunt*	*Little*	*Rivers**	*Sorvel*	*Jack/Foster*
								Ref: T Jones	Norwich slip to bottom of the table, but this was a battling display and they're unlucky not to win. Russell hits the post ten minutes from time. The clean sheet brings an end to a run of three successive losses at Gresty Road. The experienced Dane, Steen Nedergaard, 30, debuts as a sub.											
6	A	STOCKPORT	19	W		3-1	2-0	Whitley 15, Roberts 30p, 85	Marshall	Sutch	Derveld	Marshall L	Fleming	McGovern^	Roberts	Whitley	Russell	**Cottee**	Nedergaard*	Forbes/Mackay
	12/9		*5,703*	*17*	5			*Smith 52*	*Jones*	*Gibb**	*Clare*	*Woodthorpe*	*Flynn*	*Clarke*	*Cooper*	*Moore*	*Maxwell^*	*Fradin*	*Smith*	*Carrigan/Lawson*
								Ref: G Frankland	Veteran Tony Cottee arrives on loan from Leicester and gives an inspirational display. Whitley nets a superb header from a Sutch cross to grab the lead. Cottee works very well alongside Roberts. He deserves a goal, but a late effort strikes a post and rolls agonisingly along the goalline.											
7	H	CRYSTAL PALACE	20	D		0-0	0-0		Marshall	Sutch	Derveld	Marshall L	Fleming	McGovern	Roberts	Whitley^	Russell	Cottee″	Nedergaard*	Forbes/De Waard/Giallanza
	16/9		16,828	*16*	6				*Taylor*	*Black*	*Harrison*	*Austin*	*Zhiyi*	*Ruddock*	*Mullins*	*Gray**	*Morrison*	*Kitson*	*Pollock*	*McKenzie*
								Ref: U Rennie	The best goalscoring opportunity on a frustrating afternoon falls to Cottee, who, unbelievably, sends a shot over a gaping goal and high into the stands. Alan Smith's side are also shot-shy, and have now scored just once in around 370 minutes of league action. They're grateful for a point.											
8	A	WOLVERHAMPTON	20	L		**0-4**	0-3	*[Branch 70]*	Marshall	Sutch	Derveld	Marshall L	Fleming	**Walsh″**	Roberts	Whitley^	Russell	Cottee*	Forbes	Giallanza/De Waard/Mackay
	24/9		*15,105*	*13*	6			*Proudlock 21, Dinning 26, Robinson 45,*	*Oakes*	*Green*	*Naylor*	*Dinning*	*Robinson*	*Emblen*	*Bazeley*	*Branch″*	*Ketsbaia*	*Proudlock**	*Sinton^*	*Taylor/Kamara/Al-Jaber*
								Ref: S Mathieson	The live TV cameras witness what Hamilton calls a throroughly unacceptable display. Steve Walsh is the latest elderly debutant, but is not to blame for this shambles. Andy Proudlock drills the first and Tony Dinning scrambles in a corner. City end the game looking somewhat ragged.											
9	H	HUDDERSFIELD	20	D		1-1	0-0	Giallanza 80	Marshall	Sutch	Derveld	Marshall L^	Fleming	Kenton	Roberts	Whitley	Russell	Cottee*	Brady″	Giallanza/Llewllyn/Walsh
	30/9		14,499	*22*	7			*Gallen 58*	*Vaesen*	*Kozluk*	*Dyson*	*Irons*	*Lucketti*	*Armstrong*	*Thornley″*	*Gallen*	*Smith**	*Gorre^*	*Beech*	*Sellars/Baldry/Gray*
								Ref: M Warren	Pressure is building on Bryan Hamilton and the fans expect a win over bottom club Huddersfield. Kevin Gallen pounces to score for Lou Macari's men and Kenny Irons misses a sitter. Giallanza comes to City's rescue with a left-foot shot from 10 yards that is deflected into the net.											
10	A	WEST BROM	18	W		3-2	2-1	Derveld 10, Llewellyn 43, Kenton 86	Marshall	Sutch	Derveld	Marshall L	Fleming	Kenton	Roberts	Mulryne^	Russell″	Nedergaard*	Llewellyn	Mackay/Giallanza/Whitley
	14/10		*16,511*	*6*	10			*Clement 38, Hughes 65p*	*Jensen*	*Lyttle**	*Clement*	*McInnes*	*Butler*	*Chambers*	*Fox*	*Sneekes*	*Roberts″*	*Hughes*	*Van Blerk^*	*Carbon/Taylor/Jordao*
								Ref: G Laws	The big cup win at Blackpool has boosted confidence. Derveld's first Norwich goal is a marvellous solo effort. Albion's second equaliser is a controverisal penalty, apparently given for a push. Lee Marshall's free-kick is nodded on and Kenton stabs the winner with four minutes left.											
11	A	PRESTON	19	L		0-1	0-0		Marshall	Sutch	Derveld	Marshall L	Fleming	Kenton*	Roberts	Mulryne	Whitley^	Giallanza	Llewellyn″	Mackay/Cottee/Forbes
	17/10		*13,002*	*5*	10			*Gunlaugsson 90*	*Lucas*	*Alexander*	*Edwards*	*Murdock*	*Gregan*	*Appleton*	*McKenna*	*Cartwright*	*Meijer*	*Robinson*	*Anderson**	*Gunlaugsson*
								Ref: F Stretton	Newly promoted Preston are riding high under David Moyes. City give them a difficult evening and look to have done enough to win a point. Then disaster strikes three minutes into stoppage time as Bjarni Gunlaugsson grabs a dramatic winner, tucking a shot under diving Marshall.											

No	Venue / Date	Opponent	Att	Pos	Res / Pts	FT	HT	Scorers, Times, and Referees	1	2	3	4	5	6	7	8	9	10	11	Subs used
12	H	SHEFFIELD UTD		16	W	4-2	2-2	Mulryne 28, Roberts 42, Cottee 62,	Marshall	Sutch	Derveld	Marshall L	Fleming	Kenton	Roberts	Mulryne	Mackay	Giallanza*	Llewellyn	Cottee
	21/10		15,504	*8*	13			*Kelly 7, Brown 24* [Llewellyn 63]	*Tracey*	*Uhlenbeek*	*Quinn*	*Santos"*	*Murphy*	*Sandford^*	*Devlin*	*Brown**	*Bent !*	*Kelly*	*Woodhouse*	*Newby/Curle/Montgomery*
								Ref: B Knight	Euphoria after City come back from a dreadful start. Mulryne shoots the first and Giallanza sets up Roberts' equaliser. The in-form Giallanza picks up a serious knee injury before Cottee's emphatic finish. The fourth involves a slick move of 18 passes. Marcus Bent departs for dissent.											
13	H	PORTSMOUTH		17	D	0-0	0-0		Marshall	Sutch	Derveld^	Marshall L	Fleming	Kenton"	Roberts	Mulryne	Mackay	Cottee*	Llewellyn	Dalglish/Russell/McGovern
	24/10		18,772	*9*	14				*Hoult*	*Hiley*	*Edinburgh*	*Derry*	*Primus*	*Moore*	*Hughes^*	*Thorgersen*	*Bradbury**	*Claridge*	*Panopoulos*	*Nightingale/Miglioranzi*
								Ref: P Taylor	Player-manager Steve Claridge's Pompey stretch their unbeaten run. They are too well-organised for Norwich. Disappointing fare for the home fans who want the side to build on the fine win three days ago. Dalglish makes his first appearance of the season, but can't find a way through.											
14	H	TRANMERE		16	W	1-0	0-0	Roberts 52	Marshall	Sutch	**Granville**	Marshall L	Fleming	Forbes^	Roberts	Mulryne	Mackay	**Parker***	Llewellyn	Russell/Walsh
	4/11		**13,688**	*19*	17				*Murphy*	*Hazell**	*Parkinson*	*Roberts*	*Flynn*	*Challinor*	*Hill*	*Hinds*	*Taylor^*	*Allison*	*Koumas*	*Gill/Barlow*
								Ref: R Beeby	Danny Granville, loaned by Manchester C, crosses and Roberts nets after his initial effort hits a post. Scott Parker, loaned by Charlton, looks a useful capture. Cottee departs unexpectedly to take up an offer to be player-manager of Barnet - his first match is a 7-0 victory over Blackpool.											
15	H	BIRMINGHAM		13	W	1-0	1-0	Forbes 45	Marshall	Sutch	Granville	Marshall L	Fleming	Forbes^	Roberts	Mulryne	Mackay	Parker*	Llewellyn	Russell/Coote
	7/11		13,900	*3*	20				*Bennett*	*Gill"*	*Grainger*	*Holdsw'th !*	*Purse*	*Johnson*	*Eaden*	*Hughes*	*Adebola*	*Burchill**	*Lazaridis^*	*Horsfield/Johnson/Hyde*
								Ref: A Butler	Forbes misses badly, but compensates shortly afterwards when he lashes the ball into the roof of the net. A major rearguard action is required after the interval to preserve the lead, with Marshall making several superb saves. David Holdsworth is sent off for striking Coote off the ball.											
16	A	SHEFFIELD WED		13	L	2-3	1-1	Parker 42, Marshall L 90	Marshall	Sutch	Granville	Marshall L	Fleming	Forbes*	Roberts	Mulryne	Mackay	Parker"	Llewellyn^	Coote/Darveld/Russell
	11/11		*16,956*	*18*	20			*Hinchcliffe 32p, Crane 56, Di Piedi 62*	*Pressman*	*Haslam*	*Hinchcliffe*	*Lescott*	*Hendon*	*Walker*	*Cooke*	*Ekoku*	*Booth**	*Morrison*	*Crane*	*Di Piedi*
								Ref: M Jones	Former Canary Ekoku wins a highly debatable penalty, converted by Andy Hichcliffe. Parker, having an excellent game, nips in to head the equaliser. Michaelli Di Piedi fires in a 35-yard dipping shot, which proves decisive. City fight right to the end and Lee Marshall pulls one back.											
17	H	BOLTON		14	L	0-2	0-0		Marshall	Sutch	Granville	Marshall L"	Fleming	Forbes	Roberts	Mulryne	Mackay	Parker*	Llewellyn^	Russell/Darveld/Coote
	18/11		15,224	*3*	20			*Ricketts 58, Bergsson 74*	*Jaaskalainen*	*O'Kane*	*Elliott*	*Frandsen*	*Bergsson*	*Warhurst*	*Barness*	*Ricketts*	*Hansen**	*Nolan^*	*Gardner"*	*Passi/Fredga'd/Gope-Fenepej*
								Ref: J Winter	In a lively first period, Norwich go agonisingly close to opening the scoring on three occasions. After the break, Michael Ricketts and Gudni Bergsson show how to finish. Although this is their first away victory in six attempts, Sam Allardyce's men were simply too strong on the day.											
18	A	BURNLEY		14	L	0-2	0-0		Marshall	Sutch	Granville	Marshall L*	Fleming	Forbes"	Roberts	Mulryne	Mackay	Parker	Llewellyn^	Russell/De Waard/Coote
	21/11		*15,017*	*4*	20			*Payton 56, Davis 66*	*Michopoulos*	*Little**	*Briscoe"*	*Cox*	*Davis*	*Thomas*	*Ball*	*Cook^*	*Branch*	*Payton*	*Mellon*	*Weller/Mullin/Moore*
								Ref: M Pike	A third successive defeat and Hamilton is on the receiving end in the local media and from the fans. Stan Ternent's side are a tough nut to crack on their own patch. Second-half strikes by Gerry Payton and Steve Davis settle it. This will be inconsistent De Waard's final game in yellow.											
19	H	WIMBLEDON		17	L	1-2	1-1	Roberts 39	Marshall	Sutch	Granville	Derveld^	Fleming	Forbes	Roberts	Mulryne	Mackay	Parker	Llewellyn*	Coote/Marshall L
	25/11		14,059	*11*	20			*Hartson 35, Francis 46*	*Davis*	*Holloway*	*Kimble^*	*Andersen*	*Williams*	*Blackwell*	*Ardley*	*Euell*	*Hartson**	*Francis*	*Gayle*	*Agyemang/Karlsson*
								Ref: M Messias	Roberts is fouled in the box early on, but Mulryne's misses with a weak penalty. John Hartson stumbles over a chance, but recovers to score. Roberts guides a header in to level matters. Damien Francis finishes clinically straight after the restart. Kelvin Davis saves well from Roberts.											
20	A	PORTSMOUTH		20	L	0-2	0-1		Marshall	Sutch	Derveld"	Russell	Fleming	Forbes*	Roberts	Mulryne^	Mackay	**Notman**	Llewellyn	Marshall L/De Blasiis/Coote
	2/12		*13,409*	*12*	20			*Panopoulos 13, Quashie 57*	*Hoult*	*Hiley*	*Edinburgh*	*Derry*	*Crowe*	*Moore*	*Quashie*	*Thorgersen*	*Bradbury**	*Claridge*	*Panopoulos*	*Nightingale*
								Ref: U Rennie	City splash out on striker Notman from Manchester U, but the losing run goes on. Two days later, Hamilton falls on his sword after 35 games in charge, ten of which were victories. The chairman says Hamilton was a dedicated man under great pressure who didn't have time on his side.											
21	H	GILLINGHAM		17	W	1-0	0-0	Llewellyn 78	Marshall	Sutch	Jackson	Russell	Fleming	De Blasiis*	Roberts	Marshall L	Mackay	Notman	Llewellyn	Kenton
	9/12		16,725	*18*	23				*Bartram*	*Southall*	*Patterson*	*Hope*	*Ashby*	*Pennock*	*Smith*	*Saunders*	*King"*	*Thomson^*	*Browning**	*Hessenthaler/Asaba/Onoura*
								Ref: S Mathieson	Caretaker Worthington takes charge for the first time. He makes several team changes and attempts to instil some steel into a rather dispirited side. It's not pretty stuff but proves effective against Peter Taylor's outfit. Llewellyn's winning header from a Kenton cross is joyously received.											
22	A	GRIMSBY		18	L	0-2	0-1		Marshall	Sutch"	Jackson	Russell*	Fleming	Mulryne	Roberts	Marshall L	Mackay	Notman^	Llewellyn	Kenton/Forbes/**Abbey**
	16/12		***5,618***	*20*	23			*Fleming 23 (og), Nielsen 90*	*Coyne*	*Butterfield*	*Fostervold*	*Groves*	*Enhua^*	*Coldicott**	*Donovan*	*Nielsen*	*Willems*	*Campbell*	*Burnett*	*Smith D/Smith R*
								Ref: P Walton	Striker Zema Abbey signs from Cambridge U after long-term interest from Norwich. Unlucky Fleming gives a back-pass too much power and the ball ends up in his own net. Dane David Neilsen clinches the home victory when he gets a clear run on goal and gives Marshall no chance.											
23	H	BARNSLEY		18	D	0-0	0-0		Marshall	Sutch	Jackson	Russell	Fleming	Mulryne	Roberts	Marshall L^	Mackay	Notman*	Llewellyn	Abbey/Dalglish
	23/12		16,581	*14*	24				*Miller*	*Salli*	*Barker*	*Morgan*	*Chettle*	*Ward**	*Appleby*	*V der Laan*	*Shipperley*	*Sheron*	*Dyer^*	*Ripley/Bullock*
								Ref: D Crick	Lee Marshall hit the bar hits in the first half and Russell misses a great opportunity in the final minute. Dave Bassett's side escape with a point. Speculation mounts over who will get the manager's job if not Worthington. Jan Molby, Dave Jones, Ian Crook and Mel Machin are all touted.											

No	Date		Att	Pos	Pt	F-A	H-T	Scorers, Times, and Referees	SQUAD	NUMBERS	IN	USE								subs used
24	A	QP RANGERS		16	W	3-2	1-2	Roberts 41, 81, Marshall L 46	Marshall	Sutch	Jackson	Russell^	Fleming	Mulryne	Roberts	Marshall L	Mackay	Notman*	Llewellyn	Abbey"/Kenton/Coote
	26/12		16,472	24	27			*Carlisle 11, Wardley 42*	*Miklosko*	*Darlington*	*Baraclough*	*Morrow^*	*Plummer*	*Carlisle*	*Langley*	*Rose*	*Crouch*	*Wardley*	*Ngonge**	*Kiwomya/Connolly*
								Ref: M Ryan	Spirited City come from behind twice to grab a thrilling victory. Forty seconds after half-time Lee Marshall forces in the crucial equaliser. Richard Langley blunders when he attempts a spectacular overhead clearance, only to lose possession for Roberts to snatch the late winner.											
25	A	NOTT'M FOREST		17	D	0-0	0-0		Marshall	Sutch	Jackson	Russell^	Fleming	Mulryne	Roberts*	Marshall L	Mackay	Abbey"	Llewellyn	Coote/Kenton/Dalglish
	30/12		**20,108**	7	28				*Beasant*	*Olsen*	*Brennan**	*B't-Williams*	*Vaughan*	*Edwards*	*Prutton*	*John"*	*Jones*	*Harewood^*	*Williams*	*Foy/Gray/Reid*
								Ref: C Foy	An early blow for City as Roberts goes off injured after just 15 minutes. In one remarkable episode inside the Norwich area, three goalline clearances are made to keep the ball out. Stout defending throughout by City wins an impressive point against David Platt's unpredictable side.											
26	H	BLACKBURN		16	D	1-1	1-0	Forbes 32	Marshall	Sutch	Jackson	Russell	Fleming	Forbes"	Coote^	Marshall L	Mackay	Abbey*	Llewellyn	Mulryne/Notman/Dalglish
	1/1		16,695	4	29			*Bent 64*	*Filan*	*Curtis*	*Bjornbye"*	*Taylor*	*Broomes*	*Dunn*	*McAteer**	*Bent*	*Hughes !*	*Jansen^*	*Duff*	*Dailly/Ostenstad/Hignett*
								Ref: P Danson	The home fans acclaim a fine Forbes solo goal after a typical storming run into the Rovers box. Mark Hughes, already booked, flattens Russell right in front of the ref and is sent off. Marcus Bent's low drive skids under Marshall and Tony Parkes' ten-man side then wisely shut up shop.											
27	A	FULHAM		17	L	0-2	0-1		Marshall	Sutch	Jackson*	Russell	Fleming	Notman^	Roberts	Marshall L	Kenton	Mulryne"	Llewellyn	McGovern/Abbey/Dalglish
	13/1		16,052	1	29			*Saha 39, Boa Morte 90*	*Taylor*	*Finnan*	*Brevett*	*Melville*	*Symonds*	*Solcers^*	*Goldbaek*	*Betsy**	*Saha*	*Davis*	*Boa Morte*	*Sahnoun/Phelan*
								Ref: W Jordan	After one loss in six games, the board has seen enough and Worthington get the manager's job full-time. Doug Livermore will be asiistant and Steve Foley coach. In a poor match, Mulryne collects a nasty knee injury. Luis Boa Morte nets an exquisite late lob for the champions-elect.											
28	H	QP RANGERS		16	W	1-0	1-0	Abbey 33	Marshall	Sutch"	Jackson	Russell	Mackay	Abbey^	Roberts	Marshall L	Kenton	Coote*	Llewellyn	De Blasiis/Notman/Walsh
	20/1		16,472	23	32				*Miklosko*	*Darlington*	*Baraclough*	*Morrow**	*Plummer*	*Carlisle*	*Langley*	*Kiwomya*	*Crouch*	*Wardley*	*Perry^*	*Koejoe/Ngonge*
								Ref: M Clattenburg	A nervy contest is settled early by Abbey's first City goal, a thundering volley from six yards. Behind the scenes, a vote of no confidence in the board is overwhelmingly rejected after celebrity director Delia Smith stands up and makes an emotional appeal for the shareholders' backing.											
29	H	WATFORD		12	W	2-1	0-0	Nedergaard 81, Marshall L 88	Marshall	Sutch^	Jackson	De Blasiis*	Mackay	Abbey	Roberts	Marshall L	Kenton	Coote"	Llewellyn	Nederga'rd/McVeigh/Dalglish
	27/1		15,309	6	35			*Helguson 50*	*Chamberlain*	*Cox*	*Palmer*	*Vernazza*	*Page*	*Ward*	*Helguson*	*Nielsen*	*Mooney*	*N'l-Williams !*	*Hyde*	
								Ref: J Robinson	In a re-arranged match, Heidar Helguson gives Graham Taylor's men the lead with a header. Gifton Noel-Williams is sent off for two very rash tackles. Nedergaard steals in to equalise with a screamer of a shot. Lee Marshall wins the points as he buries a volley after a chaotic scramble.											
30	A	BIRMINGHAM		12	L	1-2	0-1	Llewellyn 80	Marshall	Sutch	Jackson	Russell	Mackay	Abbey	Roberts	Marshall L*	Kenton^	Nedergaard"	Llewellyn	Coote/De Blasiis/Dalglish
	3/2		18,551	5	35			*Hughes 9, Purse 62p*	*Bennett*	*Gill*	*Grainger*	*Hughes*	*Purse*	*Johnson M*	*Eaden"*	*Woodhouse*	*Adebola*	*Johnson A**	*Lazaridis^*	*Adebola/O'Connor/McCarthy*
								Ref: L Cable	Bryan Hughes fires home a Stan Lazaridis cross for the promotion-chasing Blues. Darren Purse slots home the penalty after a Lee Marshall handball. Llewellyn pulls one goal back with a stooping header from a Nedergaard cross. A late Birmingham goal is disallowed for pushing.											
31	H	CREWE		15	D	1-1	0-0	Llewellyn 88	Marshall	Sutch	Jackson	Russell	Mackay	Abbey^	McVeigh*	Marshall L	Kenton	Nedergaard	Llewellyn	Forbes/Coote
	10/2		15,164	20	36			*Jack 52*	*Bankole*	*Wright*	*Smith S*	*Walton*	*Macauley*	*Street^*	*Hulse**	*Lunt*	*Jack*	*Rivers*	*Sorvel*	*Ashton/Gannon*
								Ref: A Alcock	Dario Gradi's men are battling to pull away from the relegation zone and are no pushovers. They are gifted a goal when winger Rodney Jack rifles in at the far post. A surprise home defeat looks on the cards until Llewellyn turns neatly, surges into the box and fires in a real cracker.											
32	A	CRYSTAL PALACE		15	D	1-1	0-1	Russell 55	Marshall	Sutch	Jackson	Russell !	Mackay	Abbey	Roberts	Marshall L	Kenton	Nedergaard*	Llewellyn	Forbes
	17/2		16,417	14	37			*Forssell 34*	*Kolinko*	*Smith*	*Harrison*	*Austin*	*Gray*	*Rubins*	*Mullins*	*Rodger*	*Freedman**	*Forssell*	*Pollock !*	*Kabba*
								Ref: B Curson	Mikael Forssell, on loan from Chelsea, puts Alan Smith's men ahead, but within seconds Russell levels with a deflected shot. Russell's lunge on Jamie Smith sparks a lengthy mass brawl. When the dust settles, Jamie Pollock and Russell are red-carded. Russell's will later be rescinded.											
33	H	STOCKPORT		12	W	**4-0**	3-0	Llewellyn 15, Roberts 35, 38, 57	Marshall	Sutch	Jackson	Russell*	Mackay	Abbey"	Roberts	Marshall L	Kenton	McVeigh^	Llewellyn	Nedergaard/Dalglish/Forbes
	20/2		19,768	21	40				*Jones*	*Gibb*	*Nicholson**	*Wiss*	*Flynn*	*Grayson*	*Cooper^*	*Kuqi*	*Hurst*	*Fradin*	*Smith*	*Connelly/Carrigan*
								Ref: M North	City are not quite safe from relegation, but this one-sided affair boosts their chances no end. An excellent crowd enjoys the front three running rings round Andy Kilner's struggling side. Roberts pounces on an Ali Gibb error, floats in a header and then converts a teasing McVeigh cross.											
34	H	WOLVERHAMPTON		12	W	1-0	1-0	McVeigh 3	Marshall	Sutch	Jackson	Russell	Mackay	Abbey*	Roberts	Fleming	Kenton^	McVeigh"	Llewellyn	Nederga'rd/McGovern/Forbes
	24/2		17,288	15	43				*Oakes*	*Muscat*	*Naylor*	*Dinning*	*Pollet*	*Butler*	*Robinson**	*Andrews*	*Branch*	*Ndah*	*Sinton^*	*Ketsbaia/Roussel*
								Ref: A Jones	A great start as the promising McVeigh thumps in his first Norwich goal after a Jackson free-kick is knocked down to him by Mackay. Roberts nearly makes it two, but hits the crossbar. Kenton is carried off injured. Marshall is kept on his toes and has a fine game to keep Wolves at bay.											

35	A	HUDDERSFIELD		12	L		0-2	0-1		Marshall	Sutch	Jackson	Russell	Mackay	Abbey*	Roberts	Fleming	Nedergaard	McVeigh	Llewellyn	Forbes
	3/3		*11,122*	*23*		43			*Armstrong 8, Facey 71*	*Vaesen*	*Jenkins*	*Heary*	*Dyson*	*Lucketti*	*Armstrong*	*Thornley^*	*Irons*	*Smith*	*Gallen**	*Facey*	*Gorre/Baldry*
									Ref: M Brandwood	Winless for seven games, Lou Macari's outfit gets off to a great start when Craig Armstrong beats Marshall. Delroy Facey makes sure of the points as he is left unmarked to sweep in the second goal. This disappointing defeat leaves Norwich still some way short of a 'safe' points total.											
36	H	WEST BROM		12	L		0-1	0-1		Marshall	Kenton*	Jackson"	Russell	Mackay	Abbey^	Roberts	Fleming	Marshall L	McVeigh	Llewellyn	McGovern/Forbes/Coote
	6/3		16,372	*5*		43			*Hughes 33p*	*Hoult*	*Lyttle*	*Van Blerk*	*Sigurdsson*	*Butler*	*Clement*	*Appleton*	*Sneekes*	*Roberts^*	*Hughes**	*Fox*	*Jordao/Taylor*
									Ref: R Furnandiz	In his first year as Baggies manager, former Canary Gary Megson is bidding for promotion, but his team are made to fight all the way this evening. They take a controversial lead via a Lee Hughes penalty, after Roberts and Mackay are rather harshly accused of impeding Hughes.											
37	A	WATFORD		14	L		1-4	1-1	Forbes 7 *[Nielsen 86]*	Marshall	Sutch	Jackson	Russell	Mackay	Forbes*	Roberts	Fleming	Marshall L"	Nedergaard^	Llewellyn	McVeigh/Abbey/De Blasiis
	10/3		*15,123*	*7*		43			*Wooter 9, Smith 61, Helguson 76,*	*Baardsen*	*Cox*	*Robinson*	*Panayi*	*Vernazza*	*Ward*	*Easton*	*Nielsen*	*Mooney*	*Wooter**	*Smith*	*Helguson*
									Ref: A Kaye	Forbes nets a rare header from a Nedergaard cross to give City a fine start, but Nordin Wooter is quick to equalise. Despair for Worthington as three late goals sink City and give Graham Taylor his first win in seven matches. Miserable City fans head for the exits well before the whistle.											
38	H	PRESTON		16	L		1-2	1-1	Roberts 32	Marshall	Sutch^	Jackson	Russell	Mackay	Forbes"	Roberts	Fleming	Marshall L	McVeigh*	Llewellyn	Notman/Nedergaard/Abbey
	17/3		16,282	*5*		43			*Healy 34, Gregan 48*	*Moilanen*	*Alexander*	*Edwards*	*Murdock**	*Gregan*	*Appleton*	*McKenna*	*Rankine*	*McKenna^*	*Healy*	*Cartwright*	*Kidd/Cresswell*
									Ref: T Bates	Roberts nets a Llewellyn cross but David Healy is quick to level. Soon after the break promotion-chasing Preston go ahead as skipper Sean Gregan - not a prolific scorer - nets a sensational effort. From near halfway, he spots Marshall off his line and sends a 45-yard lob sailing in.											
39	H	GRIMSBY		14	W		2-1	1-1	Roberts 3, Llewellyn 74	Marshall	Sutch	**Drury**	**Holt**	Mackay	Forbes	Roberts	Fleming*	Mulryne	**Peschis'do^**	Llewellyn	Kenton/Abbey
	31/3		17,461	*21*		46			*Campbell 32*	*Coyne*	*McDermott*	*Gallimore*	*Groves*	*Enhua**	*Coldicott*	*Donovan*	*Pouton^*	*Cornwall"*	*Campbell*	*Jefrey*	*Smith D/Willems/Clare*
									Ref: G Frankland	Lee Marshall moves to Leicester for £600k, allowing Worthington to sign Peterborough's Drury and Kilmarnock's Holt, plus Peschisolido on loan. Nervous City pass a stern test of character, boosted by Roberts' 12-yard drive from an early corner. Forbes is voted player-of-the-match.											
40	A	GILLINGHAM		15	L		3-4	0-2	Llewellyn 58, Russell 63, Roberts 81	Green	Sutch	Drury	Holt	Mackay	Forbes*	Roberts	Jackson	Mulryne	Peschis'l'd'^	Llewellyn	Russell/Notman
	7/4		*9,608*	*14*		46			*Hope 32, Onoura 38, 47, 52*	*Bartram*	*Nosworthy*	*Patterson*	*Hope*	*Browning*	*Pennock*	*Smith*	*Shaw**	*Onoura^*	*King*	*Southall*	*Saunders/Ipoua"/James*
									Ref: R Olivier	Three headed goals, plus an Iffy Onoura tap-in, leave City four down. Llewellyn converts a poor back-pass to launch the comeback. Russell's fierce shot and Roberts' header reduce the deficit. Three desperate saves by Vince Bartram in the dying minutes prevent an historic recovery.											
41	A	SHEFFIELD UTD		15	D		1-1	0-1	Kenton 86	Green	Kenton	Drury	Russell	Mackay	Notman*	Roberts	Jackson	Mulryne	Fleming	Llewellyn	Peschisolido
	10/4		*16,072*	*9*		47			*Roberts 32 (og)*	*Talia*	*Kozluk*	*Uhlenbeek*	*Montgomery*	*Murphy*	*Curle*	*Devlin*	*Bullock**	*Asaba*	*Ndlovu^*	*Ford*	*Jagielka/Suffo*
									Ref: S Tomlin	The fighting spirit at Priestfield comes to the surface again. The Blades are on top for most of the game, but Norwich always look capable of snatching something. Roberts' inadvertently flashes a header past his own keeper. With four minutes left, Kenton guides in a Drury free-kick.											
42	A	TRANMERE		15	W		1-0	0-0	McGovern 87	Green	Kenton	Drury*	Russell	Mackay	Peschis'l'd'^	Roberts"	Jackson	Mulryne	Fleming	Llewellyn	McGovern/Notman/Forbes
	14/4		*9,303*	*24*		50				*Murphy*	*Kenna*	*Allen**	*Jobson*	*Flynn*	*Challinor*	*Hill*	*Osborn"*	*N'Diaye*	*Koumas*	*Allison^*	*Challinor/Barlow/Mellon*
									Ref: P Dowd	Both sides desperately need a win. Before kick-off City are five points above the drop-zone but have played more than most rivals. Defeat could prove fatal to Rovers. A tense affair is won in dramatic style when unlikely hero McGovern speeds into the box and drills the ball home.											
43	H	BURNLEY		16	L		2-3	2-1	Notman 13, Roberts 38p	Green	Kenton*	Drury	Russell	Mackay	Notman^	Roberts	Jackson"	Mulryne	Fleming	Llewellyn	Forbes/Peschis'do/McGovern
	16/4		17,507	*8*		50			*Ball 24, Taylor 48, Moore 62*	*Michopoulos*	*West*	*Smith**	*Weller*	*Davis*	*Armstrong*	*Ball*	*Cook^*	*Taylor*	*Little*	*Moore"*	*Briscoe/Thomas/Payton*
									Ref: M Messias	Notman bursts clear and nets a fine goal to break his duck. Kevin Ball levels with a 25-yarder that bobbles out of Green's reach. Notman is fouled for Roberts to net from the spot. A clever pass by Glen Little sets up Gareth Taylor. Ina Moore pounces on a loose ball for the winner.											
44	A	BOLTON		17	L		0-1	0-0		Green	Kenton^	Drury	Russell	Mackay	Notman"	Roberts	Jackson	Mulryne*	Fleming	Llewellyn	Holt/McGovern/Abbey
	21/4		*17,967*	*3*		50			*Holdsworth 66*	*Clarke*	*Barness*	*Elliott*	*Frandsen*	*Bergsson*	*Hendry*	*Summ'bee**	*Farrelly*	*Holdsworth*	*Marshall^*	*Gardner*	*Passi/Hansen*
									Ref: P Rejer	City make Bolton work hard and the stalemate is finally broken when Dean Holdsworth thumps in a free-kick while City are still organising their wall. Minutes later a Holdsworth header hits the bar. Mackay gets away with a handball in the area and 1-0 ends up flattering Norwich.											
45	H	SHEFFIELD WED		16	W		1-0	1-0	Mackay 18	Marshall	Kenton	Nedergaard	Russell	Mackay	Notman	Roberts	Jackson	Mulryne	Fleming	Llewellyn*	McVeigh
	28/4		**21,241**	*17*		53				*Pressman*	*Hendon*	*Harkness^*	*Lescott"*	*Westwood*	*Bromby*	*Ripley*	*Sibon*	*De Bilde**	*Ekoku*	*Soltvedt*	*Hamshaw/Geary/Donnelly*
									Ref: W Jordan	Three points will ensure City are mathematically safe from relegation. The biggest Carrow Road crowd for five years turns out, hoping for a celebration party. Mackay rises to send a Mulryne corner looping over Aaron Lescott on the line and in off the bar. The visitors lack real bite.											
46	A	WIMBLEDON		15	D		0-0	0-0		Marshall	Kenton^	Nedergaard	Russell	Mackay	Holt	Roberts*	McGovern	Mulryne	Fleming	Llewellyn"	Abbey/Sutch/McVeigh
	6/5		*7,888*	*8*		54				*Heald*	*Hawkins*	*Kimble*	*Andersen^*	*Williams*	*Gier*	*Ardley*	*Euell*	*Roberts*	*Nielsen"*	*Cooper**	*Morgan/Ainsworth/Gray*
		Home	Away						Ref: D Pugh	The result is academic for two mid-table sides, but this turns into a better match than expected. Russell fluffs a reasonable chance to win it and both sides have goals disallowed for offside. Marshall, out of contract and set to leave, says farewell to the club with a series of brilliant saves.											
Average		16,525	13,789																		

Worthington Cup			Att			F-A	H-T	Scorers, Times, and Referees	SQUAD	NUMBERS	IN	USE								subs used
1:1	H	BOURNEMOUTH		17	D	0-0	0-0		Marshall	Sutch	De Waard"	Marshall L	Fleming	Kenton	Mulryne^	Russell	Roberts	Giallanza*	Llewellyn	Forbes/McGovern/Coote
22/8			12,224	*2:16*					*Menetrier*	*Young*	*Purches*	*Grant*	*Smith*	*Tindall*	*Jorgensen*	*Fletcher C^*	*Eribenne**	*Fletcher S*	*Hughes*	*Huck/Elliott*
								Ref: A Hall	A very dour game produces little sparkle from the home side. Alarm bells are sounding about the lack of punch in City's attack. It's now well over 400 minutes of play since the Canaries last hit the opposition net. New Cherries manager Sean O'Driscoll is more than happy with a draw.											
1:2	A	BOURNEMOUTH		23	W	2-1	0-1	Giallanza 59, Russell 84	Marshall	Sutch	Derveld	Marshall L	Fleming	McGovern	Jackson	Russell	Roberts	Giallanza^	Brady*	Nedergaard/Coote
5/9			*3,634*	*2:22*				*Jorgensen 7*	*Menetrier*	*Young*	*Purches*	*Grant^*	*Smith*	*Tindall*	*Jorgensen*	*Fletcher C*	*Eribenne*	*Fletcher S*	*Hughes^*	*Hayter/Huck*
								Ref: S Bennett (Norwich win 2-1 on aggregate)	Huge relief in the Norwich camp at this result. It is certainly no classic, with the Cherries playing neat football and hard to break down after going ahead early through Claus Jorgensen. Giallanza notches the vital equaliser and is starting to look the part. Russell fires in the late winner.											
2:1	H	BLACKPOOL		20	D	3-3	3-2	Roberts 22p, Marshall L 28, Cottee 43	Marshall	Sutch	Derveld	Marshall L	Fleming	McGovern	Walsh*	Russell	Roberts	Cottee^	Nedergaard"	Forbes/Giallanza/De Waard
19/9			9,369	*2:23*				*Murphy J 28, 87, Ormerod 44*	*Barnes*	*Collins*	*Jaszczun*	*Bushell*	*Hughes*	*Jones*	*Simpson*	*Wellens*	*Ormerod*	*Murphy J*	*Coid*	
								Ref: J Brandwood	Cottee's tap-in gives City a two-goal cushion, but Brett Ormerod bundles in debutant Walsh's failed clearance. John Murphy rises to head past static Marshall to grab a deserved draw. Sutch's determination to get the ball back for a late throw leads to a mass brawl involving 19 players.											
2:2	A	BLACKPOOL		20	W	5-0	2-0	Russell 9, Giallanza 35, 64, [Roberts 49, 57]	Marshall	Sutch	Derveld	Marshall L	Fleming	Kenton	Brady	Russell^	Roberts	Giallanza	Llewellyn*	Nedergaard/Cottee
2/10			*4,038*	*2:19*					*Barnes*	*Murphy N*	*Jaszczun*	*Bushell*	*Hughes*	*Jones^*	*Collins*	*Simpson**	*Ormerod*	*Murphy J*	*Coid*	*Nowland/Wellens*
								Ref: P Dowd (Norwich win 8-3 on aggregate)	Steve McMahon's side don't know what's hit them as City create five chances and net the lot. Under-fire boss Hamilton dedicates the win to the hardy 300 travelling fans who are dancing with glee by the end. Giallanza converts a Derveld free-kick and strikes the fifth in off the post.											
3	A	DERBY		17	L	0-3	0-3		Marshall	Sutch	Mackay	Mulryne	Fleming	Kenton^	Forbes*	Russell	Roberts	Dalglish*	Llewellyn	Coote/De Waard/McVeigh
1/11			*11,273*	*P:20*				*Delap 12, Burley 16p, Christie 39*	*Poom*	*Valakari*	*Johnson*	*Riggott*	*Schnoor^*	*Delap*	*Burley*	*Elliott*	*Kinkladze*	*Christie**	*Powell*	*Morris/Higginbotham*
								Ref: C Wilkes	Jim Smith's men are rock bottom of the Premiership without a win to their name, but they cruise into a big lead by the interval. Basic defensive errors by City hand them the crucial first two goals by Rory Delap and Craig Burley. It's a very depressing evening for the 2,300 visiting fans.											

FA Cup																				
3	A	SHEFFIELD WED		16	L	1-2	0-1	Roberts 74	Marshall	Sutch"	Jackson	Russell	Fleming	Forbes^	Roberts	Marshall L	Mackay	Mulryne*	Llewellyn	Abbey/Sutch/McVeigh
6/1			*15,971*	*21*				*Hamshaw 41, Sibon 82*	*Stringer*	*Hendon*	*Harkness*	*Haslam*	*Blatsis*	*Walker*	*Hamshaw**	*Sibon*	*Ekoku*	*Lescott*	*Quinn*	*Bromby^/Crane*
								Ref: D Laws	The cup draw hands City a repeat of the third round two years ago. Young Matt Hamshaw gets his second career goal with a diving header. Roberts levels, guiding Notman's header in. Gerald Sibon's drive gives Paul Jewell his last win as manager - he will be sacked within a month.											

		P	W	D	L	F	A	W	D	L	F	A	Pts
			Home					Away					
1	Fulham	46	16	5	2	49	14	14	6	3	41	18	101
2	Blackburn	46	15	5	3	43	20	11	8	4	33	19	91
3	Bolton *	46	10	10	3	40	28	14	5	4	36	17	87
4	Preston	46	12	6	5	32	18	11	3	9	32	34	78
5	Birmingham	46	14	3	6	34	22	9	6	8	25	26	78
6	West Brom	46	13	5	5	37	23	8	6	9	23	29	74
7	Burnley	46	14	5	4	30	17	7	4	12	20	37	72
8	Wimbledon	46	7	11	5	33	26	10	7	6	38	24	69
9	Watford	46	11	6	6	46	29	9	3	11	30	38	69
10	Sheffield Utd	46	14	4	5	34	18	5	7	11	18	31	68
11	Nott'm For	46	11	3	9	28	24	9	5	9	27	29	68
12	Wolves	46	7	9	7	25	20	7	4	12	20	28	55
13	Gillingham	46	9	6	8	32	28	4	10	9	29	38	55
14	Crewe	46	12	5	6	30	24	3	5	15	17	38	55
15	NORWICH	46	10	7	6	25	18	4	5	14	21	40	54
16	Barnsley	46	11	3	9	32	26	4	6	13	17	36	54
17	Sheffield Wed	46	9	4	10	34	38	6	4	13	18	33	53
18	Grimsby	46	10	4	9	26	27	4	6	13	17	35	52
19	Stockport	46	6	11	6	29	26	5	7	11	29	39	51
20	Portsmouth	46	9	8	6	31	25	1	11	11	16	34	49
21	Crys Palace	46	6	6	11	28	34	6	7	10	29	36	49
22	Huddersfield	46	7	6	10	29	26	4	9	10	19	31	48
23	QP Rangers	46	6	9	8	24	28	1	10	12	21	47	40
24	Tranmere	46	8	7	8	30	33	1	4	18	16	44	38
		1104	247	148	157	781	592	157	148	247	592	781	1508

* promoted after play-offs

Odds & ends

Double wins: (3) QP Rangers, Stockport, Tranmere.
Double losses: (4) Bolton, Burnley, Fulham, Preston.

Won from behind: (4) QP Rangers (a), Sheffield Utd (h), Watford (h), Bournemouth (a) (LC).
Lost from in front: (3) Burnley (h), Preston (h), Watford (a).

High points: The comeback against Sheffield Utd, including an 18-pass move for the fourth goal.
The superb effort to save a point at Gillingham after being 0-4 down.
The hammering of Stockport – a rare day when City really 'clicked'.
Another rise in average home attendances.

Low points: An August nightmare – five games, no wins, two goals.
Five losses in a row in Nov-Dec – leading to Hamilton's resignation.
The departure of fans favourite Craig Bellamy in August.
The long-term injury to Gaetano Giallanza.
Finishing in the lower half of Division 1 for the fourth time in six seasons.

Player of the Year: Andy Marshall.
Ever-presents: (0).
Hat-tricks: (1) Iwan Roberts (v Stockport, h).
Hat-tricks against: (1) Iffy Onoura (v Gillingham, a).
Leading scorer: (18) Iwan Roberts.

	Appearances						Goals			
	Lge	*Sub*	LC	*Sub*	FAC	*Sub*	Lge	LC	FAC	Tot
Abbey, Zema	11	*9*					1			1
Bellamy, Craig	1									
Brady, Garry	2		2							
Coote, Adrian	3	*11*		*3*		*1*				
Cottee, Tony	5	*2*	1				1	1		2
Dalglish, Paul		*7*	1							
De Blasiis, Jean-Yves	2	*5*								
Derveld, Fernando	15	*2*	3				1			1
De Waard, Raymond		*6*	1	*2*						
Drury, Adam	6									
Fleming, Craig	39		5		1					
Forbes, Adrian	13	*16*	1	*2*	1		3			3
Granville, Danny	6									
Giallanza, Gaetano	5	*6*	3	*1*			2	3		5
Green, Robert	5									
Holt, Gary	3	*1*								
Jackson, Matt	26		1		1					
Kenton, Darren	24	*5*	3			*1*	2			2
Llewellyn, Chris	41	*1*	3		1		8			8
Mackay, Malky	34	*4*	1		1		1		1	2
Marshall, Andy	41		5		1					
Marshall, Lee	34	*2*	4	*1*	1		3	1		4
McGovern, Brian	3	*9*	2	*1*			1			1
McVeigh, Paul	6	*5*		*1*			1			1
Mulryne, Phil	27	*1*	2		1		1			1
Nedergaard, Steen	10	*5*	1	*2*			1			1
Notman, Alex	10	*5*				*1*	1			1
Parker, Scott	6						1			1
Peschisolido, Paul	3	*2*								
Roberts, Iwan	44		5		1		15	3		18
Russell, Darel	34	*7*	5		1		2	2		4
Sutch, Daryl	39	*1*	5		1					
Walsh, Steve	1	*3*	1							
Whitley, Jim	7	*1*					1			1
34 players used	**506**	***116***	**55**	***13***	**11**	***3***	**46**	**10**	**1**	**57**

No	Date		Att	Pos	Pt	F-A	H-T	Scorers, Times, and Referees	SQUAD NUMBERS IN USE											subs used
1	A	MILLWALL			L	**0-4**	0-2		Green	Kenton^	Drury	Mackay	Fleming	Mulryne	Holt	Abbey	Roberts I	**Emblen***	Llewellyn"	Russell/McGovern/**Easton**
	11/8		*14,501*		0			*Claridge 12, Reid 43, Cahill 66, Neill 90*	*Warner*	*Neill*	*Ryan*	*Cahill*	*Nethercott*	*Dyche*	*Ifill*	*Livermore*	*Claridge*	*Sadlier*	*Reid*	
								Ref: M Fletcher	Of five new signings, Mark Rivers is injured and Marc Libbra back in France after a family bereavement. New skipper Neil Emblen debuts but picks up a hamstring injury that will wreck his season. Gloom for 2,000 travelling fans as Mark McGhee's men are far too sharp for Norwich.											
2	H	MANCHESTER C		15	W	2-0	0-0	Libbra 75, McVeigh 90	Green	Nedergaard	Drury	Mackay	Fleming	Mulryne	Holt	Abbey	Roberts I^	Russell"	Llewellyn*	McVeigh/Libbra/Nedergaard
	18/8		18,745	*10*	3				*Nash"*	*Charvet*	*Granville*	*Dunne*	*Howey*	*Pearce*	*Wiekens*	*Berkovic**	*Wanchope !*	*Goater*	*Tiatto*	*Whitley^/Horlock/Weaver*
								Ref: P Taylor	Paulo Wanchope is red-carded after a rash challenge and a bizarre tangle with a ball-boy. Libbra comes on for his debut and within 20 seconds flips the ball over Steve Howey and smashes an astonishing goal. Keeper Carlo Nash and Llewellyn (broken foot) are among four carried off.											
3	A	WIMBLEDON		9	W	1-0	0-0	Libbra 89	Green	Kenton	Drury	Mackay	Fleming	Mulryne	Holt	Abbey^	Roberts I	Russell*	McVeigh"	Nedergaard/Libbra/McGovern
	25/8		*6,084*	*14*	6				*Heald*	*Darlington*	*Kimble*	*Roberts*	*Gier*	*Wilmot*	*Ardley*	*Nielsen^*	*Shipperley**	*Connolly*	*Cooper*	*Agyemang/McAnuff*
								Ref: A Hall	After the Brentford cup flop, City once again bounce back and show great spirit in the aftermath of a horror show. Terry Burton gives Joel McAnuff a debut as his side toils hard in a bid to break through. Libbra comes off the bench and does the trick again with a very late winner.											
4	H	SHEFFIELD WED		5	W	2-0	1-0	Roberts I 37, McVeigh 74	Green	Kenton	Drury	Mackay	Fleming	Mulryne	Holt	Abbey*	Roberts I"	Nedergaard^	McVeigh	Libbra/Russell/Notman
	27/8		16,820	*18*	9				*Pressman*	*Hendon^*	*Geary*	*Solvedt*	*Bromby*	*Maddix*	*Haslam*	*Sibon"*	*Ekoku*	*McLaren*	*Quinn**	*Morrison/Bonvin/Westwood*
								Ref: G Frankland	Roberts' first-half header edges City ahead against Nigel Worthington's former club. McVeigh, replacing the injured Llewellyn on the left of midfield, has a superb game and clinches the victory himself. Peter Shreeves and this famous old club look set for another season of struggle.											
5	H	NOTT'M FOREST		4	W	1-0	1-0	Abbey 14	Green	Kenton	Drury	Mackay	Fleming	Mulryne	Holt	Abbey	Roberts I^	Nedergaard	McVeigh*	Russell/Libbra
	8/9		18,061	*15*	12				*Ward*	*Louis-Jean*	*Brennan*	*B't-Williams*	*Hjelde*	*Edwards*	*Prutton"*	*Jenas*	*Johnson^*	*Harewood**	*Williams*	*John/Reid/Bopp*
								Ref: L Cable	Abbey thumps home his first of the season from 20 yards at the Barclay End, giving Darren Ward no chance. Paul Hart's young Forest outfit play neat passing football, but aren't able to find the penetration to equalise. Kiev-born youngster Eugene Bopp makes his debut in England.											
6	A	ROTHERHAM		5	D	1-1	0-0	Scott 51 (og)	Green	McGovern	Drury	Mackay	Fleming	Mulryne	Holt	Abbey*	Roberts I	Nedergaard	McVeigh^	Libbra/Russell
	15/9		*6,099*	*23*	13			*Robins 70p*	*Pollitt*	*Bryan*	*Hurst*	*Scott*	*McIntosh*	*Swailes*	*Talbot*	*Watson^*	*Lee*	*Robins*	*Miranda**	*Sedgwick/Daws*
								Ref: A Butler	Rob Scott beats his own keeper to put Norwich ahead, but the former Canary Mark Robins levels with a penalty. The latest long-term casualty is Abbey, who damages cruciate and medial knee ligaments and will be out for the season. Portuguese Jose Miranda makes his English debut.											
7	H	WATFORD		2	W	3-1	2-1	Roberts I 20, Nedergaard 25, Mackay 68	Green	McGovern	Drury	Mackay	Fleming	Mulryne*	Holt	Libbra^	Roberts I	Nedergaard"	McVeigh	Russell/Notman/**Rivers**
	18/9		17,885	*14*	16			*Vega 42*	*Baardsen*	*Cox*	*Robinson^*	*Vernazza*	*Issa*	*Vega*	*Glass*	*Hyde"*	*Gayle*	*Fisken**	*Wooter*	*Smith/Helguson/Noble*
								Ref: B Knight	Mark Rivers, signed from Crewe, debuts for City against Gianluca Vialli's big-spending Hornets. Nedergaard turns in a great display. Roberts smashes in the first off the keeper's legs and Nedergaard heads home a McVeigh cross. Mackay glances in the third from Fleming's free-kick.											
8	H	BURNLEY		2	W	2-1	1-0	Holt 4, Roberts I 55	Green	Kenton*	Drury	Mackay	Fleming	Russell	Holt	Libbra^	Roberts I	Nedergaard	McVeigh"	McGovern/Emblen/Notman
	22/9		19,849	*1*	19			*Armstrong 58*	*Michopoulos*	*West*	*Armstrong*	*Ball*	*Davis*	*Briscoe*	*Little^*	*Cook*	*Moore I"*	*Taylor*	*Moore A**	*Weller/Ellis/Payton*
								Ref: P Alcock	Holt nets his first City goal with an early thunderbolt from 25 yards. Stan Ternent's early-season pace-setters are stunned as Roberts bundles in another. Gordon Armstrong hits back and sparks a spell of intense pressure. Emblen aggravates his injury and will miss the rest of the season.											
9	A	PRESTON		3	L	**0-4**	0-4	*[Edwards 33]*	Green	Kenton	Drury	McGovern	Fleming	Russell^	Holt	Libbra*	Roberts I"	Nedergaard	McVeigh	Notman/Easton/Rivers
	26/9		*12,014*	*16*	19			*Alexander 2p, Macken 14, 45,*	*Moilanen*	*Alexander*	*Edwards*	*Jackson*	*Lucketti*	*Cartwright*	*McKenna*	*Rankine*	*Macken*	*Healy**	*Anderson^*	*Cresswell/Barry-Murphy*
								Ref: G Cain	Mackay is badly missed. It's a damage-limitation job after a dreadful first half. Fleming's obstruction after only 30 seconds concedes a disputed penalty. Two fine finishes follow from Jon Macken. A spot of head-tennis sets up Rob Edwards. City fans are drenched on the open terrace.											
10	A	SHEFFIELD UTD		4	L	1-2	0-2	Nedergaard 83	Green	Kenton	Sutch	Mackay	Fleming	Mulryne	Holt	Notman^	Roberts I	Nedergaard	Easton*	Rivers/Libbra
	29/9		*15,523*	*18*	19			*Asaba 40, Suffo 45*	*De Vogt*	*Kozluk*	*Nicholson**	*Page*	*Murphy*	*Curle*	*Tonge"*	*Brown*	*Asaba !*	*Suffo^*	*Ndlovu*	*Ford/Peschisolido/Santos*
								Ref: M Jones	City are made to pay for two lapses in concentration. Carl Asaba squeezes in a Peter Ndlovu pass and, just before the break, Patrick Suffo volleys home after a Robert Kozluk long-throw. Nedergaard's excellent free-kick flies straight in. Asaba is sent off for two late indiscretions.											
11	A	WALSALL		4	L	0-2	0-1		Green	Kenton*	Drury	Mackay	Fleming	Mulryne	Holt	Rivers	Roberts I	Nedergaard^	McVeigh	McGovern/Libbra
	9/10		*5,713*	*20*	19			*Barras 45, Byfield 53*	*Walker*	*Gadsby*	*Aranalde*	*Brightwell*	*Chettle*	*Barras*	*Herivelto"*	*Bennett*	*Leitao^*	*Byfield**	*Wrack*	*Matias/Curtis/Angell*
								Ref: M Cowburn	Darren Byfield sees a stinging shot parried out by Green and Jorge Leitao heads the ball across goal for Tony Barras to bundle it in. Vibrant Byfield's second-half snapshot makes it two for Ray Graydon's men. A late Norwich assault sees Roberts strike the bar and McVeigh the post.											

12	A	GILLINGHAM		3	W	2-0	0-0	Roberts I 81, 90	Green	Kenton	Drury	Mackay	Fleming	Mulryne	Holt	Rivers*	Roberts I	Nedergaard	McVeigh^	Llewellyn/Sutch
	13/10		9,166	18	22				Bartram	Patterson	Edge	Hope	Butters	Pennock	Smith	Browning^	Ipoua*	King	Saunders	Taylor/Osborn
								Ref: D Gallagher	The away-day blues come to an end with a very professional performance in Kent. City look tight at the back and kill off the Gills after hitting a post three times. Drury clips over a cross and Roberts stoops to head in. Roberts dummies and chips in a gem of a goal from a narrow angle.											
13	H	WEST BROM		2	W	2-0	2-0	Roberts I 13, Rivers 16	Green	Russell	Drury*	Mackay	Fleming	Mulryne	Holt	Rivers"	Roberts I	Libbra^	McVeigh	Kenton/Llewellyn/Russell
	19/10		20,465	5	25				Hoult	Chambers	Clement*	Sigurdsson	Moore	Johnson"	McInnes	Dobie	Gilchrist	Taylor	Appleton^	Cummings/Chambers/Fox
								Ref: K Hill	Ex-Canaries Gary Megson, Ruel Fox and Andy Johnson have an unhappy return. For the first 20 minutes City are rampant. Roberts buries a back-header from McVeigh's cross and Rivers nets at the far post after more good work by McVeigh. Derek McInnes' fierce shot hits the bar.											
14	H	PORTSMOUTH		4	D	0-0	0-0		Green	Nedergaard	Kenton	Mackay	Fleming	Mulryne	Holt	Rivers^	Roberts I	Libbra*	McVeigh	Notman/Llewellyn
	23/10		19,962	9	26				Beasant	Crowe	Edinburgh	Hiley	Primus	O'Neil	Barrett	Harper*	Lovell^	Bradbury	Quashie	Pitt/Vine
								Ref: B Curson	Another good crowd turns up, hoping to see the 100 per cent home record maintained. Pompey are missing star performer Robert Prosinecki, but work hard to keep City out. Rivers is guilty of a bad miss, lashing a volley over the bar from five yards. Other chances are also spurned.											
15	A	CRYSTAL PALACE		5	L	2-3	0-1	Libbra 70, Roberts I 86p	Green	Nedergaard^	Drury	Mackay	Fleming	Mulryne	Holt	Rivers"	Roberts I	Russell*	McVeigh	Libbra/Sutch/Llewellyn
	28/10		19,553	2	26			Morrison 41, 53, Freedman 65	Clarke	Smith	Gray	Austin	Popovic	Riihilahti	Mullins	Rodger*	Morrison	Freedman	Kirovski	Hopkin
								Ref: G Poll	The live TV cameras cover a Sunday afternoon thriller with a sting in the tail. Palace surge into a three-goal lead, but late City strikes mean a nail-biting end to the game. Home boss Steve Bruce wants to take over at Birmingham, but angry Palace are refusing to accept his resignation.											
16	A	GRIMSBY		4	W	2-0	1-0	Mulryne 19, 58	Green	Nedergaard	Drury	Mackay	Fleming	Mulryne	Holt	Libbra^	Roberts I	Llewellyn*	McVeigh"	Notman/Russell/Rivers
	30/10		5,489	19	29				Coyne	Chapman"	Gallimore	Beharall	Broomes	Coldicott*	Pouton	Butterfield	Allen^	Jevons	Boulding	Willems/Rowan/Thompson
								Ref: R Furnandiz	Grimsby are outclassed by a slick performance. The bar, the post, an offside flag and several good saves help keep the score down. Drury's sweeping cross is headed by Stacy Coldicott straight to Mulryne, who stabs in. Libbra sets up the same player for a well-taken second goal.											
17	H	WOLVERHAMPTON		2	W	2-0	2-0	Roberts I 7, McVeigh 33	Green	Sutch	Drury	Mackay	Fleming	Mulryne	Holt	Libbra	Roberts I	Rivers*	McVeigh	Notman
	3/11		20,335	1	32				Oakes	Muscat	Naylor	Lescott	Butler	Cameron	Newton	Rae	Blake	Branch^	Sinton*	Russell/Proudlock
								Ref: P Durkin	Another full-house enjoys a confident performance, full of slick one-touch play by Libbra and McVeigh in particular. McVeigh's jinking run finds Libbra, whose cross is laid off by Roberts for Rivers to stab home. Libbra's backheel helps set up McVeigh, who finishes off the leaders.											
18	H	BRADFORD C		3	L	1-4	0-2	McVeigh 67	Green	Nedergaard	Kenton	Mackay	Fleming	Mulryne	Holt	Libbra	Roberts I	Rivers*	McVeigh	Notman
	10/11		17,414	12	32			Jess 42, Blake 44, 64p, Bower 90	Davison	Halle	Jacobs	McCall	Atherton*	Myers	Etherington	Locke	Blake	Tod	Jess	Bower
								Ref: S Tomlin	Basking in the glow of last week, City lose the chance to go top in an open and entertaining game. Eoin Jess heads in Wayne Jacobs' cross and Robbie Blake drills in a cross-shot. Blake's penalty slips under Green. McVeigh pulls one back, but Mackay's clearance cannons in off the sub.											
19	A	STOCKPORT		4	L	1-2	0-1	Mulryne 85	Green	Nedergaard	Kenton"	Mackay	Fleming	Mulryne	Holt	Libbra*	Roberts I	Llewellyn^	McVeigh	Notman/Nedergaard
	15/11		6,551	24	32			Hurst 28, Palmer 60	Jones	Briggs	Clark	Roget	Palmer	Lescott	Gibb !	Wiss*	Wilbraham	Taylor	Hurst	Delaney
								Ref: M Brandwood	Carlton Palmer's first home match in charge sees lowly Stockport in determined mood. Another chance to go top is lost. Glynn Hurst nets a free header and Palmer volleys home after poor defending. Mulryne steers in a consolation. Ali Gibb is sent off for two yellow card offences.											
20	H	CREWE		4	D	2-2	1-1	Libbra 14, 50	Green	Sutch	Drury	Mackay	Fleming	Mulryne	Holt	Libbra^	Roberts I	Rivers*	McVeigh	Kenton/Notman
	20/11		**15,710**	18	33			Walton 6, Brammer 86	Bankole	Wright	Smith	Foster	Walton	Charnock	Hulse	Lunt	Ashton	Brammer	Thomas*	Rix
								Ref: F Stretton	Crewe boss Dario Gradi receives presentations marking his 1,000th game in charge. In an entertaining affair, David Walton powers in a header, and Libbra sweeps in a Roberts knockdown. Libbra rises high to nod another, but Mackay's stumble sets up Dave Brammer for the equaliser.											
21	H	BARNSLEY		3	W	2-1	1-0	Roberts I 30, Mulryne 82	Green	Nedergaard	Drury	Mackay	Fleming	Mulryne	Holt	Libbra	Roberts I	Rivers*	McVeigh	Notman
	24/11		17,333	23	36			Barker 56	Miller	Milligan	Barker	Morgan	Chettle	Lumsdon	Tinkler"	Bertos^	Neil*	Dyer	Barnard	Crooks/Gorre/Fallon
								Ref: D Crick	Steve Parkin has taken over the Tykes following Nigel Spackman's dismissal. Roberts bundles the ball in after a McVeigh cross. Green misses a Darren Barnard corner and Chris Barker equalises. Mulryne's winner is a neat lob over the advancing goalkeeper after Fleming's lofted pass.											
22	A	PORTSMOUTH		3	W	2-1	1-1	Roberts I 17, Tiler 85 (og)	Green	Nedergaard	Drury	Mackay	Fleming	Mulryne	Holt	Russell	Roberts I	Rivers*	McVeigh	Notman
	2/12		13,286	10	39			Harper 23	Kawaguchi	Crowe^	Vincent*	Hiley	Tiler	O'Neil	Barrett	Harper	Crouch	Bradbury	Quashie	Pitt/Lovell
								Ref: D Pugh	Sunday live TV action at Fratton Park. A great run and finish by Kevin Harper cancels out Roberts' opener. Roberts pressurises Carl Tiler into heading past his own keeper to put Norwich ahead late on. A couple of breathtaking saves are needed from Green to preserve the slender lead.											
23	A	BIRMINGHAM		4	L	**0-4**	0-2		Green	Nedergaard	Drury	Mackay	Fleming	Mulryne	Holt	Russell"	Roberts I*	Rivers^	McVeigh	Libbra/Notman/Kenton
	8/12		17,310	10	39			Mooney 30, 45, 58p, Marcelo 46	Bennett	Fleming	Burrows	Vickers	Purse	Woodhouse	Eden	O'Connor	Mooney*	Marcelo	Lazaridis	Johnson
								Ref: G Laws	The Blues are waiting for ex-Canary hero Steve Bruce to take over as manager, but he's in dispute with current club Palace. They still outplay Norwich and Tommy Mooney converts a long goalkick for the first. Mackay's foul gives him a hat-trick chance, following a looping 20 yarder.											

No	Date		Att	Pos	Pt	F-A	H-T	Scorers, Times, and Referees	SQUAD	NUMBERS	IN	USE								subs used
24	H	COVENTRY		5	W	2-0	1-0	Rivers 12, Nielsen 88	Green	Nedergaard	Drury	Mackay	Fleming	Mulryne	Holt	Libbra*	Notman	Rivers^	McVeigh	**Nielsen**/Russell
	15/12		17,889	*8*	42				*Hedman*	*Edworthy*	*Shaw*	*O'Neill*	*Konjic*	*Chippo*	*Thompson*	*Delorge^*	*Hughes**	*Mills*	*Safri*	*Joachim/Fowler*
								Ref: S Bennett	Rivers nets, aided by a deflection off Mo Konjic. Notman brings two great saves from Magnus Hedman. Seven players are booked. Nielsen, loaned from Wimbledon after the injury to leading scorer Roberts, gets off the bench to produce a superb finish, lifting his shot over Hedman.											
25	H	WIMBLEDON		4	W	2-1	1-0	Nielsen 17, Roberts I 59p	Green	Nedergaard	Drury	Mackay	Fleming	Mulryne	Holt	Nielsen^	Roberts I	Rivers*	McVeigh"	Notman/Libbra/Russell
	22/12		17,286	*14*	45			*Connolly 63p*	*Davis !*	*Darlington !*	*Holloway"*	*Andersen*	*Cunningh'm**	*Francis*	*Ardley*	*Hughes*	*Shipperley*	*Connolly*	*Cooper^*	*McAnuff/Hawkins/Feuer*
								Ref: H Webb	The Dons permit Nielsen to play against them. They pay the penalty as he nets a fine header. On a surging run, he is hauled down by Kelvin Davis, who then hurls the ball at him to ensure he gets a red card. Jermaine Darlington also departs as tempers flare. Drury concedes a penalty.											
26	A	NOTT'M FOREST		4	L	0-2	0-2		Green	Nedergaard	Drury	Mackay	Fleming	Mulryne	Holt	Nielsen"	Roberts I	Russell^	Llewellyn*	McVeigh/Notman/Libbra
	26/12		*23,003*	*15*	45			*Prutton 24, John 34*	*Ward*	*Louis-Jean*	*Brennan*	*Williams*	*Hjelde*	*Scimeca*	*Prutton*	*Jenas*	*John*	*Bopp*	*Summerbee*	
								Ref: P Walton	David Prutton is allowed time and space to convert a Jim Brennan cross. Stern John nets a comfortable header from another Brennan cross to double the lead. City are caught offside 12 times and it's a thoroughly frustrating game for the Norwich fans who make the Boxing Day trip.											
27	A	SHEFFIELD WED		4	W	**5-0**	4-0	Kenton 5, Nielsen 17, 27, McVeigh 38, [Holt 76]	Green	McGovern	Kenton	Mackay	Fleming	Mulryne	Holt	Nielsen^	Roberts I*	Sutch"	McVeigh	Notman/Rivers/Russell
	29/12		*19,205*	*23*	48				*Pressman*	*Broomes*	*Geary**	*Solvedt*	*O'Donnell^*	*Maddix*	*Haslam*	*Sibon*	*Ekoku*	*McLaren*	*Hamshaw*	*Crane/Djordic*
								Ref: R Olivier	A proud return to Hillsborough for Worthington, who spent more than ten years here as a player. The struggling home side have no answer as City power into a four-goal lead when McVeigh smashes in a far-post chance. Holt collects the ball 30 yards out and cracks in a classic fifth.											
28	H	WALSALL		4	D	1-1	1-0	Nielsen 13	Green	McGovern*	Drury	Mackay	Fleming	Mulryne	Holt	Nielsen	Rivers^	Kenton"	McVeigh	Notman/Libbra/Sutch
	1/1		19,434	*21*	49			*Tilson 56*	*Walker*	*Brightwell*	*Aranalde*	*Tilson*	*Barras*	*Carbon*	*Wrack*	*Bennett*	*Angell**	*Biancalani*	*Andre^*	*Leitao/Byfield*
								Ref: S Mathieson	The club launches its centenary year in fine style when Nielsen shoots them ahead. Nielsen had to intervene after a McVeigh cross got stuck under the feet of Rivers. Kenton sees a shot hit the underside of the bar. Frederic Biancalani's corner falls for Andy Tillson, who shoots home.											
29	A	MANCHESTER C		5	L	1-3	0-1	Nielsen 47	Green	Nedergaard^	Drury	Mackay	Fleming	Russell"	Holt	Nielsen	Notman*	Kenton	McVeigh	Libbra/Rivers/Easton
	13/1		***31,794***	*1*	49			*Berkovic 43, 66, Wanchope 62p*	*Nash*	*Wr't-Phillips*	*Tiatto !*	*Dunne*	*Howey"*	*Pearce*	*Benarbia*	*Berkovic^*	*Wanchope*	*Goater**	*Horlock*	*Huckerby/Killen/Ritchie*
								Ref: R Pearson	City pay £200k to make the Nielsen transfer permanent and he celebrates with an equaliser. Norwich are overpowered by a passionate home side. Danny Tiatto is sent off for fouling Nedergaard, who is accused of play-acting. Tiatto kicks drinks all over the Norwich bench as he exits.											
30	H	MILLWALL		7	D	0-0	0-0		**Crichton**	Nedergaard	Drury	Mackay	Fleming	Russell !	Holt	Nielsen"	Notman^	Kenton	McVeigh*	Sutch/Llewellyn/Libbra
	20/1		18,969	*3*	50				*Warner*	*Lawrence*	*Ryan^*	*Bull**	*Nethercott*	*Dyche*	*Bircham*	*Livermore*	*Claridge*	*Harris*	*Reid*	*Ifill/Ward*
								Ref: A Hall	Young goalkeeper Green is taken out of the firing line for a rest and the much-travelled custodian Paul Crichton debuts for Norwich - his 14th professional club. City are unable to provide the live TV cameras with any Sunday excitement. Russell is harshly sent off just before the break.											
31	A	CREWE		7	L	0-1	0-0		Crichton	Nedergaard	Drury*	Mackay^	Fleming	Russell	Holt	Nielsen	Notman"	Kenton	McVeigh	Sutch/**Roberts A**/Libbra
	29/1		*6,285*	*19*	50			*Ashton 74*	*Bankole*	*Wright*	*Charnock*	*Foster*	*Sodje*	*Brammer*	*Vaughan^*	*Lunt*	*Ashton*	*Jack"*	*Sorvel**	*Hulse/Collins/Rix*
								Ref: R Harris	Norwich disrupt the fluent passing game that Crewe like to employ. This spoiling ploy works until late on when Kenny Lunt's superb pass allows the much-talked-about Dean Ashton to sneak behind Mackay and send a bobbling volley past Crichton. Drury picks up a knee injury.											
32	H	SHEFFIELD UTD		6	W	2-1	0-0	Kenton 72, 74	Green	Nedergaard	Kenton	Mackay	Fleming	Roberts A	Holt	Nielsen	Libbra^	Rivers*	McVeigh	Mulryne/Notman
	3/2		17,348	*15*	53			*Brown 77*	*Tracey*	*Uhlenbeek*	*Ullathorne*	*Ford*	*Page*	*Curle*	*Tonge^*	*Brown*	*Asaba"*	*Devlin*	*Ndlovu**	*Pesch'/Montgomery/D'Jaffo*
								Ref: D Gallagher	The 1972 promotion squad has a 30th anniversary parade before kick-off. The game bursts into life with three goals in five minutes. Stand-in full-back Kenton nets the first after Notman's backheel. Kenton stoops to head in a corner. Michael Brown hits back with a 25-yard screamer.											
33	A	WEST BROM		8	L	0-1	0-1		Green	Nedergaard*	Kenton	Mackay	Fleming	Roberts A	Holt	Nielsen	**Benjamin**	Mulryne"	McVeigh^	Sutch/Rivers/Notman
	11/2		*19,115*	*3*	53			*Dichio 41*	*Hoult*	*Balis*	*Clement*	*Sigurdsson*	*Moore*	*Gilchrist*	*McInnes*	*Johnson*	*Dichio**	*Roberts*	*Chambers*	*Dobie*
								Ref: P Taylor	City are missing the injured Roberts, so Worthington recruits big Leicester striker Trevor Benjamin on loan. He provides some muscle and goes close with an ambitious 30-yarder. Danny Dichio, who is also booked, keeps Gary Megson's men flying high with the game's only goal.											
34	H	PRESTON		7	W	3-0	0-0	Roberts I 62, Alexander 81 (og), [Mulryne 88]	Green	Nedergaard	Sutch	Mackay	Fleming	Mulryne	Holt	Nielsen^	Roberts I	Rivers*	McVeigh	Notman/Benjamin
	22/2		19,506	*10*	56				*Moilanen*	*Alexander*	*Edwards*	*Keane"*	*Lucketti*	*Gregan*	*McKenna**	*Etuhu*	*Cresswell*	*Healy*	*Anderson^*	*Basham/Gudjonsson/Skora*
								Ref: B Knight	Roberts returns with a bang, heading in a Nedergaard free-kick. Graham Alexander's gentle back-pass is somehow completely missed by Teuvo Moilanen for a comical own-goal. A peach of a free-kick by Mulryne makes it three and keeps the play-off challenge going full-throttle.											

35	A	WATFORD		9	L	1-2	0-2	Roberts I 66	Green"	Nedergaard	Sutch	Mackay	Fleming	Russell	Holt	Nielsen	Roberts I	Notman*	McVeigh^	Easton/Benjamin/Crichton
	26/2		*12,622*	*11*	56			*Hyde 8, Nielsen 41*	*Chamberlain*	*Cox*	*Robinson*	*Okon*	*Galli*	*Brown*	*Nielsen*	*Hyde^*	*Gayle**	*Smith*	*Glass*	*Helguson/Hand*
								Ref: E Wosltenholme	Green dashes out of goal rashly and Micah Hyde is able to fire into an empty net from 12 yards. Allan Nielsen races on to a pass from Tommy Smith and picks his spot. Roberts bundles in a rebound off Alec Chamberlain. Green is taken off with a back problem and Crichton comes on.											
36	A	BURNLEY		8	D	1-1	0-1	Libbra 55	Crichton	Nedergaard	Kenton^	Mackay	Fleming	Mulryne	Holt	Nielsen"	Roberts I*	Roberts A	Benjamin	Libbra/Sutch/Rivers
	2/3		*14,679*	*5*	57			*Taylor 6*	*Beresford*	*West*	*Branch**	*Ball*	*Cox*	*Briscoe*	*Little*	*Cook^*	*Weller*	*Taylor*	*Moore A"*	*Davis/Moore I/Blake*
								Ref: P Jones	Norwich tackle their first Saturday league game since December and it's a crucial one in the chase for the play-offs. Gareth Taylor pounces in the early stages. City lose Roberts with a back injury. A battling second-half display is rewarded as sub Libbra strikes to win a valuable point.											
37	H	ROTHERHAM		8	D	0-0	0-0		Crichton	Nedergaard	Kenton	Mackay	Fleming	Mulryne	Holt	Nielsen^	Libbra	Roberts A*	Benjamin	McVeigh/Rivers
	5/3		18,485	*18*	58				*Pollitt*	*Bryan*	*Hurst*	*Scott*	*Branston*	*Swailes*	*Talbot**	*Daws*	*Barker*	*Robins*	*Warne*	*Mullin*
								Ref: A Butler	Ronnie Moore's men need points to stave off the drop and are in fighting mood. The ref turns down two big City penalty appeals, to the anger of players and crowd alike. A double substitution before the hour mark fails to do the trick. City are now a point outside the play-offs zone.											
38	A	COVENTRY		9	L	1-2	1-0	Libbra 45	Crichton	Nedergaard	Drury	Mackay	Fleming	Mulryne	Holt	Nielsen^	Libbra	Kenton*	Easton	Sutch/Benjamin
	9/3		*16,744*	*4*	58			*Hughes 51p, 90*	*Hedman*	*Quinn*	*Shaw*	*Breen*	*Konjic*	*Healy*	*Chippo*	*Safri*	*Hughes*	*Bothroyd*	*Thompson*	
								Ref: U Rennie	Libbra puts City ahead just before the interval, but joy turns to anger as Norwich's big play-off rivals equalise from a hotly-disputed penalty kick. A point would be a creditable achievement but, in cruel fashion, Lee Hughes jubilantly cracks home the winner deep into stoppage time.											
39	H	BIRMINGHAM		10	L	0-1	0-1		Green	Nedergaard	Drury	Mackay	Fleming	Mulryne	Holt	Nielsen	Libbra	Rivers*	Easton^	McVeigh/Llewellyn
	15/3		18,258	*7*	58			*John 22*	*Vaesen*	*Kenna*	*Grainger*	*Hughes*	*Purse*	*Johnson*	*Woodhouse*	*Devlin*	*Mooney^*	*John**	*Williams*	*Horsfield/Eden*
								Ref: M Messias	Under the Carrow Road lights, Stern John gives the Blues a first-half lead. Norwich miss a glorious chance to take a vital point when Holt has a penalty saved by Nico Vaesen. It's a crushing blow and the play-off prospects now look poor. Steve Bruce's men overtake City in the table.											
40	H	GILLINGHAM		8	W	2-1	0-1	Easton 55, Kenton 65	Green	Nedergaard	Drury	Mackay	Fleming	Mulryne	Holt	Nielsen^	Libbra*	Kenton	Easton	McVeigh/Llewellyn
	19/3		16,479	*13*	61			*Onoura 17*	*Brown*	*Nosworthy*	*Perpetuini*	*Hope*	*Butters*	*Browning"*	*Smith*	*Shaw*	*Onoura**	*King*	*Gooden^*	*Ipoua/Saunders/James*
								Ref: S Baines	Iffy Onoura inflicts more misery early on. Again the chance of a penalty equaliser is fluffed, this time after Guy Butters handled a Nielsen shot. The villain is Mulryne, whose spot-kick is easily saved. A far-post finish by Easton is swiftly followed by a fine venomous drive from Kenton.											
41	A	WOLVERHAMPTON		9	D	0-0	0-0		Green	Nedergaard	Drury	Mackay	Fleming	Mulryne	Holt	Nielsen"	McVeigh	Kenton^	Easton*	Llewellyn/Sutch/Notman
	23/3		*26,280*	*2*	62				*Oakes*	*Muscat*	*Camara*	*Lescott*	*Pollet**	*Cameron*	*Newton*	*Rae*	*Blake*	*Miller*	*Ndah*	*Connelly*
								Ref: M Ryan	A real test at Molineux and City pass with flying colours. Never-say-die defending is rewarded as the home side pile on pressure. David Jones' side are without star attackers Dean Sturridge and Mark Kennedy and are unable to find away through. City's promotion dream remains alive.											
42	H	CRYSTAL PALACE		9	W	2-1	2-0	Nielsen 42, McVeigh 45	Green	Nedergaard	Drury	Mackay	Fleming	Mulryne	Holt	Nielsen*	McVeigh^	Kenton	Easton"	Rivers/Sutch/Notman
	30/3		**21,251**	*10*	65			*Morrison 50*	*Clarke*	*Fleming*	*Granville**	*Austin*	*Murphy"*	*Riihilahti*	*Mullins*	*Thomson*	*Morrison*	*Freedman*	*Akinbiyi^*	*Gray/Kirovski/Black*
								Ref: D Pugh	The Easter celebrations begin when Mulryne's defence-splitting pass finds Nielsen and he calmly chips over Matt Clarke. Moments later and McVeigh ghosts in to net a terrific header from Nedergaard's cross. A Mackay back-header allows Clint Morrison to nip in and pull one back.											
43	A	BRADFORD C		7	W	1-0	0-0	McVeigh 86	Green	Nedergaard	Drury	Mackay	Fleming	Mulryne	Holt	Nielsen	McVeigh^	Kenton	Easton*	Rivers/Sutch
	2/4		*14,143*	*16*	68				*Combe*	*Jorgensen*	*Jacobs*	*McCall*	*Wetherall*	*Bower*	*Lawrence*	*Kearney*	*Grant**	*Cadamateri*	*Jess*	*Sharpe*
								Ref: C Foy	The race is hotting up and every point is vital. The tension shows as Norwich only manage one shot on goal in a tense and poor-quality game. The breakthrough finally arrives near the end when McVeigh pops up to stab the winner past Alan Combe and Nicky Law's Bantams are sunk.											
44	H	GRIMSBY		8	D	1-1	1-0	Mackay 4	Green	Nedergaard	Drury	Mackay	Fleming	Mulryne	Holt	Nielsen	McVeigh"	Kenton*	Easton^	Sutch/Roberts I/Rivers
	6/4		20,075	*21*	69			*Cooke 84*	*Coyne*	*McDermott^*	*Gallimore*	*Coldicott*	*Groves*	*Todd*	*Pouton*	*Butterfield*	*Falconer"*	*Robinson**	*Cooke*	*Jevons/Ford/Livingstone*
								Ref: B Jordan	After a fruitful Easter, City fans are full of optimism and, when Mackay nods in Nedeergaard's deep cross, most seem to expect the floodgates to open. But the vital second goal fails to arrive and near the end Steve Livingstone flicks on Tony Gallimore's cross and Terry Cooke scores.											
45	A	BARNSLEY		7	W	2-0	1-0	Nielsen 41, McVeigh 51	Green	Kenton	Drury	Mackay	Fleming	Mulryne	Holt	Nielsen	McVeigh"	Rivers*	Easton^	Sutch/Notman/Libbra
	13/4		*18,803*	*23*	72				*Marriott*	*Milligan*	*Gibbs*	*Morgan*	*Flynn*	*Jones*	*Lumsdon"*	*Betsy**	*Naylor^*	*Dyer*	*Gorre*	*Barker/Sheron/Neil*
								Ref: A Leake	Two wins from the final two games is a must. 4,000 fans head north as the club slashes coach fares as a thank-you gesture. The penalty hoodoo goes on with Nielsen having a spot-kick saved, but he makes amends with a close-range goal before half-time. McVeigh swoops to clinch it.											
46	H	STOCKPORT		6	W	2-0	1-0	Mulryne 45, Mackay 75	Green	Kenton	Drury	Mackay	Fleming	Mulryne	Holt	Nielsen	McVeigh	Rivers*	Easton	Notman
	21/4		20,897	*24*	75				*Dibble !*	*Thomas**	*Clark*	*Fradin*	*Challinor*	*Clare*	*Briggs*	*McLachlan*	*Daly*	*Ellison^*	*Welsh*	*Spencer/Byrne"/Williams*
		Home	Away					Ref: P Alcock	City need a better result than Burnley to make the play-offs. Andy Dibble handles outside his box and is sent off in the very first minute, to be replaced by a teenager. Mulryne shoots the first and Mackay heads in Easton's cross. It's delirium for City, for Burnley have only won by 1-0.											
Average		18,738	14,520																	

Play-offs

Play-offs		Att			F-A	H-T	Scorers, Times, and Referees	SQUAD	NUMBERS	IN	USE								subs used
SF H	WOLVERHAMPTON		6	W	3-1	0-1	Rivers 56, McVeigh 73, Mackay 90	Green	Kenton	Drury	Mackay	Fleming	Mulryne	Holt	Nielsen"	McVeigh^	Rivers*	Easton	Roberts I/Notman/Libbra
1 28/4		20,127	*3*				*Sturridge 22*	*Oakes*	*Halle*	*Camara*	*Lescott*	*Butler*	*Cameron*	*Newton^*	*Rae*	*Blake**	*Sturridge*	*Cooper*	*Proudlock/Miller*
							Ref: R Furnandiz												

Dean Sturridge slots in from Wolves' first serious attack. Worthington rallies the troops for a storming second half. Rivers fires City level and then McVeigh loops in a superb header. In the dying seconds Mackay brings the house down by rising high to head home an Easton free-kick.

Play-offs		Att			F-A	H-T	Scorers, Times, and Referees	SQUAD	NUMBERS	IN	USE								subs used
SF A	WOLVERHAMPTON		6	L	0-1	0-0		Green	Kenton	Drury	Mackay	Fleming	Mulryne	Holt	Nielsen*	McVeigh"	Rivers^	Easton	Roberts I/Sutch/Notman
2 1/5		*27,418*	*3*				*Cooper 77*	*Oakes*	*Halle**	*Camara*	*Lescott*	*Butler*	*Cameron*	*Newton^*	*Rae*	*Blake*	*Sturridge*	*Cooper*	*Kennedy/Miller*
							Ref: A Leake												
							(Norwich win 3-2 on aggregate)												

Terrific tension at Molineux, but City are determined to hang on to their advantage. Green saves superbly from a close-range Nathan Blake header. The excitement level rises as Kevin Cooper's pot-shot from 35 yards flies in. Enormous pressure is absorbed and City make the final.

Play-offs		Att			F-A	H-T	Scorers, Times, and Referees	SQUAD	NUMBERS	IN	USE								subs used
F N	BIRMINGHAM		6	D	1-1	0-0	Roberts I 91	Green	Kenton	Drury	Mackay	Fleming	Mulryne	Holt	Nielsen*	McVeigh"	Rivers^	Easton	Roberts I/Notman/Sutch
12/5		*71,597*	*5*		*aet*		*Horsfield 102*	*Vaesen*	*Kenna*	*Grainger*	*Hughes B*	*Vickers"*	*Johnson M*	*Devlin*	*Tebily*	*Horsfield^*	*John*	*Mooney**	*Lazaridis/Johnson A/Carter*
	(at Cardiff)						Ref: G Barber												
							(Norwich lose 2-4 on penalties).												

Norwich's biggest game for years is seen by 32,500 Canaries fans. After a pulsating 90 minutes ends goalless, Notman's cross is headed in by Roberts, only for Geoff Horsfield to force an equaliser. In the shoot-out drama, Mulryne and Sutch fail to score, meaning City miss promotion.

Worthington Cup

Worthington Cup		Att			F-A	H-T	Scorers, Times, and Referees	SQUAD	NUMBERS	IN	USE								subs used
1 A	BRENTFORD		15	L	0-1	0-0		Green	McGovern	Drury	Mackay	Fleming	Mulryne	Holt	Abbye	Libbra*	Russell	McVeigh	Roberts I
21/8		*4,111*	*2:5*				*O'Connor 90*	*Gottskalks'n*	*Dobson*	*Anderson**	*Ingimarsson*	*Powell*	*Price*	*Evans*	*Mahon*	*Burgess^*	*O'Connor*	*Gibbs*	*Hunt/Partridge*
							Ref: T Parkes												

In a poor-quality first-half, only Holt looks capable of unsettling Steve Coppell's well-organised, low-budget outfit. Russell goes closest for Norwich, hitting a post after 75 minutes. A stunning last-minute winner arrives when Kevin O'Connor fires home to the delight of Griffin Park.

FA Cup

FA Cup		Att			F-A	H-T	Scorers, Times, and Referees	SQUAD	NUMBERS	IN	USE								subs used
3 H	CHELSEA		4	D	0-0	0-0		Green	Kenton	Drury	Mackay	Fleming	Mulryne*	Holt	Notman	Libbra"	Nedergaard^	McVeigh	Russell/Rivers/Llewellyn
5/1		21,017	*P:6*					*Cudicini*	*Ferrer^*	*Babayaro*	*Dalla Bonna*	*Gallas*	*Desailly**	*Jokanovic*	*Forssell"*	*Hasselbaink*	*Zola*	*Le Saux*	*Terry/Melchiot/Lampard*
							Ref: P Jones												

Claudio Ranieri's cosmopolitan side play within themselves and few chances are created in the first half. After the break, City realise the game is there for the taking and pound away at the visiting defence. Carlo Cudicini has to make a series of marvellous saves to keep the scores level.

FA Cup		Att			F-A	H-T	Scorers, Times, and Referees	SQUAD	NUMBERS	IN	USE								subs used
3R A	CHELSEA		5	L	0-4	0-1	*[Forssell 89]*	Green	Kenton	Sutch	Mackay	Fleming	Russell	Holt	Notman*	Libbra"	Nedergaard	McVeigh^	Rivers/Llewellyn/Easton
16/1		*24,231*	*P:6*				*Stanic 11, Lampard 56, Zola 63,*	*Cudicini*	*Melchiot*	*Le Saux*	*Stanic*	*Gallas"*	*Desailly*	*Lampard*	*Dalla Bonna*	*Gudjohnsen**	*Zola*	*Morris^*	*Jokanovic/Forssell/Zenden*
							Ref: P Jones												

Ranieri rotates his squad and a new bunch of stars come in. Injury-hit City find Gianfranco Zola in top form. Chelsea's third goal is sublime. Zola meets a corner with a wonderful inward flick of his right foot, which sends the ball behind his left heel and screaming high into the net.

		Home					Away					
	P	W	D	L	F	A	W	D	L	F	A	Pts
1 Manchester C	46	19	3	1	63	19	12	3	8	45	33	99
2 West Brom	46	15	4	4	36	11	12	4	7	25	18	89
3 Wolves	46	13	4	6	33	18	12	7	4	43	25	86
4 Millwall	46	15	3	5	43	22	7	8	8	26	26	77
5 Birmingham*	46	14	4	5	44	20	7	9	7	26	29	76
6 NORWICH	46	15	6	2	36	16	7	3	13	24	35	75
7 Burnley	46	11	7	5	39	29	10	5	8	31	33	75
8 Preston	46	13	7	3	45	21	7	5	11	26	38	72
9 Wimbledon	46	9	8	6	30	22	9	5	9	33	35	67
10 Crys Palace	46	13	3	7	42	22	7	3	13	28	40	66
11 Coventry	46	12	4	7	33	19	8	2	13	26	34	66
12 Gillingham	46	12	5	6	38	26	6	5	12	26	41	64
13 Sheffield Utd	46	8	8	7	34	30	7	7	9	19	24	60
14 Watford	46	10	5	8	38	30	6	6	11	24	26	59
15 Bradford C	46	10	1	12	41	39	5	9	9	28	37	55
16 Nott'm For	46	7	11	5	26	21	5	7	11	24	30	54
17 Portsmouth	46	9	6	8	36	31	4	8	11	24	41	53
18 Walsall	46	10	6	7	29	27	3	6	14	22	44	51
19 Grimsby	46	9	7	7	34	28	3	7	13	16	44	50
20 Sheffield Wed	46	6	7	10	28	37	6	7	10	21	34	50
21 Rotherham	46	7	13	3	32	29	3	6	14	20	37	49
22 Crewe	46	8	8	7	23	32	4	5	14	24	44	49
23 Barnsley	46	9	9	5	37	33	2	6	15	22	53	48
24 Stockport	46	5	1	17	19	44	1	7	15	23	58	26
* promoted after play-offs	1104	259	140	153	859	626	153	140	259	626	859	1516

Odds & ends

Double wins: (4) Barnsley, Gillingham, Sheffield Wed, Wimbledon.
Double losses: (1) Birmingham.

Won from behind: (2) Gillingham (h), Wolves (h) (p/o).
Lost from in front: (1) Coventry (a).

High points: The superb second-half at home to Wolves in the play-offs.
The tension and thrills as City kept Wolves at bay in the second leg.
The drama of the last league game when a play-off place was clinched.
The marvellous day at the Millennium Stadium – until the shoot-out.
A rise in average home crowds of more than 13%.
Two classic goals: Libbra v Manchester C and Zola's at Chelsea.

Low points: The two missed penalties at the Millennium Stadium.
Losing new skipper Emblen and others to early-season injuries.
The embarrassing Worthington Cup defeat by Brentford.
Defeat at Birmingham in March – when play-off hopes looked doomed.

Player of the Year: Gary Holt.
Ever-presents: (2) Craig Fleming and Gary Holt.
Hat-tricks: (0).
Hat-tricks against: (1) Tommy Mooney (v Birmingham, a).
Leading scorer: (14) Iwan Roberts.

	Appearances								Goals			
	Lge	*Sub*	LC	*Sub*	FAC	*Sub*	PO	*Sub*	Lge	LC	FAC	Tot
Abbey, Zema	**6**		1						**1**			**1**
Benjamin, Trevor	**3**	*3*										
Crichton, Paul	**5**	*1*										
Drury, Adam	**35**		1		1		3					
Easton, Clint	**10**	*4*				*1*	3		**1**			**1**
Emblen, Neil	**1**	*1*										
Fleming, Craig	**46**		1		2		3					
Green, Robert	**41**		1		2		3					
Holt, Gary	**46**		1		2		3		**2**			**2**
Kenton, Darren	**30**	*3*			2		3		**4**			**4**
Llewellyn, Chris	**5**	*8*				*2*						
Libbra, Marc	**17**	*17*	1		2			*1*	**7**			**7**
Mackay, Malky	**44**		1		2		3		**3**		1	**4**
McGovern, Brian	**5**	*4*	1									
McVeigh, Paul	**37**	*5*	1		2		3		**9**		1	**10**
Mulryne, Phil	**39**	*6*	1		1		3		**6**			**6**
Nedergaard, Steen	**37**	*3*			2				**2**			**2**
Neilsen, David	**22**	*8*					3		**8**			**8**
Notman, Alex	**6**	*24*			2							
Rivers, Mark	**19**	*13*				*2*	3		**2**		1	**3**
Roberts, Andy	**4**	*1*										
Roberts, Iwan	**29**	*1*		*1*				*3*	**13**		1	**14**
Russell, Darel	**13**	*10*	1		1	*1*						
Sutch, Daryl	**6**	*13*			1			*2*				
(own-goals)									**2**			**2**
(24 players used)	**506**	***125***	**11**	***1***	**22**	***6***	**33**	***6***	**60**		**4**	**64**

No	Date		Att	Pos	Pt	F-A	H-T	Scorers, Times, and Referees	SQUAD	NUMBERS	IN	USE								subs used
1	H	GRIMSBY		2	W	**4-0**	2-0	Mulryne 30, 59, McVeigh 41, 70	Green	Nedergaard	Kenton	Fleming	Drury	Rivers*	Mulryne	Holt	Easton"	Roberts^	McVeigh	Notm'n/Niels'n/**Heckingbot'm**
	10/8		19,869	*23*	3				*Coyne*	*McDermott*	*Chettle"*	*Groves*	*Gallimore*	*Cooke*	*Coldicott*	*Pouton*	*Campbell^*	*Livingstone*	*Robinson**	*Rowan/Barnard/Ford*
								Ref: P Walton	Easton squares to Mulryne who converts a long-range screamer. Grimsby respond positively, but a breakaway sees McVeigh finish clinically from Easton's cross. Player-boss Paul Groves blunders to allow Mulryne in again and McVeigh and Roberts combine nicely for the fourth goal.											
2	A	ROTHERHAM		3	D	1-1	0-0	Nielsen 86	Green	Nedergaard	Kenton	Fleming	Drury	Rivers*	Mulryne	Holt	Easton^	Roberts	McVeigh"	Notm'n/Heckingbot'm/Niels'n
	13/8		*7,687*	*2*	4			*Lee 68*	*Pollitt*	*Scott*	*Hurst*	*MacIntosh*	*Swailes*	*Sedgwick*	*Talbot*	*Mullin*	*Warne*	*Byfield*	*Lee*	
								Ref: R Pearson	The Millers' pressure is rewarded when Darren Byfield's cross eludes Kenton and Alan Lee nets a simple chance. John Mullin misses a simple header, prompting Worthington to make a triple substitution. Roberts sets up sub Nielsen, who volleys a smart equaliser in the nick of time.											
3	A	BRIGHTON		2	W	2-0	0-0	McVeigh 58, Easton 67	Green	Nedergaard	Kenton	Fleming	Drury	Rivers*	Mulryne	Holt	Easton^	Roberts	McVeigh"	Notm'n/Heckingbot'm/Niels'n
	17/8		*6,730*	*11*	7				*Kuipers*	*Watson*	*Mayo*	*Cullip*	*Pethick*	*Hart*	*Oatway*	*Brooker*	*Carpenter*	*Wilkinson^*	*Zamora**	*Marney/Harding*
								Ref: D Gallagher	Seagulls star Bobby Zamora exits early with a knee problem. Michel Kuipers makes a fine save from McVeigh. Kuipers then blocks Roberts' header but McVeigh nods in the rebound. Charlie Oatway goes close with a diving header. Easton clinches the win with a sweet 18-yard shot.											
4	H	GILLINGHAM		2	W	1-0	1-0	McVeigh 40	Green	Nedergaard	Kenton	Fleming	Drury	Rivers"	Mulryne	Holt	Easton^	Roberts	McVeigh*	Heckingbot'm/Notm'n/Niels'n
	24/8		20,588	*5*	10				*Brown*	*Hope*	*Edge^*	*Smith*	*Ashby*	*Nosworthy*	*Hessenthaler*	*Osborn**	*Ipoua*	*Shaw*	*Sidibe*	*Saunders/James*
								Ref: L Cable	Gills' luck is out as Simon Osborn is stretchered off after a bad fall and player-boss Andy Hessenthaler is booked for a late tackle. Holt lofts the ball into the box and Roberts' header finds McVeigh, who volleys in. Paul Shaw hits a post with a low drive. Mulryne is booked for diving.											
5	A	STOKE		3	D	1-1	0-0	Drury 46	Green	Nedergaard	Kenton	Fleming	Drury	Rivers"	Mulryne	Holt	Easton*	Roberts	McVeigh^	Heckingbot'm/Niels'n/Notm'n
	26/8		*13,931*	*15*	11			*Commons 74*	*Cutler*	*Thomas*	*Handyside*	*Shtaniuk*	*Clarke*	*Henry**	*Gunnarsson*	*O'Connor*	*Commons*	*Cooke*	*Goodfellow^*	*Gudjonsson/Iwelumo*
								Ref: C Wilkes	Drury brings the game to life seconds after the re-start, firing home McVeigh's pass on a quick break. Kris Commons, 19 last week, beats two defenders, plays a one-two with Marc Goodfellow and shoots a picture goal to equalise. Both defences hold firm during lively late exchanges.											
6	H	WATFORD		2	W	**4-0**	1-0	McVeigh 29, Roberts 49, Mulryne 66, [Nielsen 87]	Green	Nedergaard	Kenton	Fleming	Drury	Rivers*	Mulryne	Holt	Easton"	Roberts	McVeigh^	Notm'n/Niels'n/Heckingbot'm
	31/8		20,563	*16*	14				*Chamberlain*	*Cox*	*Dyche*	*Gayle*	*Ardley*	*Hyde*	*Nielsen A*	*Glass*	*Robinson !*	*Smith*	*Foley !*	
								Ref: P Danson	A long-range effort by McVeigh is deflected in. Roberts scrambles a second. Paul Robinson is sent off for a second bookable offence and the free-kick is converted by Mulryne. Dominic Foley replicates his teammate's misdemeanours before Nielsen streaks through to loop in a fourth.											
7	H	SHEFFIELD UTD		3	L	2-3	0-3	Mackay 84, McVeigh 90	Green	Nedergaard	Kenton	Fleming*	Drury	Notman	Mulryne	Holt	Easton^	Roberts	McVeigh"	Mackay/Nielsen/Russsell
	7/9		20,074	*6*	14			*Brown 1, Tonge 5, Asaba 31p*	*Kenny*	*Kozluk*	*Murphy*	*Jagielka*	*Ullathorne*	*Tonge*	*McGovern"*	*Montgom'y^*	*McCall*	*Brown**	*Onuora !*	*Asaba/Javery/Cryan*
								Ref: P Dowd	Michael Brown curls in a free-kick and Michael Tonge knees in a corner to shock City early. Kenton brings down Tonge for Carl Asaba to net from the spot. Iffy Onuora is sent off for elbowing. United hold on till late on when McVeigh nets from close in and Mackay heads in a corner.											
8	A	IPSWICH		3	D	1-1	0-0	Mackay 79	Green	Nedergaard^	Kenton	Mackay	Drury	Notman*	Mulryne	Holt	Heck'bot'm	Roberts	McVeigh"	Russell/Emblen/Mackay
	15/9		*29,112*	*14*	15			*Counago 90*	*Marshall*	*Wright*	*Hreidarsson*	*McGreal*	*Venus*	*Clapham*	*Holland*	*Magilton^*	*Ambrose*	*Bent M**	*Bent D*	*Armstrong/Counago*
								Ref: P Durkin	McVeigh goes close trying to lob Andy Marshall with a 50-yard half-volley. Mackay heads City ahead from McVeigh's cross. Ipswich win a penalty after six minutes added time: Darren Bent hits a post, Green blocks Jamie Clapham's follow-up, Pablo Counago converts the rebound.											
9	A	READING		3	W	2-0	2-0	Mulryne 3, McVeigh 5	Green	Nedergaard	Kenton	Mackay	Drury	Russell*	Mulryne	Holt	Heck'bot'^	Roberts	McVeigh	Emblen/Easton
	18/9		*14,335*	*13*	18				*Hahnemann*	*Mackie !*	*Williams*	*Upson*	*Murty*	*Rougier*	*Hughes*	*Igoe*	*Watson**	*Salako"*	*Cureton^*	*Newman/Forster/Tyson*
								Ref: S Bennett	With Matthew Upson introduced on loan from Arsenal, Reading take a while to settle and City hit them hard early on. John Mackie misses a cross and McVeigh slots the first. Two minutes later more defensive confusion allows Mulryne to net. Mackie is sent off for a second yellow.											
10	H	PORTSMOUTH		3	W	1-0	0-0	Roberts 81	Green	Nedergaard	Kenton	Mackay	Drury	Emblen*	Mulryne	Holt	Heck'bot'm	Roberts	McVeigh^	Easton/Nielsen
	21/9		**21,335**	*1*	21				*Hislop*	*Primus*	*Festa*	*De Zeeuw*	*Harper*	*O'Neill**	*Robinson^*	*Quashie*	*Taylor*	*Merson*	*Todorov"*	*Ritchie/Burchill/Pericard*
								Ref: B Curson	Harry Redknapp's men look worthy of a point with fine displays by Paul Merson and Matty Taylor. But a full-house roars City forward and the reward comes late. Roberts powers in a header at the near post. It puts him on 83 goals, one behind Robert Fleck, third on City's all-time list.											
11	A	PRESTON		3	W	2-1	1-1	Nielsen 35, McVeigh 54	Green	Kenton	Drury	Mackay	Nielsen^	Mulryne	Holt	Emblen*	Nedergaard	McVeigh"	Heck'bot'm	**Southall**/Abbey/Fleming
	28/9		*13,550*	*16*	24			*Cresswell 32*	*Moilanen*	*Alexander*	*Lewis*	*Etuhu^*	*Broomes*	*Lucketti*	*McKenna*	*Fuller*	*Murdock*	*Cresswell*	*Skora**	*Healy/Rankine*
								Ref: P Rejer	Green is in fine form as Craig Brown's men create a host of chances. Nielsen converts Mulryne's precision pass against the run of play. Richard Cresswell curls the equaliser, but in response Emblen's throw reaches McVeigh, and his splendid overhead kick squeezes past Tepi Moilanen.											

No	V	Opponent	Att	Pos	Pt	F-A	H-T	Scorers, Times, and Referees	1	2	3	4	5	6	7	8	9	10	11	Subs used
12	H	LEICESTER		3	D	0-0	0-0		Green	Kenton	Drury	Mackay	Nielsen^	Mulryne	Holt	Emblen*	Nedergaard	McVeigh	Roberts	Southall/Llewellyn
	5/10		20,952	2	25				Walker	Sinclair	Elliott	Taggart	Davidson	Izzet	Scowcroft	McKinlay	Rogers	Dickov*	Deane^	Summerbee/Benjamin
								Ref: M Dean	A tight game of few chances and many bookings. The clearest and only genuine opportunity of the 90 minutes falls to Micky Adams' outfit when Gerry Taggart met Alan Rogers' corner unmarked, but sees his header sail over. Oustanding home performer is the terrier-like Emblen.											
13	H	MILLWALL		2	W	3-1	1-0	Nielsen 43, 59, Kenton 73	Green	Kenton	Drury	Mackay	Southall	Mulryne	Holt	Easton	Nedergaard	McVeigh*	Roberts	Nielsen
	19/10		20,448	20	28			Claridge 50	Walker	Johnson	Nethercott	Ward	Ryan	Ifill	Wise	Roberts*	Livermore	Claridge	Harris^	Braniff/Davies
								Ref: A Kaye	Nielsen comes on after McVeigh injures an ankle and shoots a fine goal past Tony Warner. Veteran Steve Claridge gets clean through to level, but Nielsen is on hand to head home Nedergaard's cross. Warner completely misses Mulryne's lofted free-kick and Kenton loops in a header.											
14	A	COVENTRY		2	D	1-1	0-1	McVeigh 89	Green	Kenton	Drury	Mackay	Southall^	Mulryne	Holt	Heck'bot'm*	Nedergaard"	Nielsen	Roberts	McVeigh/**Henderson**/Emblen
	23/10		16,409	7	29			Partridge 22	Debec	Caldwell	Konjic	Davenport	Quinn	Chippo	Safri	McAllister*	Partridge	Mills^	McSheffrey"	Eustace/Boothroyd/Pipe
								Ref: M Pike	In 46 visits here, Norwich have only won twice. Gary McAllister's men look lively in the first half and Richie Partridge gives Green no chance with a 30-yarder. City end the game with four attackers and it pays off as McVeigh breaks down the left and powers home a spectacular goal.											
15	A	BRADFORD C		2	L	1-2	0-1	Abbey 70	Green	Kenton	Drury*	Mackay	Southall	Mulryne^	Holt	McVeigh"	Nedergaard	Nielsen	Roberts	Heckingbot'm/Emblen/Abbey
	26/10		12,888	13	29			Reid 41, 55	Banks	Molenaar	Bower	Myers	Uhlenbeek	Gray	Warnock	Reid	Jacobs*	Cadamarteri	Ward	Proctor
								Ref: A Leake	Australian Paul Reid, in his second game, stuns City, rifling home two fine long-range goals. Sub Zema Abbey pulls one back, then Danny Cadamateri fouls Nedergaard in the last minute for a penalty. Loan keeper Steve Banks dives to keep out Roberts' kick and also the follow-up.											
16	H	NOTT'M FOREST		3	D	0-0	0-0		Green	Kenton	Drury	Mackay	Emblen^	Mulryne*	Holt	McVeigh	Nedergaard	Nielsen	Roberts	Rivers/Southall
	29/10		20,986	6	30				Ward	Louis-Jean	Walker	Dawson	Brennan	Scimeca	Prutton	Williams	Lester	Harewood	Johnson	
								Ref: J Ross	An entertaining contest sees Mulryne go close when his cross is bundled onto the bar and over by Darren Ward. David Johnson outpaces three, but fires straight at Green. Neilsen volleys to Southall, whose first-time effort goes just over. Paul Hart's team are entering the promotion race.											
17	A	WIMBLEDON		4	L	2-4	0-3	Henderson 71, Nielsen 79	Green	Fleming	Drury	Mackay	Heck'bot'm	Southall	Holt	McVeigh"	Nedergaard	Easton*	Roberts^	Nielsen/Abbey/Henderson
	2/11		3,908	17	30			Shipperley 24, Connolly 42, 45, 83p	Davis	Hawkins	Holloway	Liegertwood	Gier	McAnuff*	Andersen	Darlington	Reo-Coker^	Shipperley	Connolly	Francis/Morgan
								Ref: F Stretton	Dons fans continue a boycott over the club's move to Milton Keynes and City fans are in the majority at Selhurst. Neil Shipperley's volley and David Connolly's double shock off-colour City. Late goals by the subs raise hopes, but Fleming tugs Connolly's shirt for the clinching penalty.											
18	H	SHEFFIELD WED		3	W	3-0	2-0	Roberts 31p, 82, McVeigh 44	Green	Kenton	Drury	Fleming	Rivers*	Mulryne"	Holt	McVeigh	Nedergaard	Nielsen^	Roberts	Southall/Abbey/Henderson
	9/11		20,667	23	33				Pressman	Hendon	Bromby	Haslam	Geary	Owusu	McLaren	Soltvedt	Armstrong	Sibon*	Kuqi !	Knight
								Ref: S Tomlin	Under new boss Chris Turner for the first time, the Owls' Shefki Kuqi has a header superbly saved. Kuqi is sent off for handling and Roberts converts the penalty. McVeigh hooks in a second after a corner. After a long unproductive spell, City wrap it up with a cracking Roberts drive.											
19	H	CRYSTAL PALACE		3	W	2-0	1-0	McVeigh 9, Roberts 87	Green	Kenton	Drury	Fleming*	Rivers^	Mulryne	Holt	McVeigh	Nedergaard	Nielsen"	Roberts	Mackay/Southall/Abbey
	16/11		20,907	13	36				Michopoulos	Butterfield	Symons"	Powell	Granville	Black*	Thomson	Derry^	Gray	Adebola	Johnson	Williams/Riihilahti/Antwi
								Ref: E Wolstenholme	Trevor Francis' side have been on a great run lately and City are penned back early on, but against the run of play McVeigh snatches his 11th of the season. The game is scrappy at times, but Roberts ensures valuable points near the close. The top three are showing signs of pulling clear.											
20	A	BURNLEY		3	L	0-2	0-0		Green	Kenton	Drury	Fleming	Rivers^	Emblen*	Holt	McVeigh	Nedergaard	Nielsen"	Roberts	Henderson/Russell/Abbey
	23/11		16,282	9	36			McGregor 59, Little 85	Beresford	West	McGregor	Gnohere	Branch^	Briscoe	Weller	Cook*	Little	Moore	Blake	Cook/Papadopoulos
								Ref: P Prosser	McVeigh's low shot is pushed against a post by in-form Marlon Beresford. Ian Moore has a goal disallowed for offside before Mark McGregor heads in Robbie Blake's cross. City chances go begging, before the points are made safe by Glen Little, scrambling one in from close range.											
21	H	DERBY		4	W	1-0	0-0	Mackay 82	Green	Kenton	Drury	Fleming	Mackay	Rivers*	Holt	McVeigh	Nedergaard^	Mulryne	Roberts"	Henderson/Nielsen/Abbey
	30/11		20,522	16	39				Grant	Higginboth'm	Elliott	Riggott	Barton	Lee	Burley	Boertien^	Morris	Burton*	McLeod	Bolder/Evatt
								Ref: R Styles	A game of few chances bursts into life late in the day when Mackay leaps to meet McVeigh's corner with a looping header that drifts over the jumping Warren Barton on the line. Rams' coach Billy McEwan gets het up and grabs Fleming by the throat after a bad foul on Paul Boertien.											
22	A	WOLVERHAMPTON		4	L	0-1	0-1		Green	Kenton	Drury	Fleming	Mackay	Heck'bot'm^	Holt	McVeigh	Nedergaard*	Mulryne	Roberts"	Henderson/Nielsen/Abbey
	7/12		25,753	6	39			Cole 37	Murray	Edworthy	Clyde	Lescott	Irwin	Cooper	Rae*	Ince	Kennedy"	Cole	Miller^	Cameron/Sturridge/Andrews
								Ref: A D'Urso	Carlton Cole, 19, loaned from Chelsea, nets on his full debut, calmly drilling home after the ball is half-cleared. Kenton and Heckinbottom go close and Roberts constantly gives David Jones' side problems. Worthington rues another away loss and believes City were worthy of a point.											
23	A	CRYSTAL PALACE		4	L	0-2	0-2		Green	Kenton	Drury	Fleming	Mackay	Rivers	Holt	McVeigh*	Easton"	Mulryne	Roberts^	Abbey/Nielsen/Henderson
	14/12		16,791	10	39			Adebola 6, Black 27	Kolinko	Powell	Popovic*	Symons	Granville	Butterfield	Mullins	Riihilahti	Black"	Adebola^	Johnson	Derry/Gray/Williams
								Ref: P Armstrong	Lethargic City get off to a dreadful start. Lively Tommy Black crosses for Nigerian Dele Adebola to shoot in. It gets worse as the diminutive Black is given space to head a second at the far post from a cross by ex-Canary loanee Danny Granville. Norwich rarely trouble Alex Kolinko.											

No	Date		Att	Pos	Pt	F-A	H-T	Scorers, Times, and Referees	SQUAD NUMBERS IN USE											subs used
24	H	WALSALL		4	W	2-1	0-0	Mackay 55, Mulryne 60	Green	Kenton	Drury	Fleming	Mackay	Rivers	Holt	McVeigh*	Easton	Mulryne	Roberts^	Henderson/Abbey
	21/12		19,872	*19*	42			*Easton 50 (og)*	*Walker*	*Bazeley*	*Hay*	*Roper*	*Aranalde*	*Sonner*	*O'Connor*	*Corica**	*Wrack*	*Leitao*	*Junior^*	*Ainsworth ! /Birch*
								Ref: R Beeby	A drab first half is followed by three goals and a sending-off in 18 minutes. In-form Green is beaten by a deflection, but Mackay comes to the rescue with a typical header. Mulryne's free-kick winner is followed by sub Gareth Ainsworth exiting for a bad tackle straight after coming on.											
25	H	BRIGHTON		5	L	0-1	0-1		Green	Kenton^	Drury	Fleming	Mackay	Rivers	Holt	McVeigh	Easton*	Mulryne	Roberts"	Nielsen/Henderson/Abbey
	26/12		20,687	*23*	42			*Sidwell 38*	*Kuipers*	*Watson*	*Mayo*	*Cullip*	*Pethick*	*Jones*	*Carpenter*	*Rodger**	*Sidwell*	*Zamora*	*Barrett^*	*Oatway/Hart*
								Ref: K Hill	Steve Sidwell volleys home a Simon Rodger corner from seven yards with the defence in disarray. Rivers fires in a Roberts knockdown after the break, but offside is called. The unlucky Rivers turns and floats a neat 25-yard shot over Michel Kuipers, but the ball smacks the crossbar.											
26	A	GRIMSBY		4	D	1-1	0-0	Abbey 51	Green	Henderson^	Drury	Fleming	Mackay	Llewellyn	Holt	Russell	Nielsen	Mulryne	Abbey*	Heckinbottom/McVeigh
	28/12		*8,306*	*21*	43			*Oster 77*	*Coyne*	*McDermott*	*Ford*	*Santos*	*Barnard**	*Campbell*	*Groves"*	*Coldicott*	*Oster*	*Livingstone*	*Mansaram^*	*Gavin/Soames/Cooke*
								Ref: S Baines	Worthington makes wholesale changes after Boxing Day's flop. Abbey comes in for Roberts and gives City the lead as he latches on to Green's massive punt. Henderson is booked for diving. The Mariners press hard and are rewarded when John Oster's fierce shot is deflected past Green.											
27	H	ROTHERHAM		4	D	1-1	0-1	McVeigh 59	Green	Henderson^	Drury	Fleming	Mackay	Llewellyn*	Holt	Russell	Rivers	Mulryne	Abbey"	McVeigh/Nielsen/Roberts
	11/1		19,452	*11*	44			*Garner 33*	*Pollitt*	*Bryan*	*Swailes*	*McIntosh*	*Hurst*	*Sedgwick**	*Mullin*	*Daws*	*Garner*	*Byfield^*	*Barker*	*Robins/Warne*
								Ref: C Webster	Ronnie Moore's men are top away scorers in all four divisions and show why as Darren Garner crashes home a disputed free-kick from over 20 yards. Moments after his arrival as a sub, McVeigh makes space and curls in a fine equaliser. Home fans voice frustration at the failure to win.											
28	A	WATFORD		5	L	1-2	0-1	Cox 53 (og)	Green	Kenton	Drury	Fleming	Mackay	Holt	Russell"	Rivers*	Nielsen	Mulryne	Roberts^	Llewellyn/Abbey/Henderson
	19/1		*13,338*	*10*	44			*Nielsen 45, Helguson 90*	*Chamberlain*	*Ardley*	*Cox*	*Gayle*	*Robinson*	*Pennant*	*Vernazza"*	*Hyde*	*Nielsen^*	*N'l-Williams**	*Helguson*	*Smith/McNamee/Mahon*
								Ref: A Wiley	Sunday lunchtime football on a chilly day - and at times it resembles the stuff on the local parks. Micah Hyde's lay-off sets up an Alan Nielsen drive to awaken the slumbering fans. Mulryne's cross flies in off Neil Cox. Unchallenged Heidar Helguson heads in powerfully in injury-time.											
29	H	STOKE		7	D	2-2	2-0	Roberts 2, Mackay 23	Green	Kenton	Drury*	Fleming	Mackay	Holt	Russell	Rivers^	McVeigh	**Healy"**	Roberts	Llewellyn/**Briggs**/Abbey
	1/2		20,186	*21*	45			*Gunnarsson 63, Mills 88*	*Banks*	*Thomas*	*Handyside*	*Shtanuk*	*Hall*	*Richardson*	*O'Connor*	*Gunnarsson*	*Hoekstra*	*Iwelumo**	*Greenacre^*	*Mills/Marteinsson*
								Ref: R Olivier	Healy, on loan from Preston, has a shot blocked and Roberts nods home the rebound. City dominate the first half and Mackay doubles the lead. But Peter Hoekstra pulls one back and sub Lee Mills, on loan from Coventry, cracks in a 20-yard equaliser. Two points simply thrown away.											
30	A	SHEFFIELD WED		5	D	2-2	2-0	Healy 18, Roberts 43	Green	Kenton*	Drury	Fleming	Mackay	Holt	Russell	Mulryne	McVeigh"	Healy	Roberts^	Nedergaad/Nielsen/Abbey
	8/2		*19,114*	*23*	46			*Robinson 66, Quinn 76*	*Pressman*	*Westwood*	*Bar'-Murphy*	*Maddix*	*Monk*	*Powell*	*Robinson*	*Quinn*	*Johnston*	*Reddy*	*Kuqi**	*Owusu*
								Ref: M Cowburn	Loan star Healy nets a beauty and his whipped-in cross makes Roberts' second. Chris Turner's strugglers bounce back after the break and again a two-goal lead disappears. After nine league games without a win, the bookies are not the only ones losing faith in Norwich's promotion bid.											
31	A	SHEFFIELD UTD		7	W	1-0	0-0	McVeigh 69	Green	Kenton	Drury	Fleming	Mackay	Holt	Nedergaard	Easton	McVeigh	Healy*	Roberts	Henderson
	22/2		*19,020*	*5*	49				*Kenny*	*Kozluk*	*Quinn !*	*Yates^*	*Page*	*Brown*	*McCall"*	*Ndlovu !*	*Tonge**	*Allison*	*Mooney*	*Montgomery/Cryan/Morrison*
								Ref: N Ryan	Gerry Quinn and Peter Ndlovu are both sent off for second yellow card offences in the final half-hour. McVeigh scores a fine goal, collecting a difficult ball and jinking into space, before firing home a low shot. Relieved Worthington praises his side, but Blades' Neil Warnock is livid.											
32	A	GILLINGHAM		7	L	0-1	0-0		Green	Kenton	Drury	Fleming	Mackay	Nedergaard	**Sinclair^**	Easton	McVeigh	Healy*	Roberts"	Nielsen/Henderson/Abbey
	25/2		*7,935*	*11*	49			*Wallace 75*	*Brown*	*Nosworthy*	*Ashby**	*Hope*	*Edge*	*Hessenthaler*	*Smith*	*Southall*	*Shaw*	*Wallace^*	*Sidibe*	*Saunders/Perpetuini*
								Ref: C Penton	Paul Shaw hits a post with the goal gaping, but veteran Rod Wallace shows him how it's done when left unmarked. A good effort on goal by Healy leaves him with a pulled hamstring. In injury-time a Fleming goal is ruled out for pushing. Young Dean Sinclair replaces injured Holt.											
33	H	IPSWICH		7	L	0-2	0-0		Green	Kenton	Drury	Fleming*	**Bromby**	Holt	Rivers^	Easton"	McVeigh	Healy	Roberts	Mulryne/Henderson/Abbey
	2/3		21,243	*8*	49			*Wilnis 72, Bent D 90*	*Marshall*	*Makin*	*Wilnis*	*Gaardsoe*	*Holland*	*Wright*	*Miller*	*Magilton^*	*Richards*	*Ambrose**	*Bent D*	*Bowditch/Naylor*
								Ref: G Laws	Ex-Canary Marshall gets a hostile reception. To cover for suspensions, Leigh Bromby signs on loan from Sheffield Wed. In a hot atmosphere, Roberts and Fleming are lucky not to be sent off. Debutant Dean Bowditch, 16, has a hand in two late goals by Fabian Wilnis and Darren Bent.											
34	H	READING		7	L	0-1	0-0		Green	Kenton	Drury	Fleming	Nedergaard	Holt	Rivers	Easton"	McVeigh*	Mulryne	Abbey^	Nielsen/Roberts/Russell
	5/3		18,970	*3*	49			*Kenton 74 (og)*	*Hahnemann*	*Murty*	*Mackie*	*Williams**	*Shorey*	*Chadwick*	*Hughes*	*Harper*	*Sidwell*	*Tyson^*	*Forster"*	*Viveash/Salako/Henderson*
								Ref: S Baines	A serious blow to play-off hopes and another frustrating game. The lack of goals is becoming a serious problem. Alan Pardew's men hit a post through James Harper in the first half. They grab the decisive goal when Nathan Tyson's low cross is slid into his own net by unlucky Kenton.											

No	Date	Opponent / Att	Pos	Res / Pts	F-A	H-T	Scorers, Times, Referees	1	2	3	4	5	6	7	8	9	10	11	Subs used
35	A	PORTSMOUTH	8	L	2-3	0-0	Easton 58, Rivers 62	Green	Bromby	Drury	Mackay	Nedergaard^	Holt	Rivers	Easton	McVeigh*	Russell"	Abbey	Nielsen/Roberts/Emblen
	12/3	19,221	1	49			Ayegbeni 57, Todorov 59, 72	Hislop	Primus	De Zeeuw	Festa	Harper*	Sherwood	Merson"	Quashie^	Taylor	Todorov	Yakubu	O'Neill/Diabae/Foxe
							Ref: D Gallagher	Plucky City put up a great fight in a real thriller. Ayegbeni Yakubu looks offside as he gets clear to score. Just 13 seconds later, Easton hits back. Todorov slots Pompey's second, but Rivers smashes in Abbey's cross. Green's poor punch falls for Svetoslav Todorov to hit the winner.											
36	H	COVENTRY	8	W	2-0	1-0	Nedergaard 33, Drury 90	Green	Bromby	Drury	Mackay	Nedergaard	Holt	Rivers^	Easton	Russell	Healy*	Abbey	McVeigh/Sinclair
	15/3	20,099	15	52				Hyldgaard	Whing^	Shaw	Davenport	Caldwell	Partridge*	McAllister	Eustace	Chippo	Holdsworth	Joachim	Safri/Pead
							Ref: G Barber	Healy returns for a second loan spell from Preston to boost flagging play-off hopes. Nedergaard's 30-yard rocket shows his forwards how it's done after chances go astray. Norwich fade as Gary McAllister's men improve. Other contenders go down, so the play-offs remain reachable.											
37	A	MILLWALL	8	W	2-0	2-0	Mackay 8, Abbey 38	Green	Bromby	Drury	Mackay	Nedergaard	Holt	Rivers^	Easton	McVeigh	Russell	Abbey*	Roberts/Healy
	18/3	6,854	17	55				Warner	Reid	Ward^	Robinson	Bull"	Ifill	Roberts	Livermore	Kinet*	Harris	Claridge	Hearn/Nethercott/May
							Ref: A Hall	A great start as Mackay's goalbound header is cleared to him and he volleys a superb effort into the roof of the net. Moments later Abbey gets clear but Tony Warner smothers. City continue to probe dangerously and Abbey nets the vital second when Bromby's long-throw reaches him.											
38	A	NOTT'M FOREST	8	L	**0-4**	0-2	[Brennan 82]	Green	Bromby*	Drury	Mackay	Nedergaard	Holt	Rivers	Easton"	Healy	Russell	Abbey^	Kenton/Roberts/McVeigh
	22/3	27,296	5	55			Huckerby 11, Harwood 22, Williams 56,	Ward	Louis-Jean	Dawson	Hjelde	Brennan	Williams	Scimeca	Reid	Harewood	Johnson	Huckerby	
							Ref: M Riley	Paul Hart's side dominate and pacy Darren Huckerby is a constant menace. City are second best throughout and fail to create any clear scoring chances. 'We were spineless', complains Worthington. Five of the teams above City win, the other two draw. The play-offs look out of reach.											
39	H	WIMBLEDON	8	W	1-0	1-0	Healy 40	Green	Kenton	Drury	Mackay	Nedergaard	Holt	Rivers	McVeigh	Healy*	Russell	Abbey^	Nielsen/Roberts
	25/3	21,059	10	58				Davis	Volz	Nowland	Chorley	Hawkins	Tapp"	Morgan^	Reo-Coker	Darlington*	Shipperley	Connolly	Gier/Holloway/Agyemang
							Ref: M Fletcher	Green, in his 100th game, sends a huge kick downfield and Abbey's flick-on is steered home by Healy. Terry Burton's Dons go close to a late equaliser, but City deserve the win. Kenton blocks a David Connolly effort. Even keeper Kelvin Davis goes upfield and tries a header on goal.											
40	H	BRADFORD C	8	W	3-2	0-1	Rivers 49p, 86, Abbey 54	Green	Kenton	Drury	Mackay	Nedergaard	Holt	Rivers"	Easton	Russell	Nielsen^	Abbey*	Henderson/Roberts/Emblen
	29/3	**18,536**	15	61			Forrest 42, Jorgensen 68p	Davison	Uhlenbeek	Francis	Wetherall	Bower	Reid	Muirhead	Atherton	Jorgensen	Forrest	Ten Heuvel	
							Ref: P Joslin	Danny Forrest shoots a deserved opener in a drab first half. Drury is brought down for the equaliser. Abbey's fine curling shot puts Norwich ahead before Russell clatters into Ben Muirhead to concede a penalty. Rivers wins the points by cutting in and letting fly a low, bouncing shot.											
41	A	DERBY	8	L	1-2	1-1	McVeigh 10	Green	Kenton	**Shackell**^	Mackay	Nedergaard*	Holt	Rivers	Easton	Russell	McVeigh	Abbey"	Emblen/Roberts/Healy
	5/4	23,643	19	61			Burley 24, Kenton 57 (og)	Oakes	Barton	Ritchie	Eliott	Boertien	Jackson	Burley	Kinkladze	Valakari	Mooney*	Ravanelli^	McLeod/Bolder
							Ref: J Ross	New boss George Burley inspires Derby's first win in 10. He recalls his out-of-favour nephew Craig, who crashes home Paul Boertien's cross. This cancels out McVeigh's fine 25-yarder which went in off a post. A rare Green blunder sees Kenton's back-pass slip gently under his foot.											
42	H	BURNLEY	8	W	2-0	1-0	Nedergaard 2, Abbey 67	Green	Kenton	Drury	Mackay	Nedergaard	Holt	Rivers*	Russell	Healy"	McVeigh^	Abbey	Roberts/Easton/Henderson
	12/4	20,026	16	64				Michopoulos	West	Davis	McGregor	Branch	Weller	Papdopoul's"	Briscoe*	Blake	Moore	Taylor	Armstrong^/Chaplow/O'Neill
							Ref: S Tomlin	Abbey's shot is cleared off the line, but McVeigh's corner is headed in by Nedergaard. Stan Ternent's men let in seven at home last week, but it takes Abbey's second-half tap-in to subdue them. Gareth Taylor misses two of four clear Clarets chances. The slim play-off hopes remain alive.											
43	A	WALSALL	8	D	0-0	0-0		Green	Fleming	Drury	Mackay	Nedergaard	Holt	Easton*	Russell	Healy"	McVeigh	Abbey^	Mulryne/Roberts/**Jarvis**
	19/4	7,018	20	65				Walker	Roper	Barras	Carbon	Wrack	Robinson	Lawrence	Samways	Aranalde^	Junior*	Leitao	Corica/Matias
							Ref: K Hill	Colin Lee's Saddlers are battling to avoid the drop and keep a third successive clean sheet. City toil hard but lack quality and composure. Jorge Leitao goes close to a winner. One point is just not enough for Norwich. Sub Ryan Jarvis, 16, becomes the club's youngest-ever first-teamer.											
44	H	WOLVERHAMPTON	8	L	0-3	0-0		Green	Kenton	Drury	Mackay	Fleming	Holt	Rivers	Mulryne	Jarvis"	McVeigh*	Roberts^	Henderson/Abbey/Healy
	21/4	20,843	4	65			Ndah 52, Sturridge 74, Miller 90	Murray	Irwin	Butler	Lescott	Naylor	Newton^	Ince	Cameron	Kennedy	Miller	Ndah*	Sturridge/Cooper
							Ref: C Wilkes	After Kenton and Mulryne efforts are cleared off the line, Wolves cruise into the play-offs and ensure City won't make it. Dave Jones' men get revenge for last year's play-off defeat. George Ndah fires the opener, Dean Sturridge heads a killer second and Kenny Miller sweeps in late on.											
45	A	LEICESTER	8	D	1-1	0-1	Rivers 74	Green	Kenton	Drury	Shackell	Fleming	Holt	Russell	Mulryne	Henderson^	Jarvis*	Roberts	Rivers/McVeigh
	27/4	31,639	2	66			Benjamin 20	Walker	Impey	Elliott	Taggart	Rogers	Scowcroft	McKinlay	Stewart*	Dickov	Deane	Benjamin^	Summerbee"/Ashton/Wright
							Ref: R Olivier	Micky Adams' side take the lead via Trevor Benjamin, who looks offside as he stabs in Gerry Taggart's flick-on. The big crowd gets little else to enjoy as The Foxes seem to lack motivation now they are definitely promoted. Rivers nets a deserved equaliser, cracking in a low 25-yarder.											
46	H	PRESTON	8	W	2-0	0-0	Mears 46 (og), Mulryne 63	Green	Briggs	Drury	Mackay	Fleming	Holt	Rivers^	Mulryne	Henderson	McVeigh"	Roberts*	Abbey/Russell/Nielsen
	4/5	20,232	12	69				Gould	Alexander	Edwards*	Lucketti	Mears	McKenna	Etuhu	Skora"	Lewis^	Cresswell	Lynch	Broomes/Cartwright/Abbott
	Home	Away					Ref: D Crick	Tyrone Mears's attempted headed clearance is misjudged by Jonathan Gould, and it loops slowly into the net. Mulryne seals the points with a well-timed run to convert Rivers' cross. Major plans to demolish and replace the South Stand, and to build luxury apartments, are announced.											
Average	20,352	15,685																	

Worthington Cup

No	Venue	Opponent / Date	Att	Pos	Res	F-A	H-T	Scorers, Times, and Referees	SQUAD	NUMBERS	IN	USE								
1	H	CHELTENHAM		3	L	0-3	0-2		Green	Nedergaard	Drury	Kenton	Mackay	Mulryne"	Notman	Holt	Nielsen^	Roberts	Easton*	Heck'bot'm/Llewellyn/Emblen
		10/9	13,285	*2:23*				*Naylor 29, 45, McAuley 83*	*Book*	*Victory*	*Duff*	*Yates*	*Walker*	*Finnigan*	*Milton*	*Howarth*	*McAuley*	*Naylor*	*Allsop*	
								Ref: G Hegley												

Mackay and Kenton's mix-up sees Tony Naylor nip in to score. Seconds before the break the little striker repeats his neat finishing. It's a bad night for City as the visitors reach Round 2 for the first time ever. They clinch it with Hugh McAuley's curling shot after a disputed free-kick.

FA Cup

No	Venue	Opponent / Date	Att	Pos	Res	F-A	H-T	Scorers, Times, and Referees												
3	H	BRIGHTON		4	W	3-1	0-0	Mulryne 56, 81, McVeigh 81	Green	Drury	Fleming	Mackay	Holt	Russell	Rivers*	Mulryne	Abbey^	Nielsen	McVeigh	Roberts/Henderson
		15/1	17,205	*24*				*Pethick 48*	*Kuipers**	*Watson^*	*Pethick*	*Cullip*	*Mayo*	*Jones"*	*Brooker*	*Oatway*	*Carpenter*	*Barrett*	*Zamora*	*Peckham/Blackwell/Piercy*
								Ref: A Kaye												

This is a new date after the first game was halted by a power failure. Keeper Michel Kuipers comically tumbles on to his backside and goes off hurt. Robbie Pethick stabs in after a rare Green slip. City hit back well via McVeigh's cracking 20-yarder. A Mulryne free-kick is deflected in.

No	Venue	Opponent / Date	Att	Pos	Res	F-A	H-T	Scorers, Times, and Referees												
4	H	DAG & REDBRIDGE		5	W	1-0	0-0	Abbey 90	Green	Drury	Fleming	Mackay	Holt	Russell	Rivers	Mulryne	Roberts	Nielsen*	McVeigh	Abbey
		25/1	21,164	*NL*					*Roberts*	*Smith*	*Heffer*	*Matthews*	*Vickers*	*Shipp*	*Janney*	*Terry*	*McGrath**	*West*	*McDougald*	*Rooney/Stein*
								Ref: P Taylor												

One of two non-leaguers left in the cup, Garry Hill's Daggers make life hard for City. There's the odd nervous moment, but impressive Tony Roberts is by far the busiest keeper. He's one of several in tears at the end after Abbey pokes in a last-ditch winner. The heartbreak of the cup.

No	Venue	Opponent / Date	Att	Pos	Res	F-A	H-T	Scorers, Times, and Referees												
5	A	SOUTHAMPTON		7	L	0-2	0-0		Green	Drury	Fleming	Mackay !	Nedergaard	Holt	Russell	Mulryne*	Roberts	Nielsen^	McVeigh"	Abbey/Easton/Henderson
		15/2	*31,103*	*P:9*				*Svensson A 71, Tessem 74*	*Niemi*	*Telfer*	*Lundekvam*	*Svensson M*	*Higginboth'm*	*Svensson A*	*Delap**	*Oakley^*	*Marsden*	*Beattie"*	*Ormerod*	*Fernandes/Todd/Tessem*
								Ref: G Barber												

Gordon Strachan's Premiership side hit a post, but McVeigh does likewise with a curling shot. Moments later Chris Marsden's cross is nodded down and Anders Svensson converts. Sub Joe Tessem scores after Green parried a Marsden drive. Mackay departs after two bookable offences.

		Home						Away					
	P	W	D	L	F	A	W	D	L	F	A	Pts
1 Portsmouth	46	17	3	3	52	22	12	8	3	45	23	98
2 Leicester	46	16	5	2	40	12	10	9	4	33	28	92
3 Sheffield Utd	46	13	7	3	38	23	10	4	9	34	29	80
4 Reading	46	13	3	7	33	21	12	1	10	28	25	79
5 Wolves *	46	9	10	4	40	19	11	6	6	41	25	76
6 Nott'm For	46	14	7	2	57	23	6	7	10	25	27	74
7 Ipswich	46	10	5	8	49	39	9	8	6	31	25	70
8 NORWICH	46	14	4	5	36	17	5	8	10	24	32	69
9 Millwall	46	11	6	6	34	32	8	3	12	25	37	66
10 Wimbledon	46	12	5	6	39	28	6	6	11	37	45	65
11 Gillingham	46	10	6	7	33	31	6	8	9	23	34	62
12 Preston	46	11	7	5	44	29	5	6	12	24	41	61
13 Watford	46	11	5	7	33	26	6	4	13	21	44	60
14 Crys Palace	46	8	10	5	29	17	6	7	10	30	35	59
15 Rotherham	46	8	9	6	27	25	7	5	11	35	37	59
16 Burnley	46	10	4	9	35	44	5	6	12	30	45	55
17 Walsall	46	10	3	10	34	34	5	6	12	23	35	54
18 Derby	46	9	5	9	33	32	6	2	15	22	42	52
19 Bradford C	46	7	8	8	27	35	7	2	14	24	38	52
20 Coventry	46	6	6	11	23	31	6	8	9	23	31	50
21 Stoke	46	9	6	8	25	25	3	8	12	20	44	50
22 Sheffield Wed	46	7	7	9	29	32	3	9	11	27	41	46
23 Brighton	46	7	6	10	29	31	4	6	13	20	36	45
24 Grimsby	46	5	6	12	26	39	4	6	13	22	46	39
	1104	247	143	162	845	667	162	143	247	667	845	1513

* promoted after play-offs

Odds & ends

Double wins: (2) Millwall, Preston.
Double losses: (1) Wolves.

Won from behind: (3) Bradford C (h), Preston (a), Brighton (h) (FAC).
Lost from in front: (1) Derby (a).

High points: The consistency shown in the season's early weeks.
Phil Mulryne's opening goal on 10 August.
Robert Green's superb form throughout the season.
The consistently high Carrow Road attendances.
The emergence of record-breaking youngster Ryan Jarvis.

Low points: The slow but steady decline after Christmas.
The general shortage of goals from the strikers.
The home defeat by Ipswich – a serious blow to play-off hopes.
Failing to win, twice in eight days, after leading 2-0 at half-time.
The humiliating home defeat by Cheltenham in the League Cup.

Player of the Year: Adam Drury
Ever-presents: (1) Robert Green.
Hat-tricks: (0).
Hat-tricks against: (1) David Connolly (Wimbledon, a).
Leading scorer: (15) Paul McVeigh.

	Appearances						Goals			
	Lge	*Sub*	LC	*Sub*	FAC	*Sub*	Lge	LC	FAC	Tot
Abbey, Zema	**12**	*18*			1	*2*	**5**		1	**6**
Briggs, Keith	**1**	*1*								
Bromby, Leigh	**5**									
Drury, Adam	**45**		1		3		**2**			**2**
Easton, Clint	**23**	*3*	1			*1*	**2**			**2**
Emblen, Neil	**5**	*7*		*1*						
Fleming, Craig	**28**	*2*			3					
Green, Robert	**46**		1		3					
Healy, David	**10**	*2*					**2**			**2**
Heckingbottom, Paul	**7**	*8*		*1*						
Henderson, Ian	**4**	*16*				*2*	**1**			**1**
Holt, Gary	**45**		1		3					
Jarvis, Ryan	**2**	*1*								
Kenton, Darren	**36**	*1*	1				**1**			**1**
Llewellyn, Chris	**2**	*3*		*1*						
Mackay, Malky	**35**	*2*	1		3		**6**			**6**
McVeigh, Paul	**38**	*6*			3		**14**		1	**15**
Mulryne, Phil	**31**	*2*	1		3		**6**		2	**8**
Nedergaard, Steen	**34**		1		1		**2**			**2**
Nielsen, David	**11**	*22*	1		3		**6**			**6**
Notman, Alex	**2**	*6*	1							
Rivers, Mark	**28**	*3*			2		**4**			**4**
Roberts, Iwan	**33**	*10*	1		2	*1*	**7**			**7**
Russell, Darel	**16**	*5*			3					
Shackell, Jason	**2**									
Southall, Nicky	**4**	*5*								
Sinclair, Dean	**1**	*1*								
(own-goals)							**2**			**2**
(27 players used)	**506**	***124***	**11**	***3***	**33**	***6***	**60**		**4**	**64**

LIST OF SUBSCRIBERS

VOTES FOR THE MOST POPULAR NORWICH PLAYER 1972-2003

Subscriber	Vote
Steve Annels	**Chris Sutton**
Andrew Barnes	**Robert Fleck**
Mark Beardsall	**Kevin Keelan**
Michael Bird	**Martin Peters**
Lee Blackmore	**Bryan Gunn**
Richard Bland	**Ian Crook**
Richard Andrew	**Kevin Keelan**
John Brady Burgess	**Iwan Roberts**
David Burrell	**Duncan Forbes**
David Burton	**Duncan Forbes**
Matthew Bussey	**Clint Easton**
Darrell Butcher	**Malky Mackay**
David & Claire Carpenter	**Colin Suggett**
Karl Clare	**Martin O'Neill**
Cameron Clarke	**Adam Drury**
Dale Cooper	**Martin Peters**
Jonathan Cordle	**Martin Peters**
Kevin Dack	
Kevin Denmark	
Andrew Denny	**Ted MacDougall**
Julian Dimock	**Bryan Gunn**
James Distill	**Martin Peters**
Ben East	**Chris Sutton**
Tim East	**Jimmy Bone**
Tom East	**Ian Crook**
Harry John Farr	**Iwan Roberts**
Mike Felix Fields	**Kevin Reeves**
Mark Freeman	**Ian Crook**
David J Fulcher	**Robert Fleck**
Kevin George	**Steve Bruce**
Daren Gilbert	
Mark Hardy	**Darren Eadie**
George & Mary Harmer	**Craig Bellamy**
Austin Hendy	**Iwan Roberts**
Mike Hilton	**Martin Peters**
Gareth Honeywood	**Robert Fleck**
L A Hubbard	**Steen Nedergaard**
Martin James	**Kevin Keelan**
Glen Johnstone	**Robert Fleck**
Peter Kerry	**Iwan Roberts**
James Knight	**Iwan Roberts**
Stephen Leader	**Mark Bowen**
Sam Mann	**Iwan Roberts**
Mofa Meadows	**Steen Nedergaard**
Graham Murfitt	**Kevin Drinkell**
Paul Murrell	**Martin Peters**
John & Jeannette Nicholls	**Max Spriggs**
Nick Oakley	**Paul McVeigh**
Tim Powell	
Derek Pratt	**Dave Watson**
Kevin Reynor	**Steen Nedergaard**
Peter Rogers	**Ian Culverhouse**
Paul Rudd	**Jan Molby**
Jonathan Rush	**Chris Sutton**
Peter Rush	**Kevin Keelan**
George N Rutherford	**Bryan Gunn**
John Sauverin	**Martin Peters**
William Scott	**Iwan Roberts**
Colin Sendall	**Phil Boyer**
Danny Smith	**Robert Fleck**
Richard Stocken	
John Conway Stott	**Martin Peters**
Kevin William Stott	**Ian Crook**
Trevor Strange	**Tommy Bryceland**
Adrian Thomas	**Ian Crook**
Ian Thompson	**Robert Fleck**
David 'Spud' Thornhill	**Bryan Gunn**
Richard Vincent	**Robert Fleck**
Joshua Walker	**Ian Crook**
Gary Walpole	**Darren Eadie**
Geoffrey Watling	
Jon Webb	**Ulf Ottosson**
Clinton Webster	**Kevin Keelan**
Edward Wharton	**Craig Bellamy**
Stephen Whittle	**Ted MacDougall**
Teri Margaret Whittle	**Justin Fashanu**
David Whitworth	**Kevin Drinkell**
James Woodrow	

VOTES FOR MOST POPULAR PLAYER
(33 different players received votes)

1st	Martin Peters
2nd=	Robert Fleck
2nd=	Iwan Roberts
4th	Ian Crook
5th	Kevin Keelan
6th	Bryan Gunn